Lily's Story

WALKING IN LILY'S SHOES

HER EXPERIENCES

CHALLENGE

FOREIGN WORLDS,

CONFIDENCE,

AND CREATIVITY

22 stories about beauty values rippling in multicultural treks and restoring the life-force

Frances Ludmer, BA, BSc, MEd
Authorities: Social Studies, Special Needs, Generalist
&
Administrator-Certified

Series *The Forgotten Waves* - Title ID: 4787851
Created by Frances Ludmer.

ISBN-13: 978-1499328097
ISBN-10: 978-1499328095
Library of Congress Number 2014937350

First Volume

Dedication

Sarah and Raymond

"Adventure is worthwhile"[1] *said Amelia Earhart. My greatest adventures started in my childhood, journeying later with my extraordinary twins Sarah and Raymond. They traveled to many destinations with me, and because they sought my guidance, they are contributors to my extended awareness about connecting that matter and being guided by spirits that care.*

Gratitude to Amber for her exceptional support. Also, to Dan, a world traveller and adviser.

"Love is like dew that falls on both nettles and lilies."
(Swedish Proverb)

Legal Note: *Names of celebrities or persons in the media are accurate, but names of other parties have been modified to protect the privacy and security of individuals mentioned; true names have not been used.*

FOREWORD

This is an intriguing journey of one woman's adventure through countries and cultures – an insightful story that weaves through places and people. She takes us on a voyage into the eyes of a North American female. It is a world that may be imaginary for us, but markedly real for her, as she sees (images of people worldwide), speaks to them and shares her life with them. Earlier in her life story, as a bohemian child with unending curiosity and wanderlust exploring Chinatown, the author delicately explicates her personal experiences and observations through this fascinating tapestry of multicultural experience. The exposition goads us to follow a dream - one that strongly beckons us to walk alone. It reminds us of Mahatma Gandhi, who was greatly impressed by the Nobel Laureate, Rabindranath Tagore's 1905 poem on bravely following one's own call, challenging us to "be the change."[1] Epitomized in a more recent popular Hindi movie, Kahaani, the "story" of a brave woman's journey to find the truth about her missing husband, Ekla Chalo Re (in Bengali, means, Walk Alone) motivates listeners to "open their mind, walk alone; be not afraid, walk alone...If no one answers your call, then walk alone, be not afraid, walk alone my friend." Perhaps, Charles Swindoll said it well: "There is only one you... Don't you dare change just because you're outnumbered?"[2]

From her newly found childhood friend, Keiko, to her adult acquaintance, Imelda, the author embarks on a long quest for answers. With her precocious understanding of multiple identities and the search for gender equality, she faces bullying in Montreal, sees inhumane treatment at the asylum, and even marries into another culture – only to ask more questions and finding fewer answers. As she ponders, "...walking to places that were unknown," the author grapples with the lack of gender equity. This story challenges the reader to ask questions regarding how cultural improprieties purposefully signify a woman's role and constrain her identity. In her ongoing journey, Lily attempts to "humanize" the females. Just like most of us influenced by the media, the princess dreams of the ideal prince. With preconceived notions and romanticized esotericism that eventually challenges her understanding, the story is an example of everything rolled into one – courage, adventure, exploration, betrayal, broken trust, determination and survival. It even gets more personal as her machismo kin, acquires the misguided male attributes and privileges. And yet, in some cases, the reality of male privilege and double standards is evident in the adoring male philanderer who exists and crosses cultures and boundaries.

As the author transitions between cultural boundaries and wades through culture shock, the reader will be able to identify many of the experiences that are complex and multifaceted. The Aboriginal encounter in Lily's Story is a stark reminder of Freire's cautionary musings about the "oppression of the oppressor" – an unkind reversal of roles that believes in the mistaken notion that, "two wrongs make one right."[3]

This is not a scientific discourse on philosophical or moral issues; it is also not an academic dialectic. It is a well-researched story and extensively cross-referenced writing that is based on rich resources and abundant contributions. Lily's story is an authentic personal journey of an individual who is driven by curiosity, hope and adventure. Though a journey of discovery may result in excitement and fruition, the Sisyphean task of exploring one's own identity may be challenging and fraught with disconnections, ambiguity, and disillusionment. The reader is encouraged to travel with the author and make one's own observations and create his or her own journeys. Interspersed with humour, insightful comments and intuitive perceptions, the author paints a picture of colourful narratives. As she highlights male domination and privilege throughout this cross-cultural international traverse, questions of a woman's world seen through her own eyes challenges the reader to reconsider how situations affect people – especially, a woman in a developing world. The narratives also highlight the rich "foreigner" living in a world of comfort and delusion. The extravagant and conceited corporate executives and other privileged expatriates coddled within their specious intellectualism paints examples of human vanity.

There is no culture that grows in vacuum and as the "distinctiveness"[4] of any culture is only as unique as its ability to borrow and hybridize, to give and to receive from different cultures, it is obvious that cultures (in the words of Homi Bhabha and Stuart Hall) – are constantly evolving, adapting, and improvising. As a moving target, understanding a different culture further complicates the process of analyses.

The author explores fascinating cultural practices and insane military cultures. In some sense, like many traditional boardrooms, the military commander with his accoutrements and behaviour demonstrate how some domains still largely remain dominated by the male.

One main theme throughout the book highlights the historical inequality and injustice against women. With compelling evidence and personal anecdotes, the author skillfully weaves through the narratives of injustice, violence, and treachery but also shows the resilience among many women to survive and hope for a better life. Interspersed within this tale are found lessons for both female and male perspectives.

The stories of marginalized and powerless women are congruent with similar stories in other countries – especially, those lacking democracy and human rights. Nevertheless, there is the hope "to walk alone" and be resilient. Though sad, this is obvious in the case of Imelda and other women caught in the trap of violence. There exist many such "Imeldas" in the dark world of unconscionable violence. Reading about Imelda gives us more than a sense of sadness. It challenges us to take on the responsibility to share similar stories in order to sensitize individuals and perhaps, goad them into action.

The author is well travelled and has presented to innumerable audiences. She has worked with multifarious group of professionals around the world and has also lived in different cultures – allowing her to present another perspective to cross-cultural understanding. I invite the reader to walk through the eyes of Lily and experience the various emotions as one travels through various lands and cultures.

John P. Anchan, PhD

Associate Dean of Education, University of Winnipeg

Winnipeg, Manitoba. March 31, 2014.

Lily's Story

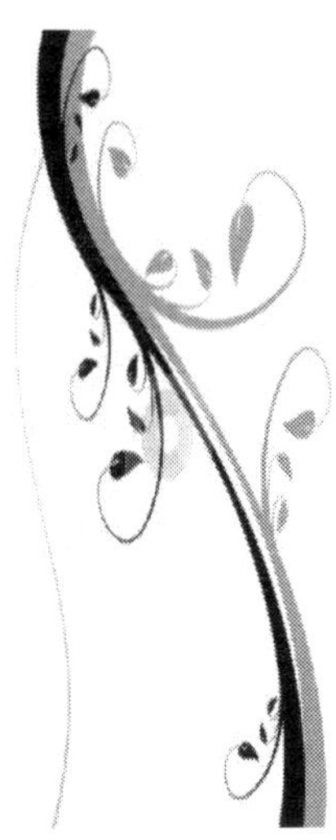

TABLE OF CONTENTS

Table of Contents....continued

REFERENCES

Cassidy Hailey, Book Cover Designer
(Calgary, Alberta)

Mia Jensen, Logo Designer
(Vancouver, British Columbia)

About the Author

Ludmer has Russian, Polish, and Mongolian ancestry. She was raised in Montreal, Canada, and has attended 15 universities. She has earned a Bachelor of Arts in Sociology, a Bachelor of Arts in History, and a Master of Education in Applied Adult Education, and has completed the coursework for a Master's in Sociology. In addition, she has done graduate work in the areas of government, psychology, administration, and teaching. She holds administration certification and teacher licenses in special needs, social studies and generalist in Canada and United States. Other coursework includes nursing, art therapy, childcare, human resources, quality management and supervision. She has also traveled extensively, conducting academic research in domestic settings, remote communities in North America, and throughout the world. Her unique background, education, and international experience have informed and inspired her writing. This has resulted in three books that offer insight into her worldly experiences, enhance our knowledge base, and invite discussion on these important topics. Her international experiences in administration, teaching, and research in local and remote North American communities (First Nations, Native Americans), provide her with a unique vision of how to see with new eyes and act accordingly to create balance and harmony in our world.

Tabart's *Jack and the Bean Stalk* is a favorite folk tale conveys that no matter how poor one is, there is a solution for every problem; we only have to grow and climb to find it. The author explores what individuals sometimes forget in the search for their pot of gold. She is a woman who has ascended mountains (rising to new heights of thinking), clambered among rose bushes (experiencing the beauty and sweetness of the petals and the pain of the thorns), and climbed scaffolds (building upon levels of consciousness). Like Jack and his bean stalk, Waters reveals how country people and giants relate to the real world today. Since diversity permeates everything we do, Ludmer's purpose is to build understanding about relationships among all types of people, whether powerless or empowered, whether intellectual or lowbrow.

PREFACE

This book dedicates to preserving values that encourage exploring new horizons, facing challenges, and learning about the unfamiliar. This book tells Lily's story to understand global mind-sets, traditions, undercurrents in thinking, and what is socially justifiable. Through an evaluation process, the content intends to define how culture-specific knowledge develops and why an individual adopts, adjusts, does something familiar, or avoids what feels or looks strange. *The Forgotten Waves* explores ways to break human patterns of thinking by walking in someone else's shoes, which gives the opportunity to surf new waves of intellect or conscious cognitive processes.

This book focuses on the real experiences of Lily and explores them in greater depth. Samplings of some of her journeys provide her visions and how she framed her thinking. Her experiences provide a sequential development of how she filters social values, her objectivity, and their results. The reader will see that social filtering reveals attitudes, approaches, **emotional intelligence,** and understanding when following the heroine's journey. As experiences amass, so do new waves of thinking. The heroine's revelations will show how objectivity and change evolve overtime, allowing the mind to absorb new experiences. This is why the author produces analysis and comparative case studies in Volume 2. This helps to explain how thinking may be similar from youth to adulthood, and provides further reflection that might be desirable. Readers will begin to understand that through excursions, challenges, and culture-specific ideologies, the unfamiliar reveals—specifically, waves of thinking that are forgotten, misunderstood, or unknown.

INTRODUCTION

Who are you? **Original** is the one real word I would use to describe myself. It means I lived through my originality, which is the part of me that is truly unique. Albeit, originality takes different forms and directions, but I wanted to realize my individual goals. This is characteristic of everybody including you (the reader). I interwove my interests and my goals to never give up and to stand out.

As an older woman raising pre-teens, I eventually came to a place where I was completely exhausted, confused, broke and utterly frustrated, and had nowhere to go. In an act of total faith, I gave myself permission to stop the cycle, and to step out from Cinderella's empty carriage. It was extremely difficult for me. I had to leave town and take time away from an exhausting schedule; disconnect myself from abusive relationships, and my network. I took years to reflect on my life's journey. I realized that two of my heroes and mentors, my art teacher and the female psychologist Dr. Naumburg, were alike. We were all creative, and open to new ideas and ways of doing things and we are all pioneers.

Facing fears is the secret to my success as an artist and thinker, and sparking passions in everyday life. This has helped me to open many doors that have led me to the most transformational outcomes and realizations.

Passions in life, gets better with time...world travels, studies and standing out. I feel like an ever-ready battery charged up to my essence, my true self. Traveling and feats carried out are how my world changed life dramatically.

I have accepted myself fully, quirks and all. Serial achieving proves I am good enough, so this has stopped. I realized something was missing and it was time for me to become my biggest fan. So, my journey of personal growth is like Rodin's "**The Thinker**" began. I let go of what others thought and tried to control the palette of my realities.

I am a woman experiencing people from all walks of life, professions, ages, race and status. My challenges have stretched me, made my imagination grow, and tested me, both personally and professionally. Once I took the steps to confront challenges, I became a woman of strong character and self-reliance. Now I would like to tell you (the reader) about journeys towards a possible awakening for you too.

My **originality** was influenced by an affection for creating artwork and an admiration for artists like Maurits Cornelis Escher, (<u>See Artwork</u>*) Luis Moreno Ocampo,* Salvador Dali* and Hieronymus Bosch.* They are in tune with my palette as I paint the realities of my life. They also began with Margaret Naumburg's psychoanalytical approach to the earliest art forms. I once was a beautiful maiden with golden flowing hair sitting in a castle waiting for my prince to come, my body shaped like a cloisonné vase with the softness of a baby's touch. Today, my locks are greying and I no longer sit in a castle. My skin has become dry and the crevices are openings for me to ponder about color and the cardinal virtues of prudence, temperance, and fortitude.

The world is spinning in front of me like a fast-paced carousel. I am trying to get off, but I am unsure because if I jump off I will fall. I moderate my thoughts, feelings and actions unlike the risky times in my youth. The strength of my mind enables me to bear past pains and combat today's trials with courage. I am wondering why I am uncomfortable in my own skin as I inspire tenets of artistic psychology. I am a humanist, creator, and reconciler of emotional conflicts with a growing self-awareness. Am I following the same path of my mother and her mother too?

I no longer have admiring men photographing my batting eyelashes and flashing hazel eyes. My skin no longer glows and I feel like Pablo Picasso's famous sculpture made of used bicycle parts held together by a cable. I guess the only reason I am not falling apart is the sinews I have and because I have changed directions. I am not only a combination of original thoughts, but of childhood rearing and multicultural journeys that led lead me to the torrential waves of reality.

I suppose because I have worked hard all my life, nature tries to slow me down. I see people feuding over history, princesses and the magical kingdom of beauty. I no longer have leverage as in earlier times. The story I would like to tell you, my story, starts with the greatest discoveries of new places, images, people humming like bees and storms moving in. Reflections of my past tell how I came to have a higher purpose to teach what is unknown or forgotten, and how transparency in society evolves.

Walk with me through the catacombs of time. Discover how the transparency of life crystallizes. From childhood glass revelations of the exotic, blind, waves of turbulence, plasticity, stiffening to an awakening. I am the female version of Auguste Rodin's sculpture "The Thinker." I dive into dangerous waters of new colonies of thinking. From high-placed dignitaries to voodoo in culture, I am sculpting emotions leading through the labyrinths of time.

I will capture the magical and enigmatic kingdom of adventure. My journeys may at first cause you to squirm, I am august as I head into new and unusual environments, mirroring a circus clown in white makeup. From an early age, I am ready for a slapstick routine. Eventually, I unmask realities and stir emotions to reach an awakening place in you.

Introducing Me, Lily

Diversity permeates everything we do. My intention is to build relationships among all types of people, whether powerless or empowered, intellectuals or not. This started because of curiosity about my parents' habits, observable differences in people's ethics, and the behavioral patterns I noticed. I wanted answers, and I began by studying a broad range of disciplines from the psychosocial dimensions of government (political science), to history, healing, education, the worlds of diplomats, corporate executives, and more. The more exposure I had, the more I seemed to confront difficult situations.

Somehow, I did not fit in, and being human, my inquisitiveness escalated. As a child, I wondered why my parents' attitudes were at times extremely rigid while at other times lenient. I realized that people have different frames of reference. I wanted to be exposed to unfamiliar situations and cope with new challenges in life. Even though I was a flower child of the seventies, I was passionate about having adventures. I assumed that by experiencing life in other worlds, I would live life to the fullest. I also imagined that I would figure out why I reacted to matters as I did. Later in life, I anticipated my discoveries revealed the truth to me, then others could also walk in my shoes and realize it too.

My name is Lily, and the name has exceptional uniqueness. Meanings are from beliefs of the past and present. For starters, the Lily of the field is a symbol of my Quebec birthplace. In 1948, the new flag of Quebec incorporated the fleur-de-lis design. It is hard to imagine that a symbol of my name was used as part of a monarchical design including the crowning of King Clovis. It also has mystical meanings. Through hearsay, I learned that the lily flower descended from heaven. These stories date to the Biblical time of the Garden of Eden and suggest that a lily was formed from Eve's tears. For the Egyptians, Lily meant life and resurrection. Without a doubt, my life can be described metaphorically as an Egyptian and as Eve. I have experienced tears and have always looked for answers as to why I rose or fell.

I discovered my name has also taken on some significance in a number of other cultures. In Hebrew and Greek, lily means purity and innocence. An English meaning of Lily relates to the number nine or a soul urge of my inner cravings to act as I have. I suppose the soul urge relates to my deeper inner desire to serve humanity than to stand alone serving none but myself. In fact, there is some truth to that. I enjoy sharing my knowledge, experiences, and creativity. There is a presumption that people with the name Lily carry the values of truth, justice, and discipline.

I found out that the Calla Lily represents grace, charisma, magnificence, dignity, and sophistication. The Madonna lily is known as a symbol of purity, and Christians assume an association with the Holy Virgin. The flower's delicacy also symbolizes a dichotomy. Lily means purity, union (wedding), fertility, and the lily flower is also placed on a grave.

Other cultures have made presumptions about the lily, too. For example, the Spaniards thought lilies had curative powers, transforming a beast back into human form.

After attending a dream workshop, I learned when a person dreams about the lily flower, it denotes a paradox. During warmer weather, it signifies amiable things such as marriage, happiness, and prosperity. During winter, the meaning is contradictory and connotes frustration of hopes, and the untimely death of a loved one. Both of these connotations perpetuate the symbolism I learned earlier.

In my research, I discovered that lilies were used in coffins symbolizing death. Keats, a renowned poet, described the lily as tombstone art and symbol. Hence, the literary implication suggests lilies restore the innocence of the soul at death. At first, I could not determine if this particular element of my name had any relation to me. When I was in Thailand, I saw the lily flower disperse its beautiful petals in the water. In South Korea, Japan, and Taiwan, I observed lilies being brought to funerals. People in these countries explained that the lily was a token. It meant that the soul of the departed automatically received the restoration of innocence after death.

This knowledge gave me the impetus to use my imagination, and I started to paint. No matter which culture, the name lily seemed to represent a universal symbol of beauty in life and death, and express an air of affluence. Themes I painted were about loveliness and comfortable circumstances. Since the meanings of flowers are a secret communication and symbolic (**Woman of Substance*), the lily flower offered two sides of the continuum: life and death. This was no different from what my artwork expressed. From medieval times, lilies have also symbolized feminine sexuality. Thus, my feminine side tells the truths that I will share. At the same time, my life experiences have been incongruent. I have seen both joy and sadness. As the meaning of lily correlates to blossoming and demise, I suspect my name choice is not a coincidence.

I am Lily "***a strong woman determined to do something others are determined not be done.***"[1] That is why most people who know me think my behavior is *not* like a lily. Instead, I might be viewed like Groucho Marx (without the mustache). Even though gender roles overlap in North America, I believe we live in a world where men dominate. They are chiefly considered to be strong and assertive in getting things done. Since I am not weak, I disliked some aspects of being female. "*A media culture created for men by men teaches women and men alike that women are valuable only to the extent to which we are useful to men.*"[2] I am goal-oriented, so I have always chosen to connect with men and be noticed in positive ways, thereby teaching men that women are equally valuable human beings, just as they are.

My journey through the unfamiliar has mirrored the lives of some famous individuals, especially men, and I compare myself to them throughout the book. The main celebrities I discuss are Dr. Patch Adams, Dr. Robert Kearns, Sir Winston Churchill, Wolfgang Amadeus Mozart, Albert Einstein, and Robin Williams. Adams is an American physician, social activist, author (and clown!), who brings humor to patients and has created an alternative health care model. Kearns is the prize-winning inventor of intermittent windshield wipers. Churchill, Mozart, and Einstein are well known as a great leader, a masterful musician, and an accomplished scientist respectively. Williams is a successful actor, director, writer, comedian, and producer.

My personality traits are not egotistical, but my trekking in life has uncanny parallels to the famed men mentioned. Adams, Kearns, Churchill, Mozart, Einstein, and Williams are all scholarly and traveled extensively, as have I. I have been called learning disabled; these men have been labeled as having visions (Adams), speech impediments (Churchill), difficulties with grammatical formations (Einstein), nervousness (Kearns), trouble coping with deafness (Mozart), and learning problems (Williams). My visions, learning preferences, and methods of coping are on par with these famed men. Even my scholastic endeavors imitate their accomplishments: They all liked to study the sciences and human nature, and all of us studied art in some form. Like Dr. Adams, I incorporated art therapy as a measure to help people laugh and learn. Churchill was a literary artist who offered words of enduring value. Einstein and Kearns used the art of logic. Mozart put into practice the art of music, while Robin Williams conducted the dramatic art of acting.

In the grandiosity of our visions, we all struggled financially. I suppose that is why I feel comfortable wearing second-hand shoes or oversized pants that a clown might wear. We all overcame adversity. I have struggled to become recognized as an intellectual and a woman, experiencing abuse and deception, and having fewer opportunities than men even though I possess an advanced university education. The most masculine aspect about me is a result of having been raised by parents reared in an autocratic society. Adams and Churchill were raised by military fathers; Kearns served in the military. The good side of the military played into the hands of Williams. In 1987, he played a military disc jockey in the film *Good Morning Vietnam*. In

2002, he went overseas to boost the morale of military personnel in Kandahar, Afghanistan. Mozart was inspired by military sounds.

We have all received awards and recognition for our feats. Adams has received awards for health models, Churchill and Einstein both received Nobel Prizes, Kearns won his patent, Mozart received global praise for his musical compositions, and Williams has received awards for acting. I have been featured in the media for helping aboriginals in poverty and for creating phenomenal programming recognized by staunch government officials in high standing and by corporate executives. We have all delivered joy where it was least expected. We have all transformed from single thinkers to spreading our thinking publicly, extending our goodwill, and generating rainbows even in the dark of the night. As a group, our accomplishments are the result of our inhibition to act on our thinking. Through our efforts, we are responsible for creating new ways of thinking and cleaning up injustices.

These men's stories have been told in films and on stage: *Patch Adams* (Dr. Adams), played by Williams, *Into the Storm* (Churchill), *Einstein's Big Ideas* (Einstein), *The Flash of Genius* (Dr. Kearns), and *The Magic Flute* [*Die Zauberflote*] (Mozart). The only story left to tell is mine. Please enjoy the D-box seat and the multi-dimensional journey I prepared.

CHAPTER 1
THE MAGIC OF CHINATOWN – 8 YEARS

My story begins in the early 1950s in Montreal, Canada. I am the middle child and one of four siblings. My parents were both survivors of World War II. My father's birthplace is Galicia, which intermittently belonged to Poland, Austria, and Russia. My mother originates in the Moldavian part of the Ukraine. Both were war veterans who served on the front lines as military officers. Despite my parents' hardships and deprivations, both of them had university education. My father graduated as a mechanical engineer, and my mother completed studies as a medical doctor. As Europeans, they were fluent in several languages.

My older siblings were infants when my parents moved from Eastern Europe to Canada. As new immigrants, my parents confronted the realities of immigrant life. They had to re-establish their qualifications and credibility. My father got his break when he repaired a broken sewing machine at the factory where he had employment for a paltry seventeen dollars a week. The owner was so impressed with my father's expertise that he proposed starting up his own business. He gladly loaned him the down payment to kick-start that venture and my father opened a business that manufactured laminated products. They included innovative designs and textured surfaces that enhanced artwork like Chagall's stained glass windows. The business eventually expanded nationally, and I was proud to tell others about it. His initiatives made me think that I should also share my creative ideas countrywide. My father also heavily invested himself in community work and public service. His conditions might have planted a seed of ambition in me to do the same.

My father behaved like a traditionalist. He vowed that no wife of his would work outside the home. This was a common attitude of that patriarchal era, but sickness challenged my father's ideal. The physicians explained that my father had contracted a rare disease that prevented proper blood coagulation and needed blood thinners. I suspect it had happened during World War II. I knew he had worked for the underground, but I did not know the details. He had photo albums of pictures taken during the war that were so atrocious they gave me nightmares.

My mother devoted herself to my father's care, and spent long hours at the hospital by his side. My family was falling apart because of my father's illness, and money was scarce. This is when my mother accepted a job as a university professor, and taught Russian literature. As a woman of that era, she had a guilt complex. My mother assumed that, while she was working, she neglected my siblings and me. She abandoned that pursuit when my father found out about her employment as a university professor, and expressed his aversion that my mother was working. She wanted to follow traditional norms and so she quit her job. In this historical time frame, what a man said, the woman followed, regardless of how professional she was. It devastated me that she accepted his undermining, and I did not want that in my life.

My parents kept traditional values in our home. Music, reading, science, and exploring the arts consistently received encouragement. My family celebrated food, and my parents bought and stored it in abundance (a reaction to the deprivation they suffered during the war). My mother developed creative culinary skills. She thrived on entertaining guests, and was so talented that members in the community praised her abilities. There were times I did not always like the food my mother prepared. Sometimes I would sit for hours with food in my mouth. In fact, food was a measure of controlling. I disliked it when my mother pushed me to eat, which always went hand-in-hand with stories about starving children.

When I was young, I was an acrobat and a ballerina. I was three or four when I started, and I continued into my teen years. My instructors were so impressed with my ability to do contortions that they asked my parents to allow me to join the circus, but my parents refused. They were too protective to let me go. I always felt that other people thought I was strange, but I was a happy child.

I was also a hugely adventurous child, and at the age of four, I hopped on a bus headed to Belmont Park, an amusement park on the opposite side of town. When my parents could not find me, they called the police who conducted a major search. I came home alone from a fun-filled day at the circus, unscathed. Another time, I found cash in my mother's purse. I took it out thinking it would be friendly to buy some treats to share with the neighborhood children, not knowing that this was the rent money. While venturing off on my own, I crossed an enormous, traffic-filled boulevard just as a large semi-truck was approaching. The driver clearly would not be able to brake in time—the truck was going to hit me. Witnesses were in amazement to see my spontaneous reaction. As a child of only three or four, I had the presence of mind to hunker down, and the truck passed right over top of me! This near-death experience led my parents to believe that my destiny was for a higher purpose.

I would say my life journey began at the age of eight, when I escaped from my parents, jumped on a subway headed for the unknown, and fell in love with Chinatown. I even dreamed that I would be the main celebrity filmed in The Magic of Chinatown.

I continued my journey, climbing down many steep steps to reach the underground subway, a public metro system. There were people pushing me and I felt like a dwarf among giants. Their collective breaths and smells were clingy and reminded me of glutinous rice with a glue-like texture that does not let go. I continued shuffling through the crowd and reached the underground subway. I saw shiny carriages linked and I heard the sparking sounds of wheels on the tracks. Someone was in the front carriage. I was unsure what they did there, but the sound of a kettle steaming on a fire was remarkably clear. That deafening sound accompanied the noise of high heels, tapping boots, and the hammering of feet behind me. The swarm of journeyers moved to the door opening of the train, and they pushed and crammed me inside like a squashed sandwich losing its filling.

The train was like a rocking chair and I was moving back and forth. I could not find a chair to sit in, and I squirmed among the commuters. Then, I squeezed between legs and found an opening. I was trying to look out of the window, but I had to stand on my tippy toes. I stretched my arms to grasp the metal overhead bar. Someone allowed me to take a seat and finally, I could look outside the train's window. I felt the train suddenly shifting and speeding ahead.

Time appeared to be static and I was not sure when I would reach Chinatown. Every time the train made a temporary halt, I could hear the loud speaker bellow the name of the stop. Time was moving slowly and places whizzed by, blurring shops and people. Then, there was an abrupt squeaking sound as the train came to a full stop. I could feel my heart pulsing faster than an Olympic racer. I had reached the end of the line.

Throngs of commuters carried me off the train and I paused as they surged around me, like water splitting around an island. This was a new world, and I stood transfixed. Overhead loomed an elaborate gateway, shimmering brightly in shades of glistening gold. The warmth of the sun reflecting on the metals brightened me and I checked my arms and legs - was I shimmering, too? Had I become magic? I felt like I had - and wondered if the magic would protect me as I moved forward to explore the unknown. The people passing by paid me no notice, and I wondered how they could not see me. Every person engulfing me was a different color, making shrill sounds I could not understand. How could they not see me, a little white child in their midst?

I kept a crisp image of being an adventurer. This was a world almost totally unknown to me because I lived in the opposite end of the city. I moved forward cautiously and stopped at a window where dead ducks twirled lazily overhead. Heat radiated up from the sidewalk. A warming sensation floated out from the door of the butcher shop. I wondered, were the ducks cooked in an oven, or by the heat surrounding them? I had no idea why, but the knives sounded like a saw cutting up my toys.

I was in an unfamiliar marketplace that looked like my mother's kitchen, but on a much grander scale. As I pulled myself up over the counter,

I saw hanging slabs of meat clinging onto a metal holder. I could not understand or believe what I was seeing. The meat had no refrigeration and flies were attacking it. Suddenly, I had a yearning to be in my mother's kitchen, but I stayed to watch one of the butchers cutting up the meat. The butcher chopped the meat so quickly, it seemed instantaneous, as if my mother was cutting onions, and I was tearing up.

Looking around, I saw goods of all kinds displayed openly. I never thought I would see clothing and toys next to hanging meat, but it was there. I was happy to see colorful toys in all shapes nearby. They almost looked like marching bands that were sleepy. Some of the toys had strings and I pulled on them. Immediately, they made beeping, clanging, and strange sounds. The vendor shouted at me for touching them, but I did not care. I continued looking at the toys. Some worked like they were robots and others were creeping or making slinky motions. Next to where I stood, there were small and large containers in bold colors. My eyes were getting dizzy from the rainbow hues. On the other side of the containers, I saw traditional tablecloths embroidered. It looked like something that might compliment the dining room table at home.

Nearby, there were countless fish displayed on wide platters. Many were still alive and their bodies were swaying as though swimming in the deep dark sea. One by one, vendors chose the fish and cut them up so quickly. I watched a man select a fish for the slaughter. I could see the gills were open, gasping, and I think I could even hear an aspiration. The eyes of the fish looked like they were popping out and staring at me, imploring help. I could not believe the man would chop the head off while it was still alive! It made me feel queasy to watch the fish slither around as if it were looking for water, turning and twisting. Then the vendor slivered the fish open. I swore I could see the heart still pounding and hear its rhythm.

I continued walking ahead, and I heard a grand splash. Someone had thrown a bucket of water downward, and it had just missed me. I was glad the water did not hit me, but thought, what if I had gotten wet? Where would I go to change, find shelter, and dry myself? I would not have known how to stop the chill and images of snow dropping down my neck came to mind. I could not imagine someone just dumping water from their window. The circumstances made me reflect. My mother would probably say, "Do not waste water."

I wondered what I would see next. I walked forward. I saw clothes hanging on lines, swaying in the wind with movements that suggested they could come alive. I disliked the reeking smell of damp clothing in the air. It brought back thoughts about the splashing water that nearly hit me before. Next, I began exploring narrow alleyways and litter was almost everywhere. I saw clumps of feces, soiled baby diapers and spoiled vegetables piled on top, also grubby cardboard and foul-smelling urine. The odors of flatulence and pungent spices give me the sensation to vomit. I felt a cat crawling next to my legs. It was smelly and I tried shooing it away. When it did not leave, I had a numbing sensation. My legs, arms, and body felt immobilized. Luckily, the cat wandered away and disappeared. As I got out of the alleyway, I saw boxes of fresh green vegetables in rows. They appeared as soldiers standing upright and crisp. These bright greeneries looked like broccoli people. There were masses of vegetables ready for sale.

Close by, people were sitting in small spaces slurping up soup noodles. I could hear the little voice of my mother telling me not to make those kinds of gurgling sounds. I was still wondering whom these people were, and why they were behaving this way, but the heavenly aroma stopped my mother's voice from echoing in my head. I wanted to gulp down the soup as noisily as they did. I suppose this is natural because human nature makes many noises. Why did my mother always underline the need to behave a certain way to have manners? The more I walked around, the more I questioned my own familiar lifestyle.

I could see squirrelly writing around me, but I had no idea what anything meant. I stopped to ask someone, but they did not answer. I was getting hungry and scared of what to expect. The flashing sign just ahead looked like a horse. I pretended to trot, thinking I would get someone's attention. No one questioned that here was a little girl, on her own, not in school. I began to wonder about this. The North American values I had taken for granted did not apply here.

Then I came across another sign. There were squirmy lines with sharp edges that went nowhere. As I squinted to make out the meaning, the pictures looked like a person eating. Probably my imagination was working overtime because I was getting hungry. I had no idea what time it was, or where I was. I did everything by instinct. I entered a small cobbled passageway, which led me into a room. There were Asian people loudly chatting, and again, I heard the sound of slurping. No Caucasians were inside. Some men were at a bar, drinking and smoking. The sounds were louder than workers fixing the road with a drill. The musty smell made me light-headed and I was uneasy, so I decided to leave.

Unexpectedly, an elderly woman came forward. Her face and neck were drooping and she had thinning skin. She had many wrinkles with blotches and dark spots on her face. The woman had missing teeth and her lips looked shrunken. As she looked down at me, she spoke in her language, and she asked me something. I could not understand her, so I did not answer. Then a feeble-looking man with a ragged, pointed beard joined her, and I became nervous. The woman touched my shoulder, and signaled me to follow. Through hand gestures, she asked me to sit down and I waited to see what would happen. Thoughts were grinding in my imagination and I thought these old people wanted to cut me up for food. Was I going to be an appetizer like the fairy tale of Hansel and Gretel? I began thinking about what it would be like to experiencing fattening and baking in an oven, so I started shaking. No one looked up, and I missed my mother's comfort. I wondered what my mother was thinking about my absence. Comforts of home did not exist in this strange, distant place. I am used to sitting in a refined dining room, with nicely drawn curtains, a shimmering chandelier, and a dining table fit for a king. This setting was the opposite and fear set in. I was in awe, and a few moments later, the old man with glistening gold teeth carried out a bowl of steaming soup. It had the same incredible aroma I had smelled earlier. It was tempting to eat, especially since my stomach was rumbling. I saw dumplings floating with some shallot pieces and surfacing spices. He also brought a beautiful arrangement of alluring food, but I was not sure what it was because it had the shape of blossoming flowers. The man placed the bowl and large plate in front of me. He gestured for me to eat. Despite my misgivings, I ate heartily.

I felt more settled, but thoughts of home ran through my mind. I could see my mother fussing at making the most appealing table imaginable. She often had fresh cut roses in a vase on the table, their aromatic smell permeating the room. Decorated plates with ornate silver cutlery would glitter in the sunshine. Spectacular food arranged like artwork. I realized the Chinese couple's generosity of giving me a simple meal was as welcoming a gesture as my mother's table setting. Shortly after, the frail looking man and woman brought me a sweet fruit. I remember my mother calling it a kiwi. An apricot gel-like dessert complimented the dinner. Even though it looked rubbery and like something fun to play with, I ate it. The taste was splendid, and I began wondering what magic these people had up their sleeves? Hospitality is extraordinarily generous. At that moment, I recognized the old couple's actions stemmed from the same parental instincts of my own parents, and I was grateful.

I had limited means and no pebbles in my pocket like Gretel might have done in the fable. I could not track where I was, but I imagined I could see my mother preparing food in the kitchen. As it was getting late, I gestured my thanks and began to walk away. The old woman ran up to me. She said something, but I could not interpret her meaning. What was she saying? Did she still want to gobble me up and grill me over the fireplace?

Shortly after that, a flood of people swarmed around me, speaking their unfamiliar words. The high-pitched tones and loudness began to hurt my ears. It sounded to me like musical instruments that needed tuning. The crackling sound of people's voices made me feel a chill. Then an English speaker came up to me. He asked me where I lived. I told him that it was faraway. He asked me if I had a telephone number, which I gave to him innocently, and he called my mother. He reassured me that I was okay and that he would take me home. I was not sure what he meant. Would he put me in the trunk of his car and send me to China? I was uncertain what would happen, but I did arrive home safely.

The thrill of being an adventurer did not stop me from going elsewhere. I also explored places such as the Saint Lawrence Boulevard, a vital artery that goes through many of Montreal's ethnic communities. I have a fascination for every culture differing from mine. I loved these explorations, perhaps because nobody judged me when I visited. I imagined I was a whip-wielding explorer of cultures, a young female version of Indiana Jones, a character who of course had yet to be created for another 30 years. However, the events of that particular day in Chinatown had a particular impact on me. That day I discovered my fascination with adventures of the unknown. Chinatown became the first setting that motivated me to travel to Asia later in life. I hopped on a train, followed the masses of people, and discovered a complex social organization full of unfamiliarity, mysticism, and color. Because people in this new world looked at me differently, I took on the role of a pioneer. Sadly, because of my tendency to wander alone, I became a mislabelled and misunderstood child, who people considered atypical.

I often reflect on that adventure, and how Chinese people and North Americans sense child care differently. As I strolled through the streets on my own in Chinatown, no one worried about me until I brought myself to somebody's attention directly. I wonder if the same kindness would be extended to a small girl in Chinatown today. I could have been taken by human traffickers, or kidnapped by a pedophile. Fortunately, I left the scene unscathed and these kind and caring Chinese people protected me. It is no coincidence that in my later years, I would question childcare, mislabelled individuals, family values, and how people react to the unfamiliar.

I entered school at age four, but when it came time for me to enter the first grade, the school authorities suggested my parents place me in a special-needs class. My parents came from autocratic societies where the voices of authority held much weight. They allowed the school to place me in a regimented, special-needs setting, and it was not the right fit. I assumed that I was doomed to be a non-achiever. To avoid ridicule, judgment, and boredom in the classroom, I spent long and peaceful hours reading or listening to the classics in the library. I manage to escape by watching when the teacher was not looking. Then I snuck out of the classroom and ran out the nearby doors, I felt free as a bird and headed to the library, where collections of books and music awaited me.

The music of Mozart was my usual escape from a confining environment. I knew the exceptional class setting was not for me. At the library, I also became fascinated with books that portrayed artwork in unusual ways. I imagined having an apperception, and fit into the Pacific world that Gauguin or other artists painted. At times, as I was listening to the melody of the music, I had an illusion of wearing a hula skirt waving my body side to side. Smells of the ocean and visions of mermaids came into my mind. I was withdrawing into the works of artists and their world. I had a 'living perspective' by capturing all the complexities that my eyes observed. I wanted to see and sense the objects in the paintings, rather than think about them.

Eventually, I wanted to get to the point where 'sight' was also 'touch.' I would take hours sometimes to ponder what the strokes meant to me, as I listened to Mozart's music drawing me into another place. The music sounds pounded loudly in a padded room and no one could get my attention. Some of the stronger strokes in paintings impelled the passion of the artist. However, the truant officer did not approve of my independent choice, and placed me under observation in an alternate environment. In a way, my journeys all came about because I did not fear harm. I needed to feel challenged and was not, which determined my choice to spend my class time in the library. By exposing me to the unfamiliar music, artwork and mesmerizing stories at my fingertips, my education continued whimsically. When I reached the seventh grade, a teacher approached me in a caring way. I was not sure what he wanted. I thought he was just going to make me jump through hoops, and I was not interested. The man smiled and assured me that his proposal would be like being in the library, so I did not resist. I was receptive to his questions, and I took a test when asked. The results revealed I was an achiever well beyond my grade level. The score was another signal that I have an extraordinary purpose.

In the library, I studied some of the great thinkers of the world. I discovered people like Dr. Robert Kearns, Dr. Patch Adams, Dr. William Glasser, and Einstein, to name a few. Throughout my life, such men make it all relevant for me to seek out thinkers. Through my studies, I found that I shared likenesses with some of these great men. As they had been when they were young, I was a mislabelled youth with unconventional thoughts and ideas. I was part of a group of youths who were, early in their lives, resolute not to be capable simply because they received labeling as learning or behaviorally challenged. Consider someone like Dr. Robert Kearns. He caught a glimpse of some new thinking on his wedding day, when he tried to open a champagne bottle and the cork blew off. Because of this mishap, he injured his eye. In addition, it gave him the idea that people can catch a partial glimpse of something, a notion which later led to his invention of windshield wipers. Because of glimpses, I too recognize things that lead me to invent new ways to wipe out matters that are troubling.

Eventually, I developed alternate coping strategies to deal with my particular idiosyncrasies, and began to excel at school. The nonconforming settings I chose, like the library, led me to question educational practices and exceptional needs environments. Because of my different approach to seeing things, I learned best through travel and exploration. I collected data by thriving through experience. I thought when I was older I might study psychiatric nursing. I had a fascination with how the human mind works. Even as a young child these early experiences beckoned questions in my mind. Why is it that people start by criticizing a person who acts or speaks differently, and assume that person to be a numbskull, criminal, mentally imbalanced, or something else?

Michelle Malkin, American political commentator and author, has talked about America 'wiping out' the strong people, implying that Americans are tossing unconventional thoughts aside. Instead, intelligent people are accepting the corrupt and the radical. Her own unconventional thoughts lead Malkin to receive profiling as a cultural radical, and some media began to refuse her an audience. Media assumed her voice to be controversial. Paul Kellogg is another syndicated contentious columnist that carried out an unprecedented, in-depth study of the industrial life, and the associated social problems that were not working. He presented some powerful and different values to the approach of governance, and like Dr. Robert Kearns, captured a glimpse of new considerations. Negative assumptions continue to address people with difference. I suspect that because I am different, and so are these people, we simply belong to another class of intellectuals.

CHAPTER 2: Newcomers

RIDING THE INFLUENTIAL WAVES: KEIKO AND CUPCAKE – 10 YEARS

I grew up in an upper middle class setting. Everyone in the community was Caucasian and lived in pleasant bungalows or semi-attached homes. Many homes had single stories with low-pitched roofs, brick exteriors, front porches, genteel-sized backyards, and plenty of space between. Some of the homes had climbing vines of wisteria or fetterbush, their blue, pink, or white blossoms clustered together over the bricks. Just taking in the colors of these vines and watching the humming birds and butterflies fluttering about created a panoramic view. The landscaping was incredible because Italian gardeners cared for most of the yards. They cut bushes and formed them into the shapes of animals, creating natural enhancers between homes. No matter where I walked, nature's beauty and friendly neighbors surrounded me. This peaceful setting had a mesmerizing effect.

The environment made me imagine I was in a small park that had babbling tones of a rambling stream or a fountain with water trickling down. The surroundings gave me inner peace and balance almost like a backdrop for staging the play of Alice in Wonderland.

A forest framed the homes in the foreground, and there I found many hiding places. The tall, dominating pine trees talked aloud. This gave me courage to look into the nearby caves. I used to imagine there were exotic fish like the ones in a pet shop called Fire Fin, the Marmalade Cat (*Metriaclima*), and Blueberry (*Metriaclima zebra*). I thought about how they were splashing about in the water. There could be treasures hiding in the caves I discovered. I remember watching red-breasted robins, fluffy rabbits, white-tailed deer, and gray squirrel feeding on seeds. I thought I was in an exciting and colorful place. Eventually, the caves I uncovered became my favorite spot, my home away from home. Of course, the caves did not compare to the semi-attached home where I lived, having multiple levels, many rooms, glorious scarlet carpets, hardwood floors, marble patio, and large backyard. My home suited an heiress. The Truth is, I had no reason to meet people in the community. My real home and make-believe home in the caves were more than satisfactory for me. I played there with my dolls and enjoyed the warmth of the surroundings. Sometimes I allowed my close friends to share my hideaway.

The first foreign girl to arrive in our community was Keiko Tachibana, a Japanese girl who had come with her family. She was the first foreigner to enter our school. No one wanted to get close to her because she looked different. She had slanted chestnut brown eyes, with hair cropped as if someone had placed a bowl on top of her head and cut around it. Keiko's expressions were odd to me, like the coldness you see at a funeral procession. Still, I was curious about her, so I introduced myself.

Since we both went to the cafeteria to have lunch, we chose to sit next to each other. Children mostly ordered their lunches, but we were unpacking what our mothers had prepared. We did this for at least a month without any conversation. We began to know each other using hand signals and facial expressions. I assumed she did not understand English. I wondered whether she could speak English, but was fearful to ask. We could not discuss her habit or my custom, but we had an understanding of some of the ways our cultures differed.

Surprisingly, Keiko had a reasonable command of written English. Her English skills gave us an opportunity to communicate on paper. She told me that in Japan, packed lunches dated to around the fifth century. People went out to hunt, farm, or wage war. They took food with them, usually dried rice, rice balls, or rice with hot water. This worked well for people working outdoors, whether they worked in the fields, on mountainsides, or on fishing boats. In town, they carried their lunches because they did not have time to go home for meals. In contemporary times, the lunch a mother prepares, called a *bento*, is unquestionably a way of communicating with her child. The meal imbues a mother's love because she puts effort into making her child smile when the lunch box opens.

My lunches looked different from other children's because my mother prepared healthy food. Most of the kids brought peanut butter and jelly sandwiches or ordered greasy food from the cafeteria. Even though, I had a paper bag like other kids, the inside ingredients were different. My mother would give me hard-boiled eggs, cold chicken, cold cuts, fried eggs with salami, salads and fresh fruit. Sometimes, she made chopped liver, and that was a turn off. I often threw out my lunch in dislike. I only looked forward to when I had fresh brownies and home-baked goodies. Unlike my packed lunch, Keiko's lunch box was metal and had several compartments. One day, she might have rice balls wrapped in dried seaweed in one section, with pickled apricots, a mixture of turnip greens, and a small fish in other sections. Another day, she might bring a Japanese omelet, broad beans, or other pickled vegetables. Of course, her lunches were incredibly different from what other children brought to school.

Keiko did not speak to me directly, which I did not like. She would avert her eyes while talking to me. It was the biggest issue I had with her. I suppose my facial expressions must have given away my dislike. This caused her concern and one day she passed me a note with her phone number, asking if I would come to her home. This was a clear sign that she understood me well. The following day my mother called her home, and told me afterward that Keiko's parents had invited me to visit her two days later. I was not sure how to feel about it, especially since Keiko hardly ever smiled.

The day arrived. Her house seemed truly empty, but at the same time, the simplicity was impressive. The living room had two transparent screen panels with flower decorum on either side. The walls and sofa were white, contrasted by one black chair. Directly above the chair was a black and white painting. In the far corner was a tall bonsai plant set in a black planter. I knew it was a striking contrast to most North American homes. I waited in silence for a while, thinking that at least an hour must have passed. The soundless atmosphere gave me an eerie feeling, as though in a funeral home. When Keiko arrived, the silence broke. I got an eye opener! I became aware that I assume much about Keiko, and that I had no idea what was in store.

There were language barriers, so first we could not play. We stared at each other, and I watched her mother do origami. I remember her folding paper, turning it diagonally and folding again. Out of just a few strokes, she created 'the heart' that left me with a real special feeling. After having *Kukicha* (茎茶), or a strange tasting twig tea, we played some games, but nothing like what I was used to. To my knowledge, after World War II, games were scarce in Japan. Therefore, we played what was available. **Otedama** was a girls' game. These were small beanbags or *ojami*. Keiko explained the beanbags come from silk kimono remnants and *azuki* beans. I was not sure what she meant, but the game was similar to playing Jacks. We scattered the *ojami* on a flat surface, then tossed one bag into the air. We tried picking the bags up one at a time by catching the tossed bags and taking turns. She also introduced me to **Donjara** or mahjong game images, also called *Ponjan*. There were 81 tiles, traditionally with pictures of boats, planes, and trains with differing colors. We took turns trying to match up the tiles. The game began with the first round called the *oya* or the parent while *KO* symbolized the child. As players, we collected points as we matched more. Somehow, playing just did not seem usual to me, but it was out of the ordinary. At the time, I felt like it was more something for her parents to see us doing together. I found it a strange sensation, for sure.

The facial expressions, movements, and overall habits of Keiko and her family were incredibly unfamiliar. They seemed linear to me, like Piet Mondrian's paintings of the 1960s. This family looked like a grid of vertical and horizontal black lines one might plaster on a wall. Their home was comparable; it gave me a creepy sensation of lines moving straight up or across. Keiko and her parents conversed as though they were a part of the painting. At times, their lines of communication faded almost as if approaching the edge of a canvas. I felt this was a stifling and cold way of being, and I did not like it, because I was a free spirit. This feeling has never left me, and I wondered if it would change growing up.

At the time, I felt carefree and happy, but Keiko's expressions always remained aloof. Each time I met her I wondered why her facial expression seemed so distant, like a corpse. I wondered what exposure she had. Did the Japanese culture teach her to alienate herself? What was uppermost in her mind? She always looked as if she was grieving, and looking away with a sense of shame. Her lips often turned downward. She would look down or to the side to avoid meeting my eyes. Keiko's eyebrows arched outwards in a nonaggressive expression. She usually kept her head tilted forward or bowed. I speculated that something was unequivocally wrong. I remembered the long wait when I first met her at her house. Was it possible that her parents scolded her often?

Keiko took pride in the Japanese *universal* philosophy of how to think. She explained that the way she appeared was associated with her cultural norms. The Japanese people have enormous concern about how they look to other people. They think of it as family honor. Whenever a person does something that might embarrass the family or other people in society, fear sets in among family members. When something worries me, I talk to my family member or a family doctor, but Keiko's family did not. Keiko had to learn to hold any conflicting thoughts within. I imagine she must have been busting inside to talk about matters that hurt. In fact, people in Japan do not usually talk to other family members, therapists, or doctors about their problems. They would feel shame to disclose that they had any problems.

These norms applied especially to their warriors, the samurai. Samurai believed that disclosure causes harm and that honor suicides, or committing *seppuku*, prove the seriousness of doing things correctly. When disobedience or fault occurs, it is the samurai's duty to kill himself to uphold his honor. Keiko's words were harsh, and while she was talking it looked like the shadow of death was following her. I suppose, if there is a breakdown of traditional social norms, people do kill themselves. This was pretty frightening to hear. Then to my disbelief, I learned from my social studies teacher that suicide is a necessary evil in Japan. Keiko had a hard time expressing herself in this area, maybe because it was a taboo subject. In fact, I learned the Japanese have a philosophy to distance themselves from foreigners. The only thing she made clear is that people in her culture do not talk about their difficulties. This left me questioning what her world was like.

Through Keiko's friendship, I discovered more about how Asians express themselves. They are typically far more subdued than Westerners are, and through association, I became more passive in my approach compared to other Westerners. Over time, I understood the Japanese try not to show their feelings of sadness, joy, or pain. They keep a conversational distance far greater than I was accustomed to. Their eye contact is indirect, and this gave me discomfort. However, Keiko's 'silent language' was purposeful. She did not want to stand out among others, and this was her way of displaying humility. All her behavior had to do with thinking about matters beforehand, and acting cautiously. The Japanese value the expression *kabe ni mimi ari, shoji ni me ari* (壁に耳あり、障子に目あり), which means "*the walls have ears, the doors have eyes.*"[3] When the Japanese are unsure of their connection with another person, they take time to watch and consider. I realized this went hand-in-hand with my feelings, too. I was becoming more cautious than ever before and internalized more thoughts for future Asian travel.

Keiko took pride in the Japanese philosophy of how to think. She introduced me to Asian social face values, and the cardinal tenet that Asians share: to save face to preserve honor and harmony within the family unit or group setting. As an observer, I thought Keiko was always pleasing her family. She conformed to their requests without question. Keiko never complained, and this set a tone where change mattered. Our perspectives were vastly different. In Keiko's household, her parents provided signals of how Keiko needed to interact. She followed their cues implicitly without thinking deeply. When I visited Keiko, it was a morbid place to visit. There was far too much politeness and conservativeness, and nothing appeared natural. Her family and friends might beg to differ, but I never saw Keiko disagreeing. To me she was like a person in solitary confinement. In Keiko's world, people did not indulge in personal wishes, but rather followed the cues of the family instead. Their practices preserve honor and harmony by sticking together. This is also how they hid realities from other people, and of course, these values impacted personal relationships. The family was responsible for all members and literally dictated choices. Keiko explained that if an Asian man or woman married a Caucasian, it would eventually cause shame for the family unit. There was no consideration to what the man or woman felt on an emotional level.

What Keiko did not share was how she the Canadian education system had impacted her. From a pragmatic standpoint, her father had come to set up a factory representing Japanese interests. I was too young to be certain, but he probably followed the same principles of behavior. I knew the family hardly mingled socially with anyone from the community, but he did business daily with Canadians. Keiko must have experienced some effects of this family behavior. Her family's norms created a conflict in my mind. I had difficulties understanding how her thinking worked. Why does this create shame? How did her father think that he could do business without getting to know people in the community? I think over time the traditional Japanese norms might have broken down in her home.

I compared Keiko and her humility to some Italians who had moved into our community. She was diametrically opposite in manner from them. The Italians were incredibly boisterous and open in their communication, stood close together, made eye contact, and used their hands a lot when speaking. These were people not afraid to show their emotions! Our community was evolving, and newcomers were adding new aspects to the landscape of our neighborhood. Even though, their ways were unfamiliar to me, it was refreshing to see new habits. The Italians picked the weeds in the open fields where I sometimes played. They would invite me to their homes to eat homemade soups, and my taste for ethnic foods and new cultures grew. The Italians' openness made me wonder what was missing in my understanding with Keiko. I often pondered about Keiko's family, and this was my first exposure to clashes in thinking with people from another culture.

In my primary years, life was first-rate, and I was pretty happy to go to school. When I returned home, I usually played with my small turtle. Sometimes I brought it to my hideaway in the house, a cold storage room. I imagined my turtle was the cashier. Together, we were taking a food inventory about what was inside. Luckily, my turtle never froze, but I suspect the chilly air did take a toll on him. At least, the turtle took the chilliness out of the association I had with Keiko.

One day, my parents surprised me! They were having a birthday party for my sisters and me because we were all born in December. My parents allowed me to invite all the neighborhood children we played with, including Keiko and a dark-skinned girl named Cupcake.

I met Cupcake a few months after Keiko's arrival. She moved into the new apartments recently erected near the school. I did not like where she lived. Her apartment was small and felt dreadfully confined compared to the open spaces of my home. Cupcake lived in a new building. Entering, I could see plenty of trash in the hallways and outside. I remember seeing some small creatures roaming around in the halls. I do not remember for certain, but I thought they were rats. I was frightened, and I chose not to visit her at her home. Instead, I invited her to play at my home, where we had tea parties with our dolls. I even remember bringing her to my favorite hideaway.

My parents sent out invitations for the party.

When the day arrived, my parents inflated balloons, set up table decorations, organized party favors, and set up food and games in our playroom where we had a large fish tank with exotic fish. My mother baked an enormous cake and had all kinds of cold cuts and salads. My parents decorated the playroom so beautifully that any artist would have said it was an astonishing place. They removed the Ping-Pong table to allow much room to play musical chairs, pin the tail on the donkey, and other games. My sisters and I wore new party dresses. I remember wearing a gray floral Taffeta dress with two crinolines underneath. The texture of the crinolines was like wearing starched gym shorts. It was itchy if I walked too quickly. On the other hand, it was a glorious feeling to wear something shimmering, colorful and new.

At 3:00 p.m., Keiko and Cupcake arrived wearing decorative clothing. Keiko wore a traditional kimono, and it was remarkable to see. It was a T-shaped, straight-lined robe worn so the hem fell to her ankle. It also had an attached collar and long, wide sleeves. The kimono wrapped around her body fastened by a belt called an Obi sash, which tied at the back. She also wore traditional Japanese footwear called Zōri or Geta and split-toe socks.

Cupcake looked quite different compared to Keiko. She wore a shiny orange floral party dress tied in the back with a red bow. The barrette in her hair matched the orange-colored dress. Cupcake had black patent leather shoes and white socks just like me. We both wore stiffened petticoats that made the skirt portion of our dresses flare out. They also gave me gifts, and it was pretty exciting to pile them up on a chair. I could not wait until later to open them up. I kept thinking that I could play with the toys they had brought.

Time moved slowly and by 3:30 p.m., no other children had arrived. Food was plentiful. Keiko, Cupcake and my sisters and I wanted to get the party going. We waited until 3:45 p.m., and then we grumbled to my mother. She began calling around to ask where the other children were. Seemingly, because Keiko and Cupcake were guests, some of the parents prompted others not to let their children attend. Community members opposed mingling with foreigners. I questioned why this was occurring. Thankfully, my mother was a persuasive and communicative person. Earlier she had practiced as a medical doctor, so she knew how to talk to the parents to get the children to come. About twenty minutes later, many children arrived. I still have fond memories of what took place, but I also recognized that I had an outstanding mother. My parents are traditionalists at heart, but thought much more liberally compared to most of our neighbors. This event made me wonder if the war caused people to judge others differently. I am not sure about that, because they often reprimanded me when I followed my own pattern.

In reality, other people thought I was a daredevil as no one else wanted to meet Keiko or venture out to meet other newcomers. I had a daring spirit, and I considered it crucial to make friends with people, regardless of whom they were or their origin. I was prominently different and this brought attention to me, much like the renowned men Patch Adams and Mozart. They began traveling early in life as I did. Adams traveled with his family to unfamiliar destinations because of his father's military career and Mozart performed in concerts throughout Europe from the age of six. This exposure gave them a unique frame of reference, as my experiences have for me. Later in life, both Adams and Mozart became renowned for having a higher purpose. They had a passion to have fun, enjoy challenges, experience travel, learn naturally, and experiment. People that knew me considered me an odd child. It gave me a good feeling to know that I was like these men in ways.

At school, I continued my escapes to the library where I would listen to Mozart's music in a soundproof room. I imagined living in worlds afar, and perhaps that is why I had no fear to meet Keiko. Through friendship, I passed on the wonder by letting her listen to Mozart's music. In turn, Keiko exposed me to Japanese conservative folk music. The sounds were incredibly unusual, and our taste for sound was essentially different. I had a zest to listen to music that relaxed me or inflected fun. Keiko's idea of musical taste did not portray the same notions as I liked. The music she presented focused on stories dating back as far back as the thirteenth century. The musicians known as 盲僧 *blind monk* performed a variety of religious and semi-religious texts used to purify households and bring good health and good luck. I did not think this was pleasurable. Some of the other themes Keiko introduced were eerie. They related to ghost stories about the blind. Even though, there were various musical genres besides what she offered, the sounds created a different pitch and I did not find it soothing. I thought I could hear an ensemble of percussion instruments that clanged like cymbals. Listening to combined musical instrumentation like flutes, drums, bells, stringed instruments, and others gave me a headache. Even some of the traditional musical instruments such as Biwa, Fue, Hichiriki, Hocchiku to name a few, sounded harsh. Keiko and her music presentations only stood out because they hurt my ears. Speculatively speaking, I thought she could not appreciate listening to Mozart's magnificent symphonies.

Despite our differences, the friendship between Keiko and me continued to grow in its own odd way. I used to ask Keiko questions about her life in Japan. I wondered if someone took care of her when her parents were away. She looked at me strangely and said that females care for all Japanese children. Keiko put in plain words that her mother and grandmother cared for her. Based on what she disclosed, it seemed as if she did not know that many children received caring in different ways. For example, Churchill and Williams had nannies, instead of female family members who cared for them. I think Keiko had trouble grasping that meeting new people were also okay. For me, meeting new people added confidence, while Keiko stepped back from knowing other people. She always acted guarded, watching her words and her appearance. I tried opening Keiko's mind to new realities, but it was hard. She even asked me why I had a nanny and not a mother caring for me. I explained that my father was ill. She misunderstood that my parents arranged a nanny to be my caregiver only during my father's rehabilitation. Her name was Irma, and when she disliked what I did, she used her knuckles and tapped on my forehead. She did this when I chose not to listen to her. Keiko listened attentively but looked at me oddly and said nothing.

As girls, we sometimes talked about what our future would look like. Keiko told me that her parents already had a spouse picked out for her. When she said that, I gasped. I could not fathom the idea of loving someone my parents picked for me, versus making a personal choice to love a mate. I told her about passionate men like Albert Einstein and Dr. Kearns. They would never put up with an arranged marriage. I explained that people are individuals, and they need to make their own choices in lovers. Einstein had an early romance with a young Serbian woman, Mileva Maric, and they fell in love. Dr. Kearns picked out a woman who infatuated him, and they married. When Keiko heard about this, she bowed down her head and said nothing. During my teenage years, I thought Keiko's parents were unreasonable. They were forcing her to accept their decision when she had the ability to make choices of her own. I was young and judgmental about Keiko coming from a collective society with different values.

Even though, community members subtly expressed their disapproval that I interacted with her, I remained good friends with Keiko for many years. After we had graduated, there was a 20-year gap before we reconnected. When we met at a reunion, we had no delusions that our cultures differed. Regardless, we cared about each other.

I was too young to recognize Cupcake's origin, but I disliked seeing her living standards. I detested the stench, the glaringly dirty environment, the crowds of people hanging around, and people talking loudly. No one had a value of privacy. These events marked for me how class differentiation begins from a young age through exposure. These scenarios left me impressionable about what I loathed. Even though, I did not like everything I saw with my friends, I became creative in adapting. I thought living peaceably with Keiko and Cupcake was still the best choice. I suppose I followed my mother's path of accepting people, whoever they were, to have intellectual capital. Something is amiss, and I question why environmental injustice exists.

I think my experiences with Cupcake and Keiko helped me to accept people of all nationalities and races readily. I remember my mother supporting my choice in having an Asian and an African girl come to my birthday party. Of course, my actions were different from other children. Most children were watching television shows about race. For example, the popular series *The Harlem Detective* was a police drama on New York City station WOR-TV. This weekly series focused on a pair of detectives (Black and White) who examined the crime in Harlem. The episodes revealed that regardless of color, people had the same condition of being human. People were talking about the lovable bigot Archie Bunker, in the series *All in the Family*. Archie was the lead character, and people listened to what he had to say, even though he had strong opinions, was uneducated, and a blue-collar worker. There were no bones about racial and political views during the late fifties and sixties. Values like these occur out of every negative stereotype imaginable. This included issues on homosexuality, women's liberation, racism, impotence, and more. The show ran on CBS and claimed to be a situational comedy. Language and insulting projections from the fifties that had previously received censorship from television, were suddenly airing again.

When Keiko and Cupcake moved away, our friendships matured and changed. At the same time, my reflections on them did not change much in later years. But through them, I first learned of cultural differences. I felt a tremendous desire to explore the world outside the community. I had no idea about the possibilities. I become curious about what I might experience and whom I would meet.

CHAPTER 3: New York City

AFRICAN AMERICANS: SCOOTING ON HARLEM'S SURFBOARDS – 14 YEARS

As mentioned earlier, my parents were traditionalists. They allowed me to earn spending money by baby-sitting, but they also expected that if I worked at night the neighbors drive me home. Since I disliked school immensely and found it unchanging, I felt a yearning to explore outside my community, at fourteen years old; I decided whimsically to visit my Great-aunt in Brooklyn. This was just after finishing baby-sitting, and I could hear the owls hooting. With money, and buses still running, I told the neighbors my mother would not mind me walking a short distance. Instead of walking home, I walked a couple of blocks to the bus station and went downtown. I got off at the central bus depot to buy a bus ticket to New York City.

I headed to the bus, and the number was easily visible and brightly illuminated. People were boarding and loading their baggage. The movement created by the carrying, pushing, and settling was disturbing. I wished the people would hurry up and find a seat, but this did not take place right away. I sat down next to the window up-front. I imagined we were already on the way on an exhilarating journey. I had no plan, but I assumed everything would fall into place. A burly, towering, dark-skinned man sat next to me. I preferred having no company, but the bus was filling up. I had no choice but to sit next to him. The man fumbled about for a while and finally settled in his seat.

I looked out the window and saw new buses arriving. I anticipated we would leave soon, and I started to feel sleepy. Although I made all efforts to keep my eyes open, the battle was futile, and I began to close my eyes. Bus movements compare to Aladdin's magic carpet as if we had been traveling for a while moving up and down in an almost Zen-like rhythm. Suddenly, I felt a nudge on my shoulder. I tried ignoring it, but the tapping was insistent. Half awake, I looked at who was poking me. It was the brawny man that sits next to me. I asked him what he wanted. He told me the customs officials would be arriving, and I needed to fill out some papers. I had no idea about that, and I asked him what it entailed. Through a brief dialogue, he helped me complete the papers, and telling authorities where I was going to stay.

I thought after completing the papers, our conversation would end. Instead, he asked me where I was going. Before responding, I started looking at what he wore and noting how he appeared. My parents always told me that I could judge a strange person by these things and by how the person behaved. The only thing I could say is that he looked like my grade seven Caucasian teacher except he has dark skin. I admired my grade seven teacher because he switched me from an unchallenging learning setting to one in which I could get challenges to learn. Both men were extremely tall. He looked a little odd to me because he was tremendously hairy, but he had a friendly, outgoing disposition. I also noticed that he wore a pinstriped suit and carried the same black bag as my teacher. I guess my gaze bewildered him. Then he asked me if I am hungry. The mere fact that he showed concern reminded me of my teacher. I felt an automatic sense to trust him. After all, he looked a lot older than me, he acted sensibly, and he did not bother me too much. The man seemed overly concerned about my well-being. I was not sure why this was so; I just assumed people display kindness, but I was naive. Our dialogue continued, and he was also going to Brooklyn, the same place I plan to go. Since we were both going to the same general area, he offered to take me to my Aunt Bessie's home.

In the late sixties, people thought little about pedophiles, kidnappers, serial killers, drug dealers, pimps, and human traffickers. During the hippie generation, people were revolutionizing their thinking. Discussions are about loving a neighbor than being wary of strangers. I had no idea that I could have been at risk. Surprisingly, the bus landed in Harlem, and this was an unsafe area for a little girl. Any number of possibilities could happen. I saw some strange looking men running towards the bus. They were banging and creating a ruckus so early in the morning. I had no idea what they were up to. Other men in the distance were wearing black leather mafia-styled hats, and the bus lights reflected on them. They were wearing many heavy looking gold, and reminded me of Mohammed Ali, Mr. T or George Foreman, prancing around in boxer shorts wearing bold, chunky, gold chains. I am not sure what they were doing, but a heated argument takes place. I began to think these were scoundrels doing something underhanded. Of course, I did not know this for sure, but I also did not want to be one of their victims and fear set in. Two men remain at the back of the bus. They might have been brothers because they looked alike. The men had broad shoulders and their faces were large and squared off. They had beady looking eyes that seemed dead. I thought this way when I turned around. I worried that they were going to steal items from passengers.

The man sitting beside me watched my nonverbal cues. He told me it would be all right and to turn forward. Since his words were reassuring, I began to feel much safer. I waited for the man to pick up my luggage, and I followed him off the bus. We arrived in darkness. I am surprised to see many people out in the streets. Unexpectedly, the setting reminded me of Cupcake's world. Some of the people were nattering about various subjects. Surprisingly, I see rats running into trash bins. There were some bizarre looking women who dressed provocatively. They revealed their breasts and wore skin-tight miniskirts. Their underwear is visible as outerwear and complimented by designer black lace panty hose with knee-high boots. They waddle from side to side as if they were an imbalanced pendulum. New York City looked thoroughly alien: hostile, dirty, and unfriendly. I was glad the man on the bus was going to escort me to my Aunt Bessie's home.

I followed the man out of the bus and walked forward. One of the men stopped me. He said, '*Hey sweet stuff, come my way.*' The broad-shouldered man from the bus said something to the man, and he went away. Then we headed to the taxi stand just around the corner. In a short while, I arrived at my Great-aunt's house. I knocked at the door, but there was no answer. I knocked again, and I could hear some sounds of movement behind the door, but still no one answered. This time I thumped at the door several times, and my Aunt Bessie answered the door. Her eyes twinkled, and her body language sparkled when she saw me. She welcomed me warmly, and was brimming with delight. Like a pot of fresh Brazilian coffee, she suddenly began percolating once I arrived at her home. The powerfully built man took note of my aunt's phone number and address. I assumed this was his way to remain connected.

The next day, I did not wake until 10:00 am. I could hear bustling sounds of Brooklyn streets. As I looked out the window, rabid happenings were taking place. Clothing designers had urban style clothing lined up on racks and mounted on heavy-duty steel rolling clothing carts, and I saw the rubber casters undulating across the streets. In a close distance, there were hipster pickle vendors. There were ginormous barrels of pickles with an array of colors and aromatic delights including spicy garlic stalks, chipotle carrots and curried squash. Some men were selling hot dogs and using pushcarts. The alchemy of pickled food products and spices, and the burning sensation of distilled whiskey made nearby was making my nostrils grow. Then I thought I detected a mild 'smoky' aroma, perhaps reminiscent of smoke from a log fire. Instead, the strong whiff came from my Great-aunt's breakfast nook. She prepared waffles, eggs, toast and freshly squeezed orange juice for breakfast. I enjoy watching her turn on the gas flames and cook. After eating what my Aunt Bessie prepared for breakfast, we both sat down to look at an old photo album. I have intrigue to see old family members, and historical fact-finding dictates my future journey.

A little while later, I heard the phone ring. It was my cousin Sheila, calling to check on my Great-aunt. This is when she discovered that I was Bessie's guest. Not long after, Sheila was on the doorstep, pacing and looking distraught at my presence. I wondered what she was so upset about, but I simply ignored her anxious movements. As though she were psychic, the phone rang just as she walked towards it. The person at the other end wanted to talk to me. The caller was the man who had guided me to my Great-aunt‘s home. He told me that my parents worry about me and that I should prepare to return home. I had no idea how or why he had called my parents. I thanked him for his call, but I had my own agenda. I wanted to stay with my Aunt Bessie, and I had just arrived.

I could not understand why so much fuss happens. My Great-aunt seemed hugely pleased that I was there, but my cousin's facial expression, full of contempt, said something else. Sheila told me that my Great-aunt was not well, and I needed to go home. I did not understand what was happening. Aunt Bessie looked more magnificent than ever. The following day, the man I had met on the bus came and said I should return home. I am disappointed that I could not spend more time with Aunt Bessie than I wanted. We did not even have a chance to go outside her door, walk in the open market, and smell the excitement in the air.

Years later, I learned that my Great-aunt had Alzheimer's disease. This is a progressive brain disorder affecting about five million Americans. It is the sixth leading cause of death that affects seniors living on their own. The problem is so severe that one in every eight older people, in the United States, becomes affected. This disease has no prevention, cure or measure to slow down, and 1 in 3 seniors die.

My parents told me Aunt Bessie had accidentally set fire to the apartment the day before I arrived. Luckily, the fire stops. I had a hard time believing this; I could not imagine they were describing the same Aunt Bessie I knew and loved. After all, she had known me when she opened her door. I will always treasure those memorable moments we had together, no matter how brief they were. At the time, I still had my doubts that she was genuinely losing her memory. I understood that this disease could cause her to forget what she was doing, but I did not like that her senses were reducing. Because I never saw any evidence in her behavior, I thought my cousin just did not want me there.

I do not know why, but then, my gut tells me that this would be my last visit with Aunt Bessie. My instincts were correct. Aunt Bessie died of Alzheimer a few months later when I was still a teenager. After I had made the trip to New York, my parents prevented me from traveling on my own again. My Great-aunt buries in the cemetery, and I am not present. All I could do was grieve. There are moments that I hang on to those precious reminiscences of our last visit. Luckily, there was a protective and caring man who brought me to see her one last time.

Surprisingly, even Dr. Robert Kearns, the brilliant inventor that battled with the world's automotive giants died of Alzheimer too. I heard Dr. Kearns last breath was in a nursing home, in Maryland. His lonely plight was in a basement, in Detroit. My Great-aunt died alone and so did Kearns, in a lone flight against the mighty world. Aunt Bessie made no monetary gains because a woman caring for family does not receive much attention. As for Dr. Kearns, he gained some vindication in the form of $30 million in settlements from Ford and Chrysler. In fact, all he wanted was the opportunity to run a factory with his six children. As a man, he receives notice for his assets (not caring), but also expires alone.

At age 14, who would think that I would get a safe, personal escort to my aunt's home? Today, it is more likely that a young girl arriving at night by bus in Harlem faces unfortunate luck. Would people today notice or care about a little girl—or any person—next to them on a bus or train? I still believe there is a loving spirit in all humanity, but this adventure provokes thought. I came to the realization that I was clueless about worlds outside my community. I had little social understanding of the world around me.

Looking out from the bus, I saw how young girls found their ways to make pocket money, although I did not fully understand what I was seeing at the time. Such exposure caused me to wonder what was taking place, what those young girls were doing in those dark places. I had urges to see the unknown, but I was naïve about shady practices. Because I journeyed late at night on a bus, people thought I was a strange child not to be at home. In later years, as an instructor, I saw girls like this in Juvenile Holding Centers, and I learned that these girls were part of human trafficking or other criminal doings. In the 1960s and 1970s, families and schools withheld information about societal demise. Thus, I am clued out about strangers, the aging progression (losing memory), criminals, and any number of such topics. I had no idea that I could cause harm to me. I realized I needed to learn more about the nature of people than I knew.

I suppose **a pivotal event in my life** was a journey taken in my mid-teen years. I have few thoughts about this, but it impacted my siblings. My father favored me because I had a like image. I enjoyed the way he spoke, as he did not come across as commandeering as my mother. If I complained that my back was sore, he made my sisters or brother clean the bath for me. As a result, siblings stressed too much favoritism occurred. I think he took pity on me, because he has guilt that I experience a non-challenging academic environment, in which he and my mother had agreed to place me. My father has involvement in the political arena. On occasion, he made trips out of the country to attend to business. When I was about sixteen years old, he took me to Chile with him, and for reasons I never understood, any of my siblings or my mother came along. During that time, I met dignitaries and saw the light in areas I knew little about. I remember moments when my father would leave me alone, and I spoke with the officials, not aware that it would be my destiny to meet with diplomats again, later in life.

Sometimes, the altitude of our travel was so high up, I was gasping for air. I tried to capture the beautiful imagery in my mind, and long after I treasured the images of the experience my father had given me. I consider this time pivotal in my life. Images became fundamental for the directions I have taken. My first true self-direction was guided by fanciful visions in art therapy (same as being on the Andes Mountains).

I resembled Margaret Naumburg as we both challenged new frontiers in vision. Naumberg became famed for instituting the professional field of art therapy. Her world and mine seemed alike as we both studied at Ivy League and reputable schools. Our thoughts mirrored reforms, and educational, intellectual, psychiatric restructuring, medical perspectives, and the impacts of nature, art and logic. I am influenced by many humanists (psychologists, psychiatrists, physicians, educators, and parapsychologists). They forge new directions in self-healing. Some of whom included John Dewey (pragmatism), Beatrice and Sidney (politics) and Maria Montessori (humanism). I prefer Charles Cooley (The Looking Glass Self). Having all of these likenesses, I felt Naumberg, and I shared the same world.

My expedition into the Arts became hugely analytical when my brother-in-Law, a psycho-pharmacologist sent me pieces of artwork done by mentally challenged patients. At the time and he worked for Ciba-Geigy and Sandoz in Basil, Switzerland. These were the world's leading pharmaceutical and specialty chemical companies. When I received the artwork, I suspected the Swiss organization had experimented with these people. I assumed they were governing drugs and assigning them art projects, but I was not certain. I am 19 years old and I grasped less about the world around me. All I recall was seeing artwork in various forms. Collages, flashing colors, and images beyond my belief. I saw how emotional distress stemming from the symptoms of psychiatric disorders expresses in the artists' work. This was a unique exposure and gave me insight into the minds of individuals with chronic mental illness, and with bizarre human behavior. I was emotional at the time, feeling uncomfortable in my own skin, seeing artwork in many forms while worrying about my art teacher and my father who were both sick.

From the powerful images of the artwork, my curiosity peaks. I wonder about the central themes of my own artwork. I began to think if my talents compare to that of others. In my pastime, I created paintings, sculptures and used a variety of art mediums. I won competitions for the artwork I created. After seeing the artwork of the mentally challenged, I began to branch my thinking. I volunteered at residences for the mentally challenged while attending a local University to acquire a Bachelor of Fine Arts. I considered myself an abstract thinker. I decided I did not need to take basic art classes, so I registered only for advanced art courses. It was then that I began disliking Fine

Arts. One professor had me create numerous exercises exploring negative and positive balance using the same form over and over again. Then I became disenchanted with the formal study of art. I was not interested in following the notions of others, and stopped my studies at the university. It was not until later in life, when I relocated to the United States that I refocused my interest in the Arts, in the direction of deep, independent study in the field of Art Therapy.

I also volunteered with at-risk youths and did the artwork with them too. Visions are abrupt, striking, and out of the ordinary, and something inside me triggers. Art therapy implies the creative method is a means of resolving emotional conflicts and fostering self-awareness and personal growth. My conviction was strong that this was how I could use my emotional intelligence to heal.

Emotional stability gives me an inner drive to do what I think is right regardless of what others think. I felt that I had individuality and cemented my belief that I was an abstract thinker. I remember when I was a child I enjoy meeting foreigners and seeing their unique clothes. I once borrowed a sari from an Indian lady I met. I put it on and walked barefoot through the center of town, and friends of my parents remarked to them that I was a nonconformist. My siblings, who were angry and jealous that my father favored me from early childhood, did not admire my eccentricity, but it also showed up in creative thinking and my artwork.

My own art therapy incited me to help others see the personal 'bridges' they access, explore and communicate about feelings and memories (including unconscious ones), as well as related psychotherapeutic issues this evoke. I have seen people from all walks of life and positions interact with their own memories including sublime conscious, but snapshots of associated thoughts and feelings that emerge. This made me more aware of people not only on an intuitive level, but I began reading people's nonverbal and visual expressions. There were valuable representational objects, symbolic self-constructs, and metaphorical transitional objects that made my own reflections integrate into theirs. It is for that reason, my studies evolved to include the many facets of behavior and therapeutic rudiments. Whether I think about Borobudur Temple in Indonesia, the Taj Mahal or the Navajo sand painting ceremonies, I see the medicine of men, but I am a woman. In the tides that roll towards me as I move into the waters of my thoughts, I create medicine for men and women alike (as does Dr. Patch Adams). Surely, you (the reader) are also becoming emotionally intelligent and growing introspectively.

CHAPTER 4: Montreal

MENTAL SURFACING & LEARNING ABOUT THE TIDES – 18 YEARS

When I was a teenager, the youths were cruel. They would put gum in my hair, call me appalling names, and tell me I was deranged. Sometime in my senior high school year, I enrolled myself into the psychiatric ward, where I stayed for three months. I did this because I no longer could deal with the emotional issues related to my dying father, the resulting chaos in my family, insensitive youths and the lack of acceptance for whom I was.

This was time for contemplation and quiet. I spent time reading books, and when I felt at peace, I took pleasure from painting, sculpturing, and listening to music. I noted patients that had obsessive habits, dressed strangely or severely medicated. I saw psychiatric nurses and doctors sometimes put people into straitjackets as if these people had no right to liberties like others. I was curious staying where I was, so there were times I walked down the halls in the ward. I noticed that some people stayed in another section of the ward, which led to another hallway. Seemingly, the most severe patients got housing elsewhere. Staff directed me to return to my area when I wandered into this section.

I managed to walk down the hall without anyone noticing me. I could hear strange sounds coming from some rooms with barred windows and locked doors. Those people were off-limits because many were 'hysterical.' On several occasions, I remember seeing some people running out of their rooms when doors were ajar. I heard these were people receiving insulin-coma therapy for drug addiction. Their behavior was erratic as if they were escaping some unknown harm. I also recall seeing group sessions where some of these people sat passive because of unconventional electroshock therapy, drug treatments or reasons unknown to me. I was fascinated by their sessions and watched from a distance. I watched nurses and doctors team together to place some patients into straitjackets by binding their hands behind their back. Many of the patients in this section rarely wore proper clothing or had nutritional meals while in the psychiatric ward. On one, occasion, I saw a nurse having sexual relations with a patient. I am shocked at what I saw and heard. Later, the pair of them were removed to an asylum.

While I was in the psychiatric ward, I decided to review Socionics. Dr. Ira Augustinian, an economist, sociologist, and psychologist, who adjusted the work of Carl Jung and Antonio Kepinski, developed Socionics in the seventies. It measures a person's psychological type, the predictability of how connections develop, and identifies a person's socio-type. The development describes common grounds with another person or group, and elaborates on what is within the normal range of other people. In Socionics, each personality type has association with a famous person or character's social roles. Examples of personalities used are Alexander the Great, Honoré de Balzac, Sandra Bullock, Rene Descartes, Fyodor Dostoyevsky, Theodore Dreisler, Alexandre Dumas, Maxim Gorky, Hamlet, Sherlock Holmes, Victor Hugo, Aldous Huxley, Jack London, Napoleon, Don Quixote, and Maximilien de Robespierre. Traits characterized by the many personality types used in this study were 'romantic' (as Sandra Bullock), 'conqueror' (as Alexander the Great), 'helper' (as Dostoyevsky), and many more.

I used the principles of Socionics to compare myself to some of the great men that I had studied. I was surprised to learn that Dr. Patch Adams journeyed an analogous path to mine. We have a sense of humor, enjoy storytelling, and take pleasure in ethnic foods. People thought I was naturally warm-hearted, and this was the same for Adams. Our character traits match Dostoyevsky. Like him, we were helpers. In our mutual adventures, we addressed helping humanity by providing free attention. Adams' focus was on medical care, and mine was on helping sensitize people to diverse conditions. Our fathers traveled, making them absent. When our fathers returned from their travels, they had a compelling need to command (a result of military training). For Adams, he traveled with his family early in life. As for me, my travels started later, but both of us discovered how cultural differences clarify thinking. In our lives, our mothers became the source for creating peaceable circumstances. Adams coped by clowning around, and I became an artist. When matters were unsettling, we reacted by having deep depression. Through our mutual vision, we saw how other people appeared. My secondary personality traits compare to Dumas (the peacemaker), Jack London (a pioneer of new thinking), and Huxley (the reporter). This is because we wanted to see better circumstances taking place and we wrote our stories.

Kearns and Adams also spent time in mental institutions. They could not deal with attachment. They felt caring often resulted in confusion and frustration. Although hard to fathom, the prosecutor for Ford Motor Company labeled Dr. Kearns an imbecile. This brilliant inventor and former intelligence officer could no longer tolerate how society cast him aside when he acted differently, and he briefly became delusional. Regardless, he found his way out of the mental institution. His 12-year journey showed that human behavior could change if one embraced new patterns of thinking. His deliberation during his trial allowed him to win his case.

Adams experienced notable difficulties when his lover rejected him. He broke down emotionally and self-enrolled into a mental institution. This spurred him to think more deeply than in earlier times. He determined that a person's idiosyncratic behavior was unquestionably an innate wish to get attention and, more often than not, accepted by society. By examining what people did, Adams went to the root to authenticate why people were there. Through his own reality, he made weighty discoveries. He thought people needed redirection to experience true happiness. Through his burning need to change societal ways of helping people, Adams decided to become a doctor. In his medical studies, he excelled above the norm, so much so people questioned his abilities. They assumed he was cheating, and they said he was unfit to be a doctor because he brought too much humor to medicine. Like Adams, when I was in the psychiatric ward, I was literally deciding who I was.

Churchill and Einstein also tie in to the way things happened for me. According to eminent psychiatrist Dr. Ronald R. Fieve's 1997 paperback *Mood Swings*, Winston Churchill had bipolar disorder. Fieve detailed a psychological study which tied Churchill to being a manic-depressive or cyclothymic (a person with intense mood swings). Intriguingly, Churchill modeled after his mother, Jennie Jerome, an heiress. Media reviews suggest Jennie is too occupied, appearing aristocratic. She acts with refinement and is coquettish. She supposedly did not care about what others thought or said. Projections of Jennie, view her as having abnormal energy, belligerence, visions of grandiosity, and a lack of restraint, which mirrored Winston's traits. This made him more empathetic than the average man and almost feminist. His tendencies portray a man driven to creating humanized personal care for both genders (the welfare system), and parallel to my world. I was empathetic to people surrounding me and did not mind what others said.

We were all travelers wanting to conquer social issues. Learning curves caused all of us to battle our own wars. Notably, Churchill empathized with humanity and later set up the welfare system. All of us had educated mothers in the arts or science. Adams' mother was a teacher and humorist. Churchill's mother was a writer who strongly voiced her opinions. Einstein's mother was a musician. My mother was a medical doctor and polyglot. Our parents were observers (Balzac), and so were we. Through watching, we also became analytical and reasoned as Descartes. Even though, there is less awareness about Kearns' mother, his probable pattern was alike. In our later years, I and the famed men (Adams, Churchill, Einstein, and Kearns) had self-discipline and sought challenges. We beat the odds through invention or creativity, the same traits as Don Quixote. These were all world-renowned men who beat the odds when receiving their Nobel Prize or headlines in the media. This includes me. I have received commendations for diversity programming for youths and adults in the past, where no comparable programming was available.

In all cultural coping, whether it is Archie Bunker stereotyping people or an Indonesian shadow play teaching morality, it is all about connecting with people. Adams employed his creativity to connect with people in novel ways. For example, he used a macaroni pool to bring smiles to a patient. Robin Williams connected with others by bringing amusement while performing live on stage. He did this by noting and mimicking traits people portrayed. As for Mozart, he put all his passion into his music and people connected naturally. His magical world of music became my escape. It brought my psyche to a dreamlike place, making it natural for me to enjoy the arts and have an instinctual passion like

Churchill. Kearns coped by having confidence in what he created. I did the same when I produced prizewinning paintings. Einstein tried to avoid areas of learning in which he failed to excel, but later found ways to improve on his weaknesses, and I did the same. I recognize that all people have limits, but I also surpassed my peers' studies by focusing on learning and spending much more effort than they were willing to put forth. The result is common for me and the famous men.

As I was a freethinker, I always knew I was not helpless, regardless of what others thought about me. I already used my creative energies to channel my visions into painting, sculpture, and diverse learning. In my senior high school years, the art classroom was where I excelled in the creative practices. I liked going to school when I could be in my own space and imaginary world. In my final year of high school, I received an award of excellence and national recognition for artwork I had produced. I created a vision of being in the forest, making the trees fade into the distance. I did this with watercolors on a large poster. It was photographed and posted in the high school yearbook.

After winning that prize, I received many other awards. The artwork I did was a combination of realism and abstract. For example, one painting in acrylics was an orchestra ensemble. Musicians' cutout shapes sprayed around the form. The spray overlapped, creating a musical sensation. I used the tip of a paintbrush to create varying sized sprays and hues. Other artwork included people in different settings, and many people commented how the lovely pastels blended so well. It was a feeling of passion no matter which piece I worked on. I told a story through my vision and add the fine-tuning of Mozart's concerto. It was almost magical because I thrived on completing artwork until the vision came to fruition.

My art teacher was my mentor. Sadly, she experienced continual thrusts of pressure in her head. Somehow, they hurt me, too. I knew something was wrong. When she became ill, my world began falling apart. She was the only individual who listened to me and did not do things blindly. When the pressure attacked her during class time, I was glad I was there for her. The ambulance came to the school, and I accompanied her to the hospital. Her pain was growing, and a brain scan revealed she had a tumor. Then, I knew nothing about tumors, and I was alarmed.

In the seventies, when people experienced mental disorders and tumors, authorities automatically took them to a mental institution. The first experience I had of this was with my art teacher. The authorities placed her in an institution, and it was terrifying. I would sit with her for hours telling her the pain would go away. My discomfort was not as severe as the aches she experienced, but I could feel how intense the pain was for her. I was a worrier, and I paced the floor. I was unsure what would take place next.

One time while visiting, some patients were sitting near my teacher. I distinctly remember seeing a man who looked vacant, as though he was not in this world. My teacher told me he was a recent arrival. Some students put lysergic acid diethylamide (LSD) in his coffee. LSD is a drug that alters perceptions, affects prominent areas in the cerebral cortex and impacts mood, cognition, and sensory perception. I have a hard time imagining the insensitivity of those students. They deliberately created harm for another human being. It was hard for me to imagine the man was only a 20-year old student. He was lucky to be alive.

Eventually, my teachers' cognitions went downhill and I was prevented from seeing her at all times. I imagine she was receiving some therapy, but I thought it was likely drug treatments that caused hallucinations, because I heard loud, shrill sounds coming from her room when I was turned away from seeing her.

This experience taught me that human beings could be cruel and even unaware of the harms they create. I wanted to understand what it was about human nature that allowed this cruelty to happen. This situation gave me the motivation to undertake studies and work voluntarily in psychiatric nursing. In the early seventies, I volunteered at the Douglas Mental Health University Institute, Lakeshore General Hospital, Mount Sinai Hospital, the Shriners Hospital–Canada, and other mental institutions. I wanted to understand conditions such as schizophrenia, mood disorders, anxiety, and suicidal tendencies.

Through observation, I saw schemes to leave people behind so others could gain. People placed in a mental institution could lose their claim to their assets if determined to be crazy. This would allow someone else to gain what was theirs. People might also be committed to a mental facility because they were too influential or vocal in society, allowing others to silence them or claim their fame. It was also during the sixties and seventies that experimentation began to take place, ostensibly to help people who were atypical. Medical practitioners could administer drugs without consent. In other words, a mental institution was a place where people with differences, including the insane, could be dealt with without culpability.

I saw patients before and after shock treatments. This was one of the measures taken in to modify behavior and alter pathological conditions. I remember seeing groups of patients herded together like animals, walking single file and linking by an ankle chain. The entire group looked like bewildered animals that had just come out of Frankenstein's laboratory. My observation was that the doctors were injecting them with an anesthetic, which was probably strong enough to check out an elephant. Nothing about it felt right or Lawful.

To cope with these feelings, I began exploring further into the possible causes of their vacant looks. Naturally, I turned to my imaginary world of the arts. The more I researched, the more I found artwork depicting the inner workings of the mind. Since mental patients do elicit impromptu imagery—whether origin, history of life, or future intent—some answers automatically become apparent in a single piece of artwork. I began looking through the eyes of many artists over the last century. I favored three artists for how they approached emotional imagery, how their work connected to what I saw in reality, and how they expressed themselves: Salvador Dali* (1904–1989), Octavia Ocampo* (born 1943), and M. C. Escher* (1898–1972).

Salvador Dali* (Domènec Felip Jacint Dalí I Domènech) was a well-known surrealistic artist influenced by the psychoanalytical work of Sigismund Schlomo Freud (1856 –1939) and Carl Gustav Jung (1875-1961). His artistic style spread worldwide. Because of how he expressed his visual imagery, his subconscious mind helped him to create art without any intent of logical comprehensibility. Dali was five years old when his parents took him to his brother's grave. They told him that he was his brother's reincarnation, an idea he came to believe. This eccentric artist cultivated an exaggerated perspective of self-admiration. He painted subjects from whimsical, to horror-like visions. This inclination could be the cause of what he saw happen to people in mental institutions. His work focused on such themes as persisting memory, changes in self, being spellbound, and mind mending. Dali's imagery reflected a person who felt alone and distant, needing love. He captured people experiencing transitions in their lives, errors in vision, forgetting, feeling impositions that make people feel helpless and obedient, not out of choice. In other words, Dali was in search of his own identity, and his expressions were not much different from the people I saw chained in the hallway of the mental hospital.

Octavio Ocampo, born in the forties, was a Mexican artist from Guanajuato, Mexico. Ocampo* had a fascination with virtuous and evil forces and created optical illusions in his visual imagery. Even though his themes were different, he came up with the same ideas as Dali. He depicted people as the beautiful petals of a flower, but with broken spirits. This was no different for me than my art teacher going through her challenges and changes. Ocampo's artwork touched on how many mental patients wished for death, but like Dali, there was no logical understanding to what he did.

M. C. Escher* was born in 1898, and he produced many woodcuts. Like Dali and Ocampo, he depicted the endless stairway of life going somewhere, but nowhere for sure. All kinds of possibilities influence artistic expression, but to me these artists had similar patterns of thinking. They saw the mental patients in their subliminal memory and captured how they appeared. Their work mirrored my thought that society was too controlling and unhealthy.

Until the 1970s, it was common practice to lobotomize mental patients and use shock treatments on them. In the 1990s, an article appeared in Freedom Magazine exposing some cases. There was unlawful behavior taking place at mental hospitals in the 1950s and 1960s. The Central Intelligence Agency, National Defense, and the Canadian Forces implemented a program known as 'MK ULTRA,' which gave psychiatric doctors the authority to conduct human experimentation on patients in mental wards, and the patients were seriously crying out for help. Information revealed that two psychiatrists named Cameron and Lehmann had experimented on people freely, many of whom died as a result. The patients I saw in the mental institutions were likely under their jurisdiction, because the hospitals where I volunteered turned out to be where Cameron and Lehmann performed. These doctors conducted hundreds of human experiments between the 1930s and the 1970s, working with chemicals such as chlorpromazine and utilising lobotomy, poisoning and shock treatment. Human psychiatric experiments were far from isolated. People experienced destruction. Too much was amiss in society. No one caught up with these wrongs until many years later. As I stood on the cusp of adulthood, the artwork of Dali, Ocampo, and Escher provided some proof for me, some examples that these realities of human cruelty existed. This discovery was incredibly spine chilling to me at the time. I became aware that humanity is capable of terrible things, and this realization was even more devastating than just the knowledge of the MK Ultra project. All this led me to wonder more about how a person becomes helpless and follows blindly. This is when I wanted to go into psychiatric nursing. I wanted to understand the issues that people had.

I also recognized that this journey related to how and why my parents influenced me. Because of my father's military career, my parents lived under authoritarian control. I experienced a militaristic lifestyle, and their approach towards me was the same. They probably had difficulties coping at times and had mental breakdowns. When they came to North America, societal norms would have differed from their ideologies. As a child, I often misunderstood their meaning, and wartime issues must have made it hard on them. My parents tried bouncing back from their experiences during the Second World War, but there were hardships they had to contend with. For example, my mother had memories of having to hide in obscure places. As a doctor, she helped many of the sick, the dying, and the depraved. On a more personal level, she watched her first husband gunned down, and her daughter died of malnutrition. My father helped with the underground, and he experienced hardships, too. His most intense memory was escaping from the Germans. He fled by giving away his diamond ring, after which he had to jump into a deep waterway while a steady stream of bullets targeted his path. Through all these reminiscences, they still kept a sense of humor, but at night these memories would come back to haunt them. My mother had a sixth sense that she could use to understand more deeply than the average person did. My father kept his worries bottled up inside, but sometimes he would explode.

Adams' mother saw how her husband's commanding ways, a result of his military career, impacted her son. As a teacher, her instinct was to offset his woes by using humor. My parent's modeling is alike. On one occasion, my mother had prepared hot chicken soup for the family. It was a wintry day, and because heat costs were high, they adapted by giving warmth in other ways. When my mother brought the soup to the table, my brother peed into my father's soup bowl—he was not wearing a diaper because we did not have the money. My father giggled when this happened and said, 'The soup will probably taste better.' This comment allowed my siblings and me to laugh aloud and kid around. My parents' sense of humor offset the days when their commanding, unassailable ways caused us fear. Adams counterbalanced his fears by acting unpretentiously, behavior that eventually brought him worldwide fame.

Churchill and Kearns both received Nobel Prizes. This happened irrespective of having impediments. Churchill learned to cope with his father's commanding ways and later followed in his footsteps—his father was a charismatic politician, too. I have little knowledge about Kearns' life in early years, but his father did work at Ford Motor Company. As the organization assembled cars, his father likely had to contend with a chain of command. I suppose both Churchill and Kearns created their own world of humor. As a child, Churchill talked to his toy soldiers and enjoyed their company. I imagine this happened because these objects did not talk back or judge him. This means that Adams, Churchill, and Kearns learned to make fun out of difficult circumstances, a sign of our mutual personality traits. We release our troubles to inanimate objects and laugh about it.

During our growing years, we also experienced the care of a stranger. When my father was sick, my mother hired a nanny. Churchill, Kearns, Adams, and Robin Williams all had a nanny or caregiver watching over them at times. Somehow, we developed some obsessive habits. Churchill turned to drinking, writing, and commanding. Society and the powers that be labelled him a manic-depressive and a rebel. Kearns became an intelligence officer and worked hard at proving he had something extraordinary to offer. Adams earned the reputation of being the unruly and clowning doctor. Williams sought drugs and drinking as a way of relief, and society called him a spoiled, rich kid who spent money freely on all the wrong effects. For me, I do not act to get people's approval. I did what I thought was justifiable whether others thought I was right or wrong. People had the opinion that I was disobedient, because I was an advocate of civil rights. This took place especially during the transforming years of the 1960s. When I fall in love with a man, my experiences reflect likeness to Adams' when he falls in love with a woman. The after effects were the same as Dr. Adams; I also became faithful to helping humanity. I addressed injustices and suffered because of it.

Additionally, we experienced separation anxiety. Einstein escaped from Nazi military control and disconnected from people he loved, but he regrouped. Kearns was in love with his wife, but his devotion to social justice issues led him astray. Naturally, these famous men and I disconnected from people close to us when we traveled. Even though people in society evaluated us as strange creatures with weird habits, we indisputably had some doubts of our own. We became knowledgeable in the arts and adjusted our unique ways of thinking.

According to beatnik poet and author William Burroughs, "*There are no coincidences and there are no accidents.*"[4] My story recounts to you, the reader. You ride along waves of what you may have overlooked or been unaware of in your own life. This may be an attribution to your own exposure, schooling, rearing, and opportunity to travel, fears, or some other reason. When I shared how common genres appear in famous paintings, this was not by coincidence. Themes are about the pendulum of life ticking away at personal worth. Even experimentation on people becomes a clear sign that people are readily disposable. People disrespect, and there is always rationale when people's rights are violated in some form. As for me and the celebrities I mention, we share the quality of feeling reduced when other people take too much control over us. Their assumptions about us are wrong. Therefore, I knew that studying more about the nature of people and their distinctive needs would help me direct my thinking about what is justifiable.

CHAPTER 5: The Family

THE MAGICAL VALUE OF CARING – 20 YEARS

Creative communication in the media highlights the current trends of the time. Even though topics change, the media still focuses on war crimes and violence taking place all around the world. The same focus is in video games and novels. In the sixties, there was an outcry over civil liberties and an accentuation that we lived-in a world of gender differentiation. Schools around the world made distinctions between boys and girls, especially what they could study. Then, North American girls learned subjects such as home economics and art. Boys gained knowledge in mechanical drafting and carpentry. These choices sent messages to society about the roles of the sexes.

When I was in school, I interpreted these North American values as a challenge to cook well. My home economics lessons began with cleaning pots and pans. I did not find it much fun surging into grime, but when the teacher explained there were secrets to making perfect, tender muffins, I became attentive. I focused on gently stirring the batter to moisten the dry ingredients as my teacher had told us to do. At first, I did not stir vigorously. Later, I could not help myself. I began swirling the batter like a tornado. Once I mixed everything, I transferred the batter to a muffin tin and set it to bake. To my surprise, about twenty minutes later, the batter I had whipped produced the most beautiful muffins imaginable. I started to believe that perhaps cooking was the epitome of what girls did best, but that was wrong.

I wanted to recreate these muffins at home, so I followed the same instructions, but substituted ingredients with what was available in our household. I waited patiently and anxiously for the results. When the buzzer on the stove rang, I took them out and was happy to see how incredible they looked. Miraculously, the ingredients I had substituted seemed to be the right ones. Nevertheless, something mysterious had happened, for when I took a bite, my front teeth almost came out because the muffins were rock hard. I acted quickly to find a hiding spot for the spoiled muffins, but I could not find a place. As I looked out the window, I had an idea. Amid winter, birds were hungry, so I thought they would gobble up the muffins no matter how awful they tasted. I thought if I put them in the backyard, the birds would certainly come to eat them. I cleaned up rapidly and did not give it much more thought. When spring came around, the snow melted, and the muffins revealed themselves. The sight of them reminded me this was not where my skills lay.

I asked to get a transfer from home economics to mechanical drawing. When I arrived, I saw the odds were against me. There were no other girls taking part in the class. I fumbled with creating the right angles, and the boys laughed at me. I could not understand their laughter. My tries to draw a family dwelling looked as if I were drawing a medieval castle instead of a contemporary home. I am not sure why that happened. Maybe I paid attention to how the angles looked in my imagination. I created a layout, but it was not acceptable. I could not understand why the teacher said the boys did well. I thought my layout had all the ingredients I wanted for my future home. Naturally, based on the coursework I took, I began to think that I did not fit into a society. I assumed that if Einstein had been one of my classmates, he would have helped angle my thoughts into new areas. Robin Williams and Dr. Patch Adams could have used these events as a comedy skit about the right and wrong of the times. My only choice was to go to the library and remind myself that whether female or male, people need to 'make their own muffins.' By doing so, they can get a taste of what substituting—values, beliefs—feels like. It all boils down to the choices people make—how they 'moisten' the dry ingredients and stir the batter up to create their own unique thinking.

I began thinking about the events of life. I questioned who seriously cares about how we express ourselves or learn except for our parents, siblings, or friends. There is no immediate muffin recipe or drafting formula for success. I only could probe further into what my true ambitions were. I decided that I was no different from other children. I had wishful thinking as they did, but I just did not like learning home economics or drafting. As a pragmatist, I preferred matters to go my way.

Indeed, my thinking did not change much over time. At age 20, I chose to live on my own. My parents did not approve. They thought a young, unmarried woman should not be out of the home. I preferred my independence and rented a studio apartment in a two-story flat. A Chinese medical resident lived downstairs. He was about 35 years old, and we met by chance one day as we both arrived in the building at the same time. He was carrying a bundle of food, and I was intent upon going to my apartment. We were both walking quickly, and we collided. I caught a glimpse of a pastel green box in his bag. When he saw me looking at it, he asked if I would like to learn how to make what was inside. The whole idea baffled me, but I thought, “Why not?” I accepted his invitation. We did live in the same building and were neighbors. I did not think it odd to visit him at his home. He was a doctor-in-training, and I assumed that, like my mother, a doctor would have the highest moral standards. As it so happened, we already had a connection. I worked at the hospital where he practiced, although we did not know it at the time.

The evening began. He took out the pastel green box and opened it, pouring the contents out onto a plate. To my surprise, transparent ovals came out. They sparkled and looked like seashells ready to adorn a Caribbean beach. Next, he took a frying pan and put some oil inside. When the oil had heated up, he placed these oval forms into the pan. In seconds, they were sizzling, bubbling up, and crisping. From transparent, plastic-looking forms, these ovals had become vibrant, multi-colored shrimp chips. A few minutes later, they were all ready to eat, with rainbow colors that looked more elegant than anything I ever ate. There was no oil residue, and they were remarkably tasty. After our first meeting, we continued to meet casually. I felt he was watching me through our conversations. Was this experience going to be like my trip to New York? I wonder if he was another protector, or a lover.

I felt a little uncomfortable guessing where this relationship would lead. It began when I found I liked listening to his stories of faraway places. It was incredibly interesting hearing about the unfamiliar customs of his homeland, and listening to him describe how much he cared about his family. Then one day he asked me where my parents lived and wanted to get their phone number. I saw no harm in providing this information, so I gave it to him. A few days later, I was surprised to get a call from my mother. She told me the doctor had paid a visit to see her and my father. He went there to tell them he would be watching over me, looking out for any lurking strangers or problems. They should not worry about me. In other words, he was like a father figure, concerned about my well-being. After finding out that he had dropped in on my parents, I asked him why he went. He said it was a necessary precaution if an emergency. I never anticipated his intent to do that for me. Later, I came to learn that this is a Chinese norm of creating a family feeling of trust. His caring compelled me to have other Chinese friends. I have found myself drawn to Chinese people because of the kindness they have projected towards me.

I had feelings towards the resident doctor, but they were changing. His behavior caused a delightful, warm feeling, and I began to wonder if he had interest in me, too. He always kept his emotions inside, which reminded me of how Keiko had kept everything secret. When I first met the Chinese doctor, he showed concern for me. I liked that he was so kind and caring. I responded with kindness in return. I hunted to find which words were right to say thanks. I wanted to become closer with him and talk intellectually, but he acted reticently when I approached him. He acted timidly, as if not wanting to know the details right away. Later his meandering eyes clued me in that he did want to know. I imagined there was more to him than met the eye. He was a brilliant resident doctor. I assumed he had many angles to the way he thought. Regrettably, his thinking did not surface right away. Instead, he confused me, especially when he contacted my parents.

I thought that when he went to see my parents, it was a sign that he had more interest in me than I had first thought. I had the inkling that he might be an incredible mate. After his visit to my parents, he decided to have open conversation. He opened up about his personal life, and told me he had a fiancée in China, and that he was to be married in a few months. As he explained these details, the color of his face flushed. He did not appear happy about the imminent event. I guess that had something to do with his invitation to meet him at his home, or coming over to mine. We started to grow closer and became more and more attached. As he spoke, his eyes expressed a yearning to be with me, and a deep sadness would come over him. He said his family had arranged his marriage before he came to study in Canada. He had never met his bride, but the marriage was forthcoming. It would take place after he finished his studies. I cannot remember how I reacted, but I felt odd. He was always smiling when we met, but when he told me this he became depressed. Since we both enjoyed being together, I asked him if he believed he should return home or stay in Canada with me. Since his future bride was at a distance, I assumed he had already changed his mind and was no longer considering marrying her. I could not understand why he held his feelings back. He hid too much from me. He said I did not understand, as I was an innocent woman, still growing. He asked me to think of him as a parent. He said he was much older than I was, and he sighed.

I interpreted his response to be a Chinese value. He had to follow his family's request to marry this woman. Regardless of his emotions, he needed to comply. I knew he was purposely avoiding telling me how much he cared. I disliked these cultural norms, but in later years, I would face a similar experience with another Chinese man. The message he sent became clearer to me when he expressed more helplessness than I imagined. He wanted to stay with me long-term, but could not. I was a woman from another culture, and he would bring shame to his family if he married me. This is an Asian family tenet that children have to follow with blind obedience regardless of their feelings.

I wonder what is the purest form of caring. The resident doctor did not mind if our association was a long-term union. Loving feelings could only be spurious without parental approval. Young Asians' personal beliefs wane in the face of the parents' wishes. Then, Asians could not get something they wanted if it ran counter to societal norms. In other words, Asian emotions are like paintings telling of other, hidden emotions. It is mastery, how they learn to distort their true feelings to appease family, and this is a settled order of society.

Based on my experience, it is the Chinese way that newcomers become part of the extended family. The Chinese have the habit to welcome a stranger. At the same time, when the Chinese emigrated to North America and other countries, they perpetuated their racial identity, ethnic pride, language, and cultural heritage. This is noticeable in viewing the Chinese and Chinatowns in many international destinations, including Cambodia, Hong Kong, Laos, Malaysia, Singapore, Taiwan, Thailand, the Philippines, and Vietnam. The Chinese expression used in greeting, '*Ni Hao Mah*' (你好吗) historically means, 'Did you eat something?' It is a commonly used expression when food was (or is) sparse for everyone. As a result, this expression communicates a family feeling of caring. When next generations migrated from China, the Chinese changed. Many of them adopted Western norms, but still saved the family ingredient. Chinese people typically revere and respect their elders, and filial piety has strong roots.

The extended family (mothers-in-Law, fathers-in-Law, grandparents) usually lived together, with grandparents nearby. Families shared meals together regularly. They would prepare platters together. After completing the preparation of dishes, they put the servings in the center of the table. There were no individual plates, only bowls filled with rice. As years passed, I understood the Chinese medical student adopted me as part of his extended family. He cared enough to oversee what would be best for me in line with his Chinese tradition. Modesty and even humility were vital to him. Further, his cultural knowledge and academic pursuits equivocated to being a good person. Through my various exposures to the Chinese, I learned the family measured success or 'wealth' not merely in financial or material terms, but also educational accomplishment and professional status. I suspect the Chinese doctor understood my background because it was the same for my family. I was more familiar with the relationship-building experience of my own culture than with another culture. When I immerse myself in another culture, I feel an expectation to buy into their customs. In other words, compromise of cultural values is less likely in foreign destinations. As a result, I misinterpreted some of the doctor's cultural traits because our expectations were unalike.

In the Chinese custom, close connections do not surface in the public. When the doctor smiled, I thought he was showing me likability. In fact, he was displaying his embarrassment that he could not hide his feelings. I had no idea he was already committed and engaged to a woman in China. He did not tell me until it was getting closer to the time he would return there. In our communication, the man always added a friendly comment. He would say, "*Mei Gguanxi*' (May gwanshee), or 'it does not matter,' when something occurred mistakenly. It was because of his gentle manner that our relationship steadily became more susceptible than other associations. The doctor chose to 'save face' by not showing his emotions as he wanted. This is because he planned to marry according to his family wishes, but he felt the necessity to tell me because he cared. When I tried asking the doctor more personal questions, he sometimes did not reply. He made the choice of not responding to reduce or remove feelings that may be harmful. He shirked off loving feelings by suggesting his concern was about what I needed to learn. He made all efforts to avoid the potential of causing shame for his family, even when he became too attached to me. Instead, he expected me to understand how crucial it was to be obedient to parents first.

Close connection with the resident doctor, and another connection with a Chinese man blossomed over the years. Whenever he felt his life was in jeopardy, he would make me aware of it. On one occasion, he phoned from South America. He wanted to say that he could hear the rumbles of an earthquake under his feet. Instead, he said I meant more to him than sinking into the ground. I was shaking with emotion and my passion heightened. I expected he might yell out in fear, but instead he held steadfast while the land underneath him moved. He understood life—it was genuinely a series of waves, and we were riding them.

Based on what the Chinese man shared, his thoughts compared to how Keiko behaved. She responded to her parents as if they were Gods, not human beings. Asian ideology does not match with implicit Western values. Despite the efforts the resident doctor made to have me obey my family's wishes, I was not necessarily obedient to my parents, even though I was respectful. This was true also for the famous men I studied. We continually engaged in our own passion and appealed to sensibility. While respecting our families, we nevertheless forged our own path.

My path followed Dr. Adams. We created happiness by connecting to people. His passion was all about bringing laughter to brighten up people's emotions, including his parents. His mother encouraged Adams to be creative. In 2006, Larry King, authored *My Dad and Me.* These were stories about Larry's famous friends, and he described Patch's relationship with his father. He said Patch did not always listen to his father. Information about Dr. Patch Doherty's autobiography is extracted from comedy-drama film in 1998. The film directed by

Tom Shadyac is based on the life story of Dr. Hunter "Patch" Adams. Patch said that it was only right before his father's death that the two had a comfortable conversation. Adams did respect his parents, which is noticeable in the philosophy of his non-profit organization, the Gesundheit Institute. Adams stipulates that his organization is "*dedicated to revolutionizing health care delivery by replacing greed and competition with generosity, compassion and interdependence*"[5] Also, his viewpoint is based on *"the belief that one cannot separate the health of the individual from the health of the family, the community."*[6] This information is from the Gesundheit Institute website. Such words project the implicit value of belonging and being respectful in a family sense. I think it is a pity that sometimes, understanding between family members does go downhill, but connections cannot be a pressure, whether with parents, siblings, friends, or others. A person develops relational understanding through exposure on how to be generous, compassionate, and interdependent. I find being thoughtful and respectful is key. With elders or parents, it is indispensable to attend to matters sensibly. This means compromising at times to keep comfortable dynamics and reduce needless anxiety. At the same time, according to William Glasser, the psychiatrist who created choice theory, people need to feel good about the choices they make.

The welfare policies created by Winston Churchill considered the importance of a well-functioning family, too. Churchill used his emotional intelligence to make all people feel good. He did not limit it only to his parents, and this was identical for me.

Robin Williams also had his unique approach. He believed that by making people laugh, they would celebrate in unison (in a sense, a family feeling). His parents were often absent and traveling. Due to these circumstances, he barely had the opportunity to get to know his parents, so obedience was not even feasible for him. Matching realities happened for me when my father became sick, and my mother traveled to the hospital, to be at his side.

I deduce that these famous men and I converged as passionate human beings without being obedient, but instead acting as shrewd thinkers. Perhaps the vision of communication needs to display some reasonable reforms. If media highlights were transparent, rather than focused on political agendas, maybe we could add to the reality of family harmony regardless of culture. The media have lost family oriented columnists like Ann Landers, who used to give advice to people about difficult associations and good manners. Perhaps asking people their opinions should matter more than merely printing a preselected editorial comment. In the sixties, there was concern about civil liberties. Today, people trust and accept the media and the values presented easily and without much thought. Sadness comes from an accentuation that we live in a world of differentiation. Rather than offer something of substance that makes people feel good or portray justice, reporting focuses on topics that create grim and tantalizing headlines with not enough time to research the facts. Their opinions reflect ignorance because of prejudice.

CHAPTER 6: Old Montreal

STILTED PERCEPTIONS: (AFRICANS, INDIANS AND GENDERS) – 20 YEARS

When I was 20, I walked into Old Montreal and found myself once again challenged in a new environment. I felt the freshness of the air. I was enjoying myself, walking around and passing the time. I even crossed through several cemeteries covered with weeds and seemingly forgotten. This included Ville-Marie's first parish cemetery. During urban development of the area, many graves had to be moved. Archaeologists were called in to study the site, and they found many historical objects. I continued walking through streets and saw a narrow pathway leading to a small black door. Rather curious, I followed my instincts to look inside.

To my surprise, it was a tiny African museum with such unique art pieces! There were small figurines displayed with intricate decorations and small crevices. These cavities were airways that allowed air to flow in or out, creating musical sounds designed for dance rituals. These African musical instruments with tiny carvings were astonishingly distinctive, and their beauty crossed the boundaries of imagination. The minuscule figurines varied in shape, pulsing their own unique spirit of joy. I did not know why, but I kept marveling at the stunning flute-like instruments. What was the original carver's real intent? Were these figurines representatives of known women like Aretha Franklin, the Queen of Soul? Barbara Jordan, congresswoman and civil rights activist from the Deep South? Maya Angelou, author of "*I Know Why the Caged Bird Sings,*" might be among many other possibilities. Perhaps Lorraine Hansberry, the African American playwright best known for *A Raisin in the Sun*?

When I began my doctoral studies in Washington, I met an African woman who reminded me of those African women figurines. She talked a lot about Obeah, a folk magic religious practice from West Africa, similar to Voodoo, that later spread to Haiti and other Caribbean destinations. The African woman addressed human nature as being a dichotomy because of the influences of the invisible world. There were both vicious and good (spells of a healing nature, love, purification, and joyous celebration). The spirits from the invisible world were responsible for invoking the harmony in nature (peace, birth, and rebirth increase a profusion of luck, material happiness, and renewed health). The male figures allowed males to be the authoritarian figures in society. According to Voodoo belief, the male spirit intervenes while a child is still in his mother's womb and identifies his destiny.

The woman I met was in search of soul connections, and at the same time, she held on to animist beliefs blindly. I suspect that her society had strongly imposed its values related to controlling nature, health, wealth, happiness, and connections with the spirit world. She respected the natural world. Nature, she explained, was telling her to go back home. The flute-like instruments were a means of calling women back to their homeland.

According to Rachael Stein, an expert on African ethnographic studies, women accept an "*inevitable degradation and drudgery*" [7] about being in their own skin. This happens when they accept their childhood rearing regardless of advanced studies elsewhere. They accept teachings regardless of whether it is morally correct. I suppose the African woman became baffled by what she discovered, because events unfolded to reveal something she did not expect.

When she returned to Africa, she arrived in the nearest town that had an airport. News traveled quickly that a former resident was coming home. The African woman's appearance was the highlight of the village. When an old friend received wind that she was on her way, a messenger came from the friend's village. The woman tells that since she had sent no communication, money, or gifts before her arrival, the friend had no need to see her. The same value reaction came from other relatives and former friends, too. They found her funny, not affording gifts, giving money, or having a cellular phone. It seemed that she was not a welcome person, because people from her childhood community rejected her.

The woman saw how the information age had changed her family and friends. They once connected *soulfully,* and now such values had been replaced by alternate practices. The tradition of caring was substituted with spending money, like on a cellular phone. Buying a cellular phone is key, because the cost of a prepaid phone was the same as food costs for a month. Since the woman expected to return to North America, she found no need to buy a local cellular phone. Regardless, her relatives insisted she get one to uphold good social standing. They experienced embarrassment that she did not have a phone. They prepared to drive her to a local vendor as a measure to uplift her image. When she resisted, the family members shrieked in bewilderment. Her response was unimaginable to them.

One day, her cousin was distraught, because she did not have the funds needed to activate her phone. When the woman asked why this was such a need, the cousin shared that the phone provided emotional satisfaction. It was instrumental for social networking and happiness. The cousin claimed that when she could not communicate with people, she would feel that matters were amiss. The woman decided to activate the phone for her cousin. When it rang, her cousin was in high spirits. In other words, her happiness came because of spending money.

The woman came to understand that the soul connection was lost. Old values had been replaced by a new set of influential people and things. Before her departure, some of her nieces and nephews requested she spend some money on toys. Since she was still a student, her budget was constrained. She told the children she would get toys another time. When her sister overheard what was said, she commented loudly that the woman *did not care about family*. In reality, she had insufficient means to buy what the children wanted. Her brother had a large home, with cars and wealth on display, because, she surmised, people were evaluating her status based on monetary wealth. People saw each other as worthy only when they had means. Even if a person were intellectually endowed, this did not add to their worth.

The woman learned that her brother had acquired his money in an unorthodox way. This made her unhappy, and she tried talking her family into doing things correctly. Her message fell on deaf ears. They did not care about doing things as before. Instead, the expatriate woman became labeled as poor and less intelligent. Influential people she encountered had the same attitude. They were influenced by other people with money. People with little or no means did not matter. The wealthy people in her village had changed the traditional mindset. There was now a belief that prosperity was the key to being connected. It was no longer about retaining old values. People were constructing their morals with a new imperative. Established ways of caring were being replaced by more global trends, where having money and assets were more vital than spiritual or emotional connection.

For me, the African woman epitomized the figurine instruments in the museum. She was a firm believer in magical attitudes. The callback musical notes sent her home, which allowed her to authenticate her realities. She was a highly suspicious thinker, often delving into beliefs that went beyond the confines of customary Voodoo (Vodoun) or tribal magic. After being 27 years in North America, something was inside of her making her reaffirm who she was. Maybe after affiliating with her family and fellow community members, she understood who she was more deeply. I surmised that my journeys in life corresponded to hers, but with a difference. Our travels brought us to understand that there was a transition taking place in the world, and I was uncertain why this was happening.

In my earlier years, I had no specific agenda as to where I was going. Sometimes I just walked to places that were unknown. One day I was walking through the cobbled streets of Old Montreal, close to the St. Lawrence River. As I walked, I came to a brick roadway that led me to another part of town. I am not sure where I was, but I saw a black door. To reach the door, I had to follow a narrow pathway and climb a large spiral staircase. The place gave me an eerie, suspicious feeling. Nevertheless, I went forward. I thought it might be another miniature museum of musical instruments, so I opened the door out of curiosity. Indeed, inside there were some small black figurines, but with some odd-looking variations in design. The dolls were female figurines covered with patterns and decorated with beads, feathers, paint, and fabric.

As I moved ahead, I could hear the sounds of singing, dancing, and strange music. Then I saw some female dolls with pins stuck in them. The dark setting and dolls were creepy. Suddenly, a high-pitched voice cried out. I stooped down rapidly to peek in. I saw women dancing ferociously, and heard bellowing notes coming from musical instruments. This was likely the customary practice of Obeah or Voodoo, practiced in both the Caribbean and West Africa that the African woman later described to me. I was frightened about what was taking place, and I panicked and ran away.

I thought about Roman mythology, where female figures become pranksters, mischievous, playful, and always up to something. There were depictions that women were planners, often cunning, conniving, and even humorous. In this scenario, something different was taking place. I gained some understanding from Jewell Parker Rhodes' book, *Voodoo Dreams: A Novel of Marie Laveau.* The ideas of figurines possibly mean the unexpected loss of a pregnancy. Thus, based on African beliefs, there would be the need to heal, get spiritual intervention, and, therefore, call up a ritual spirit. The idea of drumming up a spirit from beyond was just something I did not want to know about at age 20. In reality, the female figurines were far more prized than the male collectibles. I wondered what more I would discover.

I left this scene and walked further ahead, passing some local native Indians gathered in a tent with a variety of items on display and crafts for sale. One handcrafted doll had some writing. I looked more closely and saw there was a story attached. The artisan had created the doll in the image of

Poospatuck, an Indian prince who fell in love with an Indian princess from the Secatogue tribe. The two tribes forbade contact, so according to the story, the pair snuck out together to Lake Ronkonkoma. They took their canoe to a romantic spot well after dark to make love. Because the spirits disapproved of the pair getting together, their boat sank, their bodies fell, and the spirits pulled their souls down to the bottom of the lake. The gloomy tale perpetuates that everything has order in society, but only the right souls should mix at the right time. This repeats the value taught in Keiko's family—taught in many families—and it always appears the woman is at fault for wrongdoings. I began thinking that in subtle underlying ways, different cultures' thoughts about women matched.

Based on my experiences in Old Montreal, the Indian legend, and the story of the African woman, I began to see the fallacious thinking about women in some cultures. I used to believe there is a progression of cognitive development, where learning guides learners to what is right and essential. Nevertheless, I found out that, through social filtering, this is not necessarily true. My own experiences in life revealed hidden attitudes, often perpetuated against women. What I had learned from my childhood, from my school years, was inadequate. It was only through objectively considering the new things I was experiencing that I could evolve cognitively. Eventually, I could see matters more clearly than before. I assumed affiliating with all kinds of people was essential. In reality, this caused me to have more mental conflict. I decided to tune into the channels across the seas. I wanted to figure out the workings behind the scenes. I needed to assess how people—how men—behaved and whether their thinking was alike around the world.

When I say we live in a world of differentiation, I refer to the general behavior in society. In the sixties and seventies, I was seditious against following my parent's rules, which also meant rejecting tradition. Others think I have a gypsy spirit because I view my direction as questionable. Georg Groddeck was a psychological theorist, who allowed people's actions to be theirs alone. He said regardless of timing, there are some consistencies affecting people of all types. This happens when they have some emotional dysfunction or disorder during their lives. To shift thinking, he prescribed that people take matters into their own hands. They should figure out the best ways to be healthy. Opinion suggests anybody can do something wrong and bounce back resiliently.

Irrespective of fame, people have emotional setbacks, or make out ways to be unsound. Regardless of how well known I may be, I have had unique experiences comparable to famous men. There is a correlation between us in that we have all endured challenges to find truths, and coped with risky conditions. Sometimes this has meant dealing with extreme circumstances. In my household, my father kept hidden certain photo albums. These were wartime images, people in the concentration camps. They gave me the shivers, and impacted my vision of the world. Churchill too, saw many wartime crimes, and these likely intensified his mental pressures. Einstein saw friends and family go to the gas chamber. I imagine these men, like me, had illusions resulting from such exposure. I have tried to forget seeing gruesome photos of people in concentration camps. They were like living skeletons. I suspect that we have blocked out memories of the traumas we have seen. There is a correlation between walking an emotional line and personal greatness. A person's life compares to a patchwork quilt. There are bits and pieces of joy and sorrow, stitched in with love. It is through these intricate scenarios that we develop an assembly of new thinking. I imagine that somewhere between new and old thinking, when we mingle our emotions, equanimity comes.

As for me, I identified there is a need to correct systemic faults, especially the thinking that men undermine the worth of women. In working with people in many capacities (including the mentally challenged and the criminal), I decided to help them see their own opinions.

I aimed for studies and went to it obsessively. I worked for colleagues, which I did not mind because I was learning. People thought I was strange because of my intense focus on creativity. Regardless, I continued my pastime of enjoying the Arts. I created a porcelain doll that wore real clothing and resembled a real child. A doll so lifelike, people thought it was my real daughter. I took this doll with me everywhere I went. I held the doll in different ways, flopped it over my shoulder, and allowed people to react. Often people would stop me and tell me to handle my child with more care. People often told me to embrace or take care of my child. They did not know it was just a doll I created. I liked watching how people reacted to what I had shaped, and it further sparked my imagination. That doll became the inspiration for my therapeutic art approach of reaching people by confronting them in the least likely way. I paid attention to followers: the people with blank expressions who had lost their way and were content to follow the directions of others. There was something extremely unique about this doll. Afterwards, I would discover there was more to know than I expected.

Since I was not a follower, I was compelled to follow the ways of Dr. Adams. He entered medical school in the late sixties and during the same time, my mother, a trained medical doctor taught me about the pragmatics of medicine. Dr. Adams aimed to use medicine as a vehicle for social change, and this was part of my thinking also. Adams used his free time to study the history of health care delivery around the world, to seek out a contemporary model that matched with his own vision. He wanted to create a model that would relieve problems in the delivery of medical care. This is when Adams begins his 'war on poverty.' He assumed that a free hospital would best serve the poorest. While hospitalized in the mental institution, he saw patients cry for attention and compassion. Adams realized that intimacy was the greatest gift he could give and that medicine connects bi-directionally. In other words, both patients and care providers needed to connect in happy ways. In Dr. Patch's world, patients and staff forged friendships. The hospital is a home and a healing place, also offering a sense of community and promoting diversity. This meant that violence, injustice, unemployment, the gap between rich and poor, government corruption, the environment, and economics were all part of the medical equation for a move towards social change.

Adams' artistic style is analogous to mine. When I received acceptance to attend East Virginia Medical School (where Adams studied as a doctor), I was accepted to study art therapy. I intended to create artwork that would lessen problems in the delivery of mental care for all people, but especially women. This was a pivotal point for our minds to cross paths in the pursuit of social justice. Both of us created connections related to the performing arts, arts and crafts, the environment, nature, education, recreation, and social services—all of which were to serve people of the world. My vision focused on humanizing females. I believe that a woman is as worthy as a man. I should not face more poverty than a man. Both genders are human beings. Obviously, Adams and I have a like frame of reference. For example, when a group of gynecologists came to visit, he created a statue of women with their legs apart. It is a ghastly experience for a woman to spread her legs apart for a physician to probe. By pushing doctors to awaken to what a woman might feel like, he caused controversy. I also became a hullabaloo for men in the foreign military intelligence. I compared a woman to a cloisonné vase and this also aroused them to the unfamiliar nature of females.

Andrea A. Anderson, PhD, leader of the Aspen Institute in Washington, DC, has examined the contributions of community building and change strategies in improving social benefits. She commented that each person has a right to think the way that pleases him or her best without social barriers causing obstacle. If I am right, all state-of-affairs do not have reformation to our liking. Demanding behavior often has results such as leading a person to fame or to standing out in a crowd. I suppose that creative people drive to make changes that work for us, but this could be possible for all people, regardless of their age, discipline, financial means, or country of origin. This happens when people recognize that learning must be particular to the student.

CHAPTER 7: Thailand

STILTED PERCEPTIONS ACROSS THE OCEAN – 21 YEARS

I assumed that assessing male behavior was the key to understanding gender inequality, but human nature is not limited to this alone. In order for me to assess the truth, I also needed to consider what is culturally justifiable and peaceable. By observing habitual practices, I thought people would demonstrate their compassion and understanding, or at least their true colors, in gender relationships (male/female). I would have a cup of coffee and a donut at a coffee shop, a common daily ritual in North America. I listened to the surrounding conversations, especially after patrons had read or heard the local or international news. This let me glimpse at what was actually running through other people's minds.

A male executive once told me he had taken an opportunity to break his usual routine; he traveled to Nunavut to inspect some homes newly installed by his company. Before he arrived, he had the preconceived idea that the people in Nunavut would be enjoying their homes. The executive also assumed this venture would improve relationship building. Instead, the truth came out. The man was devastated to see the condition of the homes recently built. There was dirt everywhere, and the inhabitants had done plenty of damage. He was clueless as to why this had happened. The following day, he was invited to visit the chief and some of the Elders, including women. He came to an exceptionally large tent located in the forest. When he entered, he was amazed at what he saw. The tent was impeccably clean, and he was welcomed warmly. The executive remarked that he felt incredibly powerful, and this setting was a real contrast to his usual routine. The executive surmised that when you take people out of their usual cultural setting, they just do not know what to do. The man had never asked the Inuit people what would bring them comfort. Instead, he assumed that his perception of accommodation was the best.

This goes hand in hand with male and female relationships. All people in the world are guilty of making cultural interpretations. We are influenced by what we read, see, and know, but it takes time to understand situations truly and deeply. Many times in the travels I am about to relate, people expressed themselves in unexpected ways: the sounds of a foreign accent, the use of unfamiliar words (like hearing someone say 'toilet closet' or 'water closet' instead of bathroom or restroom), the perceptions of acceptable habits, and more. These cultural differences caused me to freeze up at times. We are in the skin we are in. We internalize our thoughts with the image presented. This may be how perceptions of our own discrepancies arise and how assumptions are formed. Mostly, it is how erroneous judgments about relationships, especially between the genders, are caused.

It is rare for any person, in whichever profession, man or woman, to pinpoint the origins of a thought. At the same time, diversity expertise might be correlated to the founding of the hippie movement in the 1960s. This is when people in society truly established a voice in local groups, associations, societies, and cultural centers, giving rise to a new human consciousness about what matters. These kinds of movements have encouraged true relationship building—moving beyond race, country of origin, gender, language, et cetera. In 2008, Jack Layton, leader of Canada's New Democratic Party, honed in on art and cultural issues in a press release. He defended diversified relationship building and freedom of expression as being central to our cultural identity. He said, "*Don't let them tell you it can't be done*!"[8] His rationale made me want to explore underlying social constructs in relation to my individual framework.

Through my experiences, I discovered what decent and productive thinking was, but I was unable to find consistent worldwide standards of morality. I also had a hard time defining whether relationship building or other factors were relevant to the patterns of having honest, culturally aware thinking. Meaning is both implicit and explicit. Researchers Li and Leonard Karakowsky have suggested the truth is all about the learned behavior of a group of people, behavior which is generally based on tradition. As a consequence, I share the understanding that there is no universal 'right way' of being human, yet there is a right way in terms of social expectations and what people learn.

According to the psychiatrist William Glasser, people's most vital needs are to feel loved and to have a sense of belonging. I suspect this is why it is no coincidence that I can relate to famous men like Adams and Churchill. Their reality is like mine. We were all newcomers to understanding people, but we encouraged daily exploration of what is socially justifiable. Certainly, we all have our own point of reference, and our own social filtering that works into our thinking. Selectively, this manifests itself in cause-and-effect relationships, reactions to criticism, laying blame, complaining, nagging, threatening, punishing, violating of rights, or other variables. For that reason, I steer you, the reader, towards my reflections of past tides (rearing, schooling, beliefs, and exposure). I expect you will shed assumption-making tendencies, gain insight, and bypass the standard *quid pro quo* that often ignores the significance of what other people have to say.

I remember how my social values grew. They became increasingly significant when changes in my environment took place. As a North American girl, I grew up dreaming of a happy Disney story ending like Cinderella or Snow White. This same glorified princess theme has been perpetuated in many parts of the world in different ways. For example, the Shah Jahan built the Taj Mahal in memory of his beautiful princess Mumtaz Mahal.

My thinking evolved over time, beginning with stories from Keiko and Cupcake, and with my Polish father always telling me that if I ate the end of a loaf of bread, I would marry a rich man. Paranormal stories stirred my imagination. Genies from Saudi Arabian stories were transformed into a magical television series called *Bewitched*. I remember watching Elizabeth Montgomery, the actress who played the part of the lovely genie Samantha, and she was a source of enchantment for me. Samantha could do anything with the twinkling of her nose. She could move the scene to another country, shift furniture up and down, make a delectable meal suddenly appear, and so on. These fantasies kept churning my reality and certainly led me to believe in the illusion that the best would also happen to me.

My parents told me that, as a child, I was a storyteller for children far and wide. All I remember is that I had a vivid imagination, and, like a rainbow, I was always flashing different colored waves of light to others. As a child of North American realities, I imagined my future to be a world of richness. I assumed people everywhere had similarly spectacular ideals. Then, when I met my Prince Charming, he would sweep me off my feet. I assumed this was a path to rich love and wealth in other forms.

My Prince Charming came from Thailand. He told me about living in faraway places, and traveling on his bicycle throughout Europe. I was impressed. He had studied engineering in Germany. In the context of my reality, I was star-struck. In a short time, I was swayed by the charisma he exuded. I would be Anna, and he the King of Siam. I imagined wearing a ballroom gown and dancing the night away.

After we had married, the picture was somewhat different. He kept telling me that his homeland was much better than where we were. I recall my parents telling me that they, too, had lived a richer lifestyle in Europe. Their home had been a palace with many rooms and servants catering to their needs, and wealth embellished by their lives. I suppose you can say they lived on easy street until the war broke out. I cannot imagine how their world changed when the conflict arose. I began thinking about their lives, and I assumed that moving would bring times of peace, and the same richness would come for me. But, at the back of my mind, I still had some hesitation about moving to Thailand. I always wondered if the Thai people were anything like the Chinese or Japanese. Would this voyage lead to kindness—or coldness?

Before heading to Thailand, I gave birth to a son in Canada. His father named him Atagone, a name that means he will always have money in his hand. Certainly, this is the truth for machismo cultures where men connect socially and for business purposes. This excludes women from participation in a male-only culture, including designated places such as the Freemasons, private Ivy League schools, and other 'Good Old Boys' clubs along the Archie-Bunker-type modeling.

When I arrived in Thailand, I found it was indeed a country of tropical flavor, but it was not at all the way I had imagined. The first day I was there, I saw a green lizard climbing the walls. I screamed, not knowing what the creepy crawlers were. I immediately wanted to leave, but I learned that these were harmless spiny-tailed geckos, common in Thailand. The second day brought dramatic rain showers, the water pouring cats and dogs. This made for a kind of damp feeling, and in between downpours, spurts of sunshine moved in. While I looked outside the window, I could even see flip-flops floating down the street. People were running after them, giggling profusely. When I ventured outside, friendly water snakes wrapped themselves around my legs. I cannot say I was thrilled, but I was told these creatures were harmless. Next, I saw the enterprising street vendors, who would set up a cluster of stalls, transforming main street corners into lively food bazaars. There was an array of products beyond anything I had ever seen. Some were pushing mini-kitchens around on wooden carts. The smell and character of the street food was tantalizing, and I wanted to eat it all. There were elaborate displays, all enveloped in sounds, colors, and aromas; chicken and pork satay barbecuing on charcoal stoves, the sizzling of fishcakes from beneath bright, colorful tarps. Vendors could broil a syrupy formula right there on the street. They grilled it into pre-molded forms creating a fabulous dessert called *Cunom Cloque.* All this was done in a matter of minutes. I enjoyed that sweet taste and wished this kind of product was available in North America, but I never saw it anywhere else.

Gray-haired grandmas in well-worn sarongs were squatting, patiently making crispy golden crepes. People here also used the squatting position when taking a bathroom break, so seeing it employed during food preparation made me uncomfortable. Not far off in the distance, a noodle man was whipping up one bowl after another of steaming hot-and-sour soup. I had some, and it was spectacular. I saw the hungry crowd moving through an open area. They sat on low stools along the landing waiting for delicacies to be presented. People were chatting, and noises came from all directions. There were clanging noises circling around in my head. Then a sharp cry announced the presence of a hefty woman, huffing and puffing down the street, carrying woven baskets neatly arranged with goodies and other indulgences. For example, the deep yellow peeled jackfruit—the smell of which was awful, but it was pretty popular among the people—and tidy packets of banana leaves filled with delicate, sweet treats. Nibbling on street food was an inexpensive way to fill my cravings, and was a pleasant change from the aloof restaurant approach in North America.

Then I saw a woman running through the streets. The police were following her. Soon after, I saw a wig come off her—no, *his*—head. It was a man dressed as a woman. How was this happening? My Prince Charming had said that Thailand is the land of honey and wealth, but my first impressions had me a little overwhelmed.

On the third day, we headed to a rural community in Saraburi, about 100 kilometers northeast of Bangkok, to visit my prince's home. The roads were bumpy, and my rear end took a beating en route. Still, I imagined I was going to see an exotic palace on a remote mountainside, rivaling the

Seven Wonders of the World. This is how my imagination worked. Instead, I arrived at a distant farming community. I was surprised to see all the houses on stilts, purposely elevated to keep them cooler. This also kept the inhabitants well above the floodwaters and the rain-soaked ground, not to mention out of the reach of dangerous animals. The space below the houses had its uses: storage for harvests (rice), livestock (kenneled chickens and roosters), and various tools, such as plows and looms. In the hot season, the shade provided a place to work or play. The open, high-pitched roofs facilitated airflow and wide overhanging eaves protected the houses from the sun and rain.

This traditional home was also modular, held together only by wooden dowels and dovetailing planks. The whole house could be taken apart in a day's time. The pieces stacked on a boat, moved elsewhere, and reassembled. The Thai are not nomadic, but a majority still relies on agriculture, making them vulnerable to the fickleness of Nature. In Thai, the word for 'move' (as in 'to settle into a new place') is *yai bahn* or 'move the house.'

Surprisingly, this home had been in this spot for over 50 years, and it was not going anywhere. The exterior was made of teak and was not elaborate in the least, except for its triangular roof. Entering the home involved climbing up a steep homemade ladder—not my idea of easy access! It was not easy for me even in my twenties, and I was extremely fit. I climbed up barefoot, worried that I would fall and hurt the bottom of my feet.

When I entered the home, I was amazed to see an almost bare room with hardly any furniture whatsoever. It was similar and yet different to Keiko's home. The colors were more earthy and classical. There was one single framed photo of the Thai monarch, King Bhumibol Adulyadej, but no family photos anywhere. There was one upright wooden storage cabinet in the center of the room. It had see-through glass doors with various trinkets on the top two shelves. The objects inside looked sensational and so intricately designed. From a distance, it looked like a silver tea set along with matching cutlery and plates. Next to this cabinet was a small radio and nothing more. Where was the rest of the furniture?

Then my prince told me his mother was approaching. She was old and grey, but she had the broadest smile possible. Was she happy to see me, or was there more to her smile? I remembered how a smile among Asians did not always mean happiness. Sometimes Asians smile because of embarrassment or to save face. I only could guess what was in her mind.

The woman appeared frail, with a narrow frame and light, barefoot steps. Her hair was silvery white and cropped short, like that of a North American man. She wore a sarong, or *teenjok,* wrapped around the bottom half of her body. Her *teenjok* was a vibrant fuchsia that glistened when she walked. The attire added color to the earthy tones of the home. The design was captivating because it had golden threaded patterns just a little above the hem and close to the waistline. On top, she wore a crisp, short-sleeved white *mudmee* silk shirt to her neckline. *Mudmee* is hand woven Thai silk that comes from the northeast of Thailand near Cambodia. The patterns are woven by traditional hand-operated looms, and the crafters do this speedily. *Pupuun,* or two tones of silk yarn, are usually intertwined to produce an iridescent fabric that is soft to touch. The weavers create motifs that are extraordinarily complicated with geometric patterns and extravagant ornamentation. His mother looked like someone you might see on a poster advertising Thailand. Then I saw his father, also wearing a sarong, but with fabric tinted in a dark blue. It had several patterns comparable to that of his mom's *teejok*. Through observation, I recognized the polite way to acknowledge their presence. I bowed my head slightly, folded my hands, and said, *Sawat-dee-kah*, the female greeting.

I walked towards the center of the room, where there was a myriad of delectable dishes laid out on the floor. Many of the dishes were made with coconut juice and local sweet fruits. The charismatic aromas and colors were indeed incredible. It was a food enthusiast's paradise—the ultimate destination for a devotee of sumptuous cuisine. I had never seen such beauty in such a stripped room. I imagined the unique and distinct flavors had been passed down through the generations, but I did not know for sure.

I was told that the food was made with local herbs, plants, and spices, most of which were unfamiliar to me. Of course, the idea of food made from flowers and plants was intriguing, but also strange. Colors ranged from the red pomegranates, to the purple-blue blossoms, to the yellow-orange egg yolks, to the green of Pandanus leaves. The invigorating fragrance in the room, I was told, came from jasmine. Other perfumed flowers had been added to create a warm atmosphere and a welcoming feeling. There were sweetly scented sparks rising in the air, and this naturally added to my temptation to want to know more, but it had been a long trip from Bangkok, and I was hungry. I was enticed by what I saw and ready to gorge down the food almost immediately. Then, on closer inspection,

I saw water bugs, worms, and grasshoppers on some plates. It was hard for me to fathom eating insects, a Thai delicacy.

Then my prince asked me to sit down on the hard wood floor and have some food with the guests. Sitting down on the floor was not my idea of comfort, but I went with what everybody else did. His father was the village head, so he had let everyone know we were arriving. Twenty-five or more neighbors had been invited, and people started coming in. These people were farmers, responsible for growing the local fragrant rice, called '*cow*' in the local language. Imagine walking around and saying, 'I would like some *cow*. Compared to my prince, and to the people in Bangkok, they were dark skinned—from working in the hot sun, I supposed. Anyway, all the people looked friendly, and they smiled when they saw me.

As the people entered the main area, music could be heard from a hammered dulcimer or *Khim*, a Thai flute called a *Kong,* a Gong, and the *Ranat*, a xylophone. These sounds were fantastically distinct and so unfamiliar to my ears. People of all ages came in, almost to the rhythm of the music. Young and old women alike were dancing and moving their hands ever so gracefully. They wore typical indigenous Thai patterned silk dresses in a variety of colors and patterns. For example, one shimmering sarong had a vast array of colors—orange, red, brown, maroon, rust, silver, yellow, gold, and charcoal gray. The designs were elaborate, using a variety of repeated shapes like squares and triangles. The wealth in design and color brought to mind the magic carpets of Aladdin. Fabrics were rich silks or cottons, ranging in texture from especially smooth to ribbed or rough. Their outfits and appearance were attention grabbing. The young women mostly had their jet-black shining hair piled on top of their heads, though some wore it loose and flowing. They wore headdresses and clanging silver hand and ankle bracelets, and a few had upper arm rings.

The men were mostly older. They also wore sarongs that were plaid, checked, or an interweaving design with darker shades of dark brown, reddish brown, and black. I always wondered how they kept the sarongs from falling down! When some of the older people smiled, their teeth were a dark red shade, like the tint of human blood. It was a turn-off for me. I only hoped they were not sick. Later, I found out that they did not brush their teeth. Instead, they chewed a betel nut, and their red-colored teeth were considered a sign of beauty.

Then the monks entered, wearing a bland yellowish-orange shade similar to saffron. For someone not exceptionally familiar with Buddhist culture, I was fascinated to see this happening before me. To my astonishment, the monks who came to the home were like beggars. According to Buddhist teachings, generosity is a meritorious deed. Offering food to the monks, particularly because of the arrival of me and my prince, was considered a gesture of goodwill. Buddhists believe in *karma*: positive actions, such as food offerings, will have positive consequences in the future. Since Buddhism professes to teach awareness or mindfulness, I wondered what these men would do. I was curious to understand if these spiritual leaders were different from priests, rabbis, or other religious guides. *Bhiksu,* Buddhist monks, supposedly live by many principles. They live by the *Vinaya* framework of monastic discipline, the basic rules of which are called the *Patimokkha*. Their lifestyle is shaped to support their spiritual practice, to live a pure and meditative life, and to attain the bliss of enlightenment. Sometimes, the people refer to this goal as reaching *Nirvana*. These monks and the people all looked so bizarre to me.

In the far corner of the room, there was an incapacitated child wrapped in grey wool blankets. She was paralyzed, and was making shrill sounds. The young girl was not allowed to join us. The idea of having a celebration with the deprived child nearby was not my idea of being mindful. I could not understand why this child was being isolated. I asked that at least she be given something to eat, but the language was a barrier, and no one answered my request. Then I communicated my thoughts to my prince. He told me that I should not worry about this. She was a member of the family, but she was injured when she was born and unable to eat normally. He said the celebration would go on and asked me to be respectful. It was hard for me to imagine leaving this child alone. I could not fathom that these people had any kind of mindfulness by allowing this child to be alone and without care. Their values did not match my perspective at all.

The merriment continued when his mother presented me with a beautifully designed emerald green silk sarong. The patterns were delicate, almost royal. Other members of the family kept looking at me, and their chattering became overwhelmingly loud. Then the father took out a 70-proof rice whiskey. The smell was toxic, but I was told it had a pleasing, mild taste. His father passed out the alcohol to all the men except the monks, who abstained from drinking. As the men drank, their volume increased, becoming exceptionally loud and offensive. I felt as though I was being watched, as a part of an inappropriate movie.

Here I was in a foreign country, with alien

ways, and my thoughts kept drifting back to the out-of-the-way female child. Finally, I got up and took some food to her. I was taken aback nearing her. The blankets reeked worse than a clan of skunks. Loudly, I asked my prince when she had last been bathed. No one paid any attention to what I was saying or doing, including the monks. For the first time, I viewed a cruel act of uncaring. I persisted in asking more about this child. Then my prince, in a rough voice, told me to leave her alone. I asked him what was wrong. He responded that she was born with incapacities, she was going to die soon anyway, and so I should stop paying attention to her. This reality impacted me hard, as if I had been hit over the head with a rock. I was not only staying in a stilted home, but also being exposed to rough-hewn perspectives. The Thai outlook was not the same as mine. Caring seemed to be only on the surface.

I focused on cultural notions related to the importance of ritualistic trivia, such as decorum, facial expressions, clothing, diet, grooming habits, bias, performances, and gatherings. When a religious order entered into the picture in the form of Buddhism, I evaluated its core principles as flawed. The people's spiritual philosophy suggested caring does take place, but undeniably, their actions did not match my thinking. In a social context, enlightenment is supposed to bring bliss or Nirvana, but based on people's merriment and excessive drinking, I did not see that taking place. Instead, I observed how people behaved towards a dysfunctional female child. I could not imagine dismissing a handicapped person as unworthy. The child was soiled, and the stench coming from her indicated that no one cared if she lived or died. Through blind obedience, other community members followed the same cues, also rejecting her. Likewise, people in the community opposed what I had to say. I was immobilized in expressing what mattered to me.

That night I slept on the floor on a mattress like a large placemat, made from the giant pods of the kapok tree. There were no blankets. The mat was handcrafted and measured about 72 inches x 42 inches, but it made me feel like I was sleeping on the grass and creepy crawlers would come in and out. There was no royal treatment here. I was not the princess worried about the pea. I just wanted to sleep in my regular bed with 12 inches of back support, a mattress, and a box spring! I had not even laid my head down to nap, it seemed, when I was awoken at the crack of dawn. I looked at my watch. It was four in the morning. I could hear the cackling of roosters and people talking. What on earth was going on? The monks were there again. This was their daily routine, to get food and provide prayers. Apparently, my prince's mother would get up as early as two a.m., to prepare food for the monks. Community offerings are how the monks are fed. I learned that time spent as a monk is a ritual all Thai boys will undertake, from as early as nine years of age.

Sunshine started to seep in, so I climbed carefully down the ladder and went outside. I saw a hammock, and following my first inclination, I lay down on it. I felt a light breeze and imagined I was dreaming. It was a peaceful place to be. As the sun warmed my eyes, I eased back to a rocking motion and fell asleep. I am not sure how long I napped, but a pinching sensation woke me up. I rubbed my eyes and saw red marks all up and down my arms and legs. Mosquitoes had been picnicking on me. I was their menu, no different from the arms and legs of the surrounding farm animals. That was a good lesson in learning to use a sheer mesh mosquito net. The only way to feel refreshed from the mosquito attack was to bathe. This became the next exciting challenge I would embrace. Bathing was extremely archaic, because the people had to pump the water up manually, but afterward I felt revitalized.

I recognized that the mosquito attack illustrated an analogy on my life's value. Even though, my prince and his family considered me healthy, and without dysfunction, they cosseted me thereafter by a mosquito net while I slept. Concurrently, the dysfunctional child was confined to her chair and was bitten by mosquitoes. Through such observations, I began to have an elevated consciousness about what wealth and caring honestly mean, whether in terms of appearance (gender), metaphysical understanding, or personal assets.

I learned I would be partaking in *Songkran*, the traditional New Year's celebration. I had little knowledge of this festive affair, but I was willing to learn. Everyone was flocking to the *Wat*, or local temple—but still the young disabled child was left alone. I could hear banging sounds, as if the tops of garbage pails were being beat. I felt the exhilaration in the air. People were adorned in their best clothes. They brought candles, Joss sticks (a type of incense), flowers, and small perfumed scented water bottles called *nam ob* with them. At the *Wat,* each devotee lit a candle. Each person placed a single flower or a bouquet in front of the Buddha's altar, which acted as a receptacle for the Joss sticks. Some uttered requests or chants before the Buddha, but from what I understood, there was no request to help the isolated child.

The worshippers were respectful to the Buddha image. They did this partly by bowing down in front of the Buddha figure in a prescribed form. They knelt down with hands placed palm to palm, and then they raised their hands to their foreheads, symbolic of kissing the earth with their **mind** (forehead) connected to **origin** (earth). The same practice can be found in other cultures, too. For example, some Aboriginals use the term *roots of origins* for 'mother earth.' The fraternal organization of Freemasons believes humankind originates from the earth, and that people use their heads for sagacity and praise. Thus, the symbolic gesture of the Thai kissing the earth is not unique. Nevertheless, how could I feel inclined to follow their prescribed ways? Certainly, I praised them for thinking in humanistic terms, but why did this not seem to apply to the young girl who was incapacitated? Each set of cultural rules is subject to the perception of the beholder; no doubt, this is the same for the Thai.

With respect to worshiping and other habits, changes take place through the generations. For example, it was customary for the family to take regular ceremonial baths. The Elder would seat himself on a broad bench. The children would assist by pouring out scented water and presenting him with the traditional candles, joss sticks, and flower emblems denoting the highest respect among the Thai. Then they would furnish him with fresh clothes to be worn after the bath. These ceremonial baths were also extended to monks, who were invariably held in high esteem. The leader in the community, the *Luang Phaw* (Great Father), guides these bathing practices. His role is comparable to a shaman or a spiritual father who is in charge of how affairs take place. The *Luang Phaw* is held to be wise. He is a doctor, astrologer, and mystical endorser all rolled into one. Thus, he is inevitably the unquestioned mediator when conflicts arise. Finally, after bathing or other ritual has taken place, he gives a sermon, often followed by blessings.

Perceptions, like habits, can also change with the generations. With that thought in my mind, a few weeks later we moved to Bangkok. Before we left, we received blessings for a house there. I could not understand all the rituals, but I respected the Thai people's ritualistic customs. At least this made for healthier relationships, which is something North Americans do not always do. It did not mean that I was buying into their ways. I went along mostly to avoid conflict and keep things pleasant wherever I was.

I was not looking forward to the bumpy ride back, but I was excited about having some privacy again. I did not like sleeping and eating in one room. We purchased rattan furniture and various decorations for our new home. There were regular beds with rattan headboards, with one customized for an infant. A heavy carved rosewood coffee table and matching chairs came next. These were solid pieces of furniture that hardly moved. The designs were unbelievable; hand-carved peacocks with matching floral motifs, hand rubbed with pure Tung oil. There were beautiful silk throw pillows placed on top. More things were coming, our home was becoming comfortable, and I was filled with feelings of well-being.

The appliances looked similar to those in North America, to some degree. A stove with two gas burners arrived, and then, surprisingly, a large white box arrived. Because most people purchase fresh items daily from the local markets, people hardly used refrigerators. Instead, this white box was a pantry for our dry goods. Large blocks of ice were available. They had to be ordered to keep perishables from going bad—even if they did drip on the food. Strangely, there was no washing machine. As I was checking the inventory of the house, I was glad to see a shower stall and a bathtub.

While I was in Thailand, no one asked for my opinion. Members of my prince's family made decisions about Atagone's care without asking me. Whilst in Saraburi they allowed him to run naked without diapers rather than be diapered and potty trained. I had a battle on my hands, and I did not like it. This difference of opinion about my son's care is what finally resulted in my prince, my son, and me, relocating to the capital of Thailand, Bangkok. And again, the family intervened, sending a young farm-hand girl, no more than 14 years old, to do the care giving for my child. Over time, I developed a rapport, but the damage from this 'caring' had already been done.

Step by step, I started to become acquainted with my new environment. There were lovely orchids and other flowers. Passers-by wore multi-colored sarongs and young women wore matching see-through sleeveless tops. These often caught the rays of sunshine, and their presence was like magical sparkling firecrackers in the air. Street vendors were calling out food offerings, and there were even monkeys swinging from house to house. The place generally reminded me of a panoramic of the Disney movie *Tarzan*. I could have been Jane ready to swing in the air, but I was still Lily, and there was still no palace.

Laundry had piled up, and without a washer. I had no idea how I would get my clothes clean. I asked the young girl in my poor Thai to show me how to wash the clothes. At first, she laughed at what I said. I was not even sure what was so funny, but she giggled pretty loudly. Then she pointed to the laundry and led me to the back of the house. She showed me that she would wash the clothing by hand. She took the clothing and began kneading with a tad of soap flakes. Her motions were brisk, and it looked like dough making for pastries, not a washing machine. I tried my hand at it, but I tired easily. How would the clothes smell? How clean would they get? In the remote farming community of Saraburi, there had been many helping hands. I had no idea how long it would take this girl to wash everything, but I ventured off to the local market while she cleaned up.

At the market, my eyes were filled with excitement as they took in all kinds of colorful wares. There was no room to pass, and people were pushing without regard. Nearby I could see a narrow Venice of the East. People were paddling in muddy waters, and the water traffic was vibrant. No matter which way I went, there was little space to go. Eventually, I was able to squeeze in and purchase the items needed for lunch. When I returned home, the young girl came running up to me. She told me that shopping was her job. This caused me more confusion than before. What is the role of a woman in Thailand?

When the young girl got close, I caught a whiff of her and felt faint. The girl was a mere child, but she smelled. When I told her to go take a shower, her eyes were questioning. I was not sure what the problem was, but I evoked a strange reaction in her. She began running away. Alarmed at her response, I ran after her and caught up. I gently tugged at her arm, and we walked back together. During our travel back, I explained I just wanted her to be clean. Then I showed her the shower again. The young girl flinched and motioned her head to say NO. It was clear that a shower was alien to her. Then I took her by the hand and brought her to the shower. I turned on the water and let her feel how it ran down and felt comfortable. She moved away abruptly, but I insisted she get in. I tried asking her a few times until I decided to push her in tenderly with all her clothes on. She might scream at first, but later she would know it was only water.

In challenging times, I would think about *The Ramakien*, Thailand's national epic (derived from the Hindu epic *Ramayana*). It is a tale about Prince Rama and his wife Sita, and their struggles between decency and wickedness. I was living in a foreign domain with lots of unfamiliarity, and defining what was virtuous or immoral was not anything like it was in North America. *The Ramakien* describes the way the Thai people take an evil opponent by the neck, push down on it, and use their knee to add extra force upwards. To me, this was much like taking an incapacitated child and isolating her. A tale like this was a wake-up call for me.

Eventually, my language skills increased, and reciprocal understanding took place. The more I was able to see, the more unfamiliar situations I encountered. I began to feel homesick, and to feel that there was nothing truly exotic about the Thai culture. There was no more novelty of being in an unfamiliar setting. My feeling now was that I was just spending my time in a far-flung culture. I did not want to be there anymore. I suppose this was the beginning of a fairy tale gone sour.

I decided we should return home to Canada, but somehow when I got back to Montreal I no longer felt the same. I still did not feel comfortable, and I began battling with the realities and reflections of what had taken place thus far in my life. My experiences with my prince and an unaccustomed culture affected my thinking. Some of my thoughts also stem from historical facts.

While trekking around the world, including Thailand, I failed to see the entrance of mysticism as a viable solution to the propagation of delusional thinking. I reverted to societal commercialism of what it meant to be happy, through the magical messages from Disney, *Arabian Nights*, and other themes of magical possibilities. I thought about how media messages in society (family, the gossip culture, and school) chain our thinking and fuel how people think. Thus, I went to Thailand with preconceived notions about what that tropical land looked like. I imagined it would be a happier adventure, like my time spent in Chinatown.

As a female, I also recognize that the **Princess theme** has been distributed worldwide. Disney has captured the idea through storytelling, songs, CDs, DVDs, costumes for resale, birthday party specials, princess toys, princess dolls, hotels for princesses, and custom designs with a princess theme in mind. The media reinforces princess marketing in the form of spreads, screenshots, official art, newspapers, magazine reviews, bulletins, flyers, telecasts, and illustrations worldwide with overly dramatized and glitzy photos. Consider as examples Britain's treatment of Princess Diana's wedding, America's retelling of Cinderella's glass slipper and Snow White's beauty in Disney movies, China's Fang Yi (the Little Princess), Egypt's Princess Ferial-Ferouk and South Korea's *Goong* (the Princess

Hours). Under these kinds of influences, I was no different from any other little girl. These resources produced imagery for me of what to expect in a relationship. As I grew up, I imagined being a princess with a happy ending, marrying a prince, even as my own father pressed me on with his story about eating the heel of the bread and marrying a rich man. I always assumed, as a child, that I would marry into wealth. My parents told me about how they had lived a life of luxury before the war broke out, which encouraged my thinking that this ideal would happen in my own life.

Naturally, realities began to set in for me, as they do for all other girls all around the world. It was not purely dressing up in fancy attire and imagining being a princess. Instead, it was about what the mind's eye conjures. Thus, when I met a man saying he came from royalty, my imagination conjured up the exotic. I always hoped that if I married a prince, and lived in a castle, the story would end happily ever after, as in the Disney tales. My prince built me a Thai-styled castle, but our thinking did not match. He had many problems in determining how to make life happy and died an unhappy alcoholic.

During my travels, I met a woman from Ohio named Anastasia. She had married a Turkish man, and she described her fantasy as similar to mine. Her parents named her after the Grand Duchess Anastasia Nikolaevna of Russia. Members of her family adored the idea of being part of a pompous royal culture. Anastasia fell in love with the idea that she would marry an exceptional man. She convinced herself that because of her fascination with ancient civilizations and the capitals of vast empires, something grand would happen. Later in life, she was fuelled to study classical and Near Eastern archaeology. This is what I did also. I imagine it was easy for her to romanticize about these lands. She was well spoken, even before she went to Turkey, but her thinking had evolved from these childhood tales. When Anastasia married, she spun out thoughts of a modern-day Ottoman princess living a fairy tale.

Storybooks and the media offer girls fallacious information. Early in life, they provide a window to the world that is more a mirage than truth. The truth lies in a patriarchal domain. It has taken me many years to recuperate from not having princess realities.

As a youth in the 1970s, I was curious to know what all the fuss was with people rebelling against social values. In my various escapades, I was always viewed as heading toward exotic doors, such as the story about Voodoo and Obeah practices I recounted in Chapter 6. When the doors in Montreal opened up, I saw people inside displaying superstitious practices. Their artwork seemed to convey distortions of the human form. Possibly this was another example of people following blindly, leading to a helpless situation. Where there is a cohesive group of followers, they often look the same, as if they are climbing around a spiral staircase that goes nowhere. This led me to the thought that artists not only have extraordinary vision, but also connect in seeing how obedient or loyal people are to fallacious thinking.

As time passed, I began to see life abroad much differently. My values about people changed, and I wondered if celebrities experienced the same shift in thinking. Symbolically, life afar represented *stilted homes* or distorted hearths (the fireplace represents the home). Almost everything appeared different from what I originally imagined or learned. Artists like Dalí,* Ocampo* and Escher* have reflected themes of helplessness and blind obedience in their work. I was helpless because I was unfamiliar in a foreign land. The more I looked, the more I saw the artwork that reinforced my thoughts. People were continually climbing upwards to the unknown.

Reflections on my life in North America and my exploration in Thailand made me remember some specifics related to the rearing of children. Some of the situations reminded me of my first adventure in Chinatown, where initially no one cared what happened to me. It was only later that nearby adults had any social consciousness about the needs of a small child.

Because he was born male, my son Atagone (เงิน มือทั้งสองข้างอย่างเต็มรูปแบบ) had privileges from the day he was born. His name "Atagone" means hands full of money. I had to work hard at supporting the family financially while my prince collected money. He said it was for our family's future well-being. My prince did not tell me that money was always available for him and our son. There were times he generously contributed to my education, but I never knew that he built a fortune and distributed funds to my son and his own birth family overseas. I discovered this only after his death, when the tax services asked me about the funds. This means trust issues between men and women are not the same. Male privilege grants unearned advantages or rights to men exclusively based on their sex. In societies with male privilege, men acquire social, economic, and political benefits simply because they are male, as I observed in Thailand with my prince, my son, and other men.

When we returned to North America, my spouse did not have the idea that I should stay home to care for Atagone. Even though I questioned this value, it did not matter. I began looking for a childcare provider by accessing database directories. I was able to discern a caregiver's personality and manner, the sanitary condition of the household, the activities available for children, and the like, but I had difficulties obtaining a trusted provider. Based on my research in both Canada and the United States, literally anyone can be on a government provider list, regardless of the care they provide. In the United States, many states offer half-day courses to be licensed as a care provider. As a consequence, I went through a number of caregivers that truly gave me grief. Unfortunately, there is still a significant gap in understanding. This relates to addressing childcare issues, including gender treatment.

Because I had difficulties locating a suitable caregiver, my prince suggested Atagone receive care from a friend's wife. Since my choices were few, I took my son to their home. I anticipated he would be well cared for, but I was surprised when I came to pick him up. My son was shaking, and he looked ghastly. I had no idea what had happened. I brought my son home, and as I removed his diaper, I saw bruising on his tiny limbs and body. He was black and blue from being hurt. When I asked what happened the following day, the friend replied that his wife had gone shopping. During her absence, Atagone became curious and started playing with a radio assembly. I suspect he did that because there were no toys in the area. The man did not want my son to touch his property. As a consequence, he explained, Atagone needed to be taught a lesson.

I was flabbergasted by what he had done. I told my prince I did not want his friends to be caregivers for our child ever again. He shirked the situation as being no fault of his own. My concern was for Atagone's welfare, but there was nowhere to go. Even though I qualified many other providers after this event, other incidents took place. During the seventies, there was no official child protection legislation or reporting, a consequence of social services amalgamation not being well supported. By the mid-1970s, some regulations had gained weight because of mishaps highlighted in the media. Dr. David Batty, a journalist and news editor at the Guardian reported that child protection against abuse or exploitation did not happen until 1989.

The catastrophe I experienced with my son's care in the seventies still happens today. I suspect this is because of current policies in place. According to British policymakers, an ideal ratio of children to adults is 3:1, with an adequate gender balance. In reality, care-giving services follow a ratio of 8:1 for smaller children and 10:1 for children up to six years old. I had constant anxiety about what would happen to my child. My agenda was to get proper care, but I had no recourse. In the 1970s, there were 67 Save the Children branches across Canada with roots in the international Save the Children Alliance. Such voices of concern were just coming up. Thus, I was never in a position to pursue social constructs that mattered to me. Certainly, there are remarkably few women chief executive officers in North America. I suspect this is because a model like the Swedish system of care still has not been instituted.

My son learned machismo attitudes from a young age. He acquired his exaggerated sense of masculinity from other men, beginning with his father and then moving to male friends, military training, and corporate relations with male executives. When I lived apart from my prince, he delivered funds to our son. My son made a deliberate choice to use the money for his own pleasure rather than give it to me to purchase essentials. My son always had money, corresponding with the meaning of the name Atagone. As my son grew older, I saw him focus more on his virility than being a good human being. He made a point of dismissing women. He would talk to male family members about his latest conquest. His discussions centered on how he toyed with women as objects of pleasure. He might meet a woman on an airplane flight and then zoom to another woman on the concourse. Although the term machismo is traditionally associated with the Latino male, my son largely thought it was okay to demean women.

In the Asiatic cultures I have visited, including the Thai culture, I have observed that males acquire a learned behavior. They have a conditioned response, taught to them via cultural forces such as local literature, religion, movies, and car styles, to name a few. I often saw manifestations of negative male behavior associated with machismo such as drunkenness, abusiveness, and rowdiness. The idea that a woman is a man's property is prevalent. When I was in Thailand, I was driven in a car by a male driver. I was told to sit in the back seat. When I questioned why this was necessary, my prince said it was a measure of protection. I could not relate to not being able to sit next to my spouse or the driver. Initially, I accepted this humbly, but I disliked being told what a female can do. Since I also had career expectations, I disliked that I was being steered by men. I was not allowed to make my own decisions. Instead, I experienced on many occasions men demonstrating their prowess or behaving as though they had superior skills.

When I was a property owner in Canada, a 20-year-old Saudi Arabian man became a tenant in my home. He rented the basement suite and began making some unreasonable demands. The man expected that, as a female landlord, I should serve his needs at his beck and call. The Saudi Arabian male anticipated that I would feed him on demand and provide him with educational support so he could get ahead. When I refused and explained this was not part of our landlord–tenant relations, he blew up and went on a rampage, taking a deliberately destructive path. He pulled out the sink in my basement suite. The pipes burst, and water flooded onto my hardwood floors. The repairs were costly. I requested he pay me for the cost of damages to recoup my losses. The tenant said he would reimburse the costs, but he never did. It is highly unlikely I could have educated him in advance about what is inappropriate. He probably grew up thinking that, as a man, he would always be in control of women.

My experiences with men have been vast, from the farmer to the diplomat, from the young to the old. Working with male decision makers has made me see that gender differences are truly a result of how women are treated by men. Unfortunately, there are too many men who dominate relationships. On the flip side, men have taught me how to be an aggressor and get my needs met. As a consequence, some women read me incorrectly, and I have to remind myself that they are not men.

Based on my experiences, men have the tendency to communicate quickly and efficiently. They do this with as little hassle as possible and often say little. It is only when they get cut off by a woman that they remember it well and talk about it a lot. I suppose this has something to do with the fact that machismo men are always looking at women rather than listening to them. In other words, men and women are often not on the same page. Matters of control often come up, especially in inclusive male settings.

Mohandas Gandhi, one of the most influential figures in the history of modern social activism, wrote a list of the seven social sins, sometimes called The Seven Blunders of the World. They are, "*Wealth without work, pleasure without conscience, knowledge without character, commerce without morality, science without humanity, worship without sacrifice, and politics without principle....Peace comes, but out of justice lived.*"[9]

In terms of understanding the values of truth, justice, and peace, Gandhi focused on peace coming from having moral values. Certainly, my travels abroad made me more sentient of what that looked like. I was able to evaluate beliefs, thoughts about humanity, work and trade ethics, entertainment norms, and political slants. These variables increased my knowledge base and were the determinants for returning to North America.

CHAPTER 8: Texas, USA

TIDES SHAKING: SPIRITUAL AND OUT-OF-BODY EXPERIENCES – 22 YEARS

Returning from Thailand to Montreal helped me to recognize that Canadians had a different set of morals and behaviors, and their patterns of personal conduct were far more relaxed. The only thing I missed about Asia was the fresh foods. No longer was I considered by others as a foreigner, but I still felt different from everyone else.

Soon after returning to Montreal, I resumed my old habits. I went back to daily ballet practices—a five-hour regime including the Arabesque, démi-plié, grand plié, and éléves. I had to exercise all formations to deliver the most beautiful poses of a ballerina. Continual practice made me tired, but it also strengthened my legs, and kept me in excellent physical shape. I wanted to reenergize as a young performer and to forget my experiences abroad.

I needed to perform in front of an audience and stand out. I remember facing many spectators, and being the object of their attention. I was in a dream-like state. Colors flashed in my mind, music was streaming through the air, and I was swirling like a tornado. I felt like I was the subject of an artist, like a painting on canvas, but the painter could wipe away the view anytime. At the same time, I no longer felt balanced. I felt as I was on a carousel feeling spinning around a cold front. In reality, the temperature in Montreal was extremely cold, often below minus 15 degrees Celsius. The snow made roads treacherous to walk. I often felt cold winds whipping my face and chilling exposed flesh. This was a clear signal that my dancing performance days had come to an end. In earlier times, I used to play the leading character in the Nutcracker Suite, a ballet presentation. I was Clara, the young girl who falls asleep and dreams about a prince. In truth, I was awakening to the identity of my prince, I accepted that cold climates were not my preference and wanted to return to a warmer climate with my prince. We decided to move to Southern United States. He went ahead of me to locate housing and meet with some friends. I planned to take an airplane to meet him, but before I headed to the United States, I decided to visit a tarot reader. I hoped she would unfold the truth with wisdom.

After all, I had just come back from a country where modernization and superstition entangle. Almost everyone I met in Thailand had superstitious beliefs. While there, I saw decisions often influenced by astrology, magic spells, superstitious beliefs, and charms. I even heard the Thai military regularly traveled as a group to visit certain monks. The locals believed in the monks' power to predict the future. In other words, many hundreds of superstitious beliefs and practices made superciliousness the Thai people's daily lives. Content is as easy as knowing what day not to cut their hair. Other superstitions determined where they stood, what they ate, when and what to do to increase luck, and so on. I remember seeing stalls set up on the streets where people were selling amulets. Outdoor shops were on every street corner and in every marketplace. Perhaps because of what I saw in Thailand, I was compelled to visit a tarot reader. I assumed that visiting this reader might help me regain some control over my life. Also, my father told me jokingly that because they traveled a lot, our family roots were *Polska Roma* or gypsy people. He explained that, in earlier years, the gypsies fled persecution because of a wave of pogroms in German territories. Later, they immigrated to Poland. Therefore, I had a curiosity about gypsies regardless of origin.

I entered the Gypsy woman's home, and she asked me to follow her to a small room. The setting was dark with some scented candles burning in the distance. These strange smells were luring me to the unfamiliar. The woman looked extraordinarily mystical, with intensely glowing eyes. This made me wonder if she had leukoderma, a rare condition of loss of pigmentation in the iris, which makes the eyes sensitive to light. When she talked to me, her voice came across like a warm hearted angel. I speculated that this woman might share a common ancestor.

There was something about her way that gave me a calming spiritual sensation. I could hear her tell me to sit down, but it came across like a sweet melody. She was a dainty woman wearing a soft pastel see-through scarf wrapped around her shoulders. Her clothing flowed around her body. There was no explanation for me feeling the way I did. I wondered if I could transform back to a simpler state. I cannot deduce any rational expression for being so compelled to meet this woman. I was glad that nothing deterred me from going through with the reading because I wanted to experience the centuries-old ritual.

Before the reading began, I had found myself gazing into the woman's soothing eyes. They were gentle and offered an extraordinary comfort that made me concentrate on her. As I looked straight at her, I began wondering if she might reveal why I also liked to roam to new places. Instead, she conducted a ritual and asked me to look at some cards. She shuffled them several times and spread them across a small table. I selected three cards. She explained that each card represented past, present, and future issues. I was not sure what she would tell me. I was curious about my life. I imagined asking her about my future wealth. I guess she must have seen that I was anxious. The woman asked me to relax and suggested we spend some quiet time together. When she asked me to close my eyes, I conjured images of a picturesque scene that might be my new environment. I had no idea what would follow. After she had explained what the cards meant, I began wondering what powers she had. Based on what she foretold, the only sure thing that I knew was that I was prepared to go to the Southern United States—Texas. Her revelations seemed daunting, and I tried releasing this from my mind. I was concerned that she had used hypnotic powers on me. When the session was over, I was left with mystical thoughts. The following day I would leave to the United States.

When arriving in Houston, Texas, the humidity was so high it felt like ocean pellets floating in the air. I am not sure if the weather triggered how I felt next, but I was feeling dizzy and off balance. I could not figure out why my body was feeling extraordinarily heavy. I imagined that this is what an elephant might feel like when pounding the ground. While I was in motion, I sensed my whole being moving into another world. I tried to resist what I was undergoing. I aimed for ballet bar exercises, but I could not do them. Instead, I experienced light-headedness. I continued walking, but there was a drumming sensation going around and around in my head. If I were Goliath from years past, I might have been awakening from a deep sleep. Something strange was happening to me. I constantly felt fatigued and nauseated, had tender breasts and felt mentally strained. I needed someone to lean on, but the people around me were in their own worlds. I no longer felt like my old self. I weighed no more than 95 pounds, but my tiny frame was falling apart.

I was living beyond my means to escape the emptiness of not having a supportive companion. I wondered if I were seeking refuge from feeling an impending disastrous affair with my prince. I was out of balance, so I decided to go to an internist. An **internist** is a doctor trained to treat diseases inside the body. These physicians have knowledge of multiple body systems, and how they interact, treating diseases of all internal organs and systems. Specialized doctors are my diagnosticians. They find out whether there are problems in my musculoskeletal system, the need for preventive medicine, and holistic patient care. I suppose these internists assumed that I must have been experiencing some toxic or metabolic processes in my brain. I guess assumptions come from my feelings. I was starting to become foggier than before. I assumed mind-altering events associated with neuro-electrical anomalies in the temporal lobes causing weaker mental connections to my body.

I had no chance to connect with my prince. I went directly to the internist‘s office. I was told to lie down on a divan designed for clients. I remember the backless sofa as being narrow and hard. Then I had an illusion that I was lying on a bed of nails. In reality, this would have improved my circulation, increased my energy level, and reduced my stress, but I was not on a bed of nails. Maybe this image came to me because of my resistance to the human body’s nervous system. As I lay there, a pressure sensation built as if I were wearing a spiky high-heeled shoe on my head. Suddenly, my head began spinning and revolving rapidly. It was as if I could hear the piercing sounds of rushing waterfalls. I swallowed and tried catching my breath, but the air was leaving me. I only knew I was falling into an unfathomable place.

Then, I recall seeing the silhouette of my body coming out of myself and moving upward. It was almost like peeling off a thin layer of an onion, casting a shadowy projection. I guess I could compare this to how shadow play or puppetry projections work. I see myself cast on a screen as if the lining of my skin is unraveling. The projection was comparable to seeing a sheer layer of transparent tissue. Afterwards, I saw myself floating above my body and looking down. I could see the doctor and several people crowding around me, but I had no idea what the fuss was about.

I became aware that a strange marvel was taking place. I was floating higher and higher, but something was holding me back. I recall feeling buoyant as if I were floating in the mystical oceans of the world. Seemingly, the doctor was working hard to wake me up. I felt there was no need because I understood that I was still connected by blood that kept me bound to the world. I could not fathom why people were working to keep me alive. I did not care about what they were doing. Instead, I wanted to enjoy the pleasure of hovering even higher. I felt a calling from an unknown place, compelling me to go higher. I did not want to cooperate with the medical staff trying to waken me because I disliked feeling people working on me. I preferred the hovering and ignored the people trying to bring me back. I was traveling upwards, but suddenly my journey came to a halt. I realized that perhaps it was not my time to go into the unknown, but rather to understand that I had a higher purpose to fulfill on the Earthly plane.

I was not sure why this was happening. I began to reflect on my earlier readings of Edgar Cayce, an American psychic who allegedly had the ability to give answers to questions on occurring strange wonders. He could prophesize the future and described the out-of-body state of consciousness as he experienced it. Cayce determined that his spirit went into a supernatural form, and his human spirit was evolving into a paranormal appearance. During out-of-body experiences, he depicted what the future would bring. I had a feeling that Cayce was by my side, and I was enabled. Cayce has recognition for many predictions including natural disasters, wars, economic collapse, and socio-political unrest. I wondered what super powers I held to be experiencing this phenomenon. I also kept in mind reading information about another well-known individual with an unusual mind. This was Nostradamus, born in Saint-Rémy-de-Provence, France. He became known, in the sixteenth century, as the author of prophecies. He was also curious about human singularities. Some happenings for Cayce match an awakening for me. In his journey of exploration, he produced a book with cryptic messages. His sixth-sense interpretations came from soulful interpretations as I had this sensation too. In the thinking of Cayce and Nostradamus, they decided the only justifiable way to find the truth was to purify the soul, and I suspected this would happen for me too.

In my own experience, I discovered that regardless of a person's upbringing, the out-of-body experience was an innate ability to envisage something unusual. It also resulted in predictive possibilities, which do not normally apply to people. I recall that my mother had exceptional abilities. She had a vision of her own mother being pushed off a rock by others, making her fall to her death. Years later, my Russian grandfather arrived in North America, and he clarified that my mother's visions were accurate. He testified to what took place because he was there. Beyond doubt, her visions were mysterious, and so were the powers they implied.

I cannot say that my abilities were on par with my mother, but I did experience a realm beyond what I could explain. Through my humanities studies, I learned that while all humans seek the same basic conditions to thrive, the gift of vision is an odd experience and an anomaly. Based on research and visits to The Edgar Cayce Institute for Intuitive Studies in Virginia, and to Saint-Rémy-de-Provence, I knew intuitively that some force was guiding me to feel more than most other people. I had instinctive visions. I understood I had a gift to see things in ways others could not. The works of both Cayce and Nostradamus related to judicial astrology; namely, the astrological judgment or assessment of events such as births, weddings, and coronations. From my perspective, judicious study of human behavior became my strength. It is also the best sign of events to take place. Therefore, I hypothesized a correlation between how people behave to where they are, and I delved to understand if this were true.

Around this time, **I started to notice** something seemingly supernatural taking place in the world. Extreme climate like the monsoon was parallel to social unrest in countries worldwide. This cycle was noticeable multiple times between 2000 and 2011. Severe weather was noticeable in China as typhoons. Earthquakes followed political unrest in Japan and Taiwan, and the United States saw freezing conditions well beyond the norm during the constant war against Iraq, and following 9/11. During this time, there were serious crop devastations, and people were paying higher prices to live. In Indonesia, Bashir, an Islamic dictator returned as a militant, and an earthquake caused a Tsunami that resulted in at least 20,000 deaths. In Iraq, the Second Gulf War and Operation Iraqi Freedom reported innumerable deaths, and windstorms ravaged the land. I wondered why these visions were penetrating my thoughts.

In reviewing happenings and people's behavior worldwide, I was seeing a pattern was emerging. It seemed that destructive weather proves a new course for how people behave. I felt this could also relate to my out of body experience, an event that mirrored being at death's door for a few seconds. There was also warning that something would be coming when I changed geographical locations from north to south. I interpreted this as meaning that new waves of experiences in travels to other destinations were to follow.

Having stayed in the cold north an extended period, I favored having a house once again, in a warm setting. We chose the southern United States as the weather was like Thailand. I assumed that my near-death experience probably took place because of humidity in Texas. At least, the doctors suggested this was the cause for my odd sensations. On the other hand, maybe I was in a hypnotic state, and only Edgar Cayce or Nostradamus might know what this mystery meant. The only surety was that I did not want to live in the cold weather any longer.

After my ordeal, I felt refreshed. I called my Thai prince on the phone, and he took a taxi to meet me. He had no idea what took place, but he wanted me to feel settled quickly. He said there was no time to spare. From there, he accompanied me to view a house on the Gulf coast about 50 miles from Houston, set in beautiful Galveston, Texas. Although at first we did not have work visas, we could still buy a home. When we entered the home, it seemed like a bolt from the blue. There were many beautiful Thai paintings on the walls. Despite the beauty, something was telling me that I needed to go away and leave this house. The house owners were an intermarried couple, whose association had fallen apart. I overheard the couple feuding over issues related to infidelity and drinking. I suspect that this was a message for me to know, and that it was no coincidence. I kept hearing a voice in my ears, forewarning me to leave that place. I took heed, and I left. I did not consider this a safe home. It was hard to fathom, but years later, in 2008, Hurricane Ike hit that area, and that house was destroyed by the lashing tides. Over 100 people in that housing area died. My sixth sense was keen and had worked well for me.

The correlation I mentioned before about adverse weather following poor behavior reflects here. All over the world, people experience bombing, torture, beheading and maiming. The human spirit worldwide is displaying as essentially self-centered. Corruption is more rampant than imaginable. I wondered if corruption and immorality are causes for houses to sink.

The reality of why thinking is so corrupt goes back to the opinions we gain in our childhood. It is the Disneyland perpetuation of false truths. As well, children model adults, even those who teach them not to tell the truth. When Walt Disney created his vision of Disneyland, the North American mind-set changed forever. People had new realities about what families needed based on Disney themes. Fantasyland, the Magic Kingdom, Space Mountain, and the World of Tomorrow are just some of the themes that have caused families exploring new streams of thought. Children imagined they had magical powers to fly like Peter Pan, shrink like Alice in Wonderland, and become a prince or a princess (no matter what). Parents and children alike saw fairy tale characters brought to life, and their imaginations blossomed.

Disney commercialization and events such as Disney on Ice, costume parties, films, recordings, stories, vacations, and more, caused escapism. In earlier times, this meant to be entertaining, but according to *Psychology Today*, this is inaccurate. Researchers have found that, "*85 percent of Disney cartoons vilify mental illness by portraying cartoon characters as crazy, mad and nuts*."[10] These stereotypes became the new basis for teaching bias and inappropriate role modeling. For example, the dim-witted Dopey in *Snow-White and the Seven Dwarfs* (1937) teaches children to laugh at fear and but also display apprehension. Based on my opinion and observations of juveniles, parents who do not take an interest in what their children watch are liable to raise children who are less analytical thinkers. Their assuming is more prone to model inappropriate behavior, and thus their potential reduces.

This raises a question. When do we gain understanding about the realities of the world? After all, I am only able to recognize that I am not a princess after learning reality. Until then, I was living life as a mere fantasy. In my childhood, I entertained myself by venturing off, playing make-believe, and returning when I was ready, without realizing the social injustices of being a female were real. Human trafficking, employment discrimination, and other acts of indiscretion are clear in the real world. Realities include closed-mindedness, racism, and superiority notions about social ranking.

Dr. Adams' mode of escapism in his early years was to misbehave at school. Adams actions nearly resulted in expulsion from school. In later years, people praised his efforts. For me, however, although I too did not enjoy school in earlier years, I did not receive recognition for entertaining people. I had a reputation as a strange girl. Later, as a grown woman, I remember diplomats shirking my tries at humor. Media representatives have reported that men get away with telling the most distasteful jokes about women, including their mothers and wives. As an actor, Williams starred in the role of Mrs. Doubtfire, where his character dresses and acts as a woman to win the job of a nanny. Mrs. Doubtfire was the best woman for the job, even though she was a man. The movie perpetuates the idea that women are less worthy than men are. Similarly, as a female, I have experienced males using trickery. Men lead me to believe they would reward me for my efforts. Instead, they received credit for the work I performed.

Winston Churchill, unlike his mother, never received public humiliation for his indiscretions; he received a Nobel Prize. Churchill's mother, Lady Randolph associates with negative controversy because she is female and not part of the Good Old Boys Club. Churchill was not subject to the same disapproval of his actions. Lady Randolph worked as a magazine editor in her early years. This is likely what influenced Churchill into writing and, in later years, tapped into his own talent. There is little information revealing Lady Randolph's writing genius. Instead, male writers undermined Lady Randolph's skills and focused on unrelated traits. Claims suggested that Randolph's maternal grandmother was

Iroquois. However, no research or evidence corroborated this to be true. In the mid-1800s, people assumed a person with aboriginal blood did not have good character. According to the Cold Lake Native Friendship Center, Views of aboriginals were unfavorable. During that time, the philosophy was "*to kill the Indian in the child*."[11] Such were the derisive remarks about Lady Randolph. Men in society chose to look for her character defects, and discredited Lady Randolph because she was female. Her character was further demoralized when she was also accused of being promiscuous and unfaithful to her spouse. Her many lovers names included "Karl, Prince Kinsky of Wchinitz."[12]

Men are not subject to the same treatment as Lady Randolph or me. A man's infidelity is often socially viewed as positive. Historical tracking of the eighteenth century revealed men like Giacomo Girolamo Casanova de Seingalt, better known as Casonova, depicted as a pleasure-seeker. He had as many as 120 sexual escapades with women and girls. His autobiography documented this information, and society viewed it as part of European social norms. A promiscuous man's image projects as a distinctive charisma. Even in the twentieth century, the same held true. Fictional characters like James Bond had many affairs of the heart. The audiences bought into the loving thrills and prowess Bond displayed. This is diametrically opposite to Lady Randolph's treatment. As a woman, Lady Randolph's sexual behavior was inexcusable. The media painted Lady Randolph as an uncaring mother, which was untrue, and society labeled Churchill inappropriately through association, but this did not damage his reputation as an extraordinary man. In fact, Lady Randolph was my hero. She strived to get her needs met regardless of what others said about her. My only regret is that she never received a Nobel Prize, and she was the true reason that Churchill got ahead.

I have seen people—as the result of natural disasters, physical and mental ailments, and drug abuse—become vulnerable. People often blindly follow cultural norms, which on the negative side can include, for example, alcohol abuse, gambling, and ill-treatment of women. When I returned to North America, I saw I was not as liberal as I expected I would feel in my own homeland. Men are in control. I think at that point in my life, I still lived in a world of illusions. I wished for marvelous events to take place, but was not confident enough to make them happen. Regrettably, some matters changed. My adventurous spirit was no longer the same. Instead, I looked for balance with family, friends, and strangers. My out-of-body experience made me feel capable, and my interests were changing. I was inclined to understand why some people, like me, are different from others. I began feeling as if I were absorbing reality more strongly than other people were, and that it was affecting me more than it did those who just went with the flow. At that point, I lost my sense of direction and balance.

I think North American behavioral models are about false judgments, expecting people to be obedient and follow the norm. There is no leverage given to the person who thinks or acts uniquely. People automatically assume that a person not complying with expectations is in need of a mental diagnosis and assigned a label. When I am labeled with a learning disability as a child, it becomes analogous to being a person with a mental problem.

I discovered that many mental health experts also labeled Dr. Patch Adams. These specialists suggested Adams disliked military rigidity and had conflicts about the make-up. Adams could not believe something was wrong with him based on others' opinions. Adams followed his instincts and self-registered as a mental patient. In reality, Adams had depression, and his time spent in a mental institution expanded his possibilities for new thinking. I think Adams was only disagreeable to the absurd criticism of others.

William Lebra was a mental health professional who also overzealously labeled Albert Einstein. He said Einstein was on two sides of the fence, proving resistance on his own. If Lebra's opinion was correct, then how is it feasible that Andrew Scull, another expert had the opposite perspective? Scull proposed labeling given to Einstein as wrong because Einstein was responsive and a genius. This variation in thinking implies people hold prejudices against people who think differently as I do.

R. D. Boyer and William Lebra were quick to label Winston Churchill, too. They portrayed Churchill as an antisocial workaholic with mental disorders. This is because Churchill repeatedly acted strangely among people. As in my scenario of labeling me as learning disabled, I succeeded in my studies beyond most people's imaginations. Churchill did the same, especially when he received a Nobel Prize.

Robin Williams is another celebrity judged as a problematic person who displays mental conditions. Adrien Daniels, Michael Foucault, and others proposed Williams to be a social deviant because of his ability to poke fun at authority figures, which was uncommon. Williams learned to express his emotions in alternate ways, and I suspect this is society's unwillingness to tolerate differences, so he became a target as I did. Robin Williams attended private schools in Chicago, where teachers determined that Williams had learning dysfunctions. For Williams, it was all about finding ways to make people happy by acting out. Williams is so much more than his original label suggests he would be.

I deduce that if a person projects differently in society because of gifts, regardless of whether they are having out-of-body experiences or reacting to events, the person becomes classified unfavorably. I suspect no matter where a person may be, the person stands out in society if they are different. Even a person's handwriting categorizes them.

Elizabeth Day, a historical journalist, studied handwriting and said Churchill had "*small, hasty script [that] demonstrates the war-time prime minister's willfulness and determination not to live by the rules.*"[13] His handwriting also showed his equilibrium in decision-making and expansive vision of independence. However, Day implied that a graphology interpretation is like looking at a "*crystal ball gazing into the past.*"[14] and is not entirely credible as in my own experience to visit the tarot reader and question of gypsy roots. This is especially true when a person discloses they have out-of-body experiences, believes in clairvoyance, or can predict events.

I think that new patterns of thinking go beyond the scope of what is now acceptable in society. Does idiosyncratic behavior warrant ostracizing or criminalizing? Are the messages Kearns and Adams received the same as what I received? Stephen King says, *"The most important things are the hardest to say because words diminish them."*[15]

To summarize, true vision overlooks issues like a person's roots, the arts of our culture, sharing globally, coping with expectations (norms, guilt, and respect), and the Law. Most people follow force. Others choose alternate direction. The human condition benefits from human nature. Some people develop cognitively and others do not. When I was a young girl, the children at my school knew I was placed in the slow learners' class. They reacted by forcing me to think I had a low aptitude. Some of the boys put tar in my hair and told me it would stick there forever. Other mean acts included spraying water at me, and name-calling. I tolerated this for a long time knowing that what they did was wrong. When I could not understand why they continued, I adapted to reality. I decided to learn in a more conducive setting, thus my rationale for going to the library.

The Stockholm Environment Institute claimed, "*Adaptation is often framed as a local or possibly regional concern,*" [16] but in reality, people who do not adapt to new directions limit their vision. Positive changes can take place because of exposure. As an example of this, Lisa Marie O'Hara, a former model was fighting terminal cancer. Having only weeks to live, she became a motivational speaker to change how people think. She believed "*anyone has the potential to exceed expectations as illustrated in her final presentation.*"[17] Isaacson, a corporate executive officer of the Aspen Institute, a nonpartisan Learning and Policy Studies Center said, "*Each person has the right to say what they think when they are pleased that there are no social barriers.*"[18]

I presume that culture-specific knowledge frames when a person adopts specific habits, adjusts, does something familiar, or avoids what feels or looks strange. I think the thought progression correlates to a child's book called "*It's a Book,*"[19] by Lane Smith. People have forgotten relevant past practices—such as reading a book or even turning a page. It is these ordinary actions that connect thoughts and developments. It is my premise that culture-specific values are personal notions that have resulted from people being blind followers.

This is one reason some people acquire the need for a soul quest. My earlier story of the African woman who returned to her village highlights what has happened to human nature. In the story, she experiences rejection because she does not have a cellular phone. In her experience, the cellular phone had replaced human soulful connections. In key continents around the world, the mobile sensation is real and growing. The cellular phone limits time to talk, because minutes cost. Results of such behavior are obvious. There was dominance of cellular use and sending text messages, especially among the global new generation. Human beings take less time to read or speak to others than before. Because of a lack of listening and connecting, **people stop thinking for themselves**. Few are not listening to false thinking. They go beyond the dictates of their own psyches.

Prior soulful leadership also is changing. Thailand's community leader, the *Luang Phaw*, was a spiritual leader and an advocate of humanity. The *Luang Phaw* united people to set up a world of peace and inner contentment. A similar value is prevalent in Aboriginal communities. I viewed firsthand that these soulful connections are reducing because people around the world do not believe in new patterns of thinking. Distrust is more prevalent than before, even between countries long allied. For example, based on a survey of 1,800 Canadians by the Historical-Dominion Institute, Canadians no longer favor American values, straining Canadian–American relations.

Distrust has replaced soulful connections. I believe this has happened for several reasons. Mainly, people are not being mindful. Instead, people are adapting through poverty, controls of echelons, elders, or authority figures, and not religiosity of the soul. No matter where I traveled in the world, I saw people losing their identity through immoral choices. Morality crops up everywhere. Sad events happen, like a young family traveling in preparation for the holiday season dying because of a drunk driver. Violence patterns the spotlight, and less an attribution to the soul connection. Businesses are stealing patents and manipulating people, there is drug experimentation, and the list goes on. There are not many soulful connections, but men like Dr. Adams still aim for social justice conferences and bring happiness to people around the world.

If people express their values, this could be a vehicle for social change. Aboriginal people have ideologies about wellness that differ from those of North Americans. I have received herbs and knowledge of spiritual healing while most North Americans typically use Western medicine and practices from their own faiths. Who decides which way is right? Each individual must accept that wellness is a common goal. Simultaneously, not everything becomes clear with observation, but it does provide a frame of reference for learning more. For example, if a man does not shake a woman's hand when meeting her, there could be a reason related to cultural traditions. Asking, or noting what others do, I think misunderstandings can clear up. Through watching, Adams learned that he could help people to feel happy. He cannot see everything. Adams lost his girlfriend because of it, so observation is a safety measure and a part of the soul search.

Since the philosophy of human rights and equity are still not prevalent in the world, it is necessary to take measures to stop needless anxiety. People need to lessen feelings of frustration and give others respect. Doing so may result in positive soul connections. This individualized approach differs from how public figures present themselves in front of the public. They choose to be superficial and fail to connect deeply at a soul level. When Kearns did not get recognition for his design, it was a tough time for him. He becomes recognized after 12 years. There were times he became sick, emotionally and physically. This is why Dr. Adams says people around the world need to be healthy by patching up hearts. Through soulful connections, transformation can take place.

In the book, *Lord of the Flies*, schoolboys end up on a deserted island alone. They have no choice but to govern themselves, and disaster arises. The book sheds light on how human nature essentially works; the strong overtake the weak. Power is the main goal that influences the Law of nations. On a soul level, we need to help victims of harm, but also recognize that fantasy Laws exist. In the Disney's production of *Peter Pan*, all the youths wanted family stability. The main female character, Wendy, symbolically becomes a mother figure. People like nurturing at a soul level, and the fantasy story nurtures the fundamental issue of having a lovely soul (learning about caring from childhood).

In my journeys of awe and challenges, the reader may see analogous impacts. The stories of Kearns battling the giants and Adams' wish to help people typify that people do have souls. People flank one another, making it more difficult to discover, portray, and preserve our own unique souls.

CHAPTER 9: Texas (Third Ward), USA

THE IMPOVERISHED SURFBOARDS AND THE MAGIC OF CARING – 25 YEARS

In my journey to the United States, I found myself in a situation that exemplified how people determine their behavior by what others do. I had neatly prepared all the required paperwork to settle and work in the United States. We just needed to cross the border to get the paperwork honored. My prince did not agree to enter the United States within the established timeframe of one year. After the year past, all the prepared paperwork automatically became nullified. When we returned to Canada, my prince entered the United States as a tourist. That meant we were only able to enter with visitor limitation; a 6-month timeframe to stay. We were not legally allowed to work or rent housing. This began an awful journey in America, a nightmare of exposure to the dark side of American living.

Our entry into the United States seemed dubious and unprincipled. Little did I know I would find out more as time passed onwards. We needed funds to enter the United States. When I asked my prince how we would meet the mandate, he told me not to worry. He conveyed the impression that there would be funds to set up a household, and there was no need to ask questions. My prince made me believe he had a conscience similar to mine. Therefore, I had no idea about his plan beforehand. I had no presumption that my prince was unlawful. As it turns out, he was accruing some mineral deposits taken from an x-ray machine, using my name without my consent as the provider of the minerals. By doing so, he could receive benefits from a privately owned organization.

The horrendous experiences began after we left the house in Galveston. My prince brought me to where he had been staying in a one-room apartment. Ten other men also lived there and I had to sleep on the floor. I was sensitive, physically and emotionally uncomfortable. Soon after my arrival in the United States, my prince found work that required him to travel to Mexico. He would not return for a full month. Fear set in almost immediately. I was alone, and I had no sense of security, no monetary or social backup. I had no one to rely on except myself. The fortune teller's reading was coming true. Without proper visas, we could not find a decent place to rent. Before he left for work, my prince arranged for us to live in an apartment complex where he left me alone and unaided.

It was a crude setting with literally no security. Many strange people lived there and many had dark skin. The setting was foreign, and it reminded me of Cupcake's home years earlier. The complex was in a terrible state of demise. There was debris everywhere, graffiti all over the walls, cracked windows, peeling paint, and locks on the doors did not work, allowing easy access. The smell in the room was rotten, as if garbage has been standing for months and spreading mold. Stained walls give a feeling of darkness. People spoke oddly. Their conversation included much slang, profanity, and heavy accents. Cockroaches, literally and metaphorically, had taken up residence. I have no way to get away from them.

One bright sunny day, the door creaked open, and I saw a shadowy figure entering. This strange man simply pushed the door open. I could hear a blaring television in the neighboring apartment. I suspect he was previously watching a favorite show as sedentary behavior with vocal media is common. I heard the door slam, and his figure grew larger as if a gargantuan beast approached. I felt like an animal about to die. I had a battle on my hands, and I fought back. Finally, I managed to make him to leave, but I was physically bruised and emotionally scarred for life. Unfortunately, these kinds of events happened all the time in this deserted place. I wanted to run away. I could not imagine why my mate had brought me here, and I hated that he had. There was no cleanliness or decency where I was. I began to question his morality. I wanted to return to my birthplace, to a familiar setting.

When I was alone with my son, I had to fend for myself in these circumstances. I noted drug sales, rapes, and violence. As mentioned earlier, it is easy for a neighbor to open the door. They could enter even if doors were locked. I recall a Black transvestite opening my door on a whim. He came in to talk to me. The man tried making the tone of his voice sound soft, but it was clear that he was male. I suppose he was coming in to have some girl chat. The transvestite was intrusive because he did not want to talk about or do anything in particular, but invade my time and space. Before I could leave those difficult circumstances, I was robbed, beaten, and violated. Unconscious feelings began to surface. I began to reminisce about the times I had seen mental patients in the psychiatric ward. People had expressionless faces, almost like blank sheets of paper. They looked helpless, obediently and blindly following the wrong way. People are not aware of outcomes. Naturally, I began to wonder what would happen to me. As William Glasser expressed, "*people make choices*"[20] (choice theory), but I felt I had no choice in sight. I became submissive to an unfamiliar setting. I felt so out of balance I eventually became delusional.

If my prince had done the right action before coming to the United States, no problems would exist. Then, I had an immediate impression that poor people automatically become associated with crime in some way, related to the unequal distribution of resources and affiliation. Thus, people in these communities often reverted to crime simply by association. I was helplessly lost in this setting, an environment in which women were often assaulted sexually or physically. I did not want to follow the blind vision that these people had. Naturally, people I knew in Canada, less used to living in poverty, judged me based on where I was living, and the associations I was making. I felt hopeless and helpless, all because my prince had not followed Laws earlier. Later, issues straightened out at a great expense. The American company that had hired him paid a steep mulct for sending him to Mexico with no visa. This became public knowledge when my prince re-entered the United States. The hiring organization's attorney prepared the right documentation, granting us legal status. With legal status, we could get decent housing, so this documentation allowed us to move and normalize our lives.

I began working as a part-time administrative assistant for a leading gas company. Later, I was referred to a small human resources company where I worked full-time as a recruiter, and my commissions were high. The only issue was that I worked long hours, and this was beginning to take a toll. At this organization, I met a woman who asked if I would like to teach disadvantaged people. I would be training individuals at a government service to gain office skills and provide knowledge for a medical assistant program. She explained it was a full-time job, but with fewer hours than I was currently working. Before I came aboard, the woman told me most the people had been criminals. Most were on probation or imprisoned; the latter attended a daytime training program.

I saw the reality of poverty even more clearly when I began this job. This was in the Third Ward, one of the six historic wards of Houston, Texas. "*The Third Ward is still a disheartened area even though efforts push to revitalize the depressed inner-city neighborhoods.*"[21] According to the 2011 Houston Market Report, the Third Ward has *"a population density of 4,568 people per square mile."* [22] The population and accommodation compared to the rest of Houston differs, where there is a *"population density of 3,639 people per square mile."*[23] The racial composition is mainly Black Americans with a handful of Hispanics. Poverty and theft are rampant and other data confirms lower literacy. "*Approximately 45% of people in the Third Ward have less than a high school education....median household income (2009) $5,328* {versus} *annual income of $42,945 in Houston.*"[24] According to research of a local non-profit organization, children were at risk because *"20.8% of the Harris County children live in poverty, 6.5 per 1,000 die before age 1, and 38% drop out of high school."*[25]

I arrived at the office and found I was the only Caucasian. Immediately I panicked, because I did not want to relive my time in the apartment complex. I was leery about what I would experience, especially since people stared at me when I entered. However, since this was a government program with first-rate benefits, I decided to evaluate further before deciding.

Matters did not start well. Since class attendance was my obligation, I had to make home visits to students who continued to be late or absent. The first time I visited the Third Ward, it reminded me of my bus trip to Harlem. The people's appearance and actions were like looking through a mirror of time. I saw houses in appalling conditions, with dirty dishes piled up, cockroaches, and all kinds of debris. During checks, some students were lethargic or asleep. They did not care where they slept. There was litter around their mattress (full of bedbugs), and small toddlers walking around without parental supervision. Overall, the students' homes were a health hazard. After several visits, I asked administration to limit my support strictly to school operations.

Initially, I was extremely enthusiastic to support the program. To make the environment conducive to learning, I even went to local businesses and implored merchants for paint donations or anything else that would enhance the environment, which they provided. Students willingly participated in helping to paint the rooms. Desks were repositioned, stationary supplies were organized, and training began a few days later.

Hardly any time had passed and subsequently, an opportune moment arrived to expand my education. I would be no longer naïve about what took place behind the scenes. The day began with the morning session, during which a large voice bellowed at the participants inside. A sizeable truck had driven up. I wondered what all the fuss was about, so I stepped outside. My presence was ignored. The truck's back door opened up, showing a load of items filled to the brim. There were new televisions, tools, radios, and other miscellaneous brand-name items inside. Everything was packaged neatly, and some even had price tags still on them. This was stolen merchandise. I could overhear discussions between the people outside and the students inside, mainly to determine which student or community member would steal which product. I heard them talking about whom would break into the boxes first and abscond with the items. People had been planted in department stores to list these items as lost inventory. The insurance company would replace the losses, the poor in the community would buy the stolen goods at a fraction of the original cost, and everyone supposedly would be happy. Such insurance scams are widespread in America according to *The Journal of Risk and Insurance.*[26] Insurance fraud comes in all sizes and forms (staged auto accidents, arson, corporate health deception, health insurance individual scam, faked death, murder for insurance, insurer schemes and property insurance rackets.

Surprisingly, the administrators were partners in these schemes, but I did not want to get involved. I was at a loss of what to do. I kept quiet, and just before I returned to go inside, one of the students asked me if I wanted any of the items. I simply let the students know they should be back in time after the break ended. Subsequently, it was so hard for me to know who could be trusted. After this event had taken place, I did not want to stay there anymore. However, I needed to get an American reference so I could obtain other employment, and, therefore, I had to stay a little longer.

It did not take long for students to get used to my style of teaching and me. I had assumed that since we were all North Americans, there would not be too many differences between us, but I had difficulties understanding the students' English. Their expressions sounded sullied and incorrect. As time moved forward, their world became familiar to some extent. However, what happened next made it clear to me that the students' habits remained unfamiliar.

This next event determined my subsequent direction. The day began at 9:00 a.m., with a fifteen-minute break at 10:30 a.m. The break sped by, but the participants did not return. I began searching for them. As I walked about the building, I saw light seeping out from a small storage room. I could hear the students inside, so I walked in. The students were sitting around a plate with a white powdery substance on it, inhaling the powder with straws. I had no idea what the powder was, but I reacted quickly. I grabbed for the plate and threw the remainder of powder away. I was clueless at the time that I was throwing away cocaine. I remember telling the students to go back to class.

We had another break in the afternoon, and I habitually had a cup of coffee at this time. The caffeine kept me alert when I had to drive home a couple of hours later in Houston's choking traffic. On this day, someone brought me a cup of coffee. I was pleased, and I did not question the kind act. Afterwards, the administrator, a colossal woman, interrupted my session. Because of her stalwart size and resounding voice, no one twitched. It was as if a magical power had stopped everyone dead in their tracks. She announced that classes would stop early because of an unscheduled board meeting. The woman was like a hippo, using her powerful bulk to whip everyone into line. The students dashed out the door, like a herd of cattle clambering to get out. I was pretty pleased to leave before the regular time, too. Most certainly, I would beat the traffic.

I went into my car and buckled up. Out of the blue, a strange feeling came over me, as if my head was circling. I managed to start my car and start moving, but I felt I was on a roller coaster ride, losing my equilibrium. A wheezy feeling overcame me and I pulled over and stopped the car. I needed to catch my breath. Suddenly, I felt as if I were flying on fast-paced water slide, the sensation of speed surging throughout my entire body, but at the same time I felt immobilized. I was terrified and thought that maybe I had been in an accident. I had no idea what was happening, where I was, or how long I had been sitting there in my car at the side of the road. Finally, the phenomenon subsided. I felt blessed that I had not driven, because I was certain something terrible would have taken place. I arrived home hours later.

This situation tapped deeply into my consciousness. It reminded me of the man I had seen in the psychiatric ward where my art teacher also stayed. The man was never the same after students put lysergic acid diethylamide (LSD) into his coffee just to see what would happen. Even though I was unaware of what the students had put in my coffee, I survived their trickery. There is no doubt that criminal tactics victimize decent people. After this incident, I left the organization and never looked back. I decided government programs were not legitimate. They served more as ways for bureaucrats to make connections. In later years, I wondered if any of these criminals had ever changed their habits.

No matter which study I looked at, there was confirmation that poverty is escalating around the globe. "*In 2005, Statistics Canada reported poverty rates were escalating, to an all-time high of nearly 9% of 10.8%."* [27]

According to **McLean's magazine**, *"The cities most associated with crime were Saskatoon, Winnipeg, and Regina."* [28] Other notable places of crime were *"Prince George (BC), 5. Chilliwack (BC), 6. Halifax (NS), 7. Vancouver (BC), 8. Surrey (BC), 9. Victoria (BC), 10. Port Coquitlam (BC)."* [29]

McClatchy, an American journalist reported poverty in America at new heights as well. "*Between 13% and 17% of the population are living below the federal poverty line... earning less than $10,000 per annum.*"[30]

Daniel Fisher, **Forbes** reporter details the highest rate of crime in United States to be in "*St. Louis (MO); 320,454, Detroit (MI); population (P) 713,239, Oakland (CA); P 395,317, Memphis (TN); P 652,725; Birmingham (AIA) P 213,258;" Atlanta (GA); P 425,433; Baltimore (MD) P 626,848; Stockton (CA), P295, 136, Cleveland (OH) P397, 106; Buffalo (NY) P 262,484.*"[31]

From a psycho-sociological and criminological perspective, scholars agree that there is a direct correlation between people in poverty and crime. The majority of the incarcerated were poor, and, therefore, resorted to crime.

Drugs, alcohol, and gambling are enormous contributors to the problem. Drugs influence young people to behave erratically. Proximity to Mexico exacerbated the situation in the Third Ward, providing a link to trafficking, distributing, and smuggling of cocaine, heroin, marijuana, and methamphetamine. In the 90s, drugs moved from

Texas to all parts of United States. Inevitably, this scenario created a significant drug abuse problem. Youths had access to literally tons of illicit drugs for consumption. During my field trips to check on tardy or absent students, I came to understand how drugs affected the way the people lived and acted. Drugs were in every nook and cranny. This is probably why the decent population had high, sturdy fences, gated communities, and guard dogs.

Alcoholism was prominent in the Third Ward. People would drive cars or operate machinery while drunk. Their acts often lead to incarceration. I encountered drunk drivers hitting my car when I conducted field trips. On one occasion, an alcoholic ran away from the scene, leaving me strapped. Luckily, he was later found and jailed. Another time, the driver was so impaired I experienced a head-on collision. It took me close to a year to heal from glass that landed in my eyes and an injury to my back. According to the Center for Disease Control and Prevention, my experiences are not unique. "*In fact, 51% of the American population over the age of 18 are regular drinkers. The number of alcohol-induced deaths, excluding accidents and homicides, was 24,518.*"[32] The National Council on Gambling reported "*the revenues from casinos and state lotteries are substantial. The gains are as much as $95 billion with a cost of $7 billion for social-related issues (addiction, bankruptcy and crime).*"[33] The Texas community of Third Ward is only one example of the massive problem that exists. Durand Jacobs, a researcher on gambling, concluded that gambling could lead to domestic violence, forgery, stolen credit cards, fencing stolen goods, tax evasion, insurance fraud, and employee theft.

These realities did not hit home until they actually happened to me. When I first came to the

United States, I had no idea that filling up my gas tank would allow criminals to duplicate my credit card information. Thus, I had to deal with the entangled mess of getting my credit straightened out when forgers used my credit card number for a purchasing spree. I was unable to leave any blank checks in my home, because thieves also made attempts to forge my handwriting. As for fencing stolen goods, the Third Ward community members were extremely proactive in this regard. They found cooperative ways to create scams and get money, including the theft of my belongings. Everyone in the community seemed to know who had done it except for me. I suspect I was an easy target for these students because I was vulnerable to their unfamiliar habits. I disliked seeing how these people were painting their lives. I think in some ways, the students approached matters the same as the Thai. In both cultures, people focused on what mattered to them and perpetuated immoral traits, which included ignoring dysfunctional people. In their impoverished settings, in the United States and Thailand, people acted against the order of nature, dismantling the brick of goodness through innumerable criminal activities.

These youths were modeling their environment. They had been exposed to poor adult role models, whether alcoholics, prostitutes, drug addicts, or criminals. When children feel cut off from relationships within the family, they seek alternate ways to make a sound family connection, such as being a gang member. Joining a gang offers a support network. This was spotlighted for me at the education center. I recall on one occasion, a prostitute mother brought her twelve-year-old son to the youth facility. She was evicting him from her family because the boy had sexually assaulted his sister. In reality, the mother had modeled her immoral behavior from the get-go. When the other youths heard about him, they ganged up on him and tried to drown him. The gang had its own morality and decided to teach him a lesson.

The youths at the juvenile holding center included runaways, gang members, murderers, petty thieves, and deviants. Most were lost in the cracks of the American system. Despite a ratio of one student to two officers, I saw little learning evolve in the classroom. I found many youths preferred to play games at the arcade. The arcade was a social arena where youths met gang members, and became exposed to the violence portrayed in the games. Parents were unavailable to support their children, so the street gangs were replacing good family modeling.

Author and lecturer Steve Nawojczyk, described the youth on the street as violent and highly intelligent. When family or friends are not supportive, social circumstances invite youths to join one of the 40 gangs (e.g. Crips, Bloods, Folk Nation, and People Nation) present in America. Youths seek supports when they do not have it from family or friends. Members only transmit information to key members. And wear identifying "*clothing, tattoos, brands, logos, body marks, and hairstyles. Graffiti is used to communicate messages, challenges, warnings, deeds achieved, and gang tra*cking."[34] I was surprised to learn that gang members also learn idiosyncratic coding (handwriting, symbols, codes, alphabets, rules, and regulations). I observed this when gang members showed up at the art classes at the holding center, where I instructed.

Aisha Muharrar is an American television writer and author of the book "*More Than a Label*"[35] addresses the labeling of youths as an unavoidable part of their social makeup. Perhaps this is why I was labeled as learning disabled. Celebrities like Albert Einstein, Winston Churchill, and others were also labeled to make life simpler for people who did not know how to cope with them as youths. Instead, they reacted to what they misunderstood by making assumptions, which allowed them to avoid connecting in positive ways. I suspect this is the same for troubled American youths, including gang members. When people are not supported, they retain harmful emotions, the impact of which becomes evident later in life. For example, Winston Churchill and Robin Williams both disliked that their parents were too busy to take care of them. They coped by "*drinking*" [36] (Churchill) or "*taking drugs*"[37] (Williams). Labeling is not limited and covers an array of mentalities.

I have heard about Jihadists where children as young as three years old model their fathers. They are trained to be killers, ready to wage war on whoever gets in their way. These young boys aim with AK-47 assault rifles. According to the Royal Canadian Mounted Police, "*parents are their children's strongest role model and greatest influence.*"[38] Parents establish the boundaries and the expectations. They are the examples for children to pattern. When there are no family supports in place, youths do not develop the necessary social skills, such as appropriate decision making. Instead, they develop their sense of personal power and purpose in alternate ways.

In my world, I learned from my parents that I needed to accept being labeled as a problem learner. They discerned this to be correct after officials told them I learned differently than most other children and needed to be placed with slow learners. In reality, the officials did not have a system set up to help diversified learners. Schools often did this in earlier times because of a lack of funding or simply because there was no know-how. I was no different from Churchill "*speech impediment*" [39] and Einstein's "*trouble with grammar constructs*,"[40] who faltered until they found their own way. When I was not challenged, I went to the library, much like the title character in Roald Dahl's book *Matilda,* a highly intelligent girl who goes to the library early in life and excels by learning on her own.

Dr. Howard Gardner, a professor of education at Harvard University, suggested that Intelligent Quotient (IQ) testing is far too restrictive to figure out where a child belongs. Maybe I was thrust into an exceptional needs class because IQ testing had poorly indicated my abilities. Gardner's theory of multiple intelligences posits that a person may be superior in one area, but not in all topics. When I was weak in mathematics, no one gave me the right support to help me catch up. Later, I excelled in university mathematics **and many other subjects**. I see this pattern **occurring** in other people, too. For example, Mozart was a fantastic musician, but he had poor social skills. Churchill's language was not comprehensible, but in later years, he excelled in writing and won a Nobel Prize. Adams and Kearns were ingenious in their discoveries, but their creativity was not in an acceptable format; therefore, they were also perceived as having learning issues.

Gardner's perspective seems to overlook the human psyche, but I believe that too much regimentation triggers learning setbacks. When I was a child, I felt the controls in my household and at school truly suppressed my creativity. My behavior was influenced by disciplinary pre-war values and other factors. On the basis of music research, perhaps we all could have benefited if music had been available at home and at school. Schools did not offer classical or other music education or exposure. According to Copper-Wiki, a community based collaboration, "*Music stimulates brainwave movement favorably, lowers blood pressure, boosts immunity, and eases muscle tension. It creates awareness about our mental and physical health.*" [41] Listening to Mozart or other musical forms at school probably would have helped me to stay alert and improve my memory. Maybe this is why I felt more relaxed at the library. There was a soundproof room where I listened to music. Eventually, I learned to decrease my impulsivity to run away. I also developed an emotional intimacy with books and found support through the librarians. This helped me later in life to excel in learning and conduct research. In addition, I applied principles of music and art therapy to my self-expression. During the 50's and 60's less was known about motivating learning. Educators were unfamiliar with how to help those who learned differently. Today, some schools and homes incorporate musical and artistic techniques to help stimulate learning. The music therapy field has expanded to include supporting persons in correctional and forensic settings, Alzheimer's patients, the mentally challenged, and students with autism spectrum disorder, are also favorably reducing crisis and trauma.

On the basis of knowledge I have acquired, I feel confident that my interpretation can be helpful to learn how to think beyond traditionalism. By this, I mean being able to think **outside the tube**, not relying on television, technology, or media alone. Instead, people need to revert to being thinkers. They should not be painted into the realities of dismal pictures such as in Salvador Dali's or other artists' artwork. Instead, they need to empower themselves and not act helplessly or blind.

CHAPTER 10: Texas USA

STILTED LIVING - KKK SQUEEZES & NO WAVES EXIST – 33 YEARS

After my prince had acquired legal status, he worked overseas routinely and returned every few weeks. It was not an ideal arrangement; in fact, it was a dreadfully unsettling experience. Once he decided he had sufficient funds, he bought some land in Texas. He did this without much discussion, as Asian men assume control of all household matters. Surprisingly, he purchased land that was rocky, inadequately graded, and poorly located, with trailers nearby. I thought he should invest in a waterfront property, but he did what he wanted. Shortly after buying the land, he asked me to find a blueprint to build a Thai-styled home. I could not imagine why he wanted to build a pier and beam structure where there was not any water. Not surprisingly, the plans available did not consider such designs. Consequently, the right planning was not done, and costs increased in no time.

For starters, the land had to be graded. The perimeter had steel wire fence, and the earth was dug up to create a sizable Koi fish pond. The land was prepped and a crew came in to pour the foundation. Creosote soaked wooden poles were set into the ground, rising 35 feet into the air. Step-by-step, the framers came in and created a massive

Thai-styled home, covered with wooden panels and at least 30 windows around the periphery. There was also a wooden western red cedar deck surrounding the entire house. The warmth of wood decking makes it a natural surrounding for a Koi pond. Carp fish were later placed inside and watching them jump up and down was captivating. The setting provided luxury, peacefulness and durability. The deck extended the living area of our home. The interior turned out to be magnificent. The living room ceiling extended 26 feet, and a loft separated the living room with two spiral staircases providing access. I remember feeling dizzy looking up at the staircases and having the feeling I was in M. C. Escher's painting (**Relativity*). There were multiple vanishing points depicting a world in which the normal Laws of gravity do not apply. In addition, there were two bathrooms, three bedrooms, and a kitchen. The kitchen cupboards were made of a rare purple heartwood mahogany imported from Brazil. In spite of all the luxurious features, my prince did not want any central heating or air-conditioning. As a result, the home did not meet basic standards for later sale. Beneath the home was a greenhouse and extra storage. This was not my dream home, but it became an attention-grabbing landmark in Southern United States.

I suspect it would have been a splendid place if the setting had been elsewhere and some design changes made. Unfortunately, my prince started to bring in rundown vehicles that needed repair, and the environment around the house soon resembled a landfill. To add further controversy, my prince did what he liked. He was growing cannabis illegally in the greenhouse without my knowledge and drank alcohol constantly.

Our enormous Thai-styled home was not like other homes in the area, and it made me feel like I did not fit in. We were positioned higher than every other home, so I also had a lofty height of awareness. It was facing M. C. Escher's reality (**Hand with Reflecting Sphere*). Our consciousness tapped into a world with metaphors and messages that take viewers decades to decipher. At the same time, it was unpleasant residing next to trailers and old cars. Furnishings were beds and a few chairs, nothing more. This setting reminded me of being in Thailand.

My prince assumed that since he had covered the building costs, he no longer had to help with any other basic expenses. Instead, my spouse acted like Prince Maha Vajiralongkorn, the Royal Son and Crown Prince of Siam. He explained that funds were being saved for our future. Later, he paid out hefty funds for his mother's funeral and to his family members as if he was royalty. Out of his hidden treasure boxes, he spent $60,000 on his mother's funeral costs—even though she was cremated! The bulk of the funds went to cover the expense of monks saying prayers and people enjoying themselves. It was vital to my prince that he portrayed a prosperous image. He gave the rest of the money to family members to buy a house and run a restaurant. In fact, no funds were allocated for our future, but I had no say in any of this. He was an alcoholic, and he began to spend a lot of money on hard liquor.

I was unhappy and uncomfortable with the living arrangement, but I had to cover food, electricity, and other necessary expenses. I found a job 30 miles away, working with mentally challenged adults between the ages of 20 and 50. The facility was a rehabilitation center where adults worked on a production line assembling packages for customers. At this center, my old feelings of uneasiness came back. Experiences of arriving in a mental institution and seeing people herded like cattle, conscious realities of Keiko and Cupcake's lifestyles, working in the Third Ward and observing all the criminal behavior, living in Thailand and seeing the neglected child. Now, at this treatment facility for the mentally challenged, the people stared at me. Their eyes followed me wherever I went, like an intense force invading my very being. The clientele appeared peculiar, with Mongoloid features I found unsettling. They were also constantly hugging staff, holding hands, and voicing their thoughts loudly. This reminded me of being confined within Ocampo's picture frame. It made me draw my attention to the formal properties that render them—such as his painting entitled, "*The Failure to Express Is Its Expression** (2002)."[42]

I am not sure why, but initially it was difficult coping with my own feelings. I could not understand why I felt disapproving toward the clients at the rehabilitation center. I had seen Asians effect disgust toward dysfunctional children because of the importance they place on saving face values. I felt I was integrating these unpleasant Asian values as my own. Because North Americans are taught not to stare at people's differences, it is a habit to dismiss people that appear disfigured in any form. I had to rekindle my spirit and remember I was also a human with imperfections. In other words, when we consider any person, we need to remember there are normative constructs that are part of our constitution as citizens of the world.

When I went to work with the mentally challenged, it seemed initially that staff at the facility was caring. Policies were in place that guided personnel to attain upstanding, moral results.

Superficially, it appeared to be a decent operation. There were partnerships with businesses to contract production requirements. The staff took me on tour to see how the assembly line flowed. Individuals were grouped at a few elongated tables. Each person was assigned to wrap some items in a box. Supervisors were on the floors watching the individuals do their tasks. Then I heard the unbelievable. These mentally challenged adults were not being paid hourly. Instead, they were paid by the completed piece. This translated to no more than 19 to 30 cents for an hour's work. I listened in disbelief and wondered who was responsible for evaluating the appropriateness of this policy.

By Law, in North America, minimum wage standards apply regardless of a person's mental ability. In the United States, the Fair Labor Standards Act (FLSA) stipulates that an employer is authorized to reduce a person's earnings only in the event the disorder actually impairs the worker's capacity to produce. This was not the case. They were not blind, severely mentally ill, physically impaired, alcoholic, or drug addicted. These lower-functioning individuals were trainable and were capable of producing what was expected, but the empowered decision-makers were not paying them correctly.

The actions of the rehabilitation facility were unacceptable to me. Years later I read a story about two developmentally disabled individuals, Burt and Barbara. At ages 88 and 72, respectively, they celebrated their twenty-fifth anniversary in 2010. It would have been their 30th anniversary, but it took five years for New York State to grant them a marriage license. This is because Burt and Barbara were institutionalized. As adolescents, they attended New York's infamous Willow Brook State School, where they both suffered intolerable conditions for a combined 43 years. The facility was shut down in the 1980s due to its blatant mistreatment of patients. There were many allegations of sexual abuse, and an investigation revealed staff members and higher-functioning residents were taking advantage of lower-functioning patients. Following Willow Brook, they met a few years later at a day program. It took a lot of work to overcome the bureaucracy, especially in regards to making sure the couple understood the concept of consensual sex, but finally the marriage was authorized. This idiosyncratic behavior made me wonder why matters happened as they did.

Officials monitoring the assembly line at the rehabilitation center were using their official position to secure unwarranted privileges. Although it was not sexual mistreatment, it was similar to what happened at Willow Brook in that staff was profiting from and taking advantage of people they were supposed to be helping. It reminded me of the 'one drop' rule applied to African Americans: anyone with any trace of African ancestry was considered black. It was as though a drop of dysfunction automatically determined years of institutionalized slavery. If African slaves ran away, they were tortured and sometimes killed. As for the lower-functioning individuals at the center, they were put out of work, shifted over a several week cycle so no one would catch up to this ploy. When I went to school, there was a quota system determining how many students needed to be labeled as having exceptional needs. When students were labeled, the school immediately acquired funding. Soon it became not about fitting students into the appropriate classroom, but about taking measures to profit monetarily. I suffered the consequences of this policy, and I only found out in the seventh grade that I had been placed incorrectly and deliberately.

I was put on the assembly line of life with the pretense that I would be molded like other people, but this is not how matters worked. I retained my individuality, I challenged assumptions, I held on to my mental imprints, and I continued my travels to mysterious places.

Around this time, I was invited to East Virginia Medical School to study art therapy, although I did not formally enroll. This field of study offers training on methods that help people manage physical and emotional problems. I knew this study area would allow me to tap into my creative side. Before learning there were no scholarship funds to enroll in a Master of Art therapy, I prepared an art portfolio and would continue studying art therapy independently. I would use art forms to help people express their emotions involving logical thinking and reasoning skills (comparison, classification, sequencing, cause/effect, analogies, and more) and inspired thinking (flexibility, imagery, associative thinking, metaphorical thinking, etc.). Adams went to the same school to become a medical doctor. He used his perception of the health care system to implement ways to help people express their emotional side in fun, imaginative ways. Therefore, our ideologies were similar.

When Adams pursued his goals, he faced a lot of resistance, especially from bureaucrats. There was a disparity in thinking. Most doctors knew little about tapping into their artistic and fun side. I imagine that Adams' exposure to different places and situations caused his understanding to parallel mine in many ways. We both learned how to accommodate others more readily because we observed diverse patterns (interpersonal relations, emotional expressions, attitudes, appreciations, and values) and meanings outside of our own world. Having these experiences helped us to synthesize our knowledge while helping others understand matters more clearly.

In 2009, at the National College of Natural Medicine, Adams spoke at a gathering. He began by addressing how embarrassed he was to be a man. He said that male behavior is atrocious, and men act as if they have a contagious disease. They conduct themselves without the necessary sensitivity. He postulated that if the government were run by women, not men, true compassion for people would be more common than it is today. This speech profoundly added to the ways in which I made a personal connection with Adams. I also liked that Adams was a down-to-earth person.

I was initially surprised that Adams saw things so differently from other North American thinkers. I found his thinking related directly to mine. There is an innate instinct that develops over time, but this does not necessarily mean appreciating all directions. Rather, it is about internalizing growth and determining what to adopt and what to cast aside. Just like the artwork of Escher,* Ocampo,* and Salvador Dali (**Persistence of Memory*), there is a need to have persistence of memory. It is like moving from the rough draft painting to the smooth portrait of understanding. It is not an automatic given that intelligence is recognized. In turn, there is potential in all of us to be in tune with our own conscious self-talk.

North Americans, I believe, have the propensity to make assumptions about all kinds of values. For example, North Americans assume people around the world brush their teeth with toothpaste to have pearly white smiles. I have found that this is not done worldwide. People from Samoa, the Indian subcontinent, and parts of Southeast Asia chew betel nut because it cleanses the gums. Other cultures use twigs from trees such as arak, areaka, cherry, neem, and oak, which contain antiseptic properties.

"*Some African cultures use the miswak or siwak, a chewing stick from the arak tree, to prevent gum disease, fight plaque and cavities, and prevent foul breath and dry mouth. In 2008, studies are conducted by Swedish researchers and information is published in the Journal of Periodontology...concluded that miswak produces beneficial antibiotics.*"[43]

When I ask North Americans what they think about brushing their teeth and smiling, they typically reiterate what the media has told them. It is crucial to have white teeth and smile. However, around the world, a smile does not always mean that a person is happy. It sometimes connotes distrust, embarrassment (Vietnam), cynicism (Thailand), or weakness (Sweden). This is only one illustration that makes me believe people can follow others blindly and obey what the media presents without looking beyond their culture.

North Americans do travel for vacation, but they never get close to the workings of the culture behind the scenes. They visit for short intervals or stay within the expatriate community. Thus, they make incorrect assumptions about others. Naturally, this is the human condition, which also influenced my parents.

When my parents traveled to North America, they planned to go to New York City. Like many immigrants, health and timing caused them to stop over in Canada, so this is where they began their new life. My mother arrived from Eastern Europe with two small children and me on the way. It probably was not easy for her to determine where to live or what to do. When decisions were made to settle down, my mother began exploring her neighborhood. Her next-door neighbor was Mrs. McGreedy, an Irish woman. The two became acquainted and bonded. My mother started to leave her door slightly ajar so that they could have their morning coffee together.

My mother had a natural intuition. She knew when something was going to go wrong. Once, when my mother needed to buy groceries, Mrs. McGreedy looked after my siblings and me. On route, my mother had the foresight that something was going to happen. A man reached out from a manhole. He had finished repairing some pipes and was pulling himself out, when he was hit by a frenzied driver. The driver had not paid attention to the warning signs. Instantly, my mother, a trained doctor, put her skills to work. She grabbed the man's injured arm and twisted it back into position. People witnessed the event, and some officials came to our home afterwards. Mrs. McGreedy assumed that my mother was in trouble, that she had done something wrong. In fact, the officials wanted to recognize good citizenship, but Mrs. McGreedy's nonverbal signals suggested otherwise to my mother. At the time, the media did not report the story, but if they had, they likely would have suggested that people need to consider potential legal implications before helping a fellow man on the street.

Like Mrs. McGreedy and my mother, the media and my family and friends also misinformed me. I was also young and inexperienced about the world around me. I did not know what to expect and followed the model of other North Americans. Fortunately, my thinking changed with new experiences.

Once, when traveling in Southern United States, I was on a dusty road about 60 miles from a major city. The day had gone well, but it was ending. The scenery changed to quaint cabins, and the road began winding, adding dusty, powdery, swirls in my path. I passed a corner store with bleak windows and a faded billboard. All I could hear were mooing sounds and the bucolic lifestyle. Suddenly, a swarm of motorcyclists came into view, their engines revving. One motorcycle sped up, and the driver started veering sharply next to my car. Another motorcyclist caught up with him, and more cyclists were moving in, pushing their way toward my car. There must have been 25 or 30 cyclists boldly invading my space. Some of the men wore strange looking hoods. Others carried knives and guns. The scene looked like something Salvador Dali might paint. I knew in my heart that these were Ku Klux Klan (KKK). The Klan was reputed to hold their rallies nearby, and I had heard people talking about them targeting motorists along this stretch of road. I became worried, but I had a sixth sense about what to do. I moved the car to the side of the road, stopped, and opened my door to apologize for being in their way. Fortunately, somehow, these words carried weight, and they left.

This situation spurred me to study how the KKK formed in Tennessee, in 1865. By the 1920s, the Klan had expanded its operations into Canada. Their hate messages in the United States and Canada were slightly different, but they were still hate messages. They sold memberships to fund their activities. These rumblings continued into the 1970s and 1980s. By the early 1990s, some new biases came to the forefront when the identity of a Cree trapper's killer, suspected to be KKK, was protected. In the mid-1990s, the media failed to report 'hate' incidents of the KKK, but attacks were no longer limited to African-Americans. Even today, rallies continue to spread globally.

I was wondering how the criminal seed was planted. I suspected a correlation happens and people become racist. All my education came from my parents, the environment, studies at school, and the exploration of art and life experience. This is so for everyone. I wondered how it would be feasible to reduce assumptions for the average North American, perhaps also reducing racism.

According to the *Huffington Post*, Georgia made history when "*Catherine Ariemma, a history teacher, allowed her students to dress up as KKK to re-enact the history of racism.*"[44] CBS, the television network, said Ariemma's approach and intent were questionable. The teacher claimed that racism could not adequately be addressed without bringing up the KKK. She said without examining KKK values, society implicitly condones their acts. The school's administration did not suggest the role-playing was wrong, but rather that Ariemma's teaching methodology was against school policy because parents had not been informed about her approach. Further, the media insinuated the youths would be exposed to harm.

Was Ariemma's approach so questionable? Teachers consider educational outcomes (future citizens in society) while providing a safe and caring environment. There was an existing trust relationship between Ariemma and her students before the incident. There appears to be no indication that she violated or compromised students' well-being. I think Ariemma's approach was less questionable than Americans might like to admit. After all, bias has been portrayed on television for years.

Earlier I mentioned Archie Bunker from *All in the Family.* That program tackled a wide variety of taboo topics, either directly or indirectly through Archie's debates with his son-in-Law Mike, among others. Topics included race relations, gender roles, homosexuality, war, economy, current events, abortion, rape, and child custody. Bunker represented the blue-collar worker in America, and when he approached controversial subjects, including the KKK, society accepted the programming. "***Good Times*** is a spin-off of ***All in the Family,*** both *receiving the highest ratings in the United States for five consecutive seasons in the 70s.*"[45] This took place even though his series portrayed Bunker as often getting into conflict with family, friends and people of different origins. The show violated many unwritten network rules, chiefly the issues that were considered unacceptable to air on public television.

Considering sociological theory, re-enactment is an option to help youths understand controversial issues. Whether there is discussion or role-playing, racism is something youths need to learn about. Otherwise, there is the potential that horrific acts repeat themselves, as Ariemma suggested, and as I experienced. A myopic vision about racism impedes students' growth and does not help future generations to understand racism's history, including the KKK. It also brings up the issue that society is failing to entrust trained professionals to handle sensitive subjects correctly. Perhaps the solution is an open airing of how racism is not being covered in schools. Ariemma's attempt should be worthy of her receiving the equivalent of the Emmys won by *All in the Family* cast members.

My overseas community experiences combined with my study of how people express themselves across borders have been incredibly helpful. As in Ariemma's role-playing of the KKK, my experiences and studies answered many questions regarding human rights, safety, thinking, and imaging. The experiences helped me to resettle into another avenue of life. Even though I gravitated towards the world of intellects, unfamiliar situations cropped up continuously. In turn, I made an effort to understand what I did not know.

Based on my observations, education has reduced the paramount issue; people need to think for themselves. I do not understand why Ariemma's job as a history teacher was in jeopardy because of her project to study the KKK. She was a thinker and provided students with an opportunity to study bias firsthand. The television series *All in the Family* exposed society's biases. In reality, there are too few social values studied. Youths often do not have the opportunity to explore social values. I believe they also lack true exposure to the deaf, the blind, the dysfunctional, and to the traumas experienced by refugees, and immigrants. This might be a result of the powers that be, which uphold a certain type of thinking and expect people in society to accept their morals. As an upshot, there is a lack of public awareness about social issues that matter. I recognize there is a breakdown of trust and a lack of acceptance of what is unfamiliar.

The hullabaloo of a woman's negated position, takes place all around the world. This is the same as my earlier observations in Harlem. The BBC News reported the headquarters of the Association for the Promotion of the Status of Women was struggling. There have been many unplanned pregnancies in Thailand. Laws in Thailand do not permit women to get abortions unless the pregnancy occurred due to rape or incest, or unless the mother's life is in danger. This puts young women in risky situations. They are often ignorant about sexual matters, so when they accidentally become pregnant, they panic. Some of the women get illegal abortions while others get debauched by poorly educated midwives. In actuality, there have been too many aborted fetuses. "*There were 2,000 aborted fetuses found behind closed doors of illegal clinics. Official statistics suggest at least 300,000 abortions have been done annually.*" [46]

In Thailand, "*The number of aborted fetuses and the care of women who have undergone the abortions is a growing concern.*"[47] This is no different from addressing the veracity of the KKK. Even though, this has prompted consideration in a conservative culture, not much is said about the dysfunctional children, as has been my experience, in Non Kae, Saraburi, Thailand.

Throughout Asia, there are poorly educated midwives. When a child is born with a disfigurement, some Asians believe they would be losing their social face in the family and the community. Similar to the story of the KKK re-enactment at the school, how the disfigured child is treated gets ignored. For example, The Children's Foundation of Thailand is a government-registered program that states these deformed children often suffer swollen stomachs and red heads. "*They are surviving by eating crusted red soil caked on the wheels of cars.*"[48] Thus, for a child to survive starvation or the youth to survive the hostilities of racism, both situations need to be exposed to help create better citizens.

CHAPTER 11: Canada

RETURNING TO FAMILIARITY; GETTING A GRIP – 38 YEARS

In my life's travels, my exposure to the unfamiliar gave me an opportunity to observe how people honestly expressed themselves behind the scenes. Issues of human rights, safety, thinking, and imaging cropped up. Whether I was in Thailand or North America, my significant partner was no different. He earned a lot of money but had no wealth of the essentials—love, caring, and emotional intelligence. He created an uncouth place to live, a place of rubbish and alcoholism. I had no comprehension why my prince valued showy extravagance, and impressing people who did not matter. For a while, I followed my prince blindly and ended up powerless. My relationship should have been about emotional well-being, not social face.

Shortly after I moved to the United States, I reflected on my father's passing. When he was alive he used to wear a Freemason ring, and as a child, I could always feel the ring staring at me. My father's association with the Freemasons seemed mystical to me. After he had died, I wanted to understand it better. In the early seventies, women were not allowed into the Freemasons, making it difficult for me to gain the information to satisfy my curiosity. I would have to come back to the matter later in life.

My thoughts moved towards grieving over the death of my father, my grandfather, and my brother-in-Law who had first brought the engaging art of the mentally ill before me. I remembered seeing my father looking strong, healthy and happy. Then, at the age of fifty-two, my father contracted a rare disease. He was in intensive care with clear plastic tubes running throughout his body, and he looked like an artificial man - in a test tube. His body had formations that looked like pustules draining, and this was shattering his energy. Suddenly, he took on the appearance of a man of ninety. He was skinnier than a rail and his medical condition became documented in health journals. My grandfather had a life of hardship on Russian soil and smoked heavily to relieve stress. These factors later lead to cancer and demise. My brother-in-Law was young, and he died accidentally on the day he acquired his doctorate in psychopharmacology.

During the time I lived in the enormous Thai house, I did artwork in my studio. I was driven by memories and feelings. As I put forth piece after piece, I felt my strength growing. Considering my state of mind, I had expected my work to reflect the images I saw from the large Swiss pharmaceutical companies. Instead, I saw a clear mind map of what mattered most to me. **Emotional intelligence**.

About ten years after my father's death I was in my early thirties, and I was settling in Texas. It was then that I had the opportunity to work with the mentally challenged, and my interest in the Arts and human behaviour grew. When I saw the creativity of the patients I worked with, I remembered the artwork my brother-in-Law had sent before. Since I lived in an elephantine-sized home, I earmarked a space to have a large art studio. Here, I created innumerable pieces of sculpture, paintings, ceramics and multi-dimensional pieces.

Some of the artwork I created was gargantuan gargoyle shapes, eclectic designs including painting several freestanding vintage bathtubs. I decorated the interior of the claw foot tubs with some eye-catching water **lilies** or *Nymphaea Caerulea*. These were the jewels in my art studio. They looked beautiful, but also became an aura of delight as they elevated out of the water's surface. The lilies spread across the water surface, filling my studio with an array of colours, vibrancy and fragrance. There were shades of peach, salmon, yellow, white, orange and pink glows with the radiance of royal blue and hues of purple. Some of the hardy lilies even changed colors as they bloomed comparable to my chameleon hazel eyes. These shallow-rooted plants needed plenty of room to grow and spread up and out across the water. Therefore, I added a few more tubs to my studio and planted some lilies also outside in the Koi pond. When I added the water lilies to the tubs, in my studio, the flowers automatically gave off a delightful fragrance, and indubitably, the scents, colors, and shapes of the Lily flowers scintillated my artistic sensations. I was particularly amazed to see the golden stamens stand upright in the center of the water lilies. I imagined they were princesses telling me I was in my own tropical Amazon setting.

My imagination emerged in this room, and I felt as if I was blossoming like night and day Lily bloomers. Even Robin McLaurin Williams says, "*People--they're kinda like flowers,"* [49] and no doubt my mind's eye was awakening. I was swimming among the vernal flowers as if I was part of Claude Monet's canvas of Water Lilies. His new approaches to art added the effects of light even when Monet suffered from cataracts. It was an indescribable feeling for me. I felt as if I were among the lily flowers blossoming mentally and spiritually and part of Dr. Patch Adams appearance in Rose Hill Gardens, Australia, when he addressed the quality of life.

Hence, these flowers become the catalyst for me to study art therapy night and day. In fact, just like the Lily flower, I also closed my mind during the late afternoon hours and slept at night.

During the daytime, I also volunteered with at-risk youths and did the artwork with them. Their visions were abrupt, striking, and out of the ordinary, and they triggered something inside of me. Applying art as therapy implies the creative process is a means of reconciling emotional conflicts. Naturally, this fosters self-awareness and personal growth. My conviction was strong that this was how I could use my emotional intelligence to heal.

Throughout my thirties, I continued producing and displaying my art, working with youths, presenting workshops, and all along my knowledge of people and the field of art therapy grew substantially. But, as the years passed, my once beautiful image had become like icy waters. My features took on a look as if I were gazing into another world rather than recognizing reality. So, in my late thirties, I decided to separate from my spouse and return to Quebec in Canada.

After wrapping up the affairs of selling the Thai home, packaging items, shipping furniture, and saying good-bye to friends, I began the long ride from the southern United States. It took a few days of driving and several stopovers before reaching the Canadian border. The scenery along the way had its own unique personality, promising distinct adventures at every turn. This scenic drive celebrated extraordinarily beautiful flat lands transforming into rolling hills. As I drove further north, I began seeing a transformation of hills into mountains. The changing landscape was charming, and marked that I was getting closer to Canada.

Finally, I reached Canadian customs and

lined up in a queue with other people. The transition from United States to Canada was smooth and a short wait time. Entering Canada, I noticed the change from the American imperial classification to the metric system. Gas was no longer gallons, but now liters. The popular 711 convenience shops or large truck stops now became Petro-Canada corner stores. Signs posted were no longer English alone, but more than one language. There were English and French postings. Even the manner of people altered from overly-friendly to a more natural soft-spoken approach. Spring was bringing the smell of the crisp, fresh air and the scent of enchanting flowers. The chill of winter was disappearing.

I knew the weather was unpredictable, but at forty-eight degrees Fahrenheit, or nine degrees Celsius, it was warm enough. Spring is an exciting time of year. Plants emerge from dormancy, and as the flora began to bloom, I, Lily, was flowering too. The expansive nation of Canada has many different climates making it suitable for a wide variety of floral species. On Quebec's east coast to British Colombia's west coast, flowers can be seen across the lands. Spring brought in blooming tulips, blue irises, and the **Madonna lily** in Quebec. My mind was in an art therapeutic mode.

I arrived in the Eastern Townships (Cantons-de-lest) where there was a profusion of picturesque traits including being the cradle for grapevines. I passed through many villages, and all seemed to be brimming with holiday resorts. It was hard for me to imagine the changes that took place. The Eastern Townships had hardly developed before I left. Suddenly it offered theatres, art galleries, antiques dealers, and eloquent dining. Luckily, there were also cozy inns where I stopped to put my feet up. This region had irresistible gourmet getaways. I remember eating combinations of natural herbs and organic food, delightfully tasty and aesthetically pleasing.

From the window of an inn, I could see the mountain horizons and broad blue lakes. This captured treasured memories of early childhood days. I used to enjoy nature trails deep in the forests, caves hiding in the interior and the aromatic smell of pine trees. There were no railway tracks or shortage of hiking trails here. Once again, I was living in harmony with nature; a place that brought serenity lost in time.

After enjoying the countryside, I took the drive to Montreal. I paused to look around and thought to myself that it is one of the most appealing cities in North America. "*Montreal has been praised by New York Times as a marvelous city in the same class as Paris, Rome, San Francisco, New York, and London.*"[50] Sidewalk cafes, remarkable cathedrals like Saint Joseph's Oratory (Mont Royal), the Notre-Dame Basilica, and Mary Queen of the World reflect the quality of life and culture. There were also remnants from Expo 67 past, including pavilions belonging to America and France. Scenery everywhere was incredibly panoramic. There were parks aplenty, lakes, ball fields, bike paths, walking paths, eclectic boutiques, high-rises, with a mix of old and new architecture.

I was taken aback to see Maison (House) Saint Gabriel, a magnificent 300-year old home in the Pointe Saint Charles neighborhood. This is one of the finest examples of traditional Quebec architecture that was later converted into a museum. It was hard for me to grasp that Chateau Ramezay was still erect. This was a structure constructed in the 18th century and once housed the governors of Montreal, the West Indies Company of France, and the Governors-General of British North America. Like

Saint-Gabriel, the Chateau was also transformed into one of the oldest private museums. The places and things of beauty I could list would go on forever.

Coming back to Montreal reminded me of when my brother lived in the well-known Habitat complex built in 1967. It was a remarkable complex that combined private homes with modern apartment buildings to create interlocking modules with gardens. My brother had a small garden and vines growing from the inside of his module and analogous to the vines of my mind. This was an interconnected community that still provided tenants with privacy and seclusion. The 158-units looked like a city in the sky. The setting resembled a curious concrete mountain of dwelling places, strikingly modern, yet reminiscent of a Taos Indian Pueblo village, or an Italian hill town. It was pretty remarkable to look at. The views were powerful, and the whole city could be seen from a bird's-eye perspective. Neighbors could look down and see someone else's terrace. The entire community was positioned in the middle of the St. Lawrence River. From what I learned from friends and family, the compound was turned into private condominiums. I guess the structural changes are similar to my brother's absence. The reflections were haunting, and thoughts remained flowering.

I continued to drive further into surrounding communities, and eventually I settled in the west end where I grew up. This area is mainly known as a middle class residential suburb of Montreal. There were lots of high-rise Apartment buildings, shopping malls and freeways, which replaced my childhood comforts of the forest and single-dwelling or attached homes. As an adult woman, I sought different things. I wanted to relax, have a new hairstyle, get my nails manicured, close my eyes and have a facial, take-in a spa, and have a fresh start.

At that time, my thoughts turned once again towards the Freemasons, and I was troubled by what I believed was unfinished business. I had once sought after answers and information about a mystical and vital part of my father's life, and I knew that particular quest was not yet finished. This desire to capture what I did not get earlier coupled with a strong conviction that I did not want to be a follower. I wanted to be me, and create new thinking for people to look beyond the scope of what they were used to.

I let these thoughts direct my path. I had an idea what drew my father to the Freemasons. I knew the men of the group favored earthenware, so I started to design mugs with the Masonic symbol, hand painted in detail with names of members in gold and silver. However, before I could present them with my talent, I had to put forth a lot of effort to get myself in. I contended with bureaucratic paperwork in order to gain access, but I succeeded. I became the first woman in Montreal to sign the Freemason guestbook and enter the male domain – the mysterious world of the Freemasons.

After gaining entrance, I found that my curiosity was not satiated. I pursued trying to understand what my father had liked so much about this society. I never did quite figure it out because it seemed to me that it was a male gossip club, and I did not learn anything numinous. It seemed there was no mysticism to know. Still, it was satisfying to see the many gaping mouths of the members as I entered an all-male club. I did not feel connected to men, but my ideas expanded by being around them.

I continued the practices of ballet and acrobatics into my adulthood. As a fit woman, I always walked on a tightrope. I worked hard at doing unexpected maneuvers in the air. I managed to move delicately on the wire and balance in a square area. People used to watch how I performed as a gymnast. They marveled at the way my body could bend into unimaginable formations. I moved like a snake, and I was able to contort my body in such ways to create geometrical designs than seemed almost inhuman. I was like a living compass moving in every direction conceivable. I suppose I would have been a fascination to Einstein because he enjoyed watching the magnetic force at work. I had an air of mystery and appeared to look like the square and compass combined. My positioning was analogous to the squaring circle. Metaphorically speaking, my body movements were like a spiritual force within a person seeking to harmonize the spiritual and physical elements together.

I thought having the ability to shape my body flexibly into a square and compass combination was a true omen. As an artist, I believed shapes and colors were prominent representatives of deeper thoughts and emotions. I remember writing my name in a green book when I visited the Freemason lodge. Initially, I did not give it much thought. Later, I saw Freemasons in light of colorful symbolism. Men wore aprons, sashes, robes, and regalia with colors that were often blinding. According to writer Leon Zeldise, colors had significant meanings. White is the original color for a Masonic apron and is considered an emblem of purity and innocence. This has been exemplified in such images as snow falling or the **white Lily**.

I wondered if there were more to understand about these men than I did before. One of the members told me that 'green' (as in the guestbook) was an ancient Egyptian color of hope. The color was adopted by the Grand Lodge of Scotland. It was also associated with immortality. I found it compelling that on that very day, one of the Freemasons told me the story of a turtle, and it had similar connotations. In my later travels, I made a correlation to Chinese symbolism too. The green turtle symbolizes a person's fulfillment, long life, and immortality.

After I had seen the journey of the Freemasons through, I was somewhat lost as to which direction I should take next. I had the option to travel the world and see all the faraway places that intrigued me. I knew I could do this by becoming a stewardess but at the same time, I thought I could cultivate myself by studying further in the areas that interested me. I received an invitation to study abroad, and one to interview as a stewardess, and I decided to accept both possibilities. I had First Class tickets on an American airline to interview. I also had confirmation to study at a university. Upon facing this new transition, I became aware that I was still emotionally set back from losing my father, brother-in-Law, and grandfather in a small timeframe. These men mattered to me, and I found myself realizing that my path aligned with men. I was among many men, impressionistic in the Poppy Field or the flower in the corporate world of North America.

Since I had never experienced a First Class air flight, I was infatuated with the offerings. I tried the extravaganza appetizers and continued to snack frequently. It was hard for me to resist having caviar with traditional garnishes, duck foie gras, chicken in aspic with celery salad to name a few. At the time, my frame was dainty, and I do not think I weighed more than a hundred pounds. When I arrived at the airport, the employees who received me immediately directed me to a large room. Apparently, my snacking did not help. I weighed half a pound over the required weight for a stewardess and was denied the position. Consequently, I took the alternative to explore the Arts and Humanities.

As explained earlier in Chapter 6, I aimed for scholarship. I wanted to investigate more about a simple occupation of flying above the ground. I found a quiet place in Texas and energized my imagination. I fancied creating the energy and exhilaration of a bird in flight. Creative art became a passion for me and through experimentation, I developed innovative and fresh thinking. I decided to create a doll that captured my vision. I had to imagine the doll had the ability to shift and have the floaty appearance of a bird. I produced a dainty and fragile doll, but not like the original porcelain dolls created for child's play. I contemplated the routines and patterns of bird-like creatures. Then I began crafting a porcelain doll from scratch. I shaped the forms for the doll's arms, legs, head, and shoulder area. By hand, I cast each piece of the doll's parts separately to ensure optimal definition of human bodily features. I twisted the corners and cleaned any plaster, carefully trimming excess material with a utility blade. Each doll part was fired in a kiln and later removed. I cut holes to attach the doll's limbs, neck and eyes, adding a movable armature. The limbs, neck, head and eyes had mobility. I prepared the rest of the body using a softer, less fragile material. I decided the doll would be a female Caucasian resembling the historical beauty of the Victorian era. I may not have been a flight attendant, but I paid attention to the details of the doll. I fashioned a doll that I thought would be my daughter. Her skin was pale, almost a shade of pastel bridal white, with rosy cheeks. I inserted natural sparkling eyes made of glass, accentuated by flurry-looking eyelashes. I used a wig that shaped a poetic ideal of Renaissance

Italy. The doll's hair was long, reddish blond and flowing. My doll creation was becoming alive. She **carries endemic memory, magic and possibilities**. If I were to film her, she would personify filming a bird flying in slow motion. Her uniqueness would be an even greater discovery later.

Even though I might think similarly to Einstein and other well-known achievers, I also recognize the way I think is different from the norm. I consider topics of lesser importance as mute to my imagination. Therefore, as you follow the paths of my journey, you may sense intangible patterns to how I think, but my focus has always been to record significant moments and the embedded feelings captured with them. My own art therapy incited me to help others find personal bridges they could use to access, explore and communicate their feelings, memories (both conscious and unconscious), and psychotherapeutic issues that may be evoked.

I have seen people from all walks of life interact with their own personal memories including sublime, conscious, but meaningful snapshots of associated thoughts and feelings that emerged. This made me more aware of people not only on an intuitive level, but I began reading peoples nonverbal and visual expressions too. There were valuable representational objects, symbolic self-constructs, and metaphorical transitional objects that made my own reflections integrate into theirs. For that reason, my studies evolved to include the behavioral and therapeutic elements of psychology, sociology, history, politics, government, anthropology and identifying unique needs. Furthermore, no matter where I went to educate people, I saw them coming together with me to understand their own visions and verbal messages. My studies in theories on human development added to my understanding, as did the nature of Lily flowers.

Hence, I can conclude the relationship between healing and the Arts is not a separate aesthetic ideal. The Arts are aspects of public life, which fits nicely with what I have learned about foreign cultures. Dancing, poetry, food, and all measurements of expression are part of the culture. Art has become an indispensable ritual for me as it also creates the magical powers of my imagination and the symbolic connections to the spiritual world as in my out-of-body experience. Whether I think about the Borobudur Temple in Indonesia, the Taj Mahal, or the Navajo sand painting ceremonies, I see the medicine of men, but I am a woman. In the tides that roll towards me as I move in the waters of my thoughts, I generate medicine for men and women alike to become emotionally intelligent by seeing within.

I shared my feelings in many forms because pain and endurance exist within an artist's frame. For example, Gauguin's artistic expressionism, or Salvador Dali's* surrealism, both exaggerate the use of color, animation, and spiritual form. As for me, I have resisted all sensible urges to control or extinguish my feelings for emotion. Through discovery, I find love can turn to hate, desire can ultimately become hostility, obsession may even trigger monastic continence or an infatuation may end in friendship, but passion demands all or nothing.

Chapter 12: The Aboriginals & Identity

New eyes: Dressing up emotions – 40 years old

Soon after I settled down in Montreal I was introduced to issues of sexual identity, and the aboriginal community. This was more about blending male and female values to be one. This variation in thinking also belongs to the Samoan, Andean, and First Nations people. They construct the ideology that a person is born with two-spirits. This seemed far-fetched compared to my out of body experience. At the same time, I would come to see patterns of Aboriginal people being obedient to this belief. No matter which Indigenous people I met, there were consistent patterns of exhibitionism, gambling, drinking, makeup, clothing, hairstyles, acrobatics, but mostly a battling of values between the sexes.

The Aboriginal people had an unusual construct, and I was unfamiliar with their chord of thinking. They argue there are two spirits in a person's body: male and female. This suggests there is a natural existence for cross-gender roles or the Chinese yin-yang balance meaning there is a propensity for a person to have both male and female traits. Thus, for the first time I met cross dressers, and this was not a familiar norm for me.

On my return from the United States, my family members greeted me when I arrived. They seemed exceedingly hospitable. It was almost as if my younger sister could read my mind. She automatically treated me to the things I liked the most. My baby sister lets me know I would be meeting someone the following day. She said Jackie was her long-time friend and her personal hairstylist.

The next day, Jackie entered my sister's home, and this is when he met me. He was there to change my hairstyle. The strange thing was that Jackie had the same birthday as me. This seemed to be an excellent omen for starters. Communication went well with Jackie, but I cannot say the same about how he styled my hair.

Jackie was an Aboriginal, and an avid homosexual with different ideas about image. He wanted to make drastic changes to my long, curly locks. He cropped off all my flowing tresses and turned my blondish feminine mane to a tapered boyish bob. It almost looked the same as Keiko's Japanese blunt-styled hairdo. I was extremely discontent because my new look was dreadfully strange. I thought Jackie fashioned my appearance into a nightmare style. It looked as if he snipped all my hair under a bowl creating a circular edge framing my head. He also created a Mondrian image. My hair appeared to be linear, with different colored blocks. One side of my hair was longer than the other appearing like a hard edge painting. When I saw myself in the mirror, I gasped at what I viewed. My face looked like Snow White's sister with hardly any hair. I tried getting used to the hairstyle, but it was hard to like it. From that time forward, I never allowed Jackie to cut my hair.

I just did not feel like myself. I did not like appearing as a boy. I also disliked the upkeep and the fuss of trimming until it grew back evenly. I still stayed in touch with Jackie because he was a riveting subject and a curiosity. We may not have seen eye to eye on hairstyles, but his conversation reminded me of a little girl I once knew. It was hard for me to imagine what my sister talked to him about, but they did have a strong bond. In reality, Jackie was a visionary, and there were similarities between us. We began relating to one another because we both enjoyed making crafts, tasting international foods, and going to neat places. Through some common likes, we eventually developed camaraderie. Simultaneously, it was difficult for me to know Jackie or pinpoint who he is.

Through observation, I began to see Jackie in different lights. When he asked me to join him in the Montreal nightlife scene, I had no idea about it. I never experienced roaming the bars or participating in the nightlife. My upbringing was more conservative than encouraging of the unusual. Therefore, I had little understanding about what nightclubs, lounges, exclusive supper clubs, wild strip clubs, or grimy dive bars were like, but I would find out. In reality, I preferred not to know much about this lifestyle because I already met bizarre people in the United States, and you might say I had my concerns about meeting more.

It did not take me long to see what Jackie's excitement was all about. When I first got a glimpse, all the nightlife settings focused on drinking alcohol or waiting for people that talked. I also noticed that bottle service or alcohol sale was also available for anyone wanting female or male attention.

Jackie seemed to be enthralled with going to the trendiest or hottest nightclubs where people flocked together. The lights were bright, and security guards monitored people as they entered. When there were groups of people, it was mostly because of envy to get into the popular crowds. The settings catered to everyone whether a connoisseur, a partygoer, or just someone wanting to meet new people. The majority of the clubs stayed open until three a.m. However, many after-hours clubs stayed open until ten in the morning. The clubs usually had popular disc jockeys, and Montreal was known for the erotic industry too. There seemed to be hundreds of nightclubs with all genres of music found, such as jazz, blues, classical, house, trance, fusion, rock, or dance. Some club scenes were purely for relaxing with a martini and a cigar or sharing a pint of booze with a group of friends. This was not my cup of tea.

My sister told me that Jackie liked going to the gay bars. As I had no idea what that actually meant, I took Jackie's invitation to experience it. This was a whole new scene for me. Muscle men were mingling with frail men, and many of them wore leather, latex, jeans, and boots. Men of all kinds mingled, and some were even dressed as women. It was a peculiar sensation when one of the men dressed like a woman asked me to dance. Their flirty behavior, regardless of their appearance, was a turn off. Some of the men chose not to keep their clothes on, and others were right in the center of the stage. It was the wildest experience I ever had in my life. I could not fathom seeing Montreal nightlife again.

Then **I saw the unthinkable**; there were men performing like any theatre work on center stage. They were dressed up, making gestures, facial expressions, modulating their voice, having odd speech patterns, and wearing unusual clothing with adornments. This confabulation all pointed to an artificial quality of life. The men were dressed in tight attire, and they swayed their body side to side as if to emphasize their body form. They caked their makeup on heavily, outlined their eyes, and false glittery eyelashes fluttered outward. The men had dramatized lips worn in glossy shades of cherry red, magenta, chartreuse, royal purple, or some other hue. The drama of vivid colors, sequins, beading, and dazzling accessories accentuated their clothing. This scenario matched Robin Williams' appearance as a cabaret owner in his movie, *The Bird Cage* (1996). The hairdos of the men were unbelievably out of the ordinary. Many looked as they had a spindle top that was ready to fly off their head. Most of the performers wore wigs in hues of pink, purple, gold, bronze, or other colors. Their hair, whether their own, or a wig puffed out, reminded me of a fluffy static helium balloon.

When the male performers came on stage, I had an eye opener. Their performances were spectacular. It may have started out simply, but extraordinary acts soon followed. For example, when a Drag Queen made his entrance, he came on stage doing the splits, accompanied by the dramatic music from the *Phantom of the Opera*. It began with soft sounding music, and the volume increased to the blaring sounds of the jungle. Themes varied from single performers to groups acting together as a bee colony, dragon, caterpillar, or another sort of assemblage.

I remember watching the performance of the unimaginable. Three men tied together inside a fantasy dragon costume, who revealed their identity revealed only after the performance finished. They wore an avant-garde blazing red, dark green, and neon yellow covering that blurred the line between art and fashion albeit in remarkably diverse ways. The three-humped sculptured wrap was a grotesque replication of a reptilian that had no rules. I was able to see a bizarre resemblance to the original Komodo dragon in terms of size. The dragon cover-up was a shimmering fabric measuring ten and half feet long. Of course, the combined weight of the three performers was at least 600 pounds, so when they came on stage, there was a prodigious rumble. On the top of the three-headed dragon, there were nine pairs of binocular formed eyes with a humongous snout giving the illusion of fire erupting. I am not sure how they came up with this novel idea, but there was some ingenuity. Even though the dragon's mouth was as narrow as a pencil, the transvestites flirted insouciantly with some construction workers in the audience ignoring what they wore. Subsequently, from the dragon's image, the three men transformed into high femme blondes suddenly wearing a tiny leather *outfit* that was about to come off. Surprisingly, they also wore spiky six-inch heels that mirrored the see-through effect of Cinderella's glass slippers, but in a size 12. The design was magical in that there was an enormous rounded front platform with a peep-toe. These amazing shoes complimented a sizzling red, chromatic spider web of sheer pantyhose signalling artists that emerged sky-high. I suspect they had anti-slip traction allowing their emaciated legs to entertain without wobbling.

When these cross dressers performed, the stage show lit up. Some of the performers came out running and screaming. Others copied the sounds of Cher, '*Back in Time*,' Marilyn Monroe, '*Diamonds are a Girl's Best Friend*,' the soundtracks of *Mrs. Doubtfire*, '*Looks like a Lady, Sounds like a Ma*n.' I was clueless as to how they came up with their ideas.

My main concern related to Jackie's nonstop drinking. It was not even an hour and Jackie consumed so much alcohol that he reeked. I was worried about how he would come out of his stupor. Jackie looked as if he were on an island of his own, a lonely planet. How was it possible that two people born on the same date were so unimaginably different?

My struggles began when Jackie had difficulties standing up. Finally, I managed to wave down a taxi. The cab dropped him off at his home. This whole experience was extremely strange, and I had no idea that Jackie would be an issue or that such eccentric entertainment existed. When Jackie asked me to go with him again, I said no. I was not in the least bit curious about seeing his irrational behavior or the strain of trying to get him to be alert enough to stand up.

I suppose Jackie was inquisitive about me too. I knew his secrets. I suspect he may have wanted to know mine. Subsequently, Jackie told he did not have a car. He asked if I would be willing to drive him to his home in Ontario. He said he had not seen his family in a long time, and he would appreciate it if I could help out. I agreed to take him there.

During our trip, he had the opportunity to know me, especially since the drive was several hours away. We set out together with a picnic basket allowing us to munch on the way. Traveling westward, Jackie began to tell me about his family. He revealed that, besides his mother, he had five brothers. All of them were drunks and heavy smokers. Jackie told me that his father was their model. He was an unemployed alcoholic, gambler, and a womanizer. He did not know much about his father except that he abandoned him at three months old. Social services had removed all the brothers, including Jackie, from their home and they had grown up in foster care. Based on Jackie's feedback, they all had an unsettling life experience. When they grew up, Jackie's brothers all returned to the reservation to stay with their mother. Jackie was the only son that lived in Montreal and visited occasionally. Even though I knew about the twin-spirit ideology, it did not fully explain why Jackie was a cross dresser intentionally. I thought maybe he had identity issues.

I began thinking about Jackie's Asiatic features and how he also looked like men in other cultures. Chinese men often play female characters or *Dan* in Chinese Opera. Culturally the Chinese explained this as a man better knows what he likes about a woman. Therefore, he can perform it better than a woman can. In that context, Jackie reminded me of *Dan Ma Dan (Tao Ma Tan),* an aggressive, forceful, female figure that wanted 'his' way. In Western Samoa (The Pacific Rim), the people would have also accepted Jackie as an '*Affine*' or feminine-man human being. The families paid more attention to the *Affine* than to a woman, because they were typically successful in everything they undertook. In South America, the Andean people believed in the blending of male and female or an androgynous creation too. Thus, the appearance of the conventional masculine and feminine traits were confusing. This gave me an impression that their sexual preferences were questionable. As for the Native artists, they drew on their rich legacy of *Nana bush*, a trickster in many First Nations' storytelling. This seams together the tale of two young men battling with their sexuality.

When I studied more about the ancient human culture or the ethnography in the Huron tribe, information about the Two-Spirit person's reality came up. These findings fit in well with how Jackie behaved. He was beautifying women as a hairdresser, but also adorning himself as a woman. His female traits led him to be attracted to men. This understanding is certainly different from what I knew as a child. I listened to him talk and share more about himself. Then I realized I must have been driving for quite a while. My thoughts continued to flow as if I were in a dreamlike state. This sensation was a result of the sun beating down heavily, and I was feeling imbalanced. Luckily, there was a sudden breeze, and this made my hair fly. The wind also alarmed and alerted Jackie. He said we were pretty close to our destination. Jackie rubbed his eyes and sat upright with flushed cheeks. I wondered why his color changed. Did he have high blood pressure? Was he drinking? What was going on with him? When we arrived at the Indian reservation, there was a sense of community. I could feel it when everyone greeted Jackie. The event was almost magical. I could see people coming to meet him. Some of the people hovered nearby while others came directly to embrace Jackie. There were a few onlookers at a distance too.

I found a water hose and began spraying the car down. I wanted to remove the dust and grime from our travels. This is when the relatives in Jackie's family laughed. They had no idea I could do a car wash for a Camaro convertible in their dusty community. Luckily, the electronic system did not break down, and it brought everyone some humor.

Jackie's family embraced him, and we all walked to his home together. His mother's home reminded me terribly of being in rural Thailand. Their house was simple and unadorned with hardly any furniture. I think there maybe was one photograph hanging up. The walls were paper thin, and the housing standard looked similar to Thailand's poor countryside.

When we first arrived in the home, Jackie's brother offered him a beer, and he joined his brothers in drinking. Soon after, all the men in Jackie's home were drunk. They started playing cards and betting small sums of money. Jackie's family members became obnoxious and extremely loud. It was during that time that I watched how the people socialized.

About two hours later, Jackie and his brothers asked me to walk with them around the reservation. People greeted us as we approached. The brothers paused briefly whenever they saw friends. Suddenly, they stopped when they reached the Bingo Hall setup in a large church vestibule. There was already a crowd of people inside feeling they would get lucky. Lots of chattering was taking place both inside and outside the hall. I had the feeling that most of these people were impulsive players because they were honestly pushing to get inside and anxious to play. I assumed this is where Jackie acquired his first gambling habit.

Before the game began, Jackie encouraged me to play. This is when he revealed his early exposure to gambling was just as a tot. He found gambling to be a reasonable way to reduce stress. Gambling also brought hope to the community at large. Everyone was wishing to win. Jackie had no idea that gambling was taboo in my family. Since I was in an unfamiliar setting, I thought trying it would reveal why my parents told me gambling was not decent. Since my car was still wet from the wash down, time favored that I try one play.

Jackie collected eight separate cards for me to play. He also obtained a handful of cards for himself. The game was about to start, and everyone became silent. People of all ages participated, and I guess there must have been the possibility to receive money for some of them.

The game began with the moderator calling out bingo numbers. Each time he called a number, a player marked its place on a square. It was difficult at times to keep up with the pace, but I managed.

Thirty minutes later after playing one game, I matched all the numbers and won sixty-five dollars. This seemed to be so much fun.

The winnings certainly would cover the gas on the return trip, but there was something about the game that caused me to pause. I did not play anymore, although we stayed late into the night. People were drinking and smoking, and I was not at all comfortable. Finally, at about two a.m. we returned to Jackie's home.

The house resembled the nursery rhyme story of *The Old Woman that Lived in the Shoe.* Jackie's mother and all her children were safe and sound in their shoe-like home. All her children were laced up in spots all around the house. Instead of Jackie's mother serving wholesome milk, she gave them some beer again. Then she whipped her boys soundly off to sleep.

This was not a comfortable setting. There were blankets everywhere on the floor, dishes piled up, a mountain of beer bottles, soiled clothes spread around, and food left out to rot. No one seemed bothered by it. They all lay down in this mess. I had little choice where to sleep, and my biggest fear was crawling insects at nightfall. Therefore, I did not go to sleep. Probably, I dozed off a few times, but as soon as the sun rose, I left their home.

Jackie was still asleep, and I knew no one would get up until a few hours later. First, I checked if the vehicle was dry, and it was. This gave me the freedom to know I could leave that day. Next, I started walking around the reservation grounds. There was a quietness comparable to a winter's silence and all the homes looked alike. I continued walking with no idea where I was going. Just ahead, I saw the forest, and I proceeded with extreme caution. I knew there were some animal traps, so I walked carefully. The traps were setup by the Indian people, allowing them to capture creatures like rabbits, deer, moose, bears, or a fox. As I walked forward, there was a fresh, crisp smell of the forest, which reminded me of my childhood.

I had awakened to the morning dew. It was wonderfully refreshing promenading through the forest compared to the stench at Jackie‘s home. It was a pleasure being in the forest. The air was warm, alive, and rich with the sweet smell of pine, cedar, and mulch. The canopy of trees shaded some of the strong heat of the sun. There was also the sound of birds chirping. They did this in their secret language, and the sunlight glowed in rays cast through the branches. It seemed like nothing could ever be calmer than the background music of the forest. There was gentle, moving water up ahead. I was not sure if there were more things to see and what to expect (a stream, creek, brook, or river?).

Shifting forward, there was a babbling brook flowing over the rocks. It created a gurgling watery sound that relaxed me. The water tumbled over the rocks, and the gentle winds were making their way waving through the forest. This was the most pleasing and relaxing sound, and an enjoyable place to be. It was far from the noisy, shouting sounds of the bingo hall, or the belching echo of beer drinkers. This is when I walked over the rocks and saw a canoe not far away.

A string loosely attached the canoe to a tree. Since there were no identifying marks to know whom it belonged to, I borrowed it. I wanted to experience the Canadian wilderness. I remembered what the Canadian Prime Minister Pierre Elliott Trudeau once said. He described the canoeing journey as something that made you feel like a *child of nature*. This gave me the inclination to get into the canoe and try it out for myself. I could see fish teeming in the translucent blue-green waters.

At first, it was a bit awkward getting into the canoe because it seemed to rock back and forward. The paddles were in the canoe, and I had no idea what to do with them. I squatted down in the center of the canoe and leaned forward. Nothing seemed to be happening. Then I took the canoe paddles out. I imagined I was a duck, and I placed the paddles in the water pushing back and forward. The canoe began moving, and the water made some gentle waves. I did not need much pressure, and the canoe glided on its own.

Traveling along the water, there were small sunlit ripples following that created unusual abstract patterns, and they were utterly beautiful. The small waves were changing patterns. They reflected a sweet gentleness patterning diamond-shaped designs. The ripples were irregularly changing into a rectangular shape. Then they moved back into a diamond form. The tiny currents flowed like a braided stream running across from one side to the other. There was absolute silence. Suddenly, I imagined I could hear sloshing footsteps as if someone were walking on the water nearby. I honestly liked this feeling of solitude and nature, so this phenomenon of the imagined footsteps frightened me a little. I was surrounded only by water, forest, and the sky above.

I took no chances, and manipulated the canoe to move forward at its own accord. Then I put the paddles back into the boat. I had an illusion that I was protected from harm's way whether by a Sequatchie, animal, or person. The sensation could have been perfect.

I have no idea how long I was out in the water. Time seemed to be infinite, and I treasured the experience. At the same time, I had no desire to remind myself that I came with Jackie. I was in a world of enchantment, and it was my own. I began to fantasize that this place was where Disney's seven dwarves wanted to stay with me in the forest. I do not remember what happened next, but it seemed as if something awakened me abruptly from my dream.

I could hear the voices of small children playing. I guessed that the canoe drifted far away because of some gusting winds. Instead, I was at the foot of a river, which was fairly close by to where Jackie's mother lived with his brothers. Suddenly, I heard footsteps cracking on some fallen twigs. Some Aboriginal people approached me. They helped me out of the canoe and brought me back to Jackie's family.

When I arrived at Jackie's home, the members of his family were awake. Astoundingly, they all seemed energetic. As I felt uncomfortable going back inside their home, I asked Jackie if he would be ready to return and get his belongings to leave.

A short while afterward, our journey homeward bound to Montreal was mostly quiet. Jackie brought up my winnings and asked me to share the gains. I did not respond and continued driving. I did not want to tolerate any more strangeness or be vulnerable to the suggestion to bring him somewhere else that might cause an additional disturbance for me. At that moment, I realized I held on to prejudice because I disliked what I saw. Even though we parted company, a curiosity about Jackie remained inside. What happened to these people? Why could they not appreciate the beautiful things in nature without turning their homes into dilapidated shoes?

During the time spent in the Aboriginal community, I learned some things of value. The Aboriginal people had a different sense of how inclusion worked. Older members of Jackie's community were called Elders. These seniors were valued for their knowledge of how to carry on past traditions and teach community members. They taught the young to trap, skin, clean, and cook the animals they caught. It could have been a deer, buffalo, or another animal. The Elders also spread stunning mystical meanings throughout the community. In later years, my travels to other Aboriginal communities were similar.

In the short time I stayed there, I observed people in prayer. They did this together in unison and out in nature. At their sweat lodge or in their homes, the natives practiced ritualistic ceremonies, and conducted song and dance. In other words, these people displayed their decent qualities and this created harmony. The feeling of being in accord with nature was part of my own philosophy too.

I recall that one of the First Nations Elders told me that everyone was a child of the Earth. He explained that all people were "*intended to live in harmony with each other.*"[51] This also meant we were to be a part of the global environment and be among all living things too. Sometimes what they said, and how they did things led me to the conclusion that their thinking was not always rational. For example, I remember seeing a lot of dirty dogs running loose. They were in search of food, some howling and others looked unfriendly. I had a hard time believing that these filthy dogs belonged to any community members. Out of the blue, expert gunmen gunned down all the dogs on the reservation. The experience on the Indian reservation gave me the opportunity to learn how chaos and nature worked in harmony too.

In terms of Jackie, his behavior was truly like a two-spirited personality. He helped me expand my horizons by learning more about the Aboriginal people than I knew before. I was his female friend, but as a homosexual, Jackie also prized his masculinity. He did this when he saw me as a friend, but also made deliberate attempts to change my appearance to appear more masculine.

This relates to picking up a piece of dirt and conceptualizing that this is where a person starts and finishes their life's journey. All the Aboriginal values were about the land providing them with their food, culture, identity, and spiritual essence. An ideology that also corresponds with the Freemason principles. There is a symbolic gesture made when men toast together with their ceramic mugs. Hence, the mugs were made of the soil, symbolically meaning all human beings come from the earth and remain a part of the land to infinity. The only variation in Aboriginal and Freemason philosophy is the belief of the female spirit. The Aboriginals believe the female spirit is astonishingly nurturing, but the Freemasons primarily focus on their fraternal brotherhood. According to freelance writer Molly Edmonds, "*the Freemasons' constitution makes it clear that no girls are allowed.*" [52]

As for Jackie, he was still trying to enhance his female side with his male partner, but they split up. I am not sure if Jackie ever figured out what he necessarily had to consider. His return to seeing his five brothers and mother may have triggered some answers. There is no certainty to what he concluded, but I know that we both had a spiritual quest about the enigmas in the world.

When I reflect about Thailand, it was their spiritual festivities that gave rise to thinking more about what **the soul needs**. The Thai celebration of *Songkram* begins their revels in April and lasts for a few days. *Songkram* represents the beginning of a new Solar year, almost like a person begins a fresh start. During this festival, everyone gets wet and cools down as this is the hottest season of the year, and is the official time that people do their spring-cleaning. Their spiritual belief implicates that anything old and useless needs to be thrown away. Otherwise, they think unpleasant luck follows the owner. During this time, the Thai bathe their Buddha images and elder men as part of their ceremony. Young people pour scented water into the hands of their Elders and parents. This marks a sign of respect while they seek blessings. Since this ceremony uses water as a purification source, it also means *Nagas*, or the symbolic belief that the soul spurs out of the water, nurturing the crops while cleansing and purifying of the mind. The idea of *Nagas* (water serpent) was borrowed from Indian mythology. In their reality, water gets offered to the Sun God and to their ancestors (*purvey)*.

On the reservation, the soul takes on a different journey, that of the two-spirited soul. I found no particular rationale why the male and female traits were blended. However, their activities such as drinking, gambling, smoking, drug use, socialization, and filthy habits intermingled. The setting was unquestionably a poverty trap, and Jackie realized it. This was a colossal contrast to the inviting peaceful land surrounding them.

The house on the reservation mirrored my experience when I resided in Thailand, Texas, the Philippines, and other localities. It was the appalling side to poverty where people literally lived as though laced up in a shoe. The wilderness symbolically presented the trappings in the lives of the people. They caught small animals like rabbits, moose, bears, and foxes, which they ate. Simultaneously, the setting drew attention that both environments were still side by side. They both brought stressors and feelings of empowerment regardless of the person's sexual identity.

In the city nightlife, I saw people also had impulsive behavior. They drank, gambled, smoked, consumed drugs, had flirtatious behavior, and employed sullied habits too. The only difference was the size of the shoes people lived in. Inadvertently, the two settings exposed me to the trappings that people confronted, and contradictions in lifestyles. In terms of the Aboriginal principles of harmonious living, both settings related to gatherings.

Regardless of setting, the reservation or the city, it does not seem to matter where a child (soul) grows up. Societies cope with established harmful norms including corruption, favoritism, human trafficking, pornography, a poorly educated population, identity issues, safety, and more. This was the same for me whether I journeyed to Chinatown, the psychiatric wards, Harlem, Third Ward, or elsewhere. These were all places where a young person might not have been safe.

Considering Jackie's roots, his parents grew up in the residential school system. This came into effect, and many Aboriginal traditions were lost. For that reason, oral history attempts to retain old traditions. This means that when I arrived on the reservation, the people saw me as a foreigner. Even though I came with Jackie, community members kept a shut door policy. They did not try to know me, and the situation worsened when I later visited reservations on my own. People turned their faces away, and there were no call backs. I had a hard time understanding the people's expectations. I grew up with a different set of values. My understanding about the Aboriginal people began with acquired knowledge about their oral traditions. The Elders and all community members shared food, habits, and trials and tribulations. The gossip culture added to their thoughts. It was only through slow stages of relationship building that some tribal members eventually accepted me. I do not think I was particularly after the people's acceptance, but my soul dictated there was a reason for me to be at Jackie's reservation and other similar settings later on.

As for traditions, they were not all lost. When I accompanied Jackie to his community, the Aboriginals burned sweet grass as their means of soul purification. The Aboriginals prayed to their Great Spirit (Creator) as a measure of natural nourishment that came from the earth. Their belief was incredibly strong, and most people carried braids of sweet grass with them or hung it on their necks as a continued connection. It was at this reservation and many others that followed that the Aboriginal people named me the ***Rainbow Lady***. The name comes from an oral story that tells of a powerful woman that disliked loud noises, liked painting, conceived twins, understood the struggle of the people, and had super potency. The Aboriginal people assumed I had a higher purpose in life.

I had no idea if my purpose was to help the Aboriginal people, but somehow I became enmeshed with their needs on more than one occasion. Through my travels, I observed many Aboriginal people in Canada and the United States. They still struggle for their basic rights, services, and respect. Many of their problems are related to North

Americans constantly trying to fix Aboriginal lifestyles to be as their own. After many historical injustices: residential schools, limiting resources, distrust, and others, the Aboriginal people are left in an exceptionally poor shape (mentality, monetary, physically).

As in Jackie's record, many Aboriginal children were deprived the opportunity to obtain an education. The original settlers took away their land and culture. It is unfortunate, but history presents a situation of demise. In all the Aboriginal settings where I went, there was extreme poverty. This is related not only to monetary assets, but the number of children born with Fetal Alcohol Syndrome is twenty-five times higher than the world average. There is a growing number of Aboriginal people that move to urban centers, like Jackie. This is in part because basic medical needs are not available on reservations. Any serious conditions require the community to have a helicopter and fly a patient to the nearest hospital. Individuals that need services such as checking for hearing loss, vision problems, and many more, are also out of luck. There is an alarming growth of emergent issues related to diseases like tuberculosis, diabetes, chronic kidney diseases, HIV/AIDS, and cancer. Thus, the Aboriginal people are caught in a dying lifestyle; hunting, trapping, and camping because North Americans continue to construct on their land, many times without their consent. Such examples are demonstrated by bombing, or tapping into resources. There have been examples of large-scale international organizations that siphoned aboriginal wealth. They placed a pipe underground to filter oil from the land, managing to bamboozle the indigenous resources by not tapping directly on the land's surface. They did this because of some technicality. As a result, the Aboriginal people are fighting back, but often with a no-win situation.

When I visited Jackie's home on the reservation, I saw a situation of paucity. Their psychological state of health was unsound. At least fifty percent of the people were living with less money than people working in the city. This gave them the impetus to leave the reservation to find work elsewhere, sustain odd jobs on the reservation to support Indian Affairs, or accept social assistance. No matter where the Aboriginal people acquired funds, they habitually consumed their money by gambling, drinking, smoking, blaming, and having other inappropriate habits. This was quite apparent when I met Jackie and his brothers. As soon as Jackie received his paycheck, he immediately spent the bulk of his earnings on gambling, drinking, drugs, and clubs. This might have been a way for him to escape his childhood realities and reduce feelings of shame about his roots. Jackie had difficulties coping with his soul connection and relationship building.

This situation is not merely a matter of providing community based social services, but a continued growing issue to gain the trust of the Elders, the Council, the Chief, and allow them to carry on their Aboriginal traditions. Even in terms of housing, North American government has taken the role of creating their accommodations. In the taking of land, they also have taken their right to allow them to live their lifestyle. The government official who built western-styled homes for the Inuit people I spoke of earlier exemplifies this issue. The official described being highly confused about how the Inuit people treated the housing. Unfortunately, when he went to assess the situation, he was in for a rude shock.

Consider what happened to the Innu Nation fairly recently. It is inopportune, but North Americans listen to the media, and miss the full story. Mostly because the media, whether in television, internet, radio, or in print, is unaware of the true struggles the Aboriginal people face or does not bother asking them what they need.

Daniel Ashini represented the Innu Nation to express his concern about his people. He said that in his densely populated communities around the Davis inlet, traditional ways of life were being jeopardized impacting 1,200 community members. It is a result of progress with the advent of industries (forestry, mining) and hydroelectric development. Ashini summarized his findings in a report called "*Between a Rock and a Hard Place.*" [53] He alludes to land assessments, land rights, and agreements not in place. This allowed mining companies to blast in areas where people lived, and disrupt hunting grounds. This also affected ancestral burial grounds, destroying and arresting their lifestyle. The Innu people were unable to use their canoes, camps, and trap lines. In addition, the military sent out NATO fighter jets that flew low to the ground. They were skimming lakes, rivers, and treetops to steer clear of radar detection and set off bombs. This left a trail of demise; pollution, burning, frightened children, and canoes tipped over with people inside. When the Innu people protested, a heavily armed Royal Canadian Mounted Police retaliated and the matter went to court to prevent further developments. Ashini's efforts failed even though he appealed to developers to keep an open mind about what they were doing. Ashini also set up the *Tshikapisik Foundation* to promote and safeguard the Innu culture. Outsiders have deliberately ignored requests to let the Aboriginal people live the life they have for years without interference. If this same situation were in Jackie's community, the reactions of people would probably appear the same. Thus, it seems their fight to retain their ways is futile. In many cases, the Aboriginals have replaced hunting with drinking, gambling, and alternate ways to gather food, leaving people in a state of demise.

When governments apply North American justice standards to people of different cultures, it does not necessarily always work, as in the case of Ashini. When I worked among the Aboriginal people, I saw their justice practices were different. When a youth did something that inappropriate, there was a consensus among Elders about what should be done. They did not employ the conventional North American justice system. People in the group used a talking stick. This allowed each Aboriginal person an opportunity to voice their opinion whether they were involved or not. It also provided the Elders a chance to hear a variety of perspectives regardless of the issue (interpersonal violence, property crimes, family problems, friction, disorder, or other forms of social tension). In other words, the Aboriginals listened to what others said. It was all about consensus building, and the Elders pointed out that the Royal Commission on Aboriginal People forced them to use the conventional justice system. According to Deprew, a social researcher, "*the justice goals of the Aboriginal people were not considered.*"[54] The North Americans have trivialized what matters to them.

When I went to a Navajo community, I saw that conventional North American ways do not work. The situation opened my eyes to the talents of these people. An Aboriginal executive introduced me to how their hiring process of a doctor operated. The man sat or stood in the center of an allocated area. Then the Shaman used his natural powers to assess if this man would be a good healer, and he determined he was not. The Shaman explained that the man had something wrong with his left eye. In addition, he had internal conflict and was not synchronized. In fact, these realities were true. The doctor checked on his eye to discover he had the early stages of cancer. Furthermore, his ex-had recently served him with divorce papers and he was in turmoil. In other words, the Shaman gave him a second chance at life. This kind of sight and justice remains uncommon for North American habits.

When I decided to support the Aboriginal people, I needed to assess assumptions, approaches, and personal constraints. I realized that helping the Aboriginal people meant that I could not assume anything regardless of my comfort level. It is because I retained an open mind that I was able to support different tribes in their direction. It was mostly about making linkages work better and more favorably than before. As for approaches, I did not use an egocentric direction. I involved the Aboriginal people in managing their needs. Based on my observations, North Americans have the tendency only to follow what the Board or their bosses tell them to do. They do not try to think for themselves and realities of other voices get dismissed, as in Ashini's case. In terms of personal constraints, I approached departments for their opinions and acquired consensus from Elders and Council. In North America, there is the tendency to let the gatekeeper decide what is essential. This reduces the opportunity to make direct contact with parties that are culpable. If I bypassed the gatekeeper to get to the party in charge, the respondent would be rude and hang up. In other words, it is all about the wrong messages people send.

With respect to the inspirational men I relate to, Dr. Patch Adams is not only an American physician, but also a social activist. Because of his efforts, Sweet grass Writer Yvonne Irene Gladue, shared "*Dr. Patch Adams received the title of Honors Chief from the Aboriginal Cree community.*" [55] Patch was visibly moved to receive this gesture in Saddle Lake, Alberta.

Einstein added that he had a passionate need for social justice too. In his 1949 publication of *The World as I See It*, he honed into capitalism causing an increasing deprivation for others, and noted that social concerns accompanied with the right education will reach social goals.

In Dr. Robert Kearns obsession with justice and his auto part creation (windshield wipers), he won his patent fight. According to the news reporter Ken Ross, Kearns said it was never about the money, but getting a justifiable end for the little guy. This corresponds to the aboriginal or the minority (the little guy) groups in North America.

Robin Williams is another example of social justice in action. On May 20, 2010, he supported the Brisbane school in the beliefs they held, by raising funding and building a health clinic for 600 students in Papua, New Guinea. Thus, as the celebrities unfold their feats, there is no coincidence that Dr. Adams and his team invited me to attend a social conference in Ecuador in 2013 to continue addressing social justice realities.

There is no doubt that the Aboriginal people have been struggling to escape a legacy of oppression, but that does not justify them feeling negative towards a foreigner. This includes feelings towards me because I was not responsible for their grief. Since there is a lack of acceptance at all times, it is time to contemplate that the dream catcher does not only have a web of complexities as in our world, but to catch the dream of being in harmonic unity for all nations.

CHAPTER 13: TRANSITION - OVERDOSE USA

FAIR DEALS: DEEPLY BURIED TREASURES – 40 YEARS

Traveling the waves of intellect to the northern United States was not as smooth as being in the southern waters, but I still managed to dip into doctoral studies. This is where I figured out what O.D. meant. It was a combination of 'organizational development' and an 'overdose.' Evaluating what *fair dealings* undoubtedly means began when I procured a fellowship to an Ivy League school in the capital of the United States. When I arrived at the school, I was taken aback to see quite a number of S and C ring wearers, and because of their presence, I would see how Ivy League Freemasons acted. The overdose aspect proved especially true in regards to coping with moralities.

I learned that this university happened to have a reputation of catering to Freemasons. I did not know this earlier except that it was a popular institution. Competition to get in was fierce. In a short while, I became knowledgeable about how the Freemasons operated within the school. They had their own virtues and inclusive ways. I imagined this was probably going to be a place where a woman's integrity would be scrutinized often. This comes from established thinking to the boundaries of the Freemason. The issue of fairness or the *Fair Deal* inevitably came up.

I learned and was fascinated that the 32nd President of the United States, Harry Truman, had every degree of a Freemason and that it was him that came up with the slogan, ***The Fair Deal.*** His values focused on supporting education, public housing, health insurance, and expanded into social benefits. Since Truman voiced the same areas of importance that I did, I imagined that the turtle's spirit was directing me to go there and experience a *fair deal* too.

The *Fair Deal* scenario was set in motion at the Ivy League university. The situation took place when a professor began challenging me to a Masonic dual. Metaphorically speaking, I assumed his sword fighting techniques would be better than mine would, but I was not interested in a match. He wanted to show me how he knew how to balance better than I did. It was almost like determining a historical connection between us. I could not figure out why he needed to be combative. After all, the Freemasons did sword fight during the Crusades in 1118. To my knowledge, sword fighting ended two centuries later and I was unsure of his agenda. As for me, I speculated that this was not personal. The man just disliked females that stiffened his intellectual collar. Apparently, this was a fight he retained for many decades. Thus, regardless of whether I desired to engage in combat or not, I became his pet peeve. I guess I must have looked and acted like a woman that caused a crimp.

Before I came to the university, I knew my hands would be full of the fellowship I had been awarded. The professor whom I was placed under did not know me, but he must have been part of the committee that reviewed and accepted my application. I am not sure what triggered him, but as in my earlier studies, I had lots of questions. Most students also queried him, but I felt he deliberately ignored me. There was no reasoning or logic for this that I could see, and I assumed he likened me to other women of an earlier time, but I decided to approach him. This did not soften the situation, but made matters worse. I continued to work hard and feigned that the turtle would continue to guide me.

I understood that the professor thought he had good morality, but his expectations seemed to be perverse. He disliked that I took the initiative and wanted me to achieve less than my male colleagues. In other words, I must have embarrassed him at some point by saying something. I just cannot be sure what I said or did to make this happen. I reflected about all that took place, and I know with certainty I used tact. Soon after, the naked truth came out. He had a stale mind comparable to a car that needs maintenance. The situation became further substantiated when he gave our group an assignment. His knowledge base was not original. I imagine this happens to professors when they do not keep up with their reading or they become lethargic. I was not sure what transpired.

The assignment required all the doctoral colleagues to discover secrets about successful international relations. We individually had to prepare a presentation of our findings and then put it in the context of how our peers thought. The objective was to come up with an innovative approach to what constituted triumph.

I began my assignment by researching various international companies and organizations that had headquarters in the northeast United States. It did not take me too long to get a listing of corporate executive officers (CEO's). Afterwards, through diligence and persistence, I managed to get through the gatekeeper and set up meetings with a few CEOs.

Luckily, I knew the strategy of the gatekeeper, who was typically a woman that for ages had held the position of guarding a man's best interests. She would gate keep or monitor access of any persons wanting to talk with or meet the CEO. I had no concern because I was one of those gatekeepers before so I understood how things worked; I eventually swayed the gatekeeper and met my first CEO. As a credible woman, I convinced the secretary to set up the meeting for me. I did this in such a way that she perceived that it was the CEO's idea. In the back of my mind, I wanted to persuade the CEO to hire me and employ me overseas. This would allow me to justify other mentalities, and I still could pursue my studies abroad. When I revealed I was getting in touch with CEOs, The professor said this would be difficult to accomplish, and he had his doubts about my outcome. His mannerism also suggested that I annoyed him, and I was not sure what was in his mind. I did not want this to be an ongoing battle, so I asked him directly to tell me why he disliked my approach and explain his rationale. Subsequently, the professor revealed some information that exposed his earlier background. He told me that he had enormous difficulties obtaining his undergraduate and graduate degrees, and that during his experience another female professor had questioned his abilities. The woman must have diminished his efforts because he suddenly became sullen. He continued to explain that she had numerous credentials and she made him the object of her negative attention. The pair dueled about many issues. Afterwards, he commented that I reminded him of her and that I acted like this woman professor. I was not his former professor, but he still made the situation next to impossible. She stopped him from progressing. I became his punching bag and the target for his revenge.

In the interim, I managed to visit three CEOs. All the men were the heads of the world's largest distributors. Among the three men were a food producer, a clothing manufacturer and software maker. Men individually found me charming. During our dialogue, there was substantial exchange, and they provided their recipe for a successful international relations. These conversations mutually affected our directions. I took the chance to explore what the men thought, and they listened carefully to what I said. This included questioning what they said when it seemed unlikely.

My efforts worked, and the food producer offered me employment, in the United States. Since I wanted to comprehend more about international regions, I asked him why this would not be an international assignment. I added that most men applying for employment were less experienced and had fewer credentials than I had. I wanted to know what spurred him to limit me to the United States instead of going to an overseas post. The CEO was vague about his rationale. He said if I worked hard for at least three years that an exceptional opportunity might come up. I gave him the benefit of the doubt at that time, but I still did not understand it.

I needed to identify clearly, why men were being shipped overseas so quickly and I was passed up. I assumed there was a personal bias related to the patriarchal values, but this was purely speculation. It was almost like a jingle in my head. It seemed societies like the Freemasons and the Ivy League Collegiate network only wanted men.

Time revealed that I would have been an encumbrance had I been sent overseas. I explore more about this in my journeys as I see women. I see women of all status are disposable commodities. For example, I remember while I was in China, I saw women became gifts for foreign and local men. It made me squirm to see this taking place. In South Korea, even the military echelons, brought me to brothels where college-educated women were ladies of the night, eventually under the thumb of men. I recall a specific incident of a woman in Taiwan. She completed graduate studies in business in the United States. Surprisingly, she was working as a secretary, and she reported to a man who had a high school education. Even as an accomplished woman, she felt happy to have a job. Women are not considered to have the same privilege as a man. I also remember meeting a Caucasian woman in Northern China. She was one of the five women in this large country that spoke Mandarin and operated a business with men. Hence, women are not considered a desirable element to a man's domain. I disliked being confronted with patriarchal norms that do not address a woman's intellectual ability. I suppose that is why so few CEO women also exist.

Naturally, women in business can change the culture. It was hard for me to fathom when an Asian woman told me that men play their games, and they learn to roll their eyes and overlook that this is anything of importance. As far as they are concerned, men play their games, but they also have a responsibility to care for the household. I asked the woman to explain further. She says when men get mistresses it is only a sensation of the moment. Women in Asia learn to accept that this is how men need to be. It is as if **history is forgotten** and there is "*linking present to past, linking the life of the soil and man.*"[56] I did not have the same thinking and I wanted to be a woman treated equitably to a man. Women accepting male behavior is metaphorically comparable to the Chinese "*taking meat from rats and foxes and selling it as lamb*" [57] to the public. After all in Aesop's Fables and Grimm's' Fairy Tales, there is inference that there is the purpose behind everything that happens in life. For me, it was not the unbelievable or magical aspect of fairy tales, but instead, the moral lessons of foxy tales that ensnared me. The stories focused on the inequalities and many boys assume they are the 'fox' or the more clever gender. Instead, my impression over the years changed. Many men have been like snake charmers as they metaphorically play the *Pungi* or an instrument that hypnotizes women. In reality, such men are not only visible in India, Pakistan, Bangladesh, Sri Lanka, Thailand, Malaysia, Egypt, Morocco, and Tunisia, but all around the world. They lure women to believe they are outstanding, but, in fact, they act as rats selling their cooing charisma, which in reality their sound projects like that of a lamb. It is as if men have become the soothing sounds of a mother's womb and bring relaxation, softness and cuddles to a woman's mind.

Regardless, I knew if I had the will, so there would be a way for me to do it later. I was somewhat bullheaded because I swept off the CEOs dusty offer and held onto my secret ammunition. I intended to find the right situation because the professor was impeding my progress and I was ready to go overseas. I honestly wanted to discover where I fit in.

Before I prepared to go to another milieu, something struck me odd. This happened when I passed by a Home for the Elderly. I saw a pulchritudinous woman in her thirties sitting in a wheelchair. She gazed at me through the window. At first, I thought she might be visiting someone, but she remained in solitude. The woman was glowing, and radiating beams of happiness when I looked back at her. In concert, her face showed so much unhappiness too. The woman's demeanor made her seem angelic and like an incredibly beautiful **water lily** painted by French Impressionist Claude Monet. She was expressing her emotional response to the environment, as does a lily. Since all of us have certain ideas about who we are and our basic self-worth as a person, I wondered what she was thinking and why she was there.

There was something truly exceptional about this woman. She reminded me of Bangladesh's national flower symbolizing life and love. The fact that she was alone led me to consider her placement. It was an incredulity that she was there; she was too young to be there without any young company. My inquisitiveness was related to why she peeked out the window of an elderly home instead of being outside with people her own age.

After entering, I found out that the young woman, named Sue, was a resident at the old-aged home. Her husband, a Freemason, left her there. Apparently, he dropped her off at the residential institution a year ago. Sue revealed that her mother came to visit her on occasion. Otherwise, no one came to drop in on her. Sadly, her children never stopped to see their Mother. Her story was exceedingly disheartening. Listening to Sue talk, I speculated what could have happened.

Sue replicated the image of a woman from the Victorian era. She resembled the leadership of Queen Victoria (1819 - 1901) with the sharp wit of Jane Austin (1775 - 1817). Sue spent time talking to me about her 'Age of Innocence' and her former life. She talked about her domestic duties, and how she often spent day after day at home. Sue was not allowed to be part of her man's world. The woman was responsible for housework, feeding the family, shopping, cooking, psychologically and materially sustaining the children and elevating her husband's image. Sue was an excellent housewife responsible for keeping the household running like clockwork. She had a daily round of fixed and unavoidable chores. They ranged from looking after babies and preschool children all-day and night, to being home to serve her husband after his shift. She also had to hold at least an agreeable view of her husband's industrial action. All these things seemed to mean she had less worth than a man did. Sue was left only to identify with other females, her mother, the nurses at the care home, and me. This did not give her many options to feel valuable. The fact that Sue sacrificed herself to her man seemed to reinforce the loss of her own significance. Sue told me about her feelings and explained how her exceptionally high ideals were an enigma. Before Sue married, she was well appreciated, but later, the novelty wore off. Cooking and caring actually became drudgery. Sue explicated that in a short while after marriage she felt lost while her husband had a life of leisure.

At the age of thirty-one, Sue contracted Multiple sclerosis (MS), an inflammation disease in which the brain and spinal cord are damaged. The

MS affected Sue's nerve cells in her brain and spinal cord. They were unable to communicate with each other. Her condition caused real duress when her body attacked other parts. Her body was imbalanced. Based on Sue's story, she had no time off from working hard and the disease was setting in. When her neurological symptom materialized as a disorder, her family abandoned her. They probably thought her ability to think and her physical state were progressing downhill far too rapidly.

Sue described what took place. Her tale sounded as a Frankenstein horror movie rather comparable to the treatment of the Thai disabled girl in the rural village where I went earlier. I suspect the family acted on their fears. They placed Sue in confinement with the elderly assuming that isolating her was the best way for them to forget about her. Since she was disabled, they likely thought she had less to offer than a healthy adult did.

Whenever I visited Sue, I saw her yearning for health and independence. It was unfortunate, but this was not happening. I empathized with her circumstance and voluntarily spent time visiting her. I did this for several months, building blocks of friendship in hopes of building her self-esteem. Her ability to think did not worsen. Rather I viewed a self-directed person who was once again building-up her sense of worth. I did not know how long her health would sustain, nor did I ask. I accepted Sue unconditionally and without question.

Through many conversations with Sue, I accepted that Sue compromised her role as a mother and wife, to be something she was not. The situation took place because of her commitment to the preservation of Victorian values. Sue had a love for family even when they chose not to come and be with her. Her spouse and children wholeheartedly believed that she needed to adapt and accommodate to new circumstances because of her health condition. Certainly, her ideas expressed a woman in a minority circumstance. Seeing this situation unfold made me question who I was. The state of Sue's affairs made it more intense and crystallized her ill-treatment as a human being.

Subsequent visits demonstrated that Sue was gaining strength. A positive image of a Sue as a modern girl was emerging. We talked, laughed, smiled about family and things that brought happenstance. When women share stories together, they get stronger. Sue gained strength and a new sense of security in our bond. But, our visits stirred thoughts about why she was forgotten. Sue often had waves of thoughts about her family and friends. They were her cherished memories. Unfortunately, because of her expectation of death, she had little to look forward to in the future. Sue's reminiscence was attaching importance to what mattered. As a result, we began to make a scrapbook together. On occasion, her mother and the nursing staff also contributed. It would be a collection of things that mattered to her. Sometimes I brought a newspaper by. I asked her to pick out an article that she liked the most, and we would cut out and paste it into the scrapbook. We talked about the content and wrote down our commentaries.

Sue was inspired to see another perspective. Thus, I was also becoming stronger in my expressions more than before. Through our interactions, I told Sue that she was more motivated about the status quo than the true world wonders. Sue listened attentively, but she was not feeling remarkably well. Her health was declining, and she was transforming into a slumbering Snow-White. I continued visiting her, but I was only like an animation moving in time. Every time I came to see Sue, I noticed her smiles were growing weaker. During these moments, her Freemason husband should have been around, but he was not there. Like the professor, his moralities, virtues and inclusion did not seem to faze him. He may have worn the Freemason S and C ring, but he was a disappointment to Sue. The man failed to carry on his spousal obligation to love her until death parted them.

During this time with Sue, I continued to be diligent in my studies, and to visit and interview CEOs. I acquired an opportunity to go overseas, and I was excited. I did not tell Sue about this, she did not need another disappointment in her life. Four weeks before departing, I decided to bring the porcelain doll I had created earlier in the Southern United States. The doll was the spitting image of a seven-year-old girl standing four feet three inches tall. The figurine unexpectedly turned out to be an extraordinarily realistic human replica. Unlike other artwork I did, I set hazel colored glass eyes, reproducing my eye color. The doll's eyes rotated, as if she has extraordinary vision like a **princess in the making**.

The initial thought to bring her was as if something nudged at my consciousness. I had to bring the doll to Sue, but I was not sure what the compelling force was. On the other hand, I knew it would bring smiles to Sue. The doll was my most precious creation. Symbolically, I intended to let Sue see that gifts come in many forms, but I wanted to keep my doll invention.

When I arrived with the doll in hand, I saw Sue gasp. I asked her what was wrong. She said nothing, but her nonverbal cues said otherwise.

Afterwards, she voiced that she had something of importance to show me. Since she could not move, I placed my doll creation on her paralyzed limbs, pushing the wheelchair into her room. Next, she asked me to take out a photo album on her night table. I had never viewed that album before. Sue asked me to open the album to the first page, and I was awestruck. I found a picture of Sue in her early childhood days, and the doll's image was a replica of her. This gave me an incredibly eerie feeling. From a gut level, my instinct was to leave the doll with her overnight. Certainly, this would give Sue pleasure. This is because I placed a higher importance for her emotional and mental stability. I also believed that the doll would provide comfort during trying times.

The following day I received a call in the morning. Sue's mother told me that she died in her sleep embracing the doll's hands. Apparently, the night before, she asked one of the nurses to place her hand into the hands of the doll. Sue had an inclination that it was her time to journey in another world. Shortly after I left, she asked the nurse to write out her last will knowing that death was knocking at her door. One of the things she specified was that the doll be left with her during passing. I was bound to comply with her last wishes, but a part of my energy went underground too. I had to let go of remembering the image of Sue embracing the doll. I am proud to say that because of the doll she holds in death, Sue's image would still be there even if she were to be exhumed. At least she had company on her journey and this treasure followed her into the world below. This was the treasured connection between Sue and me.

Sue's death was the prattle of the day. The elders in the home talked about it. Her entire family came to see Sue laid to rest, and to say their goodbyes. Her children were present for the first time. They bid her adieu, and it was mystical seeing her own creations too. In a matter of speaking, her children and the doll were generated productions. Sue's death left me with so many questions rolling in my head. Her true spirit may have sunk deeply below, but she never had a ***Fair Deal*** in life. We became linked in more ways than one can imagine.

Sue's dying battle was not the same as my sword fight with the professor. Instead, Sue mentally managed to climb the trenches and escaped the hardships of her feelings. No matter what took place, the diseases conquered Sue. Her MS illness took its toll. In Einstein's famous words, he said, "*A man should look for what is, and not for what he thinks should be.*" [58] Thus, in all fair deal making, there is a vehicle for fair deals. It just does not come when expected. In the Freemason world, Sue may not have been pivotal to her husband, but in my world, she mattered.

In my evaluation of Sue's husband and the professor's mentality, the two Freemasons, both attending Ivy League school were the same. The men illustrated their inflexibility to think favorably about women. This also compared to be the same for the corporate executive. He chose not to send me abroad. All these men had the same frame of reference. Their rationale attests to how Ivy League thinking dominates a man's thoughts. For Sue's husband it was also about the male opportunity. His wife represented a part of his social side, and she did not fit. When Sue did not accommodate her husband's image, he removed her. There seems to be no accountability that Sue sacrificed for him and the family. Sue's troublesome journey symbolically represents women in North America. She may have been accommodating, but the significant men in her life (as in my experience), were blindly obedient to the norms of Freemason and Ivy League men. He had a sense of reliance on other men rendering him helpless. Figuratively speaking, the doll became the final decision-maker for what befalls women and the justice received. Even though Sue is buried, her life exhumes the realities of **Fair Deals** not in place. I know that the compelling source within me was telling me that voices may be buried, but they are not forgotten. Through the doll's silence, I heard Sue beckoning me to go abroad and learn more.

It is commonly predictable that a person's success relies on how to get there. This corresponds with making appropriate choices. I imagine that my next adventure would position my career choices to be better. Social researchers Pamela M. Frome and Jacquelyn S. Eccles of the University of Michigan, examined "achievement-related beliefs."[59] They also examined the roles of gender and parental influences on a child's academic performance. Their findings stipulated that females are underrepresented in careers even with advanced studies. As for me, I was strongly influenced by a two-parent family. Both of my parents were professionals and I had two teachers who believed in my talents, an Art Teacher and Grade 7 Instructor. I excelled in advanced studies even when siblings said I could not achieve. Thus, my initial motive may have been to prove others wrong, but like Sue, it was all about feeling good to achieve. Through the encouragement of teachers, I was geared up to study further and felt I should receive the same opportunities as a man.

As for the famous men, they all had professional parents. This probably steered them to study more than youths not having professional parents. Simultaneously, the men had opportunities that were much greater than those of the average woman. The root of this reality comes from author, William Nelson (1830 to 1900). He says that the Mugwumps take the middle-of-the-road position to become reformers. *"They built early bureaucracies and cared less about enhancing government efficiency....* (and)...*American bureaucracy was based on a real loose structure led by men."*[60]

In assessing twenty of the greatest American revolutionists, fifteen out of twenty were associated with the Freemasons. Some of these known men included Samuel Adams, Ethan Allen, Edmund Burke, John Claypoole, William Dawes, Benjamin Franklin, John Hancock, Thomas Jefferson, John Paul Jones, Robert Livingston, James Madison, Paul Revere, Colonel Benjamin Tupper, George Washington, and Daniel Webster and Thomas Paine. This means that even though Sue's husband put her into an old age home earlier, he would have been well respected for following Freemason men. Naturally, this beckons the question why such illustrious men and reputed thinkers who created insights into reasonable human thoughts truly surface different thinking.

The term 'bureaucracy' comes from the French and the Greek. Loosely it means '*the power of the workplace*' or '*rule by office*.' Both countries in North America therefore established a framework where people follow and retain similar habits, especially for men. Simply, a bureaucrat is a government official that is viewed as overly concerned with procedural correctness. Regrettably, they lose sight of what that correctness needs to be. This is best illustrated by the Freemasons. The men are all followers employing the same protocol and procedural correctness. It is for that reason; the Freemasons are also recognized worldwide. It is irrelevant what I did as a female. Instead, these brethren carry a particular message. They influence the youths today.

I did not adhere to societal demands and always went with my gut. I recall when my father having his own business, I followed in his footsteps and so did my sisters. As for all the famous men, they also patterned their father's tracks in some way too. Even though, their mothers may have given them the impetus to explore their ways, the men ultimately get credibility for being a man.

Dr. Adams considered his father's career and used cultural knowledge gained through his travels. His mother offered him the stamina to learn and make life joyful, but less is heard about her. It is because Dr. Adams opted to do a business radically different from most males, he became ostracized. His deviated approach caused men to have concern. Therefore, Adams' humanistic approach did not get immediate acknowledgement, but years later, he received plenty of merit.

Churchill also followed the same career path as his father, but with a slight difference. He treated military operations as if it were a business and would thrive. When he followed the writing path of his mother, he was labeled as outlandish. Media reviews slandered his excellent intentions until he deliberated to convey his message to the men of the world. Thus, like Dr. Adams, he obtains credibility in the form of a Nobel Prize.

Einstein was influenced by his father's gift of direction too. This happened when he received a compass. This accessible object magnetized his thoughts as to what was relative. In a matter, of speaking he created a body of scientific expertise that was also structured (as in bureaucratic thinking). Like Adams and Churchill, he is first viewed as a problem in society. The media report an inability to learn adequately, but through affiliation, he ultimately gets his recognition too.

As for women, personal benefit does not come along as easily or in the same form. Women strive harder, but mostly they do not play along when implicated for wrong doings.

"Sherry Hunt exemplifies a woman that was not intimidated to show what was wrong (fraud and worthless investments). She would not tolerate dishonest people that changed reports to make things look better than they were. Subsequently, Hunt took her employer to court and won $31 million." [61]

In other words, the bureaucrats sent a consistent message about bureaucracy, essentially, to carry on the Ivy League or Freemason mentality to the next generation without making many changes. Whereas, all the male celebrities, thought like me; they addressed their values according to their pragmatic concerns. For example, Adams looked at humans who were not treated fairly and offered them free medical care. Churchill devised the welfare system. Einstein considered what was relevant. Mozart shared his passionate expressions for all to hear. Dr. Kearns showed that even the little man counts. Robin Williams joked about these realities to lessen tension.

I suppose my thinking is quite controversial for the Ivy League or Freemason thinking. This is because I also would not settle for less than what I needed. I remember traveling in an Asian cargo and passenger ship. I recall what the interior looked like inside. I recollect walking around a spiral parkade of eight levels. Consumers came in numbers, and there must have been at least twelve-hundred people. As I peered downwards, I began to feel dizzy. The ship accommodated the richest class on the top level and the poorest group on the bottom. Top levels offered private cabins with a sleeper, shower and a porthole to see the outside. I had a distinct impression about what that divide looked like as I went further downward. In the bottom level, everyone stayed together in a large area. There were all kinds of people from young to old. They slept on a large bamboo mat and had no lavatory facilities. The only comfort these people had was to climb to the highest level to feel empowered, and also use the toilet. There was no place to shower. Eating was based on what people brought.

The higher classes were fewer in numbers than the lower classes. There were no more than ten people who met that criteria and I was one of them. I did not know there would be such variation because I had a Mandarin speaker purchase the ticket. This is when I discovered I also would have food included in my purchase price. I did not know that the poorer status people had no toilet or showering facilities. Like Dr. Adams and Churchill, I worried about these people having inadequate basics and wanted to see fairer treatment. Through my caring, I decided to do the right thing, so I invited a number of people at the base level to use my shower. My invitation certainly changed the dynamics of communication. The ship attendants did not like what I was doing. They assumed that the lower classes needed to be treated as such. I honestly felt that the right thing had to be done. Through simple offerings, I become the person that people want to know. They looked up to me and I became their hero for offering them equity. As for the professor and the CEO, they probably would have snubbed the lower classes and never walked below. Sue might have smiled because finally there was a **Fair Deal** without demise. 

CHAPTER 14: Indonesia, Vietnam, Cambodia

BURIED TREASURES SURFACE – 44 YEARS

After Sue had died, I had empathy or '*einfuhlung,' a feeling that we were one.* I imagined what it was like walking a mile in Sue's shoes. I could feel Sue's woes when she was diagnosed with multiple sclerosis and became paralyzed from the waist down. In her early experience, she had muscle atrophy. It commenced with numbness in her legs and eventually sensations decreased. I could feel her pain especially when she described tests she took. Sue had several lumbar punctures (spinal tap) and an electroencephalogram. Multiple sclerosis affects one person out 1,600 people, and Sue was an example.

Sue's disease activated in her early thirties, and the exact cause was unknown. According to expert doctors like *"Dr. Nancy Holland"* [62] *and "Dr. Rosaline Kalib"* [63] through collaborative efforts, their books identify that multiple sclerosis affected the ways Sue thought and impaired her emotional balance. These medical specialists added that a person's ability to process information and recall memory becomes slower. In turn, there is a reduction in attention and concentration. Thus, the person with multiple sclerosis experiences some frustrating changes. Initially, I did not see all these events happening for Sue. She never seemed to have difficulties figuring out complex problems, recognizing objects, and her verbal fluency, intellect, and ability to recall or concentrate did not seem affected. I only noticed that Sue tired frequently. I saw her as a rejected woman who needed a friend to boost her self-esteem.

It is unfortunate that Sue died only a short time later. The technology of today might have saved her. I remember reading "*David Ozzello's story*."[64] He was a Multiple Sclerosis patient that just married and had an unfortunate situation. As in Sue's scenario, his spouse stood by his side initially. In David's case, when he reached his thirties, his disease went into remission. When he reached his forties, his legs started to get weak. His balance worsened, and the illness returned. He experienced having the same treatments as Sue. They both experienced some side effects, which significantly reduced the quality of life. David decided to get treatment in China. At age fifty-four, he received "five umbilical cords, blood, stem cells, and injections" that helped him recover some of the quality of life he had. He began to walk without a brace and even went skiing. I was fascinated that Ozello had his life back and investigated further. It seemed that several other patients from America also went for treatment abroad. "*Mitzi Sprague* (2009)"[65] was thirty-six years old. "*Christian Nasaudean*"[66] was thirty-seven years old. These were other patients receiving treatments from China during 2009 to 2010. They were able to move about freely with treatments and no longer confined. This technology is new and was not available earlier for Sue, so her quality of life did not improve. It was tremendously regrettable that a home for the elderly became Sue's final stopover.

Sue was, and continued to be a subject of my interest. When Sue died, I made a commitment to her that women in North America would obtain a

Fair Deal. Inspired by Sue, I made myself some promises. I would find the wonders of the world that mattered. Consideration was made to what Einstein thought. He said that *a person should not wonder, but to let the wonders come on their own*.

My thoughts did spur questions. I could not fathom why Sue's spouse stopped caring for her. He dropped her off at an institution and left her alone. As a Freemason, her husband learned that Freemasonry teaches and practices concern for people. What happened to his virtues and his pledge to her during his marriage "*until death do us part*"?

In considering the historical arrival of the Freemason, this took place over one-hundred years ago. Like Sue's husband, the men wore their signet rings (S and C). Other symbolism surfaced, and Freemason colors appeared to be significant. "*The Red color meant putting out the flames or the firemen. The Blue color represented order or the police*."[67] Also, because there is a blue lodge, I discovered this was related to their altar. These altars signified hidden crimes and sacrifice, and were where worship took place. It has also been linked as exceedingly unpleasant to the Aboriginal people.

> "*According to reporter Anne Buggins (1999), sixty aboriginal skulls were handed over by the Freemasons for Australian investigation. This quirky finding implies the Aboriginals may have been used for sacrifice,"* [68] but the claims of the Freemason suggest otherwise.

I had inkling that mysticism or the sixth sense might possibly provide the answer. All I knew is that I had to continue my search for the ***Fair Deal*** to understand how order and fire worked for the greater good. Of course, Octavio Ocampo's surrealist illusion painting that uses Lily flowers (**Woman of Substance*) or flying birds to "*create a woman's face*,"[69] and images of other famous faces such as Einstein and Don Quixote (ballet) infer *Fair Deals* might be a false impression as both are related to the duality before balance is created. Don Quixote implies the truth lies in a man's dreams, or an "*illusion of external experiences*"[70] and I had a flight of fancy to journey next to Indonesia.

Before I went, I remember reading that Freemasonry was introduced by the Dutch in the eighteenth century. As a result of colonization, their values were spread around by the Dutch East Indies in the nineteenth century. Originally, the Freemasons of Indonesia included Europeans and Indo-people, but later the Indigenous people were included. When the Indigenous people were given a Western education, they must also have been ring wearers of the S (square) and C (compass). The Indigenous people compared to Sue's husband in a way. These were men learning to cope with moralities whether they were right or wrong. I did not think too much about it because I allowed my eyes to wander to the wonders that came to me.

I packed a few bags and arrived by plane early one evening. I was enthralled to see a bright evening sky in Indonesia. I was not ready to check into a hotel right away. I felt it would be pretty safe to go to the local night market or the *Pasar Malam,* which was located in a charming residential neighborhood. As I headed towards the marketplace, I was faced with the hustle and bustle of Jakarta. The sky seemed to be quite different compared to the United States or Canada's cosmopolitan centers, but the people seemed to pace themselves the same way.

I was a doll in my own right and Sue would have been proud if she were too. I returned looking bright, shifted my arms and legs and mobilized back to North America. By doing so, I could tell everybody what happened overseas, and maybe even Sue could hear me. Mostly, I was able to reveal the realities of morality and deception just like the meaning behind the story of *Ramayana* told in Indonesia.

I recall watching the traditional Javanese dances. There were aspects of the Hindu culture that made me question how I thought. The *Wayang Klit* or shadow puppets were displayed and sold in the local marketplaces in Yogyakarta too. They were pretty far-fetched in appearance and made out of a raw hide (dried pork or beef skin). Their appearance was amazing. There were lots of detailed patterns carved to replicate clothing and facial expressions. Spontaneously, the images made me think these were live humans speaking to me. I had a healthy curiosity about the *Wayang*. In the neighboring stall, I saw some wooden three-dimensional puppets that were handmade. They had white faces with detailed slanted solid black outlined eyes, thin eyebrows, pointed noses, mostly oval faces with wisps of hair. Some of the male puppets had mustaches. Their bodies were handcrafted and made to look real in the way they moved. Their movements were created by strings attached to joints while a rod held up the base of the head. I suspect that made them move easily to project character portraits better. Handmade characters were painted with some variation in size; heavier or blunter nose, eyes and pupils that may be larger, teeth and gums sometimes exposed. I understood that their size symbolically represented a person's traits whether courageous, foolish, evil, physical strength, or other. I was allowed to touch them and move their hands, but some of the characters seemed to have royalty. The colors and crown-shaped headdress replicated what monarchy might wear. I never expected that they would come out magically, and talk to me. This foreign land was a wake-up call to see what mattered.

Some of the vendors spoke broken English. They communicated that performances take place at night. Before I checked into a hotel, I heard some odd-sounding music. This is when I asked someone nearby what was taking place. The people around me were unable to understand me. Since the sounds were not like anything I ever heard, I walked towards the direction of the noise. The closer I came to sound, the more I realized there were some shadowy-looking figures lurking nearby. It was the inquisitive beat that triggered my interest. The sounds were so weird and wonderful I decided to go closer. I could hear gongs echoing in the hollow of bamboo tubes, reminding me of a piece of paper running it down a ribbed surface. In addition, there was a bronze clanging racket, subdued by the sweet sound of a flute. I could not help myself, so I stopped to listen and watch. The puppets were telling stories that came from Indian mythology, but the stories were in the context of local gossip, and what was happening in society. All these elements were mixed together. The puppet shows were also used to teach morality.

The local people were laughing excessively, and I understood that these were hilarious skits, but I could not fully understand the humor. I guess speaking the local language might have helped especially to see the difference of how the puppets acted. At least these puppets were illustrating how ethics and untruthfulness are necessary parts of living in order to be balanced in the world today.

Even though I enjoyed the performances, I find it hard to imagine how North Americans would absorb understanding parodies executed. The performance was mighty powerful, and the locals believed that these puppets even possessed spiritual power. I watched in amazement at how the *Dalang* or puppet master worked his magic. He made the puppets move as if they were alive. These puppet masters were incredible. They had the ability to incorporate hundreds of stories, and performed sacred rituals with these puppets too. I must have watched for more than a few hours, and people around me were still staying to listen. I knew there was more to the stories than I could understand, but I finally decided to leave.

There is no doubt that these performances were far-reaching and conveyed moralities. Sue would have liked what they taught because they believed in good moralities as she did. For example, when Sue's mother came by to comfort her, her beliefs were compatible with the Hindus. There were no harsh words spoken between them, and this was an expectation. According to the Hindus, a child needs to have this temperament (not showing restlessness, or anger) with parents. There is a twist to how they think. The Hindu people emphasize that parents might be a visible representative of God. No doubt if Sue heard her mother was a representative of God, it probably would not have sat well with her. In reality, Sue was already practicing Catholic habits. In Catholicism, the Pope, religious men and males of the church are the decision-makers. This is also no different from how people often communicate in one way (male thought dominates). When I had my doubts, I reflected on Sue having deep conversations with me.

Sue said foreigners often were meandering in how they did things. I could not agree more that she was right. At the same time, there were some unexplainable differences. I disliked hearing that a son's merit has greater importance than a daughter's. Daughters get the consideration that they are pretty objects to be adorned by their fathers. Sue's father was deceased, and so I cannot weigh what he thought or if he agreed with this idea, but he did give her some jewelry when he was alive. In contrast, the Hindus spell out more that sons are of greater value than daughters are. I do not believe this is how they believed historically, but apparently, this is how they think today. Even though this did correspond with how Sue thought, her realities mirrored Hindu notions. Her husband's disregard for her might have been considered to be indecent, but invariably, preference is still being given to the man. In Sue's world, everything always evolved around her husband, but his world did not always include her. Since Sue directed her family always being in the path of love, this makes her the champion of her own story.

On the other hand, considering Sue was a devout Catholic, she would not have fared out well in Indonesia, as the majority is Muslim and not Catholics. Sue would have had issues in understanding how things worked in Indonesia. For example, when Muslims came to Rome, the Pope welcomed the construction of a mosque in Italy. It was almost completely financed by Saudi Arabian royalty, but when the Catholics wanted to consider the construction of a Church, the Saudi Arabians strictly forbid the construction in their country. The issue of religious liberty somehow did not correspond. Fighting over this matter would certainly have not been in the best interest for peaceful relations. I suppose my visit still helped me understand that regardless of a person's faith, offering uncomplicated, common, courtesies of respect do matter. In light of my findings, I recognized that saying a common expression helped to have peaceful relations.

Regardless of a person's ethnic origin in Indonesia, I found relationship building is mostly about building friendship that is lasting. Hence, I had a general expectation that I would be able to establish strong bonds with anyone by merely employing common expressions. At least, this is how I see matters being done. As in any country, relationship building is done mostly with people that are known and liked. Everything seemed to be about people in the family, people in the company, or people in general. I could say that is also how my relationship with Sue also evolved. I was getting to know another human being simply by being respectful and working towards building trust.

In the Indonesia's culture, 'Saving Face' is extremely essential. This construct seems to be an inevitable in other Asian destinations too. Every person's reputation and social standing rests on this concept (same throughout Asia). Specifically, causing embarrassment for another person justifies a *loss of face* for all parties involved. This can even be disastrous for relationships in business negotiations, and I was becoming aware that controlling emotions and remaining friendly at all times were an imperative. I remembered observing a few foreigners at the marketplace. When they brought up an unpleasant topic with an Indonesian, they were viewed unfavorably. The Indonesian people also did not like to know anyone had difficulties. If they discovered there were problems, they would usually look the other way or gossip unfavorably. Of course, the incident of the monkey was an exception.

I became familiar with people talking extended periods of silence learning not to react instantaneously. In fact, if I also had to be undoubtedly be careful about what I said or did. I chose never to speak too loud or do things without being thoughtful. Otherwise, the Indonesian people might have assumed I had a lack of self-control including shaking hands gently. Based on my observations, it seemed like I always had to be on guard in all things I did.

When I was on my way to the airport, I stopped to get directions. The person smiled at me, but their teeth colors were ghastly. They had the tint of human blood (as discovered in Thailand first). I was taken back because I was used to seeing shades of white. The colorations were so odd, but I learned later that this is how the local people like the appearance of their teeth. Their teeth were red because they chewed a betel nut mixture. This habit was something I would discover even in Cambodia, India, Laos and the Philippines. At first, seeing this man, it gave me the creeps, but I learned to accept difference. Unfortunately, the person was not helpful, and I became leery of a person's smile. This is because I was learning smiles did not necessarily mean friendliness, amusement, or approval but a sign of embarrassment, fear or shyness. I was learning to read what people actually wanted to say.

At the marketplace, I found hand painted wooden puppets or *Wayang*, arts and crafts, batik, silk paintings, exotic birds, and all kinds of animals, household items, fresh fish, vegetables, snacks, toys, shoes, and meats galore.

I paused and mulled over the *Wayang* puppets. They metaphorically appeared to represent **people being led on strings** by their masters. I questioned whether the Indonesian people were pulled in specific directions as in cultures I saw earlier. This makes me wonder if some of them were followers having an Ivy League, Machismo or the Freemason mentality.

When the *Wayang kulit* or shadow puppets were put side by side to people, they did look human. Among the Indonesian people, the Hindus told stories with the *Wayang.* They compared human behavior to a person attached to or led by male leaders. Their stories conveyed lessons of morality from a Hindu perspective. They gave an emphasis on relationship building (mother and child). The Arabic way implied some natural inequities exist among people. This is why their religious structures were in one country, but not necessarily in another place as in the conflict, in Italy. The European and other minorities had simpler demands. They liked having personal relationships more than being alone. As a consequence, they gave a welcoming feeling of trust.

I remember someone looking at me strangely when I shook hands. People had a perception that I was an aggressor. My Eastern European roots taught me to shake hands firmly as a sign of sincerity. These people (most Asians have the same value) assumed I was taking on the dominant role of a man by shaking hands firmly. Their mentality equivocated to an Ivy League, the Freemason and the Machismo state of mind. These people were followers and there were no pearly white smiles always smiling back. In fact, sometimes people had burgundy colored teeth. This allowed them to bury parts of culture not open for women to interpret. In other words, Asian women were bought and sold regardless of their teeth. They were disposable commodities just like Sue that did not get a *Fair*

Deal.

I also saw many pirated DVDs, CDs, and computer software. The environment had its quirks, leaving me on a never-ending path of delights and discoveries. I went from one group of vendors to another, and the vivid colors were something hard to forget. I luckily arrived during the *Sakaten* festival. This celebration honored a prophet, so things were pretty hectic. The excitement of bartering using hand and body signals was more exciting that the festival preparations. The people of Indonesia habitually set a high price, and I counter-offered. The haggling went back forth, and it was like watching a seesaw in the middle of the ocean. It was a bit risky in terms of getting the price I always wanted, but I had ample deals anyway. I collected many items to take back to North America. This included paintings and a number of *Wayang* puppets. I particularly liked the artwork because it was crafty and the colors were fantastic. I acquired these items at phenomenal prices after bargaining a while.

The local people were always full of smiles, but also they jumped up promptly to sell their wares to me or any other interested person. I guess they assumed approaching a foreigner was a guaranteed sale with greater profit.

Indonesia's population is bursting at the seams with nine million people. No doubt, I learned quickly to squeeze in narrow alleys, crunching through by the hair of my teeth. People were constantly occupying space, so I moved over to try some street food. The taste was incredible, and it was hard to imagine how these vendors operated. For example, one person literally carried his shop in an L-shaped rolling cart with all his food products, wood burning supplies, and dishes, and spices positioned on both sides. On the other side of the cart, there was a sizable pot of food brewing. Some had full-scale self-contained shops with several glass shelves. They were holding a variety of ready-made foods and accompanying sauces. There were paper plates, plastic wrapping and utensils all available. The marketplace was comparable to many other markets I had seen, or would see in my many travels.

When I think about my journey in Phnom Penh, Cambodia, the marketplace awakens my imagination. As in most places in Asia, women carried children on the side of their hips or back. There were numerous street vendors selling food. When I passed by, I saw meats, sausages and animal heads hanging overhead. The meat was hanging and lined up on a metal chain. To protect from attacking insects, fruits like pineapple were usually covered. Dried fish, fresh vegetables, clothing and oddities of all kinds were displayed in the same stall, in a similar style to the market in Indonesia. Setups were definitely far removed from North American style.

The appearances of the local people were customary. Women and men wore sarongs. Their image matched styles in Thailand, Vietnam and other places. The market in Indonesia was comparable to Chatuchak market in Bangkok, Thailand. The marketplace typically makes people rise early and is open on the weekend from seven a.m. until extremely late. Bangkok also had the havoc of bustling people as in Indonesia. There were anywhere from 9,000 to 15,000 stalls running up and down the narrow alleys depending on the time of day. Many stalls had an overflow of artifacts, but pricing was incredibly affordable. Costs were at least half of what most local markets charged. Probably, this was one tenth of the cost to North America. Like the Indonesian market places, the greatest fun was the bargaining. This was also quite comparable to being in Mexico and any destinations in South America too. I also was away to munch on the street food in the market. Tastes ranged from sweet to spicy to bitter. This attribute was certainly comparable to the *Wayang* puppets. People were sweet, bitter or spicy in character. The difference in Thailand relates to the youth wearing contemporary Western clothing. In Indonesia, most of the people wore traditional attire.

As I walked through the marketplace, it was a constricting feeling. There were lots of small alleyways and children playing in-between. The most alluring time was during the water festival occasion. Many flower petals and scents stimulated the air. Monks clad in saffron robes also roamed the marketplaces. Lotus-shaped rainbow-color papers held candles in the center, and there were some other artistically folded papers set afloat as well. It was eye-catching. The colors in Cambodia truly were reminiscent of my other Asian travels. Everyone was splashing gleefully. There were water pots exploding leaving misty swirls of water in the air. Muddied thongs were ubiquitous. The feeling of water almost everywhere reminded me of being in Vietnam and Thailand simultaneously. The Hoi An markets of Vietnam displayed lots of puppetry, particularly in Saigon. This is where I went to see a water puppet show at the Golden Dragon Theatre in Ho Chi Minh City. I am not sure if the Indonesia practice started as a relation with Vietnam. This is because there, the old tradition of water puppets dates to the 11th century. The variations from the *Wayang* in Indonesia to the Philippines, Malaysia, or Thailand, were more inimitable than before.

I paused to reflect how the puppet show in Vietnam impressed me. It took place in a waist-deep pool of water, and puppets are controlled from below. The mystery of how puppeteers control the puppets from beneath the water has been a closely guarded secret. Human voices along with traditional instruments produced sound effects by the sides of the pool. The sounds caused me at times to think there was buzzing in my ears. The repetitive rhythms were not particularly pleasing to me, but the themes were of interest. They were deeply rooted in rural traditions from the villages. As in the bucolic settings of Indonesia and Thailand, the puppet shows portrayed the planting of rice, fishing, and village folklore. The theatrics of the colorful puppets make me feel I was part of their lifestyle. It was a constant wonder how the performers hid beneath the water, and this kept me guessing. Like the handmade puppets of Indonesia, the Vietnamese water puppets were also handmade. They were heavy, weighing up to 30 pounds a puppet, far larger than the average human newborn. Thus, whether the *Wayang* puppet came from Indonesia or from Vietnam, people seem to be led. They have **forgotten how to intellectualize** and think on their own.

There were unusual things taking place in Asian markets. In the Vietnamese markets, I watched the local women stoop down and kill frogs. They sold the frogs for food. As for the Indonesians, they made the assumption that all tourists are rich, so they wanted to capture my attention to get their goods sold. When they could not impress me, some of the people began shouting loudly. They were making attempts to speak English to me. This was really a noisy place, so I moved to see another area of the market. As in Vietnam, I saw artists chiseling handcrafted items like Buddha statues in full view. Bicycles also passed by and shielded flat umbrellas covered most of the marketplace. In Indonesia, the people who came to the marketplace shielded their heads. Men wore the conventional Turcoman ikat hat, beanie caps, tribal headdress, beaded hats, crochet and vintage Kuban hats. Some women also wore the beanie caps and tribal headdress, but mostly, scrub hats, netted slouch head wraps and silk coverings. Naturally, the strange hat images I saw in Vietnam also went through my head. The people in Vietnam wore conical hats about sixteen inches in diameter by nine inches high. In the Indonesian and Vietnamese marketplace, people often walked barefoot. Others butchered meats, weighed products, sold eggs, displayed fish on plates, stood guard next to caged roosters or chickens for sale, or simply carrying goods in their arms. The smell of fresh-made bread in Vietnam of baguettes or *Banh Mi Tay* or the *Sima* Pita, *Roti* Pita of Indonesia created a strong whiff of delightful aromas. The scenario of some vendors that patiently waiting for customers while they enjoyed a relaxing time lying in their hammock set usually in front of their stall. The vendors were selling their products in the market and also where ever steps seem to be. In both environments, I also had a full-view of flowers and fish, both kept alive in running water. In Vietnam, the people were dancing in the streets, and the Khmer hammer dulcimer drums were beating away. This was quite similar to what was taking place in Indonesia.

My mind was illuminated and was triggered by the spherical panorama of red, green, yellow chili peppers carpeting the landscape. It was getting late, and a necessity to find a place to stay. I steered away from the Kota area, the oldest part of town. I heard it was considered the seediest. I was reminded of what Jackie had exposed me to earlier, and I wanted to forget about the karaoke bars, health clubs, brothels, and nightclubs. Based on research and dialogue with other expatriates, I went to the

Kemand district. Known for having many restaurants, cafes, embassies, and banks, it was a popular hangout for expatriates. I decided I did not want to follow that path too. Instead, I went to the nearest guest house to test out a local lifestyle.

There were twelve rooms, and only two guests were present. The people seemed friendly enough, and I checked in. When I entered the room, there seemed to be a subtle breeze coming in. In fact, the window was left open, so I planned to close it. Somewhat exhausted from traveling, I laid my head down for a moment and threw my purse on the bed. Suddenly, I was awakened by an animal sound. I was not sure if it was a whispering or a barking sound. I listened more and the sound became distinct. There were chattering monkeys gossiping in a nearby tree.

One monkey managed to get through the open window before I had a chance to close it. The monkey was screeching in delight because it successfully grabbed my bag. I suspect the monkey wanted it more than I imagined. The monkey moved so quickly, and so did my purse. The monkey was swinging from tree limb to tree limb. I became anxious and tried calling the staff in the hotel, but the phones were not working. I quickly ran downstairs to get some help, and this spurred a lot of excitement. The monkey had a head start by swinging in the trees. The locals quickly were running, and the people used a cunning strategy. They seemed to have more skills on how to deal with catching a monkey than I did. They did it in a fantastically unique way and let the monkey get caught on its own. The people cut a small hole in a coconut. It was just large enough for a monkey to put its hand in. Next, they hung the coconut on the tree and filled it up with a sweet treat. The monkey liked the smell of the treat and squeezed his hand into the coconut. When the monkey grabbed the treat, its little monkey paw was stuck. His fist would not fit through the hole, and he would not let go of the sweet. The monkey was held prisoner, and he dropped my purse. It was an enthralling time now that I had my purse back in my hands. In the words of Karrie Webb, I felt the same. "*I mean, I think it added to my excitement to playing today, and just going out there and doing the best I could, and no matter what happened, the end of the day was going to be a good end,"* [71] and then I went to sleep.

The following day, I took a train ride from Jakarta to Yogyakarta, about fifty-six miles. To get there, I mounted a rickshaw or a two-wheeled passenger vehicle and arrived in the Gambir station. I liked this mode of transportation. It was the cheapest way to travel even though it lacked the convenience a taxi has. When I went to get my ticket to travel, the price was 300.000 Rupiahs (IDR) or $33.14 Canadian dollars. I had a hard time understanding the additional costs. There was no explanation if these were taxes or other, so I concluded it was a help yourself tip, and I moved on. I managed to find the right train and arrived in Yogyakarta a few hours later.

Surprisingly when I arrived, I saw dancers performing *Ramayana*. This was an ancient Sanskrit classical story presented in broad daylight. There was no admission cost, just an incredible opportunity to see a traditional dance drama portraying the story of excellence triumphs over malevolence. The dancers were incredibly graceful. Their movements were accompanied by Gamelan, a musical orchestra of customary Javanese instruments. Background sounds were extraordinarily different for a North American ear. The music sounds were like a variety of ringing bells with different pitches. Some had clanging sounds too. Initially, hearing the same rhythm repetitively, the fascination died. There was also a female vocalist, and she was centered. The woman sang a Javanese song describing the story. At a close-up range, I saw the performers dressed in their incredible costumes. They looked fantastically remarkable with flashy brass and gold decorum, and topped by golden headdresses. The women had long, shiny, black hair creating an incredible contrast. Their costumes were in shades of brilliant blues, fuchsia, pink and golden yellows with lots of glitter. There were a number of characters being played. Some represented Gods, animals *(red and white monkeys, golden deer)* or birds *(Jatayu).* I could not help but be excited to see the graceful movements and their talent being displayed.

The great thing about traveling afar is that you get to meet people from everywhere in the world. The audience seemed to have more privileged people (dignitaries, executives, some tourists) than locals. This was exciting to see so early in the morning. Besides the dancing performance, my day began as if I were a celebrity, and would visibly be quite colorful. The air was bright and fresh, and the sounds of the marketplace were just awakening.

Before the bustle of the day, I had breakfast. I drank a glass of my favorite avocado or mangosteen juice. Then I had some *Bubur Ayam*, an Indonesian chicken porridge, followed by a glass of *Kopi Luwak* (Indonesian ['kopi 'lu.ak]), or civet coffee, one of the most expensive types in the world—better known as "cat-poop coffee."[72] I was going en route to the Seven Wonders of the World, the Borobudur Temple, but something happened.

With a full belly and the excitement of beginning my day trip with a man-powered land vehicle, I could not have felt better. The man tried to tell me a little bit about himself while taking in the sights. This is what people do to get to know you. Even though language was an obstacle, he managed to convey his thoughts. His waistline was attached to a cart, and this transportation mode was his way to support his family. He pulled the cart at a fairly rapid pace, and we were traveling like a sailing wind. Eventually, people from the city became invisible. We were taking the dusty path towards Borobudur Temple.

Suddenly, my stomach began to gurgle, and pains in my sides set in and soon became piercing. My initial thought was that there must be a corner store nearby. Certainly, stopping at a restroom might have resolved the problem. With great difficulty, I explained to the man that I needed to use the restroom. He looked at me and said, "Ma'am, I will pray to Allah." And so he did. He bowed down, and I was not sure when he was going to get up. I became rather desperate; I was worried because now my bottom had begun to rumble too. The man got up after his prayers and signaled me to follow him. He found a local residence where people would accommodate.

It was a small house, off the beaten path, and I used a local restroom. I quickly followed him, and I entered a cement room with no doors or flush toilet. There was a small hole in the far right corner of the room, and a bucket of water. With few choices, I released, only to see that my organic deposits actually churned down through a water flow and went directly to the crops. I was amazed that I could create an organic benefit—and uncertain whether the transliterated "cat-poop coffee" had done it. In fact, it seemed to be the Seventh Wonder of the World. As individuals, we could spend our lifetimes exploring our world and never imagine that we might see one of the Seven Wonders of the World (produced by ourselves). Unquestionably, the prayers worked! In fact, his soul connection appeared to be the eighth Wonder of the World.

As an individual, I spent my lifetime exploring our world. I never imagined that I would see this wonderment otherwise.

Through my journey in Indonesia and other foreign marketplaces, I discovered the common need for merriment. This was the same basic human need that Dr. Patch Adams discerned too. Whether the conditions were of the crudest form of toilet facilities to observing the colorful costumes, the experiences brought feelings of well-being. Simultaneously, even though I met prestigious people, experimented with foods and tried tropical beverages, I found respectful ways were mostly used to appease the patriarchal leaders. It was not about getting a *Fair Deal* for a woman. Even the *Wayang* or Shadow Play puppets revealed the same issues in the epic tale of *Ramayana*. The plots all relate to how humans are at opposite ends of the continuum, either exceedingly generous or wicked. This means that issues of social justice are realized, but not necessarily are they always grasped.

An Indonesian artist named Nieuwenkamp shared, "*The Borobudur Temple is remarkably like a big lotus flower bud ready to bloom, and that was once 'floating' on a lake.*"[73] Images from his reality actually turned out to be true geologically. Thus, I found the key to cultural exploration -- it is all about looking at **the base of everything**. The base of Borobudur Temple contained the story of Karmawibhangga. It may not depict human events in sequence, but there is a theme. We, as people, all get touched by magical or heavenly notions that there is tenderness and beauty to be received in the world, so as people, we are flanked by one another. It is only our perceptions that might differ. For example, the fleur-de-lis (The Lily) is the national flower of Quebec, and, in chorus, as the *puspa bangsa* or national flower for Indonesia. May be this has something to do with the fact that the lilies growing in Indonesia are atypical. The "*Minnesota dwarf trout lilies... grow before trees develop their leaves.*"[74] This is when I began feeling like I was also growing before the roots of other people. I suppose this is a correlation to me developing my roots as I was a lower height than most trees that grow.

CHAPTER 15:

China & the Ambassadors

STEAMING SMOKY TIDES – 45+

I am dedicating this section to Sue's scrapbook titled *Fair Deal*. She would have enjoyed turning the pages to see what unfolds, capturing childhood to adult impressions.

From earlier childhood, I had some distinct impressions about China. This commenced even before my voyage to Chinatown. In my imagination, I went to places around the world through fantasy. As a confident trooper, I journey out on my own. I ventured off to obtain my initial impressions, which often stretched beyond fairy tales, fables and folklore. As I became literate, print narratives help me learn with depth. Through the stories, I acquired a deep impact on my perceptions. It is because of reading and exploring, I shaped my awareness and sensitivity to develop a broader worldview.

Some of the tales I read explained that females were not permitted to have equity with men. Feng Xin-Ming, a Chinese author, addressed how women were perceived. Their portraits do not compare to the Disney version of *Mulan*, "Ballad of *Mulan* (木兰词 Mulan ci)"[75] she was not a hero. In truth, the Chinese military would never condone that kind of travesty. If women were to disguise their image to be as a man or help a man, the woman would automatically be criminalized and killed. The North American Disney group generated selective judgment. In reality, if *Mulan* were a woman that defended her country, it truly would have meant '*losing social face*' or embarrassment for the family. The worth of a woman is further exemplified in marriage rituals. The bride's side of the family has to provide plenty of gifts for the groom's family. This same custom is also in India. The gift giving, called the dowry, is a measure to entice a man to take a daughter away from her parents so as to lessen the family's burden. When the dowry is thought to be inadequate, the woman is sometimes killed. This could have been a retaliation measure because a woman was viewed as a parasite.

Can you imagine your parents thinking about you as a, parasite whether you are male or female? I think childhood impressions matter a lot. Nobody likes to think of his or her self as a parasite. Consider Sue, she felt connected to her childhood when she saw the doll I created. Sue put her passionate childhood memories into feeling worthy.

Dr. Patch Adams always was able to turn to his mother. She gave him an impression that he mattered. Subsequently, he found ways to connect to people and his vision emerged. Churchill was exposed to the classics and aesthetic beauty. Consequently, he became an amateur landscaper, painter, pilot, farmer, and bricklayer Dr. Robert Kearns acted atypically in his youth. He started off as a junior intelligence officer and these early impressions, led him to create new patterns of thinking. Mozart came from a family of musicians. That impressed him so much that at three years old, he played the harpsichord. As for me, I knew my parents had their challenges, so I always tested possibilities and seized opportunities.

Look into your own conscious, and I bet you can recognize similar patterns too. You might think that your irregularities or emotional dysfunction is less profound, but you are as worthy as Sue, the celebrities or me. Dr. Georg Groddick, a psychological theorist of *Gesellschaft*, which means *Society*, becomes published by Stroemfeld Verlag, Frankfurt am Main /Basel. He theorized that all members in society experience indiscretion, and when there is fallout, it is recognized. After this takes place, citizens of the world are capable of bouncing back resiliently. In short, it does not matter how well known a person might be, people are capable of having early impressions, becoming emotional and reacting. Some of these may not seem ordinary, especially when we feel out of balance. Therefore, it is up to you, the reader, to think about your roots, and how you gained the impressions you have. Walk in my shoes, and see what you think.

There are only two other variations that need further considerations: They are superstitious beliefs and political influences. I began wondering about this in my early twenties especially when I watched my mother burn some fire in the sink. I had no idea what she was doing, and the event frightened me. Later in life, I researched why she might have done this. I learned that even though fire can be seen as destructive, it also provides purity and protection. "*In a Russian household they refer to the fire lit in the stove as their 'dear mother.' It protects them from evil forces.*"[76] Speculatively speaking, my mother must have had an inclination that something was happening to her mother. As well, my mother probably ascribed some of her beliefs coming from my Great-grandmother, born in Mongolia. They believed in spiritual refinement with *fire, which* is also described in Hebrew scripture. My mother made attempts to steer me from knowing these mystical things, but my curiosity only grew especially when my father passed away. I wondered what happened to his soul and where he journeyed next. When I received no answers from the Freemasons or Ivy League scholars, I met some Chinese people. Their explanations were uncanny. They told me that when a person goes beyond what they need to know, it is dangerous. Further, they shared that before a person is executed, the most sumptuous food has to be given to them to satisfy the soul. If they did not adhere to providing the best of food, the person returns as a ghost to haunt. The Chinese list of superstitions was unimaginable and related to the Mandarin word, *Han.* This word not only implies the spirit, but a person's mood and the spirit of the nation. Of course, unfamiliar exposure caused me to change many of my early impressions of people I encountered.

My interpretations also considered other countries. My impressions remained fairly constant except for political influences. As a child, the word '*communism*' struck an awful chord. My parents ran away from autocratic rulers. Cultures associated with the term were automatically considered corrupt. Therefore, it is not only variables that play into my mentality, but how my intelligence was guided emotionally.

In my China journeys, politics still played into issues regarding human consideration. As an intelligent human being, I heard much talk about human rights and a litany of grievances against some governments, not only China. Country policies become their value of a *Fair Deal*. This considers punishment, freedom of press, beliefs, and labor rights as in the *Hukou* system, in China. There may be an absence of independent unions, and practices North Americans see as morally wrong, but clashes about beliefs are a historical fact. Therefore, whether China deems Liu Xiabo, a Nobel Peace Prize winner as nominated by Americans or an instigator, in his society, he may have overstepped boundaries.

I remember meeting a government official in China. Sue probably would have liked him especially because he favored blue or colorful eyes. He told me that he always envied a foreigner because of what they possessed. As a child, he took some blue ink and put the ink in his eyes. He hoped his brown eye color would turn blue. Instead, he experienced excruciating pain and reflected on the eyes of a soul. He went on to describe how some children in small villages are kidnapped. Their eyes were taken out and sold on the black market. These children were only valued for their organs. As he shared this disheartening tale, his whole disposition darkened as if a dark cloud loomed over his head. His facial expressions changed, and he appeared enormously sad. In candor, the color of our eyes is the same as our souls. In other words, some people are meant to see the entire scope and others are not. He went on to disclose that most people have the red eye syndrome. This cultural interpretation means people are envious of others for the wrong reasons.

In light of the official's story, it is irrespective the color of a person's eyes, but rather the value that gets attributed to them. According to the Chinese official, children in poverty-stricken countries were viewed as having no real need to see. I am not sure I agree with this because while I was in Texas, I wanted youth to see in good ways. Of course, this notion is a real contrast to what most North America might anticipate. In fact, seeing all is not limited to having physical eyesight, but as I said earlier, intelligence needs emotional guidance.

Therefore, sharing my truth may not correspond to North American or worldwide media revelations of Chinese men such as Wu Shishen, Li Changquing, Pang Jianming or Ching Cheong. These men supposedly crossed boundaries for speaking out. Instead, this is about my voice being in the world of China. My stories are about my peregrinating, travel by air, ocean or other modes. Therefore, I will be capture photographs that Sue might have delighted to see in a scrapbook. Pictures can identify a woman's travel and exploring what Harry Truman said, "*North Americans need a Fair Deal.*"[77]

From Indonesia, I took a flight to Dalian, China. I remembered the Chinese doctor I met when I was still twenty years old. He told me that Dalian was his place of origin, and it was in the eastern part of China. I wanted to reflect on our earlier exchanges because he told me a lot about his native land. I expected I would not be surprised, but I was.

At first, I saw hoards of peoples moving about. They looked like masses of weeds growing everywhere. It was hard to cut through or pass other people. At that precise moment, it brought childhood memories of my first adventure in Chinatown, and the unfamiliar and unpleasant smells and sights when I was a little girl unsure of direction.

Dalian did not look like the quiet town that the medical resident described. Instead, it was more like a combination of a traditional and a modern city with lots going on. I never expected to see so much smoke in the air. The smoke seemed to blend right into the harsh odors all around me appearing like a dark cloud encircling the area. Breathing became difficult. I felt as if I was climbing the ragged edges of Mount Everest. Life appeared to be toil and peoples' spirits were in flames. This was far worse than the smoke circling around and the blackening of the environment. My head felt light and even woozy. I took pictures of what hit me most. There was an influx of people and traffic 24-hours a day. People were crossing streets in danger. The foreign check-in procedure took time, and the smells were coming closer.

People were driving their bicycles everywhere. Many people carried heavy loads. I could not imagine how they could get boxes piled up several feet high and still be mobile. Others transported children and adults. Some carried large blocks of ice, food products, and other things too. Swarms of people drove their bicycles and the numbers gave me the impression of ants weaving their way through the streets. Cars and buses squeezed through, and some drivers went the wrong way. These photographs turned out to be pictures of more than a million words. I saw an abundance of people heading to a nearby local restaurant. Following the crowd, I assumed this is where I would find some scintillating food.

Inside, the people were noisy and the air was hazy. People were chattering, and many were smoking. Waitresses in black and white uniforms pushed rolling carts with the food in it. Unlike Thailand's innumerable delicacies, offerings were less dramatic in appearance. It was mostly dumplings with assorted fillings. A few variations of rice-filled soups or noodles were also part of the menu. All one had to do was wait until a waitress came by. I watched how the women carted food directly in front of me, and all I had to do was the point at what I wanted. This was wonderfully convenient. Nearby me were some unreserved men. They steadily grabbed at the women servers as if they were their commodity. The men were rude, demanding, and extremely abrasive with the women passing by. I became quite assertive when they also tried to manhandle me. I kicked at them. I would not tolerate their touching. These ladies handled it more calmly and better than I did. I suppose they were exposed to drunks, brutal yelling, reeking stench, and generally rough characters as a norm, but I was not. It seemed none of the women was treated with dignity. In other words, a woman had less worth. I moved to another seat closer to a family group, and as soon as I had my fill of food, I left.

I began walking around to look for a hotel. This is when the fun began. I had to dash across the street between bicycles, pushy taxis, rickshaws, buses, and cars without being hit. There were no traffic signs, and I felt like an animated video character zooming some place unknown.

Before I took the flight to arrive in Dalian, I received some helpful information from the Indonesian travel clerk. She told me to be careful where I went. Using my friendly Chinese translator, I saw the sign for the hotel. At least, these accommodations were near. From the outside, it did not look like a castle. I was uncertain what I would find, but it would be a local experience.

The check-in procedure was bizarre and impersonal. I was given a checklist with pictures. The attendant said the word 'Give.' I genuinely was not sure what this meant right away, but I was required to provide a passport for identification. No information about the room size was offered, only that payment was made daily at their specified rate. Questions came up. I was in a quandary trying to figure out what to do next, but I responded promptly to whatever the attendant asked. He was busy checking off information and never looked up. Finally, the procedure was complete. I was given a room key the size of a credit card. I went upstairs to the second floor to my room. Unlike any hotel I had ever stayed at, I noticed just across from my room, there were ten pairs of shoes lined up. I began to think the room I requested must have been enormous. I used my passkey to get inside, and to my surprise, I entered an unbelievably small room with an extremely low ceiling. The walls inside were faded, tides of time beating against the drab-looking wallpaper. The bed was crude and looked like bugs managed to survive in the mattress. Everything in the room appeared decrepit, but I thought I would make the best of it.

I went to use the bathroom, but I was unable to light it up. I called an assistant on the telephone, but he could not understand me. I went downstairs and gestured him to follow. He understood my meaning and came to see what was wrong. By pointing to the malfunctioning lamps, I successfully communicated the problem, and he was able to correct it. Then he took my passkey and slid it in a close by box in the room. The lights turned on, and he left. About thirty minutes later, the lights turned off again. I took the passkey and mimicked the helper's earlier action and the lights turned on once more. This place gave me an eerie feeling, and I was glad I was moving on the next day. The thirty-minute intervals of light staying on were short-lived. I became frightened when the light turned off. It also did not help when I heard the patter of footsteps across the hall. This certainly stirred my mind's eye, and I feared for the worst. What more would I encounter?

The following morning, I went downstairs to have some breakfast. There was nothing in the lobby, so I went outside to look around. Remembering how smoky everything was, I was somewhat apprehensive about what toxic things I might eat. This is when I decided to go back to my room and checked out. I walked three blocks away and saw plenty of street vendors. Finally, I opted to sit outside at a quaint shop that was serving some soup. I am still not sure what was inside the soup, but it warmed my belly. While eating, someone tapped me on the shoulder. Alarmed, I speculated the possibilities. No one knew me in a foreign place, so I was a bit edgy.

When I looked up, there was a young Chinese woman about sixteen years old. She greeted me by saying "hello." This was a pleasant surprise. I did not anticipate meeting someone so quickly. Then I asked her if she could speak English. She smiled and said she would love to practice her English with me. Hmm.... I did not expect that to happen, but it was a delightful change from being in the contaminated air and thirty-minute interval lighting.

The girl's name was Ah Kum, and this means *first-rate gold.* She said she was a senior high school student and her future plan was to study medicine. Ah Kum said both of her parents were doctors. I knew my meeting her was not a coincidence. I was in a town where there were many practicing doctors. The girl told me that she lived with her parents and her grandfather, explaining that her parents were working, and her grandfather stays at home. Since I was still digesting my soup, I asked her if she would like to join me for breakfast. She thanked me, but rejected the invitation to eat. Then she asked me if I had any plans for the day. I explained that I did not have an agenda because I did not know much about Dalian. I also told that I planned to stay the day and wanted to take a train to Beijing the next day.

I wrapped up eating breakfast and told Ah Kum she could lead me anywhere as long as I left for Beijing that night. She was pleased that I asked her to take the lead. I also liked the idea of having a personal tour guide that spoke English. I felt incredibly lucky that this chance meeting occurred. It was as if Ah Kum was golden, and an angel sent from above. I could not feel happier.

Soon after, another Chinese teenager approached. I assumed that this was Ah Kum's friend. When the other girl arrived, she introduced herself as Fang. Her name sounded peculiar because I associated 'Fang' with a long, pointed, tooth of an animal. I stayed silent. Fang explained that she was Ah Kum's cousin. Fang says her name means *fragrantly*. Maybe I am cynical, but the translation *fragrant* did not seem to match '*a sharp tooth.*' Shortly after, Ah Kum says she wants to bring me to visit her family. They live just around the corner. I did not mind meeting her family or her inclusive invitation to join her for lunch.

I was pretty content knowing there were two Chinese girls ready to support me. I began walking, and we must have passed at least twenty blocks. Ah

Kum said her home was just around the corner, but it seemed odd sauntering for quite a while already. I did not let this situation get me down. I was building up an appetite. Finally, we arrived where Ah Kum resided.

The building structure was immense and tall. Then Ah Kum told me that the building was not always like that. She explained that it was a twelve story building before. When the building was constructed, it was poorly done. There was a plan for a garage, and the locals brought equipment to remove the soil. When the dirt was removed and dug out, the soil was piled up on the other side of the building. Heavy rains caused the underground waters to seep into the ground under the building. The supporting concrete pilings snapped to the uneven lateral pressure and the colossal structure with feet of clay, toppled over. If the buildings nearby were any closer together than they were, it would have created a drastic domino effect. Her explanation made me wonder how safe the building was now.

Apparently, the collapse of buildings is not an unusual event. Beijing, Shanghai and other key cities in China had similar mishaps. When the building where Ah Kum lived tumbled down, luckily her apartment remained intact. In the surrounding area, there were seriously large blocks of flats, and massive buildings all around. When I asked Ah Kum if she knew anything about how buildings were constructed, she simply nodded. She said nothing.

There were vast numbers of apartment buildings that dotted the skyline. I suspect that the apartment buildings were erected to be uniform in appearance with other apartment complexes. They all tended to be clustered in grouped towers. Each tower in the cluster had the same floor plan. The only variation seemed to be in the number of floors.

The grounds lacked the allure of Chinese artistic expression during the Song dynasty. There were no deeply imprinted images of luxurious landscapes with images of old trees, bamboo, rocks or retreats as created by scholar-artists of the past. Instead, it was a cultivated landscape that had more a traditional Chinese motif than a contemporary look. Focus was on the building standing in front nature: the mountains, the sky, clouds and birds in flight. There was also a communal green space where plants and paths came to a junction. To add to the Chinese charm, the laundry hung out like a sore thumb. From each balcony, a metal bar stuck out where people put their laundry out to dry. There was nothing pretty about that. Then I entered Ah Kum's domain. We began climbing six flights of ironclad steps. It made a particular rattling and banging sound, but finally we reached her apartment.

The hallway was not lit up, so we fumbled part of the distance. Finally, we reached the apartment door, and I was out of breath. Then Ah Kum knocked at the door and her grandfather answered. He had a charismatic brimming smile, nodded his head and made hand gestures. He wanted me to come in and sit down.

There were no chairs, so I went to sit on the floor. I guess it was their living room. Looking around, I had memories of an earlier experience in the Thai countryside. The climb was steep, and the house was empty with one photo hanging on the bare wall. The interior had the same floor plan as a North American setup. There was a living room, kitchen, bathroom and bedroom. I was not allowed to look around the home, but I saw most of it. There was no furniture. The majority of the doors were closed, and the only source of light came from the window in the living room.

Then I asked if I could help prepare lunch, but I was told guests do not help. I watched patiently and saw a lot of movements going on. I could smell such a tremendous aroma, but I was not allowed in the kitchen. I am not sure why that was, but I sat quietly waiting. I do not know how long I was relaxing, but I observed several courses of food being brought out. Fang and Ah Kum placed the food on a small coffee table in the center of the room. Was this a celebration just to meet me or was there something else going on?

In China, eating is more of a communal activity. Therefore, I was prepared to share food with others. Fang placed a small rice bowl next to me. Other bowls were put in the center for the rest of the family. Time was flying, and Ah Kum, Fang, her parents and grandfather joined us. All meal participants picked up their rice bowls. Subsequently, Ah Kum placed pieces of chicken in my bowl. Smiles were exchanged and we took turns dipping our chopsticks into the food. Cold canned coke was handed out. The rest of the family also tried some chicken pieces. I found it strange that they spit out the chicken bones on the thin cardboard like floor. After seeing how everyone else ate, I did not ask for a side plate. Instead, I refrained from eating any more chicken to ensure others had enough to eat.

While we were still eating, the grandfather lit a cigarette. Ah Kum asked me if I wanted a cigarette too, but I politely refused. There was much food to select. I was astounded by the display. The food consisted of a myriad of sliced fish (cod, salmon, tilapia, shrimp, freshwater fish) all spread like a small pinwheel. There was also some meat (duck and chicken) topped off with some fresh fruit in a platter. When I finished drinking my coke, someone brought me a small glass of punch. This was done without asking. I drank it to be polite. Before I knew it, more punch was being served. Apparently, this was customarily how a guest was treated. I had to decline at least three times before they poured punch again. On this occasion, I left my last drink full. I learned later that this was considered decent manners. Overall, Ah Kum, Fang and their family members gave me an overwhelming introduction to China, which was extremely gratifying to experience. I especially liked being welcomed as a foreigner in their homeland.

The surroundings in the room truly contrasted the colorful food displayed. The walls were bare cheering aloud when the food arrived. There was an absence of color on the walls, and it was as if any color from the walls vanished except for the dreary grey of age, and all the pleasure centered on savoring the explosive colors of the food. I could also perceive the sounds and smell of the Yellow Sea coming alive. I could hear the tides, and there was an atmosphere of emptiness, but the food filled it up like birds in concert flying overhead. Through the window of the living room, I could see the clothes hanging out on the line just above their balcony. It was as if the clothes were waving hello and were a part of the local decorum. After our meal, we headed out to the city.

Dalian was the hometown of the Chinese medical student I met earlier. This was a city of many contrasting images, somewhat like the communication we had. Darkened areas led into lighted spots. Big spaces sometimes became small places. People ranged from startlingly gruff to warm-hearted, and sharing. My fondest memories were of Ah Kum. The homemade food was much better than local restaurants, and I took additional photos for Sue's scrapbook.

Ah Kum liked being verbose and talked about so many topics. She even addressed philosophical constructs. At one, point, I saw her facial expressions change. I remembered slipping up. I told her how teenagers in North America behaved. I explained that youths did not always listen when parents or figures of authority made demands. She questioned why youths did not listen or do what they were told. The dialogue went back and forth. Finally, Ah Kum told me that Chinese students do not talk about mistakes. I did not want to touch on political possibilities, so I clammed up and thanked her for extended hospitality. Thankfully, she arranged the train transportation. I was hopeful that she understood what I wanted, but I would soon find out. At least, Ah Kum guided me to where I was able to take the train, and I said adieu.

From Dalian to Beijing, I would become more aware about what lurked behind the scenes. It began with understanding how conversations and behavior surfaced. At first, I had a hard time comprehending what the conductor was saying. I searched for three words in my friendly English-Mandarin dictionary. Therefore, when the conductor passed by to see my ticket, I pointed to First-Class, Beijing and Cabin. I was uncertain if I said the right things, so I remained quiet. The conductor nodded as I started to look for my sleeping cabin. I could not find it, but a train employee saw me looking confused, and brought me to my assigned number.

I assumed I would have a private cabin with a shower. This is what I asked Ah Kum to arrange, but the results were different. Instead, I found out that I was bunking with three strangers. This made me feel more uncomfortable than having too much mustard on a smoked meat sandwich. These were people I did not know. The situation was like a spicy condiment of an untried situation that came to life.

People did not sleep at regular hours. In fact, there was hardly any peace or quiet. Train residents were continuously chatty, drank alcohol openly, smoked without reservation, threw paper or wrappers on the ground and never were embarrassed to spit on the floor. Some of the people ate roasted peanuts. They were cracking open the shells and throwing them directly on the floor. Every time the train stopped, people from different localities entered. Some brought small animals with them, and they varied in sizes and shapes. Chickens walked over the mounds of peanut shells and other heaps of debris. Each time the train stopped, cleaners came in. They removed the rubbish, but it grew right back like wild grass. I honestly wondered what happened to decency. These people seemed to be dreadfully dirty. As a cautionary measure, I chose not to drink any beverages. Luckily, I brought some dried foods with me, and only ate this until arriving in Beijing.

I reached Beijing's central station, in the Maojiawan *Hutong*, Dong Cheng District (东城区毛家湾胡同甲13号) where the pace of life is like a noisy conversation. There were deafening sounds coming from every direction. To add, the train station was a complex place to be in. I imagined it was because Beijing's Railway Station is a central hub of the national railway transportation. People were coming from many destinations. The tracks alone covered a vast territory. I knew the rail tracks were constantly expanded to accommodate the continual growing numbers of people.

Leaving from the train station was a mystery. I had no idea that I would be entering a grand station with a confusing network of intercommunicating paths and I was uncertain which way to go. Everyone seemed to be going upward on the escalator, and I followed. People were moving forward, and this level brought me to the main floor. Human nature here seemed different from Ah Kum's caring ways. No one seemed to have a regard for the next person. People were constantly pushing to get ahead and bumping into me. I am not sure it was deliberate, but people walked without even picking up their head. Where was everybody going?

The train station looked like it had the same architectural features as Dalian. There was a combination of traditional and modern style. The setting gave me the impression that I was a mere speck compared to the mammoth amount of people leaving or coming into Beijing. It was hard for me to imagine its magnitude. There was no contrast here to the number of people I saw in my childhood. The quantity of people was like the Titanic and sounds echoing were tantamount.

The air was still smelly when I came out on the street level. Fortunately, it was not quite as unpleasant as in Dalian. At first, I passed by the culture of *Hutong* or *Hútòng* or courtyard living. This seems to be a popular attraction for most tourists especially because of history when courtyard living dates back to the Yuan Dynasty (1271-1368). In actuality, this kind of community did not look especially comfortable. It seemed to be purely a link between passages leading to another incredibly slender lane for easier access. The housing was arranged like an orderly chessboard, but mostly like feudal living. Tourists and expatriates never went behind the heavy laden door, but I wanted to see what was behind it.

Through my readings, I had some ideas about the feudal lifestyle in China. Historically, the feudal lifestyle originated from the Zhou Dynasty when feudal order was established. Formal oaths of allegiance to the Chinese rulers were exchanged for fiefs and permission to obtain revenues and service from peasants. In return, the fief holders pledged their loyalty to their monarch and sent tribute to the capital. There used to be always a link to the monarchy. Loyalty and obedience was expected. Even though, the monarchy was no longer favored, the feudal mentality continued. I experienced this later when I lived in a *Hutong* or feudal setting. Metaphorically, I followed the orders of the *Hutong* lord. Lights were out when the feudal master said to shut them off. In other words, systems of the past may have changed names, but they are still present today.

Because of my curiosity, I courageously knocked at one of the doors. The people opened the door and looked at me strangely. At least, I managed to see what was inside. There was an exceedingly small living space and people were able to live in these infinitesimal areas. The walkway was already uncomfortable. There were narrow lanes like which measured about 32 to 44 yards. Most of the foreigners passing by were inquisitive, but they did not have the same inclination to experience what it felt like. Most of the foreigners were probing for their own amusement. They did not have a desire to know the truth of what takes place behind the *Hutong* doors. The foreigners only had a need to gossip when they returned home.

To become truly objective, I had to assess a variety of new lifestyles. I began by gathering information about being in Beijing City. This is where I found convenient lodging and accessible transportation including public and private buses, rickshaws, taxis or private vehicles. There were shops and plenty of restaurants, and lots of Western five-star hotels like the Marriot, Best Western, St. Regis, Westin, and the Friendship Center to name a few. Since I was on a budget, I opted to go elsewhere. It did not take me long to find a reasonable place to stay.

The rooms were large and airy, but the attendant kept shaking his head. I pointed to what I wanted, but instead, he brought me elsewhere. Apparently, the rooms I selected were reserved for local Chinese businessmen. The hotel receptionist took the lead and beckoned me to follow. He led me to another part of the hotel, and the walk seemed to be forever. I had no idea where I was heading. I sauntered along a narrowly winding path. Finally, we came to a halt. The hotel receptionist took out a set of keys and opened the door. To my surprise, there were at least fifty beds lined up. This was a whopping contrast compared to a reservation for four local business people. In this room, there were many beds already occupied by female foreigners. Who were these women? Where did the hotel assistant bring me?

Beside each bed was a small locker. This allowed me to place personal belongings without worries. There were two available showers not far from the room. One of them was down the hall and the other nearby. At least, the bathroom was separated. For my initial stay, I thought this would do for a day or two until I got my bearings to find a longer-term place. That night I showered, but I could hear the pipes rattling. Looking around, I was flabbergasted to see a man peeping through a hole on the floor platform. I was upset that the structure was so shabby, and I quickly dressed. Then I returned to the assigned room and retired for the evening. I kept rethinking about the matter in my head. I had no idea why the Asian men were so prying into a female Caucasian's appearance.

I had conversations with other foreign females in the room and learned people came from many countries. No one talked about the peeping man experience. Women arrived from many destinations Australia, Africa, the Ukraine, Czechoslovakia, and elsewhere. The ladies did not look out of the ordinary. Most of the women appeared to be young, Caucasian and in their thirties. Then I began wondering why so many of them were in China. Some of the women revealed they came as models, short-term visitors, as students, and all had their matchless stories. With so many women in one place, I feared that this was a collection center housing women for human trafficking. I did not want to stay, but I questioned what was taking place. I tried filtering my thoughts, but I needed to find another place to stay for a longer period than one-night or a week's layover. I was pretty grateful that someone among these women was able to refer me to an address. I speculated that this might be another *Hutong*, but out of necessity, I moved to *Hutong* living. This was a dwelling on a narrow street or alley.

I took a taxi supplying the driver with an address where to go. He took the information rapidly and responded gruffly. I had no idea what he said, but the man drove like a maniac. This cab operator complied with Beijing *Hukou* Laws. This means he had permission to drive with a residency permit on specified days. It did not confirm the driver was knowledgeable about geographical situation. In this instance, I think I did not luck out. The driver was taking an exceptionally long-time to reach my destination. I had a suspicion he did not know where he was going. I do not blame the driver. Beijing is a gigantic place that encompasses 6,500 square miles.

It has vast areas of countryside, satellite towns, and villages. Even though, the taxi driver was local, he also could lose his way.

Geographical positioning systems were rare. The only thing I could think was that the driver was giving me a grand tour of Beijing. En route, we passed several well-known landmarks like The Golden Temple, Tenement Square, The Forbidden City and Ming Tombs. Unexpectedly, the taxi came to a halt. The cab driver gestures that I get out. I hoped that this was the suggested address.

Hutong living: There was a small arched gateway, which enclosed a large red wooden door. After the taxi driver received payment, he left the scene. There was no time to check that this was the correct address, so I hoped for the best. I thumped at the door clangor, and an Oriental woman responded. Her northern Chinese appearance had subtle differences from Chinese women I met before. She had lighter skin, thinner eyes and was a little stockier. The woman nodded, and I assumed I reached the right place. I suppose she must of thought of me as strange in appearance too.

This woman was an artist that moved from Harbin City (North) to Beijing (Central). She came from the northern part of China bordering Russia. Like many other people, she was seeking a new situation, and a place of intrigue to create her artwork. In actuality, she was not allowed to stay in Beijing, and was not considered a resident of the locality. According to China's Laws, people have to produce papers to prove they were a resident of the city wherever they were. She was supposed to return home, but it seemed that no one paid attention. In other words, people were not permitted to move around China as they liked. I suppose some Laws get ignored because of the amount of people. Few people pay attention when people come from other places.

The lady responding to the door gave me a good impression that she had a tremendous vision. Before she allowed me to enter, the woman looked both ways. It seems as if she were crossing a busy intersection, but took cautionary measure. When no one was in her periphery, she signaled me to follow.

Entryway: I entered a narrow alleyway and came to a room filled with paintings. Some were completed, while others were damp and work-in-progress. The smells of the oil paintings were so strong that the odor took over. The drying oils were going through a curing phase. Because this usually takes months to complete, the oil was taking up oxygen and gaining mass. The smell of drying oil paint was not harmful, but I worried that this room is where I was going to sleep. I did not want to be situated in another toxic environment.

Mentality Determined: I kept silent and looked at her work. It was first-rate. This lady actually had real talent. Luckily, she only laid my small bag down in the room for a moment. We continued moving ahead. Again, through hand signaling she asked me to follow. The woman took me to another room about the size of a North American half bathroom. She pointed to a single bed, took my bags and placed them on the floor. I understood that this was where I was expected to stay. After all, I was going to experience living in a *Hutong* or feudal courtyard setting. There was no doubt in my mind, I was returning to the feudalism of the thirteenth century. Therefore, I assumed I would have to adopt the relationship of a Master and fief.

I assessed the situation and realized that all the people living in the courtyard had a designated small space. Each room was partitioned by the door, but this did not stop people from overstepping boundaries and coming in freely. Privacy was something that did not exist.

Public bathing was in a nearby location at the public bathhouse. This was about a block away and another experience altogether. The largest room in this courtyard belonged to the feudal lord. He designated what, when, and how much of anything was allowed. He even instructed me when to turn on or turn off the lights. Living there was extraordinarily regimented and quite uncomfortable. People would walk in and out of my room without care that I needed privacy. Since this was not extremely far from Tenement Square, I just accepted this would be the place to stay for a while. Once I settled into this new place, I knew I would learn where I had to go next.

***The Courtyard*.** There were about ten rooms forming a small square courtyard. In the center of all these rooms, was an open space to cook food. The Chinese believe that cooking where you sleep was inappropriate. They assumed that cooking smells should not filter into the rooms where people slept. Even though, the kitchen was set apart, this mentality was unheard-of. I always liked the smell of cooking scattering in a home, because it added a warm, hearty, and feeling of being at home. Instead, the Chinese people thought in contrary ways about cooking. As for basics, there was no bathroom in the courtyard. Defecation was done in a pail and removed. I could have also gone to the nearby outhouse, but I was scared what I might see. Heat in the room supposedly was there, but I never felt it. The room was as cold as an ice chest.

The Kitchen facilities: appeared dissimilar to North America. There was only one charcoal stove that looked like a smaller version of the wood burning fireplace. Perhaps this was a replica of what Benjamin Franklin may have owned. As for the designated kitchen area, I did not see where people kept their pots and pans, but in full view, I saw coals were used to heat the food. When cooking took place, I saw how the open-air kitchen concept allowed smoke to swirl around. As the food was cooking, the smoke drifted into the nearby rooms. In other words, the smells were not held back.

★

Before I went anywhere, I began my life living in a *Hutong*. It started shortly after the artist prepared something to eat. She had a small shopping bag and inside was all kinds of ingredients. I had no idea where she got water, but she filled a medium-sized pot and placed it on the burner. Then she took out some of the things she had in her bag. Soon after, she swiftly chopped up a variety of ingredients. Many of the ingredients coming out of her bag were strange to me.

The vegetables came in a rainbow of colors: green, yellow, red, purple, white, beige and orange. I could not imagine how she did it. The woman began dicing up vegetables in a space no bigger than a plate. She worked passionately, cleaning and chopping-up a lime green turnip, bamboo shoots, broccoli, garlic shoots, pea sprouts, carrots, leeks, celery and dragon beans. Next, she sliced Jalapeño peppers, sweet green cubanelles, yellow pimentos, and Ta Shih Tse orange chili peppers. The ingredients were more than enough to feed a small army. I deduced that all the colorful ingredients used, could have been stored, used later or be an imaginary palette. I am not sure what she did with leftovers, but she worked extremely enthusiastically to add some final touches. There was cilantro and other unknown spices also added.

In an incredibly short time afterwards, a heavenly aroma filled the air. She was making food fit for a king. From her bag of tricks, she took out some shredded meat, blending the meat with some egg and other ingredients that created a delightful aroma. Once again, she began the magic regime of collecting vegetables. She was whirling everything together and whipping up something sumptuous. This time the woman combined long string beans, green onions, enoki mushrooms, leeks, some radishes and miniscule yellow chili peppers together. The sizzling sound of the onions and the other elements stirred my senses. Then she served some of her final product on a platter. She gave some to me, some to a neighbor and had some for herself. The artist had a charisma of her own. One of the painting themes she employed was seeing people eating food with glee. Naturally, this clued me into whom she was. The kitchen is the place where you can find a warm heart, dry your socks and even simmer down. It was utterly different from being outside in the brisk, cold.

BATHING: The following day, the radiant rays of sun invited themselves into in my room. It was like soothing hands touching my skin. As the warm air flowed, I had an impression of being in the desert. Out of the blue, my skin started to have a grimy sensation. Maybe I was just too tired and a little delusional, but I wanted to feel cleaner. I peeked out of my window and saw the artist in the kitchen. Since she was close at hand, I went to see her. Then I hand gestured that I wanted to bathe. It almost seems to be by design that the sun and the artist struck a harmonious chord. The warmth made me aware, while the artist understood my pantomime. She must have been entertained by my mime, but she comprehended. The painter nodded and signaled to follow. We walked a block away from the *Hutong,* and she brought me to an unmarked cement building. At first, I was apprehensive about where she brought me. Instead, it turned out to be the right place. This would be my first experience of the intimacy in a Chinese bathhouse.

When I first entered, I could see some unkempt-looking women. They gave me the impression they were gruff heavy-duty boxers. There was only one woman among the group that appeared frail. These women were prancing around as if ready to spearhead a bear. If the artist could paint that picture, it would have been priceless. One of the husky women began speaking to other females. As she conversed, I saw the women glancing at me. This abruptly transformed to stares. Other women also followed as if they could sense I was a stranger, making me painfully aware I was under real scrutiny. I felt like a giraffe standing out in a crowd. I tried keeping my head down, but I stuck out like a sore thumb. I suppose the locals were shocked to see me there. In actuality, I still had a fundamental need to be accepted. I wanted to be part of the social dynamics, but I was not allowed into their circle. This made me feel strange and the locals gossiped among themselves. I suspect they were talking about me because all eyes were on me. I guessed my white skin tone and foreign appearance may have shocked them.

One of the women tapped me on the shoulder. I was unprepared to feel a strange hand, but she pointed where I should change my clothing. As I drew closer, I felt suddenly ill at ease. There were no separate, private areas to bathe, and I had to strip down naked. As a North American, I was taught in childhood to hide my body. I suppose it was a cultured expectation to feel shameful because I was used to privacy. I became incredibly self-conscious about my appearance. When I disrobed to shower, women ogled silently. They talked in Mandarin candidly remarking about the shy foreigner. Even though, I did not speak the language, their facial expressions told me what they were saying. The women were talking about the size of my breasts and skin color. Subsequently, one stalwart woman guided me to a cot hinting that I lie down. I am not sure what she had in mind, but I complied with her wish. Shortly after, I understood she intended to wash and exfoliate my skin.

The woman used a combination of solutions and creams. She wore some kind of rough-surfaced gloves and began spreading some liquid on my back. I am not sure what it was, but she proceeded to rub my back with her hands. The woman was exceptionally strong, and I could feel her pressure. As she chafed my back, she began talking to a woman nearby. Suddenly, a number of other women came by gaping at what was taking place. The women were looking that I had a collection of dirt on my body. I had no idea I had that many dead skin cells piling up. Of course, I felt extremely dirty with onlookers. At the same time, I was grateful, and I realized that people in North America have less of an idea how to get thoroughly clean. Soon after having the scrub down, I headed to the showers. I began rinsing off any debris (dead skin) and enjoyed the steamy hot water. I found it odd that the staring did not cease. Other women were looking at me intently, as though I was some kind of mermaid just coming out of the water. I was not sure, but I guess I was out of ordinary in this small locality. I learned later that I was the first foreign woman ever to visit this bathhouse. Regardless, I would visit the bathhouse regularly on a biweekly basis after this time.

The Night was setting in, and I had to get used to where I was, so I readied myself to go to sleep. In the small room allocated for me, I felt extremely confined. I had to get used to it, but I was not sure how to do it. Suddenly I heard a knock on my door. The artist gave me a heavy coat. I was not sure why she handed it over, but I would find out. Graciously, I nodded my head and took it. I got into some warm night clothing and went in the bed. The bed was cold, and this gave me reason enough to wear the coat. I wrapped myself into the coat and went under the quilted blankets. Somehow, I felt no heat penetrating. I got out of the bed and tapped on the pipes that supposedly heated the room. There was no heat coming from the pipes. I thought about asking the feudal lord to turn the heat on, but it was too late. Then I remembered the heat coming from the stove in the nearby kitchen. Since my room was just opposite the kitchen, I saw no harm relocating the wood burning stove to my room. It was not unusually large, so I moved it fairly easily. The heat began to penetrate, but the smell from the coal made it hard for me to breath. Then I heard a rapping at my door. It was the feudal lord. He looked incredibly angry and grabbed the wood burning stove from me. He put it back into the kitchen, and I had no recourse, but to stay in my room shivering. I have no idea how the people tolerated the cold. This situation was devilishly hard to endure, and I held on to treasured memories about being in my warm bed in North America. I remained freezing for many nights and had few resources. Even though, I was hopeful that this lifestyle would change to be more favorable, I had strange doubts whether I would see North America ever again.

After visiting the bathhouse, I had no idea that the local people reported a stranger was in town. I had no knowledge, but I soon discovered the local police was following me. They were monitoring my every activity, and I did not know even know it initially. Apparently, the villagers transmitted their messages through the gossip culture. As a consequence, the artist and I had to relocate somewhere else. I am not certain what happened to the artist. I knew she could be jailed for not having residency permission in order. I was also told that foreigners were not allowed to stay in quarters designated for locals. Thus, it became clear that there was a shared mentality among the locals.

There was a sublime message among the Chinese. This was a given family construct that the Chinese and Asian people learn. They are taught to associate with their own kind. This extends further to whatever they do. For example, completing their studies and reaching the highest level possible. It is all about a person's credibility in terms of social face.

In the bathing experience, the idea of social face related to the bathhouse setting. In cosmopolitan centers, the Chinese were preoccupied with more privacy, so this was not as relevant. In terms of social face, this also applies to everyday learning. No matter where I was in China, the Chinese were cut-throat. This relates to their competitive educational system, common throughout Asia.

Students are compelled to study incredibly hard. The results of their elementary and high school testing are indicators of where they can go. The high school test is an actual gauge for what a person will study. They do not have choices. Their results indicate what they will study. For that reason, many Asian students study abroad because more opportunities are open to them. Whether the Asian student is in his home country or studying abroad, they still keep close family ties. When the student studies overseas, the family also has to agree with the area of study the individual intends to do. The student is unable to change that decision without the consensus of family first. Thus, the bathhouse phenomenon was the same. All the locals pulsed with the same thinking. At least, they thought a foreigner was not part of their cohesive grouping. Based on this scenario, I truly saw enough of this lifestyle. It was time for me to find a new dwelling, and like the Chinese, I could not afford to worry about the artist's outcome.

POORER HOUSING: The following day, I looked around by foot. I began walking around and getting my bearings, but the long walk was a bone-chilling, icy feeling. I was beginning to lose grounding. I had no idea where I was because all the corrugated metal huts looked exactly alike. I started to panic and started to search for help, but no one was in view. All I saw was a bleak setting with enumerable tiny units of ribbed metal splattering across a vast space. They looked like a spotted Dalmatian's coat having hardly any gaps between. I sat down on the ground and I began weeping vociferously. I had no idea where I was or what to do. This was an extremely disheartening situation. As I reflected, it seemed to match the same poverty in Manila, Third Ward Texas, remote Indonesia rural settings and many Mexican border towns. This uncanny experience made me feel as if I were within a mirage. There were no distinct markings to identify differences. I was becoming disenchanted by the standards of living. Clearly, the locals could not afford to live like a North American. Decent housing catered only to selected prosperous groups. This truly was the epitome of not having *FAIR standards,* so I sat down and wept. I felt touched by how the poor people lived.

Suddenly, a tall-looking man appeared from nowhere. He was riding through the field on his bicycle, and he saw me. He stopped and looked at me. His colossal figure towered over me and cast a shadow. I stopped whimpering. I showed him a paper with Chinese characters. This was the recorded address where I resided. He beckoned me to climb on the back of his bicycle. At no time did he look at me with sensitivity. In fact, he looked emotionless, but he understood my dilemma. In a matter of a few minutes, he brought me to visit some of his friends. I guess I must have looked hysterical. It could have been that he brought me there to ask their advice what to do with me. The man and his friends talked together for a little while and then paused. A few minutes later a teapot was whistling. A woman went to the stove, and gave me a cup of tea. Afterwards, the man brought me back to the address, where I would stay a while longer. It was a temporary place to be while I was in transition. I guess I wandered off, with no idea that kind-hearted people were so poor compared to other worlds.

The next day, I stayed with my plan of action and headed towards the Embassy area. This is where most of the well-off expatriates lived. They had no idea where or how locals resided. Instead, most of the affluent expatriates cut off personal ties with locals except for business contact. The expatriates and the locals did not seem to care about each other. No matter whom I saw, people were trampling over another person's space. As this was commonplace, I realized this was a country of unpredictability. Subsequently, I took the necessary precautions to register at the Embassy. As a citizen, the delegates might be able to support me in the event of an uprising or a difficult circumstance, but that too was an uncertainty.

The Embassy area was in the center of Beijing. This meant I had to find some means of transportation to get there. I had a lot of choices. I could take a local or private bus, taxi, and limousine, hire a private car, or take a rickshaw. The only difference in mobility was the number of passengers taken. I weighed out the pros and cons. A taxi was pretty tricky business especially because prices were constantly on the rise. The rickshaw was too slow and dangerous in the busy traffic. Limousines or private cars for hire were pricey. Public buses reeked, and so I decided to take a private bus.

THE OUTDOORS: Everything conceivable that I can think of, actually took place. I saw a lot while I waited for the private bus to come. In the open air, people were having their hair cut and styled, their teeth pulled and products were being sold. There were also Tai Chi dancers in public. Through glass windows, I saw ducks being grilled on spittoons, and they fantastically spun around. Food vendors were everywhere, and small children were running on the streets hardly clad. Toddlers ran around without diapers. Sometimes they urinated or defecated directly on the street. These happenings gave me a new perspective on how poverty accommodated situations in new ways. This ranged from not using disposable diapers, to hustling, so as to stay alive. This scenario was a complete contrast to what I expected. I was illuminated seeing how standards illustrated affordability. As I gazed around, the private bus finally arrived.

Unfortunately, the smells on the private bus were no better than on the public. It was crowded inside including the placement of small stools positioned in the aisles. Even though, speed postings on the road were reasonable, this driver and others on the road did not follow the Laws. No matter the mode of transportation, there were steady competitions on the road. Drivers chose to take winding routes into narrow paths. They drove on nearby paths and hardly paid attention to pedestrians. The private bus acted alike, except that the driver took side streets and never made any signals. I heard through the grapevine that private buses moved wherever space was available. They did not seem to pay heed to cost. Even though, this was a few years earlier, not that much has changed except for having more complex highways. There is also the addition of tremendously speedy trains and other advanced technology too. Everything concentrated on speed or compression, and I was in a jam-packed city.

The private bus traveled along a mystery route taking circular highways steadily going up, down and in circles. It seemed as the bus tried every way feasible. The experience was nothing like I ever had. These driving techniques were unquestionably poles apart from the driving practices in North America.

Finally, I reached my destination, the Embassy area. I got off the bus and as soon as I put my feet down on the ground, there were a number of CD vendors. They seemed to come out of the woodwork. Merchants were everywhere trying to convince me to purchase CDs with no apparent name, and other oddities. These people were part of a conglomerate known as the Black market. Items such as these were smuggled in from Hong Kong. I managed to continue ahead, and I knew this was the heart of the city.

Downtown Beijing attracted all kinds of people. Fliers and colorful advertisements were all part of the local enchantment. In proximity, there were enumerable outlets: McDonalds, the Friendship Department Stores, fast food Chinese style, and chains of Western-styled stores. My inquisitiveness was stronger than ever before. I wanted to delve into things of unfamiliarity. I wondered about consumerism and social class behavior.

First, I went to see what I assumed to be familiar. I entered McDonalds and saw people waiting in a queue. The offerings on the signboard appeared to be similar to American offerings, but with some notable variations. Prices were high, but popular places of gathering were similar to those in North America. There was Baskin-Robbins, Dunkin Donuts, Kentucky Fried Chicken, McDonalds, Pizza Hut, Starbucks, and Tim Horton. In these places, I saw Chinese habits analogous to American people. Both have eating frenzies that have resulted in unthinking patterns. Pan Beilei, Consultant for Chinese State Food and Nutrition, 22% of the Chinese population are rotund with "*more than seven percent of Chinese adults are obese, constituting 60 million Chinese with unhealthy body weight.*" [78] The problem of obesity is even more severe in America. The stoutest people are "*African Americans (51%) and Hispanics (21%)* "[79] residing predominantly in "*Louisiana, West Virginia, Alabama, and Mississippi.*"[80] Canadians do not fall far behind. According to the Organization for Economic Cooperation and Development, at least "*two-thirds of the Canadian population are heavy.*"[81] This is one in every four Canadians, only about ten percent less than America's problem. The Chinese and Americans have deliberately made themselves unhealthy, likely due to "*a combination of greasy diets, little activity, and all kinds of addictive behaviors*"[82] (gaming, drinking and etcetera).

After I toured the fast food restaurants, I went into the Friendship Store and it was similar in appearance to Macy's or Bloomfield's Department stores in New York City. The most astonishing thing was the amount of products available. Items accessible were from cloisonné vases to the large-size bedroom suites. Items were all at an extremely high premiums, which should have deterred me from making buys, but it did not.

I only became disillusioned when trust issues came up while making a purchase. There had to be at least three queues before I received the item. I had to confirm wanting the product, and this was documented. A voucher was then issued to confirm the same. Then, I had to get in a lineup of people waiting to present vouchers to another clerk to confirm I was the purchaser of the item. This is where payment was made. Finally, I came to the last queue where I received the item. In each queue, there was an iron bar fencing off other queues. This genuinely made me feel on guard, and the long process seemed to be a deterrent for consumerism compared to an instant purchase in North America. As I became familiar with pricing, I realized purchasing at the local market was more cost effective, and purchases happened speedily. There were also many bins from which to choose infinite items.

In Beijing's *Dong-Hua Men* marketplace, there were many stalls near WanFujing Street. Some people ate noodle soups, and made loud slurping sounds. In the background, I could hear the voices of people on loud speakers. They were advertising products and making such blaring sounds. Music was also playing, and I found it hard to differentiate if the music were the sounds of people singing, the tapping of feet, people chattering or something else.

Food products were unimaginable. I saw items like ox's testicles, fried silkworms, goat's brain, snakes, grasshoppers, starfish, scorpions, sea horses, squid, mutton, kebab-chicken, dumplings, and candied fruits or *Tang Hu Lu*. Undoubtedly, the diet in the marketplace was unfamiliar for me. By just looking at some of the food, I became queasy. I remember Van Huis, a Scientist and Master Chef and food connoisseur saying that any adult unfamiliar with food, likely will cringe at the sight of some of the Chinese cuisine. This happens when food visions are poles apart from what an adult is used to eating. Van Huis sees this especially when he prepares Dutch-farmed bugs. I was no different from other adults. I had a hard time imagining eating insects and unfamiliar creatures: hopping grasshoppers, dogs with perked ears, or lizards with tongues sticking out ready to pierce me. No matter where I went, there seemed to be an overwhelming combination of people and food. Of course, I also searched to see what other products they had, but I did not see the *Wayang*, Figuratively speaking, people were like human puppets eating almost anything.

The air quality did not help because it was deadly. There were fumes from people smoking and factories emitted toxic gases. The traffic corresponded to the Indonesian marketplace. For a pedestrian, crossing was literally a dart across the street with hopes of being safe. Drivers used cellular phones, and many did not have formal driver training. The combination of cars, buses, pushcarts, and bicycles combined with pedestrians were lethal. Whenever I tried walking across the street, people managed to scoot ahead of me without waiting, some of them cut off anyone in their path. The outcomes were brutal because serious accidents were a daily occurrence.

Some children were carried, and others walked. Toddlers usually had an open flap at the bottom of their clothing. This allowed the children to be diaper-free because they freely peed or defecated in the marketplace or on the streets. Nearby were dentists and haircutters. They performed their task out in the open as if nothing happened. People did not have fears to do their private business publicly. This included releasing bladder or anal pressures in the vicinity of product sales, haircutting and teeth pulling. Sometimes, people brought an urn-shaped container. This allowed them to remove their organic deposit or urine. I thought I would never do this. It was not terribly unsanitary, but sometimes situations do take an alternate course.

In time, I became acquainted with the common practices, including going to the restroom. I entered a small, dark wooden hut where a series of oblong holes were dug on the floor. I had no choice but to squat and use the hole in the ground. Surprisingly, the squatting felt more comfortable. It took me some time, but I began ignoring other women that ogled at me. My travels taught me that this toilet style was also in Russia, France, Italy, Turkey, Japan, Indonesia, and other countries too. The one thing I inaugurated was to bring my own Kleenex packets because toilet paper was a luxury.

In other words, there was a spillover of Chinese culture in Indonesia and other destinations too. This certainly made me beckon the question about what occurs in a Chinese village. There was a massive amount of people. The experience in China made me reflect. It reminded me of being a child in Chinatown. This is where I was ignored or not seen, leaving me to fend for myself also as an adult.

To get at the root of *Fair Deals*, I assumed it started with dignitaries. I wanted to discover how foreign Ambassadors think, so I approached notable public figures. The Public figures were surprised at my request. None of these government officials knew where I lived. They all took it for granted that I resided close by the embassy area. My entrée into the world of foreign dignitaries was not at all what I expected.

The men truly responded in the same mechanical way. It seemed that these men shared preconceived notions about what powered a person in China. Their ideas were not about their true colors, but negativity did surface, which I suspect related to prejudice and assumptions. At first, it seemed like the officials were not interested in conversation, but in another, quite different agenda.

My purpose was to understand patterns of social thinking. It took time and eventually I honed into other people's mind-set. It was an emerging process of social consciousness. The contacts started with initial visits to the embassy, telephone calls, and faxes. I retained a consistent approach regardless of the official's origin. When I met the diplomats, I explained that I wanted to evaluate their perspective on challenges in China. I left them to discern what they wanted to address. At least, I had a common ground with officials because we were both foreigners in China.

There was a prelude to actual relevant dialogue with the officials. Typically, we met at a pricey restaurant instead of their embassy location. I was not sure why they would do this, but it seemed as they were trying to impress me. I had thoughts that the men were attempting to captivate me like Salvador Dali's* painting, *The Spellbound*. I assessed the situation and I had no intention of being blind to their intent. I was extremely forward and made my request known from the start. I did not come to them out of a need nor was I helpless. Instead, the men wanted a more personal attachment. They presumed regardless of a woman's nationality, they could be used and be disposable. Based on interviews and experiences that followed, I questioned the morality of these men. Even though, the men had established boundaries, there were moral slips and issues of disrespect particularly notable among African, Asian and South American leaders. Through trial and error, I found genuine conversations more likely when I met dignitaries at their embassies.

At our meetings, these men exposed their realities and others asked me to support their internal training objectives for staff. Discussions usually began by them revealing their background. The majority of the diplomats had traveled to at least 30 to 40 foreign destinations. Their careers were mostly initiated by family influence from very young ages. These diplomats were very savvy about international settings.

At the beginning of conversations with the diplomats, I asked that they clarify any possible misinterpretations. I provided an illustration by asking them to discern their meaning of the Chinese saying *God's favored one*. Most of the diplomats suggested this was a mockery of Western values corresponding to dismissing monotheism. I explained that cultural interpretation is honestly personal, but that this expression dated back many years. The Chinese mean that few students becomes successful, and they had a god's favor. Historically, the average Chinese person did not complete elementary school. Therefore, when someone managed to finish their studies, the person was considered incredibly magnificent because they had *mighty powers*. Even though, a Chinese student's success has increased over the years, the context has not changed. The issues come up as a result of literal translation and generalities are then made. This means intended meanings often get distorted and cause offense. Ergo, in this regard I asked people to hold their personal prejudice.

I assumed dining and conversations would be lighter than business dealings. Most of the dialogues took place in an exclusive club or five-star hotel restaurant setting. As suggested earlier, when I met envoys at their embassy, there seemed to be a greater value in what they said. I think dining in posh locations acted as a deterrent for honest exchange. Regardless, conversations usually flowed because we shared a common interest in the Chinese. Some of the officials acted with snobbery because they assumed I had no business in a man's world. In fact, one of the Asian diplomats cancelled meetings with me several times. When I finally met him, the truth came out. I listened attentively to his words, but he was determined to convey that I would never wear his pants, and became offensive. There was no need to deliberate further, so I left the scenario. Naturally, the rhythm of my dialogues depended on the individuals I spoke to.

Carlos, the Cuban Ambassador had a Latin tempo. He illustrated more about virtuous relationship building than I knew before. He was immensely creative in how he communicated and placed spotlights on the feeling impact between people. He started by treating me with the highest regard.

The Cuban Ambassador was a colossal man shaped like an earthquake, but he never imposed his size to intimidate others. During my initial wait for him to arrive, his staff treated me to the best of imported Cuban dessert possible, complimented by the finest brewed coffee. His welcoming reception made me reflect that a person is not about size, but character.

Initially, I was fearful of Carlos's massive size. He trotted down the stairs, creating rumbling sounds, and perceptible earthshaking. Then he gently walked closer to meet me and gave me a warm hug. He said that an ethnographic interpreter is a refreshing change from whom he usually meets. This was a veritable icebreaker, and our conversation was stimulating. Carlos talked openly about many subjects. He alluded to loving baseball, learning about people around the world, and how he overcame obstacles. His passion to communicate effectively helped me realize gaps in my own communication. After, we met a few more times; my first favorable impression remained the same. He talked about how he adapted in tough situations and told these stories with zest, sincerity and passion. Carlos looked at each country as a new learning challenge, and he never overlooked the people he associated with.

Carlos saw imperfections in life as an opportunity to perfect them. He talked directly about things that caused difficulties in China compared to other countries, and he did not use blame as a solution. He chose to use innovative ways to make his own path. He explained that it took him time to figure matters out. He described a nagging circumstance when asked to wear something like other officials. Since he thought it did not suit him, he felt like a walrus wearing clothing fit for a dwarf. When his clothing was too tight, he described his dancing and standing out above all the other walruses. Even though, his size intimidated smaller people, he waddled about without concern of having a sea lion status. This made him extremely likeable.

Arif was the Ambassador of Sierra Leona, Africa. His stories evoked an entirely different perspective. I arrived at the embassy, and there was a small child climbing up the stairs. An embassy staff member instructed the boy to stay out of sight, and allow his father to wrap up a conversation with another official. I was asked by his staff to wait in the lobby.

When the Ambassador was ready, we sat face to face across from each other. He initiated the conversation as a man proud of his African heritage. He told me some historical information about his country roots. Arif conveyed details about obstacles his country had faced and how they were overcome. I listened attentively to what he had to say. Afterwards, he seemed to be more receptive to talking at a heart level. It seemed my patience, manner, and regard for learning about his country determined how he would open up and communicate.

Our conversation continued when I asked where the small child went to school. He explained that this child was his pride and joy. Numerous people were brought in to teach him, and he did not attend a regular school. Subsequently, Arif told me that he had other children too. There were three other children that lived downstairs. They were from an earlier relation while married to his wife.

He was open to talk about African moralities, explaining they are not the same as people in North America or China. Arif said women in Africa accept marriage with relatives even when there is an extreme age gap. In one, situation, a woman asked him to stop marriage proceedings to her younger nephew. She appealed to him because he had the authority to prevent the union. Arif granted the woman her wish with a condition. She had to have coital relations with him. In his official capacity, no one would question what he did, but there were exceptions that came later.

Arif dwelled on the issue of whether we need to define morality. At 72 years old, he saw people of his own status assuming they had something to offer. They alleged others would get joy from their actions, so he had the same feelings, especially when he met the opposite sex. This was regardless of the woman's race or color. He paused to fuel his thoughts and said occasions arose when he lacked discipline. He had a natural tendency to get into trouble with the opposite sex and blamed it on human weakness. Arif had trouble drawing the line of what was acceptable and made moral slips. He probed over the issue, questioning when a person actually is immoral. Arif became intense on the topic of women engaging in intellectualization. He said, "There are possible consequences because a woman may do the wrong things." His comments did not disturb me. I understood he had some dilemmas to deal with as a result of his debauched actions. Robert Louis Stevenson also agrees with me. He says, "Everybody*, sooner or later, sits down to a banquet of consequences.*"[82]

The dialogue moved forward to hostile and prejudicial experiences in England, where he had feelings of hardship because people disliked his dark skin. They made biased remarks openly while he was at the bar. Their actions made him believe these people were cold and uncaring. He shifted his thoughts to the Chinese people. He compared the attitudes they held. Arif was a married polygamous man. In respect to his harem, he felt an obligation to care for all the women equitably. This means providing the same standard of housing, gifts, treatment etcetera. This gave him the impetus to also have a relationship with a Chinese woman. Through his communication with a Chinese lady he desired, he discovered that the Chinese reacted the same as the English. I made no judgments and waited for closure. At the end of our conversation, I empathized that people sometimes forget about human needs. I did not add any more. Arif gave me the opportunity to teach his staff and son on a weekly basis. I honed into helping others understand Western culture. In turn, he referred me to other embassies to do the same.

I set a goal to meet at least forty dignitaries, and I changed my place of residence out of necessity. This truly posed a problem because regulations limited the number of places foreigners were allowed to stay, including the exclusion of local apartments. Therefore, only through the right connection with a Chinese dignitary, accommodation was found.

I felt so out of the ordinary when I was told to sneak into the building, late at night to avoid others seeing me come in. I wondered how I would handle this daily. In addition, I was faced with numerous obstacles. The building structure had imperfections and safety hazards.

When I first approached the building, there were no exterior lights. The inside of the building was the same, and I had to grope my way around. I guess this was a security measure so no one would know a foreigner was living in the building. I am not sure about their reasoning, but it was an intensely, demanding journey along a long dark hallway. I was terrified that I might bump into something. Cautiously, I entered the first floor, but there was only one window at the end of the hall. At least, the small amount of light helped me endure the difficulties. I did not tumble until I reached the end of the hall. This is where I saw a door entrance with an added step. Circumspectly, I headed to the doorway, which led to the next floor, and in a step-by-step movement, I went upstairs. The flight upwards was dreadful because the handrail was shaky. I had no idea when it might break. Fortunately, I did not fall and managed to reach the sixth floor where the apartment was located.

I fumbled about in the darkness finding the key to open the door. Unfortunately, it was not an easy key lock, and there were two locks to open. Finally, I opened the door and searched for the light switch. I grappled along the wall feeling for a light switch, but I could not find one. Somehow, I caught a glimpse of a light switch, but it was a few feet higher than I expected. Awkwardly, I found a chair and reached the light switch. I was elated that the light turned on and amazed to see three light switches next to each other. At least, the apartment was lit up, and I looked around.

The rooms were unembellished with the exception of some furniture. There was a bed in one room, and a small table with some chairs in a kitchen area. There were no curtains, allowing anyone to see me in the dwelling. This seemed to defeat the purpose of me coming in the dark. Anyway, I looked around for some linen and covered the bare windows promptly. I finally managed to get matters in place when I heard some strange sounds coming from across the hall. I was not sure what these sounds could be, but I would find out later.

I headed for the bathroom and had another startle. I sat down to use the toilet, and I pulled a string thinking this would flush the toilet. Instead, the shower came on. I was wet. I think the Chinese people must have a sense of humor because the place was built for an elephant. There was plenty of water to fill a trunk and with little need for much more. Regardless, I let the water pour down, showered and jumped into some warm clothing I had with me. As I sat down on the floor, it was affable and cozy because warm air was shooting up directly to my body. This made me feel safe, but the shrilly noise across the hall kept me awake late into the night.

Morning came rapidly, and the sun shone through the windows. I looked outside and saw a local market. Before heading downstairs, I rapidly groomed myself. I paced myself quickly and soon arrived at the market. The breakfast options were new for me. There were crepes or *Jianbing* in full view. Since it seemed to be pretty popular for the crowd, I thought maybe this would be good to eat. Before I made my decision, I watched how the *Jianbing* was made.

There was one person standing over a metal barrel that stood upright. The top of the barrel had an aluminum surface, and a gas heater was underneath. The vendor took some prepared batter and spread it around like a mammoth pancake. The *Jianbing* cooked rapidly, and an egg was cracked on the surface. The Chef spread the egg with a spatula and flipped the *Jianbing* over. Some plum sauce and a red pimento spread were placed on top. Some additions topped the *Jianbing,* like shallot pieces, cilantro, cabbage strips, sesame seeds and fried crackers. Within a few seconds, the vendor took out a flat stick, and folded the crepe into three sections and placed it into a bag. The ingredients and the way it was prepared seemed pretty novel, and I ordered one. It had a scrumptious taste, and I continued to walk around the market.

I could not believe my eyes. I saw shoes that I paid sixty dollars for in North America for less than one dollar. The most expensive pair of shoes was no more than five American dollars. Probably even these prices were inflated because I was a foreigner. It made me realize that anyone importing Chinese products can get rich almost instantly with these kinds of costs. There were so many products available, and the marketplaces actually became the highlight of my day.

After handling my affairs with the diplomats, I began meeting some Corporate Executives. Once again, I became connected through government officials, and I met many expatriate men in high status. They mostly came from Australia, New Zealand, South Africa or the United States. Somehow, I understood that these men knew about their own world, but appeared blind to the real world of China.

The expatriates lived-in eloquently furnished homes with an array of servants. There were drivers, gardeners, cooks and caregivers. They did not have to drive in the vicious traffic alone. Their landscape and children were attended. Errands were run at the snap of fingers while the cooks made delightful meals and magically did laundry too. In other words, they could get almost anything they desired. These men and their families were pampered and clueless about how the locals lived.

The executive expatriates were all about status. Before I was even able to express my intent, most of the men blared out information about their exquisite homes. They described their furnishings and locality. Interestingly, they never invited me to their homes to meet their families. All conversations took place in business settings. I suspect they held onto an Ivy League or Good Old Boys' mentality, which promoted whom they were. These men made it a point that they had an exclusive membership to how they lived, and I did not fit into the scheme of things.

The men were verbose and primarily spent time talking about their prestige. They made sure I heard the things that mattered to them, including salaries earned, lifestyle and their reputed image. Naturally, there was a monumental disparity with local executives and the people of China. I am not certain what compelled these men to exhibit their dull monologue conversations. They did not try to understand anything around them including what I had to say. I suppose this is why they only related with locals on an as needed basis. Their attitude was like the Washington professor or Sue's spouse. Thus, there were conflicts because these men were incapable of producing truths to me, or for that matter, to generate truth in a Corporate Social Responsibility Report. These expatriate executives were unwilling to see matters behind the scenes. They were overly confident in all they did. It was then that I came to recognize how the corporate executive officers in the United States seriously were. They were also diametrically opposite from local executives in lifestyle and attitude.

One of the executives rented Beijing's Golf Palace. He paid 38,000 Yuan or an equivalent to $6,034.29 U.S. dollars. This lodging covered approximately 3,300 square feet. Most of the expatriate managers rented an apartment. They paid at least 22,000 Yuan or $3,500.00 U.S. dollars monthly, whereas the local executive made about 5,000 Yuan, which is not much more than $800 U.S. dollars monthly. The local farmer made 22,000 Yuan or $350.00 U.S. annually. Naturally, the difference in spending and cultural interpretation was unalike.

When I conversed with a Corporate Executive Officer (CEO) from an international food producing company, the Executive focused on what was wrong with China. He targeted how corruption was involved related to paying fees to government officials. These people had the power to put a halt to project development, or make it happen. Another CEO focused on how they connected to Chinese officials at exclusive clubs. Their conversations were primarily about capital gain and not intellectual exchanges. This certainly leads me to question how these executives were able to address Corporate Social Responsibility reporting. They did not have anything pleasant to talk about. I can only imagine what they might say about a Chinese operation when they reported to headquarters. There was such a mammoth contrast in understanding. Then, I began interviewing several local executives and the gap was exceedingly pronounced. Social values were vastly different.

When I first met a Chinese executive, he was working at a leading hotel chain that spread across China. The executive was well groomed and in his late thirties. Throughout our entire conversation, he never made reference to where he lived. Initially, he focused on positive attributes and even addressed his desire to have blue eyes like Caucasians. He shifted from his fascination from being able to see through blue eyes, to the harm of having no eyes. The executive suddenly looked sullen and talked about disappearing children. He knew they were captured for their eyes and body parts. When he told me the story, I began to gasp. His realities came out, and then he suddenly stopped talking.

The second, Chinese CEO, was in his late forties. He had done a lot of foreign travel, having been to enumerable destinations including New Zealand, England and the United States. He also spent considerable time in Australia. He held a graduate degree from the United States and used extensive English in his technology business. Thus, he had a better grasp of what vendors required. We conversed at a fine restaurant in Beijing where Imperial Cuisine cooking took place. This was an eloquent decision, but symbolically implied he was offering me the highest honors possible. I was not sure of his intent, but I took a chance to meet him. The food was indeed marvelous, superbly prepared for monarchy, with appealing colors. The dishes were even named after royalty. For example, *Yu Feng Huan Chao* means a jade phoenix or returning to royalty. It was the preferred food of the Qing Dynasty during 1644 to 1911.

We went to the Beijing Grand View Garden Hotel. The restaurant was right next to the Grand View Garden and it was truly something. This elaborate setting was depicted like a famous Chinese novel called *The Dream of Red Mansions*. I was flabbergasted to see this elaborate setting with as much as 500 people present. The decorum reminded me of centuries past where dragon and phoenix designs were everywhere. It was hard for me to imagine the cost of my meal, but I paid close attention to what the CEO was saying. Before long, he made overtures that he liked me. I ignored his advances and asked him to tell me about his international experiences with CEOs. He changed the subject and reverted to talking about kind women. He remarked about an American woman that helped him in a time of need when he first came to California. I understood that he had other interests in me. Again, I changed the conversation to focus on situations in business. He kept trying to switch the topic, and I had to thank him for his time and say goodbye.

A few months later, one of the Chinese nationals gave my contact information to a Corporate Executive Officer. They heard that I came from Canada, and automatically assumed I spoke French. I found it quite funny that I became the representative for a French university. I did not mind the attention, being called Chairman Lily, but there was a palpably cultural gap. The Chinese presented me in the medium, and I was glorified with flower and attention. I let the scenario pass my eyes. I watched people in merriment. They were drinking wine, smoking, and laughing loudly.

The events that followed were also astounding. The company hiring me to be Chairman Lily paid for a nearby Chinese hotel. There was a lot of excitement taking place, but I finally reached my room. As I took the steps up, I saw many Chinese women accompanying foreign men. They seemed to be very closely attached, and I could tell relations were going on between them. Entering my room, I overheard a conversation. Foreign men were receiving local prostitutes as gifts from their Chinese hosts. This explained why the Chinese CEO might have behaved as he did. The bulk of these expatriate guests were married men. It was not my business to preach to them about what they were doing, but this kind of behavior does impact Western men. There seems to be an increasing notion that women are commodities. Men, that were faithful, were now coming home as infidels. The Chinese imposed their practices on discouraging monogamy. Based on the glory of being in the medium, I suppose being in the bright lights hurt my eyes.

SHANXI: In this setting, the local Chinese nationals were tremendously friendly. A local executive invited me to meet his family and friends. When I arrived, I was treated like part of the family, which made me feel like an honored guest. Through this connection, I was able to see more about how local people lived. I traveled with a friend to areas where foreigners never went. Some of the places were noxious environments, while other places were peaceful. During my journey, I saw unexpected performances that demonstrated how passionate people inject traditional culture into the community. I experienced the pure joys of feeling the warmth and energy of the people around me. I found that this does not compare to North American people, who have another idea of being wined, dined and entertained outside their home. They do not necessarily extend it to their fellow man, unless the person or people are part of their Ivy League exclusive club.

I traveled along the Taihang Mountains neighboring Hebei, Henan, Shanxi and Inner Mongolia. I was going with a friend to pass out some red envelopes. The intent of these envelopes is to reconcile friendship, forget grudges and sincerely wish peaceful relationships for the Chinese New Year. I assumed it was going to be an exciting journey as we were taking the sleeper bus, which is not crowded and offers greater comfort. When I got into the bus, I was astounded to see there were only 16 passengers. The setup allowed us to eat, relax and sleep along the way. The most satisfying part, there was privacy including blackened out windows.

After arriving in comfort, I would see the flip side. The 32 million, massive population was heading in the same direction as we were. I was heading towards Taiyuan City. This is known for being part of the coal mining industry. I heard it was the most toxic, deadliest place to be and I was a bit nervous. My friend assured me that it was out of harm's way so I came along. I was walking through the streets and I could feel a filmy mist surrounding me. The air was like a sandy mixture. I had trouble breathing and felt dizzy. I stopped in a small shop where I was able to get some cold bottled water.

There were a lot of advocacy campaigns addressing protecting people, improving their equipment, and retaining standards. In fact, this was a truly sheltered culture where more tons of sulfur dioxide was being discharged than imaginable. I was whiffing the smells of poisonous gases in the air and the promoters did not convey something sound. The journey became difficult for me. My Chinese friend kept insisting I walk, so I did. Out of the blue, a troupe of Chinese dancers came out to perform in the middle of the street. Their performance took my breath away in the brisk winter weather.

There were at least 10 people dressed in flamboyant colors of shining bright yellow, flashy orange and scarlet red with gold trimmings. They were performing the Dragon dance and these people were fantastically swift on their feet. Some were acrobats and others did dangerous stunts. This was undoubtedly an exceptional contrast from the black soot to crisp, bright, colors.

Walking along, I saw red signs placated on doors. I was told that these signs were notices to wish people well. Finally, we reached our destination. As I entered my friend's home, I was shocked when I looked in the mirror. My face was black and full of soot while the house was sparkling clean with avant-garde furniture. I certainly questioned how the contrast was possible. After washing up, I was invited to eat an elaborate vegetarian meal served with uncut noodles that represented a long life. Sweets and dried fruit goods were centered on the table. Most of the items were stored in red Chinese candy boxes.

That night I spread a blanket on the floor. It was a comfortable rest because the under floor electric heating kept me warm. The next morning I thought about traveling through the coal environment again, but the thought of Mary Poppins came to my mind. If there were only a way that I could fly above the dirt and cover up, this might work well. I imagined that my smile acted as an umbrella and the dirt caused me no harm. Instead, I took a train to go to northern China, Julin province.

JULIN: This time I traveled first class with a private shower and single cot. It was as if I were a designated government official because this was uncommon for locals. Getting out of the train station, I was freezing from the cold. The air was becoming extremely brisk, and my feet and hands felt refrigerated. There were lots of men wearing hats that covered their ears. These hats were called *ushanka,* named from the Russian word for 'ears.' The hat protected my ears, jaw, and lower chin from the cold. My legs and upper chest were chilly, and never felt that coldness in Canada. My friend had an extra pair of leg warmers, and I put them on. I still was nippy, and wanted to feel the heat. I had no idea what my friend's family would think about me especially I had a dire need to feel the warmth.

Of course, the amount of people coming together would probably make me feel warm. Then, I noticed many other men wearing furry, warm-looking, hats. This clued me in on a way to get warmer. Concurrently, the local men were staring and following me everywhere. This made me feel quite uncomfortable, but the amount of people dwindled as I arrived at my friend's quarters. This is where I was able to embody the true spirit of the Chinese family's character. People did not feel cold because they were accustomed to the weather. Also because, family joined together making Jiaozi (Chinese: 餃子) or dumplings.

I did not even have time to put my bags down, but it was fun getting into it. I watched how quickly some of the people made it, but my fingers were not as nimble as theirs. It seemed people were coming from every direction and helping out. Then, I noticed a large-framed woman with tiny feet. She was my friend's grandmother, and one of the million women who had her feet bound, which was a status symbol years earlier. This practice caused her serious harm. The woman's arch was broken, and her own foot grew closer to her heel. The grandmother was struggling and mostly hobbling on her feet. It was hard to fathom that breaking the foot became a passport to social mobility and increased wealth in the past. If Sue were alive, maybe she would have condoned this vain act because this sounds like an Ivy League mentality. Women during those times were expected to style their appearance with certain standards. Regrettably, the old woman had a large frame and her tiny feet did not match with a large body.

I felt awful about this older grandmother, but there was not much I could say or do. I continued preparing the *Jiaozi,* placing them into a large boiling pot. The aroma began to fill the air, and I finally had a moment to put down my bags.

There were only three people that lived in this self-contained dwelling. Rooms were undecorated and plain cement walls separating the kitchen. There were also three bedrooms and a large open courtyard. As the guest of honor, I was put in a room with a heated bed or *Kang*. This bed is usually reserved for the entire family especially during the New Year where family ate together. The *Kang* was otherwise kept for elders. It turned out that the *Kang* bed was multifunctional. It was easy to place items to cook over the *Kang* bed including boiling water for tea. As this was the primary source of heat for the family, everyone gathered around to talk, tell stories, and sing during the cold winter nights. In the past, it was pretty common for the entire family to sleep on the *Kang* bed together. Also, this was where marriage ceremonies and mourning services took place, thus; I understood that giving me the *Kang* bed was extremely out of the ordinary. The rest of the family went to sleep on what appeared to be large place mats. They probably were not as incredibly warm as I was, so I received exceptional treatment. While I slept, someone from the household came by to put coal under the bed. This ensured that all members of the family were kept warm including me.

The *Kang* was primarily a sleeping platform, which is widely seen in the villages of Northern China. These are steadily fading out, but the rectangular construction was actually a bed built out of bricks or cheaply fired clay. The *Kang* consisted of a stove for fuel, the bed itself, and a chimney. This was entirely heated by coal and covered with a heavy quilt. I particularly liked how the heat from the stove was directed through the flues under the bed.

The only thing missing in their home was the rest room, but the family used an outhouse nearby. The family members knew I was unaccustomed to going to an outhouse, but I tried. When I entered the outhouse, women, and small girls were squatting down on a wooden platform. There were eight holes side by side and all the Chinese females present, looked up.

I felt incredibly strange to be there, but mostly I had a fear to fall in the hole. The whole opening was fairly wide. The women in the outhouse began chatting and glanced back and forth at me. I had an uneasy feeling. The stench was making me nauseous. I returned, but I suppose the family was concerned about my presence becoming the gossip in the small village. Since my friend's father was head of the village, people needed to be halted before any officials found out I was there. Apparently, there was never a foreigner in that vicinity before. I did not have official permission to go there, but since my friend's family did not want matters to get out of hand, they asked that I do my bodily functions in a pail. Then, a family member removed it so that villagers would not see me in the outhouse and talk about me. Even though, my friend's family was friendly, I was relieved to return to the privacy of my apartment in Beijing.

RETURN TO BEIJING: I never experienced any comfort squatting down nearby other females in Julin, so I was thankful to use a toilet again. I was pleased to be back in the Beijing apartment. After all, the fifteenth day of the New Year's celebration was too overwhelming. Simultaneously, I began to think superstitiously like the Chinese. If you feel satisfied, then something magnificent is bound to happen. Therefore, I assumed that having a fantastic time was a bright omen for my future.

Unfortunately, the word got out that I lived nearby in an apartment. Since it was not designated for foreigners, I had no idea what problems might follow. People in Beijing gossiped excessively, and problems came up. I guess I should have retained my original beliefs because superstitious beliefs brought me nowhere. I had some blissful times, so changing housing would give another opportunity to intellectualize with people from around the world. The experiences of the *Kang* bed brought warm memories of being a part of an extended family among the Chinese, but it was time to move on. I did not want the apartment owner, who was a doctor to experience problems, so I left on my own volition.

Before leaving the rented apartment, I had a real curiosity about what was making a racket just opposite my door. I knocked at the door, and a Chinese person answered. I could not fathom what I saw inside. It was undoubtedly a small bird and monkey sanctuary. There were many cages lined up, and I suppose the people inside were breeding them. This explained the piercing sounds I heard. The birds and monkeys were calling out, but their howling was most disquieting. It was a combination of birds marking their territory and monkeys screeching for attention. The neighbors were breeding these creatures even when they made unusually strident sounds. The Chinese people never comment on the more bizarre practices of their neighbors. For all I knew, there could have been a small mental asylum where people were chained up just down the hall. I only imagined that behind other black doors, other unimaginable things must have also been taking place. Between the sounds of the birds and the monkeys, the greatest racket came from the Chinese gossip culture (the black doors). The people rattled and screamed about me, a quiet, unobtrusive foreigner, when there were beasts shrieking in the apartment across the hall. They disliked the idea that a foreigner was living in their precious complex. Anyway, my bags were packed, and I planned to go to Shanghai with brief stopovers in Liaoning and Tianjin.

The Great Wall: I visited Shenyang, Liaoning earlier but now I could see the Great Wall on my own. This incredible wall was a 2,000-year-old strategic masterpiece, with over 6,000 kilometers to explore, if I wanted to see all of the Great Wall of China. In reality, walking up on its steep path, the wall looked no different at any angle, but I could see many rolling mountain ranges in the background. People may rave at what they see, but the climb is not so exhilarating. I was constantly catching my breath and dealing with mixed climbing difficulties. I often thought that if I was not careful I could suffer severe injury or death, as the steep rocky paths were getting more difficult and not easy on my feet. I made sequential moves that were challenging and required perseverance. Often I had to put my hands and feet onto the rocks to get to the next plateau. All I knew is that I was high above the world of civilization. Once I reached peak areas, I was able to pause to see the natural world ruled by nature and her raw beauty. Indeed, the scenery was breathtaking, and I saw deep river valleys, broad basins, rolling plains and terraced hills.

I continued to walk along the Great Wall where I saw locals wearing traditional clothing. The men wore replicas of ancient times, a two-piece ceremonial outfit with an armored hat and sword. These individuals liked being photographed chiefly because foreigners paid for it. Other locals were selling souvenirs, beverages and food products. In the Liaoning area, there were two restored portions in Hushan and Dandong. These were the newer portions of the Great Wall. When I went there, there were fewer visitors. I suspect it was a less popular spot than for tourists to go, as it was a remote location.

From Liaoning port, I connected to Tianjin, a northern port along the coast of the Bohai Gulf. It was officially opened to the outside world in 1860. As this was one of the earliest foreign trading posts in China, seeing foreigners was pretty common. From this destination, I could have taken a ship to Russia, South Korea or Japan. It was an ideal junction and gave me a reason to check around the area. It was in this location that I booked a fare for Shanghai.

Shanghai: Since I was going through considerable changes in my residence and life, I stopped to reflect on the lives of the Chinese. I wondered what my ancestors would have done. Through the eyes of an inexperienced ship traveler, I was about to embark on a local ship heading to a new destination. I treated this like a unique challenge, boarding a large Chinese cruise and cargo ship headed towards Shanghai. It was exciting because I could view the ship getting ready to disembark. This reminded me of romantic movies where lovers bid each other adieu before setting off to sail. Peering further, I could see a number of ships docked. There were some military vessels, cruise liners, and other cargo or passenger ships.

People were still walking into the ship, and the inside was like an enormous Noah's Ark. The Chinese people were mostly coming in pairs. They brought various items with them as if they were going to a faraway place. As I came aboard, two stewards greeted me. I truly had no idea what I would see.

I watched a massive amount of people entering the ship. The people went into single-file, not by choice. They were pushing each other to go ahead. One of the stewards directed me to my cabin. I remember taking a long circular walk until I found my lodging. In order to get there, I walked past many bare white walls. Then I peered down, and I saw at least five or six levels below me. It made my head feel dizzy just looking at the layers in this monumental ship. I am sure it had the capacity to carry more than a thousand people and also held lots of bulky cargo. Finally, I reached my cabin and saw a small porthole. I looked out, and there was a sundeck. I put my baggage away and heard people chattering just outside my door. Then, I heard a strong knock on my door. The steward was calling me to do something. When I was about to respond to the attendant, he spoke aloud. He said, "You Go." I was not sure if he meant I needed to go out or go with him. To avoid confusion, I nodded, and followed him.

The attendant was directing me to another room to eat breakfast. I thought it might have been too early, but apparently, everything was prepared. The ship was already in motion, and only a handful of people were seated to eat. I suppose this is the advantage associated with my booking. There were steamed stuffed buns, deep-fried twisted dough sticks, and various other steamed snacks made from wheat flour. The dishes were called *Youtiao* and *Baozi*, both famous breakfast snacks. Besides this, I had some *Zongzi*. This was food wrapped up in pyramid-shaped leaves, and the inside was made of sticky rice with some sweet red bean filling. Besides that, there were condiments and side dishes. These side dishes could be added to a chicken gruel as part of the main course. It seemed more than unusual that, with hundreds of people aboard, there were no more than nine people eating breakfast with me. After having my fill, I allowed my food to settle.

From the breakfast dining, I went on deck. I watched the water rise and fall. When the waves peaked upwards, the foam curved in such a way as if to say hello. I was beginning to feel I had the importance of a celebrity like Mozart. The passionate rush of the waves brought the sounds and smells of sea creatures, the ocean's music and the faint sound of background echoing from the seagulls. I could not see where all the living things were going. I closed my eyes and just imagined. I pretended I was a mermaid, submerged in the water. Then I had the vision of all the living creatures swimming in many places. Some fish headed for the caves. Others went behind the moss, in the seaweed and elsewhere. A chilly breeze circling brought me back to being human, and my large floating castle in the sea. There was also something ringing in my ears. What was it?

Unexpectedly, a large fish appeared out of the water. There were dolphins that swished in the water using their tails with much force. The strength of their tails enabled them to reach high speeds in and out of the water. There were at least six dolphins leaping in the air. Soon after jumping up, they quickly dove downwards to enormous depths. What were they doing? Were they mating or chasing their food? I had no idea what was going on. One of the bystanders spoke English. She said dolphins beat their tails as a warning to others that danger is close. I was concerned, because I saw the dolphins swimming upwards and close to each other. They circled around in rhythmic movements. This was their way to have social discourse. When they did not want to see other fish, they dived into the water. From a distance, it was hard to imagine which were the adults or the children dolphins, because their appearance looked similar in size. I guess I did not know quite how to look at them carefully because no two dolphin fins are identical. Their fins are the same as a human fingerprint; each is unique to a dolphin. Anyway, after being entertained by the dolphin's social dance, I went back inside. I was more curious about what the other levels of the ship looked like than seeing first class.

I walked down to see what was below. The levels spiraled downward, and it was like a concentric path. The journey below reminded me of a Medicine Wheel in Aboriginal tradition. Would this be a healing place or a place of discovery for me? I only knew that the ship's design mirrored a mystical message that I had *a* **higher purpose**, and it was related to the fair dealings of healing.

I descended downwards reminding myself that this was intended design, much like a Western parkade. Each level was clearly different. The accommodations were beginning to look like chalk and cheese. It all was based on what people paid. The shift clearly was a progression of different classes. I had a private room, and the next class was semiprivate cabins with four to ten people sharing a room. Finally, an open-area space where there was no privacy whatsoever.

At each level, I smiled to the people. I enjoyed that they tried saying, "Hello, how are you," in English. When I came to the actual last level, I saw families cluttered together. They had prepared food, and some ate together. Others slept in a small space. I saw a young mother breastfeeding her infant. Nearby were some old men playing a strategic board game and it looked like a Chinese chess Board. The groups of people were active in their own way, I still reflected on who the Chinese people were. When I saw so many people gathered together, and without a shower or toilet facilities, I took it to heart. It must have been difficult for them. I began wondering why paying more or less money should matter so much. This did not seem like a *Fair Deal*. These people had the same needs as me. Shortly after, I gestured some of them to follow me. The people came with their towels, following my lead.

We all climbed upward together. I brought them to my room and took a picture for Sue's scrapbook. Subsequently, I let a handful of people use my shower. The people were exceptionally happy to have this chance. Some of the people offered me their food, but I did not want anything in return. I refused them gently. I wanted to please the people. I kept thinking about the hardship I experienced earlier, and something inside of me kept muttering that I needed to help more people rather than ignore the situation. I went back down again, and got more people to come to my cabin and shower. Maybe I reached at least 20 people, and I became another Dr. Patch Adams, and the talk of the ship.

Unexpectedly, I heard a large knock at my door. The greeters who met me initially were steaming angrily. They said, "No, No, No, No." The attendants were complaining about the water consumption. I smiled and understood their meaning. I was at incredible risk to continue helping people. This was a society where everything is regulated in a certain way. If a person has status, people look the other way. If I did not stop, I knew it could lead to unfavorable consequences. At least, I gave several people the opportunity to feel clean and morality was as high as the dolphin's dance. All I remember is the people's faces. After showering, each person would come out smiling. It was the language of the face that said it all. If Dr. Kearns were present, he probably would invent a "wiping away the mist" for showers.

Shanghai - Learning Evolves and Tides Settle: The ship docked for two days in Shanghai. This was a stopover before heading to Hong Kong.

I had to make the best out of the time I had. Getting off the ship, there were two women who I had spent time talking with earlier. The women were both doctors. I suppose Sue would have been proud that I kept bumping into female medical experts. Anyway, I learned that they were both retiring from the profession. They seemed young to retire. One woman was 50 years old. The other woman was 55 years old. This was an awakening call. I was hearing that aging defines a person to be less worthy than much younger people. I did not get into a discussion about it, but we all relaxed together. We spent some time together enjoying the sun shining down on us on the deck. Our entertainments were the dolphins socializing in harmony. Maybe that is why they had the idea that I join them to see Shanghai together.

The women grabbed hold of my hand. This was their way of showing friendship and a customary practice throughout Asia. When I experienced this the first time, it certainly created discomfort. Eventually, I was happy to be carefree to see another place with newfound friends. I allowed them to hold my hand, and we walked together. As we walked offshore, I saw human rickshaws just like on my trip in Indonesia. The traffic was extremely terrible, but it was no different from other cities in China. Even though, we seemed to wander aimlessly, we knew we had to be faster than the wind to cross the roads. Riders of motorcycles and bicycles often ignored traffic lights. Like other cities, drivers weaved their way in and out of traffic. Vehicle drivers were just as reckless. They cut each other off, no different from other Asian cities. Motorists who missed their exit became a hazard. They threw their gears into reverse and backed up even when it was unsafe. Many of the drivers on the street refused even to stop or yield when they made turns. This forced my friends and me to get out of their way. Drivers of all kinds routinely barreled down the wrong side of the street. I often feared for my life, and wondered whether I would be able to make it across the street safely.

In the midst of all this chaos, I was taken aback to see people dancing in the streets. They did not fear the potential for harm, so I went to a park bench to watch. My fervor as a youngster to be a ballet dancer was reenergized. The situation undoubtedly gave rise to extreme dramatic moments. They were performing the sleeves and ribbon dance. The dancers used long silk sleeves to accentuate their hand and arm movements. They whirled around like banners or ribbons and snapped as whips. Their extra-long sleeves were associated with moral conduct. They were there to promote their upcoming performance. It was incredible watching them move. Their sleeves were an extension of their hands. When they threw back their sleeves, it revealed the sensitive and beautiful hand movements of the dancers. Incredibly, the long white silk cuffs, or "*water sleeve*,"[84] became a functional extension of a person's ordinary sleeve. The water sleeves were as long as two feet. I watched the dancers make sweeping pheasant plumes and manipulating movements. The dancers did this by holding plumes between their first and middle fingers in each hand. I had no idea that this kind of fantastic performance could be held on a street and at no cost. It was so stimulating to watch each woman move like the **gentle waves** of the ocean. What a fabulous occasion to be! I was exceptionally lucky to see how breathtakingly they performed. There was something about the dancers. Their moving hands were the grace of what I experience, the moving tides of a person's journey. Simultaneously, this was a culture where the hand truly was an extension of friendship and grace.

There were a few more extraordinary things that also became visible. For example, a man is carrying many heavy ice blocks on the back of his bicycle, a woman transporting a myriad of boxes on her head. There was a businessman dressed in a suit driving a bicycle. He managed to haul a pile of bricks on his moving rickshaw. The Shanghai Paparazzi followed and offered photos to be taken, but I do not think Sue would have approved. There were many more phenomenon's' taking place, but I waited for Shanghai to reveal itself to me.

Like other places in Asia, everything starts with the cyclopean amount of people. They were everywhere, and there was hardly any space to move around. As in other Chinese cities, there was terrific street food. The same crepes I saw in Beijing were also here. There were also many kinds of floating fried dough with different filling. Some square grilled dough was cut-up with dessert, rolled treats, and more variations that I ever saw in North America. I found it to be pretty astonishing to see so much available. This even included sparrows that were skewered, roasted and fried, and served on sticks. I saw people eating every bone. Some of the people sipped beer in street side stalls. Like in Thailand, I also saw silkworms, grasshoppers, seahorses, scorpions, snakehead soup, and more. There were even **Lily** bulbs and deer penis for sale. There were so many eating choices, but not many were my preference.

Strolling along, I assumed some local vendors were trying to appeal to foreign visitors. I had that impression when I saw some menus written in English for public viewing, but what was written sometimes was humorous. I saw many examples of menus including goat genitals soup, pig's hoof gruel, fried goose intestines, chicken without a sexual life, beef with no fur, drunken shrimps, and the list goes on. The food delicacies were making my head spin, so I looked around at the architecture.

There were many buildings with European and Asiatic styling. My friends moseyed together with me. I could hear feet clicking along the cobbled streets, and this signaled that the world of Shanghai would shine on me.

There were all kinds of colorful things in the air. Products for sale, people laughing, smiling, dancing, and carrying on and much more than I truly wanted to see. The open marketplaces were naturally exposed. There were traditional and contemporary restaurants, clothing, medicine shops describing that they could *kill the terrible or ugly pain*. Shanghai was indeed a tribute to another breed of thinking. After touring for a while, I returned to the ship. Tomorrow would be another day in Shanghai.

That evening presented a new talent too. I learned that the Chinese people's favorite activity on land or at sea was karaoke. People were singing all kinds of tunes, but they did this mostly to entertain each other. I had a hard time appreciating the people that could not carry a melody. I was too embarrassed to try. I knew my notes sounded like a croaking frog. People on the ship continued to sing into the wee hours. This did not allow me much rest, so I was certainly looking forward to the next day without hearing another wretched tune. I wanted to see the dolphins, more dancers, and whatever else I did not see before.

The next day, I left bright and early. This time I went on my own. I heard the boat dancers were going to perform. I hoped this would be a mobile Chinese opera, but it was different from I expected. The dancers wore a boat-shaped prop around their waist. They covered their legs with pieces of silk. The procession of dancers began. Some were singing while other dancers imitated boat movements. Then a man dressed as a boat followed the group. The inventiveness of their movements was distinctive. I could not follow how they moved. This entertainment was certainly a decent opener for the day. The performance lasted at least an hour or maybe more.

The weather in Shanghai was beautiful in May. I wanted to stroll along and thought about my friends, but they had other plans. They were going to an annual film festival, which attracted international audiences, so I was not interested. I was walking alone along a fenced area, and right behind the fencing was the Yangtze River. I could hear birds cackling, and then remembered the superstitions of the Chinese. If the bird screeching turned out to be a magpie, this would be a perfectly brilliant sign. The Chinese believed that the magpie symbolized *a bird of superb luck and happiness*. Surprisingly, when I glimpsed at the birds, they were magpies. These were black and white birds, mostly covered in black. It was as if I had to see things in black and white. It was lovely to have a tremendous omen happen. I supposed I lucked out to see quite a number of magpies gathering near the water. I sat down on a nearby park bench, and a young girl approached me. She sat next to me while her grandmother looked on. They were both smiling at me. I liked the warm-hearted smiles they presented. It gave me a sense of peaceful things to be.

I started to walk lackadaisically because I was not in a rush to go anywhere. Moving along the rail fencing of the Yangtze River, I saw some small shops nearby. I never saw anything like what I viewed at that time. The chefs were cooking and working so quickly behind clear glass windows. I was able to see every movement they made while preparing food. Freshly made dough was formed into noodles and fried. All kinds of ingredients were rolled together. There were fresh ducks; fish cut open and prepared to look like grapes. The pork was diced up into small cubes, and savory sauces were placed on top. The lychees were a small round Chinese fruit, rather sumptuous to see blended with a prawn mixture. It was incredible watching knives moving at a pace my eyes hardly could follow. They were preparing different dishes, and they did not mind that people were watching. In fact, showcasing of food is done that way in China. The glass windows allow anybody to watch and determine if they want to go inside.

I saw groups of people eating together. They seemed to be enjoying themselves. Two of the people were gesturing me to come inside. I did not know these people, but apparently, they wanted me to join them. I had nothing to lose, so I went inside. There were about 10 people gathered around a large communal cookout. I liked being invited by a friendly crowd. I found it better to be introduced to the unfamiliar than being left unaware. I saw some food brewing on a Mongolian copper stove. This same dish fascinated me earlier when I had some in Beijing. This time it was a lot more fun joining a group who was eating and laughing together. It gave me the chance to learn how the locals enjoyed themselves, while trying something new. I liked the idea that the Chinese people asked me to attend their gathering without reservations. This made me wonder about values I learned in North America, where this kind of manner was not recognizable.

The group of people was eating together and the dish was called *Mongolian* or *Chinese Hot Pot*. This cooking style originated from the Mongolians when nomadic tribes gathered around the cooking fires and prepared ordinary meals. Chunks of meat were speared and cooked in a stew, bubbling in their primitive cauldron. The Beijing and Shanghai people modified this cooking style. They used lamb and a variety of vegetables to create a more tantalizing dish than Western food. The food is placed in a copper pot, and heated up by a tube with hot charcoal inside. This allows the ingredients to diffuse evenly, cook throughout, and heat up quickly. I enjoyed this popular cooking style. I tried the Hot Pot cooked in its original style, (not stainless steel) and it was yummy. I wonder if that is how my great grandmother ate. Were the traditions the same years ago?

The most intriguing part is the brewing pot ingredients and sauce naturally partitions. They looked like yin yang, the complimentary forces in the universe (male and female), so the food both looks and tastes magical. On one side of the pot, the sauce is white, referred to as *Yang*. The other side of the pot, the sauce is salmon-colored, called *Yin*. **Yang** represents everything that is positive and masculine. **Yin** signified the feminine and the negative. Either force (*Ying or Yang*) is not considered better than the other. Instead, both are needed for balance. Synchronously, the yin / yang construct does present some contradiction. Based on equitable notions, I cannot understand why men are still the favored gender. Regardless, the groups inviting me were mostly men and two women.

I suppose the Chinese party invited me to have a greater sense of balance. When I participated in their group, I followed the cues of other people. Everyone took turns picking up all kinds of vegetables, so I followed. There were two plates with loosely piled strips of lamb meat. I watched the people dunk the meat or vegetable into the sauce of their choice. I did the same thing and the person speaking English told me the true meaning. He said the sauces are associated with an intuitive side all people have. Since the group had to head back to work, sadly, I bid them good-bye.

The experience of eating together certainly reminded me of how Asiatic people can be. There is typically one leader, and everyone follows the leader's prompt. No one seems to move in a different direction. In a collective group of people, people do lose their individuality, but they also feel closer collectively. No one seems left out, and that is far more vital than feeling alienated. I saw that self-centeredness does not usually take place. At first, I thought this could not be right, everybody seemed happy. Indubitably, this made me feel more like being a part of a group than alone, especially after I ate together with the group. When I followed the Chinese ways, I saw everyone pulling together. It was quite opposite from habit I saw in North America. People are more sensitive of the next person, and no one argues. The feeling made me think this is how warm feelings need to develop. Everyone seemed fantastically relaxed, and it did not seem like people expressed any artificial emotions. In reality, every person had his or her chosen built-in point of reference filters that allow us to be selective. It was then that I realized it was up to me not to react to criticism, stop finding blame, cease complaining, reduce nagging, and avoid punishment or other. Of course, this makes me question if there are other possibilities that I need to consider. I knew I was not holding onto an Ivy League mentality even though, I went to Ivy League school. Instead, this overseas experience taught me to discern how to help myself by taking away the good from any situation. Thus, I did not have to follow people blindly. Also, the notions of helplessness and blindness as in Bosch's painting *The Garden of Earthly Delights,* is a depiction of people's behavior. The painting attributed to societal conditioning stemming from the media, the gossip culture, local acculturation, family rearing, exposure and schooling.

I paused to have a reflective moment. I conceptualized that all behavior certainly relates to how we speak the language. When I first started speaking another language, I transferred my thoughts into that language. Some things just cannot be translated. In other words, interpreting a person's intent is actually what counts. Paying attention to a person's tone of voice, facial expressions, and body language matters. Such factors helped me to determine what was truly meant.

I lingered at the restaurant a little longer even though the group left. I wanted to try some sweet dessert, and I watched how peoples' eyes still supervene where I went. I kept thinking I was being followed as in my earlier experience, in the bathhouse, but I was wrong. Mostly, people were curious what I was doing because I was acting individually and not as before, collectively. Anyway, it was time to move on and I continued walking.

I went to the old city section next to Chenghuangmia area. This location was considered to be exquisitely lavish with finest Chinese gardens in the region. It was gratifying to see a garden of flourishing flowers because I was a true Lily anyway. My imagination started stirring, and I made-belief that I was in Alice in Wonderland's world. No matter where I went, I felt as if I was being chased by a rabbit and following an illusionary tunnel. I was moving towards the Queen of Hearts, but time was running out. Suddenly, it began raining, and the tides were about to take me somewhere else.

The ship moved out of Shanghai, and the waters rippled towards Hong Kong. The tides were exceptionally serene, and I did not get to see the dolphins while heading out, but I reflected. I grasped that China was truly like being *spellbound** as in Dali's painting. There were so many things that mesmerized me. Even when I paid close attention to how dolphins socially interacted, I saw similarities to human nature. Specifically, Male dolphins engaged in acts of aggression apparently for the same reasons as humans. There were disputes between companions and competition for females. At least, I did photograph this for Sue. The dolphins were part of the *Fair Deal*, too. They provided more understanding about how genders behaved.

Hong Kong: Thoughts continued to flow, and I was fascinated to see the waters moving. I imagined ballerinas dancing. They were casting shadows against the sunlight while the ship moved ahead. It seemed like only a matter of a few hours until I arrived at the port of Hong Kong. This was an exceptionally busy place, and hardly any room to walk among the people. I guess this is a reality because Hong Kong is a small island. Obtaining space is just like grabbing gold.

Once I hit land, I had to travel along alleyways just to capture a little bit of breathing space. Hong Kong was a commercial hot spot, so passing by; I could see an array of products such as DVDs, 24-carat gold jewelry, elaborate trinkets and more. I believed if I made any wrong turn, it might have led to the immoral side of town or human trade. I knew that anyone might lose their way easily, because life in these woods has little meaning where so many people get lost. I took more precaution than before. I preferred going to smaller populated areas whenever possible.

As far as accommodation goes, Hong Kong is so space-starved that many people complain about the high rents and steep hotel rates. This reality is for tourists, entrepreneurs, vexed university students, and locals. The settings were undoubtedly created by fearless people. They took a small piece of land and made it their own, naming a number of heroes. I had no inclination to be known as Hong Kong's hero.

The activities in Hong Kong were many, and so were their heroes. I was reminded of my childhood upbringing. I remember my mother telling me that I could not have any pets at home unless they were incredibly small. I had little money to purchase much of anything, but I decided to use my cake box and collect a mouse. When I asked the shopkeeper if I had enough money to buy one, she smiled. The merchant said she would give me two mice for the price of one. That day I came home and took my two mice with me. I tucked them carefully under my bed, and they magically multiplied. This is parallel to the people in South China. They like to bargain especially if they can get two for the price of one. Like the motions of the mice, the people of Hong Kong had their adventures in small spaces too. Their businesses were also trapped in small spaces. Businesses of all kinds seemed to be scurrying in all directions and, so was the nightlife. The hustle and bustle was a 24-hour showplace.

When I decided to take a bus in Hong Kong, I found this to be quite the challenge. There were large numbers of people that had to be pushed into buses and trains. This was mostly because of the amount of people. No one had time to monitor what was taking place because even the police were busy pushing people inside. People did not line up in a single queue. Instead, they formed a vague line. As soon as it was time to get on the bus, the race was which person gets there first. Men pushed in front of women and children. Even though I did get on, the bus ride was uncomfortable. Therefore, I looked out the window as best I could and saw how incredible Hong Kong certainly was. This was an implausible place to be. There were thousands of skyscrapers, putting the city at the top of world rankings. Thirty-six of the world's 100 tallest residential buildings are in Hong Kong. In fact, more people in Hong Kong live or work above the 14th floor than anywhere else on Earth, making it the world's most vertical city. This is when I knew that no matter where I would go, I always had to look up at least from time to time. When I stopped looking up, something changed.

There was a rooster walking near my feet. I had no idea where the owner went. As I strode along the street, I noticed the rooster was following. Not far away, I could hear some people giggling, and cheering. The noises were getting stronger. I tried walking ahead, but never thought the rooster would keep pace with me. It was hard for me to fathom that the rooster was still nearby even when I walked quickly. Somehow, the rooster was shadowing me and became my squawking partner.

I proceeded ahead, and the noises were getting stronger. I tried keeping pace with most people around me and unbelievably, the rooster was still tagging along. Someone tried pushing in front of me, so I let them go first. In reality, the rooster adopted me as his pet. Soon after, I saw a large sign with the picture of a rooster. This made me remember the same kind of pictures in Thailand. People over there went to see roosters boxing together. They placed bets to see which rooster would remain alive. I was not particularly interested to get in to see what was going on. I knew if the trailing rooster were caught, he would have to fight. This was prodigious business in Asia, and I was unsure what I should do. The creature continued to shadow me. I marveled that this was taking place, but I realized that the rooster was smiling on me.

I tiptoed to see what was going on, and went around the building. I found a peephole in the wooden slats and looked in. From a distance, I could see two roosters walking around a circle. Roosters were kept in hand-strewn kennels in a kind of a dome shape. They were released to dual. I realized that, as I was observing, the trainers could be out to get another rooster. I watched the trainers take a rooster and put it into suspenders. The trainer would move the rooster up and down deliberately to get them motivated to fight. Then, I saw the men put some spandex bands around their legs. This was done to strengthen their legs. Men certainly took their rooster fighting sport seriously. They would bet on which rooster would win and let them fight to the death. Like Thailand, the men put their bets down.

The rooster neared me and then unexpectedly, he began chuckling. I knew what the consequences might be. I hoped no one heard him. Therefore, I spoke to the rooster as if he were human and would understand. This was a trick I learned from the aboriginal people. They used to say if you talk to an animal's spirit, they could understand you. I told the rooster if he continued to sing, he would be put back into the kennels. Possibly, the rooster pal might be in a boxing show. I asked the rooster if that is what he wished to happen. Suddenly, the rooster calmed down. After viewing what was taking place, I got up to leave. The rooster continued to straddle nearby. I knew this gambling sport was unlawful, but it is practiced throughout Asia, Mexico and other places too. This sport has already been outlawed in Brazil, Europe and the United States. I think the rooster was listening to what I was saying. The creature understood that people in Hong Kong were boxers of another kind. I moved ahead, and the rooster walked with me into the crowded streets. I saw the rooster for quite a while and then it vanished. I suspect he went to a rooster conference to tell them what I said.

I continued walking into the congested streets. In passing, I met a blonde-haired American woman that came from California. She lived in Hong Kong for years and was briefing me about affordable lodging. I thanked her and continued my journey. Even though, it was not easy to find the lodging, I managed to get there by foot. I was a little confused at the directions. This was a soaring high-rise building with no markings. I was uncertain where I was entering. I thought the information might be a mistake. I kept looking up at the building. This made me quite light-headed. There must have been at least 60 or more stories of one-story flats. I decided to check it out and pressed the elevator button. When the elevator stopped, a handful of people came out. The elevator only accommodated about 10 people. Some other people were hanging around to get on the elevator, so, I let them go first. I waited for the elevator to come back down, but it had taken at least ten minutes before it returned. This time I was fearful to go up. My destination was on the 56th floor. People were cramming into a dreadfully small space, but I was being lifted to new heights. The elevator began to rise higher than expected. I felt I was in an airplane ready for takeoff. As the elevator moved higher, the air was getting denser. Finally, my stop came, and I got out. The woman was right, I reached a protected area, and this was where I would lodge.

When I arrived, the attendant was glad to take my American dollars. The man showed me my partitioned spot where I would sleep. There was no separated room. Instead, a sleeping area separated by a thin white sheet. No locker was visible, but many foreign people were staying there too. The bathroom and shower were down the hall, and I became familiar with my surroundings. I was rather alarmed to see a massive amount of people in the same sleep area as me. I was thankful that I was going to another destination and accommodations would be better.

After securing my lodging, I began my plight to see more of Hong Kong's attractions. Unfortunately, there was nothing particularly quick because I had to muddle through a huge crowd of people. There was only one elevator going up and down. Even taking a ride from a few floors above, took an incredible time. Then, the most unimaginable thing happened. I approached the elevator, but it was being repaired. It could have been an opportune time for sightseeing, but I could do nothing.

I saw the light on floor 43, and I assumed the repairman halted the elevator there. I heard from the attendant that he was installing a gearing machine. This was to correct the traction drive wheel and adjusting the movements of the heavy steel cables to be steadier. At least, once it was repaired, maybe the journey moving up or down would be quicker, but at the same time, being so high up truly posed some problems. This was the precise elevator car that I rode up in. I speculated what would happen if the elevator car halted when I was inside. What if the hydraulic plunger faltered? The elevator car could have dropped down like a falling star. I did not want to think about it, but these thoughts came to my mind. I kept holding onto the belief that everything would work out.

There was only one man working on the elevator. Hundreds of people wanted to get down while plenty of people were waiting to go up too. There were all kinds of possibilities of what might take place. There could have been a failure to move in any direction, electrical shocks, sudden jerks, but I hoped for the best. I went back to my designated spot and lay down for about thirty minutes. I was restless and I began pacing the hall, but that did not make the repairs any quicker. Perhaps, thirty minutes later, the elevator was restored and it functioned normally.

When I was on the elevator, I had the flighty feeling. This made me ponder why the Hong Kong people had no fear of heights. What if an earthquake rumbled and several of these tall buildings came crashing down? I felt pessimistic about these buildings, remembering what took place in Dalian. I guess I was becoming a fatalist. I thought fate had a plan. Maybe I was right, to come out of the elevator when I did. I saw a sign that Hong Kong Disneyland was being built. I imagined that I was Sally Field, and I came to cut the ribbon for the opening Disneyland ceremony. I thought about Sally because she acted in the movie, *Places in the Heart*. In other words, her world was mine. Both of us interchanged our lives to see how places in our heart feels elsewhere.

Two days later, my contact in Taiwan introduced me to a business client. I was instructed to meet him at a restaurant. This man was planning to set up a technology branch in America, so he wanted to hear about possibilities. As a woman, I had to take more safeguards than a man did. I had to alter my appearance by wearing clothing to match a woman of prestige. Otherwise, the possibility of being labeled as a less worthy woman may have come up. In the context of business, I always had to keep in mind a person's beliefs, superstitions, philosophy, gender, business practices, etc. even if the dialogue would be brief. In addition, I had to use my feminine charisma to make a man think he thought it out himself. I was prepared, and I went to meet my party.

To begin with, I gave the businessman my business card and introduced myself with a light handshake. I could tell that he was not comfortable dealing with a woman in business, but he seemed approachable. He was looking at what was listed on my business card. My name was listed as Lily Gem (百合寶石), Agent (代理). In English, I listed my motto "*Places in the Heart of Business*" and he smiled. When I smiled back, this automatically provided a calming effect. Smiles were a way of breaking the ice or showing embarrassment. My objective was to cultivate "*Guan xi*," or give him a "*place in the heart*" so that he could share some connection.

I did not wear my **Lily**-white clothes because this could have been a turn off. In Asia, 'white' usually means mourning or a death. I did not want to start off on the wrong foot. I allowed him to take the next step. He passed his business card to me and also smiled.

I remembered the Cuban Ambassador telling me that person-to-person relationships are practiced in South America, but it was ubiquitous also in Asia. I took slow steps and let the businessman take the lead even when ordering food. He understood I knew how matters worked and then our conversation began.

I kept an open mind and lightly touched on principles he would meet in Taiwan at our next business meeting. I cautioned talking too much during our meeting, but I did add a personal touch by wishing that he started the New Year with luck. This made him smile again. At least, he was acknowledging my presence, and I thrived on making him feel he would be lucky too. First, we had some *pak choi* or stirred fried beef together. He seemed delighted that I could handle the chopsticks. He glanced at me several times, but never gave me direct eye contact. During our dining, I spoke occasionally allowing him to respond. When I talked, I paced myself to be moderate. This allowed the Asian man to grasp concepts more clearly. At times, he looked at me with a blank expression. I let him light up his cigarette even though I did not smoke. This allowed him to feel he was in control. Conversations were almost like creating a marriage. It would soon be a time for the two branches to operate in synchronization, like two families coming together. This would ensure we worked in unison, while enhancing operations. The people associated with his Hong Kong operation and America would give mutual respect when meeting in Taiwan. Omens would also establish a sense of prosperity, social and financial obligations for both branches.

We continued to dine, but also discussed what was necessary. We made arrangements to meet some Chinese Americans in Taiwan. I added that when he would be in Taiwan, I would personally introduce him to the Chinese Americans. This was a necessary measure because centuries of dynastic histories have conditioned the Chinese people to obey their socio-political leaders the same way they obey their parents. The upcoming situation in Taiwan was to create a business betrothal. There would be extensive gift-giving etiquette in Taiwan. The American Chinese business 'family' with the Hong Kong 'family' would have recurring elements.

In regards to the preliminary consultation, it must have been odd for him. He was used to dealing directly with male company. I was pleased that he placed trust in me through the Taiwan company introduction. I acted as a buffer between his Hong Kong operation, connections in Taiwan, and America. The Agenda for the business meeting was now established. My role compared to a real estate agent. I created a positive illusion that the situation would be bright. I listened attentively to what he wanted to make the business get-together work.

Before we closed our deal, I also made sure he understood the motto on my business card. I reviewed that my motto on the card, "*Places in the heart of Business.*" was a colloquial English expression to make business work well. I stated this while he sipped on Hong Kong styled milk tea (part of the Hong Kong tea culture). At that point, I bid him adieu and looked forward to seeing him in Taiwan soon. This set the stage for discussion about productive business possibilities on the horizon. After I made my exit, I magically continued to dance to my own beat.

My luck was beginning to change favorably. No longer did I think about the elevator. I also had no need to walk among Hong Kong's wall-to-wall people. As I left the restaurant, I was surprised to see people dancing together as a flash mob. There were at least one-hundred teenagers mimicking Michael Jackson's dance steps while the music in the background played "*Beat It*."[83] Hands went up and down, to the side, left and right, and bodies rolled in every direction. All the youths were gyrating in the same way that Michael does it. Inadvertently, I became a part of a group that had to stop, look, and listen.

It was not a choice situation, but a phenomenon that came out of the blue. I had no idea there would be a colossal number of people nearby the restaurant. It seemed as if thousands of people were chattering and moving every which way. Then suddenly the dynamics of dancing stopped. Everyone scattered into many directions. It was an incredibly thrilling moments.

The lyrics started with, "*They told him don't you ever come around here,*" and the chorus repeated, "*It doesn't matter who's wrong or right.*" I thought this situation was actually symbolic. I was here in the beat of Hong Kong. It was time to settle my thoughts. The contemporary background music that played allowed me to come back to the reality of the patriarchal world. I was more conscious about my higher purpose, and this corresponded with looking up to see the next *Deal.*

Hong Kong is actually a small island. It was renowned for its impressive panoramic skyline and natural setting, but the flood of people and items made it less desirable for my taste. No matter where I walked, I saw a deluge of people and items galore. The whiff of Chinese southern food and 24-karat gold were noticeable items. Food was available in all places, and the taste was much sweeter than eating in the northern parts of China. In this small area of 428 square miles, Hong Kong is the most densely populated area in the world, and I genuinely felt closed in. The population of seven million people made me feel as though I was being squeezed out of the tube. I hardly had breathing room, and this was compounded by the excessive debris, visible almost all over the place. There were some relatively cleaner spots. These were designated for tourists as market friendly. In reality, just staying near the market was a death defying experience.

Since everyone gets hungry and needs supplies, I went to the night market. It was a truly, bustling event. People pushed and shoved while talking boisterously. No one seemed to worry about their *social face* and I headed out to Temple Street. As in other marketplaces, there were lots of commodities. The biggest difference was seeing open displays 24-karat gold, sparkling and innovative jewelry. Nothing was locked up. There were the occasional thieves that ran away with stolen goods, but I suspect that included mostly chickens. At least, the revolving sounds of the sirens were not normally heard. Sometimes, a police officer would be on the chase and this might stir the attention of onlookers. I must say I was allured by the many golden accessories and gems. The quality of the gold shined exceptionally brightly. For a moment, it almost made me believe I was close to the sun.

I had finished all I had wanted to do in China, and it was time for another journey elsewhere. I needed fulfillment on another level. I decided to head to India; the land of yoga, and spiritualism, where Mohandas Gandhi offered words aimed at complete harmony of thought. I particularly like that Gandhi said, "*Freedom is not worth having if it does not include the freedom to make mistakes.*"[85] Naturally, this applies to me, but in the last minute, there was a change of plans and I headed to Taiwan.

CHAPTER 16: Taiwan

CELEBRITIES, BUSINESS & THE BATHHOUSE SPLASHES – 20 YEARS

In the vertical city of Hong Kong, I thought about my dining experience with the businessman. He is unusually obese, and reminded me of concerns in the United States about eating habits there. When I was in Louisiana, I learned people there love foods like crayfish and spicy Creole sausages or *boudin.* This is a favorite sausage eaten in the Acadian cultural region of Louisiana, Lafayette, and Lake St. Charles (nearby vicinities). I often watched them eat *boudin, crayfish* and more. People spread out huge amounts of food and eat it all. A business leader I met in Hong Kong was the same. He ate almost in frenzy, and his weight was an issue. According to the State of Louisiana, Department of Health and Hospitals, the obesity reports specify, "*64.9% of all adults in Louisiana are heavy.*"[86] Data from school-based health centers point out obesity is also a problem in children. It is hard to imagine, but 13,000 children, ages 2-19 years assessments to be overweight. I assumed that this Hong Kong man's family suffered the medical effects of obesity. In 2010, The Center for Disease Control and Protection report obesity in the Hong Kong Population is rising. "*Thirty-one percent of men and 18.8% of women and children are also obese.*"[87] This eating trend coincides with drinking and gambling obsessions. In 2012, "*233 gamblers commit suicide in Hong Kong.*"[88] They have difficulty coping with their addictions.

Throughout my travels in Asia, obsession was a consistent and I worried about what the Hong Kong man might expect.

Knowing that people in Hong Kong and the United States have enormous appetites, I decided to find out what happened in the past. In the 18th century, manners were a weighty issue. Even the American President George Washington set up rules of civility. Men like William Penn and Benjamin Oilskin were models for social behavior. In the 20th century, etiquette promotion continues. In 1896, the book entitled *Youth's Educator for Home and Society,* focused on conducting one's affairs decently. In 2012, losing weight and coping with pressure matches me treading in patriarchal waters, so I decide to test them.

I suspect there is a definite correlation between being female, and how men divide their thinking when respecting norms. I discover when two countries have unalike thinking; each country offers their own answers to what sets up linkage. For example, executives between countries accept their relations to be worthwhile. They presume there are some common interests and trust. For example, the Vietnamese assume because China's has military build-up, the Americans see eye-to-eye with them about the possibilities of country relations. History leads to the conclusion the Americans and the Vietnamese both want to dominate the region of the South China Seas. The same thinking works when Norway and Sweden are compatible when they launch a "*common market to trade renewable energy certificates with the goal of adding a total 26.4 terawatt-hours (TWh) of new power production.*"[89] In Vietnam, America, Norway and Sweden, the men have like-minded interests. They influence politically, get along and work out details to normalize understanding.

Of course, building success is not always one-sided. There is patriarchal thinking that men need to dominate women. Men having a Machismo or patriarchal outlook, belong to the Good Old Boys clubs (the Freemasons, the Ivy League Schools). Their cultural model is still alive and "*set above all, a symbolic organization of behavior.*" [90]

This implies that women-owned businesses are fewer than male-owned businesses. Their revenues are 27% of the average compared to most male-owned businesses. Most women therefore, work in fields where they readily accept. Human services fields in medicine and care giving have become more popular for women. Therefore, "*men take other men in business areas more seriously than they would a woman in the same position.*"[91] Walsh Borkowski of LaSalle University in Philadelphia, Pennsylvania backs up. He conducted a study of gender difference in the medical and human services profession. His study revealed there is variance in health care administration career development and university administrators between the genders. Borowski's report number 101143035, inferred that "*base salaries at the start are the same for both genders.*"[92] Sadly, the promotion and financial benefits decrease for women. Findings imply precluding women. Instead, males are the primary benefactor in the business facet.

In 2013, Mercer *reported an increasing trend for people to move around the world* as a result of "*increasing the number of international positions for expatriate workers.*[93] Companies offer international opportunities and the expatriate population booms. I become aware most arriving females do not arrive through an intra-company transfer (promotions for men). Rather, women come as tourists, through studies, marriage or as teachers. As a female expatriate, I cannot avoid many problems, as I am not fully aware of the male mind-set. My reactions to what takes place range from clamor to silence.

First, I am uncertain what to expect. There are gender expectations about grooming (bathing to hairstyles), food, and approaches (to language, immigration, health clearances, contracts, housing, and country rituals). In business, I have to build a rapport compatible with cultural lifestyles. Women not traveling abroad have misinformation about what takes place. Men overseas become infidel. North American marriages (Chinese, American and other ethnic males) are on the fast track. Las Vegas lifestyle is about cashing into 'love' or settling in divorce. Love rating is landing more people in divorce, it seems male habits are becoming alike. During my stay abroad, I am unclear what to expect. Moisés Román serves as the Diversity in Action Chair for the California Association for the Education of Young Children. As a speaker (state, national), he presents a variety of topics such as Men in Education. Roman says "*that learning the right way is about capturing a teachable moment.*"[94] Moral lessons of all kinds occur in teachable moments. In considering these thoughts, I am also able to make presumptions about Asians if I listen to Archie Bunker, Disney messages or the medium. Luckily, through social research and direct observation, my truths get clearer. I feel confident in my findings. My premise about male behaviors match Dr. Madeline Van Hecke, clinical psychologist and an adjunct faculty member at North Central College in Naperville, Illinois; says people get their truths from direct observation of the "*media, television, radio, newspapers, newsmagazines, documentaries, books and other people.*"[95] Dr. Hecke does not specify the proportion of people overseas, but I see there are a lower number of females working in business. The psychologist draws on research addressing "*critical thinking, child development, education, and philosophy.*"[96] She recognizes that even the smartest people have blind spots. They do not always stop to think, hold biases, and adopt society's labeling of individuals and groups.

While I am overseas, I see most foreign travelers are tourists. As for the executives and diplomats, they live a more lavish lifestyle than in North America. It is unavoidable the expatriates (executives, diplomats, teachers, marriage partners and tourists) also have fewer exposure to cultural realities. Overseas meetings and observations, the expatriates (North Americans, Australians, New Zealanders, Europeans and South Africans) have become less able to think on their own than in the past. They conform to Dr. Heck's findings and the conclusion I make. People need to have a greater awakening about their prejudice and blind spots.

Blind spots and prejudice are also visible in North American learning. This is a result of limits understanding patriarchies work. In Canada, there are three expatriate associations (Ontario, British Columbia and Alberta). In the United States, there are ten networks (southwest, southeast and central states). These expatriate groups get to share cross-cultural information. Their mission statements include topics like career opportunities, visas, immigration, taxes, banking, financial planning and investment. Associations have no interest in expanding their knowledge. Instead, they are an inclusive society with prominent male business thinking. Their purpose is getting profitability from people that stay overseas. Based on observations, most expatriates interact with locals for profit and socialization is slight.

My truths about the locals grow when I live and meet people behind the scenes. I mainly contact locals and communicate with expatriates on as need basis. My greatest challenges come when I meet men from Africa, South America, Southeast Asia and the United States. I come to realization that I must communicate without creating fireworks. Through trial and error, I listen mostly to affairs of the heart and business.

Abrupt changes constantly follow. As I need to be alert meeting, I get some rest before. I do this by napping in the daylight, an ordinary practice for Asians. They believe having forty winks is helpful as a person's energy and spirit increases, heightening mental performance. From now, when I take a flight to Taipei, the short trip allows for slumber time to refresh my thoughts.

Air travel from Hong Kong to Taipei becomes another whirlwind of events. Birds in the air are making gentle whooshing sounds, and I have a feeling of indescribable weightlessness. I feel free, as if there are no restraints when I am. I feel like I am also flying with wings, but the sensation is short. The airplane nears Taiwan, and I get an aerial view of the land.

I can see the island of Taiwan getting bigger. There are mountains, forests, hills, tranquil flatlands, shimmering lakes, and exquisite beaches. Far, near, high, the views are coming into sight. I do not know which skyscraper I am seeing first. Public buildings are zealous. Buildings like Taipei 101 built, in 2004. The Sky Tuntex Tower construction is in 1998. The Shin Kong Life Tower erected, in 1993. The Han-Lai New World Center invention is in 1995. They all have ardent interests in aiming for people to visit and reach new heights. During my stopover, I come to learn that Taiwan officially ranks as having the world's tallest buildings. Thus, angling in towards Taipei makes me wonder if this is another vertical city like Hong Kong.

As I look out the window, a young Taiwanese man takes the seat next to me. He taps my shoulder and says, "Hi." I like it that he is friendlier than the Hong Kong people I have previously met. This man wants to practice English and share information about his experiences in Hong Kong. I listen to what he says. His thoughts mirror mine and that makes me smile. Our conversation goes satisfactorily. Before we land, he starts to talk about his clothing.

I look at what he is wearing, and his clothes confirm that he belongs to the younger generation. His outfit is far more outlandish than that of the flower power generation. I tell him that photographers took many snapshots of me during my youth. There are snapshots of me at several leading photographers' studios in downtown Montreal. I describe myself as having flawless skin, stunning hazel eyes, long, wavy lashes, golden blonde curls and a remarkable figure. As for my clothing, I remember wearing an Indian sari and many bangles and walking barefoot. I suppose this is what captures a photographer's interest. Mostly, I am promenading on the main street in my hometown. I am part of the hippie generation, or the Age of the **Lily** (Flower Child). I become the center of attention because I choose to dance when I hear my favorite song, *Boogie Wonderland,* the music of *Earth, Wind and Fire* in 1979. The lyrics start off with, *"Do you remember,*"[97] and I realize I was chasing my dreams. The young man smiles as he listens.

He wants to know my thoughts about his long green hair with pink highlights. I reply he is modish. I suggest the dark purple and violet improvements might be more becoming and match the incredible beauty of Elizabeth Taylor's eyes. The young man listens attentively. He is uncertain about whether his style suits him. I assure him that he appears wildly wonderful, and he sniggers.

His apparel matches his hair. He wears a jacket with flared lapels and matching navy blue and aqua pointed shoes. The color and pattern selection compares to Jeff Koon's artwork.* The young man looks like a huge *blue diamond*. In fact, he also wears a matching diamond-shaped ring and a snowy white top hat with an aqua and navy ribbon trim. He inspires blissful memories of the time I also dressed radically. I ask to look at his hat, which has satin lining and custom-made. The man's overall image is artistic. I am curious and ask if he designs his own clothing. He nods and. I think he is exceptional, eccentric and probably an entertainer.

We do not have much more time to share, but he tells me that he is, like me, an unconventional person. He makes a few suggestions where I should visit when we arrive, and then I hear the propellers as the plane swoops downward. I have a great feeling about this young man's inspiring spirit, although I cannot pinpoint just what it is that he has. Suddenly the attendant taps me on the shoulder and asks me to put on my seat belt. As the plane angles more sharply, the young man hands me an envelope. Suddenly, there is an intrusive series of bumps. As the plane rolls ahead, I can see Taipei City from the small window. It looks much cleaner than Hong Kong. I hold on as the bumps get stronger, and finally the knocking stops and I wonder again is inside the envelope.

People are getting off the airplane. Then I head towards customs clearance to enter Taipei. I expect a long queue to do documentation processing, but then something out of the ordinary takes place. Shortly after coming out of the airplane and on the way to customs, I hear girls screaming. Police scramble all over the place, and camera operators are flashing their lights because a rock star has landed. I feel my heart pounding, especially when I learn it is the young man who sat next to me on the flight. We leave the airplane together. The rock star tells me to remain calm and prompts me to follow him, and I do so.

I dislike the commotion, mostly because I fear the worst that might happen. The teenage crowd idolizes this man. The youths are getting too close, and I am afraid they are getting ready to seize something. Flashbacks of the Indonesian monkeys grabbing my purse come to mind. I am not sure what to do. Luckily, the performer steers me away from the crowd. We go through an unexpected passageway and escape the scene. Going ahead of me, he says, "Lily, you are the center of attention again! You can feel free to dance to your favorite tune once more."

After we exit the passageway, we see a black limousine waiting nearby to pick up the rock star. The young man asks me to come along. The celebrity says he is going to drop me off where I need to be. This incredible new acquaintance is allowing me to experience a marvelous day!

I am off to meet a long-time friend, but she does not even know I am coming. I want to startle her with delight. I ask the rock star if he can drop me off in the Da An Park. I imagine I will also stroll around in downtown Taipei before meeting my friend. I want to savor the glory of this day. Silently, I think about a lover that once had my full attention. He has the fervor to sing aloud and he is enchanting. The performer's smile reminds me of this person from my past.

I get in the limousine, and the traffic reminds me of the masses of people in motion in mainland China. Bountiful numbers of people and scooters are everywhere. Various cyclists are carrying different sized loads as they crank their small motors. The scooters, sandwiched between buses and cars, create a buzz in the streets. Traffic patterns regulate better than in mainland China. At least, people here obey the traffic lights. This place is like Singapore, hardly any debris on the roadway. The police appear uniform as if they are overseeing all traffic and so unalike Mainland China and other Asian countries.

Many motorized cyclists and scooters pass, I hear them grinding their gears and wheels are spinning and sounds like a jeweler correcting the imperfections on the surface of a diamond. I look out the car window and see signs overhead. I am amazed to see Taipei's metro transit. Since the tracks are so high, I am a little fearing a train might fall off them. I pass so many buildings while catching a glimpse of Taipei's ultramodern high-speed train. It speeds by like a wind on fire. As we continue our route, I am getting some high quality snapshots of Taipei. Suddenly the limousine halts as we arrive at the Da An Park. As I bid the young man farewell, he places his top hat on my head and the car quickly pulls away.

Sadly, the exciting experience vanishes as if he had waved a magic wand. I begin walking towards a park bench and remember the envelope he gave me earlier. Just as I am about to open it, I hear footsteps approaching. I wonder who is following. I guess I am a little paranoid, but then I hear the rustling of some leaves and realize that they were the "footsteps." I suppose being alone in a strange city does that to a person. I calm myself and open the envelope. I am dumbfounded. Inside, complimentary vouchers for a week's stay at the hotel across the street! I cannot believe such kindness. Then I start looking closely at the hat the young man gave me. I feel something bumpy and search in the lining. Was it a blue diamond? Instead, a piece of paper slides out and I find the rock star's business card inside. He is the owner of the hotel for the vouchers he has provided. On his business card, he writes, "Lily, you are the flower that matters in the world." When I read this, I am ecstatic because dream interpreters say that *dreaming of the Lily "leads to family gladness. Your children will be beautiful, healthy, clever and obedient.*"[98]

Even in this unfamiliar setting, I can watch significant commercial enterprises, education institutions, and a cultural center. In fact, the name ***Daan*** *has consistency in spelling and foreign names* district translates as *enormous peace and great safety.*

The young Taiwanese man has extraordinary ability. He could bridge the gap between our generations, and he positioned me in a perfect location. I am near several major universities, most shopping, ponds and the Tonghua Night Market. After seeing this pleasing area, I head toward the gargantuan Park Taipei Hotel.

At first, it is hard to believe that I am in this luxurious hotel with so many rooms just opposite the park. The procedure for check-in is ordinary. My room is on the 12th floor and I settle in quickly. This is the city where I feel most like I a woman in the rough or a *blue diamond.** Later, I try to figure out where to go next. I am not sure what the best course of action is, but I decide that taking a stroll outside is better than staying inside. After promenading, I notice the environment is becoming greener.

I arrive at the botanical gardens fitting a Queen. There are flowers of all colors blooming and naturally blending, in harmony with nature. My imagination begins to flutter as if I am in flower power times. Fascinatingly, I see a pond of "*blossoms floating on the water with the support of its* ***lily pads****. The white lotus (Nymphaea lotus) is called the Egyptian white water lily or the tiger lotus.*" [99] The unique lily is also an aquarium plant. The flowers also spread their scent and their aroma gently whirls, making this place heavenly. This pond brings me to a reflective moment. I see the lotus sinks its roots deeply in the muddy water while the blossom rises and shines. This is just like being part of nature. If I sit in the mud long enough, I guess I get clarity. These refreshing words stem from Buddhist philosophy, that a person's true nature is unclear first and rising to clarity of enlightenment. It makes me ponder what this value means. In the words of the Dalai Lama, after asking a Buddhist follower about his understanding, he says, it is about getting "*the biggest threat or danger.*" The man describes when he experiences imprisonment. He learns about forgiveness and limits that some people have. His deep thoughts drive me to think about the moral question of waterlogging. I imagine being when I am in meeting the Thailand Ambassador or living in China's feudal court, I do question how people exercise love, justice, atonement and forgiveness. Interpretation of *karma* of the force a person acts on is unescapable. I am **Lily**, a person of peace, forgiving, suggesting and viewing the reactions of others. At least, I feel balance in nature, so I continue walking around the garden. To my amazement, I face a sign reading, 'this bathhouse receives one million visitors in 2009.' Hmm...

Learning the ways of another culture is never easy. I have no experience with public bathhouses in Taiwan. I assume it is like the bathhouses in China. After all, the young man in the car recommended spas as exceptional places to get skin therapy because they draw out toxins from the skin. I am eager to see if this place is helpful. As I enter, I see a grand pump room that reminds me of the ones used in the Roman times. I am directed to follow a winding pathway, which leads to the main opening. There I am alarmed by the sight of women and small boys unclad. I am uncertain what to expect, but somehow I sense this place offers something different. The smell of human sweat and water mingle, giving off a taxing scent (the roots of a growing lotus). Women scrub backs of other females. Women wash their private parts in full view. I stand for a moment overcome by discomfort, when several women pin me with their gazes.

In the bathhouse, I experience firsthand knowledge that bathing is natural to do. Statures of women are visible. No one worries what they look like. Old and young alike are gathering in ritualistic bathing. Afterwards, I go into a Jacuzzi. I follow my instincts, go to another room, and see a spa with no one. I think it is superb to have heat warming my toes. The sensation was spinning upward throughout my entire body. Beginning to feel tranquil, there was a sudden gush of water. It came from two women splashing their way into the water.

I guess finding privacy is just not something common in a place with so many people. The women had no idea who I am, but then they are gazing at me. I glance back and see the two Asian women whispering. One of them speaks loudly, and her appearance strikes my attention. Her hair has a soft divide with bangs. The hair descends past the corners of her eyes and hangs limply, draping her shoulders. The other woman has a short, shaggy, hairstyle, which partially covers her eyes. I do not like the intrusion, but they come in anyway. They ask me if I can speak English.

I am in the Jacuzzi, but two other women enter. I do not know them, but we begin to have a rapport. Conversation reveals that earlier, one woman studies in America. The other woman tours the United States and Canada several times. The woman with short hair says her two brothers undoubtedly prefer North American women to Asians. After hearing what they say, I affirm liking people from all countries. Our conversation continues, but the two women act like two small tittering girls having a secret. A woman apologizes for murmuring. She says a person has a need to speak in the native tongue. This allows for a clearer understanding. She addresses topics that are of interest to her. They focus on what most Asian women ponder. They think about a North American Caucasian female. The women disclose their inner secrets. Women in Taiwan prefer a Caucasian woman's colorful, eyes, fair skin and plump breasts. I am startled by their comments.

They continue to say that Taiwan women get surgery just to have their eyes look like a North American woman. The women also tell that fair skin color is exotic, so they have a habit of covering their skin and stay away from the sun to remain white. As for breasts, they make no comments.

I am flabbergasted to hear what the women say. I think that Oriental **eyes** have an exaggerated charisma. I have admiration for their slanted eyes as they offer intrigue especially when I choose to paint women as subjects. As for their **skin color**, I consider women in Asia shade themselves with umbrellas and rub on bleaching creams. I see this also in other Southeast Asian countries. I get the impression that Southeast Asian women regard having a white porcelain-looking skin tone as the highest standard of beauty. I suspect this belief is long-standing from history. The elite class and royalty do not have to work in the sun, so their skin remains pale. Lower class people work in the fields for hours. The heat of the sun makes their skin darker. As a result, paler skin stands for higher classes and has become a value of gorgeousness. Therefore, Asian opinion consensus infers a lighter skinned woman has better breeding and class. Their ideology makes me reflect on a meeting with a handful of Chinese women. They stare at my fair skin and assume I model. Besides, women in their early thirties have breasts no bigger than two dainty flat buttons, so I suppose they have a feeling of inferiority from viewing too many commercials. Sadly, women see themselves as Caucasian women.

I keep silent and wait to hear if the women want to add something else. They voice that women in North America are far luckier than Taiwanese women. I invite them to clarify. One woman reveals she has an infidel husband. I try to be tactful in commenting. I share that North American women take vows to accept what their husbands do, but infidelity is unacceptable. She tells that some Taiwanese women live apart from their spouses and prefer this arrangement. Other women accept the Machismo culture and only a handful of women fervently oppose infidelity. Taiwanese women say that it is about a man's competency. If the man provides monetary benefits, that is plenty. Other habits of unfaithfulness are likely consistent for all men. I gasp at what the woman tells. Later, the other woman says this is part of Taiwanese culture. Of course, it is hard to swallow because it raises the question of moralities, deceptive practices, obstacles and gender bias. The Taiwanese women are dissatisfied with men in society. They opt for more equity. Kristen McCabe, journalist reports, "*There are 358,000 Taiwanese immigrants living in the United States*" [100] and the majority own their own homes. The implication suggests Taiwanese women are opting to be in other countries. North America is where Taiwanese women can find out their own identity and professionalism. The women grasp their needs. They can have less grief with an American man than with a Taiwanese man. On the flip side, a North American man has preconceived notions about having a Taiwanese woman. They think she is a deal because there is "*no questioning of a man's actions*"[101] as a North American woman might, and they lavish a man with attention.

I learn it is natural for me to presume that corporate social responsibility reporting has a male focus in Taiwan. Personal and housing probably fit into the same scheme of thinking, so I save notions. Instead, I realize I am in the water for a while. My skin is beginning to dry out and feel wrinkly. I grab a towel and dry up. I am going to head back to the hotel. As I get up to leave, one of the women remarks that her brother thinks North American women have curvier **bodies** than Taiwanese women. Even though Asian women are often more tiny than North American women, a woman's anatomy remains the same. I listen to what they state and thank them for the opportunity to converse, and leave.

Thinking about what transpires, I think a woman in business does become questionable in Taiwan because men are prizes. I also gauge my thoughts about Taiwanese culture based on correspondence I have with my Taiwanese female friend. She often addresses difficulties in coping with men in high-ranking positions. Men lack the same education. She tells about daily morals and control issues with men, so these values weigh heavily on my mind.

When I return to the hotel, I start mapping out where I will go next. I want to see and experience some of the Taiwan scenery before I meet the Taiwan acquaintance. I decide going to the natural hot springs of *Wulai*. It is a bright day, and I grab a light breakfast at a convenience story. Surprisingly, I find 711 just before heading out to take the train. This popular American convenience store has over "*5,000 shops spread throughout Taiwan*."[102] I am astonished to see their inventory. Items are incredibly similar to the setup in the United States. Snack variations are great. Products include typical American items like freshly brewed coffee, sandwiches, dairy products, drinks, tobacco, magazines and cleaners. Besides the North American products, there are quick tasty Chinese style pickups for breakfast.

I buy tea eggs, a Chinese bun, flavored egg rolls, and have some strawberry flavored soybean milk or *Dou Jiang*. There were so many cookie styles and snacks I never see in America. Taiwan is unbelievably a booming place with mostly Western commerce. Soon after, I return to the hotel. I tell the staff to keep my bags until I return. Then, I take the train heading for *Wulai*.

The travel time to *Wulai* takes about an hour. As the train moves forward, I see the countryside. The setting appears much tidier than I expect. The train passes a few spotlights including murals, water trickling, valleys, rolling mountains, shrines, houses and some commercial buildings. I find the most breathtaking part is seeing an incredible waterfall. When I reach *Wulai,* there is with a signpost for no cars access making the air crisp and fresh. I no longer have a feeling that I am in contaminated air, but in the open bucolic air. This is when I take a mini-train to reach the sky mobile unit. Once I am seated, I am moving across a steep valley. Viewing is implausible, so I think this place is for soul healing.

I arrive in Wulai, and see many bathhouses having connection by a passage. The water comes from the town's subterranean network of thermal springs and the waters are therapeutic. Access is at street level and by taking steps downward, I can to see the waterworks at river level below. I pay for privacy and have a private room. It is hard for me to fathom having a single bathtub with water piped up from the mineral spring waters, and soft music playing in the background. These practices come from the influence of the Japanese, a custom dating 300 years ago. Some old features remain including tall stained glass windows. As well, pleasure-seeking practices still exist.

I begin feeling an unfamiliar culture becoming more familiar to me than before. I find it also easier to interpret cultural expectations. I am getting used to seeing new places, know what to do or say, and the best items to buy. I also enjoy watching how the food sellers entice people to get nearer. For example, I see a Taiwanese aboriginal man dressed in traditional clothing. He is performing a dance in rhythmic motion and spinning to the beat of the clanging music. The man sways his body to the left and right and moves forward. He does this while spreading sauces on *satay* and grilling small pieces of beef on a stick. People are enjoying themselves.

Through chattering, I also hear people talk about Zhonshans (野柳) National park. Clearly, this place had a meandering stone pathway leading to a place where lily ponds spread throughout the park. My name Lily is following my tracks. After I feel refreshment from the hot springs, I return to the hotel but I think about going to the national park later. Time is fleeting and I am now getting keen to see my Taiwanese friend.

I have memories of good conversations I have with my Taiwanese compadre. I recall having frequent business and emotional discussions. When I studied earlier in the United States, she studies commerce while my center of attention is the humanities. As our common aim understands people behavior, I stay in touch. Later, my Taiwanese buddy offers me a business opportunity. Before I begin making exchanges, we talk about general expectations. She thinks because of my unique background, we can agree to go forward. Our goal is to secure placement for about 150 students. They want to study Master of Business Administration in North America. Since I am familiar with educational contacts and she is familiar with the business end, we combine our expertise. I make easy the education and social networking part while she handles the business on sound ground. I seek out a volume discount for students wishing to attend. The arrangement seems sensible. I begin contacting institutions that I think can be a fit. I explore some international schools that do this training. My friend Ms. Yen introduces me to her contacts in Taiwan and moving forward, some preliminaries take place.

Ms. Yen spends much time factoring issues that matter. Considerations include school ranking, training timeline, course offerings, tuition schedules, housing and other details. Once I receive some information from Ms. Yen, I identify a handful of relevant schools that have these features. I measure reputation, the possibilities for discount and other. Before any information releases to Ms. Yen's party, I setup agreements with Ms. Yen's contact. I know I can trust Ms. Yen, but something unexpected takes place. Agreement goes downhill. She tells that Taiwanese people are not being trustworthy and the deal falls through. Naturally, some ethos does not take place. Precautions are a consideration, but the Law favors amoral men. Therefore, I am a little eager about what might take place when I see Ms. Yen, but I have no grudges.

I begin mulling in my mind and reassess real causes for failure. For starters, Taiwan has a long-term orientation reflecting Chinese culture. Credibility matters and the first issue is a collective society versus me acting as an individual, alone, in North America. Because I am not part of the collective decision-making in Taiwan, the local Taiwanese probably feel offended because I do not come to join them in person, so the issue of trust causes ambivalence. I see the most senior ranking individual does not know me, so I am out of the loop. The second issue is I am female. During my meeting with a man from Hong Kong, Chinese Americans and the Taiwanese, the men behave according to norms. They do not consider a female in business to be serious and this includes Ms. Yen. Therefore, the business transaction takes place in secrecy with men only.

In Taiwan, considerations on the surface appear enormously western, but dealing is disparate. Corporate Social Responsibility reporting (CSRR) is the hottest issue in business today. The social model in business depends on social norms and local expectations. As a North American, I construe this to mean there are inescapable responsibilities for an enterprise, the community and society. However, this does not necessarily agree to the Taiwan business model. CSRR practices represent their best idea about how it needs to work. This is a male inclusive group.

Through building, I understand Taiwanese or foreign women are not as worthy as men. Women never are in positions of authority, which is why Mrs. Yen is not privy. As a result, the research that Ms. Yen does is a benefit for male decision makers and their accomplices. Therefore, I realize that any commitments or promises come from the most senior decision maker first. Social investment to include women is not tangible in collective decision-making. The business players all have their specific roles. As for the Hong Kong and American Chinese businessmen, I am only a token of exchanges about to take place. I am just another woman that can serve the needs of men. I chalk the business dealing up to experience and look forward to seeing Ms. Yen.

Ms. Yen marries and has two children. We address childcare and troubles in the home front. Her husband's parents cared for their children when she works. Of course, in contrast to North America, childcare is a benefit and does not cost any money. Unfortunately, Ms. Yen is not happy with this arrangement. When her in-Laws take care of her children, there is an automatic expectation that Ms. Yen will take care of her in-Laws when they become too old to work. I think that can be a sensible arrangement, but rearing values cause issues. Today, I am going to see her and I hope she has overcome most issues. Before I meet Ms. Yen, I prepare some gifts in advance and call. Finally, the arrangements transpire.

I arrive at a high-rise apartment complex where Ms. Yen lives on the seventeenth floor. As I ride up the elevator, I recall old memories when I am vexed to rely on an elevator. I finally reach Ms. Yen's floor and I walk around the corner to apartment number 1707. I knock and at first, her family is apprehensive about the person at the door. Providentially, I happily know her family. They make my stay incredibly comfortable. We talk about earlier times, but mostly tour Taiwan. I especially enjoy visiting the tofu and night market. There is incredible food and an unimaginable array of products. I am overwhelmed by the strong garlic pong as I near the stinky tofu (臭豆腐) section, so I do not try it. When I go to the night market, I see the fermented tofu on display. Ms. Yen and her family cultivate a taste for the tofu varieties, but I do not. I also go with the Yen family to see some art galleries and museums. I find the artwork and exhibitions are like seeing through shadows. The artwork I view gives me a mindboggling sensation of creative people enjoying diverse expression. I see some of these ideologies also at the Shung Ye Museum of Formosan Aborigines (順益台灣原住民博物館). I view some landmarks like Story House, Chiang Kai-Shek Memorial and Martyr's Shrine (忠烈祠). I get pleasure from visiting the Grand Hotel (圓山大飯店), and catching entertainment like the Chinese opera, public dancing and much more. I have a good time with the Yen family. It is tricky trying to understand why we visit so many places. Was the Yen family trying to say something more than just giving a good impression?

My most favorite event is when I make a brief visit with Ms. Yen to the *Huashan* or Hua Mountain area or the centralized location for the Arabic coffee-growing industry. Coffee shops in this area spring up throughout the region. Even though, the coffee industry flourishes, I notice an auspicious sign in the window of a small shop; a fortune-telling advertisement lists a Turkish reader. Ms. Yen watches my curiosity and encourages that we go inside. She also reminds that my destiny has resolve when I grow in my mother's womb. I listen attentively because I know I have a **higher purpose**. My thinking and Ms. Yen does not happen in a vacuum. When I am in my 20s, I have an out-of-body state of consciousness. This is when I see colorful dreams of this event happening. I create mind-blowing artwork, but in reality, my consciousness speaks aloud through my artwork. I only know I will enter the home of the psychic and something special is going to take place.

I enter the psychic's home with Ms. Yen. She asks us to follow her to a smaller room. After I go into the next room, I feel there is a sense of darkness. Candles are burning in the distance and some reputable smells allure me to the unfamiliar. I am not sure why, but the woman appears uncommonly mystical. Her eyes are as intense as a Siamese cat. Even when the woman talks aloud, her mellow voice comes across like a purring sound of a cat. She signals me to sit down and Ms. Yen sits in the other room. The large-figured woman makes me feel as if I am in a trance. She tells that I am embarking on secrets only found in a coffee cup reading.

Before The Reading begins, I find myself looking intently at the woman's eyes. Her eyes beam like a flashing yellowish green light and I concentrate on the fierceness of her gaze. Then, the woman asks me to drink some coffee. She says sip it only to one side. I follow her directives and she places the saucer on top of the cup. The fortune-teller asks me to make a wish. A saucer tops the cup. Then, the woman takes the mug and holds it against her chest. She turns the beaker counter clockwise a few times.

I am unsure what to expect as the gypsy woman hovers over the cup. She reminds me of an eagle ready to pounce on its prey. She turns the cup over leaving residual coffee grinds in the cup, and turns it upside down. The coffee cools and the gadabout begins her interpretation by viewing shapes at various angles in the cup. As she casts her eyes downward, she looks hard at the leftover grinds. I am fascinated when she says the shapes show what to expect. The reading ends and she flips the saucer over once. The fortune-teller finds out whether my wishes can come true. Then I shift positions with Ms. Yen. She is enthusiastic to receive explanation. In fact, we are like two small girls at a pajama party having a girl's day out.

The entertaining time comes to end and I part company with Ms. Yen. I put on my top hat the young man gave me earlier and I cloak thinking in the hat. Reading reveals a life force that always keeps us having a connection. A person in reality speaks indistinctly and so does the gypsy woman. She typifies people hide. Covering compares to lilies growing from the mud. Finally, I take a small boat and ride the tides to imagine the sea caves in the southern part of Taiwan. These caves represent human traces of many years ago. It helps me redirect my **thinking about people in more purposeful ways**. Do you think this is the same for you when you look at traces of years ago? Come along on the Forgotten Waves to see what happens next.

CHAPTER 17: The Philippines

LAS VEGAS BANKING INTELLIGENCE – TSUNAMI SWEEP-UP

After taking the wavy waters from south Taiwan to the Philippines, my head is drowning in intellectual thought. I have a constant need to receive a steady supply of oxygenated thinking. I am trying to determine what constitutes cleverness. Perhaps, it is the buoyancy of the waves at sea.

As a North American baby boomer, I was born into an era that guaranteed work through education. Lamentably, mental power seems to be shifting. I am not sure if this is a consequence of newcomers arriving in the 1960s creating competition or something else. When the immigrants come from the Philippines and other countries, the public reacts with bias. This is extremely noticeable in the media as described earlier about the television series "*All in the Family.*" [103] Mind-sets are changing as issues of Human Rights advocacy and immigration come to the forefront. By the 1970s, I observe people becoming far more self-centered than before. In fact, having an independent streak unexpectedly has become highly valued. During this period, people also make assumptions about what is liberal thinking. Naturally, this leads into new assessments and people are being labeled in degrees of intelligence. The impact hits personages of from various settings. I may not be famous, but I am also included in this grouping. Having a new dimension of thinking determines fluctuations in societal categories. This includes people with dysfunctions and magnates like Dr. Patch Adams (medicine), Winston Churchill (politician), Dr. Kearns, Einstein (scientists), Mozart (musician), and Robin Williams, Cher, Sylvester Stallone (entertainers) to name a few. They are not considered to be in synchronization with societal norms.

During the 1970s, I remember being told not to laugh too much. Loud sounding mirth is considered to be not ladylike, but is sometimes acceptable as part of the in-group. No matter how I look at it, scorning is not sensible. When Dr. Adams and Robin Williams are young, they are cast aside when they clown around. Today, their humor is celebrated whether entertaining in the Philippines or elsewhere. When people laugh at me, or my Japanese friend Keiko, I disliked it. I suppose it is because we looked or acted differently than other children. One-hundred years ago, stories about Winston Churchill playing with his toy soldiers' commentary is alike. In 1870s, people make fun of Churchill. He is ostracized for not having any unique talent except for marching his toy soldiers even as a grown man. As a sensitive woman, I do not want to live during times where laughter has borders. Will the Philippines be a place of laughter?

I am somewhat nervous about this new destination. I hope people will not be judgmental, but I already have some insight about Filipino thinking when I meet the Ambassador of the Philippines while I am in China. He has the same notions as Ninotchka Rosca, writer. She coins the phrase "*If I can't have it, neither can you.*"[104] The Filipino emissary metaphorically describes people as individual crabs that fight to escape the heat of the pot. Among the crabs, only one crab can reach the top and the others are put to rest. His attitude sounded like what

Bruce Springsteen sings in his new hit called the *Wrecking Ball.* The track starts off with '*Taking Care of Your Own.*"[105]

My expedition begins when I take a flight from Taipei to Kaohsiung. I briefly make a stopover in South Taiwan to see the Eight Immortals Caves, and capture childhood memories of being a whip wielding archaeologist. This is where I discover human traces dating 50,000 years ago. From the southern part of Taiwan, the cargo ship sets sail to Luzon Island where 9.9 million people reside. After arriving in the far most northern point in the Philippines, I travel south by bus for about four and half hours heading to Manila City.

When I arrive in the thriving capital city, people approach me for money and handouts. I am unsafe and I have to watch my purse carefully. It is extremely difficult crawling out of the crowd, but I manage. There are some helpful police officers standing nearby. They are pushing the crowds back, directing them to move away and provide leeway to get out. As I inch out of the crowd, I look around and see a parked vehicle that catches my eye. Luckily, the driver also spots me. He is the shuttle hotel driver. As I near the car, I see an unusual landscape. There are religious slogans placated everywhere on Lorries, buses and jeepneys. Some of the signs read *Jesus Saves; God Loves You, Mercy* and so on. Where there is so much religious commercialization, it immediately makes me think something is wrong.

I ask the driver to bring me to the hotel in downtown Manila. As we move along, I have no idea that the ride will be like a jungle. I am in a genre where the music of the city incorporates the hard-core sounds of animals running. The tempo synthesizes the clicking sounds. There are long pitch snare rolls and drumming beats. The rhythms are deep bass melodies while people zigzag intermittently across the road. No one seems to care about the next person. I am speechless when drivers are careless and pedestrians get hurt. As the car moves through the traffic, it becomes a beating, rudimentary ride as if I am journeying to Thailand's bumpy countryside. From the back seat, I catch the view. The driver is struggling to get through the traffic. Cars are cutting in-between and frequently edging their way into the next lane. Bigger vehicles are even worse. They move over and push right in. Then a car blocks two entire lanes causing more time to lag. The pathway finally becomes clear. Traffic lights are meaningless because drivers ignore signals to move or stop. After traveling through the havoc for a while, I arrive at the hotel. This is when I experience a prelude to the flip side of goodness.

Once I approach Manila's center, I am baffled. It seems as if I am in Las Vegas, Nevada, the honeymoon capital of the United States. Couples are visible everywhere. The main street imitates the cityscape of Las Vegas Strip. There are luxurious hotels, InterContinental hotel chains, The Linden Suites, New World, Dusit Thani, Diamond, Heritage and Pan Pacific. There are plenty of money exchange outlets, a galore of residential high-rises and deluxe cars. The drama in the city is accentuated with Spanish architecture, lavish restaurants, and many souvenir shops. Shopping concourses (Harrison Plaza, Greenhill Shopping Center, Robinsons Place, Ortigas Center, and Ali Mall), Crystal Arcade, Marikina Shoe Expo, skyscrapers, leading department stores (Aguinaldo, Landmark, and Unitop), spas, clubs, theaters continue as if endless. The lights are flashing brightly like a strobe emitting a continuous blinking light. I wonder if this was the entrée for an

Elvis Presley impersonator to gyrate his body for center attention. It was almost as if I arrived in a Filipino ocean of excitement, but I settled in the hotel for the night.

The following day I embark on a new expedition. I plan to exchange American dollars for the local peso currency at a bank. As I move forward, someone is following me. At first, I assume my imagination is playing tricks on me. When I turn around, I see an individual inching ahead, so I stop dead in my tracks. This is a fearful moment and I go to a nearby coffee shop to order a fruit dessert on the menu. It is a tropical concoction of tapioca balls and jelly cubes combination. The blend is crunching and sweet and I think it will keep my mind off the person following me.

I finish my hors d'oeuvre and I look around. I am convinced the person is no longer there, so I continue walking. I head towards a bank to exchange American dollars. I want to make some local purchases. Just as I am about to enter, an old woman approaches me. She says, "Lady, I have a much better deal than any bank. I have been helping foreigners like you for a long-time. I am able to get you the best rate of exchange." I look at her directly, and she seems quite sincere. Since I conclude I have nothing to lose, I agree to exchange $25 American dollars. I saunter with the old woman for a few blocks, but I sense something is out of the ordinary. This is when I tell the woman I am not going any further. She tells me not to worry because there are only a few more steps. Then I see DHL Worldwide Courier Service, and my apprehensions calm down. I believe the aged woman. I presume she is bringing me to a legitimate place. Instead of going to the DHL Courier, however, she diverts the path and goes to a food vendor across the street. I am thinking that something is bizarre. The woman has $25 American dollars in her hands. I see her make a transaction, but she does it extremely quickly. I am excited to get the better rate offered than the bank exchange, but I have some doubts. Since there is a souvenir shop nearby, I plan to check it out after the transaction. The woman hands me a packet, and I go to shop.

Inside the shop, there are colorful knickknacks and nicely hand-painted wooden fish. There are so many souvenirs that my eyes begin bubbling with excitement. It does not take me long, and I make my selection. As I head to the cashier, I open the packet the old woman gave me earlier. I am shocked at what I see. There are about four American dollars inside. The true money is on the right and left side of the package. The rest of the weight is in the center and a pile of cut newspaper. I am scammed, and I rapidly look out the window to find the old woman, but she has vanished.

The following day, I ask the hotel attendant to contact the local police. She tells me that there is no need, because I can walk across the street. Since I am unfamiliar with what to expect, I ask the attendant to call the police to report theft. I want to capture the woman bandit. About thirty minutes later, the police officer arrives. He listens attentively to what I tell him. Subsequently, the officer assures me the thief can be found soon. The officer tells me that it takes time and effort, casually disclosing that he needs a retainer to begin the investigation. I am somewhat confused, so I ask him to clarify again. The police officer says he needs money. I explain that I am the victim, and he goes into a long soliloquy about the efforts he has to make. I understand that this situation is a setup, and the involvement includes the police. After experiencing this mishap, I become far more cautious than before. I decide not to trust the local people, regardless of their age, position or occupation. My experience of deceit (*the fixer culture)* compares to a déjà vu that Dr. Robert Kearns may have had.

Of course, I am not in the greatest spirit after this takes place, so I find a diversion. I take a walk towards some large shopping malls. This is where I see handcrafted products. I particularly keen on admiring the *Barong Tagalog. The* formal lady's garment *is* extremely lightweight. It is made from banana or pineapple (Piña) fibers. The shop clerk explains it is hand-loomed directly from the leaves, but the craft is becoming a scarce commodity. Mechanical weaving has almost replaced all traditional talent. Instead, banana silk or *abaca* is employed. In another section, there are *barongs* designed for men. Legend has it that the Spaniards made the Filipinos wear a *barong* to distinguish them from the ruling class. The translucent fabric allegedly helps the Spaniards by seeing if the wearer carries weapons and shows their lower status.

After seeing so many rainbow colored *barongs* for sale, I am not sure what is believable. Regardless, I purchase a *barong* because I like the smooth surface and its appeal. Afterwards, I have some regrets wearing it outside when a large truck swoops by. The truck splatters mud on the gorgeous *barong* and it needs cleaning. I head to a nearby restroom and I try rubbing the dirt off with liquid soap and water. Unfortunately, it only leaves a stain. I return to the merchant and explain what happens. The seller does not make an exchange, but suggests I bring the *barong* to a local dry cleaner. As I have no choice, I follow the advice. A day later, the *barong* comes back looking resplendent, but with a major problem. The binding is unraveling at the seams and the life of the *barong* is short-lived because it was shoddily made.

Metaphorically, the word *barong* also corresponds to an Indonesian myth. The *barong* symbolizes a lion-like creature that is the King of Good Spirits. It is also the enemy of Rangda, the demon queen. According to the traditions of Bali, Indonesia, the *barong* comes from entertainment. The *barong* is a local dance and symbolically means society has a continuous **struggle between morality and wickedness**. That is why; it seems no matter where I go the issue of ethics and evil crop up.

Of course, there are some notable Filipino women that portray two sides of the coin. Women like Imelda Marcos and Maria Corazon Sumulong Cojuangco-Aquino are well-known dignitaries. Their portraits depict better than males in official positions.

Maria Corazon receives her education in the United States. She has an extensive background in the humanities and Law. After attending several Ivy League schools, she acquires a doctorate in Law and Humane Letters. Her prestige and learning implies she is a decent human being as is Imelda Marcos, a college-educated teacher.

Maria Corazon and Imelda Marcos, both define themselves in the milieu of a male-dominated Asian society. In the existing patriarchal framework where men are in the lead, even prominent women have to mêlée to get respect. The women are unable defeat the patriarchal system. Men intervene in the lives of both women and their outcomes are dismal. Their images are tarnished through association with men deemed unworthy. Maria Corazon's husband is murdered and Imelda Marcos is driven out of the country with her former dictator spouse. Corazon's spouse becomes a primary target for the dispute about the country's ideology. He represents the Democratic Party after Marcos rules. Since he is in opposition to the Military tribunals, he becomes a target to be assassinated. According to the New York Times, Ferdinand E. Marcos and Imelda are indicted for corruption and embezzling millions of dollars from the Philippine Government. The couple buys *"three buildings in New York City."* [106]

No matter what I see or hear, my gender truly makes a difference in the reverence I receive. It is during these times, I reminiscence about Sue's world. She is a firm, devout Catholic believer, the same as many Filipinos. Sue's husband is also the head of their household. When Sue is alive, her spouse heads their affairs. Otherwise, she has less important. It is for that reason; I am clipping out articles about the celebrated Filipino women. I am pasting articles about the women that obtain prestige. The photos of these prestigious women and expository become part of Sue's scrapbook. This is my symbolic effort to commemorate Sue and deserving women.

Lilia Quindoza Santiago, writer and researcher discovers there is no lack of courageous women in the Philippines. Santiago's findings are backed by the Canadian International Development Agency and Hasik Incorporated. They confirm women in the past "*played an important role*" [107] There women are known to be warriors, innovators and fighters for justice. Some of these women include Melchora Aquino, General Agueda Kahabagan, known as the Joan of Arc of the Philippines. In 1905, Gregoria de Jesus and Concepcion Felix lay the foundation for feminism (Asosacion Feminista). Darlene Magnolia Antonino Custodio is a Congresswoman for the district of South Cotabato.

She fights against mismanagement. In fact, the amount of notable women still is few, so the Filipino culture favors men and trusts women less.

As a female, I like seeing what womanly objects I might buy. I fancy seeing some shoe choices so when a shoe manufacturer's sign comes up, I go inside. It is beyond my imagination seeing so many shoes. There are boots, sandals, Oxfords, loafers, pumps, flip-flops, clogs, lace-ups, sneakers and other styles. The shoes are made out of a variety of materials. They include leather, faux suede, felt, faux fur, mesh, canvas, fur-lined linen, and canvas. Needless to say, I glimpse at shoes Imelda Marcos may have worn. After all, she owned 3,000 pairs of shoes while in office as the former tenth president of the Philippines.

I continue looking around and become famished. As in other Asian countries, I fill my cravings with local street food. I have an aberration that I am in Mexico. This is because the Filipino street food is lined up with Mexican food - *burritos, tacos, quesadillas, nachos, relleno, morcon, paella, callos, embutido* and *caldereta*. Indubitably, there is a Mexican flavor, but culinary influences also include Spain, Malays, Arabs and the Chinese.

It is unfortunate, but I find the Filipinos' adaptation of other country's foods to be simply not authentic. I experience this especially when I go to Davao Chinatown in Manila. I get there by a trotting, horse-driven carriage. I see plenty of signs advertising popular Chinese noodle dishes. Names like *bihon, Miki, sotanghon, Mami, Lomi, miswa* or *pancit*. I choose having some *pancit* and lumpier spring rolls. When I eat the food, the taste is absolutely dreadful. Before I judge too quickly, I try other shops. Unfortunately, my impression remains the same. After eating foods that are unpleasant, combined with congested traffic, I decide to leave.

I avoid carrying excess luggage, so I repack my three bags into one. When I get into the taxi, I experience some arthritic pain in my fingers and take off all my rings to relieve the pressure in my fingers. There are rings for every finger, some conferring honorarium and university graduation, to collectibles I obtain during travel. I mistakenly take them off just before realizing the taxi driver is watching my movements. When I go to pick up the larger bag just on the outside of the door, the driver speeds off before I get wind and gather my rings. I did take precautions based on my earlier mishap. I luckily recorded the driver's name, but regardless, I experience paroxysmal. I lost all my rings that I cherished. Since that time, I have trusted my instinct that misfortune is part of my learning journey. Even though I am devastated, only the wind and the ocean hear my cries. Now, *the rings are in the possession of the forgotten waves.* After this takes place, I am exceptionally solemn. I hear the ringing of the church bells before leaving. Perhaps Sue must have known I called out to tell her.

I am not especially content about the earlier incident. Invariably, intelligence seems to be like the tides that move up or down. I begin thinking about what happened. I see too many poor people in the Philippines. They have no option in life. They have to steal to survive. Traveling back to the Philippines several more times, I have the realization that the poor need to strategize how to get money. Sometimes, I see the locals skim off takings wherever possible. Even the restaurant workers replace the stock in-house with their own produce at night. I know it is not always obvious which industries are affected, but this is the habit in the Philippines. This also explains why some of the food tasted more terrible than the authentic dishes. Ingredients or prepared products are absent. Like the terrible muffins I made as a girl, substitutes do not suffice. Even the local fish breeders often experience people fattening their plates by stealing fish once they start swimming. The local children are also exposed to criminal elements daily. They face vulnerability not only to theft, but also prostitution, drug addiction, and so many other kinds of crime. In fact, most of the street children and the elderly become thieves, because they live in pitiable circumstances. As in my earlier experiences, I suspect syndicates force local Filipino people into other criminal activities. This is why so many Filipinos do not have decent jobs or gain reasonable compensation.

Sadly, young people have become the scapegoats for most of the crime that takes place. Timothy Austin, Department of Criminology, Indiana University of Pennsylvania clarifies about the Filipino mentality when he researches street theft among Filipino youth. He describes the phenomenon as an Oliver Twist-style. Youths come from low socio-economic environments and survive by begging or conning outsiders. It is survival of the fittest or the ***crab mentality***. Many of the youths are jailed before the tourist season starts for vagrancy Laws. Austin's research augments "youths *are criminalized and stigmatized forno obvious crime committed*."[108] The Filipino children are truly in the worst predicament. There are 1000s of children arrested, detained, tortured, raped, or experience some other forms of inhumane treatment. I want to grab as many children as possible and save them, but I cannot.

The Filipino economics continuously appear miserable. Pertinent factors involve corruption, mismanagement, and stealing from the poor. Relief donations typically never reach the poor. Therefore, as proposed by the Ambassador of the Philippines, the ***crab mentality*** is quite prevalent. Hence, the crab behavior is embedded in the Filipino culture, so I experience the "fixer" or crab mentality culture. I am not a wealthy North American woman, but I am a blend of many cultures. Therefore, I can contribute my thoughts about what takes place to evoke more of a true emotional picture than Austin's research. My rings and money are part of the *Forgotten Waves* culture, but this reality also happens elsewhere. In Russia, I remember my parents sending money to my grandparents. They never receive the funds. Since I understand the dilemma of the underprivileged, my anger leaves me. My reoccurring visits to the Philippines make me reflect about people calling themselves humanists. It is when I experience deprivation in Texas and China; I walk in the shoes of the Filipinos. I suspect the North American wealthy and middle classes have little or no knowledge about what it feels like inside.

On a political note, my earlier discussions with the Ambassador results in a later invitation to get together. During encounter, we talk about how travels cause issues of trust to evolve. He briefs me on events that take place during World War II. He explains how people were in the past. In Manila City, people trust neighbors, friends and strangers. In the role of a child, he receives protection from his parents, but he comes to fear the Japanese invaders, and the impact they create. There is no television or media to direct his thinking. It is only through experiences with American GI's that make a profound influence on his values. The GIs represent goodies to strive for as a human being. He adds that in his earlier years, he is imbued with American values. This happens when he attends a local Filipino school. The American Jesuits educate him with their values, and they attach their dreams. Events after wartime cause many people to leave the country. He is dismayed by their exit, but understands they feel insignificant and see no future. Many of the Filipinos wind up in the United States. Some become doctors, shopkeepers, or clerks. These are many of the brightest people that abscond. They leave the country high and dry. The scenario mirrors what happens in Venezuela when the government also changes hands.

Years pass and his impression about Westerners changes. The Ambassador of the Philippines says North American people are unable to understand the position of Asian countries. They do not try to walk in the shoes of the Filipinos and consistently judge incongruously because they hold on to different values.

Learning the full truth takes times, so I continue to explore more about the past and hear what is said. The Filipino government advocates the best human welfare, but contrast discussion I have with enumerable Filipino people. They offer their opinions, but ask to be anonymous. Generally, they are in disagreement. They assume there are too many existing unlawful practices. In the smaller communities, some issues include bogus birth registration, falsifying academic credentials, fake driver‘s licenses and other. As an Asian orientated country, people have collective norms. They are of the same opinion as the Ambassador of the Philippines. North Americans keep track of a person's importance in an unalike fashion to Filipinos. Some examples include birth records and education. Details follow.

Birth Records - North Americans count a person's age after the child is born. In the Philippines and other Asian countries, the age of a child begins when the child is conceived and grows in the mother's womb. For that reason, a child is considered to be a year old at birth. In smaller communities, birth records are produced by a group of Elders that act as witnesses. The older people go by memory, so information is often inaccurate. This is an accepted pattern of community life. Naturally, there is a discrepancy in birth documentation.

Education - Learning about any subject boils down to accruing facts and application. In the past, local universities produced manual records on a demand basis. It is not a given that a person attending school can get a transcript or any kind of record. To obtain such records means sending gifts to do this. As for the standard of the elite in the Philippines, they have another criterion. Some of the reputable institutions providing documentation do it at a premium cost. This might include known universities as the University of the Philippines Diliman, University of the Philippines Los Baños, De La Salle University Manila, Ateneo de Manila University, to name a few.

According to the World CIA Fact book, literacy rates are higher in the Philippines compared to other countries. In 2000, the national Filipino census states 92.6 percent of youths 15 years and over are able "*to read and write.*"[109] There is only one problem with the fact-finding. If there are so many educated people, then why do the poorer people tolerate inequity in learning what is right? May be the root of the problem corresponds with culture. It seems so much is loaned from other cultures. In fact, it makes me question if the Filipino people truly have a distinct culture of their own.

If Dr. Patch Adams were in the Philippines, there might be some positive archangelic changes. The 65-year-old physician dresses in motley psychedelic outfits and cares about making changes to the situations of poverty. He does this by hugging and being a social activist. Certainly, when the Filipinos see a beatific model as Adams, they probably will behave felicitously.

Instead, the Filipinos act as if they are parts of Bosch's painting, in *The Garden of Earthly Delights*. The artwork symbolically demonstrates part of human existence. There are negative messages of maltreatment of people, so reverting to the Filipino waters might be the solution. The Philippines and Sri Lanka have the world's richest marine life. There are clams, corals, algae, sea grasses, crustaceans, mollusks, sponges, jellyfish, sea urchins and thousands of other organisms. When a person decides to ride one sea turtle, behavior will definitely change. These amazing sea creatures not only wear eloquence on their tortoiseshell, but they take pleasure in swimming swiftly away from the demise on land. Hence, if people put on their flippers and become like sea turtles, they obtain the inspiration under the water. In fact, it is only a matter of paddling and the flow of rushing water inspires betterment.

In my journey on the back of a turtle, I am traveling towards Japan. I see the bridge where Claude Monet made his famous painting. In 1899, Monet spends thirty years of his life painting the water lilies in different compositions. Hence, as my name is **Lily**, I know there is something significant. Therefore, if all people learn about biodiversity and human nature, they also can join the travel because Lily in Japan translates to mean "*lots of numbers.*"[110]

CHAPTER 18: Japan

BANKING ON PERSONAL INTELLIGENCE

Flying from the Philippines, I soar with the birds. When a gust of wind swirls in my path, feathers seem to be floating, and others plummet. All my life I have tried to pluck the feathers of a bird, but in only an instant, bird feathers are fluttering everywhere. They are temporarily obliterating my sight, and I arrive in the miasma of Fukuyama, Japan.

Fukuyama has an unwholesome atmosphere as a result of decaying organic matter from a garbage factory nearby. There is also smog from other factories in the vicinity. I feel nauseous from the toxicity, and sense there is a menacing atmosphere. My impression stays with me even when I encounter the custom officer that shows little warmth. He makes me feel as if I am a shear see-through piece of glass, and I feel uneasy.

The officer's facial reactions and coyness is reminiscent of Keiko. She was the first foreigner to come into a Caucasian community. Her father comes to setup a scientific factory in Montreal. Keiko is the only Oriental person in the school, and no one wants to know her. I do not mind making her acquaintance even when I cannot understand why there is a difference. Now, I feel I am in Keiko's shoes when the officer acts with disdain. I imagine his behavior is analogous to how Keiko might have felt years earlier. Everyone treated her with derision, especially poking fun at her features. These memories are disturbing and I get the impression that nothing changes in how people react to someone that appears disparate.

In reality, this does not impact all people. In fact, the Japanese Medical Attaché name is Hideo (英夫). This means "a splendid *man*" [110] and this is not a coincidence. Hideo hears from other dignitaries that I am exploring ethnographic perspectives at a number of embassies. I am uncertain what he thinks, but Hideo acts eloquently when we meet. Initially, he invites me to dine with him, while I am in China. At that time, we have some general conversations and Hideo gives the impression of condign recognition. I want to understand his mind more deeply, so we arrange a meeting time and place, in the outskirts of Fukuyama, Japan. There, I like to address his values because he perks my curiosity. He tells there is a universal way of thinking, so I am anxious to know what that means more clearly.

Luckily, the officer grants clearance and I enter Japan. I look for a taxi, but it is hard to find in the misty weather. Somehow, I stumble on a cab and give the driver a slip of paper. The Japanese writing provides a destination and the note comes from Hideo. The driver spins his wheels and I am heading to the unknown. The ride is particularly quiet passing by the Seto Inland Sea National Park. The ride is rather long, but I catch sight of Shodoshima. This is a place of natural beauty and stunning sea views. At least, I am on the path of the *Forgotten Waves.* From my window, I also distinguish the mountain top has crisscrossed walking trails, There are also many plants flourishing, but no conversation takes place. The driver gives me a copycat impression of the officer. I suppose my presence causes him to react in a chilly manner. Regardless, I cope with the silence. Finally, I reach the hotel that Hideo recommended. When I arrive, the staff informs that Hideo makes arrangements for a limousine to pick me up later. I have about three hours before

Hideo's driver arrives. At least, the gap in the time allows me to look around in the town.

As I look in the area, there are enumerable color signs advertising noodle soups and appetizers. I head into one of the shops, and the entryway is a little unusual. There are at least fifteen vertical plastic see-through slats in the doorway. The slats are about four inches wide, which initially blocks entry and other shops have it too. I imagine the slats allow the air to flow more easily. Anyway, I push through the slats and go into the shop. I could see a few tables eloquently spread and the people inside are quiet. Not a soul draws their eyes to look at me. Everyone seems to be eating or reading. When I sit down at a table, the waitress gives me a menu. Then, I show her a picture of shumai steamed shrimp dumplings. I think this appetizer will tide me over until Hideo arrives. Even though, there are few tables inside the shop, no one comes to sit beside me. I savor the hors d'oeuvre peacefully and without interruption.

After having an enjoyable, light, taste, I continue looking around. Somehow, I have a feeling that Sue's spirit is hovering athwart, and has a clear view. I could see one shop that has life-sized dolls. The shop owner tells me that the dolls or traditional ningyōare exported worldwide. I imagine the meaning signifies a sign from the world beyond. I reflect on my earlier handmade doll that Sue still embraces. I think there is no happenstance in what takes place. The .Japanese handmade doll represents the inner workings of the Ying Yang principle. These porcelain dolls are exquisitely handcrafted. They have a hollow interior that correlates to a person's fragile soul. The hollow serves to contain the spirit in just another form. In retrospect, this resembles Dr. Robert Kearn's principle of windshield wiper vision. As people, we all capture a glimpse to develop new patterns of thinking. The idea about what to think, received tacit knowledge, before getting wiped away. I imagine that if there is an exhumation of Sue's remains, the created doll and her delicate soul still thrives. Sue was an incredible woman that had multiple sclerosis. Unfortunately, she sank sweetly below into the earth with my doll creation. I suspect that because of my act, Sue is still balancing the positive ions of her spirit upward and nearby. Somehow, I also have a sensation of light-headedness. As I whiff the air, my energy becomes re-boosted. This event rekindles memories of the out-of-body experience I had. At the time, my energy is tolerable. Such thinking sways in my mind, but I decide it is time to head back to the hotel for my appointment.

I had few details about my rendezvous. I only know I am going to an exclusive club in Shinbashi District. I have a favorable impression of Hideo's actions. He has given me, so much consideration. Hideo's talents as a gastroenterologist, also gives a digesting feeling. The Medical Attaché receives his training in Japan, Australia and the United States. Hideo also holds a doctor of philosophy from an American Ivy League school. Incredibly, Hideo also lives in 35 foreign countries, so he knows how to make a favorable impression. Indubitably, the man has outstanding savvy about international human relations.

Time speeds quickly, and the limousine arrives. The chauffeur brings me to Aragawa, an exclusive Japanese club. When I met Hideo, he tells me his nickname is "Akira."[111] The name means a person that is extremely intelligent, so I have no doubt that Hideo, Akira, can do no wrong. He is intelligent and gives a magnificent impression. He greets me with a smile and tells that return transportation is arranged after our meeting concludes.

This hidden club is tucked away among high-end restaurants. Apparently, even though Hideo Akira is a member of the club, it is excruciatingly hard for most people to get inside. The Medical Attaché has an exceptional ability to pick up the phone and tell the staff who is going to accompany him. Even though, the Japanese are exceptionally picky about their customers, Akira is a favored, trusted, customer and any company of his does not receive questioning.

When we arrive, a hostess brings us to a table where menus are already there. I am inquisitive about what was inside the menu. As I open the menu, I am in awe what I see. The average meal cost is $370 American dollars or 32,352.80 Yen. I worry about the pricing and Akira notices my concern. He assures me that my meal is complimentary. Before our conversation begins, I am served some Kobe or beef prepared with mustard and pepper. There are also other fabulous food items that arrive. Soon after, our conversation takes off with a dialogue about Japan's core thinking. He refers to this as the **universal way** to conduct affairs in life. The Hideo Akira says his values come from the Shinto tradition, the state religion. His words automatically cause me to reflect about my first encounter with Keiko. Ultimately, it is through our discussion, I gain a clearer understanding about the universal way.

Akira adds the Japanese people are nationalistic. They feel there is no threat to their universal thinking from outsiders especially missionaries. At the same time, the Japanese society imposes certain expectations from members in the society. This includes having a calm composure, being self-reflective and marching loyalty to their Emperor. As Akira speaks, his emotional expressions are minimized. He goes on to explain the Japanese people have full control. They connect on a soul level even with their past ancestors. The Japanese people replicate the same model their parents employ. Hence, from an early age, he is learns to **self-sacrifice** for his nation. Akira also confirms that he is always cautious about what to say or how to act. By doing so, this reaffirms his personal **morality** or the 'universal way' to conduct life satisfactorily. I think he means that the family dominates the direction of an adult. This is irrespective if the person is happy about choices. I know the same core value is also something that the Chinese and other Asians also portray. I remember the medical student I met earlier times. He accepts an arranged marriage, but does not seem content.

Akira shares that whenever people communicate with a person that is unfamiliar or foreign; there is the potential for misunderstanding. Therefore, conversation usually commences with "*the **silent culture** or the amae, the assertion and acceptance in communication*"[112] and recognizable through facial expressions. The silent culture suggests the Japanese are more loyal within their familiar group than to an outsider that might cause harm to take place. This reality is also highlighted by Professor Miyake, a social psychologist at the Michigan Medical Innovation Center University. Miyake considers Darwin's premise that facial expressions are "*genetically programmed into our species.*"[113] He determines that people incorporate their own thoughts about regulation. They do this to reduce possible discrepancies between a person's actual and ideal self. Certainly, this explains the behavior of the custom officer and the taxi driver too.

The Japanese also keep to themselves for another reason. This relates to my earlier description about China's social face constructs. The Japanese and other Asian countries practice this as well. The people avoid having conflict to be a part of the in-group. This perspective also matches with other conservative cultures such as the Netherlands. People there also are part of the in-group. They do not claim individual identity. Hence, this makes me think that the Japanese and the Dutch are less sensitive than a North American might be.

To substantiate further, social face looks like what David Matsumoto, Professor of Psychology and Director of the Culture and Emotion Research Laboratory at San Francisco State University describes. The Japanese explore the innuendos behind expressions. He brings to mind that there are "*micro-expressions associated with the intensity of a person's emotions.* "[114] These expressions even discern when a person is deceptive, all factoring into being part of the in-group.

Our conversation, then takes a twist. I notice Akira is staring at me. Was he expressing some consternation about intellectualizing with a woman? Many thoughts run through my mind. I assume he has memories of Japanese women from an earlier time and is intent on the women in his life. From Akira's childhood, he receives instructions about the obligation of women. Young girls from poor families acquire training to be a Geisha. During their apprentice, they first work as maids. Later, they acquire knowledge of entertainment skills. This includes learning musical instruments as the *samisen*, traditional singing, classical dance, the preparation of tea ceremonies, flower arranging or *kebana*, composing poetry and literature. Since these women learn how to better deal with men and their rapport, maybe Akira is raised to think women with skills, regardless of origin, fall into a Geisha category. Even though, modern geishas are no longer bought or brought into geisha houses as children, they are still considered to be women that entertain men behind closed doors. This is not to be confused with a Japanese prostitute. They desire changing their image to have the same prestige as a Geisha. I conjecture that he thinks even I fall into a Geisha category. I pause for a moment. Akira seems to have the uncanny ability to see-through a person. He begins to make me feel edgy particularly, when he says nothing. Later, I catch him off guard. At that point, I understand his deeper prejudicial notions. He inadvertently, sputters out distasteful English words when he changes talking about the changing world.

Akira addresses international marriage or *kokusai kekkon.* He says this takes place historically when there is a shortage of Japanese brides. The *nakǒdo hǒshǒkin* or 'arrangements for brides' is the result. He emphasizes that there is a *"gender division of labor, age differences, and insider-outsider relations within the ie."* [115] and impacts the position of a female in Japanese society. From his tête-à-tête, I understood that men are in control and have a higher status than women have. This includes the husband is above his wife. As our conversation progresses, his nonverbal cues change. Perhaps, Dr. Matsumoto's "*Subtle Expression Recognition*"[116] charting is accurate because I sense Akira's deception. He may have come to a realization why he is staring at me and possibly, doubts the Japanese philosophy. I imagine it is difficult for him to be comfortable intellectualizing with me, a foreign woman.

The topic shifts to intermarriage in current times. Akira immediately frowns and blames the Japanese women for changing the dynamics within the country. He says the Japanese women are marrying men from foreign lands. This includes America, Australia, China, the Philippines, Korea, Thailand and Brazil. His realities are on target. The Japanese women do choose to marry other nationalities.

Social researcher, Denman, substantiates with facts. He says there is an agreement between the Australian and Japanese government analysis about intermarriage. "*Sixty-three percent of Japanese migrant women marry Australian nationals. In 2003, there were 36,039 international marriages between Japanese and non-Japanese.*"[117] Akira's bias appears to be deeply rooted. There is also evidentiary documentation from the Asian-American research study of "*Shinagawa and Pang.*"[118] They determine there has been a lower frequency of intermarriage because of miscegenation Laws and segregation principles that are in place. Because of changing Laws, Akira is right to affirm that traditionalism is becoming a wave of past thinking. Our dialogue closes on that note. Subsequently, the limousine driver returns me to the hotel.

My sixth sense is guiding me. I decide not to stay in the hotel. I take a walk and unsure where it leads me. I come to an unmarked concrete building. In appearance, this is identical to Hong Kong's rooster sport or China's bathhouse. Instead, the entryway leading me into a dim-looking room with wooden shelves, I see something unbelievable. Inside, there are canisters lying out on the wooden planks with Japanese wording under each container. I have no knowledge what it says. As I walk closer, I think this must be a sacred place. I have no idea where I am or what else is inside. Suddenly, the door creaks open, and I get startled. A young, attractive, Japanese woman enters. Since I see her come in as a shadow, I believe Sue's spirit orchestrates her coming for things **I NEED TO KNOW**.

At first, she sits for a few moments in a meditative or '*za-zen*'state "za" (sitting) and "Zen" (deep absorption)] and gains consciousness. It is her way of clearing her mind to discover something of significance. Her speech is deliberate. The woman begins by talking aloud in a broken English addressing religiosity philosophical perspectives and a person's final journey. She explains that whether a person is alive or dead, their journey needs to be bare and have no clutter. These words also recap how Akira, the custom officer, the taxi driver and Keiko respond too. They all look like they are clearing their mind more than before. Then, the woman reveals we are, in the memorial section of the temple, called the columbarium. It is the place where human ashes are placed soon after someone is cremated.

There are numerous shelves that hold urns containing human remains. The ashes of a female weigh about four pounds (1.8 kilograms) while a male weighs close to six pounds (2.7 kilograms). Symbolically, this room depicts a person's life from sunrise to sunset. The urns do not stay in only one room. They move from room to room. Each movement is purposeful and corresponds to how the spirit moves after death. This movement continues sequentially until the spirit is settled on the burial grounds of the Zen temple.

I sense that her conveyance of the spirit is also an extension of Japanese ideology. Specifically, the soul becomes harmoniously balanced and corresponds with the *yin yang* belief. The Japanese have Eastern thinking. This evolves from the Chinese thought of two forces being opposing and complementary or male and female. This is the make up for the phenomena of life. Since this relates to the living spirit, the implication impacts every aspect of thought including "*astrology, divination, medicine, art, and government.*"[119] Thus, Asian people avoids conflict and seeks directions that are congruent with established standards.

The Japanese principles seem to be a complex mixture of ideas and doctrines. When I review how contemporary military training or *seishin kiyoiku* adapts to spiritual training, standards support the Samurai code. Specifically, the Japanese listen to commands of people in authority and adhere without question. The same application is among the simple farmer to workers that labor rigorously. The Japanese willingly accept conditions that are extremely harsh. At the same time, they internalize this is how to obtain balance. I do not agree with this value. I think some people in positions of authority are not experts. No doubt, this become a time for me to question matters of logic.

As I listen to the Japanese woman, I also capture a chilly expression appearing on her face. I began wondering why she is holding back what she likes to say. After all, we are alone in a columbarium. This is where commemorating a loved one or speaking aloud, matters. The Japanese woman coughs slightly and continues to address Japanese practices. She explains that when a person passes into the next world, the Japanese people make a monetary contribution for the costs of the funeral. The offering varies and depends on the age of the dead person and their reputation in society. She says when a colleague dies, the amount given ranges from 3,000 to 20,000 Yen (1 USD = 88.18445 ¥) or $34.02

to 226.80 US dollars. As for relatives, they visit the grave and also offer prayers using a small alter or *Butsudan* in their home. This signifies that the spirit of the deceased still lives with family and watches over kin. The commemorating process is lengthy, so regard stays for years.

I listen attentively and hear her explain that customs also include the purification of the soul. Some of these practices spell out the actual time to visit, and practices. She tells that the Japanese people follow these rituals implicitly. For example, *Chiju-ku Nichi* is a prescribed feast offered for the deceased on the 49th day. During this time, water is the purifying source for the soul. According to the Japanese beliefs, the soul submerges into water and come in contact with a deity. Then, the soul takes on the sacred properties of water. Therefore, the Japanese pay their respects also using water by washing down tombstone. By virtue of the washing act, it becomes a purification process. Water rituals offer desirable relief for almost any event in a person's life including making birthing easier, recovering from illness, successes in an examination or a new job. Water also has the propensity to **remove** evil, luck and everyday spiritual grime. Because of water, there are also propitious outcomes such as moving into a house, acquiring more money, having good eyesight and longevity and so on.

I was astonished when she also brings up the importance of a '**lily**' flower (my name). She said a lily is commonly associated with funeral services because there is a symbolic association of innocence. When the soul is departed, the lily is believed to restore the soul. She differentiates between the white stargazer lily and the white chrysanthemum. The stargazer lily denotes sympathy while the white chrysanthemum is emblematic of death and grief. This fuels me to think about the soul's mission. I knew I had an inevitable **higher purpose**, but I was uncertain what could it be.

The answer came when the door creaks open again. This time, a young man with red curly hair enters. He does not stop to think the woman was in conversation with me. Instead, he makes demands on the woman in the columbarium. As the woman turns towards him, she introduces the man to me. He is the Japanese woman's fiancé. They met in Italy six years earlier.

Apparently, the couple is feuding before entering the temple. The Japanese woman avoids confrontation and goes into another part of the building. The young man is persistent because he wants to bring their disagreement to resolution. The couple's nonverbal expressions exaggerate their tension and their discord comes where there is already human demise.

The mixed couple replicates the impression that I had about Sue's relationship with her husband. In both situations, the couples collided because the men sought perfection from their point of view. The men conceded in unnatural ways by holding onto a Machismo mentality. In other words, Sue's husband diminishes her value because he wants his wife's image to be full-bodied, functioning and obedient to him. Instead, Sue and the Japanese woman, both neutralize their stressful situations by retaining a blank look. Sue and the Japanese lady do not match male expectations. It is at that moment, I believe Sue sends me a spiritual message. She focuses on the legitimacy of a woman's social status. As for the Japanese woman, the subject of intermarriage and equity comes up while we tour the rest of the temple.

It is my distinct impression that all relationships in Japan are about one-size fits all philosophy. As I promenade together with the couple, I hear their opinions about how it works in a Japanese family. The Japanese woman's father and the Medical Attaché have identical thinking. The men both assume a Japanese woman marries and goes along with what a Japanese man tells. I think the Japanese woman also has the same embedded reality. When the Japanese woman resides in Italy, her conscious values remain sublimely. The situation takes a turn when she returns to her homeland and old thinking resurfaces. Her reality probably becomes more pronounced even, in the columbarium. Even though, she had an emotional and happy attachment to her foreign Italian fiancée, she abruptly changes to follow the dictates of her father.

The Japanese woman's reasoning is no longer logical for the Italian man. The female refuses consciously to admit that she left Japan to get away from inequitable gender treatment. Even the history of Japan illustrates historically that women are perceived to be a man's commodity. This influence affects the local, Japanese women and women originating from other places in South East Asia too. Territories include China, Indonesia, Japan, Korea, Malaysia, the Philippines, Taiwan, Thailand, Vietnam and the Pacific region.

Essentially, in Japan, women regardless of their origin, appear to be there for male **comfort**. Although, a 'comfort woman' is a euphemism for women that work in military brothels, decent women experience being coerced into prostitution during World War II. There are as many as 200,000 women involved also from other countries (China, French Indochina, Hong Kong, Japan, Korea, Macau, Malaysia, and New Guinea, Philippines, Thailand,

Vietnam and other Japanese-occupied territories). Young women were abducted to satisfy the needs of men. They were taken from their homes during Japanese imperial control. The New York Times comment that it was a time when "*the sex slaves issue remains highly emotional,*"[120] particularly impacting women.

I suspect the Japanese woman truly escapes feeling like an object of pleasure too and rationale to be in Italy. When the Japanese woman is in her fiancée's country, she has a real chance of being happy. Regrettably, something makes her resist. She deals with the dichotomy between her father's control issues and her mother's modeling. Her mother is hardwired to think Japanese men are empowered before any women. Such a philosophy nurtures the woman to think her father is right and simultaneously, she obtains maternal love from her mother.

From the dark columbarium to the bright outdoors, the couple addresses the ever-changing Japanese culture, as does the Military Attaché. The couple invites me to spend the rest of the day together. I let them do most of the talking. I become their sounding board to echo their thinking. I listen to the airing of their problems throughout the course of their relationship. The Japanese woman tells she is formerly a student in Italy, while her fiancé is a businessman. They are both accepted in Italy as a couple, but family acceptance issues are unalike in Japan. When the Italian man speaks, I catch a glimpse of the Japanese woman remaining quiet. She reminds me of how Keiko might be. Her reservation seems almost to be untouched by the man's expressions. She makes no direct eye contact. Instead, the Japanese woman, models norms of family obedience and listening to what her parents think is correct. According to the Japanese woman's fiancée, she does precisely what her father tells her to do. Eventually, the Japanese woman speaks aloud about misgivings she has. The couple assumes they brought their legitimate points in the open, but it mostly relates to social stability between them and the family.

On a personal level, the couple's confusion relates to their constructs of love. The Japanese tend to be like the Chinese. The issue of social face is far more critical than a person's emotional well-being. Core thinking reflects on handling of personal situations. Years earlier in North America, when I fell in love with an Asian man, I experience the same. Even though, marriage is a consideration, the Asian family dislikes the relationship. This is because the Asians have precise expectations about what to do. The couple's situation mirrors the rationale of what Akira describes. The Japanese constructs of universal thinking has been described by the Medical Attaché, but a journalist, William Lidwell substantiates how this works. He uses the analogy of the art of the traditional Japanese garden saying. "*Principles are interconnected and overlap.*" [121]

Lidwell used an analytical perspective to include "*the principles of Kanso* (簡素), *Fukinsei* (不均整), *Shibui/Shibumi* (渋味), *Shizen* (自然), *Yugen* (幽玄), *Datsuzoku* (脱俗) and *Seijaku* (静寂)."[122] In terms of the personal relationship of the couple, my interpretation following incorporates Lidwell's principles,

Kanso occurs when there is exclusion of the nonessentials, namely, reject the foreigner; the Italian man. *Fukinsei* speaks about the idea of controlling balance in any composition. This takes place when nature's innate beauty duplicates. Specifically, a couple stays together with people in the same grouping or race. *Shibui/Shibumi* hones into having no elaboration. In context of the couple's relationships, there is an expectation that there are no other possibilities and questioning should not occur. *Shizen* infers there are no pretenses and nothing occurs accidentally. Therefore, the relationship between the Japanese woman and the Italian man allow them to both see there is not a fit in values. This is regardless that the father imposes his thinking. *Yugen* is a collection of subtleties and symbolic elements. As for the couple, the *yugen* shows them how the couple gravitates to what is familiar for them. It becomes a clear indicator that their thinking does not match. *Datsuzoku* conjectures that naturalism does include attraction. In this case, the magnetic force pulls them apart. *Seijaku* communicates that having tranquil thinking. This equivocates to the energized calm, stillness and solitude of the Japanese woman's reaction in the columbarium. Whereas, the Italian man has a portrait that is diametrically opposite, there is disturbance. In the Japanese woman's mind, she naturally accepts the family's lead how to proceed in life. The couple does gravitate to what is familiar to them. By staying in Japan, they come to grips with specific social obligations. They change from following their hearts to battling over the perfect direction. The couple constructs different ideas about 'love.' They both seemed to be blind to their own shortcomings, while trusting their story with me.

Years earlier, Keiko tells me that a Japanese woman has expectations to be subordinate to father's wishes. Her future husband also has to follow the same pattern. Akira also addresses the consequence of mixed marriages or *Kokusai Kekkon.* Hence, there is an expectation that relations are uniform. These values fuel paramount concern towards ethnic preferences as in the universal thinking design.

Furthermore, the Japanese particularly are in discord with the appearance of Black people. Anti-miscegenation Laws are instituted because of it. Specifically, the Japanese have marriage customs that caution mixtures. They prevent Blacks to have relationships with the Japanese. The Medical Attaché summarizes his perspective. He says that when a couple's relationship fails, this is usually attributed to not adhering to Japanese philosophy or the universal design. The dignitary adds that Japanese women are culpable for marriage traditions changing. In fact, In the 1950s, the first Japanese intermarriages occur. In current times, changes are a consequence of younger Japanese women choosing to marry outsiders from other countries. Even though, aesthetic thinking or the universal design is becoming ignored. This left the couple in a quandary over their union perspectives and Japanese universal reality. They either have to follow the Japanese trappings or be absorbed into Bosch painting, which depicts "*the progression of sin*"[123] in *The Garden of Earthly Delights*.

As a North American woman, I reflect on all the couple says. I suspect the Japanese woman and others like her, probably are searching for something unique. They are seeking something than looks different from what they know. This can be because of doubts, hearsay, literature or situational exposure. As a consequence, some of the women search for answers, others intermarry and the remainder follows tradition. Regarding the couple's reactions, as individuals, they are infatuated and intrigued by difference. Initially, they both like how difference triggers their imagination. It is only a matter of time that they confront the subliminal conscious. In Japan, they relive childhood rearing principles. The Japanese woman becomes obedient to her parents, while the Italian man discovers how his familiar values conflict with the constructs of Japanese universal ideals. Hence, when the couple falls in love earlier, they are oblivious to the disparity and gaps surface. Speculatively speaking, the Japanese woman does not want to hurt her parents, so she reverts to traditional ways of accepted wisdom. The Italian man sees his fiancé shifting from the way she is in Italy. He feels emotionally imbalanced by her decision and the dynamics between them are problematic.

I expect that the couple probably never discuss possible social problems beforehand. This makes them both ill prepared to cope when differences actually surface. As for the Italian man, he is familiar sharing with other men. He does this on a personal and business level. Therefore, he has expectations that his future father-in-Law relates in a like manner. When his future father-in-Law creates conflict and discomfort by expecting the Italian man to follow his dictates, everything in his mind shatters. He no longer feels worthy; his prestige, honor and reputation are destroyed. If the couple stays in Japan, the pair has to live under the guise of Japanese habits. On the other hand, staying in Italy might be an easier lifestyle for the pair. Regardless, it is time for me to surf new waves.

I am heading to Tokyo to take the Shinkansen bullet train. It goes at an incredible speed of 220 kilometers per hour. The pace and the crowd of people also match what takes place in Beijing, China. My only concern is how everyone can fit inside the train. Before I know what is taking place, I hear a bellowing sound coming from some nearby speakers. The voice lets everyone know that the train is arriving. Unexpectedly, I see lots of police officers surrounding the area. Their edging into the area makes me uneasy. I have no idea what is taking place. The train approaches and comes to a screeching halt. The doors open and people are pushing to get inside the train. They behave like herded wild animals. There are many more eyes, ears and noses to spot you than when you walk civil. The sounds of the people resemble the motions of an earthquake. There are rumbling noises of rapidly moving feet and extraordinarily piercing. People are pressing onwards to get inside. As the train loads the people in the units, the police officers approach, using their full force. They are impelling people to move forward and abruptly, the doors close. People are tightly squeezing against me. I feel like a trapped sardine in a heated crammed area. The heat is stifling and there is only standing room. The experience is exhausting, but finally, the train arrives in Tokyo in record time.

From feeling total confinement as part of a herd, I am glad that I can get out of the train to be an individual. I get my bearings once again, and enter the hub of Tokyo City. As I look ahead, I have a weird sensation. The streets are spotlessly clean and hardly any people are in sight. I cannot imagine what is happening. I walk ahead, but there is absolutely no debris visible anywhere and there is a sudden silence. In a flash of the moment, I realize the Japanese habit mirrors what I see in Singapore. Shops are all neatly lined up, and the national flag in its colors of red and white are often detectable. Items on the street showcase what is inside the premises. Clothing, food and most products have extremely high costs. I have no idea why there is a sudden lull. Perhaps, the banshee or the spirit of death briefly passes through.

The scene hastily changes from feeling a ghost town to a warm, radiating feeling when I see the Cherry blossoms or *Sakura* trees. They are brightening up the environment ubiquitously. Seedling trees are planted during earlier days of the Imperial Court. The Japanese produce the trees as an effort to bring forth a convivial feeling. Rumor has it that the *Hanami* festivities exhibit the most exceptional cherry tree blossoms during springtime. In spite of the blossoming cherries, there are flourish buds. They are giving off the scent of a lovely aroma. This scenario amazingly reminds me of travels in fantasy destinations. Indubitably, the cherry blossoms symbolize **friendship**, so this is a nice change from the harsh realities of the train and universal constructs. This still does not change how the Japanese people appear. They portray an emotionless expression when the encounter another human being. Fortunately, the sweet spirit of affability takes over as the chromatic, red cherries, shimmer their gorgeous coats. It is almost as if the cherries are tantalizing spirits to be wish makers and change expressions on faces.

I suppose my excitement shows. Out of the blue, a Japanese lady speaks in English. She says dreams do come true. They are an avenue to explore inner realities. The lady tells me to take a small piece of paper and write a wish. On the flip side of the paper, I am to write my name. Once I complete these tasks, she instructs that I wrap the message around the twig of a cherry tree. I am told by the woman that following instructions can turn out to be pleasing. At least, I make a wish for everything to go well, but her explanation is enchanting.

I continue walking, passing the Tsukiji Fish Market. This is a sushi Mecca for visitors and also the center of fashion. Surprisingly, there are also fruits, vegetables and other products for sale. The marketplace is known to be the largest bazaar in the world. I hear from the locals that fish is in strong demand. In fact, seventeen percent of the entire world's total fish catch is at this market. I try moving ahead, but I am caught between people bargaining. This gives me opportunity to listen to the buzzing power of the fishmongers and the consumers negotiating. I find this place to be fun. Surprisingly, the Tsukiji Fish market opens at 5 a.m. but I do not arrive until late morning. I expect the market is going to close soon. As providence has it, I follow the crowd and steer away from the market haggling, finally, the noise dies down and I continued traveling. I feel I am in a maze, but I reach a popular street in the center of town.

I continue looking around in the general vicinity when a stranger suggests I head towards Fukagawa. Apparently, this is closer to my intended lodging. First, I pass the merchant district in the old City of Edo. It is there that the present mood seems to reflect much of its surrounding. The environment is unlike other parts of Japan. The area appears to be spacious, but the layout mirrors other places in Japan. I do not like the sense that I am in a hospital environment of sterile cleanliness. Colors are also subdued, and buildings offer a few rough edges. As I stroll ahead, I pass by the exquisite Kiyosumi Teien Gardens and a number of parks. I also sight a myriad of beautiful temples. Once I turn the corner, I am startled to see an *obaasan* or grandmother (おばあちゃん) sweeping the street. She wears an eloquent kimono with hair cropped high on her head. The *obaasan* abruptly stops what she was doing when she sees me. The grandmother motions that I head north. I am not sure about her meaning, but I continue to travel up the hill. Some local people pass me by as I hike up the mountain. They smile and gesture greetings. Their actions certainly make me feel welcome. This is a precious moment when I feel a connection to the Japanese people. Apparently, the lodging I selected is in a residential community. I have a few more heavy steps upwards and I am there.

I enter into the guesthouse and I am greeted by a heavyset Japanese lady. She signals that I remove my shoes. I follow her directions. Initially, I handle the usual issues of making payment to get getting a passkey, so I can enter the premises. Afterwards, I move to my room anticipating a private single space. Instead, I have a roommate. Her image is unlike any conventional Japanese woman. I am in awe to see a Japanese woman with green hair. This is almost like a flashback of the green-headed pop star I meet in Taiwan. I am unsure what I might expect next. I keep thinking where I put my top hat. I guess it is tucked away safely. Regardless, my meeting this woman is not a fluke.

The Japanese roommate wears European clothing accessorized with lots of silver and gold bangles. As I enter the sleeping area, I make her acquaintance. The woman responds in a sociable way and there is an instant connection. We begin by talking about our travels. She tells me about her European and Asian tour and stopovers to meet her boyfriend. The green-headed gal is loquacious. She divulges stories of different countries and does it with astonishing passion. Her emotional expressions immediately put me at ease. The contemporary Japanese woman makes me feel as if I were at a pajama party. I have so much fun listening to her gabbing.

Before nightfall sets in, I decide to take a shower. I head to the bathroom and discover peculiarity. There is no toilet in the bathroom. Instead, the toilet is in an entirely separate room. Apparently, the Japanese people consider washing the human body to be quite separate from bodily functions. As I stand in one room, I see another room behind a glass partition. There is one entrance room where I undress. This room has a sink, while the other room has a shower and an extraordinarily deep bathtub. I am not sure what to do, but my Japanese roommate helps me understand practices. She tells me to first rinse myself using the washbowl. The Japanese woman says I should not rinse off in the bathtub. This way the tub remains clean, but I can soak in the steamy hot water.

The temperature of the tub is relatively hot for Western bathing standards. Regardless, I enjoy the sensation of the sizzling water. My roommate asks that I leave residual water in the wooden tub or the *Gyōzui* for her use. She explains this is traditional bathing practices and I comply with her wish. After I soak in the water for a while, I shower. Unfortunately, the steamy water lasts only a short time as the water is timed to shut off. I have to get out quickly before I feel a chill. At least, I do not have to contend with traditional family bathing practices of sentō or bathing in mixed company for too long.

I return to the room and my roommate give details that bathing is considered less luxurious than in North America. The small tub gets used by each family member in order of seniority, traditionally starting with the oldest male. As for babies and toddlers, they are bathed by both parents. When a child grows older, the individual is still bathed by one of the parents. When there is a guest in a

Japanese home, the visitor receives priority. It is only because of the advent of tourism, public bathing now separates male and female bathing facilities. As in China, the Japanese have an expectation to disrobe in front of family members. She continues talking about common practice and says reserving water is a family tradition. This certainly is a wave of different thinking in contrast to my upbringing.

The partitioned space between bathing and the sleeping room is ultra- small. I am so surprised that the minuscule space I have, is priced at premium rates. The allocated space reminds me of being in Hong Kong, but the aesthetics in Japan are far superlative to Hong Kong. The rooms in the guesthouse provide sufficient legroom, but not much else. Soon after, I dry myself, dress into my pajamas and head to sleep.

In the morning, I try a traditional Japanese breakfast. Food consists of steamed rice, miso soup, and various side dishes. Some of these side dishes include grilled fish, a rolled omelet or *tamagoyaki*, *Onsen tamago*, *tsukemono*salty pickles, some dried *nori* or seaweed. This is probably the same food selection that Keiko has at school in earlier years. My roommate sits next to me in the dining area. She demonstrates eating customs and placement of rice on the left side while the miso soup goes on the right side. As in my earlier impressions, Japanese etiquette is regimented. I am unable at all times to figure out what to do. The information is useful because dining issues come up again.

As I peer out the window, I see businesses galore at a distance. I know there are multinational corporations attracted to this cosmopolitan city. The companies are worldwide. Some of the known companies are Pfizer Incorporation, BASF, Bosch Corporation, Merrill Lynch, Texas Instruments, to name a few. Products are in health care, chemicals, communication systems and are part of an array of others. These companies are only representative samples of the many multinational entities situated in Tokyo. It seems truly odd that I can see this from a residential setting. I suspect the locals and foreigners alike obtain new perspectives. At the same time, I think sensitivity tune-ups and better ways to listen can also be helpful. My roommate says the Japanese express acceptance of communication as "*sasshi,*" [124] with an emphasis on focusing to the listener at all times.

I was rethinking how the Italian fiancé might be playing a role in business. I have a brief impression that the Japanese men lack true ingenuity. This is because the Japanese people have a reliance on other Japanese people to handle matters collectively. Times are changing and the Japanese men having lifetime careers are clued out how to work in another function. Maybe the Italian man's future father-in-Law will become more flexible. I am not sure, but I do know that I am perceived to be lower than the Japanese. Naturally, relationship building draws on the same problems that the Italian man talks about. Formerly, Japanese businessmen make the assumption that people automatically follow their cue, but changes are taking place. The Japanese discover new approaches that do not correspond to past conventional thinking. There is a restructuring of thinking taking place and one size no longer fits all.

During my visit to Japan, I am working as a female consultant. Therefore, I am already clued into patriarchal attitudes. The men seem to dislike having me in their business world, so I rectify the problem by using psychological tactics. I allow the men to believe they are in the lead. Naturally, I reduce some of the rigidity, but old habits do not totally die. In the collective society, the Japanese accept the influence of total quality management. They model what Proctor & Gamble (P & G) establishes when they set up their operations in Japan in the 70s. I suppose this is a parallel to what Keiko's father sets up in Canada. The Japanese are proactive and manage to light up the world in the midst of economic storms. They use a forward-looking approach in business. Business executives shift their thinking from a centered business philosophy to making social investments. The Japanese consider world consumers and make a positive difference to reach new market niches.

As I head out to smell the fresh, sweet air, I feel the state of affairs in Japan is like a rubber cap topping a jar. All the people within the jar hear commercialism matters. In all their habits from handmade items to fabrications, there is an exceptional phenomenon. Just by giving a whiff of Wasabior spicy green horseradish, people sense there are new delights. They come out of the jar to see Mount Fuji's tallest mountains. In reaction, they elevate their meditation to the highest level as if they are on top of Mount Fuji. They put turmoil aside and consider this as the rest of the world or *zenjo*. This kind of thinking allows reading between the lines and drawing alternate conclusions. Even though, the Japanese attitude truly corresponds to the earlier lifestyles of people in isolation, their universal design is a catalyst for their sense of order (scheduling routines) and emotional expressions (killing live animals or pushed in trains). Their **one size philosophy fits all**; at least, there is accommodation for a wide range of appeals and sizes. Now, I am heading to the waters of South Korea where there is to another world of differing idealism.

CHAPTER 19: Republic of Korea

TIDYING UP INTELLIGENCE & GENDER VALUES

Japan's "*one* ***size fits all*** philosophy also matches capturing the full moon. This impacts people having patronage to the full moon. Even Dr. Patch Adams maneuvers the "*one size fits all*" philosophy by considering the light of the moon naturally. He assembles people "*from all across Japan to have a fun-raiser.*" [125] This takes place right under the night of the autumn's full moon when there is usually a gravitational pull. Instead, this event pulls people together. Considering my instincts, I create my own fun by heading to South Korea for "*Chuseok festival.*"[126] I am going to see another full moon and wonder what might take place. I do know that I am going to meet another prominent man. I get an introduction to him, in Japan, under the auspices the full moon. He is refers to me by the Japanese Medical Attaché and an arrangement to meet later in Seoul, South Korea.

From the waning night sky, I travel from Tokyo to Sakaiminato and to Pusan, Donghae port. I spend time overnight and during this time, I see something strange taking place. People are leaving Japan in masses resounding like lambs. They are resounding as if they are a herd of sheep saying "bah bah bah." They want to be first, and shuffle their belongings to inch closer by pushing their bags forward. Eventually, the lineup becomes long with piles of bags between people. The Japanese and Korean travelers going to South Korea act analogous to the drivers in mainland China. They shove into each other, cut in the queue, take risks and have little regard for the next person. To add further grief, the crew takes forever to arrive. Finally, the ship staff enters and people board the ship by pushing and heaving into one level remaining thoughtless. All the passengers shift into one large room where sleeping mats already spread out. People find their spot and lie down, as this is a short overnight trip. In the morning, I arrive in Pusan.

The sun is rising, and I enter the second largest metropolis, Pusan City. This conurbation happens to be the gateway city connecting the Eurasian continent with the ocean. I come to Pusan having no any expectations, but this port city is like revisiting San Francisco, California. Pusan City is scenic. I hear the birds above in the sky, while below, the city is landscaped with an entrancing coastline and beautiful blue flowing waters. There are towering mountains connections with the Diamond Bridge almost as if I am at the Golden Gate Bridge. Just as if I were in San Francisco Bay, the gentle wind tickles my shoulders. The atmosphere is delightful and it makes me wonder if Sue's spirit is rising to tell me to look around.

Moving along, I see a signposted near the metro entrance; the Dongnae spa waters. I see this on par with San Francisco's Japanese earmarked area. In contrast to Japan, South Korea has many similar traits such as the Kabuki spas and Japanese-styled communal bathing. The major difference is less hygiene and a lesser allure.

As I walk around, I have flashbacks seeing Jackie. The Aboriginal man has strong projecting facial features similar in appearance to the Koreans. Even their sporting habits of gambling, drinking smoking, arcade playing and partying are identical with some exceptions.

Night Habits: The Koreans like gambling and going to the casinos, while many Aboriginals Chiefs own casinos. The Koreans bet with cash, while the Aboriginals mainly make their wager with beer. In both cultures, there is need for sensual relations, so the Koreans and Aboriginals mix company with prostitutes. Korean and Aboriginal males spend time cruising the bars and hotel lounges. This is where drinking strong alcoholic beverages are dominant. The Koreans prefer *Makkolli* or *Soju*.

Day Habits: The two cultures enjoy shopping in malls and spend great time enjoying roasted fresh shop. In Korea, the coffee shop or *Tabang* and the Internet café is popular. On the other hand, the aboriginals also enjoy coffee flavors, but artwork displays create their atmosphere. To recap, the coffee culture is alike for all people. In fact, coffee shop meetings are becoming widespread globally.

Pusan port is the hub for sailors worldwide. This compares to the Aboriginal beliefs. They welcome people from ports all around the world. Pusan mostly receives guests from nearby destinations such as China, Guam, Japan, and Russia.

I take the local trains or bus to get around. I take the Korean train, but I find it is less contemporary in contrast to Taiwan, China, Britain and Japan's metro. From the high-speed trains, Pusan's transport is like a turtle's dawdling pace, but stopovers for street food are ubiquitously an appeal. I see mostly young foreigners and the Elders excited by what they grasp. I cannot blame people for enjoying the mouth-watering food. I ask, "Can you tell me, what that is?" He responds, "It is delicate, blood sausages filled with rice." My stomach is churning and I think he means it is a delicacy. Then I point to another item and he says, "The best food ever! Pig intestines and *Mandu, Ho Ddeok (dumplings).*

Traveling, munching and nauseated, I pay attention to the time. I have to be on time to meet the South Korean executive. He is expecting me to meet him in Seoul, so I begin trekking north by bus. I pass cities; Gwangiu, Daegu, Daejeon and the scenery remains unchanged. Consistently, I view plenty of high-rise buildings and sellers on the streets. There are popular department stores (Sampoong, Shinsegae, Hyundai, and Lotte World) with dazzling markets offering goods for sale. As I pass by malls, the coffee shops, there are signs that light-up. Some advertisements have comical cartoon figures waving their hands. Other signs show children playing, but the traffic remains chaotic. Traffic patterns match being in the Philippines, Taiwan, Hong Kong and China. From the crammed snail-pace movement of cars weaving in and out of traffic, drivers create their own directions. They have no concern if they make illegal U-turns, change lanes or shift ahead. Scooters wind between the cars. No one adheres to traffic Laws regardless that cities regulate traffic lights. The police officers remind me of being in the Philippines. They close their eyes when people drive, do something wrong and allow drivers to use cellular phones. The worst event occurs when I arrive in Seoul City. I ask the driver, "What's wrong?" He does not reply, but I notice when arriving at the Gyeong Bokgung Palace I arrive in downtown Seoul and check into the magnificent Lotte Hotel. I heard this is a five-star-rated hotel known not only for lodging, but also for having a theme park included. I am marveling at the beautiful places to stay, but I am also excited to learn there is exceptional bathing or the *Jingjaebongs* ---hot, cold and herbal. There are also masseuses on-site taking out any muscle cramps. As I explore the hotel, I am astounded to see a multi-junction leading to the train, museums, restaurants, movie theaters, bookstores, swap meets, karaoke outlets, luxurious hair shops, dentists, musicians, extravagant shopping. I like conveniences in one spot. Like other Southeast Asian travel destinations, there is only one downfall, too many people --- hordes of commuters, students and families. People are pouring into this center like colonies of ants marching in and comparative to the worlds of Southeast Asia. This demands automated snacks and drinks at almost every corner.

I am at the junction for thirteen subway lines that connect. Passengers in the millions, stop by. People come from surrounding neighborhoods like Inchon, Gyenggi-do, and Gangwan-do. Obviously, there are plenty of available rest rooms to house the masses. The only peculiarity is that I never see any toilet paper. For that reason, I quickly learn to carry Kleenex. Along the way, I see almost every uniformed high school student using a cellular phone. Since English is the common second language learned in school, I stop to ask a student how they can you afford a cell phone. I hear the government promotes the use of cell phones at a low cost for students. Later that day, I buy a cell phone to contact Mr. Kim. After completing the telephone buy and catching glimpses of Seoul City, I return to my hotel suite.

The following day, I contact Mr. Kim and arrange a meeting. In conversation with the executive, he let me know that he has been in touch with the Military Intelligence. I am not sure of his plans, but Mr. Kim shares that the Korean defense is in collaboration with the United States military. I think he means partnership arrangements, which ensure humanitarian disaster relief efforts as part of South Korea's role in international affairs. He tells men belong to Special Forces and Peacekeeping. These men are in charge of military intelligence. There are diving specialists to snipers, peacekeeping initiatives, and rescue of men, bomb specialists and etcetera and routinely face brutal environments.

I am not sure what Mr. Kim has up his sleeve, but clearly he has connection to the Military. During our conversation, he tells linkages to larger Korean organizations. This includes include the Korean Government, Seoul Metropolitan Government, LG Group, Pohang Steel, Hanjung, Daehong Communication, Korea Telecom and government officials. I am uncertain how Mr. Kim connects with everyone. During conversations with Akira, I discover that Mr. Kim delivers customized management programs for various establishments. He has traveled to many destinations including China, Germany, India, Japan, Taiwan, South Africa, and the United Kingdom. I am perplexed how Mr. Kim manages his business affairs, as his language skills are not as skillful as Akira's are, but he makes himself understandable. Mr. Kim's expressions or words often come out awkwardly.

When I meet Mr. Kim in Japan, he stresses he is a family man and says the same on the telephone. I suppose Mr. Kim wants the opinion of family members whether to aim at offering an opportunity to work with intelligence staff.

Contrary to Akira's transport arrangements in Japan, Mr. Kim makes a personal effort to pick-me-up in his luxury Sedan. I am amiss to see the different styles of a diplomat and a businessman. Concurrently, I am pleasantly surprised to meet his family, his wife, son and daughter. They are all smiling at me, and their inviting eyes signal me to come inside the car. At least, I am going experience being a part of Mr. Kim's family for a short time. I know this can help me to understand the mysteries about of rapport in a South Korean family.

Mr. Kim drives the car to a suburban area that has sprawling high-rises and pleasant landscaping. After parking the car is in the high-rise building, I am directed to the main floor of a 60-story building to take an elevator. Pressing floor twenty-seven, I reach the home of Mr. Kim's family. In a short time frame, I realize that Mr. Kim is the head of the household. He makes all the decisions and values resulting from Confucianism, in 130 A.D. These are principles of order and authority representing the hallmark of how Mr. Kim thinks and acts. He is in-charge of the family and they are obedient.

My journey begins with unfamiliarity. Family members bow to Mr. Kim as a common measure of greeting and respect. I copy the habit to ensure peaceable relations. As I lower my head, I realize that following creates a strong connection with the Kim family. Symbolically, I become part of the extended family and communication flows easily. Mr. Kim's facial reactions also show he has pleasure that I shadow the Korean tradition. In discussion, Mr. Kim invites me to stay with his family until he negotiates agreements with the Military. Seemingly, he is alike to Akira.

Korean Home Life: Staying with the Kim family becomes an advantage to understand the normative behavior of a Korean family. I learn the normal practices of family order; beliefs, educational models, philosophy, routines, social expectations, routines and eating habits. I view food preparation, layouts, the manner of facial expressions and other practices.

The day starts with the glorious smell of food and I come into the kitchen. Mrs. Kim has already prepared some breakfast. The food arrangement is beautiful on the table and is not comparable to a North American breakfast (eggs, cereal, toast, juice and coffee). Instead, there are bowls of soup and many side dishes or *banchan*. The side dishes include *Kimchi* (fermented cabbage), spicy *cucumber* with a mixture of red chili pepper powder. The *spinach* cooking is with sesame oil and soy sauce toppings. This serving is icy cold. Other dishes are *bean sprouts* boiled and spiced up. There is *seaweed laver* or salted small squares. The local vegetable *aubergine*, and *tofujorim* go with dry sardines, and desiccated *cuttlefish*. The breakfast meal overall appears festive. The colors, shapes, and display are a real treat. The table is incredible to look at, but nothing is eaten before Mr. Kim arrives in the dining area.

Mr. Kim arrives wearing his business clothes, a black suit, crisp-looking white shirt and polished black leather shoes. As he enters the dining area, his wife bows and he sits down at the head of the table. Then all the members take their place and only start eating after Mr. Kim begins. The table is silent and no one speaks. Later, Mr. Kim tells his wife to expect visitors at their home in the evening. After everyone eats their food, I see the daughter and mother staring at me. The mother says something aloud and Mr. Kim translates. He says, "You are a beautiful woman, but females in South Korea do not compare." Mr. Kim continues to explain that his wife and daughter both had plastic surgery to look better. The South Koreans have visual expectations of how a woman needs to appear. Soon after I hear the information, Mr. Kim asks that I provide a photograph to present to the military personnel.

After eating breakfast and there is discussing of image, Mr. Kim leaves his home early about 8 a.m. I am uncertain what I need to do, so I watch what Mrs. Kim does. She is busy cleaning the dishes and preparing various foods in the kitchen. Two hours pass, and I hear knocking. Mrs. Kim responds to the thump and opens the door. There is an elderly couple, and Mrs. Kim bows when she sees them. She motions the couple to enter her home bowing as the same to her husband; the traditional bow is also for the Elders. It displays veneration as part of the Korea's pecking order. When the elderly man begins to speak, Mrs. Kim put her head down to listen. This is her way of following a man's directions. As the elderly woman has more years than Mrs. Kim, she also puts her head down when listening to her. Eventually, words between exchanges. Then the older couple looks at me, and I also lower my head downward. Soon after, the older couple and Mrs. Kim resume their conversation for about forty-five minutes. After, the elderly couple takes leave. Mrs. Kim returns to the kitchen and continues to prepare dishes in the kitchen. I cannot do much because there are barriers in communication, but I learn to roll the rice into dry salted seaweed leaver.

School Routines: The day moves speedily, and the Kim family's teenagers do not return from school for suppertime. I wonder where they are. The executive and his wife sit down at the table to eat supper. They do not have worries about their children's whereabouts. At 10:00 p.m., Mr. Kim's children return home. I find this abnormal because I know my mother would never have allowed me to stay out that late on a school night. I am unclear what is taking place, but I assume the youths tire and head to sleep right away. Instead, they first come to eat and do not retire for the evening. I get up at 3:00 a.m. to use the rest room. The light is still shining in the children's rooms. The following morning I ask Mr. Kim why his teenagers do not go to sleep earlier on a school night. He replies that they are preparing to bet into a well-known university. Mr. Kim says competition is fierce and a need to study exhaustingly to enter university. He adds the whole family moved to a smaller house to be nearby the school allowing their schooling routines to go mysteriously at 6:00 a.m. They go to school early in the morning to receive tutorials. Then they attend classes and afterwards do their homework. The Korean youths have little time to relax. His words contradict patterns I see when I go outside. Teenagers socialize at the shopping malls, but the Kim children act differently. Are they an exception?

Korean Lifestyle (Outside): Apart from the Korean home life, I see what takes place outside the household. I pay attention to how the children and youths get instruction. Through conversation, I learn what they think – from the influence of technology, advanced education and beliefs.

In passing, I see some Korean elders frowning at a foreign couple having a romantic attachment. They kiss is in the public subway. Some of the youths watching, remain quiet. They do not appear distraught by what they see. People pass by and do not take notice. As culture has its blemishes, I notice

South Korean youths are noisy and long-winded. Their behavior compares to a copy of Chinese youths. I also see many young women wearing the shortest pants possible. They are showing off their long, thin legs. Strangely, the young women do not have low necklines, but their dressing style infers there is a double standard of modesty.

Outside the Kim family, Korean behavior seems consistent. Elderly people have reservation in what they say. They try not to disagree in public, but occasionally there are public outbursts such as domestic abuse or drunks. As a rule of thumb, people do not behave rowdily for too long. Arguments stop quickly. Surprisingly, young people approach me as if I am a novelty. In fact, they want to practice their English skills. Their expressions are difficult to understand. They are usually too wordy or they speak indirectly. I suspect this comes from cultural interpretation. They avoid offending another person.

Assuming habits I detect, I keep thoughts within. Sometimes, I hear oddities about girls getting cosmetic surgery. *The Korean Herald*, an English publication, also addresses that thirty-percent undergo plastic surgery. Appearances are an emphasis. I find this uncomfortable for everyday conversation including getting a job. The Koreans consume too much time addressing image. In fact, youths attach their photograph to their resume stressing appearance. Scrutiny of a person's image becomes the basis of evaluating a person's opinion. In South Korean society, a person's snapshot becomes the focal point of consideration. Hobbies are also sensitive. They also highlight the opinions of people including Mr. Kim. He also asks my photograph.

Gaining Trust: I stay at the Kim's home almost one week. I want to know the position of the military intelligence. I hesitate to question him right away, as he provides a key to access their home. I can come and go freely. As I start absorbing more about the Korean culture than before, I am wondering how long I need to stay before gaining a contract to work for the military. I think I am going to approach Mr. Kim in week two. At least I have the opportunity to further check the surroundings around Seoul City.

On Sunday, Mr. Kim asks me to follow him and his family. I have no idea where I am going or what to expect. Since his children spend long school hours from Monday to Saturday studying, I think the family must be going to a retreat. I hold my thoughts from speaking aloud and follow the Kim family to their car. Mr. Kim drives about thirty minutes before he comes to a full halt. Next, the executive takes out a bunch of pamphlets written in Hangul. These are religious fliers asking people to attend his church. It is then I discover Mr. Kim has an expectation of me. He asks that I hand out these pamphlets to any passerby. I am in an awkward position. Mr. Kim's beliefs are not my faith. As I am staying at the Kim's home, I have a tie to handing out the fliers. I do not understand what it means, but Mr. Kim draws pleasure that I follow his directives, but I am subjected to parental control. Time to readdress positioning in the military. I wait for the right moment, and I ask Mr. Kim directly. He tells the South Korean military men are coming again the next day for follow-up, so I need to be patient.

Military Intelligence: During the 1990s, a woman's role in the armed forces has limits because of the Korean constitution and cultural restraints. In the early 1990s, there is abolition of the Women's Army Corps in South Korea. As a result, women assignments go to various corps of the army, the navy and the air force usually as nurses or office support. Therefore, if I am accepted to serve military men as contracted consultant and educator, I will be an exception. I am in South Korea in the mid-1990s and if I am accepted, I will be the first Caucasian woman living and working with the military. Naturally, social representation, cultural integration of women occurs in the male division.

Mr. Kim arranges that I meet the military personnel. Two uniformed military men arrive that evening at Mr. Kim's home. They are wearing prescribed South Korean uniforms with medals, badges and patches. The reflection from their achievements reflects pride, but their stone-faced appearance gives me slink. The men are tall, at least six feet three to five inches in height with a 50-inch chest. Both men weigh about 220 to 250 pounds (100-115 kg). The men arrive, Mr. Kim motions that I go to the kitchen with Mrs. Kim. The three men are in the living room area talking alone.

Mrs. Kim is busily preparing some traditional tea and biscuits. She signals me to bring them in the living room area where the three men are talking. I enter the living room, and it is clear the men are part of an inclusive society. As I draw closer, I wonder what they are thinking about me.

Mr. Kim gestures that I sit down with the men. The military men and Mr. Kim receive a cup of traditional *omij-hwachae* tea. I also drink a cup of the tea. I prefer this tea to the usual brewed grained teas made of corn and barley. I become an integral part of the man's group. This is significant for a female Also, drinking of the Korean tea stands for the chi (energy) surfaces creating links to nature (same as Japan). This meeting settles the result.

Through conversation with the military men, I discover that Mr. Kim is a by-product of what the Korean military model. He is wealthy and has a powerful father formally a Colonel in the military. Mr. Kim connects on my behalf making an impression earlier that these discussions take place before I arrive in Seoul.

Two weeks later, a man of important height dresses in military clothes and knocks at the door. He is a messenger providing notice that my paperwork is complete. I am accepted to work for the military intelligence serving the peacekeeping and Special Forces units. Instructions are in English. I am to report to the Admiral 대장 (大將 at named time and date. Even though, I am unfamiliar with the military, I am ready to start a new challenge.

I take the opportunity to thank Mr. Kim and two days later, Mr. Kim drives me to the military base. I take my luggage and bow to Mr. and Mrs. Kim before going.

As I arrive, the soldier at the gate asks Mr. Kim to halt. The soldier has a surprise to see me. Regardless, there are preliminaries that Mr. Kim has to do before I can enter. I take around fifteen minutes, and I am granted clearance to enter. I am directed to bring my belongings to where there is housing. Mr. Kim does not have permission to go past the gate. At that point, I am escorted by military personnel to the housing unit. Mr. Kim shakes my hand, says good-bye and leaves.

My housing sets apart from other men by a few feet. This gives me the first clear sign that treatment is also going to be different. The lodging is acceptable and images a North American one-bedroom suite with a balcony.

As I stick my head out the window, I can see wall-to-wall men. I did not even have ten minutes to settle in, and a military man knocks at my door. The man is burly-looking. He is the first greeter and delivers a rota of personnel that I would support, instructions and my schedule. The directives read that my assignment begins in two days. This time frame allows me to get some grocery shopping, so I can buy a few basic supplies.

The distinguished treatment shows up swiftly after I make necessary buys. I leave the military base to buy groceries and setup a household. I walk about twenty-five minutes to get transport to go shopping. Later, I return with a taxi, as the items are heavy. Unfortunately, the driver does not have permission to enter the military base. I have to heave my bags for a fair distance before I reach my home. It takes three trips to bring back all my belongings. I am getting tired walking and carrying heavy items, but the military men drive their vehicles directly into the premise without issues. No one on the base comes to help me. The third trip, I ride with one of the military men. They bring the rest of the items to my lodging, and an exasperating experience.

I am becoming aware of military routines. They are mostly learning to wake up at ungodly hours or using the rest room cautiously while men are still on duty. Of course, this does create some discomfort. The regime or military lifestyle starts before my shift begins. At 4:00 a.m. I am awakened by the sound of a bugle. I hear the patter of marching feet. Men exercise while it is still dark outside. There are an enormous number of men in motion, but I need more rest before fully waking up. I find it problematic to fall asleep with a racket taking place, but I am getting used to military existence.

Today is my first day, and I begin preparing myself to meet the men. The new turf is frightening as I am the only woman on the base. As I lock the door, some of the men are already causing a disturbance. Men whistle because I am female and others are muttering something under their breath. Some men are deliberately bumping into me. I do not like the distinguished treatment, but I cope. No matter where I walk, strange expectations come up. Men expect that I would be answerable to them at a whim. The military men call on the phone continuously. I find it difficult to get some rest. Then an event takes place that indisputably make me realize these men are not intelligent.

When the phone rings, at first, I answer it. The caller is a man that wants me to meet him. I explain it is after hours and discussion will be later. The man's voice expresses disappointment, but I hang up the phone. Then, a barrage of phone calls continues. I choose not to answer the calls. Nightfall comes quickly, and again at 4:00 a.m. I am awakened by the rooster's cackling and marching feet at the break of dawn. Is it my outstanding rooster friend that comes from Hong Kong? Regrettably, it is the marching military men.

On the first day, I introduce who I am and start with training. Afterwards, I return to my apartment. This repeats what takes place the day before. The phone continues to read and the buzzing sound does not end. The following day, I tell the men to respect my private time after work and not to call. After work, I leave the military base and go into the City to buy an answering machine. I am going to put a halt to the constant calling.

I return to the military base, thinking that men do not assume I am at their beckon call. The military men do not respond as I expect. Many men are aloof and act frosty. They behave like their Japanese counterparts assuming I can be a "comfort woman." They are unaware that I am Lily and I put a stop to their calling, and new for the men.

My role in the military is to provide an opportunity for men going to English-speaking domains, to become aware of cultural expectations. I am there to strengthen communications and bridge cultural gaps. I help men understand cultural protocols, especially gender relations. I help to handle the move and practices abroad (food buys, schooling, academic affairs, staffing including family, workplace practices, driving) and address other business-related topics too. I am also culpable for reviewing relevant materials the military provides and offer opinion. I am also asked to assess psychological military-related strategies and create customized training sessions. Later, I get permission to develop a pilot program. This is to introduce military men to dignitaries.

Gender Relations: In dealing with the unfamiliar, there are times I experience awkwardness. There is no separate rest room for a female. I have to wait until the rest room is clear before I can go inside. I bravely enter the male domain and I never know for certain if a man is inside. Since the issue of comfort presents itself, I decide to customize a session on gender relations. This session covers two groups of men. They are coming from the Peacekeeping and Special Forces units. These men have a superb command of the English language. They range in age from twenty to fifty-five years old. Some younger men are friendly. I overlook advances because no other women on the base. I am not influenced by their flighty behavior. Instead, I pay heed to their competitive behavior and how to reach them. The men usually get their way with women. I am not one of their typical women. I customize programming for men, contrary to what women usually do in South Korea. I begin with a probing discussion addressing a woman's image in North America. I ask them what they think about the women in their lives. I receive responses from the men in their twenties and thirties. They comment how they love their girlfriends, fiancés or marriage partners. Also, they say the women in their lives are beautiful. The men put their women on a pedestal. As for the older group, men in their forties and fifties, their responses are drastically different. They champion the idea there are radical changes taking place in their lives. The men share they do not appreciate the women in their lives as before. The older men highlight that as a woman ages her image is less attractive.

After hearing the men of different ages respond so differently, I decide to use an analogy to help them understand a different belief. At our session, I start by showing the group a beautifully adorned cloisonné vase. I ask the men to imagine the cloisonné vase symbolizes the form of a woman. I briefly explain the vase has equal appeal, shape, color, texture and to satisfy what is inside.

I query a few men on gender-related issues and oversee their replies on a whiteboard. I make the men tell what they are thinking about when they first meet girlfriends, wives or significant women. I record the information and chart the findings by defining the data into three columns. In column 1, I record the age of the military men. In column 2, I document the place they meet a woman whether in public or private. In column 3, I register information about the degree of likability they experience with a woman or women. The data forms patterns and a discussion follows.

The men give varying responses. The largest inconsistency is in column 1 and defines age. Most men claim their new female acquaintance regardless of age, is extraordinary. In column 2, the common places for meeting women include employment settings, on campus at school, the marketplace, a preferred restaurant or a religious setting. In column 3, the men rate likability of their woman on a scale from 1 to 10. One is least likable. Ten is most desirable. When I receive all the data, I compare the results.

I reiterate the cloisonné vase symbolically represents the beauty of a woman. I explain a woman's image, interior or outward, is alike over the years. Extra cracking lines, and breaks overtime, happens when the cloisonné vase experiences tampering. The cloisonné vase has the tendency to change depending on what men pass on.

The men digress about loving a woman. They voice that love is intense in their youth, but changes result unfavorably over time. I go on to clarify the internal hollow shape of the cloisonné vase symbolically is the spirit of a woman. Spiritual connections men hold with a woman or the metaphorical vase. I want them to deduce what they put into the cloisonné vase (the woman) is what they get.

Unfortunately, the older men continue to focus on how an aging woman's facial and body features changes are reasons for death. Men in the late forties and early fifties fail to grasp that they are also changing in appearance too. The forty plus group forms a consensus. They share a younger woman changes the vibrancy. Youthful women please and demand less than their spouses or significant other. The older Korean men stipulate that women are also less worthy than men. They say a woman is a commodity for men. The discussion continues and I explain North American opinions about healthy couple relations. People remain loyal because they believe in making vows to stay together in good and or bad times. Men that become infidel consider being indecent and violate the basic understanding. I continue by sharing a woman in North America receives instruction to get a partner that cares about her throughout their life. She makes a choice as does a man to be together.

The men in the group think understanding is bidirectional. They want to prove their thinking, and invite me to see their ritualistic practices, in the evening. I am curious what the men will show me and how they keep their affairs private. The men want me to see their emotional and personal side, so I accept. I am only one woman among a large group of men. The oldest man in the group takes the lead. There are six taxis heading with twenty-four men assembled. As I enter the taxi, I am the twenty-fifth person. I tell the men that a lady goes first in Western society. The men smile, and allow me to enter before them. The taxis stop at an odd place, a narrow alleyway. The men and I walk on a thoroughfare. Somehow, I believe something strange is going to happen. There is a long, winding trek. My feet are getting sore, and the trail begins to curve. Finally, a man shouts that we are about to arrive. Everyone stops in front of a heavy iron-cast door, and the leader clangs at the knocker. A man responds to the knocking sound, and he directs us to go ahead. Our group heads into a large room. This is where I expect to meet the significant women in the military men's lives.

Someone is directing the men and me to a large room. Inside, there are several long tables. The tables have an array of aesthetically pleasing food without any plates or cutlery. A few minutes later, several women enter the room. They come in modeling, and I am uncertain what is going on. I am having doubts that these are the women that usually partner with the military men.

Soon after, a young woman speaks to me in English. She is a college student and asks me what I am doing there. I am perplexed by her question and ask her the same. We converse for a brief time, and I learn I am in a brothel. This is a place where women make their living by entertaining men, so I gasp. As I am in a crisis, so I decide to watch what takes place. Women continue to arrive in the room and model. Each man in the room selects a woman. Clearly, the men have a ravenous appetite. They want to secure a woman for the night. They begin by eating dazzling food and enjoy the company of the women they choose. Marital status is irrelevant.

I sit quietly and nibble on some grapes while viewing what takes place. Then, a man approaches me. He places his hand on my shoulder. I remove his hand and tell him there are many women to choose from, but I am not one of them. I see men choosing women and they are getting too close for comfort. I speak to the nearby women. Most tell they do this for a living because there are no other jobs for them. Men become too friendly. I thank them for their kindness and leave the scene. I know this is going to be a challenge the next day in class.

I have to offset what I know to keep the military men's attention. Since I do not consider myself a magician, I am wishing for a miraculous answer. I have to unravel the mindset of these military men. Indisputably, they act much like the Freemasons and Ivy League males. They all follow their leaders and their outlook surfaces as a happy-go-lucky fraternity that plays together. I bet Robin

Williams would have a field day creating a comic skit for this military base.

The next day I get with the men at intelligence school. I convince men of different expectations in English-speaking domains. I consider that an early clarification might put a halt to cultural gaps, at least temporarily. Regrettably, it does not stop there. The word gets around that I am curious about what the men think and this forms new interest in who I am.

The following day, I receive a gruff knock at the door. At first, I do not respond, but the rapping at the door continues. The knocking does not come to end. Instead, it becomes harsher. Finally, I go to see who is behind the peephole, I see a pacing soldier. He is rambling some words, but his soliloquy is noisy, so I open the door. The soldier gives an impression he is rehearsing Hamlet's monologue from William Shakespeare's play. The military man must be saying "*Whether 'tis nobler in the mind to suffer*"[125] or wait until I answer the door. I answer the door and the soldier glares at me with anger. He says I need to get ready to meet the demands of the Commander. I tell him to go away. I gently close the door. The soldier does not leave. He waits for five minutes to pass. Again, he knocks curtly on the door. His primitive urges are like an ape. He continues hitting the door several times again. I turn on my CD player and begin listening to Mozart's classical music. I hear him finally walking away, and I am at ease.

A few days later, after work, I hear a hammering sound. I looked outside and head to the balcony. Next, I check if the sound comes from the front door. I peer through the peephole and this time there is a Peacekeeping Officer. He politely asks that I respond by opening the door. I unfasten the latch on my door and open it slightly. I ask him what he wants. I also question him why he is creating a raucous during my off-duty time. He apologizes profusely, but explains this visit comes from the commander's order. He tells there is an Order for me to see the commander and an arranged limousine to pick-me-up in the next ten minutes. The man stresses to adhere to his directive. Of course, I am leery, but because I think it is richly serious, I follow the command. I ask the soldier to wait outside as I dress-up rapidly. I have no idea what the commander wants. I pause wondering if this has to do with Mr. Kim. I reason there is something wrong.

I dress conservatively and consider it is warm weather. The peacekeeping officer escorts me into the commander's Bentley; a luxurious imported car. The chauffeur drives about fifteen minutes, and the car halts.

I arrive at the commander's house. I can see a beautifully festooned array of flowers. Flowers are prolific for any gift-giving occasion. Interestingly, there are white **lilies**, stargazer lilies, tulips and other flowers. As I get out of the car, I am greeted by the commander's butler. He hands me a white lily flower and says this comes from the commander. Based on rumor, South Koreans believe the white lily flower means a person is regal, so I am flattered.

I am unsure about the truth, but the legitimacy is soon to unravel. At first, I am in awe seeing the butler wear his traditional South Korean clothing. The clothing is colorful with a *Cheogori* top reaching waist length. He wears a shiny red color band tied across his chest with loose matching pants. His outfit is appealing and surely the attire of an upper class. The butler wears one of the five traditional colors in Oriental cosmology. The red matches strength and fire. I am in mystification when the butler presents me with a **lily** flower.

The butler directs me to the waiting room. He tells the commander is expecting me. He is coming to join shortly. I follow the butler's lead and pass by a large dining room with a profusion of food, so I wonder what is the occasion. The banquet suggests other guests are coming. I see another car pull up. The commander approaches, I will soon find out the purpose of this meeting.

The commander is wearing his military garb and he has plenty of adornments and military insignia. I find this impressive and I am honored to be in his presence. At that moment, the commander asks that I remain seated. Then, he says in impeccable English, he wants me to join him for supper. I am surprised at the commander's invitation. I ask when the other guests are coming. He smiles, and says no one else is coming. I am startled. I ask him where is his wife, and why the immediate invitation. He explains that his wife has some personal shopping and is returning later. The commander tells that he prefers to immediately meet two military attachés from Canada and the United States. He knows that I can be obliging and fulfill his need, adding that I may launch a pilot project intended for military men to meet diplomats. He says I have ideas to heighten communication and understanding. The commander approves that I can go forward. He voices the opportunity for military is worthwhile. They need to be proper introduction to diplomats. Based on his response, I accept his supper invitation and agree to carry forward his needs. I add that following proper protocol is a need as he is the model for many military men on the base. Therefore, his compliance is also a need to regular proper manner. I ask that in future, he give enough notice for meetings that conduct afterwards.

I also stipulate that after dining, I expect his driver to bring me back to my home. He nods agreeing.

We advance to dine. The food is scrumptious. As I complete the meal, I thank the commander and tell him I must leave. He asks that I stay a little longer because he has something exceptional to present. I am calm and silent, and I wait to see what comes up. His butler arrives with a box that has a pink wrapper. I am immediately alerted. In South Korea, the pink color stands for happiness and love. Naturally, this wrapping infers something inappropriate, but the meaning depends on the giver. As the commander is a married man, his present automatically suggests his wish for a love affair. Further, he pleads I open the packaged gift instantly. I know his presentation goes against the traditional grain of South Korean protocol. Opening the gift in front of the giver is disrespectful.

Since the commander travels to many foreign destinations, I assume my sixth sense is wrong. Therefore, I open the box. I am immediately astonished by what I see. A 24-karat bracelet with an exquisite design. I know this must have been expensive, so I lift my eyes and look at the commander directly. I tell him that I cannot receive such a gift, but I have an expectation that his wife wear this bracelet. In fact, I tell him that she must wear the bracelet the next day or I will let her know that he had ill intent. I explain if he chooses not to follow my mandate, I am not going to arrange a meeting with the military attachés. I tell him gift giving is for a lover (wife or a mistress). My gut instincts confirm he knows. He has to comply with my wishes and respect follows. In turn, I arrange for him to meet the military personages.

The pattern of how men treat women in South Korea almost flows in the mainstream of society. This is no different from what the officers show me earlier, in Korea's past. The expectations are that that women obey their spouses. A husband abuses (physically or mentally) or has another woman. The commander models this behavior. He is typifies how women are toys.

History of South Korean Male Behavior: In reality, I often see Korean men acting aggressively. I recall a Korean man beating his wife in public. He probably drank excessively. The man did not stop assaulting her and I had no idea how to stop such atrocity. No one dared to step in. A woman howls from a man's brutality, and the scene is unbearable.

In the past, South Korea documentaries underline the acceptable treatment towards a female. An example includes sexual abuse in "*the Hanguk's story.*" [126] During my contract with the military, the men share an archived video in collection. The story depicts a wealthy woman a few hundred years ago. The woman is unattractive, and a marriageable age. Her parents arrange for her to marry a Korean man in a nearby village. This man cavorts with many women. He is uncouth and a gambler. A handsome man is not a match for a rich, caring woman. Irrespective, the man's family decides he should marry the woman because his gambling reduces to poverty. The film discloses the man's character. He has no wish to be with this rich woman. He only likes that he can become instantaneously rich and gain control of all her assets. Once, the man marries, his gains entitle him to her wealth. Soon after, his true colors show. He gambles all the woman's assets and fornicates with other women in her presence. When the woman no longer can tolerate his abuse, she returns home, hungry. The father decides to teach her a lesson. He beats her and says she is the property of her husband. This video authenticates what generation to generation learns.

In World War II, Korean women receive force to be the comfort women for Japanese men. In 2009, the escape of "*Bang Mi Sung* " [127] from North Korea. She was a former actress and fled male abuse. In 2010, the movie *Harmony* gets promotion in South Korean theaters. Another good story of a woman physically receiving abuse. In all these settings, I am not in position to change history or handle public abuse, but to have empathy.

Outcomes of Male Behavior: These events cause me legitimate concern. I research and discover there are ubiquitous patterns in female treatment, in South Korea. Women celebrities are even best known for killing themselves because of abuse. They include Korean Lee Eun-Joo on Feb. 2005. In 2007, *Yuni, Jan and Jeong Da-bin.*In 2008, *Ahn Jae-hwan"* [128] and "*Choi Jin Sil is the country's cinematic sweetheart"* [129] Choi Jin Sil is a recent symbol of the difficulties that women face in South Korea, in a technologically-savvy society. The amounts of female deaths are astronomical. Deng Shasta, journalist reports *"South Korea has the highest rate of female suicide among the member countries of the Organization for Economic Cooperation and Development."* [130] This information comes directly from the Finance Ministry and Statistics Korea. In 2008, Shasta extracts data reporting that 18.7 out of every 100,000 South Korean women commit suicide. Thus, the female gender identity issue is a serious problem for society. No doubt, shady contributions are *a result of trade relations with other patriarchal countries that also treat women as inferior.*

My head spins with endless grief in South Korea. To some extent, I am enjoying being among the South Korean men, although, I change my mind when I experience disrespect. I understand the men have desensitization to care. Thankfully, I am not a South Korean woman, but this outlook is widespread even in North America.

Social Models: The social attitude is *Kibun.* Namely, a group consensus to have a harmonious atmosphere. This expectation extends into all facets of Korean lifestyle. Korean expectation of harmony means even telling a *white lie* (a lesser feint) to avoid conflict. Therefore, I have to be on guard as I am still viewed as a woman irrespective of origin. I am prone to concern always. I know whatever I say can be a misinterpretation. I do feel a hindrance when I realize the Koreans are always watching how I or other people follow the group to be part of the in-group.

When I receive an invitation from the military men to visit the Wollyubong Mountain, I accept and this is when I see how *Kibun* works. First, I head out to the scenic flower festival on the road to Hwagae Villages in Gyeongsangnam-do Province. Coincidentally, "*Hwagae*" (花開: blooming flowers) means "a village where flowers bloom."[131] The cherry blossoms are one of the top five cherry flower spots in Korea. No doubt, the cherries came from Japan as an offering of friendship. In chasing wishes, I can wrap my fortune around a cherry tree.

Naturally, the fragrance of the ripe on the mountains and hillsides offer some picturesque decorum. I shadow the men and enjoy the cherry blossom road, almost like catching some sweetness. As in Japan, there are some incredible Shrines and I pass by Ssanggyesa Temple. As I hike along the mountain trail, I reach Bulilpokpo Cascade. This is an attractive spot when I pass Jirisan Mountains. The cherries are hiding in a narrow valley and the sound of stream water is refreshing. As I get to Wollyubong Mountain, I seize sight of the royal azalea flowers. They are visible everywhere with brilliant bright flaming red flowers, sometimes, referred to as Ruby Princesses and Mandarin lights. There are hues of mauve, bubble-gum pink, orange, and white. The landscape has the same reflection of Katya Gridaeva Sherpard's still life paintings. This artist has a like distinction to reality depicting life as beautiful in its ever-changing beauty, with all its diversity of color signifying life everlasting. Were the Korean men trying to suggest something more to me than I imagined?

As I follow the men, their path takes a turn to an eloquent restaurant. As a guest of the Korean men, I follow their tradition by removing my shoes. I walk on the slippery hardwood floor and think I am on a skating ring. My imagination flickers back and forth as I watch the men and women of all sizes sit down directly on the floor's surface. The men put their legs under a low-leveled Tea Table and slide on the floor to seat comfortably. I go with the men and I wait for the leader of the military men to arrive. Then, lower our heads as a sign of respect to Mr. Park, the oldest man. His invitation brings delight to all participants.

As in Mr. Kim's home, there are many small silver dishes with colorful items being served. They include dozens of spicy vegetables that grace the table. Some variations include *Kim chibokkeum* and dried squid. There are anchovies, *joijim*, steamed fish, *Jpachae* translucent starch noodles and *Bolgogim,* a marinated grilled steak dish. The server brings long stainless steel chopsticks or *jeokkarak* (젓가락). These are more practical and sanitary compared to the Chinese and Japanese chopsticks, but I find them slippery and harder to eat food. Once Mr. Kim begins to eat, I am stirred to taste all the splendid flavors.

The men relish the food they eat. They are also drinking a strong alcohol beverage and becoming exceptionally rowdy. I am not sure what to do. The headwaiter brings in *Soju* and the men steadily change for the worse. They are drinking a ten to twenty-five percent proof colorless alcohol. I am offered to try it. The taste corresponds to Japanese *Sake*, or rice whiskey in Thailand, Vietnam, China, Taiwan and other Asian countries. Unfortunately, the *Soju* is creating gusto for the men. They are laughing hysterically and start babbling in foul tongues as they eat without end. The alcohol keeps making its rounds. Some of the men look in my direction and call me *Azumah.* I think they have forgotten who I am. Their merriment continues. A soldier passes *Soju* to me again. I do not want to be impolite, so I taste it quickly. As I drink the alcohol, the tang is sharp. It gives off a burning sensation and after a few sips, my head begins to gyrate. My reaction is not pleasing, so when the men continue to offer *Soju*, I refuse. I know my toleration level. The men dislike that I do not trail them. They use inappropriate language, so I worry what might take place next. I know it is time for me to leave, but the men keep drinking.

The smell coming from drunken men is ghastly. Some fireworks hit and men already behave erratically. Luckily, I leave and go to the famous kiln sauna or the *Han jeung mak*. This is where I try to release stress from the *Kibun* experience. While I am at the sauna, the earlier crisis makes me reflect on the time I spent in China because the women in South Korea also appear rough looking. These women wear lacy bras and matching underwear, but their body frames is powerful and large. They probably can easily squash me and I mull that some might be men in disguise. I do not take on any grueling routines they might do, but at least this place is where Korean women can go. I try to reduce anxieties, while the Korean women get extremes beautification massages. I guess they are trying to perfect themselves for their mates. After I feel refreshed from the spa, I decide to exit.

I take path where I think there are no people. Suddenly, I hear a deafening, howling, sound. I am curious where the sound originates. It is getting stronger and sharper as I walk forward. Then, I hear some barking dogs. At a distance, I can see bunches of wolf-like dogs crunched together in kennels. They transport dogs into a truck. I am not sure where they are going. As I turn around, I bump into some military men from the base. I ask them where the canines going. The military men look at me strangely. They say, "These are not pets." Three soldiers bring me closer to see what is taking place. I am a leery what to expect. I am overcome at what I see next.

Shockingly, the dogs are hanging upside down and a man beat the dog with a whip. A man is lashing the dogs repeatedly and the dog is howling in pain. Simultaneously, the man uses a soldering iron to burn the animal's skin while the creature is alive. I have a hard time tolerating what is taking place. I ask the man to stop burning the dog, but he laughs. The man continues striking the dog ferociously. My mind races because I think about dogs as pets. Horror suggests 'uncaring' crops up again. The Korean men treating or transporting the dogs imply the canines are worthless. Harming dogs easily equates to being able to torture humans without difficulty. I feel faint and gasp for air, but this does not change what takes place.

After I view the cruelty to animals, I can understand that being heartless to woman is a cultural habit. I have flashbacks of Sue's husband. He isolated her in their home. Later, Sue's placement is in a home for Elderly. There were no friends or family around to support her. This scenario seems equally callous and without mercy. Sue's treatment is equitable to warehousing a dog. She is forgotten as laudable and no different from a dog. She experiences butchering and burying as these dogs. The soldier adds the dogs are to create a brew. They mixture supposedly increases male prowess acts. They obviously mirror Machismo, the Ivy League, the Good Old Boys Club and the Freemason outlook of comradely supporters.

Pilot Program – Introduction to Diplomats: Since the commander asks earlier to create new patterns of thinking, I am about to adventure into new terrain, as does Dr. Kearns. I realize that some of the officials lack understanding about otherworld frame of references. Therefore, I am determined to create a pilot program that matters. I want the military men to get a glance of how to build success with dignitaries. Therefore, I arrange meetings with government officials to ensure access to personages coming to the military base. During my first contact with diplomats, I explain the intent and the projected result of the pilot project. I am confident that this project will reduce some of the men's preconceived notions. In tries, I also plan to expose them to diverse appearances and customary practices. I consider distinguished individuals that have varying hues of skin and hair.

To introduce my prime intent, I begin by visiting various Embassies. I arrange appointments and talk directly to Ambassadors. I explain people often misread intent. Therefore, I hanker after creating **new patterns of thinking** as Dr. Robert Kearns might do. A few Ambassadors agree and I fix the date, and time.

The day arrives and I group twenty select-military men at five separate tables. I arrange one dignitary at each table to represent diverse country norms. I start the program with introductions. I explain to all taking part that this is a first time effort to collaborate and gain better understanding compared to what they may know. As I am culpable for all the Ambassadors arriving, I am also viewed by the men to address any unfamiliar issues arising.

Limousines with country insignia arrive one-by-one. Each driver stops at the entry gate for security clearance. Then, they come to connect with the military men in a fixed location for this setting. Diplomats from Hungary, Canada, Ecuador, and Italy check in. A diplomat from Nigeria does not arrive. There is blockage for him to access the military base. The soldier follows instructions. He does not allow the Nigerian Ambassador access. I have no idea why this happens. I checked with the commander and high-ranking military men to gain approval earlier. The authorities make an earlier agreement to allow entry, but they change their mind in the last minute. They do not let me know why and I am at loss for words what to say or do.

I begin to evaluate what are the possibilities for exclusion. Nigeria has two-hundred and fifty ethnic tribes. I question if one of these ethnic tribes cause offense unintentionally to the South Koreans, I receive no answers, so this remains to be an enigma. Could it have been the most dominant ethnic groups like *Hausa, Yoruba orIgbo* caused harm? Tension harbors and the Nigerian Ambassador leaves on his own.

The incident creates some undue havoc for all the other parties present and sways the mood for the military men. One Korean military man guesses the Ambassador does not have the right to come. He has dark-skin. This damaging thinking is an oxymoron for peacekeeping and intelligence. Another man vocalizes the Nigerian man is not suitable. He clarifies that races compare to cookies baked in the oven. The white color or the Caucasian race is too pale. They do not compare to the dark cookies because they are an extreme hue. He postulates the only perfect cookie is the shade between as Asians, the preferential race. Regardless, the notion is as harmful as a Nazi philosophy.

I oversee what follows to ensure there are clear deductions about varying cultural expectations and habits such as family values. Unpredictably, I discover the men are much less aware about other people's nationalities than I conjure. They hold onto deep prejudice more than I envisage. I did not foresee that I had to act as a referee to avoid flare-ups or clashes that come up. Instead, the men are engaging with a foreigner government emissary.

Table One - There is a Canadian diplomat telling the Korean Military Attaché he does not have Korean roots. The Korean man is insistent the Canadian envoy must be akin to Koreans. The hostility between the men heightens. The Korean colonel insists on telling the Canadian-Italian that he has Korean blood. The Korean places his hands on the head of the Canadian. He tells the Canadian legate that his hair is as black as his own. Their exchange causes rage when opinion differs. The Canadian dignitary also takes offense to the Korean man touching his hair and it is nerve-wracking. The man repeats himself. As a result, I redirect thinking to focus not a person's origin, but to identify what they have in common. I change their conversation by focusing on their common interest. When the transition does not go smoothly, I suggest the Korean colonel address what kinship means to him. This creates a shift in their discussion allowing conversation to flow easily. I ask them to use soft tones in their speaking and to keep their hands to themselves. I know grown men should understand but I have to explain touching is punishable by Law in some countries. Their conversation comes to a lull; I direct one of the Koreans to talk about the famous park in Seoul. In this park, people's names connect. Before he begins, I ask the Canadian to think about his family members, and what might impact emotional expressions favorably. The interjection allows the men to pause for thought. Thus, I redirect the men's beliefs to have camaraderie. In candor, these adult men behave similar to children in their terrible twos.

Table Two - The Hungarian Ambassador reacts poorly when the Korean asks him to sit down on the floor. The Hungarian dignitary dislikes the Korean etiquette because he is uncomfortable. The luminary is a heavyset man that probably feels awkward sitting on the floor under a low Table. I picture that he worries about knocking legs or tipping the balance for others when getting up. At this point, I intervene. I suggest that both men be compromising by sitting in the Korean traditional style. I suggest the next time, Korean man uphold the Hungarian tradition of sitting in a manner of the emissary's choice. I explain being respectable is important. Their facial expressions show they are not content. They display increasing anger and do not want to control their emotions. I scale down their sentiment by raising my eyebrows, wrinkling my forehead and have a troublesome look. There are no words spoken, but the men realize.

Afterwards, I pull out a Korean Yearbook from the institute with many photos. This automatically opens the lines of communication. The Korean officer takes the initiative to explain the photos when he is younger. In turn, the Hungarian man takes out snapshots of his family. Through the simple introduction of visual frames, the men sit contently together on the floor. They find a common ground and the men are at ease. Their conversations move along well. The men tune into being respectful.

Table Three - Two of the men do not wait for my presence. Instead, they begin discussing women. The men start the conversation while I am checking on what is occurring for the Nigerian Ambassador. When I arrive at this table, the Ecuadorian man is already agreeing with the Korean colonel. They say, "American women are far too aggressive," so they focus on Machismo values. When I hear what is taking place, I remind both men that they have lovely wives. I ask them to take out photos of their family members and this spurs positive as in table two. Thankfully, I sidetrack their negative thinking to introduce interest in family rearing, schooling, and sports.

Three tables have a jump to talk when I have to check on the last dignitary. Naturally, political issues raised tension. Therefore, I maneuver bias thinking to achieve the immediate aim, namely, gearing a favorable exchange of ideas between human beings. I have an inclination that I an Olympic runner holding a torch in the air and running several laps, but I cannot make all the strides I crave. Concurrently, the pilot project does help the men better and understand something more about different nationalities than before. Of course, political issues remained on edge. I may not soothe this problem, but forward thinking is starting to take place.

I contend that it is step-by-step to look for **new patterns of positive thinking**. At least, the project also decides when bureaucracy, politics, stereotyping, and how people respond, it is best to produce new directions of thinking satisfactorily. The men do improve their channels of communication from earlier times. Notably, when personal connections prove, at least, the local bathhouse as a congenial place for all the men to have fraternal connections.

To sum up, the reality of communicating effectively, regardless of people of prestige, it boils down to having the **right mediation tools**. I suppose this works well when embracing good thinking. I discover later that I also incorporated the success model the Canadian Forces Conflict Management design uses. Immediate consideration is the organization and the countries draws on. In the military base, the principles are of obedience and ethos.

In 2011, the Canadian Forces show their perspective when Mohammed Ibrahim, organizer of the Taliban movement and Lieutenant Colonel Hope, of Canada both has an interest-based communication. As in the interpretation I make, the men have common interests. Discussion is on farming, their children, and hopes they have for them. Communication turns out to be rewarding. Both men discuss deeper values and what motivates them. The private conversation cements a foundation of deeper trust. Ibrahim sends favorable messages to his group to renounce rebels and thanks the Canadians. It is hard to fathom the pilot program I develop in the mid-1990s copies what I do in 2011 in the Canadian

Forces. Potential for re-humanization and team-building and exchange of ideas. The men learn to understand through exchanges (body language, arbitration tools). The men work out their own **interest-based** conversations regardless that they are both warriors. Therefore, the humanity issues make a difference when there are lessons that teach men tolerance and awareness. Foreign trade and international trade Canada continue to focus on several conflict prevention and mediation initiatives. Was I instrumental in creating a chain of thinking from the mid-1990s? I consider "*in trial and error diplomacy*— (there is) *better management of shared borders.*"[132]

As for Table 4 and Table 5, I interpret that awareness of the men is a result of parental influence. This is comparable to all the famous men – Dr. Patch Adams, Winston Churchill, Albert Einstein, Dr. Robert Kearns, Mozart and Robin Williams. They all discover new angles of thinking, and because of it, they become creative people. Challenges lead individuals to become fighters for what they believe. From here, all the celebrities add strength for people to think using new patterns of thinking. I have an innate force and so do you (the reader) to experience a greater awareness than before.

Several years later, I return to South Korea to receive two incredible gifts. I gave birth to lovely twins and I have a dual soul connection with them. The memories of my adorable twins and the military regimentation keep circulating in my mind. At the hospital, I face a crude awakening. No matter how common men may feel, they still undermine women. It is during the delivery of my twins, I am stripped naked. I have no cover going to surgery. I miss my privacy, but now, I am the same as a Korean woman. Instead, I am an object of study and experimentation for men.

I am placed on a rolling bed and several male medical students push me rapidly through a moving tunnel. There is a light projection coming ahead and the anesthetic is kicking-in. I am becoming light-headed and a strange sensation takes place. The male doctor has hesitation to tell the gender of my children. I am fearful if a child or the twins are going to live. I am a female in a foreign land. I have no choice, but to adhere to what the doctor does. Will he remove the female fetus that I might be bearing?

Opinion does not count. Children's souls are uncontrollable. I am going to surgery unsteady. I imagine surfing above the water. I remember the foundation is the opinion of men. The deeper trust between men and women do not exist. Therefore, I let my soul take course, and luckily, I deliver a baby girl and boy. Thankfully, their soul connections cultivate on their own.

In the South Korean tradition, *daeboreum*, the children born in the first month of the lunar calendar and *Chuseok* marks celebrating the full moon and a mass departure for Koreans. They return to their hometowns to pay respects to the spirits of their ancestors. Thus, when I gave birth to my twins during the *Chuseok*, harvest, I receive the blessing of spirits. Therefore, I commemorate the birth of my twins to be the next photo in Sue's scrapbook. As "*in trial and error diplomacy,*" [133] the tiny eyes of my children greet the unity of all human races. I am the incubator of children and the creator of the pilot program under the protection of the moon and cherry blooms coming.

CHAPTER 20: The Northern Lights

ABORIGINALS SHIMMERING OVER THE WATERS

LEARNING TO TRUST

As a child, I learned to trust men like police officers, executives, and officials. There are many meetings with men, and I come to trust fewer males. Journalist Holly Buchanan says the issue of trust happens after a woman "*trusts (having) common experience.*"[132] Men, however, automatically trust authority, especially when they become a part of a regimented organization as the military.

I read what Buchanan implies about women. She suggests women make it a habit to tell their personal stories about their experiences. This makes a woman's reality more believable. Men need convincing proof to consider data trustworthy. In assessing Buchanan's commentaries, unquestionably you (the reader) can decide both the stories and the credulity offer the foundation to trust. In adding facts to the cloisonné vase story, I realize there is a challenge to open minds. I think analogy of metaphorical nurturing vase asks you (the reader) to judge if the chiefs of indigenous people also have the same self-interests as the men I introduce. You (reader) decide whether the facts or the story are believable.

To briefly recap, the cloisonné vase symbolizes the Spirit connection contained in the vase. The Naskapi call themselves Nenenot, meaning "*true, real people.*"[133] of the world. Naturally, implication of the most trusted people in the earth. Kiana is a writer for the Inupiat people. She argues that survival is the test of time. Getting to meaning has to do with connection to the spiritual world. The Inupiat Ilitqusiat movement understands that societal values change from the concern of people-at-large to having 'self-centered' thinking. This presents the issue of trust, and begins from family modeling. Regardless of gender, a child needs to feel the passion and even discipline. Stephen Corry of Survival International, reveals more than half the world's one-hundred indigenous groups have had no contact with the outside world. In fact, the most recent example is the Panoan Indian tribe. They live in the remotest parts of the Amazon rain forest, in Brazil's Acre State. In 2008, photographers publish pictures revealing red-daubed Indians wielding their bows and arrows. When the helicopters fly overhead and close to the ground, the sound probably scares them, disrupting their lifestyle. Simultaneously, the Panoan tribe compares to the likeness of aboriginal voice. The Inuit leader Ashini says the Inuit people experience intrusion on the people's lifestyle drawing question about the world's last no-contact tribe or the indigenous people of today. At least, I can decide what is more trustworthy and help you (reader) decide.

The aboriginal people tell a story that has effect on me. It begins when I meet many tribes. They all tell me that I am a child from "Mother Earth." All humans **live in harmony with every living creature** in the environment. In fact, the aboriginal people have a sixth sense. Their abilities track back to the jungle-dwelling Mayans. Prophesies allude to human behavior (bias, close-mindedness, altered awareness, egotistical attitudes values and changes). Even the Hopi natives tell that we live in the "*Age of Purification.*" [134] It is the time when three forces combine and end into total beginnings or extinction. The Lakota Sioux add their perspective. They foretell the birth of a "***Rainbow Tribe*** *that saves the earth from environmental destruction."* [135]

After meeting the Shaman priests or priestesses, I think the indigenous people believe in what they say about the future. They disclose dream interpretation and their power to heal the sick from the earliest known people. From collecting aboriginal thinking, I assume there is a common thread with Nostradamus and Edgar Casey. They deduce events of time in a cultural context and carry out spiritual practices, as well. Historically, the aboriginal people keep their secret knowledge. This is alike other cultures that correlate mystical beliefs, the Eye of Providence, the Holy Spirit, the universal way and nirvana to name a few. I recognize an aboriginal person having supernatural vision, likely has a spiritual guide. There is no limit to staying in concealment, just as the cloisonné vase stands alone.

The first time I meet the aboriginal people, I enjoy caring about them and sharing food. I am in amazement that when a family member kills a moose or large animal, the raw meat gets split up among as many families as possible. Before an animal dies, hunters claim having a connection with the animal spirit. The hunter asks permission from the animal to sacrifice their life and give food to the people. It is rituals such as sharing food to help confirm a balance in nature. Caring causes a sense of trust, especially when I feast with an aboriginal family. This comes from the strong bond among family members through warmth and trust. Since I am an outsider, the locals probably have difficulties understanding who I am, regardless that I come to help tribes in need. At least, I listen to what community members say. Apprehensions of outsiders come from reliving history and passing down the value to the next generation. Their rooted thinking considers how people see, expectations, how they fit in and the sixth sense.

SIGHT - Regardless, which tribe I come to offer a helping hand, the aboriginals see me as the Rainbow lady. Tribal story variations still keep the same content. They depict me as a powerful woman that is caring and a warm-spirited mother. Shamans tell community members envisaging the Spirit is guiding and helping me through all challenges. Eventually, I embark on my own journey with my twins. They say that my children never have any worries when they are with me. The aboriginal people say the almighty spirits know that I also come from the Rainbow tribe of past generations.

EXPECTATIONS - As for Aboriginal expectations, I do not recognize having any Spirit connection to a past tribe. It is hard for me to imagine the people think I am a Goddess. At the same time, I do feel a maternal love is growing. The related facts come from "*the Hawaiian petroglyphs of the "Anuenue Wahine {Rainbow Woman} known as ...the woman who sees all.*" The Cree nation says a "*Great Spirit....tells... why.*" [136]

FITTING IN - I begin marveling how the Aboriginals decide I fit into the scheme of their culture. The Shamans make public that I come deliberately to share a higher purpose. Assumption that humans (native and nonnative blood) get together as a tribe of people. This means I understand the transitions of colorful spirits and I have wisdom. The legend of the Rainbow woman does have slight variations depending on the tribe I meet. Essentially, it is a tale that describes the First woman Goddess creation. Men want the woman, but she prefers the Sun God. Naturally, she radiates from the rays of sunshine. The aboriginal people imply that I always carry the Sun God. In fact, an Eastern man fathers my twins while the Sun God arises from the East.

Interpretation does correlate with my life. I am attractive to men when I am young. Intriguing twist to the aboriginal legend complements their tale. In the East, the biological father accompanies me to a shop. I find a pair of twin porcelain dolls (a boy and a girl). I genuinely feel a magnetic pull. The doll pair gravitates interest because their images are blemish-free, so I buy the dolls. During this time, the father smiles at the choice I make. When we return to our house, he dubs the dolls a fertility wish, and hides them from me. He places the dolls in a dark closet. About a week after, I am pregnant with twins.

The aboriginals settle that I best compare to the Rainbow Lady. This makes me think about Charles Horton Cooley's theory. "*The concept is based on how we think others judge us the way we look and act.*"[137] Cooley intimates the workings of humanity are parts that fit together. People do not think alone. Instead, they reflect together and the aboriginal people's presentation of the tale causes pause to think.

THE MAGIC OF THE 6TH SENSE - I connect to Dr. Patch Adams bonding notions of love for all people. We are part of a magical quilt. Patches combine our expressions on a blanket. Maternal love is fewer as mothers are not present. Maternal or nurturing love counts the most! At least, the only replacements I can think about might be Disneyland's Nanny Mary Poppins, Nanny McPhee, or Franny the Nanny (Dreschler in the 1990s) are all female figures depicting maternal love. They are role models for fostering the magic of a child's life and the origin of my story starts with my journey to the aboriginal people.

I travel with my children on a meandering path of unpaved road for eighty-two jagged kilometers to get into the community. On occasion, there are enormous logging trucks swishing by. They leave blinding dusty trails resembling a tornado that swirls in our pathway. Immediately, my heart thumps, and I move my car to the far side of the shoulder. When the dust clears, I imagine hearing ghostlike cries. Instead, there is a deadly silence with gravestone markers. Trees stand upright as if they are the force of the magnificent Xian soldiers that rise from the underground. It is an eerie feeling seeing the stark nakedness of the forest. The dry bark remains because of an earlier forest fire, and trees freeze at the root. As I drive further on the road, the scenery changes. There are pockets of green spruce trees and blueberries flourishing. The images of sprawling trees and berries also mirror reflections in the lakes. The sky plays tricks as it creates cloudy portraits of people, places and children playing. As the nightfall draws closer, there is a mistiness that captures glowing dreamy hues. Trees and wildlife emerge as an image. The petrified trees, wildlife and land almost carry an impression of the Group of Seven landscape paintings.

A few hours later, I arrive in a small community where a handful of people gaze as I approach. I am unfamiliar with this setting. I recall someone telling me to go to a large greenhouse. When I see the home, I step out of my Car to see an elderly bearded man approaches. He introduces himself, and tells I am near my destination. The aboriginal man guides me to go down another sandy pathway, eventually leading to a house about five-hundred feet away from a small school.

I follow his directions and I detect the house in a desolate area with no people around. Two trailers nearby are in decrepit condition with boards covering windows. Trees tower over the house and the wind blows angrily leaving the house alone next to an empty lake. A close cavern likely once is rich in minerals. I carefully take steps around the backside of the house. As I mount some steps, I hear a crunch. The steps are rotten, but I manage to reach the door safely. Wind blowing continues with little effort as if to unfasten the door.

I enter the house, stunned to see a present-day home, in this countrified setting. Commercial carpets and linoleum tile are part of the layout. There are modern appliances for cooking, laundering, and refrigerating food. The windows have vertical blind coverings. Security wires snap off. There is no furniture inside except for a musty-looking orange couch ready for Halloween guests.

After a long drive, I am beat, and I prefer to lie down. Unfortunately, the beds I ordered earlier have not arrived. Luckily, I bring some cots, and this is where I briefly nap. Sixth sense tells me a spirit is in the dwelling. I hear a natural whooshing sound echoing in the air, and I imagine that Mother Wind is speaking to me in subdued tones. In chorus, I can hear the gentle sound of the rain pattering against the window and sounds of birds flying overhead and nature puts me to sleep.

In the morning, I am alerted by a loud knocking at the door. I am unsure, but I think maybe the winds reveal the marching sound of a stone-like Xian soldier surfacing, and I am not sure what the soldier wants to tell. I come to the door and there are two lively young people. These youths come to welcome us into the community. There is a twelve-year old boy. His sister is twenty-three years old. The boy is incredibly tall, appearing as the main character in the television show "*The Friendly Giant (1958-1985)*"[138] years earlier. Missing is seeing him in a huge castle and having Rusty the Rooster and Jerome the Giraffe nearby. The young boy says his name is Bob. His name matches the star's name in *The Friendly Giant*. Bob's voice sounds like a small child, but his welcoming actions show caring. He extends invitation to experience fishing, a magnificent to gain familiarity of the surroundings. After agreeing to attend, I prepare some sandwiches to take along and head toward the lake. Bob brings fishing rods, bait, and buys fuel.

We get into a large-sized motorboat fortuitously holding all of us. As we set out, the speed of the boat makes larger the thrill of adventure about to take place. The boat is pacing like a mammoth fish exhilarated by the sensation of the wavy waters. The weather sets the mood to relax and enjoy nature. The motorboat moves along the water. I can see gradients of brown, green and blue hues blending colors to be transparent, as if in a painting. As the boat picks up speed, the waves form foaming caps. Trees and bushes reflect their charm in the water. Seagulls and ducks take their places in the surroundings, adding sounds of nature in the distance. I can hear the screeching sounds of the seagulls acting as background music and a loon cries out.

Bob is a risk-taker as he stands up in the boat fearlessly. He balances and never fears the boat will tip over. He bellows mimicking the loon as a signal of spirits from above balance is in nature.

Afterwards, Bob sits down and slows the speed of the motorboat. Suddenly, halts and spreads out three baited rods. He sets them all into the water. In a short time, jerking on the fishing lines. The schoolboy begins tugging at the line. There is a fight taking place and combat lasts when a cyclopean-sized fish surfaces. His sister grabs the net and hauls the fish in the boat. Incredibly, this is a forty-pound trout and a prize catch. Bob holds up the fish, beaming with pride. His sister snaps a picture to keep the memory of the huge trophy fish. Unfortunately, according to Law, fish oversize goes back into the water. I take another photo for Sue's album. I think she would have a hard time believing how nature sometimes works.

Fish returning to the depth of the water need readiness of mind and the fish does not want to return home. Bob puts the fish back into the water, but the fish stays afloat. Seemingly, I picture the fish is weary from its earlier wrestle. The fish lies buoyantly as if it dies. The fish is so weary, but Bob persists to guide the fish downwards. He steers the fish into the lowest point of the water possible making several tries maneuvering the fish to gravitate into the depths of the water. The fish refuses to go. Bob repeatedly moves the fish until it finally immerses Bob's big catch. He decides to return to the land.

I am uncertain why the fish skirmish alone inclines Bob to return. Regardless, we return to land and with rocking motion, I can get back on land. Slowly, I mount the rocky surface and I head into my car. I transport Bob and his sister, May. Riding to their home is full of huge lumps and bumps on the way. I have to steer carefully and I think I am once again in the backwoods of Thailand.

I arrive at their worsened home. It is a simple wooden framed shelter. The property is rundown with unpainted slats, no indoor heat or plumbing. Unhealthy dogs run around in the neighborhood. I also see some construction trailers, where some families live for extended periods. Aboriginal people live alone, so their habits are also unalike from most North Americans.

Bob introduces me to his brother Mark as I pull into their property. May is cynical when she describes her older brother. She says he has fatal attractions to the wrong women. This is why he never completes his schooling. May continues to vocalize that her brother, Mark still experiences mishaps. He becomes especially unhealthy when there are influences from a woman that gains shamanistic practices from her father. He teaches her what he knows, and she uses magic inappropriately on Mark. Through association, her brother becomes different. His skin texture changes from being smooth and clear, to rough and having massive boils spreading all over his face. May appears upset and shifts to talking about another older brother. She says he is handling a forest fire nearby. Indisputably, the introduction helps me to know members in the community. I thank her for sharing and return to my home.

Following day, a heavy knocking is at my door. I find this rather spooky, so at first, I assume it is the rustle of the wind. Sounds come from the empty cavern and there is a booming sound ensuing. May be the real spirits are nearby. In fact, May calls late and tells about a legend. She says there is an old miner spirit buried in closeness to where I stay. I am not sure why she tells the story, but I think the likelihood of ghost does come to visit. I cannot imagine why this ghost might return, but some answers come the next day.

Morning expectation is students will register for school. There is something portentous taking place because absenteeism is excessive. Seemingly, the spirits the night before take action. They remove another soul to the spirit world. A youth becomes deceased in the early hours. Speculation is that a logging truck passes at high speeds. The dead man is merely twenty-three years old, and greatly liked by community members. Locals voice all possibilities for what occur. The storytelling is rampant with no certainty of the truth.

As I am the school administrator, from the window, I see some Royal Canadian Mounted Police. They are spinning their wheels in the area, and looking and marking terrain where the accident occurred.

I have no idea what transpires, so I call a trustee to ask if they know what has come to pass. There is no answer. I try to grasp what is going on. Nearby the school, there is a yellow marking outlining the shape of a human being and crime scene police examine. Then, the police authenticates that a young man dies and the body comes to the large green home. Local nurse identifies the young man. Afterwards, body flies by helicopter out of the community. Officials are going to conduct an autopsy, and police take a suspect into protection. According to the grapevine, the police track down the tire markings. They belong to Mark, Bob's older brother.

Gossip in the town spreads rapidly about what takes place. Some people blame it on the speeding logging trucks. Others connect Bob's older brother as being high on drugs. Aboriginals say partying and drinking gets out of hand. A drunk stabs the young man. Irrespective of the truth, the result is poignant and heartbreaking.

The school closes. I make a trip to the local store to get some milk. On the way, I see a group of people gathering. I continue driving and after a short distance, a community member stops me. I halt the car and listen to what he has to say. The man does not share too much, but says there is an earlier incident of a thirty-four year old youth. The adolescent drinks himself to death and incontrovertible toxic thinking is circling in the community.

No matter where I go, I hear community members rattling about the misfortune. They speak among themselves, and hardly look at me. At that point, I am considered to be an outsider. Discussion about the man is inclusive for family and community members. Information about the man's death spreads to nearby Indian communities. Earlier along my path before entering the community, I realize that a ferocious fire consumes many of the trees. This incident is like the news of a fire spreading ferocity, leaving only darkness and dismal picture.

A local hotel owner tells thirty years earlier, with a difference. This town is a prosperous mining community with about one-thousand five-hundred people. The community size changes when investments deplete. People pack up and move to other places. Homes are on sleds and shifts to a nearby reservation leaving a scanty seventy or eighty families remaining. Remnants of the past buildings still stand. There is a general store, a firehouse, a community hall and two recreational lodges.

The arrival of death leads people to believe the community is not memorable. The fact remains the young man dies on the same land where he becomes alive. Residents and former inhabitants in the neighboring towns and reservations come. The people arrive from a distance to give their reverence. Friends grieve and there is no doubt a dreary mood sets in. The dead man leaves a young wife and two children to fend for themselves. When I hear this news, I do not feel as if I am the powerful Rainbow Lady.

The relatives arrange a grieving spot where a vehicle hits the man. This happens to be nearby where I stay. It comes to mind when I hear strange sounds echoing, it could have been spirits the night before. The miner's spirit and elders come to take the young man with them. The hit-and-run incident happens so quickly. People set up the location and sit in a circle on hard chairs. Aboriginal custom compares to the practice of Shiva in the Jewish faith. The primary difference is that members in the community bring warm food for the grievers where an incident takes place and in the open.

In front of lamenting people, there is a large pyre of wood stacked up into a pyramid shape. The tradition of northern aboriginal people is to add composites to the wood to set it aflame. Locals tell that this represents passing the young man's spirit. Also, symbolically the spirit receives cleaning and compares to be similar to the customs of Japan's Zen temple. Earlier, the Japanese woman I meet at the temple told me the soul takes a journey for cleaning. I continue viewing. Some people bring sweet grass as an addition to the burning flame. Ceremonially, the sweet grass means purification. Supposedly, the sweet grass replaces the negative energy of the soul to have positive ions.

Symbolically, the sweet grass also suggests the hair of *Ogashiinan* or **Mother Earth** is significant. Chippewa mythology and the Anishinaabe have traditional secretive animistic beliefs. They practice three distinct visionary groups, namely, the Midewiwin, the *Midewiwin* or *Mide* and Waabanowin. As time progresses, some of their practices change. Yet, the emotions of people step up when sweet grass is aflame. The smoke spirals, and the scent of death is visible. Clearly, the misfortune inflicts pain on community members. Through this gathering, the grievers outpour favorable memories about the deceased man and people are cut-off from reality.

I like to bring the colors of the rainbow back into the Little Red Schoolhouse, but the dusty air continues to swirl from the ashes releasing from the pyre. Community members use this time to also gossip, and I become the center of their conversation. I am the newcomer. Unhealthy whispers zoom among the aboriginals spreading from ear to ear. I stop by the grieving area and offer condolences. I suspect this causes the people to hush their negative thoughts and I receive a visit that night.

At 11:00 p.m., I hear knocking at the door. I assume a drunk is at the door. Pounding continues with an expectation that I will respond. People in the community stay up late. I do not have this habit, so when the hitting sound becomes impossible, I come to the door. There is an aboriginal woman in her late thirties. She asks me to get microphones from the school in preparation for the memorial service the next day. Also, she asks I prepare some food and bring it to the community hall for a feat. Preparing the feast represents the dead man's final journey. This brings back memories of when I attend a funeral service in Thailand. Food preparation for feasting and gaiety seems so strange. I cannot handle this event as a joyful occasion. As I do not know the man, I decide to attend the memorial service but not the feast. I do not want old feelings of anxiety that I have of Thailand's funeral arrangements to return.

The following day, I query the school custodian. I ask for the whereabouts of the microphones. He utters there is no need to get them.

Some people bring their own loud speakers, impacting the children's schooling. They are not attending school and parents overlook their behavior as acceptable. Aboriginal community members commemorate the dead to be more significant than being present at school. Thinking reinstates when a handful of students arrive at 9:00 a.m. These children range in age from five years to twelve years old. Most of the children are blood relations, so no introductions necessary. The children's parents come from different occupations including lodge owners, guardians, local employees, and a handful of officials from the Indian council.

I pay attention to arriving children. They look similar in appearance to Asians. They have Asian features; jet-black eyes and hair with olive complexions. The children are enjoying playing outside, frolicking when I allow a small puppy in the playground. Children are no different. They are sliding, jumping or racing and all have a keen sense of social bonding. Then I realize playing and education is a tie-in.

During a difficult time and happiness, Conflicts still arise and it is political. It starts when a six-year-old child shows his wit. People in the community ostracize the child's inconsistent presence. Community members say the mother is a drinker and dislikes to bring the child to school regularly. Other people in the community think their child's education is far more critical than any government-run program. Parents are in disagreement about children going to school when a funeral takes place. Parents send children schooling while others do not. Finally, the majority wins and the children do not attend school. My opinions do not matter because I represent a government educational program that has lesser priority in their lives.

There are different personalities among the community members. I am amid a civil war. The political tension is compellingly forceful. There are clearly two distinct sides in the community. People party to the aboriginal network or unacceptable. Lodge owners, a couple in their thirties, elaborates. This couple belongs to the opposite side. This couple comes to the community after the man's mother commits suicide. The lodge owners expand about unhappiness taking place. The woman is lengthy in explanation, while the husband remains silent. On occasion, he nods his head. I hear more **nepotism** that takes place. Unfortunately, hiring of suitable talent to support community or the school supports are inadequate. I have to deal with available people that have few qualifications, an elementary grade three level or fewer. In 2010, the research of Andrew Sharpe and Jean-Francois Arsenault confirm the average aboriginal Canadian has a low standard of education. It is "*much lower educational attainment than their non-Aboriginal counterparts, with 43.7 percent not holding any certificate, diploma or degree.*"[139] I suppose this is why the former principal has only a high school education. As for the support staff, the natives hardly complete elementary school.

I know I have my hands full. I am dumbfounded by the difficult politics. People have shortages and only few understand learning objectives. I have no doubt the aboriginal children learn differently than most Canadians. I find reality about the youths traveling outside their community. I try to bring sunshine into the lives of these children, but I come to the realization I am an outsider. Locals gravitate in a world excluding an outsider. I feel like a turtle in a shell, not being able to prove the truth they need to accept.

I take a step further by analyzing the opinions of many indigenous people in the area. In reviewing a prepared 1994 document E/CN.4/Sub.2/ 1994/2/Add.1, I understand the Aboriginal people propose specific educational rights intentionally representing their own concerns. They want a legitimate guidance for locals and not include outsiders. The document infers the aboriginal people make their own educational choices. The intentional Law specifies "*the right of indigenous families and communities to retain shared responsibility for the upbringing, training, education and well-being of their children*"[140] is in conflict with getting better learning standards. Almost the aboriginal people have a lower educational attainment from start. Therefore, the Law does not consider the best interest for all parties. Also, their need to idealize me as the Rainbow Lady is also dead issue.

Among the children in the community, I watch how the children learn. In a classroom session, I ask them to expand about human origin. Aboriginal children cannot grasp how origins begin. Therefore, children easily take offense when features spotlight "attractiveness," but not necessarily the features of the first people. The young boy tells his parents that learning about a person's features is vindictive. The opinions of parents are different. Instead, they assume learning about other people is a deliberate to invoke racial slurs. The parents assume outsiders are evil. They believe aboriginal child are accurate and refuse to have faith in learning about humanity. Exploring human features is basic. Unfortunately, the parent's misinterpretation intensifies with no understanding. There is no likeliness to correct learning patterns and looks more like Bob's prize fish. Matters do not immerse downward immediately. They are buoyant, but new learning is dead. For that reason, a North American seeing cannot ignore the adult aboriginal modeling. Matters worsen and explaining this to parents that cannot read past grade three is a difference.

Positively, the children have interest in their environment. At least, they play in the dirt and go hunting. This is their preference rather than attending school run by the government. Thus, the children's education only adheres to ignoring outsiders and listening to parents and community members. Their core thinking is in synchronization with Asia's social face. The adults refuse to tell their children that they are not learning correctly to avoid conflict, but they also think lying is acceptable. People in the small community enjoy fighting overpower regardless of deprivation in learning or the result of death.

After seeing what takes place, I think it is time for me to introduce shadow play and exotic music. There is no rainbow in the sky, so I am uncertain what to do. People in the community habitually keep their heads down. Shoulders evidence posture sloping and out of balance. Aboriginal expressions are somber and without secrets. Here, the gossip culture assumes they are correct and an outsider is always wrong. Constancy is people dying because of mishaps or ignorance. The aboriginals remain on the edge.

Soon, all the people in smaller, remote aboriginal communities connect more with other aboriginals than listening to the media or any outsiders. Happily, I experience an occasion that a woman from a remote community strikes up a conversation. She is cooking her breakfast on a portable gas stove and approaches me. Aboriginal woman says it's a real enigma for a youth to be with the creator. The lady wants to share her beliefs, so I listen attentively. By recognizing her feelings, she tries to raise a spiritual connection. Through sharing, her emotional issues settles in her mind. At least, we have a common understanding. Our common emotional intelligence impacts, especially when there is a loss of a young man. The woman continues to tell me about her "vision quest" or what she envisages when looking into the fire. She says, there are images that speak to her. Naturally, the flames can pierce the imagination and the aboriginal woman remains in a confusion. She cannot understand why people cause harm. The implications clearly infer the young man's death should cause a person regret for destroying a young life. I remain humble and allow her to thinks about voicing what else is on her mind, but she says stops to say anything else.

By the communication the aboriginal woman shares, unquestionably some issues remain to be ambivalent. I am not sure if she means the death of the man is **a deliberate act of outsiders**. Regardless, I assure her that life is something that is unpredictable. The crisis weighs heavily. I leave the community to get some basic supplies about one-hundred and fifty kilometers away from the reservation. I leave early in the morning passing by the sleeping grievers and continue to trek. Noticeably, I also see the aboriginal people erect a teepee formation on the left side of where they sleep. The dead man's picture is on the right side. I keep this vision in my mind as I exit the reservation.

It am living as if I am an alien community. The road has a rock-strewn foundation, and I am experiencing the tides in the ocean of the aboriginal world. As I surf the road, there are increasing bumpy peaks. I move ahead, and part of my body is juggling. I am coasting the twisty path ahead and not certain what else comes up. I genuinely aspire to go quicker, but the tides of the road hold me back and so does progress. There are moments the steering cause's shiftiness and swerving along the meandering path. Then I come to a standstill. I am reliving my Thailand experiences in Saraburi, Non Kae, but this is more treacherous than I expect. I continue to travel forward. I see small, stormy clouds of dust scattering in the air leaving a sandy path for drivers behind. I am unfamiliar in this terrain, so I use a radio transmitter. I am ensuring there are no logging trucks ahead that can blow the car off into oblivion. Bumpy road ends. The dust scatters. Out-of-the-blue, a gorgeous horizon is in view. Hues of reds, blues, violets, and gold are radiating as if to beckon the **Rainbow Lady**, to stop and look. A whimpering puppy comes along for the expedition. I do not mind and pause to capture the horizon. Some hopping rabbits come into vision. Rabbits move quickly scurrying into the bush. The puppy continues whining, but I am uncertain why. I let the puppy frolic among the greenery for a little while, and eventually, I return the puppy to the car. Surprisingly, the puppy begins whining again. I almost come to the end of the gravel thoroughfare, and I stop to place the puppy among the greenery and eventually I return the puppy to the car. Bolting from out the blue, a fox stands right in front of the car. The creature acts like a royal king as if to say, *"I am first on this road."* The fox's arrogance startles me, when I see its beautiful coat. It has many shades of silver, copper, gray, and black. The orange tinges of the animal's coat instantaneously brighten an incredulous exquisiteness. At that moment, I recall the large greenhouse on the reservation. The owners invite me to see their taxidermy collection and a fox is on display. The stuffed dead animal does not have the same allure as the live fox I am now facing. Life far more radiant when presents itself. Then the fox delicately trots away, and its shimmering fur moves toward the bush.

Memories of the fox are now fading as I continue my trip. Finally, I reach a quaint old-fashioned city. Street names are unusual in the center of the western city. At least, I find basics in town that takes me to the old days of the west one-hundred years earlier. Outlet names of shops are also different. Shops lineup in a horizontal path with only a few streets spreading outwardly. In contrast to the remote community of the aboriginals, I experience paved roads, local beggars and drunks. On the favorable side, people act a little friendlier than a large, cosmopolitan, city, but with less commodities. Local places such as a bar are now the Canadian Liquor Commission. Missing are the dancing girls of the old west.

After I get needs, I wonder what in-store at the reservation is. As I begin a return journey, I realize there is a mist rising from the waters. The haze of a natural spa creates a foggy pathway. It becomes hardly visible to drive. The mist makes me feel like I am driving into *The Wonderful World of Oz* as if a curiosity into the patterns in life. I have no expectations, but I tumble from visions of the water to nature calling me to experience more than before. Am I going to tumble into a Queen like Jackie?

On the return trip, I take an expedition on the lake. I get a canoe and I think back about my earlier experience with Jackie, the aboriginal man from Montreal. I want to experience the same peaceful moment I had. There are no crowds or clutter. I get into the canoe wearing a life jacket. The boat begins rocking and rolling. Steadily, I push the small vessel into the water and head toward the wilderness.

Beginning the voyage is an intrigue. I see long grass strewn into the water looking like streamers floating to make a spread. Compared to the earlier motor boat travel experience, the water shades are gradients of gray and brown. There is an interesting contrast to the deep, dark blackness. This view is affable. This spurs a craving inwardly. I yearn to paint this scene, but I cannot. The wind oozes anger and becomes a forceful force. The motions are far too strong to even hold an imaginary paintbrush. I concentrate on getting the oars to move. Finally, I cross the waterway. People from a distance shout out. They are glad to see an outsider in distress, but I paddle forward. The aboriginals are laughing heartily. Their unruly sounding echoes through the air, but I continue rowing. I dislike the noisy sounds they make.

I am struggling with the water current. It is tedious work out to keep the oars moving in synchronization. Clouds are edging closer together. I think the rain might decant gently soon and the possibility of a heavy downpour speaks loudly. Turbulent water causes the canoe's pace to be robust. I can feel the spirits of humanity coming alive when I see the fox earlier as an omen. Challenges of this journey reminds me of what comes. In fact, the Northern aboriginal people believe a fox is a symbol of wisdom. Such sighting is intense and agrees with the Chinese belief of a "*fox* [狐狸, hu-li]"[141] sighting to be a signal from the spirits of deceased "*beautiful young girls*" [142] Other Chinese legends repeat the theme. Fox is a creature "*seen emerging from coffins or graves....* (and are) *the transmigrated souls of deceased human beings.*"[143] Spiritual vision is also a realization of beautiful souls.

I imagine the deceased man must have come

to tell me something. I am uncertain what I will next. On my return, I am on my way to visit Bob and his family. Instead, there is a procession of at least one-hundred cars. Varying sizes of vehicles put their headlights on as respect for the corpse. I follow the long-line, but I am uncertain where everybody is heading. As I drive forward, the pathway becomes muddier. Finally, all the cars stop. Friends, relatives and neighbors come from many places. They all want to reach the burial grounds and pay their respects to the deceased. Some are friends, relatives and guests. I come to an awareness the dead man wants me to be present. Therefore, I see the entire picture of aboriginal life fleeting by.

The burial grounds are small. Grave markings of deceased with a flood of white crosses are visible. Some footstones have a pictorial image of the late person. Burial ceremony starts when the pallbearers carry the casket from a truck. There is no hearse or horse drawn carriage. Instead, the pall bearers bring the casket to a mounted stand that frames a wooden box. Nearby the stand, there is a mound of the earth with long stemmed roses piled on top. Roses offer the scent of sweetness. There is also traditional healing that occurs earlier. This comes from the "*crushed bulb of Onion* ***lilies***"[144] and cleanses the dead man's infection while he is alive, but the aroma remains.

People in the ceremony pass out a single red or yellow rose. These colors represent the transcendence of love and respect to the deceased. I also recall reading Jennifer Kyrnin' aboriginal interpretation for the meaning of **red** to *"represent the land."* [145] Among the Apache Indians, **yellow** means "*the sun rises.*" [146] Community members are passing around the flowers, I am in my imagination is judicious as Dante's stained glass colors are another sign of the sun. This also rivals vision of the Rainbow Lady.

As the flowers circulate, I think about the Freemasons. The **red** color likens to "*armor (connected with the idea of sacrifice and struggle*"[147] and the people question why there is an early death. The **yellow** symbolizes "*the gold* (the sun)"[148] and cherishes the golden memory of the deceased. In turn, individuals come one at a time to place flowers in the wooden box. Besides the flower-giving, there are some long pieces of sweet grass people put inside the wooden box. The flowers and the sweet grass jointly symbolize the final offering to the dead man. The aboriginal intent is for the expired man to have a pleasant passage to his afterlife. The pure act of giving roses and sweet grass are reverent. Sweetness of flowers scatters when set aflame. Smoke rises into the air creating a spiraling upward trail. Extra roses are on top of the coffin. The pall bearer then begin nailing down the wooden box. They position the coffin into the dugout grave. Individuals grab some soil from the mound. They throw it into the grave. Afterwards, many hands of the earth landing descend. The coffin's journey compares to Bob's fish as if there is a sinkhole.

Before the funeral proceedings completes, some of the people leave early. The locals do not find this to be offensive as they come from long distances. Aboriginals coming from a distance, need to return before it is dark. Many leave before the ceremony completes. The rest of the people are getting ready to engage in the community feast. Members of the community assemble to offer their final condolences to the deceased in spirit of digesting memories.

Close knit aboriginal societies glue their thinking to be alike as a feudal outlook. Some people do not come to the funeral because of distrust between families holding onto an old feud. Politics brewing behind the scenes. Attitudes do not change favorably regardless of a death in the community. People return to their old habits. They act like the conniving foxes that come into the neighborhood. The closer the fox comes to the school property, the more idiosyncrasies appear.

The funniest incident occurs when the fox comes on the school grounds. The teacher's assistant gives the fox some bubble gum. The fox chomp down and chews steadily. As he masticates, the fox offers a lesson on digestion, Parents like the idea of their children running freely when a fox is present. The fathers and mothers do not see this as danger, but as natural learning. I do not want to distinguish if the aboriginal people have poor standards, but their ideas are different from normative learning for North Americans. So, when children are absent from school, they are usually in the woods hunting and valuing nature.

I try to ease emotions in the community by visiting families and members in the community. I make my presence known. I yearn for the aboriginal community to be more trusting. I recall while I was in another aboriginal community, the parents shut the doors in tries to reduce truancy. Fathers and mothers mostly fear that I was going to take their children from them. In both settings, the community members did not have pleasure that an outsider takes interest. At least I try and that is what I think the deceased spirit seeks. He wants me to know the Northern Lights are shaping a new aura. Illumination glimmers, and many lights glow in the sky. Sparks of the light collide between the electrically-charged particles from the **sun**. They are entering the earth's atmosphere, so I am once again the **Rainbow Lady** inspiring the array of colors to display--- green, pink (most common), shades of red, yellow, green, blue and violet too. This rainbow is an enlightenment of the human condition and a valuable addition when I make snapshots for Sue's scrapbook.

In 2006, Larue Barnes, writer for Cleburne Times-Review describes Karen Parr's meeting with Dr. Patch (Hunter) Adams. She joins him at a Health Care Justice Gathering. Parr happens to be one of thirty medical students across the nation to take part. Parr receives the grounding to help people of all nations. In 2013, I am not a medical doctor, but there is plea from Dr. Adams. He asks that I go to a Justice Gathering in Guatemala. I cannot join the Gathering, but he tells here are only eighteen clown or medical doctors coming from seven countries. Perhaps, I am more privileged than Parr to be a part of the caring patch quilt. At least, the patches are elementary for his direction and for the aboriginal people. As for me, I am still putting the patches together for you (the reader) to authenticate that we are now in the times of Tsunami tales.

In closing, the Freemason describe the Lily as "*symbolic of purity and peace.*"[149] In the stories I tell you (reader), I have been in prominent places among the ornaments of Temple, an observer of rituals. I draw nutrients from the earth. The nutrition comes from the rising water to absorb the rays of the sun. Therefore, I remain to consecrate a higher purpose, namely, help you (reader) to blossom and sleep well at night.

CHAPTER 21:

BOTTLED OCEANIC MESSAGES

THE WOMEN WRAPPED IN THE TIDES

OVERSEAS -- EGYPT, PAKISTAN, INDIA, GERMANY & NORTH AMERICA

Spirit connections occur when arrival of a newborn child, a long-time friendship, meeting a person for the first time, or a "déjà-vu" (the feeling that you have been there before and know that person). I discovered the importance of the mind, body, and spirit meshing when I connected to Sue, Keiko, and others. There was a mutual opportunity to hear, feel, and internalize because women are natural sharers. As a woman, I experience a vast combination of feelings ranging from having tender compassion towards people to complete unabashed passion in other circumstances. I am in tune with my instincts, nature, human behavior, and worldly matters. Through my strength to learn ancient practices, I have regard for the sacred. My wish is to go where few people go. I gain knowledge in the least likely places, I believe there is the essence in every woman, a flowering **Lily** waiting to be free, to see, and hear. As a woman, I experienced passage into the man's world of patriarchy. I faced varying intellects wavering from *hot* favors or *cold* injustices. New realities were unfolding, and they did not always match with my upbringing. I wondered how my experiences compared to the experiences of other women. Then I remembered tying a wish to a cherry tree in Japan and thinking about it in Korea's once Wollyubong Mountain. I wanted women, including myself, to bring vision and experiences to the surface. Thus, I evolved in response to CHERRY SEEDLINGS changes starting in Japan and extending friendship globally to North America (United States), South America (Curbita), Africa (Egypt) culture, Asia (Pakistan), and Europe (Germany). These sprouts send a measure of friendship and worldly exposure.

THE MIDDLE EAST: *EGYPT*

During my European travels, I meet a woman who comes from Cairo, Egypt. She tells about memories of the picturesque cerulean blue sky in Egypt. There are no visible clouds, but because of high levels of pollution, the environment changes. The-once-blossoming array of flowers makes her think the colonists and Pharaohs planted tree seedlings thousands of years ago. She holds a reasonable snapshot of the scenery. A woman reveals when the factories move in, so does the toxicity. The pollution becomes widespread and creates a winding path that targets blossoming **cherry flowers**.

When the woman enlightens me what happens in her country, the setting reminds me of earlier times in Japan when I make a wish. It is the times the cherry buds spread their sweet fragrance and flourishing everywhere. Wishes tie to the twigs of a cherry tree. Wishes become happy realities and others do not. The sky peeps as twinkling sapphire gems with no clouds. Years later, the torrential weather strikes Japan and plenty of Japanese spread their wings settling and fleeing to other places. No matter where the Japanese head, they bring some cherry seedlings with them. In turn, the Japanese carry the sprouts to many faraway destinations.

Because of the Japanese, cherry budding makes an entryway into Brazil, Canada, China, Germany, and other journey's end. It is almost as the Egyptian woman says, "the pharaohs of old Egypt restructure their pyramids of joy." The woman telling "Aahmas"[150] means "the child of the moon." Therefore, I journey to the moon.

Aahmas's revelations begin on a cloudless day while the Egyptians were soaking in the warm rays of the sun. Traffic is heaviest because Egyptian workers return in the hundreds from Libya, Tunisia, Jordan, Syria, and Yemen. There is no work for them in Egypt, so they drive to nearby places to visit friends. They pleasure in the social smoke of the *Sheisha* water pipe or the *hookahs* and they share stories. Workers such as the police, teachers, and archaeologists gather in the Tahrir Square. They come in numbers and demand higher wages and safety for the antiquities. Present government rules disallow strikes. Of course, people come out in the thousands to show their disagreement. People are complaining, leaving something hovering in the air, because societal norms are not working effectively. Since Egypt's environment is changing, the woman's story intertwines with my realities in South America.

Aahmas's tale reprints my travels to Curbita, Brazil, even though, the temperature in Curbita is at the opposite extreme from Cairo's blazing heat. Curbita is colder than the Arctic. I am living high in the mountains in a different environment than I know. Atmospheric pressure is thinner in the peak of the mountain compared to the lower regions where oxygen was plentiful. This setting makes breathing rate hasten and red blood cell production increases, creating an increase in the oxygen flow to my brain and muscles. My ear pressure is unequal, and I am in extreme pain. It takes me a few weeks to adapt, and I experience changes in appetite. Swelling of my hands, feet, and knees, and I have a temporary condition of breathlessness. Body affects are straining. I am uncomfortable and a crisis occurs.

As in the Egyptian tale, people also assemble to overcome obstacles. I try warming up at a public gathering at Garibaldi Square, the most strategic location of the country and central. This place is where ordinary citizens of the country seeing many changes taking place in the 1960s. I am uncomfortable and in lethal circumstance. The tales of these two countries mutually account for people congregating in the cities of Cairo (Egypt) and Curbita (Brazil), overcoming obstacles.

I am trying to warm up at Garibaldi Square while the Egyptian woman experiences crisis in Tahrir square, also known as the Martyr Square. The Squares (Tahrir and Garibaldi) are strategic locations in Egypt and Brazil. Ordinary citizens can see changes taking place. Transformations in the particular places happen during a rise in social awareness and an awakening.

When I am in Curbita, Brazil during the 1960s, there is a romantic revolution. People protest, in the wake of cultural changes. Curbita becomes a charming place and people socialize the same as in Cairo. There are radical changes taking place and most people think Curbita is a backward town, a place to sojourn and buy tobacco on their way to São Paulo. This matches the Shisha water pipe social time in Cairo, Egypt. In the 1940s, Curbita's small population grows to well over one-hundred thousand inhabitants. By the 1960s, the city has three-hundred thousand residents, so the entire country is evolving. Curbita also mirrors the effects of Cairo's snarling traffic. In both cities, the air is growing thick with car fumes. It is clear the time comes to modernize. In

Curbita, revolution begins with planting the **cherry blossoms**. In 1980s, the environment has many blossoms, so Pharaoh's era of fragrances returns.

Curbita's main streets get widener. Workers lay out cobblestones. Streetlights and kiosks erect. Thousands of flowers glorify the landscape. This makes Curbita one of the world's famous cities. Curbita City is a copycat of Cairo City. Both cities are strategically in position as a charming locality for commercial glamour. Both Curbita City and Cairo City are fairly provincial places as measured for livability. According to Aahmas and the experiences I gain on this trek, Curbita City and Cairo City become classic examples of a decent environment.

I consider that Curbita City has too uncanny likenesses to Cairo. This creates an overwhelming moment of happiness. Also, Aahmas's name relates to an ancient Egyptian belief the "*crescent moon.... brings good luck.*" [151]

Aahmas continues her story. She describes more about Maadi City, another Egyptian locality that neighbors Cairo City. Maadi is a rural area about twelve kilometers south of Cairo's center. The town has roughly three-hundred thousand to five-hundred thousand inhabitants. Maadi is originally setup as an idyllic model for Egypt. The town has its wide boulevards, villas and panoramic scene catering to higher and middle class Egyptians residents. Expatriates also

Expatriates gravitate to Maadi, which has large links to Cairo. The cities both have many high-rise buildings, villas and flats. Their wide boulevards make Maadi attractive and originally the British own businesses and embassies situate there. It is a town never experiencing the same unrest as in Cairo's Tahir Square.

Aahmas's describes a warm place that becomes happier as Curbita does, but there are some changes. She tells the local people return working regular hours in Cairo. Most of the United States Aid workers resume their life in Maadi. The Egyptian people are excited about their future. There are at least ten presidential candidates waiting to be the people's choice. The Deputy Chief of Party resigns, and his duties become delegated. The staff she works for in Cairo City is strong, faithful, and has devotion, but a difference crops up. Aahmas cannot travel outside Cairo to visit Maddi because there is chaos. People are protesting at Tahrir Square. Arguments continue, and some killings take place. Egyptian army tanks and soldiers head into the city. They want to stop the violence between antigovernment activists and the supporters of the president. The two-sided battle with rocks, sticks, bottles and firebombs. There are hours of automatic gunfire. Many soldiers move towards the front line. Four tanks clear a highway overpass. This is where presidential supporters are hurling rocks and firebombs onto the protesters. The assaults and demonstrators step up. People are receiving whippings, and the violence continues. These events evoke Aahmas to leave Egypt. She finds out from friends that her brother experiences harm in Tahrir Square. Aahmas panics when she cannot find her brother. Then she gets wind that he escapes, and he is well.

When Aahmas seeks refuge, the fighting starts. She is on the run and hopes to find her brother. During this time, she nearly experiences harm. There are firing guns and rocks flying several times in her direction. Somehow, she manages to near the army tanks. They are heading towards a clearing. Tanks advance to Ismailia. Aahmas jumps off the tank and reaches a passing ferry. Supercargo boats are also passing by. Once Aahmas reaches the other side, she gets car transport to connect to a bordering town along the Mediterranean Seacoast. She lands in Said City, but Aahmas is still not sure how she can meet her brother. Somehow, the **magic of the blooming cherry buds** make it happen.

Aahmas finds a passage aboard a plane heading to Washington, the District of Columbia in the United States. Eventually this is where her brother meets her and the same city Sue lives before. Aahmas is also like a pliable doll as she can be a package covered by pink wrappings. The woman is strong, but I can imagine that her heart is beating like the passion I have when I meet a new challenge. Aahmas's spirit almost magically fly and she comes safely from harm's way to America. She gains a sense that America is country that offers social justice. In reality, I think she is unsure what to expect.

Aahmas's spirit is remarkably fervent as if she is beckoning Sue to arise from the ground. I meet Aahmas when she arrives first in New York City. This is where I meet her first. We are both viewing the Statue of Liberty, a female statue that holds a torch for freedom fighters. Statue of Liberty symbolizes for the power of light over darkness and hope over despair. I am in amazement that even the Statue of Liberty's physical features imply being a free woman and being safe country away from revolt and cruelty.

The meeting with Aahmas causes reflection on challenges I experience. As I view the Status of Liberty, I see some facts that cause amazement. The stone-faced sculpture has "*Seven rays on her crown, representing the seven continents.....twenty-five windows in her crown stand for gemstones found on the Earth and heaven's rays shining over the world*."[152] The rings I lose in the Philippines are now the shining gems in the crown of the Statue of Liberty. Aahmas and I both successfully escape the atrocities of indecent behavior.

Luckily, Aahmas and I land in cities where there are more than three-thousand (3,000) cherry blossom trees blooming. Beyond imagination, Cairo and Curbita are cities that receive the cherry blossoms from the Japanese. Cherry blossoms metaphorically are present in all the states. Thus, friendship symbolism spreads globally and appears at the turn of the twentieth century. There are precise spots in the city where women can celebrate their blooming success. As for Aahmas and me, we manage to escape some hardships and chase our dreams. I decide my **higher purpose** in life is the same. I meet Aahmas, and I realize it is a junction in my life to go forward and expose beauty and humanitarian modeling.

I marvel that my meeting Aahmas becomes decisive and a metaphysical connection I hear her stories to discover that we share mutual realities that go beyond what is perceptible to the senses. In light of what takes place, I know I have a humanitarian mission to help people. I am not sure exactly what is clear or abstruse, but in time I am going to find out. I only know that because of the cherry seedlings, they make their way into the cities where Aahmas and I land. The purpose of cherries becomes clear, spreading healthy friendships from out of thorny circumstances, to get a sense of contentment. At the same time, I wonder if men and women stop thinking that external beauty is not the end all, and then it is the time to celebrate sweet cherry endings.

From an artistic perspective, there is emotional healing from artists as they all convey the same philosophy and higher purpose as I do.

In the 1400s, Hieronymus Bosch's (1400s) medieval triptych, *The Garden of Earthly delights* the artist metaphorically portrays life as a bowl of cherries. Terry Tempest Williams, author of *Finding Beauty in a Broken World* infers that Bosch mediates his higher purpose. He reaches a heightened level of **spiritual awareness** when he paints. The cherries figuratively come direct from the earth. The fruit captures the sensations of beauty and delight that feed on souls. They appeal to senses of lust and pleasure, apathy and bleeding sentiments. The Cherries depict elated emotions --- floating in the sky, bouncing on the water, fondling and reveling in the spirit as it spills out the red juices.

In the late 1800s, M.C. Escher depicts a metamorphism of changing **beauty realities** in his painting of a *Pair of Sweet Gradient Mesh Cherries.* Hence, "beauty" becomes a genuine crystalline image.

In the 1940s, Octavio Ocampo's creates illusionary artwork of *The Cherry Tree and the Horse, A Woman of Substance** and *The Ecstasy of the Lilies.** He also has a higher purpose to show women are in fact, blossoming cherries. They flourish in society, but **their true beauty** is often not something people see.

In 1969, Salvador Dali* creates a gouache watercolor of *Cerises Pierrot* or Pierrot Cherries. The painting takes on an anthropomorphic quality as does the other artists. He is a natural art **therapeutic healer**. He tells humanity, people are deserve the sweetness or "cherry blossoming" in life.

Historically, these artists display consistent opinion of human intellect from the 1400s to the twentieth century humanists, but their opinions are often unheeded.

SOUTHEAST ASIA: *PAKISTAN & INDIA*

I accept that being a humanist does not necessarily always have **cherry beginnings**. Indisputably, I have to rely on my sixth sense, logic and knowledge especially when I meet a Pakistani woman. She comes from the Baltistan region of Northern Pakistan, which neighbors the territories of Jammu and Kashmir. This magnificent area has influence from the Tibetans. I assume the high altitudes might be a parallel to Curbita travels in South America, but I am not sure. Instead, focus is on a woman that feels the heat coming from the moon. According to Pakistani belief, there is a famous folktale that implies a female snow leopard lived partially on land and water, but the leopard only comes out when there is a full moon. The myth symbolizes the leopard is mystical because nature *"does not necessarily seek rational explanations."* [153]

Pakistani Habits: The Pakistani woman, named Mehreen comes from Southeast Asia. Her name means "*two moons*... (and has a) *loving nature."* [154] She is not a mythological character, but her behavior displays an illogical nature. Does she live partially on land and water or is she running from telling the truth?

The meeting of the Egyptian woman is like discussions with Mehreen. She also gives an account of her own. She is a talented mathematician and tells that she comes from India. Undoubtedly, I marvel at how knowledgeable she is, but I have doubts about her birthplace. Her eye contact is a giveaway that causes me to question what she wants from me.

Mehreen is deceptive. She is introduces herself as coming from India, but her birthplace is in Pakistan. I ponder that she provides wrong information because images of Pakistan are not as good as India. Her reasoning likely has a political slant. In 2010, North Americans do not help the Pakistani people with relief when there is severe flooding. Instead, the North Americans and the international media describe Pakistan as the hub of terrorism. Canada dubs Pakistan as "*the most dangerous country in the world,*"[155] while Britain and the United States also find fault. Since India does not have the same portrait, Mehreen probably rationalizes that she should not divulge her origin to be Pakistani. She discloses her origin is from India. I guess Mehreen thinks this to be a better chance for a productive rapport. At least, India has an economic partnership with North Americans. In fact, there are Indian campaigns against terrorism in Asia. Therefore, Mehreen begins with a lie.

Mehreen is a survivor, but her misleading habit of not telling the truth remains consistent. Thinking origins are a continuing battle between Pakistan and India. The two neighboring countries habitually camouflage the truth. In current times, these countries amplify indecent behaviors that do not change. There are issues of ceasefire, political designs, and falsification of identity, but the people in India and Pakistan internalize cultural-learned behavior.

I meet Mehreen at an academic institution. Then, she describes a sob story. She cannot bathe or shower because of economic burden imposed by an Indian agency. Mehreen gives details of hiring practice for a mathematics instructor, but the

Agency's fees reduce any opportunity to survive. Earnings mostly cover fees payable to the agency. I am unsure what to believe, but I am empathetic that she has no access to bathing. I am vulnerable and I give her permission to stay in where I live.

I am renting a small one-bedroom apartment. By allowing Mehreen to stay temporarily, there is confinement. I have two dependent children and adding another person makes matters difficult. Mehreen deliberately pretends to be oblivious. Soon afterwards, Mehreen assumes I need exposure to her beliefs, and she introduces her Temple of faith.

Naturally, her **beliefs** are a part of her world and a place where people from Pakistan swarm. They pool common interests dressing in traditional garbs. Women with beautiful brown eyes, silken hair, wear marvelous, exotic-looking clothing. They men also have customary clothing. According to her custom, the temple separates the men from the women. As I am in the room with other women, I hear chanting and humming sounds that echoes throughout the temple. My children's eyes are open and in mystification of what they see. After the prayers complete, we advance into a large room.

The Pakistan people sit along the side panel of the room wherever space is available. The women in the community provide foods including Chicken (*Barfii, Karahi, KaQuorma, Marachi, Rulao, and Tikka), Gulab Jamun, Halwa Poori, Kala Kand, Laddo, Mutton Kunna, Palakm, Ras Malai, Seekh Kabab, Gal Gappay* dishes. In an adjoining room, the women prepare the platters and serve the food on the floor. People are salivating when the food arrives. They compete to get a paper plate and load up with food. People instantly eat food with their hands, lick their fingers and delight even when there is a pasty substance. Their habits are unfamiliar. I am uncomfortable and

I assume the Pakistani people will splash water to clean their hands, but they do not. Mehreen is not an exception; she eats as others do.

During the time people eat, Mehreen and community members talk loquaciously without an end in sight. In fact, when Mehreen is at my home, she spends hours on a cellular phone. She communicates to people in her homeland. I find it astounding that Mehreen loses sense of reality and time. Her habit is to spend money on telephone calls. At no time does she offer to subsidize the cost of where I rent. Since the comforts of my children are at risk and her spending is extreme for cellular calling, I ask her to leave. I am no longer vulnerable to her lies, but I help out with some costs. She chooses not to help. I move to a larger place. I do not invite her to come and she finds housing somewhere else.

A few months pass and Mehreen unearths where I live. Once again, she pleads me for a chance to stay. I resist her pleading, but I do not have the heart to tell her no. I allow Mehreen to stay for one week. During that time, she creates unlucky accidents. Mehreen manages to ruin my vehicle by bumping into it accidentally, but she hides the truth. The neighbors tell about the incident because they hear a crashing noise. They explain that Mehreen backed her car causing a huge dent in the van. I find it difficult to be generous to Mehreen, so I put a halt to her deceitful ways. I want to teach her about honest practices of giving and taking. Unfortunately, an ugly situation presents itself.

Mehreen makes an effort to show she has virtue. During her shift work, she supposedly watches my children. When I return home, Mehreen is not present. My son tells she leaves early and the children are without care. Of course, I am anxious and when Mehreen returns, she lies again. She claims to care for the children and her departure is only a few minutes early. I have trouble trusting her words.

Mehreen is a prime example of the old deceptive woman I meet in the Philippines. On the surface, the women both appear trustworthy. Therefore, I decide that Mehreen's behavior is from her roots. I envisage that Mehreen has a never-ending battle about what to say to remain safe as if she resides in Pakistan. Her responses are a composite of conscience thinking and disastrous habits. Mehreen does not understand the words of Abraham Lincoln. He says, "No *man has a good enough memory to make a successful liar*."[156]

In rumination, many cultures view Mehreen as having faults because she comes from Pakistan. North Americans often assume she is inept than them because many develop their opinions from the media, childhood rearing and exposure. In fact, the people I work with have no idea that an unfamiliar setting or action does not justify a person being a low achiever. I suspect Mehreen met people from around the world, but remains uncaring. She comes from a society where men are in power and fervently oppose policies that dignify her as a woman. Mehreen does not have a normal life and learns that dishonesty goes a far distance. She learns to be submissive and humble because the Laws in her country are unsound.

Through discovery, I learn that Mehreen whips into a fraudulent lifestyle, not much different from the canine in South Korea. When she is a Pakistan wife, she experiences brutal abuse from her spouse. He kicks often and uses an iron to burn areas of her body. The practice in Pakistan compels a woman to have three male witnesses to testify against the wrongdoings of her husband. She has no witnesses, so in the eyes of men, she is a criminal because and brings shame to her family. There is no bearing when she does something wrong. She lives with the opinions of men that judge her because she is a woman. The Laws in Pakistan add no sympathy for women victims. As I am emotionally black-and-blue from an Asian, domineering spouse, I understand her feelings.

I am taken aback when Mehreen has a greater understanding than I assume realizing much about Western culture. I gain knowledge that earlier in her career she worked as a feudal serf to pay off debts. Her **conscience thinking** is clear when she stays at my home. It is through her views, reactions and sense of right and wrong that I came to realization about this Pakistani woman.

It does not matter if Mehreen escapes her journey in Pakistan, or the Egyptian woman escapes harm, or a well-versed female expatriate confront abuse, there is a common thread. Women are still escaping abuse from humankind.

From the Egyptian and Pakistani women, they communicate that a woman's private and public life is not always easy. Women carry the fear that their private life might become public. Egyptian and Pakistani lifestyles, dignity and independence in the community are fewer for women. Inequity is part of family-ordered traditions, which compel women to have fewer choices in their lives than men. Regretfully, their reflections often connote physical or mental abuse from a significant male or another male attacker.

In 2010, I hear there is a terrorist attack taking place in Mumbai, India. People's atrocious behavior matches the Pakistanis. Some friends of mine staying there, die even though, Pakistan's Hunza (Gojal) and Nagar valley areas have panoramic views to enjoy the blossoming cherry season with over seven-thousand meters. Remaining cherry blossoms give off an indelible scent. Mehreen's ephemeral nature of lying flowers immortalizes the "*ephemeral nature of life.*" [157] As I am Lily, a woman, I cannot forget that I am a fragrant blossom that grows vigorously. My higher purpose is encouraging women to flower truthfully as blossoms.

EUROPE: ***GERMANY***

Moon Beliefs: I continue a humanistic path because I want to help people understand there are alternatives open to them. To my bewilderment, their beliefs still floating around the moon exerts a strange influence on people. In 1995, psychiatrist According Vance, said, "*Mental health professionals comprise a large percentage of people believing that full moon alters a person's behavior*"[158] because of association with the moon's gravitational pull, which is also connected with causing floods. Other people surmise that when the moonrises, it automatically connects to madness. In the artwork of Hieronymus Bosch,* M.C. Escher,* Octavio Ocampo* and Salvador Dali,* they all create illusions. Did they have the same belief that when "*people stayed up later and slept less*"[159] it can "*induce mania*?" [160]

I ponder about Winston Churchill, Dr. Robert Kearns and other celebrities' disposition including mine. Intensities reflect the anxieties of the times. Sleep deprivation links to manic-depressive traits. Eccentricities are mood swings. Other times, they could manifest as blank expressions, excessive diligence and belligerence. These personas cause someone crazy to lose their credibility. What do you (reader) think?

In the 1830s, Ewald Hering, a German psychologist judges the full moon increases mania. Hering correlates his thinking to the events at the Bethlehem Hospital in London. Inmates are in chains and receiving whippings during certain phases of the moon. This takes place likely to thwart mental patients from becoming violent.

In the twentieth century, Arnold Lieber's authors *The Lunar Effect.* He guesses that human emotions connect to madness. Thirty years later, Lieber's theory debunks. Resulting studies follow. Questioning peculiarities matters. Disabled adults, superstitions or synodic cycles do not cause madness. Opinion about the moon's impact might change with the story following.

The Moon Lady

Imelda introduces herself as being a former government employee in a coffee shop. She is a poetic presenter and her opening statement causes me to pause. Her poems are about how life shifts when the moon influences leaders around the world. Imelda employs an admirable symbolism that credits energies influencing the lunar cycle. She says the lunar influence belongs to all thoughts and emotions formed by the community. Imelda imagines marriage between the community and the moon. She takes pleasure in how the bride (Imelda) and bridegroom (moon) exchange full cups of glowing rainbows, the silver lining of the moon, and the community's mystical embrace with the couple. Later, she adds that government officials are culpable for changing her life's path and so is the moon.

She uses a lyrical emotion and revelations of beauty that begin. Imelda responds to her bridegroom, but later follows the community's command without question. During her reading, she

Increases her energy level, .and is in a euphoric mood. Suddenly she talks about how government officials are no longer the silver lining of goodness and she cannot concentrate well. She becomes easily distracted and has poor judgment when cynical people are in the audience. When she gets no response, she becomes irritable and describes her acute panic from effort to commit suicide. Imelda has a compelling need to share her belief. The lunar cycle causes harm because of society's ruin.

Imelda's name originates from Old German and Italian and means a *universal battle*. Imelda has a widespread clash with people in the audience. Her "excessive behavior" matches the first lady, Imelda Marcos want for owning an abundance of shoes in the Philippines. I wonder why I am meeting Imelda. Is she a controversial blossom that dropped from the moon?

Imelda's Story

Imelda's story takes place in the Altes Land Orchard in Germany. This is where cherry trees produce tens of thousands of spectators to come to view the blossoming cherries every spring. Imelda's birthplace is where the cherries spread. Lamentably, her story talks to flowers that wither away and the confusing path that her life takes. She moves from Germany and immigrates to America, but her direction in life has little relevance to the moon.

I meet Imelda in the 1980s and she is in her 30s. Notes in her file suggest she is a nightclub singer and a humanitarian. My colleagues tell that in earlier times, people have admiration for her extraordinary contributions to society. She comes for a scheduled appointment and I ask her how an intelligent woman is on probation. Imelda asserts the justice system imprisons her for no clear reason. She says, "There is a new vogue in society and innocent people are in jail." I inquire to tell the history of events leading up to probation. Imelda explains her tension links to the moon's gravitational pull. I think this is bizarre. I let her continue her story, but this makes me speculate if she resembles Cher (Cherilyn Sarkisiana) the diva philanthropist with learning dysfunctions.

Justice Projections: Finally, Imelda settles down and says societal values have changed. She talks about an elite group of politicians are *the untouchables.* These people play God and create a new set of rules. They contrive theft, and criminality of their own. When she has a clash with some of these people, they expect her to bend backwards, forwards and sideways for their benefit. She is unwilling to aid their needs. She sees them change their colors to suit their need. Next, they consider Imelda harmful. Imelda adds the oldies (righteous people) are no longer the goodies (indecent). Replacements occur and people experience entrapment into the new justice world.

During discussion, Imelda is smoking heavily. I flip through the case notes and note violations for having too many cocktails as a social lubricant. Her nonverbal cues cause closer observance. A colleague intervenes briefly and Imelda becomes an exhibitionist. She is taking off her clothes and she is in her own exclusive fantasy world. I insist she have a cup of coffee, redress and continue with her story.

Imelda clarifies that history rewrites are by politicians and questionable people. Then she asks if I want to know the truth. I respond that I do and add to be straightforward. I am probing to know more about her unconscionable thinking.

Her story begins with her talking with an intellectual crowd. She gives a poetry presentation and people applaud her talent. As she reads aloud, her words offer magnificent reflections. An agent approaches Imelda to sell her writings. Soon after, her outspoken poetry becomes fashionable. She offends countless people and does not try to make amends for what she says. Concurrently, she is reaps monetary gain and helps people in need. Her motivations are good, but with a twist of events - sales of her work goes downhill. She works obsessively to gain control back, but less radiance comes out. At this point, I probe further delving into her childhood. Imelda's story unravels two major catastrophes and the cherry pits that take place.

The first calamity occurs at age 6. A drunk crashes into her world. Her mother and sister are in the front seats of the family's car, and Imelda in the backseat. She remembers the car spiraling, turning and whirling as if a tornado strikes. Imelda wakes up in the hospital. She learns from the nurse there was an accident her mother and sister died and Imelda survives.

The second mishap occurs because of her exposure to warped realities of living with an abusive father. Her life begins with disillusionments when her biological father rapes her at age eight. She tells the family about what happens. Her father's is stronger. No one believes what Imelda says. Her father has good standing in the community. From now, people in society assume Imelda is insane.

Imelda is a little girl crying out for her mother and sister. Instead, she deals with an abusive father and childhood memories of embitterment. Afterwards, I invite her to tell me what happens as she grows up.

She reveals working in high-powered justice and world affairs. Imelda says she worked with government officials in the military, and the Central Intelligence Agency. She claims that justice officials are corrupt and confronts too much violence. Imelda bemoans her life.

Imelda does not cope well and turns to drinking and chain-smoking. Her story does not compare to the millionaire military man, Chuck Feeney. He makes a bundle on mail orders for liquor and cigarettes. However, Imelda is the consumer of his products. The woman clearly makes Feeney richer, but like him, she is "the anonymous donor." To help penurious people, Imelda and Feeney's entire fortune commits to "giving while living," In 1982, Feeney gives away billions. Simultaneously, Imelda bestows time and money to deprived women.

When Imelda no longer copes with her emotions, she laments aloud. People stop listening to her, so she becomes a Lawbreaker. The court summons her to take part in group psychiatric sessions. This is an initiative to ease her pains and help her balance because appendages (drugs, alcohol) are genuine.

Emotional Assessment: Imelda is an inventive person, but her life takes a toll. Her challenging confrontations are analogous to what emerges in Japan. She experiences wars, earthquakes, Tsunamis matching Hiroshima. Imelda comes about as a Lawbreaker and her habits get worse. She no longer keeps promises, stops dressing in business suits, and acts insensibly. In fact, the idea of gift giving or the Japanese act of *Senbetsu* is no longer part of her earlier practice. Imelda reacts to people as if she is a stone sculpture. I try reaching her, but she reflects a howling canine I see in South Korea. Imelda and the dog have extreme pain with no comfort in sight. She claims other people are iniquitous and at fault. Nevertheless, truth disentangles.

I have concern for her well-being, so I ask how she is doing. She does not respond. When I rise from my chair, I tell her to wait. Before I leave the cubicle, Imelda stares as if inane. I quickly go to another part of the building, but I am inattentive to leave a journal on my desk. I excuse myself to get some forms to address Imelda's needs. During time-off, Imelda finds the journal on the desk. Inside the cover, there are details carrying my whereabouts and telephone contact in case of loss. I return in less than five minutes and Imelda is blankly looking at the wall.

It is 1:30 a.m. and I unexpectedly, get a call from Imelda. I think she loses all sense of time, but she wants to talk. I tell her it is too late and I take the phone off the hook. She repeats her actions for several days, so I change my telephone number. Imelda no longer rests at night. Instead, Imelda fits the archetype of a mentally ill person and I report what happens. The Court issues a mandate that Imelda take part in art therapy.

At the next appointment, I tell the tidings. I am hoping Imelda likes to join in, but she despairingly tells a wish to be dead.

In a follow-up session, Imelda, brings some of her artwork. Her feelings are inescapably present in the paintings she makes. Her choices of colors are bland, dreary and unalike for a person living in the world. Her artwork depicts a person with a severe mental disorder. I decide Imelda fits into a select group of modern impressionistic artists. Her artwork resembles Mark Rothko when he expresses emotions of doom of her creativity compare to Edvard Munch. He has frightening themes such as "*The Scream,*" and *"Anxiety."* Her collages also replicate Bernard Buffet's portraits of "*The Witness*," and "*Jo Jo the Clown*." There is no doubt in my mind that artists;

Rothko (1903-1970), Munch (1863-1944) and Buffet (1928-1999) express the same psychotic state of mind as Imelda.

Her depression reproduces canvases of psychotic perceptions; barred windows, cemeteries, gardens filled with the darkness of nightfall. Dr. Rustin Bauth tells in a psychosocial medical review that emotional addictions are visible in a person's artwork. They couple with a "*psychiatric disorder.*"[161] Imelda lives with delusions and escapes through obsessive acts of chain-smoking, excessive drinking and self-mutilation. Sue might have been an inspiration to inspire her world to live irrespective of hardships.

At the next appointment, Imelda creates her own place of solitary confinement. She does not communicate, but sits staring at the wall. I expect Imelda cremates her spirit and there is no return. I reflect on my own childhood. When I am in Chinatown, people ignore me. At the age of 10, I make friendship with a girl named Kathy. Her paintings match Imelda, and her dress style reprints the Gothic fashion. Kathy has a pale complexion, black hair, and black lips. She also wears glaringly dark and puzzling clothing. Her style comes from the times of the Victorians and the Elizabethans, so I make a snapshot for Sue's scrapbook. Are Kathy and Imelda's events reflective of the dangers of trouble in life? In reality, you (the reader) need to probe if the undercurrent of what happens to Imelda, a young girl that cries out for help. Is Imelda's reality the same as the young dysfunctional girl I describe in Thailand?

I mull over what happens to Kathy and Sue. Sue dies of Multiple Sclerosis and Kathy commits suicide. Death and the absence of a warm heart results.

In 1970s, Imelda is an ideal subject for psychopharmacology experimentation. I am uncertain whether she ever meets psychiatrists, Dr. Cameron and Dr. Lehman. Although it is conceivable that Imelda has a lobotomy or shock treatment because she never fits in society. I am pondering if society allows experimentation to go too far, if a little girl that cries out.

Imelda's lifestyle and the history of psychopharmacology match. CIBA, Sandoz, Geigy, pharmaceutical organizations, claim drugs solve traumatic issues. In fact, Herbert Y. Meltzer of Princeton University reasons drug experimentation is a necessity to transform minds. He says, historians *of* science are now recognizing that former drug experimentation. He believes "that the key thing that has happened over the last 10 years is that [improving the] cognitive deficit has been identified as the key to improving outcome in schizophrenia." [162]

Does Imelda, Kathy, Sue, the dysfunctional girl in Thailand, get a cure at the expense of human experimentation or is something missing?

Imelda never experiences the fun raising that Dr. Patch Adams does in Japan. In Imelda's early life, she never sees how necessary "*social control mechanisms*" [163] can be to reduce "*feelings of emptiness and disengagement from society.*"[164] Frankly speaking, Imelda's experiences are parallel to Gandhi Nagar. She is a five-year old girl raped in Delhi, India by an adult male. No doubt the cries of this little girl raises the questions about the perpetrators. Has global society become so blind and helpless? They cannot see the fallacy in the Good Old Boys Clubs, the Freemason fraternity, the Ivy League or Machismo mentality.

Validation: In 2010, research authenticates parts of Imelda's story. Dobson-Smith representative of the Citizens Commission on Human Rights reports thousands of people suffer from experimentation, injustices, and are consequential to despoiled ethics.

It is hard to assume that drugs experimentation has been the leading cause of mental breakdowns. This calls the question of why Imelda takes a nosedive. Does Imelda experience poison, insulin, nitrous oxide injections, shock therapy or a lobotomy? After all, medical doctors like Dr. Cameron and Dr. Lehman are culpable for such events. Then, Imelda is a productive citizen. The National Institute of Mental Health and Quebec's Ombudsman added disturbing information. They confirm past treatment of humans during the 70s and earlier are degrading. Psychiatrists cover tracks of their colleagues even when errors result.

In summary, at all the meetings I have with Imelda, talks about corporeality debauchery and injustices. As a child, she does cry-out for help. In later years, her remarks reflect an emphasis on criminalizing a person who really is a victim. Imelda's issue cause thinking about a young girl (*The Forgotten Waves*). As for her perpetrator, Hoda Mazloomian, and Bruce Moon, art therapist, enlighten interpretation of Imelda as a rape victim. They psycho-analyze the work of male rapists. These male violators produce "*Images from Purgatory...* (Revealing a diagnosis of) "*Mental illness and were themselves victims of sexual abuse.*" [165] I conclude that people like Imelda are part of what Hieronymus Bosch intends society to see. His artwork predates to the 1400s, but the truth about human existence is the symbolic depiction of "*The Ship of Fools*" [166] or people not seeing what is necessary. These reflections even mirror what happens to beautiful, female actors that commit suicide in South Korea.

I am empathetic to Imelda and part of a higher purpose. Little girls identifying with her enlighten men about women matching the analogy of the cloisonné vase.

EMPOWERED WOMEN

Before I settle my opinions about relevant reflections, there are two more women on my journey. Their names are Buttercup and Blossom. These ladies oppose each other in what results they wish to achieve. Buttercup manages Adult Probation, while Blossom is the psychiatrist. They contribute to the meaning behind empowered women and social justice.

BUTTERCUP

Buttercup is another addition to flowering women and an addition to princesses as a "*Bride*" [167] or a nurturing source. I am not sure whom she marries and nurtures, but she is unlike most women I know. She assumes that modeling male behavior is worthwhile. Buttercup is time-sensitive, but ignores when more moments are necessary. She is not so happy when I spend time with probationers like Imelda. In fact, I am curious about Imelda's description about chameleon men. Buttercup repeatedly says a good probation office capitalizes on gains. Her ideology is not the regality of a Princess, but more like cherry pits already in a trash can.

I have to succor ethical actions for both genders in adult probation. At first, Buttercup praises me for aiding another client. On another day, she tells "new thinking" is not desirable. She says "social justice is a world where large corporations buy and promote intellectual capital, and my kind of caring is not a necessity." Buttercup thinks all adults on probation are a pressing burden on the justice system. They weigh as an albatrosses in a Machismo-run corporation. In fact, Buttercup does not idealize the portrait of being a nurturing woman. She reacts like a hollowed-out log and has no feeling for penurious people. I do not fit her example of a Machismo-minded adult probation officer and I am stopped. Simultaneously, I agree with Imelda, there are people like the chameleon men and *the untouchables*.

Buttercup's behavior impacts other women when she models manliness. As well, her conduct poses an ethical dilemma when she perpetuates the interests of a self-centered man inflicting pain on a woman. Unfortunately, less caring is allowable and Imelda's experiences surmount. She tries to commit suicide.

Buttercup acts more manly than I expect. She overlooks that a woman in a man's domain includes more males in Justice too. There are more gentlemen judges than lady judges. In 2003, the Right Honorable Beverley McLachlin, P.C. and Chief Justice of Canada confirms feelings about gender differentiation. In the grand scheme, her position stresses there are slight differences between men and women. In fact, both genders are creative. Women receive less pay and praise. Thus, a woman's identity needs more reinforcement. In fact, there is still no female Chief Justice in the United States. For seventeen Chief Justices, they are all Caucasian male. In 2012, the tables change when 20 female Chief Justices receive nomination, in the United States. Irrespective that female judges are on board; there are still more male Chief Justices in 2013.

Blossom

Blossom is another flowering woman. She is a mental health professional and diametrically opposite to Buttercup. I meet her when Imelda is in the hospital after making attempts on her life. I come to the hospital to check how Imelda is doing and Blossom is Imelda's nurse.

I open discussion with Blossom on how Imelda is acting. I learn Imelda receives an evaluation, and there is constant checking to prevent self-injury from taking place. Blossom communicates with the family, significant other and shows me the Treatment plan in place. This includes a rotation of staff checking on Imelda.

After seeing Imelda in the hospital on several occasions, Blossom asks that I have a cup of coffee with her. She is off-duty in about ten minutes. I meet her at the coffee shop in the hospital. During our gathering, she tells there is another nurse assigned to Imelda. Because of legal dispute, she leaves.

Blossom invites conversation over coffee and wants advice about troubles she has. Blossom reveals there is a prominent doctor wanting to retaliate when she refuses to court him. Her career is at stake because she ignores the man's advances. Since Blossom's family lives two-thousand miles away, I do not mind listening to what transpires. I get a snapshot of what emerges and I recognize she is no different from me, Imelda or other women projecting their gentle image. I agree that matters expand because of fraternal associations (Ivy League, Freemason, and Good Old Boys Club). They supposedly protect the outstanding men in the community, whether a doctor or other another professional. I cannot help. I offer moral support for her to have a successful result.

In listening to the Egyptian, Pakistani, German and North America female voices, it makes me marvel when women rise above their difficulties. In the political world of advocacy, ethics definitively link with empowered white males and Blossom's position is not an exception. Because I travel, I recognize there is an enormous amount of trafficking women and girls across international borders. They come mostly from China, Thailand, Vietnam and Latin America. Regardless of culture, there is unspoken toleration between women from all everywhere including Blossom. They all want the same as I do, namely, freedom of opinion, the idea of being self-reliant and respectable. Despite tacit understanding, **my soul search stops.** I feel as if I am the Statue of Liberty. I am tipping the scales of justice while voyaging on rough waters.

THE MEN WRAPPED IN THE TIDES

AMERICAN REGIMENTATION

As I travel to countless unfamiliar cultures, fear reduces and I have greater ease to head to another destination. I am over the moon myths and off to exploring the **higher purpose** as do men.

First, my thoughts give rise to the rigid men I meet in South Korea. Their actions mimic the leader in Libya in how they rule, and their expectation that others obey orders implicitly. Tens of thousands of people escape violence in Libya, but the state of affairs fit what the Egyptians experience. The country management of Libya and Egypt typify everyday business and strict practices among men. Organizations strive to check policies that best work in synchronization.

I am a rare woman because I blend into government and corporations. Therefore, I am privy to see men giving allowances to other men first and treating a woman as if she is invisible. I ponder on this, and envisage men as subjects in the artwork of **Salvador Dali**.* He strives to improve diverse styles of art into something unique by incorporating light sensations, illusions, and out-of-the-ordinary interpretations to strengthen his emotional intelligence needs. **Octavio Ocampo*** adds hidden emotional meanings, while **M. C. Escher*** attaches trickeries and repetitive geometric designs. It is almost like a cryptic coding for how moods occur, tides move, dreams and nightmares follow.

Most women cannot cope with male abuse. Imelda copes by consuming alcohol. Women like Anna Nicole Smith, and Whitney Houston are exemplary examples. **Smith** is 39 years old, and a former playmate. **Houston** is 48 years old and an American celebrity. Their circumstances are public record. Both of these women revert to addiction (alcohol, drugs, smoking). Just like Imelda, they have vacant emotions and do not feel any gratitude, so they stop coping. Sadly, Smith dies in poverty because no one believes she deserves as much as her billionaire spouse. Instead of thinking, she is a devoted wife; the media exposes her to be a manipulator of a rich man. As for Houston, she no longer wants abuse she has a compelling feeling to take the final leap out of life. Considering what happens to Imelda, Smith, Houston and Jackie, I stay clear from joining men or women in their social cocktail hours.

I am a stalwart, powerful woman in contrast to Imelda, Houston, and Smith. As a female, I am not confused about my identity like Jackie. Instead,

I carry out three full-time jobs: motherhood, career and student. I did not need a wealthy spouse to tell me how I should be. As a full-time mother, I support my children's needs. Sometimes, I work double shifts and juggle my schedule while my significant men hoard their earnings. I have above-average intelligence so I discover cryptic coding of a man's moods, the moves he makes, and underhanded ingenuity. I am also the cryptic encoder for their emotional intelligence.

I have plenty of experience because the men in my life teach that they have no inclination to share their wages, equity or hocus-pocuses. Men catering to Imelda, Houston, Smith and Jackie, all try to control, but fail. Among ethnic cultures, a dowry supposedly reduces the load of the family when a female leaves. Laws in many countries protect men, and not necessarily women. In fact, male doctors even have greater control over my body than I do when I am in South Korea. I tune into my own social construct to tune out what I see (Machismo and patriarchal attitudes).

I begin surging to the next challenging destination. I tap deeply into subconscious feelings, but my mind is racing especially when I am about to meet delinquent youths.

I have flashbacks of studies in history, social organization and human experimentation. In 1930 to 1972, six hundred African-American sharecroppers contract syphilis. They take part in the United States Public Health, Tuskegee Syphilis study in Macon County, Alabama. Men receive conditioning they are healthy, but they are not. The syphilis remains untreated. If the Africans easily buy in, then it is guesswork knowing if Black youths are in trouble.

In another study, in Canberra, Australia, Kathleen Mills of *The Stolen Generations Alliance* tells a Senate Query that aboriginal children with leprosy receive injections with serums to assess their reactions. They become human guinea pigs for leprosy cures done without adult consent. Like all the experimenters and researchers, deaths result. Cruelty results in death dying of tumors, heart disease, paralysis, blindness and insanity. Does this confirm future happenings for aboriginal youths?

My mind is pirouetting as if I am performing acrobatic ballet. I wonder why these images are coming to mind. Imagination can act like an ingenious ticking bomb. Then, I receive introduction to the Juvenile Holding Center.

Ryan is the manager of the youth holding center, and the make-up of youths includes runaways, delinquents and serious criminals. From the start, I learn Ryan is a man that masks the facts. Probably, Ryan's enforcement training leads him to work here; especially his previous experiences are exposure to violence, corruption and immorality. Was Ryan reacting to his instincts? Probably, his backgrounds matches Imelda's father. He sees continuous horror as a soldier of the war. No doubt, Ryan and Imelda's father have similar personality traits. For the Egyptian and Pakistani woman, both flee from men of destruction. I affirm that Ryan's police regimentation schooling makes for rigidity. In fact, I am wary that he echoes the tapping sound of a cloisonné vase when he commands.

Ryan's schooling exposes him to other enforcement personnel (armed forces, navy, air force, prosecutors). Men having these exposures receive training to act in twisty, labyrinthine circumstances. Unlike expert men or scholars, Ryan receives protection from enforcement leaders when he fits their rigid, molded lifestyle. In fact, the most influential leaders in world history weigh on Ryan's thinking. These leaders do not come from churches, the halls of governments, or the scholastic centers, but from the ranks of soldiers receiving **enforcement** training.

Throughout time, people believe men with enforcement training whether in the military or the police academy are leaders. These men are innovators in warfare like Winston Churchill. Transferring information and exchanging opinion becomes identical with the men in the South Korean military or any men in the armed forces. Like other men of enforcement, Ryan has a high school education. He is the preserver of the "Good Old Boys Club," their traditions and Machismo attitudes. Ryan is one man of many that receive opportunities to control enumerable people. I work under his Supervision as a trainer for the youths-at-risk.

I consider that a woman's opinion differs from men, so I decide to step back. I record cautiously before going full-speed ahead. In all my educational training, I begin questioning if the scholastic organization causes inconsistency in thinking. You (the reader) need to make the interpretation.

The Juvenile Holding Center contains youth from the ages of ten to seventeen years. They are all labeled as wrongdoers. Naturally, these children have fathers of capricious backgrounds. They have various backgrounds (for example laborers, white-collar workers or other). Other Dads are absent. They defend the country, absconding their bond to care for their child, and are missing. As for the mothers, I need to search for answers.

My adventure begins when I come to work, in the Criminal Justice as a schoolteacher. I want to assess whether my presence increases positivism and steers the youth in better direction. In reality, I have no idea what to expect after I meet Ryan. His nickname is **Berthold**. His name means "*bright strength; renowned leader.*"[168] Youths say Berhold is the muscle in the Criminal Justice operation. It is through a competition; Ryan successfully advances his education at the Police Academy. This materializes when he is physically fit; conducts routine workouts, and does his drills. He mirrors all training military. Ryan takes some courses in criminology, which supposedly gives him the leading edge on understanding felonious minds. In light of his position, he has the same powerful rank as the commander in the South Korean military intelligence operations where I work earlier. His supervisory title has clout. One year later, Ryan becomes the Director of Youth Programs only after one year.

I make it a goal to examine Ryan's ideas. I am curious how he sets up learning. I want to evaluate current affairs and changes. I am also naive about the justice practices in America. I come with the ideals to promote well-being.

When I arrive at the Juvenile Holding Center, I suddenly have a panic attack to see many security gates as precaution. The Justice precautions cause claustrophobic. As I enter the building, there are many clanging closures. I pass seven or eight safekeeping gates, before arriving at the Center. The experience feels as I am in a mini-Alcatraz. The environment unquestionably is capturing, and my world ends.

After passing all the clearances, I am given a large loop with many dangling keys. These are the resounding lock solutions to entering and closing gates. The doors cross the threshold, and I am apprehensive to step into the youth holding setting. Ryan opens each entry. Every time a gate opens, there is a resounding echo. Sounds alone are eerie and match the Philippines where I lose all my **rings**. This is a reflective place that ricochets something terrible as ghouls haunting the environment. The clanging sounds become audible everywhere to all people's ears. As each door closes, the clinking sound is also resonant of the movie *Silence of the Lambs* produced as an American thriller. In 1991, the movie comes out. It is about the same time I am supporting the criminal holding center. The film revolves around the central character, Hannibal Lecter. He is a brilliant psychiatrist and cannibalistic serial killer. Perhaps, he is one of the mental professionals that believe in the moon influence, but I am not sure. Simultaneously, the movie thriller makes me question whether Blossom's opinion about men genuinely suits to this setting. The institutional surroundings are a backdrop stage for frightening events to detonate. I try to be tolerant about the unfamiliar atmosphere, but some youths assemble. I have no idea about origins of the young men here. Their appearances scare me. They are mature beyond their years. Youths are colossal in size and remarkably strong. I wonder if they are related to American boxer professionals Mike Tyson or Mohammed Ali. Unquestionably, the youth's knockout rate is a stunner.

From the corner of my eye, I see a handful of youths trying to pick a fight. The guards are moving-in. They mirror the actions of the police force when I try to get into the subway, in Japan. Law enforcers push commuters inside. This is the same steadfast hold that criminal justice support workers have with the door keys they hold and keeps the youths from getting out. This location makes me fearful about what might materialize, so I am also unsure how long I plan to stay.

Later, I arrive in the Juvenile Holding Center's lockdown. It is a circular room framed by at least fifty sealed-off doors. The individual rooms have a small window reproducing a mental institution. I hear some of these young people are newcomers in confinement. When the class time bell rings, there is a bellowing sound roaring out like a lion's fiery. Doors link to the framed and open in synchronization. Afterwards, a harrowing sound summons. The youths leave their rooms and assemble. They come out of rooms from all angles.

Ryan takes the lead and orders his staff to scan each youth for weapons. Youth checking youth is individually. Once checking is complete, the youth move ahead in the queue. The security officers use handheld scanners. They detect if any youth carries illegal weaponry. Every officer employs a scanner that runs up and down a child's body. Then, another security officer conducts random physical checks. Officers feel for bumps and lumps. Sometimes nothing shows in the first scanning. When something appears suspicious, the youth sits alone. Then a body cavity search. On the first day I arrive, the officers discover there is a boy carrying a dagger. The long blade is in his anal opening.

Among the participants are murderers, runaways, thieves, and criminals of veering degrees. Some youths look like neighborhood children, but the majority has a fiercer appearance.

I hear chattering among the youths. Their latest buzz is about a new entrant. He arrives the day before. Gang members ambush a thirteen-year-old boy. They team up and try drowning him in the toilet.

Conversation about the thirteen-year-old boy reveals his mother turns him in because he sexually abuses his sister. Through hearsay, I learn that his mother is a prostitute and a drug addict, so I assume his sister role models Mother. She probably has vulgar behavior too. Thus, I deduce the boy has confusion about what role he needs to play at home.

Youths see the teenager perpetrator in need of lesson. I see him as a child in need of help. The gang members reveal their plot to destroy him. Ten youths successfully pounce on him. They force the boy's head into the toilet bowl. They are almost successful, but one of the officers intervenes to save him as the Director (*Berthold)* intercedes. He tells the officer the dirty work is efficacious as they gloat. Rumor has it the new entrant moves to isolation. The boys boldly talk about what happens. They have no fear of repercussions.

Twenty or more guards surround the delinquent and not visible in a traditional school setting. The ratio is one officer for two youths.

The boys and girls wear what they like, except gang insignia is not permissible. The youths mostly wear regular clothing; blue jeans, shorts, and large tea shirts. Youths have handcuffs. Others wear heavy anchors around their ankles. The delinquents have sizable tattoos or identifying marks denoting power and gang membership.

Youths continue talking about the incident of the thirteen-year-old boy. Soon afterwards, the new entrant comes out. He is wearing a straitjacket that binds his arms. The new enrollee is immobile. His image is analogous to a patient in the critical mental ward in an insane asylum. The guards are removing his bindings as he wears a straitjacket as he goes to the back of the line. As I watch the boys group, I see some of the youths staring at me. I watch their gaze and officers telling them to look forward. They are heading to the classroom.

Degenerates receive escort to the classroom. Youths take a seat one at a time. As students enter, a dilemma takes place. Seven security guards are at the front. Remaining seven guards stay at the back of the room. One of the youths nudges me as I pass by. I look back and ask what he wants. He inquires if there is any news about his pending murder trial. I recognize his presence and say nothing. He seems upset, but I continue moving to the front of the room. Briefly, I walk around to assess the environment. I detect that it is best to do plenty of overseeing. I also check if there are ample supplies—books, papers and pencils for each desk. When pencils are missing, I tell Ryan I need some writing tools. He says the pencils will arrive later. I go ahead with the lesson, but uncomfortable the necessary tools are not on hand.

Juveniles shuffle into the classroom as a herd of animals. The officers treat the adolescences appallingly. They use rough language and strike them in line when they make a peep. I reckon the justice personnel consider this to be proper as these youngsters are excluded from society.

The delinquents take seats in the classroom. Then the last child enters. He is a ten-year-old mulatto boy with an escort. The tall officer seats the boy in the far corner of the room.

The classroom separates the genders. I am in the all-boys classroom. The tension in the air increases. I mull how to teach these youths – lingering adverse mood and too many officers in the classroom for an effective outcome. I suppose there are reasons for many officers. I compete for the boys' attention as officers steadily vie for turmoil.

Regardless of the difficulties, I open discussion why people need to understand their environment. Dialogue progresses well. Some of the youths have remarkably attention-worthy responses. The other adolescents bring back memories of adult criminals when I administer training before.

The bulk of these minors act aggressively. They push and demand to be ahead. Their behavior compares to my travels on ferries when I am overseas. People were racing ahead. They do not care about the next person and often cause harm. In this setting, the youths make attempts to sidetrack. They are steadily pushing and becoming louder. Their behavior spurs small problems, but it is unpredictable what might occur. Changes are drastic when officer react to youth acting-out. I am certain the teens are testing the waters before learning launches. Officers intrude in the lesson. They voice their opinions too vociferously. The justice personnel are already impeding the learning process by being too vocal. Learning does not seem conducive to study. I am prepared to address learning issues with Ryan.

Class Time: The first hour ends. Then I switch the subject from environmental studies to mathematics. Then, I ask the security personnel to bring the pencils. This is a necessary tool to complete calculations. An officer calls on his radio. He says the pencils are on their way.

The mathematics lesson begins when I write out some exercises on the chalkboard. I design the exercises for age-specific groupings. Afterwards, I work row by row to support learners of all ages. I want to ensure they grasp the assigned exercises.

I continue to check student's work, when the ten-year-old mulatto boy captivates my attention. He is fond of learning and is enthusiastic. I try giving him as much attention as possible, but I also circulate to support others too. The boys immerse into studying and have good manner. Unfortunately, a rumble takes place. Two boys are brutally hitting the new delinquent enrollee previously wearing a straitjacket. The guards take hold of both youths and separate them from the classroom. I am not sure what abounds in the juvenile hall, but I do not see the boys for the rest of the day.

I work at the Center regularly. I am there every day for five hours from Monday to Friday. Then I begin noticing how the young mulatto boy, named Bonbons continues to excel in his learning. He is content that someone cares about his learning. For that reason, I decide to devote extra time to Bonbons. I tutor him for one hour, three times a week. During our sessions, I learn more about Bonbons than I expect.

Bonbons comes from a broken home. In earlier years, his housing is with fifteen other siblings. The boy later gets placements in countless foster homes. He tells the conditions are pathetic. Bonbons experiences abuse and often food deprivation. I am empathetic to what he says.

Undoubtedly, I began wondering what the crux of the problem is for Bonbons as he is only ten years old. I plan to review case notes, but I cannot see his file in the office. Before I address the matter with Ryan, he comes into the classroom where I am training Bonbons. He says, “Stay away from this child because he is trouble. Do not continue giving him extra attention.” His remarks are an enigma. I cannot understand why he thinks this child to be unworthy. After all, he is a minor in trouble and can use the added support I offer. I am surprised that Ryan thinks this to be correct. The following day, I tell Ryan I cannot find Bonbons file. He does not explain. Instead, he is steadfast in his belief and says Bonbons is none of my business. He defies basic understanding, as it is common protocol for an educator to review case notes and education history. Bonbons is part of my responsibility and I need to understand his learning shortfalls. Therefore, I tell Ryan that this is standard procedure and I like to see the file. Even though, I give Ryan a reasonable explanation, he insists the boy's file is off-limits. I am not sure why he protects the information, but the matter surfaces later.

The matter of Bonbons file becomes an emotional hardship. I sense that this small boy is powerless. I want to boost his self-esteem. I am puzzled that Ryan holds up information about his educational history Then, I have an idea. I bring my old computer for repair. When the computer works, I donate the unit and some software (mathematics, writing tools) to the Correctional Center for Youths. I do this with the intent of pleasing deserving students.

I place the computer in front of the classroom after the technicians confirm it is fully functioning to their satisfaction. Thus, I put into practice the reward system as a measure of successful learning results. I confirm my intent to the supporting staff.

The following day, the class routine continues. When Bonbons does well in his studies, I allow him time on the computer. Then something outlandish occurs. Five security officers abruptly come into the classroom. Officers tell Bonbons to stop what he is doing. I do not like the intrusion. I ask the officers why they intrude because I am in charge of the classroom. He tells there are directives from Ryan. Bonbons suddenly flinches and is enraged. This is the first time I see something in

Bonbons's eyes. He lashes out at the officer. There are no pleasantries. Several guards grab Bonbons and remove him from the classroom with providing a reason. Later, some officers tell Bonbons is alone.

The next day, there is bad news. I hear from Criminal Justice personnel that Ryan is in the hospital. When I probe to find out what transpires, a security officer clarifies. He says, "There is a conflict between Ryan and Bonbons. Their altercation heightens and Bonbons runs away. Therefore, removal is necessary correct an earlier dispute." A chain of events ensues and I cannot understand the enigma.

Bonbons recurrently outshines other classmates. Therefore, he goes to the computer. Ryan dislikes that Bonbons is poles apart in the classroom. Ryan has determination to have the last word. Therefore, he manipulates the reward system to his advantage. He assumes that if he disallows Bonbons computer privilege, he can settle the score.

I hear rumors that Bonbons is not obedient to Ryan. Thus, when the computer arrives, the incident takes place deliberately. Seemingly, this is a new trigger for Bonbons. He struggles with his emotions, and cannot release his frustration, so he acts violently. Unknowingly, the boy hides a pencil he has for doing classroom tasks. Earlier, Ryan and Bonbons feud, but the mulatto boy may not tolerate the state of affairs. Bonbons pent up anger transforms from being a good student using a pencil to an aggressive delinquent that uses the pencil as a forceful tool. In turn, Bonbons gouges out one of Ryan's eyeballs. I am not sure what occurs. No one offers details, so I may not find out the truth, but I speculate that something is unquestionably sneaky.

Conclusions

No doubt, the relation between Ryan and Bonbons are unsavory. Anger issues of the boy are unclear. I deduce there are multiple reasons. In addition, there was no need for several bodybuilding type guards to remove a ten-year-old child. The combat between Bonbons and Ryan are a clear signal for patterns occurring in the justice holding center.

To recap, I have no information about the mulatto child's background. For all I know, he could have been Ryan's biological son. I never have access to Bonbons case file, so I do not know the particulate about the. Boy's idiosyncratic needs. Earlier, when I ask for the case file, there is neglect to my request. Regardless of the events that take place, Ryan's attitude remarkably matches Buttercup. He is my boss, and he has expectations. I suppose I must adhere to Ryan's command whether it is right or wrong.

I am uncertain about Ryan's background, but I surmise he has similar traits to Winston Churchill and Robin Williams. The staff says Ryan is a drinker just like Churchill and Williams.

Anthony Storr, psychiatrist and historian discovers Churchill is a rebel and is manic-depressive. He determines Churchill's personality traits give the answer. These traits include no restraint, having abnormal energy, spendthrift, prolific writer and visions of grandiosity. As for Ryan, his responses and bring positive reviews. Simultaneously, his addictive habits say something else.

Ryan's acumen causes me to doubt his capacities. Further, when the justice personnel buy-into Ryan is an effective leader, I have misgivings. Bonbons life is an enigma. I promote his civil rights, but there is no solution. Logic dictates the *flower children* of the 1970s and 1980s era might contribute the moon is to blame. In reality, the moon has no bearing to the importance. There are no blossoming flowers growing in "*The Garden of Youth*" at the juvenile holding center. Instead, there needs to be planted promising flowers in places other than Hieronymus Bosch's gothic artwork in "*The Garden of Earthly Delight.*" * (Bosch' artwork)

I consider the illustrious men. They receive notables worldwide (Nobel prizes and global awards). Perhaps, Bonbons is deserves merits too. On the other hand, Bonbons shows two sides of his personality -- the witty child and the fierce reactionary. I think like Dr. Kearns. There is a necessity to create new designs. What do you (the reader) think? Is pioneering something innovative in an impossible circumstance?

William S. Burroughs says, "*There are no accidents in the universe.*"[169] His quote infers this incident is worth assessing. Personnel and youths reach high level of keenness. They create remarkable feats like celebrities regardless of their age. Brian Cox adds, "*Everything is connected with everything else and everything can be explained by everything else.*" [170] In the words of Leonardo Da Vinci, we are all the painters of events in the cosmos." [171] The result is the "*mind and hands*

From the beginning of tales told in Chinatown, I gain emotional intelligence. According to Patricia McFadden, former preschool teacher, I have an "*ability to understand, empathize and* *respond appropriately to others.*"[172] Skills of caring and knowing how to respond in healthy and positive ways, takes practice, especially to resolve conflict. When the caring (gentleness, quiet talking, turn-taking, or other requisites such as real life affairs) is less in early years, it can cause a setback for Bonbons, Ryan or someone else. Therefore, with proper supports, it can reduce dismissive feelings.

Juvenile holding center and adult incarceration do not rehabilitate and teach **caring**. In the book, "*Game Over*" [173] authored by Bud Allen and Diana Bosta, there are a number of designs to redirect deceptive habits. The authors' clarify on setting limits. They address avoiding criminal manipulation. Also, they target the criminal belief or attitude of the offender's behavior (lying, dissimulation and manipulation). Unfortunately, focus is mostly on cooperating within the justice system boundaries. It fails to address real-life settings according to "*the justice system behavioral statistics.*" [174] Bosta and Allen offer inadequate everyday 'normal' habits in "*Game Over.*" They do not adequately deal with life outside imprisonment.

In terms of cooperative conduct, I detect emotional impediments among workers, and leaders. I consider Ryan. He has less exposure to academics. Therefore, when he confronts an academic expert like me, the advice I give becomes vague. Criminal justice statistics say forty-seven percent of workers have a decreasing attitude towards youth in the holding centers. I realize it is a challenge to change attitudes. Indisputably, justice workers are burned-out before positivism occurs.

Data from justice research also identify the workers have feelings of **exclusion** towards youth. The statistical information confirms there is a natural bias correlation of thirty-six percent. This means officers and support staff are recurrently cynical. This exemplifies when the new juvenile enrollee enters the holding center. He has no protection from harm and nearly drowns. The staff treats the boy as deserving.

In all relationships, people bring their baggage whether moral or immoral. In 2008, the numbers of juvenile youths held in detention centers continues to rise. An illustrative example is in New Mexico's detention center in Bernalillo County 26,000 youths present on any given day. Countable youths in New Mexico are a mere speck of many detention center spreads throughout the United States. In most of the centers, the youths suffer from **mental health problems**. Combining statisticians and criminologists Kathleen Skowyra, Dr. Cocozza, all confirm my findings. "*It is a well-established fact that the majority of youths in the juvenile justice system have mental health disorders.*"[175] It is reasonable for justice workers to be expressive positively. Then they can aid youths to have emotional balance. Statistics authenticate fifty percent of worker attitudes are negative. Half of workers cannot be encouraging for youths. The results infer that no one in criminal justice facilities want to hear about promoting true rehabilitation. Erstwhile, the copycat value of the Good Old Boys attitude and Buttercup.

Plenty of **unethical behaviors** also occurs and a part of human nature. I agree that justice workers are ignorant of knowhow. As importance, at least thirty-nine percent of justice workers do not follow through to provide suitable tasks for the delinquents. Besides, snitches become a source of information for justice staff. Credit goes to youth who are fully compliant even when wrongdoings. Adolescents model "mistaken" instructions, so they remain dishonest. Justice statistics confirm this fact at thirty-nine percent. Hence, the misgivings I have about Ryan are probably true.

I also assume dishonesty comes from strict disciplined training. This is further substantiated by the mission statement of Thunderbird Regimented Training in Oklahoma also known as Bravo Company. The youth program designed for ages twelve to eighteen and the name incorporates the word '**regimented**.' "*The Bravo Company has a contract between the Oklahoma Military Department (OMD) and the Office of Juvenile Affairs (OJA) to provide residential placements and the treatment of OJA custody juveniles.*" [176] The program focuses on social skills and leadership style for both genders. In 1998, there are 497 male enrollees with 441 graduates. Female enrollment is less. There are 175 female enrollees with 159 graduates. Therefore, I close that males have a higher criminal rate than females.

In learner maneuvering, whether the Bravo Company or another program catering to juveniles, it goes with leaders. They also come through the controlling ranks. Most leaders are males. Their academic backgrounds are more meager than experts in criminology or sociology fields. Instead, many of these leaders receive upgrading of their skills. These leaders have a superficial sense of superiority through fraternal association. Habitually they are defensive. They likely get rid of any potential rivals that might be worthier than they are. Largely, long-term effects are pitiable.

The Associated Press comments that people supporting the system are truly becoming questionable characters. For example, "*Tony Simmons, a former counselor for New York City's Department of Juvenile Justice used his job as an advantage.*" [177] He extracts sexual favors from underage girls. The setting is obviously not safe. Personnel does not undergo proper scrutiny or upgrade negative attitudes.

I hanker after understanding whether the criminal justice holding center actually resembles other leaders with regimented training too, so I will share another story about a Caucasian military man named Randeep.

Randeep

His name originates from the Hindu meaning "to *outshine in battle*."[178] As I gain understanding, I find out that his name truly reflects the appropriateness of the operation.

Randeep comes from the military ranks, and he takes full charge of educational processes. Instead, he plants the seed for a criminal approach. He matches Ryan's ways when he also does not follow protocols. Randeep makes his own rules. He also has a likeness to Tony Simmons' behavior when he extracts favors from women who work for him.

Randeep begins his career as an American military soldier. He acquires a few more courses after high school, but his intellect has the semblance of Ryan. Through friendship connections, he acquires his first job as a support worker supporting adolescents. Randeep knows the drills and has the street smarts. His awareness gets him through systems. Most people find Randeep pleasant especially he is always smiling. When Randeep is fresh out of school, his manner rings a bell in the hearts of people. His blue eyes gravitate on whoever rings his bell. I listen to what other people tell me, but there is something about his appearance that makes him look naive. He has blonde hair that glows like the sunshine. Simultaneously, his charisma is like an Elvis Presley magnet.

Randeep performs in the same fashion as his army buddies and men receiving enforcement training (same as Ryan). He has a wife and wishes much like the women I introduce earlier. They all want a white picket fence and a dream house. Randeep's aims to get all he needs no matter at what cost.

Many of his high school colleagues go to college, but Randeep stays in the military and gains basic training. His ideas change through the push pull techniques gained in military drills. I am not sure if he starts out believing he can get all his needs by being flexible in moral ways. I am only certain he learns over time what is necessary and acts accordingly. I reckon he is pliable because he bends backwards, forwards, and any which direction he has too. Randeep manages to appeal to people in authority, so he receives many promotions and excels.

I detect the American Military and all armed forces prize their individuals especially when they are manageable and compliant. Whether I enter the United States military base, congressional office, embassy, border patrol, I have a similar impression. The men and women in these organizations conform by following their leaders blindly even when injustices is recognizable. This is the same as the comradely organizations identified earlier (The Freemasons, the Ivy League males, the Good Old Boys Club).

Based on how Randeep runs his ship, I assume the American military practice matches foreign military cultures too. At least, Winston Churchill provides historical evidence that all the men follow their leaders. Over time, I see Imelda's commentaries about military men are correct. She says, "Military men that stray become fragments." Randeep's position is no different. He keeps values in his memory bank. He knows precisely what he has to do and reserves some thinking in buffer memory. Therefore, I deduce that Ryan also handles his routines and strategies mirroring the practices of Randeep.

Randeep is a man that follows the same thinking as "*It's a Book*"[179] authored by Smith. Even though, the storybook is designed for young children, Randeep's vision has the copycat structure. He **chooses to forget memories of past importance** and flips the pages to whatever is necessary. The man cannot grasp content. He hardly reads any books. Instead, he learns through his personal journey and male associations.

His values are a transmission of what he learns from the influential eyes of the military. He assumes that unacceptable behavior is occurs. Randeep's habit is like Dr. Cameron and Dr. Lehman. They support men and cover their tracks even when there are wrongdoings. Military habits of soldiers around the world are alike. Men from various military bases come to other domains. They image includes being unruly, obnoxious, partygoers, alcoholics, scandal creators, public nuisances and criminal. As in the juvenile holding center, Randeep's facilities operate identically. Any individuals that fail to comply with mandates get phasing-out.

Randeep initiates his operation by selecting people he favors. He conscientiously selects the people that shadow his directives. People in Randeep's operation become his subjects and they showcase him as a celebrated star. Their academic standards are similar to Randeep. The men are self-taught with superegos.

Randeep's social constructs compare to *social face*. He avoids all possible conflicts and affiliates with people in his select network. This includes other military men, Lawyers, judges, corporate executives, and chameleons. These are the people within his network that instinctively behave alike. There is no variation, in how his associates think. It is a world of fabrication, distrust and of things that Imelda describes earlier.

Randeep's expectations also employ military and political strategies. His protective links are his ringleaders as they are crucial to the welfare of the foundation. When matters of unfamiliarity arise, he ignores policy that dictates a need for an academic undergraduate background because he has the supports of his ringleaders. Thus, he makes headway dishonestly.

Randeep is in charge of an organization responsible for a few thousand people. He has limits when it comes to knowhow, so he relies on affiliates that do it for him. Randeep carries on blindly as do many men.

His management team meets behind closed doors. They decide which way to go and who should be inside they clique. People questioning Randeep or his group members are immediate targets to be cast aside. If a person or a group works particularly hard and does not make Randeep shine, his immediate impulse is to get rid of them.

Randeep is hugely receptive to the *Lady Gaga* women (stage name for Stefani Joanne Angelina Germanotta). *Lady Gaga* women are sexually provocative in appearance. They are as tantalizing as an American Apple-pie serving. As long as these women have a frontal image, expose their body parts, or complimentary to his personal style, they win positions of authority in the establishment. Sometimes, these women give their sweet favors. Regardless, Randeep has no concern for their qualifications as long as they serve his needs. He selects blonde, blue-eyed women. Some of these femme fatales or dangerous women are Marilyn Monroe's twin or the Playmate of the Month for Playboy Magazine. There are a few women he chooses having dark-hair. They mirror Sally Fields' bedroom image and his most promising choices.

These selective women walk the floors of the company. They allow the eyes of male workers to be as erect as stiff penises. If you (the reader) talk to these women, they are adept to speaking profanity and idiocy. They have little ethical understanding, so it is not strange to hear that some of these women cause dramatic incidents, or scandals. Rumor has it that scandals occur Randeep is not discrete. When he gets wind there are echoes of trouble, he usually sweeps these uncouth ladies underneath his carpet using the "*just-in-time*" quality principle.

When I come into the picture, Randeep meets me with his peers. They ask that I conduct customized training and design distinctive programming onsite. After Randeep knows who I am, he prefers I am not there. The only reason he retains me is that whatever I do, he gets credit as an exceptional leader.

Eventually, Randeep adds another member to his management team. The man is not a military brat, but he meets Randeep's needs. He is a hand-selected man in his late twenties and goes by the name Jason. He has a Senator looking appearance that is laudable, polished, prim and proper. Randeep discovers Jason as at a political rally when operations close down. He is asked by Randeep to be his right hand.

When Jason arrives, he makes his demands known. He uses the same push-pull and an abysmal approach as does Randeep. Jason always assumes that his priorities are greater than mine are, especially since he is Randeep's right hand. This young man becomes a living contradiction for men favoring women as equitable.

My work environment was unlike Jason. I have a large space that has toxic smells and appears a grand piano playing "*clutter of dirt.*" Musical notes sound off residual dust and debris. There are art supplies and piles of wood scatterings. I imagine that this is where Mozart's classical concert of waves sometimes plays. If Dr. Robert Kearns, the inventor of windshield wipers is around, he could have produced grime-wipers for this setting. Consequentially, the environment needs shaping for therapeutic learning. The graffiti decorum comes out from hiding. Wrinkles wipeout with paint in a Piet Mondrian style. Cabinets get a new design. The face board has an abstract grid-like format of solid colors. The block patterns create congenial vibrations for the youths to learn in the future.

Then the real intrigue comes when I watch how Randeep performs. Randeep's lethal partners follow his directives. They hire friends, family, and people they know as if part of a Pac Man game grouping. In Randeep's eyes, movements go forward as a genuine arcade. Beeping sounds for people to pass and others get beat. Randeep realizes how a hooked-up game plan in life works. During Randeep's reign, there are a few conditions, which create torrential waves. Select individuals receive public scolding and a metaphorical mist of water pours into the environment. Regardless of truths, there are many people that experience game over as they are not compatible to Randeep's direction.

In the architectural construction of the building, Randeep makes many changes. The rooms he selects, bow to his command. Because Randeep's knowhow has limits, he is unfamiliar about importance. Beams holding up the foundation are jittery. Luckily, other people support Randeep because several hundred people are at stake. Randeep never admits he is culpable for making errors. If Blossom is present, she will describe him as a narcissistic man and comparable to the physician troubling her earlier. Randeep assumes he is the greatest, self-made, military man that hires men just like him.

Based on the perspectives of the women I encounter from Egypt, Germany, Pakistan and North America and life experiences, it is a grueling task to understand men ignoring nurturing women and causing undue harm. I think it is dubious to assume all men mirror this manner, but the men trained in enforcement compare to be alike. They are unaware how to create a cloisonné vase that showcases intelligent women. Instead, Ryan and Randeep types are excellent shattering beauty as it needs to appear.

Chapter 22

REFLECTIONS IN MY LOOKING GLASS

REFLECTIONS IN MY LOOKING GLASS

I gain privilege when the Chinese artist paints me. I imagined that like measuring and mixing the ingredients called for in her delightful stir-fry recipe, she mixed colors in her palette to bring realism to life. She succeeded magnificently at her goal of portraying an extraordinary image and painted an idiosyncratic reflection of me in my looking glass.

I am sitting in crystal-clear blue water in the Jiuzhaigou Valley's national park, in the Sichuan province of northern China. I am standing at the water's edge wearing a dress made of water splashes. I am wavering my feet at the bottom of the waterfall while enjoying the flowing river water. I am holding a lily flower (genus Lilium) in my hands. In the background, an astonishing double rainbow represents transforming spirituality and wealth. As I peer at the angles of the portrait, I see a trace of immortality. This is when I see the mirroring traits of the famous men. My golden blonde hair spikes up like a firecracker, mimicking Einstein's wiry hair, only longer. The artist depicts me as having a majestic beauty, perhaps as Michelangelo illustrates in his painting. Although I am fully clothed, wearing a businesswoman's clothes, I have the same cantankerous appearance as Dr. Robert Kearns, who is always seeking justice. In my hair I wear a bow, just as Winston Churchill dressed in a crisp shirt and wore a bow tie. My eyes appear small and beady, my lips are thin, and my long nose looks like that of the actor Robin Williams. Because I am portrayed as unconventional, my figure looks like Dr. Patch Adams, the humanitarian medical doctor known to make people healthy and feel happy. I be in contemplation. This mien matches Rodin's sculpture *The Thinker* and has a rational presence. I wonder what she imagined when she painted me.

Watered-Down Images

"*Splashdown is the method of landing a spacecraft by parachute in a body of water.*"[180] In my wet and wild, I am engrossed in thought. When I worked with the mentally challenged, the individuals were sensitive to cues. They are far more caring and displayed greater concern for others than the average North American adult. The mentally challenged took the time to talk to their neighbors, whereas most North Americans were far more self-centered, wherever they were. They forget how to be caring and friendly. They were more hostile and more likely to take legal action against a neighbor, co-worker, or even a stranger rather than discuss matters openly and come for worthwhile resolutions.

Despite people that bring to kindness to mind, society has forgotten that warmth in communication goes a long way. Communication with people from all walks of life has taught me to keep my individuality, avoid assuming, and attach importance to mental imprints. In traveling, I experience a few surprises. Largely, I am woman among men in control. The women I meet also view themselves so differently from me. I internalize it is my education.

I felt as though my thoughts were swimming around like a school of fish. Was the artist influenced by Salvador Dali when her subconscious mind helped her to create art without logical comprehensibility? Is it probable that Dali's artwork reflects a mental institution where he has alike memory to my art teacher? Did she think I was making a transformation and becoming lily? Is it possible that she saw me as a lady who felt alone and distant, needing love? I experience transition, and I cannot forget what I saw. I envisage faults in society because of wrongdoings causing helpless and obedience, but not by choice.

My visions crystallize messages I need to know. People form opinions by the media (news, movies, bulletins, broadcasts). They filter thinking from family rearing, education, and experience. Woman's beautiful image is of the utmost importance. I remember seeing Araya Hargate on the cover of *Maxim*. She is a mixture of British and Thai. She gets votes as "*Thailand's sexiest women.*" [181] The media and the public hone into beauty. Anything that is ugly, poor, or deformed casts aside.

As a North American female, I grow up believing I am a princess. I receive pampering from my parents. Disney media gives notions about beautiful princesses. Last, my Ivy League education teaches to be comfortable in my skin, luxuriating bathing, and intellectualization. This is my thinking before I take tides to go overseas. In reality, these are pretentious pompous North American views. The worldwide media and reputed schools offer fantasy images of a woman's appearance, clothing, style, skin color, manner, and language. The most admired women are Caucasian, fair skinned, young, and thin.

I was not receptive to the media reviews that presumed that beauty is unattainable for a woman unless she uses the right cosmetics or has surgery to reduce her imperfections. I have heard a barrage of messages on how a refined woman is like a princess. Such refinement is also the visions of Henri de Toulouse-Lautrec (1864-1901). The French artist uses an image of woman in oil painting "*in the act of combing....hair in the toilette*"[182] and a princess sitting on a throne. Metaphorically, the toilette is a princess's throne taking care of beauty in privacy. I thought that I must be an *ordinary* woman, because the mass media insinuated that all women in some way needed "adjustment*."* The so-called adjustment matches to Ivy League schools and Freemasons outlook. In other words, beauty association is for a select crowd that offers entrance into a world of exclusivity and private clubs—a membership that never expires. Ivy League schools and Freemason clubs had specific expectations, which included clothing and overall image. When a woman did not follow their ways, the members considered her blind and helpless. Specifically, treating women are unalike men. They do not belong to the Good Old Boys club, and not allowed into the exclusive gender group. These values were about machismo and buy-in expectations.

Deluge

While I was in Indonesia, I met a Filipino young woman who matched the Ivy League and Disney model. She grew up thinking that she was a princess, and the pampering from her parents led her to believe this was true. She happened to have a beautiful appearance, but she lived-in another world. She had "Ivy League style" and wore spiky, red high heels that flashed like rubies and diamonds. Perhaps she thinks about shoes as does the former

Philippine First Lady Imelda Marcos. She "*owned three thousand pairs of shoes.*"[183] This contrasted with her classic gray, pinstripe Gucci suit with Jacquard stitching, probably priced at $2,500 or more. Her haircuts cost more than $200. Her makeup was faultless. Her appearance was a visible and silent testimony of her North American values. She was a media-soaked rat who presumed that people should admire her for her wealth, power, and social status.

She often took out her mirror to see that she was perfect (making her an ideal subject for Toulouse-Lautrec to paint). She told me about her education. She attended the American International School in many locations. This gave her the ability to read and speak eloquently while following American norms. I have interest to hear about her travels and ask her to describe them. She told me about her experience in Indonesia and said that she lived-in an extravagant, beautiful home and many servants cater to her. She did not leave the boundaries of her picturesque home to associate with locals.

I asked her if she had visited the local Indonesian people. I wondered if she saw the good hearts of the locals even when they lived-in minuscule spaces and pitiable conditions. She looked at me peculiarly and did not respond. She has no reason to see the locals because of her beliefs gained at American institutions. Members of the revered institutions felt honor setting them apart from other people. The Filipino woman gets pressure to believe she does not fit in with *the untouchables*—people who live outside her colonized area, which she defines as unsafe and not intellectual. She says "a natural boundary exists for people of status. Locals experience less exposure to the intellectualization, so her experiences are not worthy of local attention." She described herself as a refined, polished woman who held a high status, claiming that she was a female of privilege who deserved respect. Her assumptions caught up with her when she traveled to North America. She said the females in North America choose not to talk to her. I asked her why she thought they had responded as they did. She had no answer. I asked her what made her so distinct from the local people. She said her lifestyle was different from theirs. She would never cross that boundary because of prejudice she holds. She said that in conversation with them, she was in disbelief. They assumed she did not speak English. She thinks everyone knows the first language in the Philippines is English. She was aghast to learn that because her skin tone was darker than Caucasians, North American women assumed that she was inferior and did not want to associate with her.

Her realities were not outrageous to me because I remembered experiencing prejudice in my twenties. I face a horrible snowstorm leaving snow rising above the doorsteps. The extreme and unpleasant weather inspired a dream within me to live in the tropical climate of Australia. I applied to The Department of Immigration and Citizenship as an immigrant to Australia, and received a shocking reply—a Letter of Decline. The letter tells that non-Caucasians are receiving admission. I explain I am Caucasian, but my application stands the same. I am uncertain about their outlook. In the 1960s, during the Civil Rights era, the Immigration authorities do not consider me a full-fledged Caucasian. I suppose it has to do with my parent's origin.

The reality of the Filipino woman reminded me of that strange moment in my life. The North Americans did not consider her a full-fledged, knowledgeable English speaker, worthy of their attention. The Australians and North Americans made inaccurate determinations about whom we were.

These assumptions came from Western societal values based on presumed phenotype. In reality, I was so white that some doctors thought I was anemic. As for the Filipino woman, she had an olive complexion. People receive conditioning to think about strangers in certain ways. This included a person's cultural heritage, education, and experience.

I experienced many variations in how people thought about me. Like Ocampo,* I had a fascination seeing the virtuous and evil forces in society create optical illusions of reality. There are times, I have become the beautiful petal of a lily flower and alternately a lily with a withered spirit, like other women in the United States.

When I returned to my familiar roots in Canada, I saw how it was different from the United States. I knew Canada to be a place that valued women and supported a female's drive for success and personal improvement. I had had my fill of indecent behavior such as poverty, theft, violence, drugs, and profanity, Now, I needed to find a sense of decency and peacefulness. I recalled what an Aboriginal once told me. He said that people make journeys in different directions purposefully. This gives the human spirit opportunity to gain the lessons that are necessary.

Traveling helps me realize the term "beauty" is almost on par with other countries around the globe. There were consistent patterns in what people thought about beauty.

Luxuriating at a public bathhouse gives insight. There, I confront my shyness and the shame I learn in North America. I cloak my body most of my life. I am self-conscious. I worry about weight. I am conscious about the texture and lines in my skin. In my first experiences at a bathhouse in Asia, I undressed to shower. The women ogled me in silence, and then they talked in foreign languages and continuously glanced at my breasts, eyes, and nose. I assume they were addressing their values of beauty of how fair I was.

During my reflective moments, I deliberated on beauty models in Asia. Women viewed me as different and suspicious. I am a foreigner, and values conflict. I find it almost impossible to get hot water for a bath. People usually drink boiling water and do not bathe in it. They preferred showering to cool off, especially in the warmer season. Foreign countries make it hard for me to judge whether I am a striking beauty or worthless in the eyes of other women and men.

China's Mermaid Challenges

I admired Chinese women, because they spoke to me frankly, no matter where I was. I came across women at restaurants, parks, and all kinds of public places. When we met, they told me that I was much more attractive than Chinese people. They are admiring my whiteness. I discovered that my fairness was an essential beauty part. I am in amazement to see skin whiteners in many Asian marketplaces. Cupcake, the black female, unquestionably is not venerable. Instead, beauty themes about whiteness are throughout Asia.

During my searches for quiet moments, I indulged in a bathhouse or went to a beauty salon. I found pampering treatments to be a delightful sensation for little money. Beauty treatments are unimaginable in contrast to North America. Here, there is a historical tradition of luculent beauty and relaxation practices. To my astonishment, the greatest learning occurred at the bathhouse. It was a place for women to soak and relish hours of female company. I imagined I was Disney's mermaid comparable to the "*Middle English interpretation of from the sea*."[184] By trading news and gossip, I learned the local ideology about beauty and being a woman. At first, I found my entrée into the bathhouse shocking. Asian women felt no reserve about uncovering, but I did. I guess if I were "*a legendary aquatic creature with the upper body of a female human and the tail of a fish*"[185] there would be no problem.

Some of my experiences in Chinese spas included pulse light wave therapy. It removed unattractive skin conditions or covered up sun damage. The light waives stimulated the collagen in my skin and improved elasticity while warding off wrinkles. To promote a relaxing and therapeutic experience, the workers used circular rollers made of jade. Treatment helped the circulation in my face. The body scrub and the hot stone massage did wonders for my skin and blood flow. Women giving treatments were rough and a measure to get rid of damaged skin. I remember a Chinese woman telling me that hot stone massages mimicked the reenergizing properties of hot spring baths. I could get hot stone-massages any time I went to the beauty salon or public bathhouse.

The beautician tried to dye my hair. I am not sure what she used, but my hair turned an algae seaweed green with emerald highlights. I laughed, saying the color is nutritional, but I asked to have hair changed back. The woman looked aghast. She could not correct the mess. It took months before my hair normalized.

They tried to put me at ease. They say "*my outer beauty needed improvement.*" Mishaps occur because organs need detoxification. They offer aid with another treatment. They trump up a mixture of herbs. Supposedly it acted harmoniously with my body, but it made me feel like vomiting. I went to a Chinese herbal shop and met a German herbalist who was studying Chinese medicine. She claimed salubrious benefits when I discard greasy or spicy foods, and my outside would be fresher. The German herbalist did not act like the Filipino lady. The German woman considered that no person is better than the next. An exception is only when an individual has an official government position or owns a custom-made Philippe Patek watch ticking at time.

Reflecting on my portrait painting, I ponder about the endless stairway of life. I am not sure where I am heading. I often see people appearing as mental patients, as does M. C. Escher. Escher's* subliminal memory mirrors my thinking. Society is too controlling and unhealthy.

My first overseas visit was to China. In 1989, there is no beauty. Instead there is a student uprising at Tiananmen Square. Public surveys on the mainland suggest corruption fuels social unrest. In reality, too many people panic.

Because countries like China have become plagued by conflict, poverty, and destruction, so I keep thoughts about what beautiful means. It seems the Chinese failed to show reasonable accountability, justice, solidarity or humanity. Instead, they show people metaphorically as part of Hieronymus Bosch's *The Garden of Earthly Delights* painting. Each individual portrays a unique, artistic style whether it is beauty or the temptation or immorality. These include the principles of order, social justice, and fair dealings.

Rodin's Sculpture – *The Thinker* Distends

The portrait painting of me and Rodin's sculpture match a thinker's outlooks, global travel and favor being in front of educational institutions. This reflection has symbolic meanings on several levels. I and Rodin ponder about cardinal virtues such as prudence, temperance, and fortitude. When *The Thinker* and I are in front of financial buildings, trade and data centers, Law buildings, libraries, medical centers, museums, castles, and places of pleasure, unquestionably thinking is about the human condition. Background sounds and smells of the environment are relevant whether the air pressure drops in Iceland or rises in the subtropics. This makes us (I and *The Thinker)* adept at seeing what most people cannot.

We (I and *The Thinker)* tolerate climate in the background. Science explains background happenings, but it does not reveal the emotions of a sculpture, or human diverse-thinking. Science overlooks how human are destructive worldwide. Science does not explain why *The Thinker's* placement is in funerary settings and a reason I am not there. Rodin creates a stone sculpture that is silent, attractive and without human thoughts.

Like *The Thinker,* I (Lily) have conquered a moral crisis. Thinking takes action and sitting down does not cut it. It also does not compare to being in funerary setting because no thinking exists. I see immorality attacking like the rush of waves. The bitter waters of life surge, six feet from clandestine graves. Sue, the woman that dies of multiple sclerosis might be calling out *transparency international.* Her words capture the essence of the paintings of Bosch. His paintings depict empowering images of life's complexity. Painting portray creation and the innocence of the first couple to paradise lost. From a pure state of bliss, I think Sue wants a snapshot on how people have changed from beautiful flowering or "Garden" thinking to a society in jeopardy.

Transparency

"*Transparency International (TI)*" [186] is an organization that has not forgotten the picture that remains untold. TI helps to monitor what society has sculpted. It presents information that readily identifies human beings as corrupt and immoral. TI defines immoral human behavior. The Corruption Perceptions Index (CPI) are recordings of iniquity in opinions. The CPI records contain data from surveys, freewill reporting and many other wrongdoings. TI is organized by educated members of society and presents facts.

The TI advisement board consists of crown agents, academic scholars, trial court judges, ministers of foreign affairs, and attorney generals, to name a few. The information from TI is a credible source to identify human destructive patterns. "*Transparency international were created 1993 in Berlin friends engaged by the former director of World Bank Peter Eigen.*"[187] An introduction of TI's ideals come from "*report number one in corporate reporting, January 2013, (ISBN number 978-91-980090-9-5).*"[188] Data confirms around 175 of the largest companies in the world. Data is publicly available in the organization's annual reports, websites, surveys about the organization's structure and country-by-country reporting. For example, Transparency International Canada Incorporated have sponsorship from major companies. They include Bennett Jones LLP, Deloitte LLP, Export Development Canada, Nexen Inc. and Siemens Canada. Thus, the information following includes TI reporting from 2001 to current. Refer to chart 1. You (reader) can view patterns. The Corruption Perception Index (CPI) rating ranges from zero (amply corrupt) to ten ("squeaky-clean"). Five is borderline behavior. I assume this added insight does not capture what is beautiful. Specifically, indecent human behavior is not an action of beauty. Instead, I see a relation in China and other terrains to the climate.

The information I present is not a twist of fate but what China experiences. Flooding catastrophes come when uprisings also occur. In 2010, the TI identified China's CPI score as 3.5. Rest assured, it not pleasurable to ponder what may take place next. Landslide (physical and mental) moves in without a way to improve accountability, justice, solidarity, or humanity. This causes thinking about what is **beautiful** about destructive human behavior. Does the man-made environment create weather catastrophes? I wonder why there are scores of deaths, injuries and missing parties in China in 1989, 2008, and 2010.

In **1989**, geomagnetic forces in southeastern United States and Puerto Rico increased. Hurricane Hugo also rips into the lives of thousands of people in both territories making me wonder what happened. In twelve years, there is corruption scandals in the education system in Atlanta, Georgia. There were "*35 former teachers and administrators...charged with 65 counts*"[189] of corruption as judged by a grand jury, of wrong behavior. In Puerto Rico, identity theft was widespread, and incidences showed a moral decline.

In **2008**, nine tropical cyclones impacted Queensland, Australia. Concurrently, domestic violence data soared. Children face destructive psychological and emotional weight. Research agreed "*Rome was very much a male dominated society; so* *much so that in the Roman Republic a man could legally kill his wife or daughter if they questioned his authority."* [190] Information gathered from the Middle East and the Indian subcontinent, share fundamental ideologies about the status of women. They all punish a woman to *"keep her in place, and a husband must therefore be vigilant in his control of his wife lest she challenge his authority."* [191] Same male patterns existed in Australia (CPI 7.8) and Indonesia (CPI 2.2). Domestic violence and other horrific acts are forms of male behavior and the underpinnings of Roman and Greek beliefs. It is not surprising that Indonesia experiences threats of cataclysmic weather (landslides, and tsunamis). In South and North Korea, fighting continued between the territories. Drowning of military men takes place in South Korea (CPI 5.6) while North Koreans deny actions conduct *"Third nuclear bomb."* [192] (CPI 1.0).

In 2010, bad behavior in Haiti reproduces the Koreans. The former dictator Jean-Claude Duvalier returned after twenty-five years of caustic behavior (CPI 2.2) that was even worse than China. Approximately five hundred thousand Haitians relocated to Florida, Montreal, and New York City. In the same year, the most severe earthquakes in two hundred years struck Haiti. More than three hundred thousand people died or were displaced or injured.

I am sure *The Thinker* would agree that healthy thoughts do not coincide with inhaling too much volcanic ash. I am heading to new waters in hope of getting cleaned up and recapture the essence of beauty.

India's Oceanic Currents

Public bathhouses are one form available to me to do just that. Mostly men and women bathe wherever water is available. I do not jump in any water because of safety. I thought I that could find other ways to find out about their norms of beauty. I tracked down some literary extracts and found that a "stunning" woman had dark hair, light-colored skin, large hips, a thin waist, large breasts, and lotus petal-shaped eyes. According to Rajini Vaidyanathan, a BBC News reporter, "*the skin whitening was one example of how women could appear beautiful.*"[193] This value stemmed back centuries. It gave rise to the skin-whitening industry that encouraged women to bleach more than their hands and face. Surprisingly, noticeable in Nigeria. Women are "*using skin lightening agents in the search for beauty.*"[194]

The artistic treasures of Mughal paintings in 1680 gave rise to the ideas of what formed a woman's beauty. "*Women's beauty is seen as unclothed; collecting water and bathing.*"[195] In 1998, Jyotsna Kamut presents historical research on bathing in Karnataka at the Sirsi History Conference. He basis his findings on temple sculptures and period paintings in ancient times.

During the Indus civilization, the caste system distinguished female beauty. This was visible in the paintings and sculptures I saw in Bangalore, Bombay, Chennai, Delhi, Gurjarat Kolkata, and Mumbai. Women of beauty were "*spotlighted washing their hair, drying themselves or looking into a mirro.*"[196] having "*unique about the Goddess Lakshmi.*"[197] I learned that she was a favorite goddess among women. The Indian society worships this Goddess daily. They see her as a beautiful, golden-complexioned woman.

The goddess Lakshmi has four hands. These represent the epitomy of desire, wealth, liberation, and the cycle of birth and death. She sits in a full-bloomed Lotus (Lily) position, which grabbed my attention. Her position matched my name, and this gave fuel for thought about whom I was. The

Nymphaea caerulea, also known as the Blue Egyptian Water Lily or sacred blue, grew near the base of the Nile River. Flowers rise to the surface of the water. In the morning the flower opens and closes at dusk. The whole "business of beauty" makes me rise in the wee hours of the morning to apply makeup to my face, which removes my naturalness. In the eyes of outsiders, my original beauty wipes out at night. I learned how to use the Indian beauty prescription including how to care for my skin (masala-spiked dishes or beauty masks), hair (avocado hair mask, castor oil, vinegar, and coconut oil), and red lipstick. Ingredients come from the kitchen. Like the Egyptian water lily, my body shut down for a beauty rest at sundown, but this did not prevent me from dreaming about what I saw.

I see human sewage or dead bodies in the Ganges River. The faces of beautiful people were gone, and I closed my eyes **to forget**. Unfortunately, my dreams came to fruition. In 2007, unforeseen occur. The dead people I see in my dreams become reality when they are killings by torture, kidnappings, terrorism, and bombings (CPI 3.3). In 2010, killing of 166 people takes place during a bomb strike. Concurrently, freezing weather struck the Adakh region (CPI 3.1). My eyes were no longer blurry. I tried to cleanse my thoughts as I bathed in Indonesia.

Indonesia's and Nigeria's Images Whet

At least I no longer saw the Ganges River. I came to a peaceable setting, but bathing was not luxurious. I washed myself in the local well. I keenly sense that I am dancing, but I am not allowed to stay too long because the local well water is for drinking in Indonesia (Jakarta, Surabaya, Bandung,

and other). I realize drinking and bathing in the same water poses serious health concerns, and the conditions are unsatisfactory. (This was why the Filipino woman never crossed the boundary to meet the locals.) Too much need to upgrade bathing.
I talked openly and used hand signals to understand the local women. I met them face-to-face, but their ideology of beauty was hush-hush and unspoken. Women mostly chose not to respond to my questions because of language barriers or the social and cultural cost associated with speaking aloud. They carried on the Asian idea of avoiding controversy. The women shaped their beauty by being susceptible to the rules of physical attractiveness stipulated by men.

In 2008, UNICEF Innocenti Research Center confirms female genital mutilation is for beauteous appearance. Also, "*ensures a girl's or woman's status, marriageability, chastity, health, beauty, and family honor.*"[198] Abigail Haworth was one of the few Western journalists who see "*young girls being circumcised.*"[199] I had no desire to see the horrific act of female genital mutilation (FGM). It violated the premises of beauty. I knew it was taking place, but I was afraid and steered away. FGM is a procedure for all women, including small girls. Society presumes women without FGM, are not beautiful. In reality, FGM is the destruction of natural beauty and many women die. It was a measure that men used to control women. I am in horror to see the realities of the practice. FGM took place in Africa (thirty countries), Central Asian (undetermined countries), Eastern Europe (nine regions), and the Middle East (eleven countries). I tried to keep in mind that the countries and entertainment practices were ravishing. As a woman, I became more aware of what impacted the local females, and I decided to leave.

After seeing innumerable signboards that advertised lingerie, I did not want to be a Caucasian puppet (*Wayang Kilt)* or shadow play to teach moralities. I understand a Caucasian woman is like a volcano on the verge of exploding to see unacceptable images of women.

I imagine that because Indonesia is a land of exploding colors and exquisite loveliness, there are discrepancies. There is greater emphasis on female compliance to male rules in all associations and images.

In 2007, angry outbursts do not have limits to gender relations alone. Trouble brews among ethnic groups. Locals Indonesians resent the Chinese. Hatred intensifies and turns to horror. In the same year, torrential rains affect Central and East Java. (Refer to Chart 1 – CPI 2.3)

In 2009, Nigeria also has ethnic conflict. The Yoruba and Hausa tribe conflicts sent thousands of people to their grave. I do not believe if *The Thinker* becomes human, he likes to be in Nigeria's funerary setting with so many burials. Simultaneously, Nigeria experiences outbreak of meningitis. This affected nearby territories, and two-thirds of Nigeria's states were affected. According to UNICEF, "*In Africa, 276,000 women die a year from maternal deaths. This constitutes 51% of the total maternal deaths in the world. West and Central Africa accounts for 30% of these deaths while East, and South Africa account for 19% and northern Africa accounts for 2%.*" [200] Deaths results because of malaria and "*meningitis.*"[201] The human behavior in Indonesia struck a similar chord according to the World Health Organization (WHO). "*Indonesians were beset by avian influenza virus, and it became pandemic in 2009.*"[202] The smell of death enlarges in Indonesia like Nigeria when the country has threats of landslides and tsunamis.

In 2010, Nigeria became a heat and dust trap. Flights delay and cancellations take place. The climate in Indonesia were just as horrible when Mount Gahunggung erupted. The lahars and pyroclastic flows spread into West Java. There is no chance Indonesia's CPI is 2.8 and compares to be like Nigeria's CPI of 2.4. (Refer to Chart 1) The CPI scores for Indonesia and Nigeria are at levels of extreme corruption, which corresponds to dangerous weather.

Prophecies

Ghastly natural disasters became meteorological phenomena and were coeval in their impacts. Did this mean that the predictions of Edgar Cayce and Nostradamus, prophecy teller revealed what is true?

Cayce's friends, family, and associates claimed that he did not read much scientific data. He did not have a grasp of the scientific phenomena of the world and never claimed to have an eidetic memory, but he did help people with severe problems in primitive times. Cayce, the soothsayer was unlike psychiatrist Dr. Cameron who hurt and killed people without conscience, and more like Dr. Patch Adams. Michael Mandeville's book, *The Return of the Phoenix*, records thousands of testimonials proving a high consistency. Minor inconsistencies about dates are the exception. Casey's information provides abounding parallels. Obvious ties are in cultural, archaeological, and geological facts in the world today. His "*psychic accuracy was demonstrated repeatedly.*" [203]

In 1555, Nostradamus's first book of *Quatrains*, or four-line predictions, publishes details such as the disappearance of the rainbow, parts of the earth becoming dry as a bone while other areas flood. Other information records earthquakes, burning, weapons of destruction, and other catastrophic prophecies.

The prophecies elucidate reasonable presentations of facts. The TI conducted judicious research on countries around the world, and the findings agree with predictions of M. C. Escher, Ocampo, Salvador Dali, Bosch, and others. They all question humanity and environmental situations. The sampling of people in upset also has association with TI's corruption research. For example, in 2012, the TI assessed176 countries. Seventy percent of all countries score less than 50 out of 100. The average score is 4.3, which is worse than borderline behavior. In 2007, environmental phenomena ties to current times. The chart following shows the pattern.

Chart 1 (following) also infers that "beauty" in a world's context is superficial. The "beauty constructs" are commercials of male voice. This means women worldwide are uncomfortable in their own skin. In 2009, Newswire reports worldwide statistics of plastic surgery backing patterns. Cosmetic surgery (CS) lists the top 24 countries (Refer to Chart 1). Rankings are results from the *"ISAPS Biennial Global Survey* of plastic surgeons."[204] The United States is number 1 and represents 75% of all procedures. The most common surgical procedures include liposuction, breast augmentation, belpharoplasty, rhinoplasty, and abdominoplasty. Besides, cosmetic procedures, female genital mutilation (FGM) is popular surgical procedure for beautification too (Refer to Chart 1).

The term **Mother** alludes to a goddess. She represents the scope of mortal life (nurturing, fertility, creation). As well (**Mother Earth**) the sphere of spiritual life (embodying the Earth). When I equate society's habits, I see decadence among people and the environment. The following chart portrays a sampling of immorality (sexual abuse - human trafficking, harassment, decreased female image), debauchery and shamelessness in human behavior. The Chart also ties into caustic climatic patterns, which destroy people in its pathway. Details follow.

Chart 1 –

Comparison of Beauty, Corruption, Weather and Health

CODING

*** = repeated patterns**

x – refers to the year, s = south,

c = central

id = indecent behavior.
Chart follows.

Note: *Today, 31 countries (Involved in Cocaine) 1.1 CPI 2.4 CPI 2009 – Conflicts and Ethnic clashes & Laws against women*

Country	Locality	Weather	CPI 2007	CPI 2008	CPI 2009	CPI 2010
AFRICA	*30 county's Nigeria Syrte Somalia	Drought Landslides Heat & Dust	*FMG 1,5 - 5,4 (All CPI Countries in Africa) Bush **war**	* (30 countries below 3.0) 1.0 (Somalia)	*++ See Note p. 561	
AUSTRA LIA CS-21	Queens land New South Wales	Tropical Cyclones Drought	Aboriginal chronic Emotional & social; **Human Rights**	8.7 *Binge Drinkers **Alcohol**	8.7 *	Cost $13.6 billion **family fero-city** (2011) *
CANADA CS-15	Toronto	Snow Squall	**Fewer female <u>CEOs</u>** Sexual **Abuse** cost $4.2 billion	8.7 *	8.7 *	8.9 * Cost for abuse $14.3 Sub-stance Abuse
CARIBB EAN	Costa Rica	Volcanic Eruption	Drugs*	5.1 *	*	5.3 *
	Haiti Barbados	Earthquak e	Absence of Law& Order*	1.4 * 7.4	*	2.2 **Despot erratic cruelty**
CHINA – CS - 2	Tagus River	Drought Flooding Mudslides		3.6		3.5
EUROPE	Den mark	Sandstorm		9.3		9.3
CS-19 (Greece)	Eastern *9 Regions		**FMG***	4.7 * (Greece)	*	3.5 * (Greece)
CS-14 (France)	France	Lightening		6.9	6.9	6.8

COUNTRY CS-8 (Germany)						
 CS-10 (Spain)	**Location** Iceland	**Weather** Landslides	**CPI** **2007**	**CPI** **2008** 8.9	**CPI** **2009**	
CS-12 (Russia)	Italy	Flooding		4.8		
CS-13 (Italy) CS-24 (Nether- lands	Poland	Flooding			- (2010) 3.9 9.2	
MIDDLE EAST CS-9 (Turkey) **UNITED ARAB EMIRA-TES**	Iraq *11 countries	Sandstorm	FMG* Cosmetic Surgery **Honor Killings**	1.3 *	 * 6.5	
CS-23	Saudi Arabia	Sandstorm			(2010) 4.7	
C. AMER-ICA CS-4 (Mexico) **S. AMER-ICA** CS-18 CS-11 (Argentina) CS – 3 CS-22 (Venezuela	Columbia Brazil Ecuador	Hail Storm	**Drugs** - **Altering mindset** **Traffic Human*** * * *	*	* (2010) 2.1 * (2010) 2.5	

	Location Peru (2003)	**Weather** Earth quake	**CPI 2007** Violence	**CPI 2008**	**CPI 2009**	**CPI 2010**
S.E. ASIA – CS 4 (India)	India	Monsoons	3.3 **Terrorism**	3.4		3.3 Dead afloat **Not Clean** (CPI 2.8)
	Indonesia	Volcanic eruption Freezes	Ethnic clashes CPI 2.3 (2007)		Avian Flu	
	Japan	Landslides Tsunamis		7.7		
CS-5	Taiwan	Flooding	3.5 (2007)	5.6	5.6	
CS-16						(2011)
	Pakistan		**Hudood Law (1979)**	**Murders** (Honor killings)		
	Philippines	Typhoons		2.3		
CS-7	South Korea	Typhoons **Weather**		5.6		5.4
CS-20	Thailand	Tsunami		**Drowning** 3.5		3.5
UNITED STATES 600 women experience violence daily	Criminality (2011) jump 18% in USA	Tidal Bore		181 murders against women (2005)	7.5	7.1
	Alaska					
CS-1	California	Landslide				
	Chicago	Wind Bursts				
(2007)	Colorado Florida	Water short Floods				
	Kentucky Minnesota	Storms Wind Bursts				
	Missouri	Tornados				
	New York	Blizzard				

	Location	Weather			CPi 2009	
	Oklahoma	Tornados				
	Texas	Tornados				
U.K. CS-17	Britain	Dust Storms			7.7 (2010) 7.6	

The CPI' below 5 represents extreme immoral human behavior. It is no coincidence there is risky climatic conditions too. As for the countries with a higher CPI, their human behavior speaks aloud. Australia, Canada, and the United States have higher CPI ratings. They are responsible for destroying the aboriginal lifestyle. They create residential schools and conduct human experimentation on the aboriginals. Findings from the extreme north and south send a message to humanity. It comes "*from Australia's sky when it has double rainbows in Victoria"* [205] and "*the shimmering opus.... in Anchorage, Alaska...(as) nature's perfect backdrop for the dancing northern lights (the aurora borealis).*"[206]

Japanese Exemplary Adorning

While visiting several areas in Japan, I saw the Japanese advertise using Caucasian female models. I see the same practice in Malaysia and Indonesia. The models posing are not like what Japanese women would be doing in public. The images of the Caucasian females were at times distasteful. If Keiko, an early Japanese childhood friend was present, she probably would not have made a comment. Her "universal" teaching made me understand. She thought about me in perverse ways, and it startled me how she deliberated. I am also upset to see women from the West on signboards as sensual and willing females. Their portraits display less value than a Japanese woman. It was hard for me to fathom seeing Caucasian women wearing only lingerie or as shady characters. Even expressions about Caucasian women appeared more defiant and independent compared to those about Japanese women. Recently, Japanese women have become human advertisers. They are "*draped in sign boards plastered with deals for discount suits....sticker-like advertisements—wait for it—on their thighs....the first advertising scheme to objectify women's bodies as thigh boards.*"[207]

When I saw photos of women in magazines, it confirmed the Japanese constructs of beauty. Caucasian women were displayed as objects of sexual stimulation, whereas the Japanese "next door" classic girl was coy and uncommunicative. Based on social constructivism, Berger (1972), a sociologist, suggests "*women in advertising is built on the feminist argument that media are patriarchal, and that in patriarchal societies, men watch women and women watch men watching women.*"[208]

I saw patterns of these opinions. Based on my experience with Keiko's mother and Japanese female performers, I see women wear a kimono, a full-length robe made of silk. Because the women are covered, I suspect this is why they act conservatively. Muslim women and orthodox Jewish women also cover up. In Muslim countries and in Japan, the woman's ceremonial outfits are bold and vibrant. No doubt colorful wear is an expression of a culture's love of color and nature, not promiscuity. Orthodox Jewish women typically are modest and do not necessarily choose bright colored clothing.

When I walked the streets of Japan, the women were more formal than women in North America. They did not wear jeans and running shoes in an office or shorts or brightly colored clothes in the street. I do not remember ever seeing a Japanese young woman trying to look older or an elder Japanese woman copying the style of a hip teenager. In current times, fashion has changed. Naturally, beauty regimes are also different. Japanese customary practices of the Japanese Misogi or Shinto ceremonial purification ritual are of high value. Preparation is with water and displays modest thinking.

I do not remember Keiko ever wearing makeup. Perhaps she thought she was too pure. I remember her telling me that makeup was a traditional art of the geisha. These women wore makeup to create exotic and time-honored exquisiteness. Keiko gained beauty notions from her script for femininity, which is part of the Japanese culture. It was also why I thought she looked more ghostly than beautiful. From Keiko's perspective, she was modest. Even her hair has a blunt cut—nothing fancy or gorgeous. Keiko was more demure in appearance, and there was nothing sexually suggestive in what she wore or did. I suspect that when she saw Western women wearing makeup, she may have equated it with prostitution. Her nonverbal cues were priceless. There were times when I could read her clearly. I expect when the anime princess comes out on Japanese television, she thinks Western women like to transform themselves into plastic princess dolls coming alive Unquestionably, princesses, always have a high price in association with their image. Princess Margaret of England's home was remade in 2013 for the coming princess heir (William and Kate). This came at "*a cost of one million pounds to the taxpayers.*"[208]

Japan's Crown Princess Masako is less public than the British team. Yet, the Japanese Princess Peace dolls slates for release in October 2013 (with a suggested retail price of 5,250 yen or US $52.71) standing at 120 mm. Makkiko Tanaka, the first female minister of foreign affairs, was costly to Japan (CPI 7.1). She managed to clean up money scandals and made numerous radical reforms.

"*In the 1980s and 1990s, Japan's corporate culture of lifetime careers for men was lauded as a permanent competitive advantage*," [209] but it ceases, and there was a growing anti-immigrant sentiment. In 2010, human messes accrue as a result of freezes and landslides. In 2011, catastrophes result from tsunamis and nuclear explosions (CPI 8.0).

Bangladesh, Malaysia, and Iran Desiccated

When I meet women in these countries, I cannot understand their opinions because they are so covered up. The women wear the *hijab* (head covering), *abaya* (a cloak or a loose over garment), or *baju melayu* (a loose-fit tunic worn over trousers). I want to understand the benefits and their mentality. I purchase a *baju melayu* to wear for comfort. The material is beautiful in color and shiny. I have an attraction to the bold, imperial turquoise fabric with Moroccan embroidery of a white floral vine design. The color gives serenity and calmness and is the color of communication. Amulets also often contain turquoise hues and supposedly provide protection, health, confidence, and strength. When I wear the clothing, it seems the Bengali and Malaysian women automatically respond to my presence.

As I look at the women in Malaysia, they seem happy when I flatter them. Reactions parallel the Filipino woman. A compliment goes a far way, and their faces light up. Unquestionably, I find the same pattern globally. Women are anxious about their appearance regardless of whether they are heavily or scantily clad. Findings in Chart 1 further support and so do Malaysian beauty treatments. They include cream bathing, traditional facials, milk baths, floral baths, and herbal body scrubs.

Because I had experienced public bathhouses in other parts of Asia, I wanted to see what it was like elsewhere, so I decided to get a bathhouse service. I went to the bathhouse assuming other women come for the same purpose as I do. I immerse my body in the water for personal hygiene, but the Malaysian women tell me bathing is for much more - religious rituals, therapeutic purposes, and recreational. As I interact in closeness, I detect what they think. Their beauty lies in their décolleté and waistlines. The Muslim women opened up, and some of them shared how they feel about images of beauty. Their values match other women worldwide. A woman's discomfort is accepting her own skin. I suspect this is a result of mediating, parental influence, and religious models.

Malaysian women have preoccupation with their appearance. Surprisingly, I hear a story on National Public Radio that cosmetic surgery for women is increasing. In 2006, it is hard for me to imagine there are at least twenty thousand cosmetic procedures (nip, tuck, and nose) in Shanghai. The most frequent cosmetic surgeries are for women from Afghanistan. I learn "*the demand for plastic surgery is growing*."[210] Women from Iran and Malaysia prefer to go to Shanghai, China to alter their characteristics, even though they must wear clothes hiding most of their features. "*Three million procedures performed in China annually...the second largest executor of cosmetic surgeries in the world. The United States currently holds the first position, and Brazil follows at a close third according to the International Society of Aesthetic Plastic Surgery*."[211]

In 1979, Pakistan introduced the Hudood Ordinance Law, and the same Law was applied in

Bangladesh, Afghanistan, Iran and Nigeria. These Laws did not focus on a woman's beautiful image. Instead, they put females in difficult positions merely because of their gender. A woman in a Bangladesh village receives punishment for adultery after becoming pregnant. Her punishment is a beating. A man uses a cane striking her one-hundred and one times. In Afghanistan, Pakistan, Iran and Nigeria, a woman's punishment for adultery is stoning to death or execution. Society tolerates a woman that pleases her man, but other realities also say something else. In 1986-90, studies of violent behaviors (rape and domestic assault rates) compare to Coker and Stastny's study number 6558 in Ohio. The research confirms crimes against women are high. In all these countries, realities of violent behavior compares to dirty toilets and women suffocating behind closed doors. Women are unsafe in a man's world. As a consequence, women experience sizzling (torture), dripping sweat (fear), crates (human trafficking), and collapse for thousands of females. These unethical practices affect women in Ecuador, Bolivia, and Peru. Women hardly have an incentive to complain about men. Laws in effect in these places protect males much more than women. These extreme triumphs of licentious behavior also include poisoning climate. Thus, there is a correlation between extreme climate and indecent human behavior, especially values of beauty. I surmise the construct of "beauty" boils down to superficiality. I believe it is no coincidence that we see Cyclonic storms in the Bay of Bengal in Bangladesh. Afghanistan suffered an earthquake in 1998; Peru was gripped by cold waves in 2003. Malaysia's flash flooding was part of regular natural disasters that happen annually during the monsoon season.

Taiwan's Rainy Season

When I was in Taipei, Kaohsiung, Taichung, Tainan, Chaiyi, Hsinchui, and Keelung, I learned the women wanted their skin to be fairer, their eyes larger, and their breasts bigger. The females I met in Asia appeared to feel more anxiety than North American women. I discovered this when I dated an Asian man. Later, I met a male friend's sister in a public bathhouse. During my meet, I saw her talking to her friend about me. She saw photographs of me and wanted to see my beauty in person. I found this odd, but in Taiwan, snapshots of women get attached to their resumes and private membership cards, and they were representative of social standing.

I am in amazement at the enormous amounts of money big cities spend on advertising campaigns or broadcasts encouraging women to improve their appearance, face, hair, or body. There are far too many advertisements displaying a Western woman with deep set, wide eyes. In conversation with Taiwanese women, they describe the need of surgical eye shaping.

When I had had enough of the intrusive social setting, I went to an inexpensive hot springs as Yangmingshan. I immersed in a natural mineral hot spring. It becomes a real pleasure feeling the heated water as it rises from deep underground. There are times that cold gushing water surges in causing a unique sensation. I steadily wake up, as if I am a dormant volcano about to release all I learn about beauty.

The "reign" of beauty is afloat. Natural disasters are a consequence of natural hazards and the human condition. In 2007, consider wind speeds are excessive when the weather unleashes its power around the globe (Refer to Chart 1). There is no beauty in destruction. The weather leaves scores of dead, hundreds missing, and whole villages like Hsiao-lin buried. Some culpable human contributors come from the former President Chen Shui-pian and family members. The previous Lawyer, politician and president of the Republic of China (Taiwan) from 2000 to 2008, graduated with highest honors from its Law department. He later changes his behavior and accepts bribes, launders money. The corruption perception index confirms beauty patterns decrease and corruption rises. In 2007, the CPI is 3.2 and increases CPI over 5.6, but by 2010, the CPI slopes to 2.8. This concurs that indecent behavior and climatic changes are evident. This means the definition of "beauty" is crumbling. (Refer to Chart 1)

South Korea Watering

I continue to realize the model of beauty is dominated by male outlooks. Men think of themselves as protectors, and responsible to create *moyoktang* or public baths. I suppose this represents male interests to toy with a clean woman. I find out more about their thinking when I work with high-ranking military leaders, corporate executives, and diplomats.

I mostly ignore their illicit messages when I am propositioned for sex. After a long, stressful day, I find there is nothing like a steamy sauna and bath to wash away my troubles. I go on my scooter and find a *moyoktang*or a Korean bathhouse. They are everywhere in South Korean cities. Costs range from $2 to $10 American dollars. I enjoy going to luxuriant *moyoktang* in a five-star hotel. I pamper myself to feel clean and comfortable.

I remember showering before entering the hot tub, pool, or saunas. The different tanks of water, whether hot, cold, or herbal, provided an amazingly refreshing feeling. Like in China or Taiwan, masseuses were available. At first, I find their scrubbing too harsh. It is like an S.O.S. scrubbing pad, rubbing my skin off, and it makes me feel raw. The women are strong and place excessive pressure on my skin making me uncomfortable. During the massage or *ji-ap*, hot water and scouring cloths are part of the treatment. I feel all traces of grime disappear. In American and Canadian cities, there is a reproduction of *mooting* styles. Unfortunately, the cost is steep and less affordable. Interestingly, North American saunas propose beauty procedures have multiple benefits. They allude to treatments relieving stress, improving circulation, increasing the heart rate, easing joints and muscles, and effecting weight loss. Manipulating "beauty" modeling is a commercial venture of expatriates taking advantage.

When I go to two popular spa locations at Heosimcheong and Itaewon Land, the hot spas are usually packed. They have soaking tubs jam-packed with people. At Itaewon, I try the luxurious green-tea beauty treatments. There are benefits to using green tea because it is rich in antioxidants. Treatments are a measure of protecting "beauty" or against aging appearance. Unquestionably, the green-tea acts as a soothing spritzer, but other benefits make me wonder. Advertisements suggest the green-tea properties prevent bad breath and reduce weight.

The beauty issues remain prevalent in Korea. I see women almost everywhere checking their appearance. They are looking at their reflection continuously in a mirror. Their behavior heightens the meaning of "beauty." Advertising media waves the importance of beauty in women's faces worldwide. The South Korean women carry "beauty" to the length of tying it to a woman's sense of worth.

The Koreans mutter among themselves and

comment that I have big eyes, a small face, and a good-looking nose. Preoccupation with "beauty" is extreme. Many describe having plastic surgery even when very young. Generally speaking, the women have dissatisfaction with their features. They claim being pretty or *Jong-in* (꽤) means having the right features. South Koreans aim for "*small faces and big, round eyes*."[212] Korea's plastic surgery obsession causes enormous concern over what "beauty" means.

In 1995, I have a flashback of being in the demilitarized zone (2.5 miles wide). I projected my beauty, accidentally, and I moved forward. A North Korean soldier aimed at me in an effort to kill. Years later, in 2010, there was heavy flooding in North Korea, and the North Koreans (CPI 1.1) experienced serious food shortages. Hence, having beauty women seem pointless if men behave so inappropriately with the slightest wrong move.

Thailand's Beauty and the Beast Ads

Like many modern Southeast Asian cities, Bangkok is a behemoth of blaring traffic, gleaming shopping centers, international sensibilities interwoven with devout Buddhism, and the beauty business, which is the largest income source. I was drawn to the glorious beaches because they were stunning and hedonistic. I saw that many Westerners liked tanning on the sandy beaches, especially in Pataya, the southern part of Thailand. Like other North Americans, I wanted a bronzed image while the local Thai women shied away from the sun. Women in Thailand protect their skin from the sun with an umbrella and a part of an Asian woman's psyche. They allege they would be more beautiful with skin lighter than their own skin tone. Some of them openly told me that they wanted to look like

Western women. I suspected that this related to the commercialization of beauty that was dominated by male opinion. This was notable in magazines, flyers, billboards, and advertisements. The women thought that having fairer skin was more radiant.

In my experience, women in Thailand bathe out of necessity. A country girl would flee from a Western-styled shower. Bathing is not for leisure, but also for religious purposes like the *Um Phra Dam Nam* ceremony. Unquestionably, my servant girl had a fear of showering water.

In the stories told about Thailand, there are weathering (wuthering) heights. The environment in Thailand to the metaphor comparable to *Wuthering Heights,* written by Emily Brontë in the mid-1800s. "*The book's core theme is the destructive effect that jealousy and vengefulness have, both on the jealous or vengeful individuals and on their communities.*"[213] Perhaps the conditions in Thailand are ripe for "wuthering heights." People gossip because of jealousy. The Thai people become retaliatory when they do not have their way. Therefore, tsunamis strike Thailand along the Andaman Sea, causing death and destruction from the northern border of Burma to the southern border of Malaysia.

Estonia, Turkey: Inculcating Fantasy

When I go to the Estonian saunas (the *Haman* in Turkey), it is like revisiting history. I see the traditional Turkish Iznik Chini tile artwork also in palaces during the Ottoman Empire. The splendorous setting creates a social atmosphere for conversing, sanitation, religious rituals, and building friendly and business relationships. This is where I see women entirely nude. Some older women wear towels or the woven cloth of the *peshtemal*, wrapped around their waists. Sometimes there is friendly teasing when they compare body sizes, shapes, or degree of sagginess, but it later becomes a comfortable place for refreshment and releasing tension. The bathhouse becomes a social experience. Women talk to me about skin color, eye shape, and breast size. Other discussions revolve around men. Some women talk about their intimate relations including unfavorable times. They explain that their men have other female partners. The women learn to roll their eyes and ignore it, and the same conversation is elsewhere. I suspect the bathhouse is a safe place to address infidelity and cope with emotions. They share the general belief that a woman's image is vital to holding onto a significant male partner (boyfriend, fiancé, and husband).

I do not know what it means to have a great partner. If I think about "turkey" maybe I cannot have a great partner. Further, I evaluate how similar it is to the Turkish people, I can say their habits correspond to climate. The Turkey (bird) and people are alike. Declining decent behavior ties to Turkey's earthquakes. Landslide hits in the northern provinces of Giresun and Trabzon. Dreadful weather causes paralysis in the Istanbul City. In Taiwan, heavy rainfall causes multiple deaths. Red Cross crews uncover people under the rubble of their homes and debris. In Estonia, the snowstorm weather is fierce. I am wondering is there a messages in the sky like in Alaska or Australia. Is the double rainbow in Australia or the Northern Lights in Alaska indicators of beauty? (Refer to Chart 1)

The Cascades of South America, Central America, Africa, and Europe

Images of women seem to predominantly consider **external beauty.** As discerned by Asia's Human Rights News, there are inequalities between male and female, and during my travels, I confronted gender bias. The household division of labor created many issues for Asian women. The mortality rate of females, particularly in North Africa, China, and South Asia, is much higher than that of males; much of this is attributed to FGM.

The longer I stayed in Asia, the more it felt like my head was spinning on a carousel. Ownership is not equal and a world phenomenon. Inequality was visible in North America, Asia, Africa, and Latin America. No matter which country I go to, English misunderstandings exist. English takes on a different twist in other languages. Hence, the interpretation is often bizarre. Signs and notices worldwide illustrated errors. There always is emphasis as to where a woman "fits." For example, when I was in Thailand, I memorized two English expressions that were written by people in Thailand. "No foreign women are allowed to impersonate a man" and "It is forbidden to enter a woman into a man." I suppose the two phrases emphasize men only and no transvestites allowed.

There were some commonalities throughout Asia related to social values and image. South American, Central American, and African cultures followed ascribed ways. I recalled meeting with male officials in Thailand, the United States and other countries and although we had similar degrees of education, the male official had more credibility than I did. In the Middle East, religious values regulated relationship-building, but I was unwilling to accept it when men needing my academic support felt they could made demands of me specifically because I was a woman. I steered them away and opted not to help them.

In Europe (North or South), social values related to image varied by country. For example, North Denmark had more liberal ideas. "Social face" or the positive social value a person projects equality for men and women. "Image" affects all members of the society. No person shines more than another. In southern Italy, men are typically the breadwinners. A family experiences disgrace if a woman overrides her husband's career by being more successful than he is. Women wanting alternatives have limits. Traditional families comply with the wishes of the head of the household (the father).

Global ideals of appearance or social face outlook images on the surface as an expression. The term "beautiful" no longer matches to how people internalize their truth about "beauty." My love for Asian men typifies a need to look deeper at my own psychological and theoretical framework.

Gushing Lady Rodin

When I read about the Parent Support Services Society in British Columbia, I realize that exposure to traditional and present-day values spell out differences. In 2011, the society's findings point out children "*left their home when differences arose*."[214] This is identical with what I did when I went to Chinatown. Later, I have my own apartment. According to the society, "*youths become assertive and disobedient to parental traditions*."[215] Choices to merge with other cultures have limits. For example, I cohabit with a male to save on lodging costs because my female roommate turns out to be underage. When my parents learn about this, they compel me to marry my male roommate. There is a specific mandate to follow traditions of the old country (country of origin) when people immigrated to North America. This can be seen in the example of "honor killings," which take place even in Canada when Middle Eastern women consort with men without consent. Traditions tie with the Order of Canada's motto "*Desiderates Meliorem Patriam,*"[216] speaking of a desire for a better country, but meanings are various.

In the spirit of theory, women imagine themselves in three categories. First, the feminist theory, guided by Western liberalism and human rights. Second, the globalization perspective, having to do with rights about women's bodies and how it may be displayed. Third, the marketing theory. Countries around the world show favor for a white face over a dark one. The "fair" skin sells better in magazines like *Vogue India, Vogue China,* and *Maxim.* Consider Araya Hargate-Chompoo of Thailand. She is fair, and is a "Western brunette." In all these images, I find women like me are no different than other women, a disposable commodity even in marketing.

Careers of women including mine can be dismal even with an education. Women around the world experience forced labor in agriculture, domestic service, construction work, sweatshops, and prostitution. A woman's origin or ability makes no difference. Women have no voice. Northern Europe could be an exception. Women are Lawmakers and part of the cabinet. There are also the rare exceptions like American woman Oprah Winfrey, who becomes a billionaire by an early age. Few North American women are in the same capacity!

In my experiences, I see the worst outcome for Asian women. I remember being in China and seeing women of various origins. I had no idea what they were doing there, but I have suspicion they are going to other destinations for human trafficking. In 2007, the Human Trafficking Report confirms

"*Women come from Burma, East Timor, Japan, Laos, Malaysia, Mongolia, the Philippines, Singapore, South Korea, and Taiwan.....14,500 women being trafficked annually.*" [217] Their image is powdered, sweet, and wrapped up not unlike a man's Turkish delight.

I am certain many women around the world have low feelings of worth. I attribute this somewhat to a woman's birthplace. I recall feeling indignity when questions were directed to my male partner and not me. In South Korea, I am in the hospital about to deliver my twins, and no one asks if I want privacy. I am in an awkward position. I have no covering when I go to surgery. Men can stare at me and do what they like. I am in a country where patriarchalism matters, I have to keep silent. Ovaries are cut without my permission. The doctor asks my significant other if he wants my female child to be born. These are values unacceptable to me.

I was not surprised to see "Mukhtar Mai's"[218] case make international headlines when she became the victim of gang rape. Mukhtar explained predilections established for sons. This kind of mentality has allowed females to be neglected and murdered. In China, India, South Korea, and other Asian countries, many women chose to terminate their pregnancy when they found out that they were expecting a daughter. If they knew it was a son, the woman carried the pregnancy to full term.

Doo Seung Hong of Korea, conducts research at the East West Center. In 1960, the United States establishes and funds a cooperative study, research, and dialogue. This purposely enhances the understanding between the United States, Asia and the Pacific region. Doo Seung Hong examines low fertility rates in South Korea. The study infers that cultural restraints make Asian women different from North American women. He "*examines the changing role of women in the Korean armed forces and explores the issue of gender integration in the military. During the past half-century, the utilization of women in the armed forces has been limited in Korea due to constitutional and cultural restraints.*"[219]

In the mid-Nineties, I am the only woman on a South Korean military base. I provide training and consultation to military specialty personnel and men in peacekeeping, Special Forces, and echelon posts. In Korea, there is speculation that women will become more common on military bases and increase five percent by 2020. I think this is still a long while off because male domination likely remains prevalent. Whether American or South Korean, Sam Grove, past military officer, says the military puts "*women in situations where they may find themselves captured and possibly sexually abused.*"[220] I experienced the truth of his words.

Male domination corresponds to what is happening in North America. It is worthwhile to note that the Canadian military is now made up of "*15 percent women with over 7,900 female personnel currently serving in the regular force and more than 4,800 women serving in the primary reserve.*"[221] In the Royal Canadian Mounted Police (RCMP), the number of females is minuscule compared to males. There is now "an RCMP class action suit (2012) for "*alleged maltreatment of women on the job.*"[222] *The Globe and Mail* reports that one-hundred females are involved. Women are "*seeking damages in the millions from sexual harassment complaints and a zero-tolerance attitude in the workplace.*"[223] British Columbia's Solicitor-General Shirley Bond says, "*Sexual harassment has profound and damaging impacts on people's lives.*"[224] I think a favorable outcome is highly unlikely because of the para-militaristic hierarchy that exists. Few women criticize men in positions of authority, because it leads to more trouble. I know this from experience.

In a war-stricken country like Afghanistan, women had beauty procedures that deal with injuries from decades of conflict. Because of their fear, most women opted to ameliorate men in authority. Even women in Afghanistan focused on having an appealing image for men. "*There is an increase in surgical procedures... from treatments ranging from eyebrow lifting to reducing the look of wrinkles and removing unwanted hair.*"[225]

Today's world population estimates are at 7,029,111,773. The population is growing more than 1 percent daily. According to Geohive population studies, "*countries with the highest population, ranked in order, are China, India, Indonesia, Brazil, Pakistan, Nigeria, Bangladesh, Russia and Japan.*"[226] The female population are almost equal to men. Women are no longer the genuine minority, but they are still differentiated. I experienced this when I approached the largest known fraternal organization, the Freemasons. I was a minority.

Fortune 500 companies also relate that women in key roles are the minority. "*Women like Meg Whitman from Hewlett Packard or Virginia M. Rometty of IBM*" [227] are notable women. Whitman becomes the company's ninth CEO and the first woman in that role. The total number of powerful women remains small, because women matter less than males.

Women generally take directions from males and work below skill level (as I have). Women in mainland China may be an exception. There are many women given positions of authority. In reality, "*they mostly make up the backbone of production-line workers in China's private, export-oriented factories.*"[228] Even though, they gravitate to medicine, journalism, and teaching, the number of women in the political ranks are few. Women have "*lower economic power and wealth than men in China.*"[229]

Women's earnings are also lower. In 2004, studies in America reveal that women receive an average of seventy-five percent (75%) less than males in comparable positions. In 2007, "*women's earnings were lower than men's earnings in all in the United States and the District of Columbia according to the Income, Earnings, and Poverty Data From the 2007 American Community Survey by the United States Census Bureau. The national female-to-male earnings ratio was 77.5 percent.*"[230]

In 2009, David R. Hekman and colleagues study the issue of gender equity. The findings confirm white males get preference over equally performing women. Simultaneously, the Credit Suisse Research Institute confirms after "*testing the performance of 2,360 companies globally over the last six years...analysis shows that it would on average have been better to have invested in corporations with **women on their management boards** than in those without... More women on the board have delivered higher average returns on equity.*"[231]

On a positive note, Irene Natividad, president of the Global Summit of Women, says women "*own approximately thirty percent (30%) percent of the world's wealth today.*"[232] She alludes to celebrities like Lady Gaga, Sally Fields, Sandra Bullock, Oprah Winfrey, and Marilyn Monroe. Women are now coming from leading companies such as "*BT, Xerox, Nielsen, Siemens, Goldman Sachs, Coca-Cola Company, Shell Foundation, NBC Universal, MasterCard, Oracle, KPMG,*" [233] and others.

Whether exploring psychological or theoretical frameworks, it is relevant to consider sociological studies. Findings of the Canadian Research Institute for the Advancement of Women indicate women experience more criminal acts against them from men compared to men experiencing misconduct from women.

"*The physical and sexual abuse of girls and women costs the Canadian economy $4.2 billion dollars each year, factoring into account social services, criminal justice, lost employment days, and health care interventions. Nearly 90% of the financial cost is borne by government - your tax dollars. Your taxes go into cleaning up the mess that abusers leave behind....Children who witness violence against their mothers are significantly more likely to develop aggressive behavior (bullying ,fighting), emotional disturbances (depression, continual fear, anxiety), criminal activity (destroying property, theft and vandalism) and experience negative effects.*" [234]

Females are unequal to their male counterparts. Women are in awkward positions because of men. They are part of the human trafficking operation, where men are in-charge. Women also play the roles of caregivers, sweatshop workers, and prostitutes. By having less (or no) human rights, they have exposure to drugs, gangs, hatred, poverty, and mental and physical abuse (as I experienced). Women have inequitable opportunities in contrast to men. Men are the primary policymakers. There has never been a female Canadian prime minister or American president. Men historically deny women the same opportunities as men

In the 1600s, Sor Juana Ines de la Cruz lived as a Mexican scholar. She was a poet and taught herself Latin before she was ten years old. To continue studying she had to become a nun. She did not have a choice and gave up her extensive library to avoid prosecution. Women like Yentl Mendel, a Jewish girl living in an Ashkenazi Orthodox Jewish society rebel against patriarchal norms. She also avoided consequences by disguising herself as a man.

In World War I and II, Lise Meitner, "*a female, is responsible for unearthing the physics of nuclear fission. This Jewish woman was robbed of her Nobel Prize.*" [235]

Debunking women or males celebrities (Adams, Churchill, Einstein, Kearns, Mozart, Williams) as some point second-rate citizens is not easy to do. Later, male celebrities receive notice, but females get negative notice as Churchill's mother does.

Dr. Susan Love is an American doctor. She is an American surgeon for preventive breast cancer and the president of Dr. Susan Love Research Foundation, a charity institute founded in 1983. Like Dr. Adams who said that women deserve better chances, "*Dr. Susan Love, is (also) committed to the health of women.*"[236]

I agree with Mary Wollstonecraft Shelly, the author of *Frankenstein*, that "*I do not wish women to have power over men, but over themselves.*"[237] Vickie Mallazo, a nurse, was cited as saying, "*You may never think like Albert Einstein, but new patterns, new thinking and new behaviors will nudge the genius within you.*"[238] I see two neighbors fighting, but it only takes a few minutes to say, "Love your neighbor." I determine the fighting among neighbors is primarily men. Even Barry Hugman's Encyclopedia for the Barry Hugman History of Boxing confirms fighting is among men first in 1870 to current times. In 2012, the amount of male boxers exceeds that of women.

From the watery images at the start of this chapter, comes biblical history of flooding and Noah's Ark. A man saves humanity and coupled animals. This leaves me to travel the undulating tides and see many oceanic currents. I voyage on the India's oceanic currents (Indonesia) that whets my imagination. I cogitate what needs adoration (Japan), desiccation (Bangladesh, Malaysia, and Iran) or precipitation (Taiwan, South Korea). Through the media, I discover the elements of **beauty and the beast** (Thailand) while inculcating fantasies of being on a magic carpet (Turkey, Estonia). I am falling with the flow of cascades (South America, Central America, Africa, and Europe) and come to a standstill. It is here that I see Rodin's sculptor, *The Thinker* but also I sculpt whom I am. I am a female emulating the rainbow colors of **Lily**.

Because the lily plant grows in abundance in the Semi Won area of South Korea, it is worthwhile to mention a Korean proverb: "*One will cleanse their mind by looking at the water lily.*"[239] In 2002, Ye-eun is born in Seoul, South Korea. If there is truth to the proverb, I cannot understand why the young South Korean girl, Ye-eun experiences abandonment. She is "*born without eyes...abandoned by parents.*"[240] She is a prodigy like Mozart with no formal piano training. At three years old, she is able to play songs after listening only one time. People lack the emotional intelligence to determine Ye-eun, a female is **worthy**. Instead, society figuratively continues to embrace catastrophic weather (fire, brutal storms, tornadoes, and flooding) and say it is not their fault. Societies worldwide do not figure out **unethical** behavior is not a good song to sing. Ye-eun removes her blinders and plays songs after listening once, how about you?

In reality, all the bath houses I visited were often in exclusive or remote areas, providing illusionary impacts. Bathhouses were not a place to cleanse the mind, but ponder issues of the unavoidable. For example, a retreat area in Liepaja, Latvia is breathtaking at 10,500 feet and easy to fall down. In Roman times, the public bath house was the place where people went to socialize and do business as well as getting clean. Also, the large roomy entrance or meeting area was a place where visitors could walk and talk or sit on seats around two large fountains. During the Nazi era, and today, the bathhouse becomes the place to socialize and get clean. Spacing is alike, but in reality, it is a place to disguise intent. Women go to the bathhouse to improve their image and clean-up. The same premise exists to exploit women's image as for humankind in the gas chambers. Historically, during the Roman times men created the architecture or archetype of what women unconsciously should copy. Similar to Rene Magritte's surrealistic perspective in painting number 5. Women are like beautiful nighties hanging up in an armoire and visible only for accentuated sexual parts. Therefore, communication between the genders is a rebellious act, as in painting number 4.

According to Robin Williams, ""*If women ran the world we wouldn't have wars, just intense negotiations every 28 days.*" [241]

My greatest discoveries happened when I change directions, and return to North America. As I open the door to the next world in Texas, I am in astonishment to see a hardback turtle, recently escaped from a national park, and is a delightful omen.

"*Cultures in the Orient believe that a turtle 'represents creation, endurance, strength, stability, longevity, symbols of motherhood and innocence. The Turtle also provides protection and Feng-shui symbols, and brings happiness."* [242]

In contrast, in aboriginal *"American Indian culture, the turtle represents the caring wisdom of the ancient ones and is respected for its protective strength....the most sacred symbol of the Anishinabe and Haudenosaunee people. They believed that North America was created on the back of a turtle."*[243]

I pick up the reptile and stroke its back. Then put him down and let him go. The turtle shows me (a tellurian) where I need to go. Heading out to a nearby national park, I strap the turtle into a car seat. I come to the park's grounds and talk to the turtle's spirit. I thank him for leading me to a better way. I take off my blinders and obey my instincts. I am off to another lily adventure. I am sculpting the path to intellectualize with other people (Lilies) as I am my own new sculpture *The Female Thinker* (Lily).

THE END

References

BIOGRAPHICAL SKETCH OF FOREWORD CONTRIBUTOR

DR. JOHN P. ANCHAN, Associate Dean of Education, University of Winnipeg

Dr. John P. Anchan is Professor of Education and Associate Dean of the Faculty of Education, at the University of Winnipeg, in Manitoba, Canada. Some of his teaching assignments have been at a community college in Tumkur, India, the Embassy School in Abu Dhabi, U.A.E., the University of Alberta, and the University of Winnipeg. He worked as the Executive Director of Edmonton Immigrant Services Association (a non-profit, charitable, settlement organization). He served as the Executive Director of the University's Centre for Teaching, Learning & Technology from 2006 to 2011. Dr. Anchan has 33 years of teaching experience and is fluent in four languages. Anchan's areas of research interests and expertise include information technology, technology and education, cross-cultural education, global education, culture studies, history of Canadian education, and contemporary sociological issues in education. Professor Anchan is a Research Affiliate of Metropolis International and has been involved in a large-scale Metropolis national study on the health of immigrant children in Canada. His publications focus on global education and transitions. Dr. Anchan is the current President of The International Higher Education Teaching & Learning Association focusing on issues of immigration, race, and settlement. http://anchan.ca

ARTWORK GALLERY

Escher- 1. *Escher*- 2.

.3. *Ocampo - Artwork "Woman of Substance" follows.*

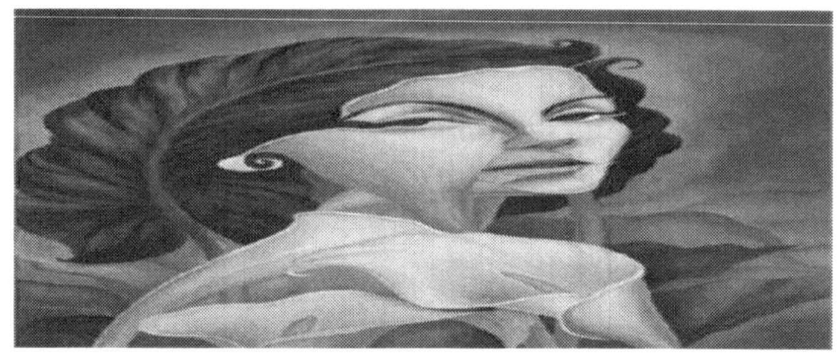

Magritte - 4. *Magritte - 5.*

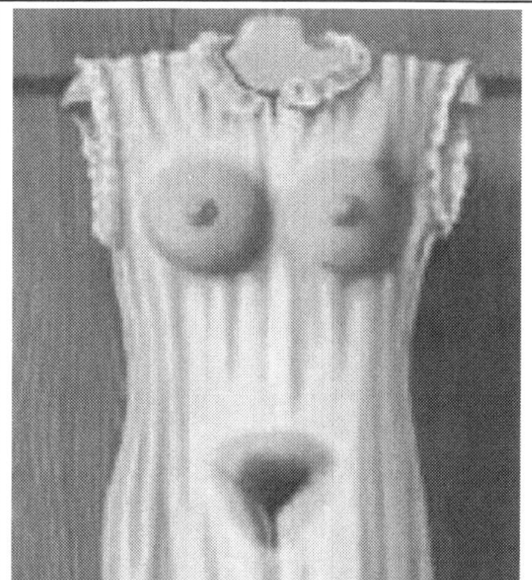

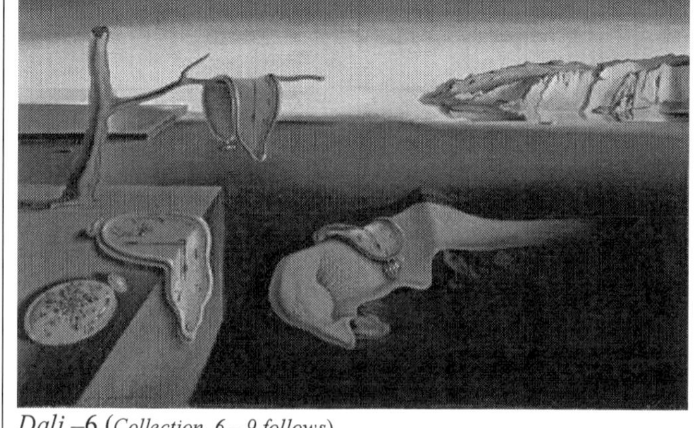

Dali –6 (*Collection 6 – 9 follows*)

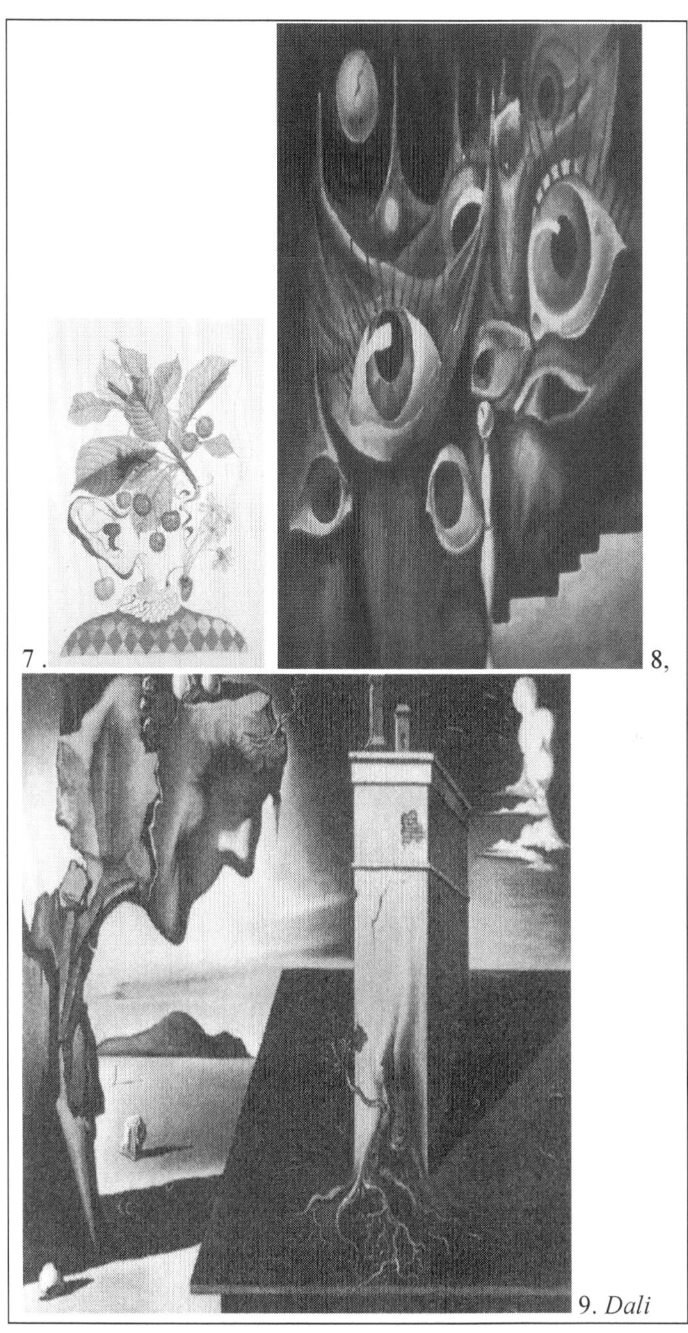

7 . 8, 9. *Dali*

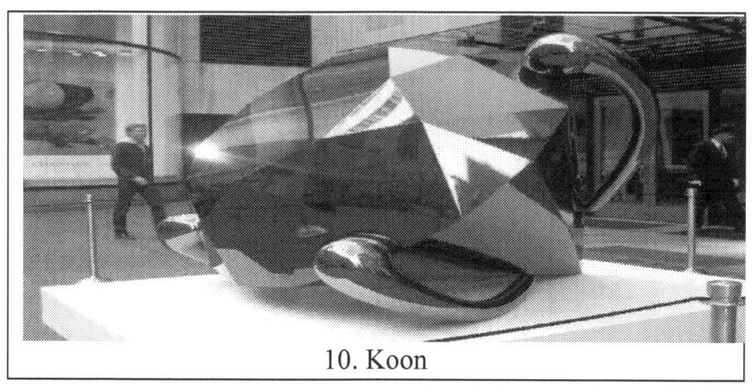
10. Koon

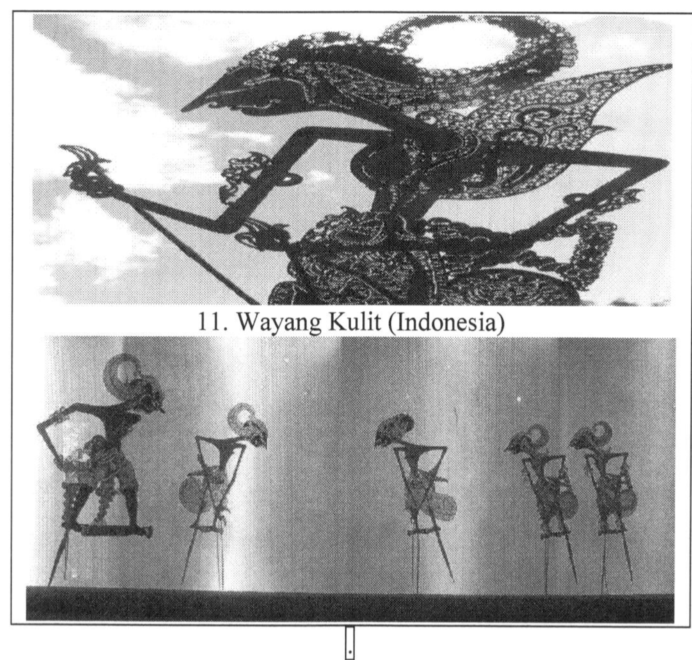
11. Wayang Kulit (Indonesia)

(12) Hieronymus Bosch

(13)

Title: *Garden of Earthly Delights* by Hieronymus Bosch

CITATIONS OF ARTWORK

1. M. C. Escher (1953) 23 October. *Relativity*. (Lithograph) Jav Rivera. Updated 21010 by Christopher Noland in his film, "Inception" http://www.2ndfirstlook.com/2010/10/mc-escher.html

2. M. C. Escher (1935) 23 October. *Hand with Reflecting Sphere*. (Lithograph) Jav Rivera. Updated October 23, 2010. http://www.2ndfirstlook.com/2010/10/mc-escher.html

3. Octavio Ocampo *Woman of Substance* (Watercolor), n.d. Visions Fine Art Gallery. Sedona, Arizona. Signed Giclee. Updated 2012. http://www.visionsfineart.com/ocampo/woman_of_substance.html

4. Rene Magritte (2008) 02 February. *The Art of Rebellion Sexuality and Love in the Arts* (Painting), n.d. http://sexualityinart.wordpress.com/2008/02/02/the-art-of-rebellion/

5. Rene Magritte (1962) *The Philosophy in the Bedroom* (Paintings), Freud, Sigmund. "The uncanny." first published (1919): 339-76. http://web.mit.edu/allanmc/www/freud1.pdf and Levy, Silvano. "Magritte: The Uncanny and the Image." French Studies Bulletin 13.46 (1993): 15-17. http://fsb.oxfordjournals.org/content/13/46/15.full.pdf http://surrealismfall2012.wordpress.com/2012/11/28/rene-magrittes-the-philosophy-in-the-bedroom/

6. Salvador Dali (1931) *The Persistence of Memory* (Painting). The Musuem of Modern Art, New York, NY.http://en.wikipedia.org/wiki/The_Persistence_of_Memory

7. Salvidor Dali *Spellbound* (Oil on Canvas), n.d. The Stratton Foundation. http://ca.search.yahoo.com/search;_ylt=Ail.HsqrQyc.LiZMaFazLe0t17V_?p=salvador+dali+spellbound&toggle=1&cop=mss&ei=UTF-8&fr=yfp-t-715

8. Salvador Dali (1945) Spellbound (painting) n.d. http://ca.search.yahoo.com/search;_ylt=Ail.HsqrQyc.LiZMaFazLe0t17V_?p=salvador+dali+spellbound&toggle=1&cop=mss&ei=UTF-8&fr=yfp-t-715

9. Hieronymus Bosch (c.1500) *The Garden of Earthly Delights* (Oil on wood panel) Museo del Prado,Madrid.http://25.media.tumblr.com/91e18cb6793fda4a5d585669f8a42617/tumblr_mutbrfHBQl1ssmm02o4_500.jpg

10. Jeff Koon (2007) 13 November. *Diamond Blue*. http://artobserved.com/2007/09/jeff-koons-turn-to-bling-blue-diamond-up-for-grabs-november-13/

11. Wayang Kulit (2014) *Pandawa. Indonesian dalang puppet master Ki Mantbe Sudharsono.*https://www.google.ca/search?q=image+wayang+kulit&oq=wayang+image&aqs=chrome.2.69i57j0l5.8174j0j9&sourceid=chrome&espv=2&es_sm=93&ie=UTF-8

12. Hieronymus Bosch (1480 and 1505) *Saint Anthony and the Garden of Earthly Delights* (Oil on wood panel), n.d. Updated 2011. http://en.wikipedia.org/wiki/File:The_Garden_of_Earthly_Delights_by_Bosch_High_Resolution.jpg

13. Salvidor Dali (1969) *Cerises Pierrot* (water color, gouache and 19th century stipple engraving)https://artsy.net/artist/salvador-dali/auction-result/51cb229d4c91c6103201f69a

ENDNOTES

Dedication
[**1**] Amelia Earhart. Brainy Quote. Last modified 2013. http://www.brainyquote.com/quotes/quotes/a/ameliaearh130007.html
[**2**] Anonymous. Swedish Proverb. http://www.searchquotes.com/quotation/Love_is_like_dew_that_falls_on_both_nettles_and_lilies/14939/

Content
[**1**] Brainy Quote. Quote by Marge Piercy. Media network. http://www.brainyquote.com/quotes/quotes/m/margepierc100505.html
[**2**]Anonymous. The Victoria's Secret 'Fashion Show' – A Feminist Rant**.** Last modified June 17, 2013. http://peacehopetrees.tumblr.com/post/13542440036/the-victorias-secret-fashion-show-a-feminist-rant
[**3**] Kotowaza and Sayings. Serenori. Last modified 2009. http://thejapanesepage.com/kotowaza.htm and D.E. Marvin. "Footnote" *Curiosities in Proverbs. 1916*. Last modified May 24, 2013. ttp://www.bartleby.com/346/2.html
[**4**] William S. Burroughs "Footnote," *Quote*. Goodreads Inc. Last modified April 115, 2013. http://www.goodreads.com/quotes/255064-in-the-magical-universe-there-are-no-coincidences-and-there
[**5**] Patch Adams, M.D. *Green Shadow Cabinet*. Last modified April 22, 2013. http://www.greenshadowcabinet.us/statements/adams-replacing-greed-generosity
[**6**] Patch Adams, M.D. Gesundheit Institute. Last modified October 2007. http://www.patchadams.org/
[**7**] Rachael Stein. *Remembering the Sacred Tree: Black Women, Nature and Voodooin in Zoara Neale Hurston's Tell My Horse and Their Eyes Were Watching God* (New York: Siena College) Last modified September 1, 2010. http://www.scribd.com/doc/36745263/Black-Women-Nature-and-Voodoo
{**8**] Jack Layton. "Footnote" *Jack Layton 2003-2011*. Last modified 2012. http://www.ndp.ca/history

[**9**] Mahatma Gandi "Footnote" Quote. Last modified 2013. Goodreads Inc.
http://www.goodreads.com/quotes/76987-the-roots-of-violence-wealth-without-work-pleasure-without-conscience
[**10**] Neil Parmar. *Lunatic Toons: Disney films may denigrate the mentally ill by portraying cartoon characters as "crazy" and "nuts."* Last modified December 02, 2004. Psychology Today.
http://www.psychologytoday.com/articles/200412/lunatic-toons
[**11**] J. Cochrane. May 1992. First Nations Health Commission. INAC File E6757-18, Volume 13. *History of Indian Residential Schools: Effects on Native Child-Rearing Practices.* Canadian Journal of Native Education 18.
http://clfns.com/images/people/documents/history_of_indian_residential_schools.pdf
[**12**] Elizabeth Snell. 1996-97. *Churchill Had Iroquois Ancestors.* Number 93. Journal of the Churchill Center and the International Churchill Societies. (London: The Churchill Centre: Museum, Churchill War Rooms).
http//www.winstonchurchill.org/learn/myths/myths/he-had-iroquois-ancestors
[**13**] Elizabeth Day. December 5, 2004. *Arrogant, pig-headed and willful - what handwriting says about Henry VIII, Churchill and Charles Dickens.*
http://www.telegraph.co.uk/news/uknews/1478257/Arrogant-pig-headed-and-wilful-what-handwriting-says-about-Henry-VIII-Churchill-and-Charles-Dicken.html
[**14**] Ibid 13.
[**15**] Stephen King. Quote. Last modified June 17, 2013.
http://www.searchquotes.com/quotation/The_most_important_things_are_the_hardest_to_say_because_words_diminish_them/230209/
[**16**] Stockholm Environment Institute. 2013. Timeline 1989-2010. (New York: SEI's team)
http://www.seiinternational.org/mediamanager/documents/Publications/Policyinstitutions/%20social_learning_wp_091112.pdf Note: People who do not adapt to new directions limit their vision.
[**17**] Lisa Marie O'Hara. December 16, 2012. *Final Inspirational Goodbye Talk.* Notes: Motivational Speaker, Part 1; dying from cancer.
http://www.youtube.com/watch?v=LCgcN7b6tTE

[**18**] The Aspen Foundation. 2013. *Mission and About the Institute: Mission.* Notes: Relates to current principles and nonpartisan venues to eliminate barriers in thinking. http://www.aspeninstitute.org/sites/default/files/content/docs/bsp/3_PREPARINGBIZLEADERS.PDF
[**19**] Lane Smith. August 16, 2010. It's a Book. MacMillan Children. (New York: Roaring Book Press) http://www.youtube.com/watch?v=x4BK_2VULCU
[**20**] William Glasser. 1998. *Social Choice Theory: A New Psychology of Personal Freedom.* (United Kingdom: Harper Collins). Notes: Wikipedia comments on theory March 30, 2013. Last modified June 11, 2013. (CA. Wikipedia)
http://en.wikipedia.org/wiki/Social_choice_theory
[**21**] Rick Lowe. Founder Project Row Houses. Last modified 2012. Notes: A documentary in 2007 depicts housing, real estate, artwork of Black Americans in this area, distributed by New Day Films.
http://projectrowhouses.org/about/
[**22**] Texas A & M University, Real Estate Center. 2011. *Texas Metro Market Report*. Note: density of Houston's population.
http://recenter.tamu.edu/mreports/2011/DallasFWArl.pdf
[**23**] Harris County Texas. Statistics and data on Harris County. City of Houston and Wikipedia.
Noterofile of 77004 Third Ward neighborhood. Data shows consistency re: unemployment, crime rate, education and low socio-economic situation.
http://www.city-data.com/city/Houston-Texas.html Last modified 2012, Advameg, Inc. and http://en.wikipedia.org/wiki/Harris_County,_Texas Last modified June 16, 2013 and http://www.city-data.com/neighborhood/Third-Ward-Houston-TX.html Last modified 2009. City-Data.com.
[**24**] Ibid 23.
[**25**] Harris County Texas. Statistics and data on Harris County. Notes: Report from Children-at-Risk, a non-profit organization; well-being.
http://en.wikipedia.org/wiki/Harris_County,_Texas
[**26**]David Rowell and Luke B. Connelly. December 2012. Journal of Risk and Insurance. Volume 79, Issue 4, pages 1051-1075. First publication February 8, 2012 online.
[**27**] Ligaya Amina. November 12, 2007. *The Debate over Canada's Poverty Line*. CBC News. Last modified 2013. http://www.cbc.ca/news/background/economy/povert

y-line.html
[**28**] Ken MacQueen. March 12, 2008. *The most dangerous cities in Canada.* (Wordpress.com VIP) http://www.macleans.ca/canada/national/article.jsp?content=20080312_110944_110944
[**29**] Ibid 27.
[**30**] Daniel Fisher. 2012. *Detroit Tops The 2012 List Of America's Most Dangerous Cities. Last modification 2013.* http://www.forbes.com/pictures/mlj45jggj/1-detroit/
[**31**] Macleans March 4, 2009. *The Most Dangerous Cities in Canada: Overall crime score—by rank.* 2009 Maclean's National Crime Rankings. Canadian Center for Justice Statistics. Last modification 2013. http://www2.macleans.ca/2009/03/04/the-most-dangerous-cities-in-canada-overall-crime-score%E2%80%94by-rank/
[**32**] Center for Disease Control November *7, 2012. Alcohol and Public Health.* ttp://www.cdc.gov/alcohol/faqs.htm
[**33**] National Council on Problem Gambling. (2013) *Problem Gamblers.* http://www.ncpgambling.org/i4a/pages/index.cfm?pageid=1
[**34**] Steven Nawojczyk, Steven May 2013. *Parent/Career Resource Guide*. Purple Youth Limited. Notes: Emotional issues related to you and why they participate in gangs. http://pages.123-reg.co.uk/purple17-709240/sitebuildercontent/sitebuilderfiles/gangsparents.pdf
[**35**] *Aisha Muharrar, February 2, 2013. Book on More Than a Label. (San Francisco, CA* Wikipedia*).* http://en.wikipedia.org/wiki/Aisha_Muharrar
[**36**] Michael Richards, January 19, 2009. *Alcohol Abuser.* The Churchill Centre and Museum at the Churchill War Rooms, London. http://www.winstonchurchill.org/learn/myths/myths/he-was-an-alcohol-abuser
[**37**] Robin Williams. Mar 31, 2010. *Robin Williams, talks about drugs, as an older man.* http://www.youtube.com/watch?v=PNuDJddS4EE
[**38**] Royal Canadian Mounted Police (2013). *The Power of Parents: Role Model.* http://www.rcmp-grc.gc.ca/docas-ssdco/guide-kid-enf/page3-eng.htm
[**39**] John Mather, M.D. 17 November, 2002. *Churchill's Speech Impediment was stuttering.* The Churchill Centre

& Museum, Churchill War Rooms, London. Baltimore Sun. http://www.winstonchurchill.org/learn/myths/myths/he-stuttered

[**40**] *Answers.com. Did Albert Einstein have poor grammar? Last modified 2013.* http://wiki.answers.com/Q/Did_Albert_Eistein_have_poor_grammar

[**41**] Copperwiki February16, 2012. *The Mozart Effect.* http://www.copperwiki.org/index.php?title=Mozart_effect

[**42**] Susan Gibb, July/August 2013. *Never Give Up Before it's Too Late - Manuel Ocampo. Art Asia Pacific.* http://artasiapacific.com/Magazine/79/NeverGiveUpBeforeItsTooLateManuelOcampo

[**43**] Dr. M. Ragaii El-Mostehy. *Forget about your Toothbrush! Try Miswak.* Quran and Science. Last modified 2010. http://www.quranandscience.com/plants/211-siwak-an-oral-health-device-.html?start=1

[**44**] Donna Walker. May 24, 2010. *Catherine Ariemma, Georgia History Teacher, Let Students Wear Klan Outfits. Huff Post Politics.* *http://www.huffingtonpost.com/2010/05/24/catherine-ariemma-students-klan-outfits-video_n_588065.html*

[**45**] Norman Lear Sitcom. 2013. *Series: All In the Family is a story of a 'loveable' bigot. The series runs from January 12, 1971 to 1983.* TV Tropes Foundation, LLC. Good Times runs on CBS from 1974-1979. The show followed the lives of the Evans family, a poor black family living in the high-rise projects of Chicago. Rating links: *Good Times.* http://en.wikipedia.org/wiki/Good_Times and *All in the Family* http://en.wikipedia.org/wiki/All_in_the_Family. http://tvtropes.org/pmwiki/pmwiki.php/Series/GoodTimes?from=Main.GoodTimes

[**46**] Robert Horn. November 23, 2010. *Thailand: Discovery of Fetuses Sparks Abortion Debate* http://www.time.com/time/world/article/0,8599,2032414,00.html#ixzz2SSJL7sSl

[**47**] Rachel Harvey. November 27, 2010. *Thailand Fetus find breaks abortion taboo.* BBC News, Bangkok. Asia-Pacific Last modified 2013. http://www.bbc.co.uk/news/world-asia-pacific-11845572

[**48**] School for Life (2004) *The Children's Stories: The Red Soil. Jamy "Jimmy" Jator, nine-years-old.* INA.

http://www.school-for-life.org/en/children_stories/index.html
[**49**] *Robin McLaurim Williams. September 18, 2012. Wikiquote.* Last modified May 24, 2013. http://en.wikiquote.org/wiki/Robin_Williams
[**50**] Montreal. April 2013. *Living a Wonderful Life in a North American Gem of a City.* http://www.lovelettertomontreal.com/
[**51**] Karlton Douglas. 2003 *American Indian Philosophy.* ISBN 0-196439-07-8. Last modified 2012. http://www.melungeons.com/articles/american.htm
[**52**] Molly Edmonds. 18 March, 2010. *How to Become a Freemason If You're a Woman.* Last modified 2010. http://blogs.howstuffworks.com/2010/03/18/how-to-become-a-freemason-if-youre-a-woman/
[**53**] Daniel Ashini. September 12, 1999. *Between a Rock and a Hard Place: Aboriginal Communities and Mining. Innu Nation / Mining Watch Canada.* http://www.miningwatch.ca/keynote-speech-daniel-ashini-between-rock-and-hard-place-aboriginal-communities-and-mining
[**54**] Robert C. Depew.1996. *Popular Justice and Aboriginal Communities; Some Preliminary considerations;* 36 J. Legal Pluralism & Unofficial L. 21, http://heinonline.org/HOL/LandingPage?collection=journals&handle=hein.journals/jlpul36&div=8&id=&page=
[**55**] Yvonne Irene Gladue, 2003. *Patch Adams named Honorary Chief at Powwow. Vol. 10, Issue 8.* Alberta Aboriginal News Publication: Sweet Grass. Saddle Lake, Alberta. http://www.ammsa.com/node/25917
[**56**] Craig A. *Lockard. 2008. Southeast Asia in World History. World History Connected.* University of Wisconsin-Green Bay. World History Connected. http://worldhistoryconnected.press.illinois.edu/5.1/lockard.html
[**57**] The Canadian Press. May 03, 2013. *Rat meat sold as lamb in latest China food safety scandal; top court beefs up food safety Laws.* Extracted from The Associated Press. http://ca.news.yahoo.com/rat-meat-sold-lamb-latest-china-food-safety-162211645.html
[**58**] Alberta Einstein. Brainy Quote. Last modification 2013. http://www.brainyquote.com/quotes/quotes/a/alberteins148819.html

[**59**] M. Frome and Jacquelynne S. Eccles. 1998. *Parents Influence on Children's Achievement Related Perceptions. Journal of Personality and Social Psychology.* University of Michigan. Reference 0022-351498. American Psychological Vl. 74, No.2, 435-452.http://www.rcgd.isr.umich.edu/garp/articles/eccles98q.pdf
[**60**] William E. Nelson. 2006. *The Roots of American Bureaucracy: 1830 – 1900.* http://www.beardbooks.com/beardbooks/the_roots_of_american_bureaucracy.html
[**61**] Biggins. June 16, 2012. *Non-Intimidated Woman Wins $31 Million; Sherry Hunt.* http://bigginsblog.wordpress.com/2012/06/16/non-intimidated-woman-31-million-dollars-15/
[**62**] Nancy Holland and June Halper. *Multiple Sclerosis: A Self-Care Guide to Wellness, Second Edition.* Last modification 2013. http://www.barnesandnoble.com/w/multiple-sclerosis-nancy-holland-mscn-edd/1114875392?ean=9781932603071
[**63**] Rosalind Kalb. *Multiple Sclerosis: A Guide for Families, Third Edition. Last modification 2013.* http://www.barnesandnoble.com/w/multiple-sclerosis-nancy-holland-mscn-edd/1114875392?ean=9781932603071
[**64**] China Stem Cell News (2010) 19 April, *Multiple Sclerosis. David Ozzello Age 54, USA: Multiple Sclerosis.* http://www.stemcellschina.com/index.php/en/patient-experiences/multiple-sclerosis
[**65**] Hakim, A.A. M.D., Ph.D. (2013) 10 May. *Stem Cell Egypt - Mitzi Sprague, Age 36, USA.* http://stemcellsegypt.com/?page_id=370
[**66**] China Stem Cell News (2009) 17 December. *Multiple Sclerosis: Cristian Nasaudean - Romania, Age 37.* http://stemcellschina.com/en/patient-experiences/multiple-sclerosis/1233-cris-ms
[**67**] Zeldis, Leon (2012) *Color Symbolism in Freemasonry.* http://www.masonicworld.com/education/files/apr02/include/colour_symbolism_in_freemasonry.htm
[**68**] Ann Buggins. July 22, 1999. Freemasons Hand Over 60 Skulls for Police Tests. The West Australian. PEN-L:11978. http://archives.econ.utah.edu/archives/pen-l/1999m09.e/msg00267.html

[**69**] Mayhem & Muse (2012) August. *The Hidden Faces of Octavio Ocampo's Illusion Art. Last modified 2013.*http://mayhemandmuse.com/the-hidden-faces-of-octavio-ocampos-illusion-ar/
[**70**] Miguel de Cervantes. *Themes in Don Quixote.* http://www.cliffsnotes.com/literature/d/don-quixote/critical-essays/themes-in-don-quixoteNotes: No longer online, but information about ideals were extracted. *The Duality of Don Quixote: The Antihero and the Epitome of Renaissance Ideals*. http://fysm-149.wp.trincoll.edu/2009/10/03/the-duality-of-don-quixote-the-antihero-and-the-epitome-of-renaissance-ideals/
[**71**] Karrie Webb. (2013) *Brainy Quotes.* http://www.brainyquote.com/quotes/authors/k/karrie_webb.html
[**72**] Wikipedia. June 17, 2013. *Kopi Luwak.* http://en.wikipedia.org/wiki/Kopi_Luwak
[**73**] Tripod. History of Borobudar. Extracted May 2012. http://borobudur7.tripod.com/id1.html and Wikipedia. 2012 - Extracted. *Borobudur ancient lake*. Last modified April 24, 2013. http://en.wikipedia.org/wiki/Borobudur_ancient_lake
[**74**] The Nature of the Conservatory (2013) 11 May. *Minnesota Trout Lily Preserve.* http://www.nature.org/ourinitiatives/regions/northamerica/unitedstates/minnesota/placesweprotect/trout-lily-preserve.xml
[**75**] Wikipedia. (1998) Plot Summary: Mulan. Last modified 2013. http://www.imdb.com/title/tt0120762/plotsummary
[**76**] Wikipedia. Russian Traditions and Superstitions. Last modified June 21, 2013. http://en.wikipedia.org/wiki/Russian_traditions_and_superstitions
[**77**] Harry Truman. 1946-to present. Announcement of the 'Fair Deal.' Rejection of National Health Insurance. Employment Practices. Note: The inference is that all 'Fair Deals' making logical sense, needs consideration. Refers to first 3 links. By definition, fair deal and by definition is "*a continuation largely of a continuation and development of the principles of the New Deal.*" http://www.americaslibrary.gov/jb/modern/jb_modern_fairdeal_1.html and http://www.americaslibrary.gov/jb/modern/jb_modern_fairdeal_2.html

http://www.americaslibrary.gov/jb/modern/jb_modern_fairdeal_3.html
http://dictionary.reference.com/browse/fair+deal
[**78**] National Center for Policy Analysis. November 8, 2006. Ideas Changing the World: *60 MILLION CHINESE ARE CONSIDERED OBESE. Last modified 2010.*
http://www.ncpa.org/sub/dpd/index.php?Article_ID=13747
[**79**] d, Garcia R, Dankwa CM, Young T, Lipsky MS. May-June 2008. *Overweight and obese prevalence rates in African American and Hispanic children: an analysis of data from the 2003-2004 National Survey of Children's Health.* Department of Family and Community Medicine, University of Illinois College of Medicine at Rockford, Rockford, Illinois. US National Library of Medicine National Institutes of Health.
http://www.ncbi.nlm.nih.gov/pubmed/18467530
[**80**] Leah Goldman and Gus Lubin. July 7, 2011. Business Insider. *The Ten Fattest States in America*. Last modified 2013. http://www.businessinsider.com/fattest-states-in-america-2011-7?op=1
[**81**] OECD *Obesity Update 2012*. Notes: p.6 (Adults), p. 7 (Children) http://www.oecd.org/health/49716427.pdf
[**82**] Robert Louis Stevenson. 2012. Cited by Dr. Stephanie Sarkis. Psychology Today. Sarkis Media, LLC. Last modification 2013.
http://www.psychologytoday.com/blog/here-there-and-everywhere/201204/50-quotes-consequences
[**83**]Michael Jackson. March 29, 2013. *Beat It.*
http://www.youtube.com/watch?v=6B2wtC91_0U
[**84**] About Cultural China. *Shuixiu (Water Sleeves)*. Last modification 2010.
http://arts.cultural-china.com/en/87Arts7305.html
[**85**] Mahatma Gandhi Quote: # 28993.
http://www.quotationspage.com/quote/28993.html
[**86**] Department of Health and Hospitals. State of Louisiana.
http://www.ncpa.org/sub/dpd/index.php?Article_ID=13747
[**87**] United States Government. February 16, 2011. *Overweight and Obesity Trends Among Adults.* Center for Disease Control and Protection. Atlanta, GA and http://www.cdc.gov/obesity/data/index.html
[**88**] Chris Wright. 2013. *How Gambling Can Kill You Faster Than Drug Abuse or Alcoholism:*

1 in 5 problem gamblers try to kill themselves. Why gambling may be the most dangerous addiction of all. Alter.net. http://www.alternet.org/how-gambling-can-kill-you-faster-drug-abuse-or-alcoholism

[**89**] Reuters. February 19, 2013. *Norway's consumers may end up subsidizing renewables in Sweden.* http://www.reuters.com/article/2013/02/21/norway-renewables-idUSL5N0BEEZU20130221

[**90**] John Zerzan. April 13, 2010. *Patriarchy, Civilization and the Origins of Gender.* http://theanarchistlibrary.org/library/john-zerzan-patriarchy-civilization-and-the-origins-of-gender

[**91**] The Wall Street Journal. May 17, 2010. *Why Are Women-Owned Firms Smaller Than Men-Owned Ones?* http://online.wsj.com/article/SB10001424052748704688604575125543191609632.html

[**92**] Borowkowski, Julia (2014) 11 April. http://www.freedomworks.org/content/real-talk-julie-borowski-episode-2-equal-pay-debate-1

[**93**] Mercer. April 26, 2014. Expatriate positions rise worldwide. Expatica.com http://www.expatica.com/ch/news/news_focus/Global-employee-mobility-Expatriate-positions-rise-worldwide_263219.html

[**94**] A Place of Our Own. Learning Areas. Press Relations Jessica Robinson. Moises Roman.
Press Relations.
http://aplaceofourown.org/question_detail.php?id=599

[**95**] Madeleine L. Van, PhD. 2007. *Blind Spots*. Prometheus Books. Amherst, NY. http://www.ebay.com/ctg/Blind-Spots-Why-Smart-People-Do-Dumb-Things-by-Madeleine-L-Van-Hecke-2007-Paperback

[**96**] Ibid 95.

[**97**] Earth, Wind and Fire band. May 1, 2007. Lyrics. Not Available for viewing in Canada. http://www.youtube.com/watch?v=nfLEc09tTjI

[**98**] The Interpretation of Dreams. 2013. http://eofdreams.com/lily-of-valley.html

[**99**] Maya Health. 2013. Lotus and Water Lilies. Notes: Images. http://pinterest.com/isiscat/lotus-water-lilies/

[**100**] Aileen McCabe. October 8, 2010. Asia Correspondent, Post media News http://www.canada.com/news/Canada+congratulates+imprisoned+Chinese+Nobel+Prize+winner/3642953/story.h

tml
[**101**] Mckinsey & Company (2012) June. *Women Matter: An Asian Perspective. Harnessing Female talent to raise corporate performance*.
file:///C:/Users/IC/Downloads/Women_Matter_An_Asian_perspective.pdf and Government of Taiwan. Promoting Cultural Sensitivity. Chinese Guide: Overview of Chinese Culture. Chapter 2. P.16.
http://www.cdc.gov/tb/publications/guidestoolkits/ethnographicguides/China/chapters/chapter2.pdf
[**102**] Sophia Liu. 2011 - *7 Reasons Why We Love 7-Eleven in Taiwan*. Taipei43.
http://taipei543.com/2011/12/08/7-reasons-why-we-love-7-eleven-in-taiwan/
[**103**] ID. (1971-79*] All in the Family*. Last modification 2013.
http://www.imdb.com/title/tt0066626/
[**104**] Crab Mentality. May 22, 2013. Wikipedia
http://en.wikipedia.org/wiki/Crab_mentality
[**105**] Bruce Springstein. 2013.
http://www.lyricsfreak.com/b/bruce+springsteen/we+take+care+of+our+own_20999721.html
[**106**] Arnold H. Lubasch. 1998. *Marcos and wife, 8 others charged by U.S. with Fraud.*
http://www.nytimes.com/1988/10/22/world/marcos-and-wife-8-others-charged-by-us-with-fraud.html
[**107**] Lilia Quindoza Santiago. February 2005. *Famous Filipino Women*. Diwata Foundation, Hasik Incorporated and the Canadian International Development Agency.
http://jeanrojas.tripod.com/id13.html
[**108**] Timothy Austin. *Street Theft in the Philippines. Indiana University of Pennsylvania, the Department of Criminology.*
http://www.iup.edu/newsItem.aspx?id=126092&
[**109**] The World Fact book, Central Intelligence Agency. The World Fact Book. *Literacy - Philippines* ISSN 1553-8133.
https://www.cia.gov/library/publications/the-world-factbook/fields/2103.html
[**110**] Tact-all. 2006-2012. *Lily/ Yuri. Japanese Kanji Images.* Wikipedia Foundation Inc. San Francisco, CA.
http://japanesekanji.nobody.jp/flower/lily.htm
[**111**] Google (1989) *Male Japanese Names*.
http://www.20000-names.com/male_japanese_names_02.htm
[**112**]Yoshitaka Miike. 2005. Japanese Enryo-Sasshi Communication and the Psychology of Amae:

Reconsideration and Reconceptualization. Keio Communication Review No, 25
http://www.mediacom.keio.ac.jp/publication/pdf2003/review25/7.pdf

[**113**] Zeepedia. April 2012. Social Psychology. *No. 13 Person Perception: Impression Formation, Facial Expression.*http://www.zeepedia.com/read.php?person_perception_impression_formation_facial_expressions_social_psychology&b=95&c=13

[**114**] David Matsumoto, *Social Psychologist Subtle Expression Recognition Training: Original and Advanced Micro-expression Recognition Training (MiX).* Last modification 2013.
http://www.davidmatsumoto.com/research.php

[**115**] Nobue Suzuki. 2003. Critical Asian Studies, Routledge. *Transgressing 'Victims' Reading Narratives of 'Filipina Brides' in Japan,* 35:3, 399-420
http://www.academia.edu/295633/Transgressing_Victims_Reading_Narratives_of_Filipina_Brides_in_Japan

[**116**] Dr. David Matsumoto and Dr. Hyi Sung Hwang. Subtle Expression Recognition Training:
Matsumoto Method to learn Subtle Expressions. Humintell.
http://www.humintell.com/subtle-expression-recognition-training/

[**117**] Jared Denman. 2010. *Japanese wives in Japanese-Australian intermarriages,*
The University of Queensland. Australia
http://www.jpf.org.au/newvoices/3/chapter4.pdf

[**118**] Shinagawa and Pang. *An Asian American Study on Race and Identity.* Chapter 6. P.137. Rutgers University Press. New Brunswick, New Jersey. ISBN 0-8135-2464-4.

[**119**] Encyclopedia Britannica. 2004. *Yin and Yang.* Last modification 2013.
http://www.religionfacts.com/chinese_religion/beliefs/yin_yang.htm

[**120**] New York Times. December 27, 2012. *Will Japan Un-apologize to 'Comfort Women'? The International Herald Tribune.* The Comfort Women issue
http://rendezvous.blogs.nytimes.com/2012/12/27/will-japan-unapologize-for-comfort-women/

[**121**] Dan Pink. September 07, 2009. Rethinking the ideology of carrots and sticks. 10 Design Lessons from the art of Ikebam and 7 Japanese aesthetic principles to change your thinking.http://www.presentationzen.com/presentationze

n/2009/09/exposing-ourselves-to-traditional-japanese-aesthetic-ideas-notions-that-may-seem-quite-foreign-to-most-of-us-is-a-goo.html

[**122**] William Lidwell. October 1, 2003. Universal Principles of Design. Rockport Publishers. http://www.goodreads.com/book/show/130730.Universal_Principles_of_Design

[**123**] Nocholas Pioch. October 14, 2002. Painting - Bosch, Hieronymus: *The Garden of Earthly Delight*. Web Museum Paris. Central Panel. BMW Foundation. http://www.ibiblio.org/wm/paint/auth/bosch/delight/

[**124**] Ibid 112.

[**125**] Chi Moriya. September 24, 2008. *Japan: Autumn Moon Fun-raiser in Tokyo*. Gusenheidt Institute. Dr. Patch Adams' Event. http://www.patchadams.org/taxonomy/term/45

[**126**] Wikipedia. April 21, 2013. Chuseok. Note: Moon superstitions South Korea. http://en.wikipedia.org/wiki/Chuseok

[**125**] William Shakespeare. 2012. Monologue. http://www.monologuearchive.com/s/shakespeare_001.html

[**126**] Hankuk Story. September 10, 2012. *North Korean Female Soldiers Sexually Abused*! The Treatment of Women http://hangukstory.blogspot.ca/2012/09/north-korean-female-soldiers-sexually.html

[**127**] Kristin Butler. May 06, 2009. *North Korean Bride Trafficking: When Escape Becomes Bondage* Last modification 2013. Salem Web Network. http://www.religiontoday.com/articles/north-korean-bride-trafficking-when-escape-becomes-bondage-11603283.html

[**128**] Wikipedia. Suicide in South Korea. Notes: Female celebrities commit suicide. Last modification June 20, 2013. http://en.wikipedia.org/wiki/Suicide_in_South_Korea

[**129**] Jennifer Veale. October 06, 2008. *South Koreans Are Shaken by a Celebrity Suicide:* Choi Jin Sil. Time. http://www.time.com/time/world/article/0,8599,1847437,00.html#ixzz2X9OXNSkT

[**130**]Deng Shasta. July 8, 2010. *South Korea Sees World's Highest Female Suicide. English News.* http://news.xinhuanet.com/english2010/world/2010-07/08/c_13390330.htm

[**131**] John B. Hay. May 16, 2011.*The Dubai Process: Lessons learned and implications for third-party engagement in managing cross-border challenges in other regions.* The Norman Paterson School of International Affairs: Carleton University.http://www1.carleton.ca/npsia/ccms/wp-content/ccms-files/Dubai-Process-Evaluation.pdf

[**132**] Holly Buchanan. May 11, 2010. *Word Of Mouth: Men Trust Authority, Women Trust Common Experience.*http://marketingtowomenonline.typepad.com/blog/2010/05/word-of-mouth-men-trust-authority-women-trust-common-experience.html

[**133**] Encyclopedia Britannica. 2013. *Innu.* http://www.britannica.com/EBchecked/topic/1071428/Innu

[**134**] Dan Katchongva and Sun Clan. Excerpts from "*Teachings, History, and Prophecies of the Hopi People*" Notes: the data is discovered in 1865 and translated in 1972 by Danagyumptewa. http://apocalypse-soon.com/prophecies_of_hopi_indians.htm

[**135**] Manataka American Indian Council. 2013. Cree Prophecy: *Warriors of the Rainbow.* http://www.manataka.org/page235.html#CREE PROPHECY

[**136**] Ibid 135.

[**137**] Theories of Socialization. Education and Science. Sociology and Anthropology: Social Theory. Last modification December 23, 2012. http://dilipchandra12.hubpages.com/hub/Theories-of-Socialization

[**138**] Yours to Celebrate. The Friendly Giant. CBC. Last modification 2013. http://www.cbc.ca/75/2011/11/the-friendly-giant-1.html

[**139**] CSLS. February 2010. Investing in Aboriginal Education in Canada: An Economic Perspective. Ottawa, ON. Note: Aboriginal academic level http://www.csls.ca/reports/csls2010-03.pdf

[**140**] University Minnesota. Human Rights Library. Draft Declaration on the Rights of Indigenous Peoples, U.N. Doc. E/CN.4/Sub.2/1994/2/Add.1 (1994). Aboriginal Educational premises http://www1.umn.edu/humanrts/instree/declra.htm

[**141**]Thomas Watters. The Takao Club: Chinese Fox Myths. Pu Song-ling [蒲松齡]. *Collection: The Strange Tales from a Chinese Studio.*

http://www.takaoclub.com/foxmyths/chinese_fox_myths.htm
[**142**] E.T.C. Werner. March 4, 2005. *The Project Gutenberg EBook of Myths and Legends of China. Chapter XV. Legends of the Fox.*
http://www.gutenberg.org/files/15250/15250-h/15250-h.htm#d0e5705
[**143**] Ibid 142.
[**144**] Traditional Aboriginal Bush Medicine. 2000.
http://www.aboriginalartonline.com/culture/medicine.php
[**145**]Jennifer Kyrnin. 2013. *Visual Color Symbolism Chart by Culture: What Different Colors Mean in Different Cultures.*http://webdesign.about.com/od/colorcharts/l/bl_colorculture.htm#yellow and http://webdesign.about.com/od/colorcharts/l/bl_colorculture.htm#red
[**146**] Ibid 145.
[**147**] Leon Zeldis. 1992. *Color Symbolism in Freemasonry* "The Israel Freemason." Vol. IO5, Ars Quatuor Coronatorum Transactions.
http://www.masonicworld.com/education/files/apr02/include/colour_symbolism_in_freemasonry.htm
[**148**] Ibid.
[**149**] Ibid.
[**150**]Name meaning Aahmas.
http://www.20000names.com/origin_of_baby_names/etymology_A_female/meaning_of_the_name_aahmas.htm
[**151**] Buzzle. 2012. Superstitions and their Origins.
http://www.buzzle.com/articles/superstitions-and-their-origins.html
[**152**] Cicely A. Richard. 2012. *Description of the Statue of Liberty*. USA Today. Notes: Travel Tips. Symbolism of the Statue of Liberty
http://traveltips.usatoday.com/description-statue-liberty-11766.html
[**153**] Snow Leopard Conservancy. Myths and Legends. 2011. The Otter and the Snow Leopard. Note: Popular Pakistan folktale
http://www.snowleopardconservancy.org/text/myth/pakmyths2.htm
[**154**]. 2012. *Mehreen*. Persian word meaning
http://www.babynology.com/meaning-mehreen-f44.html

[**155**] En Rammohan. April 19, 2013. *Pakistan: The most dangerous country in the world*
Uday India. Indian Defense Review
http://www.indiandefencereview.com/spotlights/pakistan-the-most-dangerous-country-in-the-world/
[**156**] Abraham Lincoln. 2013. Quote World. Note: Lincoln's birthdate: February 12, 1809. Last modification 2012. http://www.quoteworld.org/quotes/10274
[**157**] Jackie Fitzpatrick. April 5, 2011. Cherry Blossom: The Ephermeral Nature of Life.
http://yourdreamcareercoach.com/cherry-blossom-the-ephemeral-nature-of-life/
[**158**] Alina Losif and Bruce Ballon. March 22, 2007. *Senior Resident in Psychiatry. Bad Moon Rising: the persistent belief in lunar connections to madness. , University of Toronto, Toronto General Hospital; Assistant Professor of Psychiatry, University of Toronto, Toronto, Ont.* Note: Moon Beliefs.
http://www.biology-online.org/articles/moon_rising_persistent_belief.html
[**159**] Terry A. Rustin. July 8, 2008. 5: Doc07. *Using artwork to understand the experience of mental illness: Mainstream artists and Outsider artists.* PMCID: PMC2736519. Note: Mental illness and artists. Psycho-Social Medicine. http://www.ncbi.nlm.nih.gov/pmc/articles/PMC2736519/
[**160**] CINP History of Psycho-pharmacology and the CNIP As told in Autobiography. pp.1, 13, 22
ttp://search.babylon.com/?q=ciba+geigy+psychopharmcology+basel+switzerland+psychotic+depression&s=web&as=2&rlz=0&babsrc=SP_ss
[**161**] Terry A. Rustin. July 8, 2008. *Using Artwork to understand the experience of mental illness: Mainstream artists and outsider artist*. School of Nursing, University of Texas at Houston Health Science Center. Houston, TX. Excerpts from GMS Psycho-Social Medicine. Corporate Journal of German scientific society in psychosocial medicine. Electronic version.
http://www.egms.de/en/journals/psm/2008-5/psm000052.shtml
[**162**] Psychopharmacologic Innovations in the Treatment of Schizophrenia, Past and Present: An Expert Interview with Herbert Y. Meltzer, M.D. *Medscape*. Jan 20, 2006.
http://www.medscape.com/viewarticle/519981#2
[**163**] Sutapa Deb. April 27, 2013. *What makes someone rape a child? NTDV.*

http://www.ndtv.com/article/india/what-makes-someone-rape-a-child-359599
[**164**] Ibid 163.
[**165**] Hoda; Moon, Bruce L. 2007. *Images from Purgatory: Art Therapy with Male Adolescent Sexual Abusers. Art Therapy: Journal of the American Art Therapy Association*, v24 n1 p16-21. Alexandria, VA 22304. E777019. American Art Therapy Association http://www.eric.ed.gov/ERICWebPortal/search/detailmini.jsp?_nfpb=true&_&ERICExtSearch_SearchValue_0=EJ777019&ERICExtSearch_SearchType_0=no&accno=EJ777019
[**166**] Nicholas Pioch. October 14, 2002.
Bosch. Ship of Fools.
http://www.ibiblio.org/wm/paint/auth/bosch/fools/
[**167**] Nameberry. 2012. Meaning of Buttercup.
http://nameberry.com/babyname/Buttercup
[**168**] Nameberry. 2012. Meaning of Berthold.
http://nameberry.com/babyname/berthold
[**169**] Denis Haley. 2013. Quotes. Daddy.
http://www.quotesdaddy.com/quote/1400386/denis-healey/world-events-do-not-occur-by-accident-they-are-made
[**170**] iseemydestiny. February 21, 2012. *Quantum Physics and How Everything Is Connected To Everything Else: Achieving Zen with mindful random.*
http://scriblinmind.wordpress.com/2012/02/21/quantum-physics-and-how-everything-is-connected-to-everything-else/
[**171**] Leonardo da Vince. 2013. Quote. Goodreads.
http://www.goodreads.com/author/quotes/13560.Leonardo_da_Vinci
[**172**] Patricia McFadden. March 25, 2013. *Emotional Intelligence in Early Childhood*
http://suite101.com/article/emotional-intelligence-in-early-childhood-a192691
[**173**] Dr. Bill Elliott and Dr. Verdeyen. October 3. 2003. *Strategies to redirecting inmate deception. Game Over! Strategies for Redirecting Inmate Deception. The Free Library. Last modification 2010.*
http://www.thefreelibrary.com/Game+Over!+Strategies+for+Redirecting+Inmate+Deception.-a0121937641
[**174**] Sabol, William J., PhD. Heather C. West, PhD. December 15, 2011. Prisoners 2009. Bureau of Justice Statistics. Behavioral statistics in justice systems. NCJ 231675.

http://bjs.ojp.usdoj.gov/index.cfm?ty=pbdetail&iid=2232
[**175**] Kathleen Skowyra and Joseph J. Cocozza, PhD. June 2006. A Blueprint for Change: Improving the System Response to Youth with Mental Health Needs Involved with the Juvenile Justice System. National Center for Mental Health and Juvenile Justice.
http://www.ncmhjj.com/Blueprint/pdfs/ProgramBrief_06_06.pdf
[**176**] Thunderbird. *Regimented Training Program*. Pryor, OK. 2012. Note: Military style of Training. http://www.philliproy.com/pdfs/tunderbird.pdf and http://www.okkids.org/OJSO/Facility%20HTML/Facility%20Reports/Thunderbird_Youth_Academy_Bravo_Company/03%20October%2014%202005.pdf
[**177**] John Eligon. February 1, 2011. *Court Counselor Sentenced to Four Years for Sex Assaults. Note:* Dubious criminal justice employees.
http://cityroom.blogs.nytimes.com/2011/02/01/family-court-counselor-sentenced-to-four-years-for-sex-assaults/
[**178**] Top 100 Baby Names. 2005. Randeep. Note: Name Meaning.
http://www.top-100-baby-names-search.com/funny-baby-names.html
[**179**] *It's a Book*. Lane Smith. 2012.
http://www.amazon.ca/ItsBookLaneSmith/dp/1596436069/ref=sr_1_1?s=books&ie=UTF8&qid=1372437887&sr=1-1&keywords=it%27s+a+book+lane+smith
[**180**] Wikipedia. May, 14, 2013. *Splashdown - Spacecraft Landing*. Wikipedia Foundation Inc. San Francisco, CA.
http://en.wikipedia.org/wiki/Splashdown_(spacecraft_landing)
[**181**] Goggle. 2006. Araya *Hargate - Thailand's Sexiest Women on the Cover of Maxim*. Google.
http://www.asiansweetheart.net/Thai_Beauty/Covers/cover_maxim_araya.html
[**182**] Toulouse-Lautrec. 1891. Painting: *The Toilette (Combing her hair)* Reference: Dortu P.389 The Ashmolean Museum, Oxford Bequeathed by Frank Hindley Smith, 1939.
http://nga.gov.au/Exhibition/TOULOUSE/Default.cfm?IRN=221589&BioArtistIRN=16815&MnuID=3&GalID=5&ViewID=2
[**183**] Amy Oliver. September 23, 2012. *Imelda Marcos' famous collection of 3,000 shoes partly destroyed by termites and floods after lying in storage in the Philippines*

for 26 years since she exiled. Mail-online.
http://www.dailymail.co.uk/news/article-2207353/Imelda-Marcos-legendary-3-000-plus-shoe-collection-destroyed-termites-floods-neglect.html
[**184**] Mermaid. New World Encyclopedia.*Mermaids and Mermen in Myth and Legends.*
Last modified May 10, 2009.
http://www.newworldencyclopedia.org/entry/Mermaid
[**185**] Wikipedia. May 13, 2013. *Mermaid.* Wikipedia Foundation Inc. San Francisco, CA.
http://en.wikipedia.org/wiki/Mermaid
[**186**] Erik G. Jansen 2010-2011. *Evaluation of Transparency International. ISBN: 978-82-7548-545-6.*
Norwegian Agency for Development Corporation. 2010-11. Report 8 and Channel Research.
http://www.norad.no/en/evaluation/news/_attachment/268518?_download
[**187]** Wikipedia. Transparency International.
http://wikipedia.qwika.com/de2en/Transparency_International
[**188]** Transparency International Sweden. January 2013. Transparency in Corporate Reporting No. 1 Sverige.
http://www.transparency-se.org/4_ENG_TI_Transparens-i-foeretagens-rapportering_978-91-980090-9-5_EN.pdf
[**189**] Anne Campbell. April 16, 2013. *The Atlanta scandal: standardized testing and the corruption of US education.*
http://www.transparency.org/topic/detail/education
[**190**] Spartacus Educational. 2013. *Women in the Roman Empire.*
http://www.spartacus.schoolnet.co.uk/ROMwomen.htm
[**191**] Lloyd Lewelly-Jones. October 24, 2011. Domestic Abuse & Violence against Women Greece. P.250, #68495
http://www.academia.edu/1169194/Domestic_Abuse_and_Violence_Against_Women_in_Ancient_Greece
[**192**] Justin McCurry and Tania Branigan. February 12, 2013. *North Korea stages nuclear test in defiance of bans.* The Guardian.
http://www.guardian.co.uk/world/2013/feb/12/north-korea-nuclear-test-earthquake
[**193**] Rajini Vaidyanathan June 5, 2012. *Has skin whitening in India gone too far? (India:* BBC News Mumbai). Last modified 2013. http://www.bbc.co.uk/news/magazine-18268914
[**194**]Mohammed Adrow. April 6, 2013. *Nigeria's dangerous skin whitening obsession: Nigeria has the*

world's highest percentage of women using skin lightening agents in the quest for "beauty." http://www.aljazeera.com/indepth/features/2013/04/20134514845907984.html
[**195**] Christie. Krishna Watching the Gopis Bathe. #1180 http://www.christies.com/lotfinder/paintings/krishna-watching-the-gopis-bathe-the-painting-5668168-details.aspx
[**196**] Jyotsna Kamat. 1998. *History of Bathing in Karnataka.*http://www.kamat.com/kalranga/ancient/bathing/inkar.htmBathing Scenes
[**197**] Celestial Journey Therapy. *Who Is Goddess Lakshmi.*http://www.pyramidcompany.com/CJT/index_Page5013.htm
[**198**]UNICEF. 2005. *Changing a Harmful Social Convention: Female Genital Mutilation/Cutting.* Innocent Research Centre. Additional Research Contributions: Miller, Michael, Moeti, Francesca and Landini, Camila. Notes: Information extracted from research. http://www.unicef-irc.org/publications/pdf/fgm_eng.pdf
[**199**] Abigail Haworth, November 26, 2012. *The day I saw 248 girls suffering genital mutilation.* http://incitytimesworcester.org/2012/11/page/2/
[**200**] UNICIEF. 2009. *Africa Facts and Statistics. World Vision.* http://www.worldvision.de/_downloads/allgemein/Africa_fact_sheet.pdf?mysid=acpc3uq0p3id1ckojnq1spseqmb28slg
[**201**] ABC. March 5, 2013. *Meningitis Outbreak Kills 333 in Nigeria.* http://www.abc.net.au/news/2009-03-05/meningitis-outbreak-kills-333-in-nigeria/1609582
[**202**] World Health Organization. 2013. *Disease Outbreak by Country: Indonesia.* http://www.who.int/csr/don/archive/country/idn/en/
[**203**] Association for Research and Enlightenment. 2013. *Edgar Cayce Readings on Ancient Mysteries*http://www.edgarcayce.org/are/ancient_mysteries.aspx

[**204**]PR News Wire. July 24, 2013. *Worldwide Plastic Surgery Statistics Available for the First Time* http://www.prnewswire.com/news-releases/worldwide-plastic-surgery-statistics-available-for-the-first-time-100248404.html
[**205**]ABC News. May 6, 2012. Double Rainbow in Victoria. http://www.abc.net.au/news/2012-05-06/double-rainbow-in-victoria/3993886
[**206**] Aurora Collection. July 2013. *See Northern Lights in Anchorage.* http://www.anchorage.net/articles/northern-lights-anchorage-alaska
[**207**] Katie McDonough. March 07, 2013. *Japanese ad firm turns women's thighs into billboards: A new trend in Japan is taking human advertising in a slightly more risqué direction*. Salon. Last modified 2013. http://www.salon.com/2013/03/07/japanese_ad_firm_turns_womens_thighs_into_billboards/
[**208**] Mail Online. July 22, 2013. *Kate and William's home makeover costs taxpayer £1m: Couple and new baby to move in to Kensington Palace in the autumn*. http://www.dailymail.co.uk/news/article-2349635/Kate-Middleton-Prince-Williams-Kensington-Palace-home-makeover-cost-taxpayer-1m.html
[**209**]McKinsey & Company. July 2013. *A 20-year Road Map for the Future.* http://www.mckinsey.com/features/reimagining_japan/20_year_road_map
[**210**]Colin Cayer. 2013. *Getting under the Skin of Shanghai's Cosmetic Surgery Scene. Shanghai Expatriate.* http://www.shanghaiexpat.com/article/getting-under-skin-shanghai-s-cosmetic-surgery-scene-18238.html
[**211**] Aesthetics. 2009. ISAPS Releases Study Results. http://www.aestheticsjournal.com/news/item/isaps-releases-study-results
[**212**] Eun Jee Park. February 16, 2012. *Korea's plastic surgery obsession sparks concern. Reuters.* http://www.reuters.com/article/2012/02/16/korea-surgery-cosmetic-idUSL3E8CC06K20120216?goback=%2Egde_4058649_member_95825834
[**213**] Top Ten Hut. 2013. *Wuthering Heights.* http://www.top10hut.com/education/books/top-10-books-of-all-time.html/

[**214**] Parents Support Service Society of BC. November 9, 2011.*2010-2011 Annual Report.* 37th General Annual. *Meeting.*http://www.parentsupportbc.ca/uploads/3e/8d/3e8d37a2de26b57e3440c836c91f30c9/AR_2010_2011.pdf
[**215**] Ibid.
[**216**] Dr. Bryan Walls, Abolition of Slavery in Canada: *Freedom Marker: Integrity and Spirituality.* Notes: The motto of the Order of Canada is "Desiderates Meliorem Patriam," means "They Desire a Better Country." http://www.pbs.org/wned/underground-railroad/stories-of-freedom/abolition-slavery-canada/
[**217**] Human Trafficking Statistics. 2007. Polaris Project. Washington, DC. http://www.cicatelli.org/titlex/downloadable/human%20trafficking%20statistics.pdf
[**218**] Catriona Davies. February 21, 2013. *Muktar Mai's Struggle for Reform: Gang rape victim fights back for girls' education.* CNN. http://www.cnn.com/2013/02/19/world/asia/mukhtar-mai-pakistan-gang-rape
[**219**] Doo Seung Heung. Ph.D. 1980. *Sociology Research: Women in the South Korean Military. Areas of Research and Teaching: Social Stratifications, Sociology of the Military, Social Research Analysis. Seoul National University. College of Social Science.* http://csi.sagepub.com/content/50/5/729.abstract
[**220**] Sam Grover. July 9, 2010. *The Disadvantages of Women in the Military.* http://www.ehow.com/list_6714669_disavatages-woomen-military.html
[**221**]CBC News. May 30, 2008. *Canada Military: Women in the Canadian Military.* http://www.cbc.ca/news/background/cdnmilitary/women-cdnmilitary.html
[**222**] Colin Freeze and Bailey, Ian. November 9, 2011. *A female RCMP officer's damning indictment of her employer The Global Mail.* http://www.theglobeandmail.com/news/national/british-columbia/a-female-rcmp-officers-damning-indictment-of-her-employer/article2231489/
[**223**]Gary Mason. January 20, 2012. *Dozens of female Royal Canadian Mounted Police officers seek justice through class-action Lawsuit.* Globe and Mail. http://www.rcmpwatch.com/dozens-of-female-rcmp-

officers-seek-justice-through-class-action-Lawsuit/
[**224**] Colin Freeze and Ian Bailey. September 6, 2012. A Female RCMP Officer's damning indictment of her employer.http://www.theglobeandmail.com/news/british-columbia/a-female-rcmp-officers-damning-indictment-of-her-employer/article4181592/
[**225**] Khali Noori, December 07, 2012. *Afghanistan's growing demand for plastic surgery.* BBC News, Kabul. http://www.bbc.co.uk/news/world-asia-20638975
[**226**] Geohive. Population Studies. Notes: United Nations designations. http://www.geohive.com/cntry/
[**227**] Knowledge Center. January 1, 2013. *Corporate Governance, Women in Leadership: Women CEOs of the Fortune 1000*. Catalyst. Last modification June 18, 2013. http://www.catalyst.org/knowledge/women-ceos-fortune-1000
[**228**] Lucy Hornby. March 8, 2010. *China's women struggle for a foothold in power.* http://uk.reuters.com/article/2010/03/08/china-parliament-women-idUKLNE62704W20100308
[**229**] Ibid 228.
[**230**] Wikipedia. May 05, 2013.*Male–female income disparity in the United States. (*San Francisco, CA. Wikipedia Foundation Inc.) http://en.wikipedia.org/wiki/Male%E2%80%93female_income_disparity_in_the_United_States
[**231**] Credit Suisse. August 2012. *Thought leadership from Credit Suisse Research & the world's foremost experts.* http://www.fortefoundation.org/site/DocServer/cs_women_in_leading_positions_FINAL.pdf?docID=17902
[**232**] Anne Ravona. May 19, 2013. *Women sphere Europe Summit 2013: Creating the Future - Europe and the World.* http://www.globalleaderpost.com/womens-progress1.html
[**233**] Ibid 232.
[**234**]Canadian Research Institute for the Advancement of Women. 2013. *Violence against Women and Girls. http://criaw-icref.ca/ViolenceagainstWomenandGirls*
[**235**]Ruth Lewin Sime. 1996. *Lise Meitner: A Life in Physics .Lise Meitner: A Battle for Ultimate Truth*/University of California Press. http://www.sdsc.edu/ScienceWomen/meitner.html
[**236**] Susan's Blog. 2013. Advocates 4 Breast Cancer. Dr. Susan Love's Research Foundation..

http://a4bc.wordpress.com/2013/01/24/dr-susan-love-is-back-in-action/
[**237**]Mary Wollstonecraft Shelley. Brainy Quote. *http://www.brainyquote.com/quotes/quotes/m/marywollst144756.html*
[**238**]Vickie Milazzo. 2013. *What Was Albert Einstein Thinking?* ESL Teacher's Board.http://www.eslteachersboard.com/cgi-bin/motivation/index.pl?page=4;read=671
[**239**] Water Lily Database. 2011-12. *Sem-iwon, South Korea – Experience the Healing of Nature.* http://waterlilydatabase.com/recent-news/semiwon-south-korea/
[**240**] Huffington Post. July 28, 2008. *Blind Piano Prodigy from S Korea only 5 years old, can play any song.* http://www.huffingtonpost.com/2008/07/13/blind-piano-prodigy-from_n_112387.html
[**241**] Robin Williams. 2012. *Brainy Quote about women.* http://www.brainyquote.com/quotes/quotes/r/robinwilli385566.html
[**242**] Squidoo, LLC. 2013. *Turtle Symbolism and Lore.* http://www.squidoo.com/turtle_gifts
[**243**] Native American Legends: The Creation Story (Iroquois)
http://www.firstpeople.us/FP-Html-Legends/TheCreationStory-Iroquois.html

Chart References

Information has been extracted from Transparency International, listed in date sequence and media broadcasts by countries as related to Transparency International. In addition, there are media weather reports and the balance is listed in miscellaneous and the Bibliography. Details follow.

Date Sequenced – Transparency International

[**2002**] Transparency International. 2002 *Corruption Perception Index. List of All Countries. Last modified 2003.* http://www.middle-east-info.org/league/corruptionindex.pdf
[2003] Transparency International. 2003 *Corruption Perception Index. List of All Countries. Last modified 2004.* http://gcb.transparency.org/gcb201011/results/
[**2004**] Transparency International 2004. Archive Press Release.

http://archive.transparency.org/news_room/latest_news/press_releases_nc/2004/12_10_2004_australia_corruption_study
[**2004**] Transparency International 2004 Corruption Perception Index.
http://www.integriteitoverheid.nl/fileadmin/BIOS/data/Publicaties/Downloads/Corruption%20Perception%20Index%20_Transparancy%20International_2004.pdf
[2006] Transparency International. *2006. Corruption Perception Index. List of All Countries. Last modified 2007.*
http://abcnews.go.com/images/International/CPI_release_061103.pdf
[2007] Transparency International. 2007. *Corruption Perception Index. List of All Countries. Last modified 2008.*
http://www.infoplease.com/world/statistics/2007-transparency-international-corruption-perceptions.html
&http://www.infoplease.com/world/statistics/2007transparencyinternationalcorruptionperceptions.html#ixzz2TZBRjSHg
[2008] Transparency International. *2008 Corruption Perception Index. List of All Countries. Last modified 2009. Regional Highlights: Asia-Pacific - Countries/Territories Ranked: 32.*
http://www.transparencia.org.es/IPC%C2%B4s/IPC_2008/Asia-Pac%C3%ADfico.pdf
[**2008**] Australian Institute of Criminology. October 2005. *Corruption Perceptions Index 2005: Australia and selected countries.* Crime facts info no. 109. ISSN 1445-7288.
http://www.aic.gov.au/publications/current%20series/cfi/101-120/cfi109.html
[**2008**] High Beam Research. 2008. *Most and Least Corrupt Nations* Info Please.Transparency International Archive Site.
http://www.infoplease.com/world/statistics/2008-transparency-international-corruption-perceptions.html
http://archive.transparency.org/news_room/in_focus/2008/cpi2008/cpi_2008_table
[**2009**] Transparency International. 2009 *Corruption Perception* Index. List of All Countries. Last modified 2010.
http://www.bibliotecapleyades.net/sociopolitica/sociopol_globalization80.htm
[2010] Transparency International. 2010 *Corruption Perception Index*. List of All Countries. Last modified 2011.
http://www.locationselector.com/images/stories/feature

d_reports/CPI_report_ForWeb.pdf
[**2010**] Transparency International. *Corruptions Perceptions Index 2010. Last modified 2011.* http://www.transparency.org/policy_research/surveys_indices/cpi/2010
[**2010/11**] Transparency International. *Global Corruption Barometer 2010/11. Last modified 2012.* http://gcb.transparency.org/gcb201011/results/
[**2011**] Transparency International. 2011. *Corruption index 2010: how each country compares*. Last modified 2013. http://www.guardian.co.uk/news/datablog/2010/oct/26/corruption-index-2010-transparency-international
[**2011**] Transparency International. 2011 *Corruption Perceptions Index* 2011 Slide Share. Last modified 2012. http://www.slideshare.net/kanhema/corruption-perceptions-index-2011
[**2011**]Corruption Perceptions Index 2011. http://issuu.com/transparencyinternational/docs/ti_cpi2011_report_print?mode=window&pageNumber=6
[**2012**] Transparency International. *2012 CPI Brochure: Corruption Perception 2012. Last modified 2013.* http://files.transparency.org/content/download/537/2229/file/2012_CPI_brochure_EN.pdf
[**2012**] Transparency International. *2012 ISSUU Corruption Perceptions*. Last modified 2013. http://issuu.com/transparencyinternational/docs/cpi_2012_report

Country Specific Weather - Destructive Paths

[**Afghanistan**] David Smith. May 9, 2011. *The 2010 Corruption Perceptions Index (CPI): Afghanistan sits near the top of the list. "There are two reasons why pouring billions of dollars into Iraq and Afghanistan has made them more corrupt"* Rawa News. http://www.rawa.org/temp/runews/2011/05/09/world-corruption-special-report.html#ixzz2TbIU6NHP
[**Afghanistan**] Global Edge May 2013. *Afghanistan Indices.* 1994 - 2013 Michigan State University. http://globaledge.msu.edu/countries/afghanistan/indices
[**Africa**] Investigative Africa. *Corruption Perceptions Index 2011.* http://www.slideshare.net/kanhema/corruption-perceptions-index-2011
[**Africa South**] Bridget Johnson. World News: Definition of Apartheid. Last modification 2013. Note: Information of

groupings are extracted.
http://worldnews.about.com/od/ad/g/apartheid.htm
[**Africa**: Nigeria] Olukorede Yishau. February 12, 2011. *Transparency International ranks Nigeria 143th on corruption index. The Nation.* http://www.thenationonlineng.net/2011/index.php/news/28348-transparency-international-ranks-nigeria-143th-on-corruption-index.html

[**America**] Feuer, Alan March 19, 2008. *Dentist Pleads Guilty to Stealing and Selling Body Parts. New York Times.* http://www.nytimes.com/2008/03/19/nyregion/thecity/19bones.html

[**America**] Juan A. Lozana, January 11, 2011. *Once powerful Congressman jailed for money laundering*. The Associated Press. Section B2, Reprint Chronicle Herald.

[**America**] Juan Carlos Llorca. March 1, 2013. US seeks $2.5 million in El Paso Lawyer's money laundering case. *The Associated Press. Last modification 2013.* http://www.elpasotimes.com/newupdated/ci_22697803/us-seeks-2-5-million-el-paso-Lawyers

[**America**] BBC News. June 21, 2007. *Profile: Michael Bloomberg* http://news.bbc.co.uk/2/hi/americas/1640778.stm

[**America**]Ann L. Coker and Elizabeth A. Stasny. October 01, 1996. *Adjusting the National Crime Victimization Survey's Estimates of Rape and Domestic Violence for Gag Factors*, 1986-1990. University of South Carolina, School of Public Health, Department of Epidemiology and Biostatistics and .Ohio State University, Department of Statistics. Refer to the National Archive of Criminal Justice Data, Study 6558.http://www.icpsr.umich.edu/icpsrweb/NACJD/studies/6558/detail

[**Bangladesh**]Luke Harding, April 28, 2013. The Guardian. *Bangladeshi garment factory death toll rises as owner arrested on border Syed Zin Al-Mahmood.* http://www.guardian.co.uk/world/2013/apr/28/bangladesh-garment-factory-collapse-owner-held

[**Brazil**] Euro News. July 2004. *Former Brazilian President Lula da Silva under investigation. Last modification 2013.* http://www.euronews.com/2013/04/07/former-brazilian-president-lula-da-silva-under-investigation/

[**Canada**] Kevin Dougherty. March 19, 2004. *Former refugee board judge charged in alleged fraud*

RCMP claims group sought $8,000-$15,000 from immigrant applicants. The Montreal Gazette http://www.canadianjusticereviewboard.ca/article-judge%20charged%20with%20fraud.htm

[**Canada**] Carlito Pablo. February 10, 2010. *B.C. NDP, Liberal leadership candidates target ethnic communities. Last modification 2013.* http://www.straight.com/article-373731/vancouver/candidates-target-ethnic-communities

[**Canada**] Linda Gyulai. September 18, 2009, *Eerie Pattern of Corruption Scandals in Montreal Politics,* Montreal Gazette.http://communities.canada.com/montrealgazette/blogs/cityeye/archive/2009/09/18/eery-pattern-of-corruption-scandals-in-montreal-politics.aspx

[**Chile**] Wikipedia, 2004. Domestic Violence in Chile. (CA: Wikipedia Foundation Inc.) http://en.wikipedia.org/wiki/Domestic_violence_in_Chile

[**Chile**] The Guardian and Media Limited. August 5, 2011. Franklin, Jonathan. Chile *student protests explode into violence. Article: Franklin, Jonathan.* http://www.guardian.co.uk/world/2011/aug/05/chile-student-protests-violence

[**China**] CNN Turner Broadcasting System (2008) 3 August. *Leaky toilet exposes corrupt China official.* http://articles.cnn.com/2008-08-03/world/china.toilet_1_yuan-bribes-toilet?_s=PM:WORLD

[**China**] Eastern. July 1, 2004. *China selling organs of executed prisoners Falun Gong sect accuses Beijing of torture, theft, sale of body parts.* http://www.wnd.com/?pageId=25362#ixzz1HKNyFGei

[**Georgia**] United States Department of State. June 2012. Report: *Investment Climate Statement.* Bureau of Economic and Business Affairs. http://www.state.gov/e/eb/rls/othr/ics/2012/191153.htm

[**Georgia**] Civil.GE. December 5, 2012. *Georgia in TI's Corruption Perception Index.* Daily News Online. http://civil.ge/eng/article.php?id=25516

[**Haiti**] The Telegraph. 2013. *Haiti's former dictator Jean-Claude 'Baby Doc' Duvalier charged with corruption in Haiti.*http://www.telegraph.co.uk/news/worldnews/centralamericaandthecaribbean/haiti/8268169/Haitis-former-dictator-Jean-Claude-Baby-Doc-Duvalier-charged-with-corruption-in-Haiti.html

[**Haiti**] Latin America Public Opinion Project. May 2013. *Study of Haiti.* Vanderbilt University. Nashville Tennessee.

http://www.vanderbilt.edu/lapop/contact.phpand http://www.vanderbilt.edu/lapop/

[**Haiti**] Alex Stepick, Carol Dutton Stepick and Philip Kretesedemas. October 2001. *Civic Engagement of Haitian Immigrants and Haitian Americans in Miami-Dade County.* Hatian American Foundation, Inc. partnering with Florida International University and Ryerson University. A Study conducted by Immigration and Ethnicity Institute, Center for Labor Research & Studies.

[**Haiti**] Danica Coto and Trenton Daniel. May 06, 2013. *Haiti Immigrants Using Puerto Rico as Gateway to U.S. In New Migrant Route.* Associated Press. http://www.huffingtonpost.com/2013/05/06/haitian-immigrants-puerto-rico-_n_3225298.html

[**Haiti**] Aaron Terrazas. 2010. *Migration Information Source: Hatian Immigrants in the United States.* Migration Policy Institute. ISSN 1946-4037. Last modified 2013. http://www.migrationinformation.org/usfocus/display.cfm?id=770

[**Haiti**] Global Edge May 2013. *Haiti Indices.* 1994 - 2013 Michigan State University. Last modified 2013. https://globaledge.msu.edu/countries/haiti/indices

[**India**] The Wall Street Journal India. December 01, 2011. *India Sinks Lower in Corruption Index.* http://blogs.wsj.com/indiarealtime/2011/12/01/india-sinks-lower-in-corruption-index

[**India**] The Wa David Rowell and Luke B. Connelly. Street Journal India. December 01, 2011. *India Sinks Lower in Corruption Index.* http://blogs.wsj.com/indiarealtime/2011/12/01/india-sinks-lower-in-corruption-index/

[**India**] The Indian Express. May 23, 2010. *7/11 blasts trial to resume tomorrow.* http://www.indianexpress.com/news/711-blasts-trial-to-resume-tomorrow/622569/

[**India**] The Associated Press. November 20, 2011. *India hangs gunman from 2008 Mumbai attack - Mohammed Ajmal Kasab hung in secrecy at a jail in Pune.* Last modification November 21, 2012. The Associated Press. http://www.cbc.ca/news/world/story/2012/11/20/india-mumbai-attack-hanging.html

[**India**] Huff Post. 29 December 2010. *India Gripped By Freezing Weather.* Up dated 25 May 2011. http://www.huffingtonpost.com/2010/12/29/india-gripped-by-freezing_n_802273.html#s216360

[**Indonesia**] International Federation of Red Cross and Red Crescent Society
January 5, 2008. *Indonesia: Floods and Landslides.* Information Bulletin No. 2.
http://www.ifrc.org/docs/appeals/rpts08/IDFLIB02-050108.pdf
[**Indonesia**] Desi Utomo. May 24, 2000. *Indonesia: Discrimination against ethnic Chinese. GWL Issue 406. GreenLeft.* http://www.greenleft.org.au/node/22266
[**Indonesia**] Murni. May 2013. *Wayang Kulit: shadow puppet performances. Ubud, Bali.*
http://www.murnis.com/culture/articlewayangkulit.htm
[**Indonesia**] Indra Harsaputra. December 30, 2005.'*Nyi' Sumiati highlights role of women in 'Wayang.'*
http://www.thejakartapost.com/news/2005/12/30/039nyi039-sumiati-highlights-role-women-039wayang039.html
[**Indonesia**] Endy M. Bayuni, November 24, 2010.The Jakarta Post. *In the current slave trade, Indonesia the largest exporter. Last modified 2012.*
http://www.thejakartapost.com/news/2010/11/24/in-current-slave-trade-indonesia-largest-exporter.html
[**Indonesia**] Gulf Times. *Indonesian envoy's residence hosts Batik workshop in Doha. Last modification 2012.*
http://www.gulf-times.com/qatar/178/details/352400/indonesian-envoy%E2%80%99s-residence-hosts-batik-workshop-in-doha
[**Indonesia**] The Jakarta Post. December 1, 2011. *RI ranks 100th in 2011 Corruption Perception Index*. Last modified 2012.
http://www.thejakartapost.com/news/2011/12/01/ri-ranks-100th-2011-corruption-perception-index.html
[**Japan**] Naohisa Murakami. February-April 2002. *How the rise and fall of Ms.Tanaka was reported or ignored in the English-language press —case study of depth of analysis in news article.* http://www.economist.com/node/624016
[**Japan**] Axel Brodsky. June 2002. *Corruption and Bribery in Japan's Ministry of Foreign Affairs: The Case of Muneo Suzuki.* Japan Policy Research Institute. Paper No. 86.
http://www.jpri.org/publications/workingpapers/wp86.html
[**Mexico**] Belinda Luscombe. October 17, 2011. *10 Questions for Mexican President Felipe Calderón.* Time World.http://www.time.com/time/world/article/0,8599,2096353,00.html Notes: Information Extracted also from

http://www.romereports.com/palio/benedict-xvi-meets-with-mexicos-president-felipe-calderon-english-6370.html

[**Nigeria**] Adele Bamgbose. May 26, 2009. *IDPs: Case studies of Nigeria´s bomb blast and the Yoruba-Hausa ethnic conflict in Lagos, Nigeria.* Journal of Humanitarian Assistance. http://reliefweb.int/report/nigeria/idps-case-studies-nigeria%C2%B4s-bomb-blast-and-yoruba-hausa-ethnic-conflict-lagos-nigeria

[**North Korea**] Kim-Il Sun, *Biography. A+E Television Networks, LLC. Last modification 2013.* http://www.biography.com/people/kim-jong-il-201050

[**Pakistan**]Sadie Bass. January 8, 2010. *Anti-American Sentiment Grows in Pakistan* ABC News. http://abcnews.go.com/blogs/headlines/2010/01/antiamerican-sentiment-grows-in-pakistan/

[**Pakistan**] Irene Watson and Shaila Abdullah. 2005. *Pakistani Women Struggle to Find Their Individualities. Academic Essentials. Last modification 2012.*http://theacademicessentials.com/11034.html

[**Pakistan**] Thomas Reuters Foundation. 2012. *Pakistan Violence at a Glance. Last modification 2013.* http://www.trust.org/spotlight/pakistan-violence/

[**Pakistan**] The Associated Press. 12 September. 2012. *Death toll in Pakistan factory fires rises over 300 Workers suffocated behind locked doors, fire official says. CBC News World. http://www.cbc.ca/news/world/story/2012/09/12/pakistan-factory-fires.html*

*[**Peru**] DW Academie. 2013. Peru: Preventing Violence against Women. http://www.dw.de/peru-preventing-violence-against-women/a-6340262*

[**Philippines**] Wikipedia. May 1, 2013. *Violence against Women in the Philippines.* Modified June 13, 2013. http://en.wikipedia.org/wiki/Violence_against_women_in_the_philippines

[**Phiippines**] Wikipilipinas. December 2, 2010. *Benigno "Noynoy" Aquino III.*http://en.wikipilipinas.org/index.php?title=Benigno_%22Noynoy%22_Aquino_III

[**Singapore**] Russell Flannery. May 5, 2012. *Asia's Richest Man Li Ka-shing Reaffirms Succession Plan, Says Son Richard in Acquisition Talks.* http://www.forbes.com/profile/ka-shing-li/

[**South Korea**] Weird Asia News. 2011. *Yoo Ye-eun. A 5 year-old South Korean girl is being talked about as though she might be the next Mozart: South Korea: Blind 5 Year-Old Pianist Next Mozart?* http://www.weirdasianews.com/2008/08/03/blind-5-year-old-pianist-next-mozart/
[**United Kingdom**] BBC News. May 11, 2007. *Body parts sale man avoids jail* http://news.bbc.co.uk/2/hi/6646467.stm?lsm

Weather - Destructive Paths

[**Myths**] Benjamin Radford, April 21, 2006. *Voice of Reason: The Myth of Tsunami Survivors' Sixth Sense.* http://www.livescience.com/209-voice-reason-myth-tsunami-survivors-sixth-sense.html
[**Cancellation**] Bohan, Caren. December 3, 2010. *Obama in Afghanistan, Kabul trip canceled by weather.Yahoo.*http://www.reuters.com/article/2010/12/03/afghanistan-usa-obama-kabulidUSN0310491620101203?feedType=RSS
[**Predictions**] Anthony Cornelius, weather Moderator. January 5-12, 2011.The Weather Zone. http://forum.weatherzone.com.au/ubbthreads.php/ubb/printthread/Board/22/main/19597/type/thread
[**Cold Front**] Before it's News. July 26, 2010. *Peru Government Declares Cold Wave Emergency as death toll exceeds 400. Last modified 2012.* http://beforeitsnews.com/weather/2010/07/peru-government-declares-cold-wave-emergency-as-death-toll-exceeds-400-113664.html *and Notes: Article about the Catastrophe.* http://www.laht.com/article.asp?ArticleId=361111&CategoryId=14095
[**Cyclones**] *2007-8 Australian Region Cyclone Season.* Last modified May 20, 2013. http://en.wikipedia.org/wiki/2007%E2%80%9308_Australian_region_cyclone_season
[**Disasters]** Wikipedia. February 28, 2011. *List of disasters in Canada.* Wikipedia Foundation Inc. San Francisco, CA. Goggle. http://en.wikipedia.org/wiki/List_of_disasters_in_Canada.
[**Earthquake**] Department of the Interior. U.S. Geological Survey. Earthquake Hazard Program. 2005. Last modified July 30, 2010. http://earthquake.usgs.gov/earthquakes/eqarchives/ye

ar/2005/
[**Earthquake**] Kerr than. January 13, 2010. *Haiti Earthquake "Strange," Strongest in 200 Years.* National Geographic. http://news.nationalgeographic.com/news/2010/01/100113-haiti-earthquake-red-cross/
[**Earthquake**] United States Department of the Interior. December 03, 2012.Earthquake Hazard Program. United States Geological Survey. http://earthquake.usgs.gov/earthquakes/world/most_destructive.php
[**Earthquake**] Wikipedia. 2013. (CA: The Wikipedia Foundation) Last modified June 9, 2013. *2010 Haiti Earthquake.* http://en.wikipedia.org/wiki/2010_Haiti_earthquake
[**Floods**] John Hogue. January 19, 2011. *2011 The Year of the Great Floods.* http://www.hogueprophecy.com/2011/01/2011-the-year-of-the-great-floods/
[**Floods**] Mceer. 2009. *Pakistan Floods 2010: Latest Facts, News, Photos & Maps.* State University of New York at Buffalo. Last modified 2010. http://mceer.buffalo.edu/infoservice/disasters/pakistan-floods-2010.asp
[**Floods**] Asia-One. October 26, 2010. *South Korea Flood Relief Aid for North Korea Delayed by Bad Weather.* http://www.asiaone.com/News/Latest%2BNews/Asia/Story/A1Story20101026-244177.html
[**Floods**] Peter Walker, November 17, 2010. *Millions of North Koreans face hunger after bad weather hits harvest* http://www.guardian.co.uk/world/2010/nov/17/north-korea-harvest-food-shortage
[Floods] Karamjit Kaur. April 16, 2012. *Bad weather leading to more flight delays at Changi Airport. More disruptions expected because of wet conditions.* http://www.straitstimes.com/BreakingNews/Singapore/Story/STIStory_789270.html
[**Freezing**] Kevin Carter. April 27, 2010.*Frost on Tulips: Severe Weather Team 9 Blog.*http://www.wtov9.com/weather/23766541/detail.html
[**Freezing**] Daily Champion. March 29, 2010. *Nigeria Unusual Weather Conditions.* http://allafrica.com/stories/201003290481.html

[**Freezing**] Dunning. November 30, 2010. *The big freeze,* Independent.ie Photo Gallery http://photos.independent.ie/gallery/The_big_freeze/slideshow/DUNNING%2C_UNITED_KINGDOM_NOVEMBER_30%3A__People_walk_through_the_snow_on_November_30%2C_2010_in/03drdlvd8ge0R

[**Landslides**] CBC News. May 11, 2010. *Family of 4 found dead in Quebec landslide: Area prone to landslides.* http://www.cbc.ca/canada/montreal/story/2010/05/11/quebec-landslide.html

[**Modeling**] Government of Canada. Environment. *Dr. Nathan Gillett, Research Scientist. Canadian Centre for Climate Modeling and Analysis (Victoria, BC)* Last modified May 30, 2013. http://www.ec.gc.ca/ccmac-cccma/default.asp?lang=En&n=4A642EDE-1

[Rain BBC News. July 23, 2007. *Humans affect global rainfall*. http://news.bbc.co.uk/2/hi/6912527.stm

[Rain & Smog] Los Angeles Times. July 3, 1999. *Weather Northeastern United States.* http://articles.latimes.com/keyword/weather-northeastern-united-states

[**Rain & Winds**] Fox News. November 11, 2008. *Official: Brazil Blackout Caused by Bad Weather.* http://www.foxnews.com/world/2009/11/11/official-brazil-blackout-caused-bad-weather/

[Snow] Tim Ballisty. August 2, 2011. *Meteorologist: Snow Makes a Return Visit in the South. Yahoo.* http://www.weather.com/outlook/weather-news/news/articles/tracking-snow-across-south_2011-02-08

[**Storms**] SABC. June 2, 2013. *Cape Town to step up relief efforts amid bad weather.* http://www.sabc.co.za/news/a/ad6bbe804fd808c1abcaeb0b5d39e4bb/Cape-Town-to-step-up-relief-efforts-amid-bad-weather-20130602

[**Tornadoes**] Wikipedia. List of Tornadoes. Last modified June 7, 2013. Notes: Information about North American tornadoes was extracted and summarized. http://en.wikipedia.org/wiki/List_of_tornadoes_striking_downtown_areas_of_large_cities

[Tornadoes] Environment Canada. December 29, 2009, *Canada's Top Ten Weather Stories for 2009.* http://www.ec.gc.ca/meteo-weather/default.asp?lang=En&n=627B5C83-1
[**Tsunami**] MapXL.Inc. December 26, 2004. *Tsunami Thailand.* http://www.mapsofworld.com/world-news/26-12-2004-thailand.html

Miscellaneous

[**Definition**] Google. 2013. Definition of Transparency International. http://www.google.ca/search?sourceid=navclient&aq=&oq=transparency+international&ie=UTF8&rlz=1T4RNSM_enCA392CA393&q=transparency+international&gs_l=hp...0l5j41l2.0.0.0.3329.......0.lSkHqS88KdY
[**Healthcare**] Hedley Galt. April 01, 2013. *A passion for change.*Yaffa Publishing Group. http://www.natureandhealth.com.au/news/a-passion-for-change
[**Lily:** Australia] Fact Sheet: Grampians Pincushion Lily (*Borya mirabilis*) *Environment Australia,* lovely lily is close to extinction. http://www.environment.gov.au/biodiversity/threatened/publications/pincushion-lily.html
[**Lily:** China] Lauren Mack. 2013. *Chinese Flower: Lily.*http://chineseculture.about.com/od/chinesefestivals/g/Chinese-Flower-Lily.htm
[**Lily:** Philippines] Dave's Garden. *Plant Files: Philippine Lily Lilium Philippinense.* Last updated 2013. http://davesgarden.com/guides/pf/go/1050/
[**The Thinker**]] The Thinker. Wikipedia. Last modified June 1, 2013. http://en.wikipedia.org/wiki/List_of_Thinker_sculptures

BIBLIOGRAPHY

Agtmael, Antoine van (2007) *The Emerging Markets Century: How a New Breed of World-Class Companies is Overtaking the World.* Free Press. New York, NY.
Ali, Muhammad (1996) *Healing: A Journal of Tolerance and Understanding* Collins, San Francisco, CA.
Arsenault, Dan (2011) 31 January. *The Video that made Headlines,* Chronicle Herald, A3 - Crime Reporter. Halifax, NS.

Ashman Anastasia M. and Cokmen Eaton (2006) *Tales from the Expatriate Harem: Foreign Women in Modern Turkey*. Seal Press, Emeryville, CA.

Bernstein, Joanne, (1981) *Dmitry: A Young Soviet Immigrant*. Clarion books, New York, NY.

Bhabha, H. (1994). The Location of Culture. New York: Routledge. Foreword.[4]

Browne, Malcolm W. (1993) *Muddy Boots and Red Socks: A Reporter's Life.* The New York Times, New York, NY.

Blumenfeld, Robert (2006) *Tools& Techniques for Character Interpretation,* Amadeus Press, Pompton Plains, NJ.

Bullard, Sara (1996) *Teaching Tolerance: Raising Open-Minded, Empathetic Children,* Doubleday, NY, NY.

Capodagli, Bill and Jackson, Lynn (1993) *Innovate The Pixar Way,* McGraw Hill, New York, NY.

Carr, William, Kemmis. Stephen, and Farmer, Routledge. Deakin University Press 1986. Notes: No content has been extracted except for the theme in the construct presented, namely 'Becoming Critical: Education, knowledge and action research.' New York, NY.

David, Jay, (1999) *The Life and Humor of Robin Williams,* p1, 69, 114-115 Quill/William Morrow, New York, NY.

Davene, Jeffrey and Colley, Borden Sherri (2011) 11 March. *Calder found guilty: Long time criminal Lawyer convicted of struggling drugs in Dartmouth jail,* The Chronicle Herald.

Davene, Jeffrey (2011) 16 March, *Concert cash scandal,* The Chronicle Herald.

Edwards, Julia (1988) *Women of the World: The Great Foreign Correspondents,* Houghton Mifflin Company. Boston, MA.

Fairclough, Ian (2011) 1 March. *Gambler Suing Casino*. The Chronicle Herald. A1.

Farnsworth, Robert M. (1996) *From Vagabond to Journalist: Edgar Snow in Asia* 1928-1941, University of Missouri Press, Columbia, MO.

Fetherling, Douglas (1990) *Year of the Horse: A Journey Through Russia & China One: False Starts, Final Edition,* the Whig - Standard, Sept 29, p 1, Kingston, ON.

Fraser, Laura (2011) 3 March. *Immigration: Royal Canadian Mounted Police Allege Fraud in Citizens' Bids,* Section A7, The Chronicle Herald.

Freire, P. (1968). Pedagogia do Oprimido (English translation by Myra Bergman Ramos – Pedagogy of the

Oppressed). Foreword.[3]

Glaser, Judith E. (2007) *Creating We: Change I-Thinking to We-Thinking,* Platinum Press, Avon, MA.

Gruber, Ruth (2003) *Inside of Time: My Journey from Alaska to Israel,* Carroll & Graff Publishers, New York, NY.

Hajkatwala, Minal (2009) *Leaving India*. Houghton Mifflin Harcourt, New York, NY.

Harrens, Margaret ET. Al. (2010) *Refugees: Opposing Viewpoints Series,* Greenhaven Press, Farmington Hills, MI.

Hughes, Lesley (2003) *Good New or No News: The Conflict in Iraq Hovers like a Poisonous Cloud*. Spring 2003, Vol. 10, Iss: 1, Canadian Association of Journalist.

Jackson, David (2011) 4 *Charged in expense scandal: fraud-related allegations after Royal Canadian Mounted Police probe* Hurlburt, MacKinnon, Wilson Zinck face 52 , The Chronicle Herald, Halifax, Nova Scotia.

Kahaani (2012). Produced by Sujoy Ghosh and Kushal Kantilal Gada and Directed by Sujoy Ghosh. Viacom 18 Motion Pictures Pen India Pvt. Ltd. Foreword.

Klein, Freada Kapor (2008) *Giving Notice: Why the Best and the Brightest Leave the Workplace and How You Can Help Them Stay, Jossey*-Bass, San Francisco, CA.

Morley, D. & Chen, K. (Eds.) (1996). Stuart Hall – Critical Dialogues in Cultural Studies. New York: Routledge.

Lesley, Hughes (2003) *Good News or No News: The Conflict in Iraq Hovers like a Poisonous Cloud*. Vol. 10, Iss.1,
Spring, Ottawa, ON.

Li & Karakowsky (2001). *Do We See Eye-to-Eye? Implications of Cultural Differences for Cross-Cultural Management Research and Practice*. The Journal of Psychology, *135*(5), 501-517.
http://www.tamu.edu/faculty/choudhury/culture.html

Majer, Chris and Brant, John (2009) *The Power to Transform,* Rodale Books, New York, NY.

McCracken, Grant (2009) *Chief Culture Officer: How to Create a Living, Breathing Corporation*.
Basic Books, Philadelphia, PA.

McGill, Michael (2003) *Global News: Perspectives on the Information Age*. Vol. 28, Iss: 3, p. 380
Canadian Journal of Communication, Toronto, ON.

McMartin, Pete (2004) *New Yorker Gives Us Rare Review: Final Edition*. p. B.1 Vancouver Sun, BC.

McQuigge, Michelle (2011) 3 March. *One in Four Canadians Obese: Researchers say rates will soon match those of U.S. if action isn't taken,* B3, Canadian Press.

Moorehad, Caroline (2003) *Matha Gellhorn: A Life,* Chatto & Windus, London, UK.

Muharrar, Aisha (2002) *More Than a Label*. Free Spirit Publishing Inc., Minneapolis, MN.

Pitarakis, Leferis (2011) 25 February, *Chaos rules in Libya In focus*. The Associated Press, Reprint Chronicle Herald B1.

Shea, Gregory and Gunther, Robert (2009) *The Job Survival Guide*. Pearson Education Inc., Upper Saddle River, NJ.

Stoffman, Daniel (1997) *Masters of Change: Profiles of Canadian Businesses Thriving in Turbulent Times.* McGraw-Hill Ryerson, Toronto, ON.

Staff (2011) 16 March. *Officials estimate more than 10,000 dead in Japan,*The Associated Press. Reprint Chronicle Herald March 16, 2011

Staff (2011) 17 March. *Workers dubbed modern samurai: Nuclear plant employees race to avert disaster.* The Associated Press, Reprint Chronicle Herald.

Sullivan, Cheryle, MD (2008) *Brain Injury: Survival Kit*. Demos Medical Publishing. New York, NY. Foreword.

Swindoll, C. (1983). Growing Strong in the Seasons of Life. Multnomah Press – A Division of Random House, Inc. Foreword.[2]

Tagore, R. (1905). Ekla Chalo Re. Original in Bengali. H. Bose Swadeshi Records, India. Foreword.[1]

Taschen. (2012) Rene Magritte1898-1967. Throught Render visible. Homage to Mack Sennett, 1937. P.56. Los Angeles, California. Original Edition 1994 Benedikt Taschen Verlag GrabH. Paris, France.

Taxin, Amy (2011) 16 March. *Canadian American authorities close in on massacre suspects.* The Associated Press, Reprint Chronicle Herald.

Teacher (2011) March. *Province unveils cuts to public education.* Volume 49, Number 5. Nova Scotia Teachers Union.

Twenge, Jean M. (2006) *Generation Me*. Free Press. New York, NY.

Thatchernkery, Tojo & Metzker, C. (2006), *Appreciative Intelligence,* Berre-Koehler Publishers Inc. San Francisco, CA.

Ward, John and O'Hanlon, Martin (2011) 1 March 2011, *Canadians Escape Violence in Libya,* Canadian Press.

Wiesenthal, Simon. (1998) 07 April 7. The Sunflower: On the Possibilities and Limits of Forgiveness. P.130. Shocken Books Inc. New York, New York. | Note: the Book provides rationale that challenges define a person's beliefs about justice, compassion, and human responsibility. |

Weiss, David S. (1999) *High Impact HR: Transforming Human Resources for Competitive Advantage,* John Wiley & Sons Canada Ltd, Etobecoke, ON.

Wilson-Smith, Anthony (1999) *Why Canadian Eyes Matter: Great Correspondents All Have a Mysterious Alchemy that Produces the Right Mix of Passion and Perspective.* Macleans, Vol. 112, Iss. 16; p.9, Toronto, ON.

WORKS CITED

Abma, Derek (2011) 24 January. *Almost half of Canadians feel racism on the rise: Survey.* http://www.canada.com/business/Almost+half+Canadians+feel+racism+rise+Survey/4156024/story.html

Academy for Educational Development (2008). *China National Plan of Action on Combating Trafficking in Women and Children.* http://www.humantrafficking.org/countries/china

Adams, Douglas (2011) 3 March 2011. http://thinkexist.com/quotes/with/keyword/dolphins/Quotes.

Adams, Patch (2010) 18 November, *Autobiography*. 03 February 2011. http://www.streetlevelconsulting.ca/biographies/patchadams.htm

Adams, Patch 03 February 2011. *A Fringe Dweller: Alive and Well in the Movies: Robin Williams' Initiation, Transformation, & Meta-comedic Journey in Patch Adams.* http://home.earthlink.net/~jvcody/data/RobinWilliamsPatch/PatchAdams.html#anchor313678

Ader, David (2011) *Indigenous Poverty in Chile: Variance by Group and Region Rural Sociological Society.*http://ww.allacademic.com/meta/p_mla_apa_research_citation/2/4/6/3/6/p246368_index.html

Aerin (2010) 21 September. *Slash and Burn,* http://texasimpact.org/node/934

American Sociological Association (2010) 7 December. *Research exposes racial discrimination against Asian American men in job market.* http://www.sciencecodex.com/research_exposes_racial

_discrimination_against_asian_american_men_in_job_market

Andrews Don A. (2004) 17 June: *Recidivism Is Predictable and Can Be Influenced: Using Risk Assessments to Reduce Recidivism, Study of Correctional Service Canada, Department of Psychology,* Carleton Universityhttp://www.nipissingu.ca/faculty/ianm/imhome/predicting.htm

Albert Einstein Society Archive: *Einstein's biography.* 27 December 2010. http://www.einstein-website.de/z_kids/biography/kids.html

American Institute of Physics (2011). *Formative Years IV Einstein. The Center for History of Physics.* http://www.aip.org/history/einstein/early4.htm

American Music Therapy Association (2012) March. *Music Therapy and Music-based interventions in the treatment and management of pain: selected references and key findings.* http://www.musictherapy.org/assets/1/7/MT_Pain_2010.pdf

American Obesity Rates (2008) November. *Eating Disorders.* http://www.lilith-ezine.com/articles/health/American-Obesity-Rates.html

Anonymous (2011) *Ancient Roman Baths.* http://www.crystalinks.com/romebaths.html

Anonymous (2003) 22 February, *Officials Say Priest Sex Abuse Suit Settled to Ease Pain* http://yourLawyer.com/articles/read4763

Anonymous (2011) *Original Charcoal Drawing - Franklin Roosevelt President & Biography.* http://www.bonanza.com/booths/OriginalsByRobert/items/Original_Charcoal_Drawing Franklin_Roosevelt_President Ch

Anonymous (2005) 24 December, *Robin Williams serves the troops: It's Christmas Eve! Do You Know Who's Who? http://www.robin-williams.net/interviews/uso/07-12b.php*

Anonymous (2011) Vaults of Erowid. *Betel Nut.* http://www.erowid.org/plants/betel/betel.shtml

Answers.com 23 December 2010. *The Churchill Cigar.* http://wiki.answers.com/Q/Is_the_Churchill_cigar_named_after_Winston_Churchill

Answers.com (2011) *Countries in the Southern Hemisphere.* http://wiki.answers.com/Q/Asian_countries_in_the_southern_hemisphere

Aroq Limited - Just-Food (2010) *China Fast Food Analysis.* http://www.just-food.com/market-research/china-fast-food-analysis_id68416.aspx

ArtQuotes.net (2011). *Robin Williams Quotes.* We're all worms, but I do believe I'm a glow worm. http://www.artquotes.net/entertainment-quotes/famous-actors/robin-williams.htm

Ashbury, Susan (2007), update: 2010 11 May. *Taiwan.* http://www.multicsd.org/doku.php?id=taiwan

Ashford, Jenny (2008) 17 December. *Wolfgang Amadeus Mozart & Leopold Mozart: A Bitter Father-son Relationship.* http://www.suite1010.com/content/wolfgang-amadeus-mozart-leopold-mozart-a84982

Ashini, Daniel (1999) 12 September. *Between a Rock and a Hard Place: Aboriginal Communities and Mining.* Innu Nation/ Mining Watch Canada Ottawa. http://www.miningwatch.ca/en/keynote-speech-daniel-ashini-between-rock-and-hard-place-aboriginal-communities-and-mining

Ask.com (2007) *Definition of Diplomacy.* http://www.ask.com/wiki/Diplomacy

Atlantic Halfway House Association (2007) Canada. http://atlantichalfwayhouses.com/about/our_mission_values/

Australian Government (2011) 03 June. *Grampians Pincushion Lily (Borya mirabilis).* http://www.environment.gov.au/biodiversity/threatened/publications/pincushion-lily.html

Australian Institute of Criminology (2005) October. *Corruption Perceptions Index 2005: Australia and selected countries. Crime facts info no. 109*, ISSN 1445-7288, Canberra.

Authors - Multiple. February 18, 2012. *Women and the Media SP 2012* Notes: Overall View about Women and the subject of Gazes; Author's Names after Titles. *Who's Vision's Who's Fantasy: Are we seeing?* (Shay); *Take a Look. Women and Society. Reflexion of Society (Sofija);* Ways of seeing, viewing (Ian Jensen); Male Gaze (Jason Gonzales); Scopophilia "love of looking" (Danielle); The Male Gaze and The Oppositional Glaze (Diana Golde and Shin Wen Tan); Gazes (Anonymous); A Powerful Look

(Shira Benhamou); Whey Gaze (Julian);The Male Gaze and Oppositional Gaze; The World Could Use a New Lens (Pablo Dominique).
http://womenandmediasp2012.blogspot.ca/2012_02_01_archive.html

Ayers, William, Dohen, Bernard and Ayers, Rick (2002) *Zero Tolerance,* The New Press, New York, NY.

Baker, Greg (and Marquand, Robert 2001) 6 August. *Taken Down: Chinese police detain a Falun Gong protester in Tiananmen Square July 20, two years after the sect was banned.*
http://www.cesnur.org/2001/falun_aug01.htm#Anchor-49575

Banderas News (2006) December. *South Texas Drug Bust is Hugs: News from Around the Americas.* ksatcom.
http://www.banderasnews.com/0612/nw-drugbust.htm

Baseball Canada (2011) *Baseball Ottawa, ON.*
http://www.baseball.ca/eng_home.cfm

Bawden, Tom and Shalvey, Kevin (2011) *Era of 'Owned by China.* The Guardian.
http://www.guardian.co.uk/business/2011/jan/12/era-of-owned-by-china

BBC News (2008) 30 May. *Isolated tribe spotted in Brazil.*
http://news.bbc.co.uk/2/hi/americas/7426794.stm

BBC News (2005) 7 September. *Musharraf concern about women's' image.*
http://news.bbc.co.uk/2/hi/south_asia/4222400.stm

BBC News (2011) 24 June. *Profile: Thaksin Shinawatra.*
http://www.bbc.co.uk/news/world-asia-pacific-13891650

Beaver County Times (2012) May. *Weather Deaths double in 1983.*
http://news.google.com/newspapers?nid=2002&dat=19840823&id=xl8tAAAAIBAJ&sjid=kdoFAAAAIBAJ&pg=5294,4327216

Beijing Review (2008) 4 February. *The Year of the Rat.*
http://www.china.org.cn/english/culture/242072.htm

Bell, Thomas (2008) 22 July. *Cambodia on Brink of War with Thailand.*
http://www.telegraph.co.uk/news/worldnews/asia/cambodia/2445052/Cambodia-on-brink-of-war-with-Thailand.html

Berman, Lee Jay (2009) January. *Interest-Based Communication in a Regimented World: Recession Advice for Mediators.*
http://www.adrontario.ca/media/ADRIOSpring2009Newsl

etter.pdf
Bernardo, Jesusa (2008) 12 November. *Continuing Negatives of Gloria Arroyo - Pulse Asia Survey.* http://jesusabernardo.newsvine.com/_news/2008/11/12/2102757-continuing-negatives-of-gloria-arroyo-pulse-asia-survey

Bertone, Andrea (2011) *Empowerment through Knowledge,* Academy for Educational Development. Washington, DC. http://www.humantrafficking.org/countries/united_stated_of_America

Bierly, Mandi (2011) 16 November. *Robin Williams talks drugs on Discovery's 'Curiosity' -- Exclusive Outtakes. EW.Com.* http://insidetv.ew.com/2011/11/16/robin-williams-talks-drugs-on-discoverys-curiosity-exclusive-outtakes/

Biography Robert Kearns. *True Knowledge, Internet Answer Engine.* http://www.trueknowledge.com/robert_kearns_biography

Blogger (2009) 31 January. *Literacy Rates in Japan.* http://facts-aboutjapan.blogspot.com/2009/01/literacy-rates-in-japan.html

Bodo Lifespace Series (2011) 21 February. *The Bodo Store.* http://www.bodo.ca/far-infrared-saunas/#id=album-10&num=52

Bonander, Ross (2011) *How To Navigate Bureaucracy.* http://ca.askmen.com/money/how_to_300/361_how_to.html

Books, Peck (2011) 25 January. *Messi fined for wishing his mother a happy birthday.* http://ca.sports.yahoo.com/soccer/blog/dirty-tackle/post/Messi-fined-for-wishing-his-mother-a-happy-birth?urn-sow312467

Bornrich (2012) March. *Most expensive shoes for men.* http://www.bornrich.com/entry/most-expensive-shoes-for-men/

Breitbart (2011) 2 November. *Canadians still 'distrust' United States: poll.* http://www.breitbart.com/article.php?id=CNG.6b2c7e71c384e4ab229e57736dcbe1f8.691&show_article=1

Brian Koslow (2011) *Quotes.* http://www.brainyquote.com/quotes/quotes/b/briankoslo162723.html

Brodie, T.D. Brodie (2009) January. *Interest-Based Communication in a Regimented World: Can these two concepts co-exist?* http://www.adrontario.ca/media/ADRIOSpring2009Newsletter.pdf

Brooks-Arenburg, Patricia and Wynne, Eric (2011) 03 February. *Why did they do it? Burning (Bias)* http://www.citizendia.org/Interacial_marriage/Africa

Brooks, Marcus (2008) 08 April. *Understanding gang mentality and why people join them.* http://www.helium.com/items/982440-understanding-gang-mentality-and-why-people-join-them

Bumberger-Scott, Barbara (2006) August. *Mozart.* www.curledup.com/mozartpg.htm

Buzzle.com (2010) 17 October. *Ancient China Zhou Dynasty.* http://www.buzzle.com/articles/ancient-china-zhou-dynasty.html

CanadaVisa.com (2010) 27 June. *About Canada Immigration Lawyer David Cohen.* http://www.canadavisa.com/immigration-attorney-david-cohen.html

Campanella, Eduardo (2010) 14 July. *Beware Italy's intergenerational conflict: With a gerontocracy that locks the young out of its economy and politics, Italy may be a canary in the mine for other nations.* http://www.guardian.co.uk/commentisfree/2010/jul/14/italy-gerontocracy-intergenerational-conflict

Canadian Literacy Learning Network (2011) 15 March. http://www.literacy.ca/

Canadian Union Public Employees (2005) June. *Strong Communities: Aboriginal Peoples.* http://communities.cupe.ca/updir/communities/RSC_aboriginal.pdf

Canwest News Service (2008) 31, January. *Mob-connected man shot to death at halfway house: Police released the name Thursday of a former professional football star with ties to the mafia who was shot to death inside a halfway house in Brampton, Ont., just west of Toronto.* National Post. http://www.canada.com/ch/chchnews/story.html?id=fb6703c2-4aee-4f88-b2cc-edc07d1ff1b8&k=24300

Cassaro, Richard (2012) *Sacred Science of Three, "Prehistoric Roots"* Freemasonry's Lost Sacred Science: Volume 1, Article 2.
http://www.deepertruth.com/journal/article-2.html
Cave, Damien (2012) 11 January. *Mexico Updates Death Toll in Drug War to 47,515, but Critics Dispute the Data.* New York Times.
http://www.nytimes.com/2012/01/12/world/americas/mexico-updates-drug-war-death-toll-but-critics-dispute-data.html
CBC News (2004) 21 August. *B.C. to close halfway house tied to murders.*
http://www.cbc.ca/canada/story/2004/08/20/halfway_house040820.html
CBC News (2007) 1 March. *Crime victims suffer injury, loss, emotional fallout study: CBC News.*
http://www.cbc.ca/canada/story/2007/03/01/victims-study.html
CBC News (2003) November. *In-Depth Gambling. Betting the Farm: An Overview of Gambling. Addiction.*
http://www.cbc.ca/news/background/gambling/addiction.html
CBC News (2010) 11 March. *Bingo halls turn to tech to stem decline.*
http://www.cbc.ca/consumer/story/2010/03/10/f-charity-bingo-electronic.html
CBC News (2008) 3 November. *Gap found in kidney disease treatment for aboriginal Canadians.*
http://www.cbc.ca/health/story/2008/11/03/kidney-aboriginal.html
CBC News (2010) 07 May. *MLA spending scandal prompts expense changes.*
http://www.cbc.ca/canada/nova-scotia/story/2010/05/07/ns-spending-mla-regulations.html
CBC News (2011) 18 February. *MLA spending probe in Nova Scotia gets four charged.*
http://www.cbc.ca/news/canada/nova-scotia/story/2011/02/14/ns-rcmp-mla-spending.html
CBC News (2010) 14 December. *N.B. slashes capital budget in 2011-12.*
http://www.cbc.ca/news/canada/new-brunswick/story/2010/12/14/nb-capital-budget-1245.html
CBC News (2009) 11 June. *Regina jail official charged with child pornography offence.*
http://www.cbc.ca/canada/saskatchewan/story/2009/0

6/11/jail-official-charged.html
CBC News (2011) 01 December. *Canada slips in corruption-ranking measure.* http://www.cbc.ca/news/canada/story/2011/12/01/corruption-index-canada.html
CBC Radio Canada (2013) *Friendly Giant.* http://www.cbc.ca/75/2011/11/the-friendly-giant-1.html
Center for Computer Forensics (2011) http://www.computer-forensics.net/home.php*Tier One Automotive Supplier – IP theft to China Intellectual Property Theft - International.* Southfield, MI.
CFA Institute (2011) *Robin Williams loses $6 million Lawsuit.* http://www.reuters.com/article/2010/02/05/us-williams-idUSTRE6141F320100205
Cha Cha Search Inc. (2011) *Who played George Washington in the new Dodge commercial?* http://www.chacha.com/question/who-played-george-washington-in-the-new-dodge-commercial
Chandra, D. (2013) *Theories of Socialization*. Hub Pages. http://dilipchandra12.hubpages.com/hub/Theories-of-Socialization
Chang, Shirley (2011) *Chinese Wedding Customs: Traditional Chinese Wedding Customs.* http://www.chinese-poems.com/wedcus.html
Channe4.com-News (2003) September. *Social Justice.* http://www2islandnet.com/mikezimmer/theprogressivemind/tpminfo/justice/2005_09_01_tpmsocialjustice_archive.html
Children's Shelter Home Union (2012) *Social Welfare in Thailand founded by Thaneen Joy Worrawittayakun.* Chiang Mai Thailand. http://www.childrens-shelter.com/childrenstories.htm
China Fact Tours (2010) 28 March, *Chinese Eating Customs.* http://www.chinafacttours.com/facts/tradition/chinese-eating-custom.html
ChinaTravelGuide.com (2008) 5 January, *Restrooms and Asian-Style Squat Toilets.* http://chinatravelguide.com/ctgwiki/Restrooms_and_Asian-Style_Squat_Toilets
Chinese Horoscopes (2011) *The Rat.* http://www.usbridalguide.com/special/chinesehoroscopes/Rat.htm

Churchill, Winston. Bi-Polar Lives.com. (2010) 28 December,
Winston Churchill and manic depression: The great statesman's mental health, and in particular Winston Churchill's manic depression, is still generating controversy today.
http://www.bipolar-lives.com/winston-churchill-and-manic-depression.html

CIA World Fact Book (2011). *News from Nigeria.* http://www.africa.com/nigeria/leaders

Circle Tengerism (2011) *The Preservation of Siberian and Mongolian Shamanism.*
http://www.tengerism.org/becoming_a_shaman.html 03 August 2011.

Clairmont, Donald (1996) *Alternative Justice Issues for Aboriginal Justice.*
http://jlp.bham.ac.uk/volumes/36/clairmont-art.pdf

Clothing and Fashion Encyclopedia 20 March (2010) *Brooks Brothers: Clothing & Fashion.*
http://angelasancartier.net/brooks-brothers

Cochrane, Johanne, Chen, Hanhui, Conigrave, Katherine M. and Hao, Wei, (2012) March.
Alcohol and Alcoholism: Alcohol use in China. Volume 38, Issue 6, pp. 537-542
http://alcalc.oxfordjournals.org/content/38/6/537.full

Cold Lake Friendship Center and the Cold Lake Community Reconciliation and Healing Project (2012) March. *History of Indian Residential Schools.*
http://clfns.com/images/people/documents/history_of_indian_residential_schools.pdf

Colgate Palmolive (2011), Advertisement *Max White: Get the Smile,*Colgate,http://www.colgate.co.uk/app/PDP/ColgateMaxWhite/UK/UK_Promo.cvsp

Colgate Palmolive (2011). Advertisement: *Whiten Up Your Smile*: Colgate,
http://www.colgate.com.au/app/PDP/ColgateMaxWhite/AU/HomePage.cvsp

Cooper, Tom (2003) 13 November. *Civil War in Nigeria (Biafra), 1967-1970.*
http://www.acig.org/artman/publish/article_351.shtml

Conservapedia.Com (2010) 28 December.
http://www.conservapedia.com/Winston_Churchill

Council on Foreign Relations (2011) 22 January 2011. *Culture: Destiny, The Myth of Asia's Anti-Democratic*

*Values.*http://www.foreignaffairs.com/articles/50557/kim-dae-jung/is-culture-destiny-the-myth-ofasiasantidemocratic-values
Council on Foreign Relations (2012) 21 May. *The Global Nuclear Non-proliferation Regime Issue Brief: Scope of the Challenge.*http://www.cfr.org/proliferation/global-nuclear-nonproliferation-regime/p18984
Cox Brian (2012) 21 February. *Quantum Physics and How Everything Is Connected To Everything Else* http://scriblinmind.wordpress.com/2012/02/21/quantum-physics-and-how-everything-is-connected-to-everything-else/
Crunchbase (2012) 11 November. *Li Ka-shing.* http://www.crunchbase.com/person/li-ka-shing
Counseling Association Japan (2010) 14 December *Newsletter 2005. No. 1.* http://counselingjapan.com/eng/cs_tokyo_japan_ml20051.php
Craft, Carri**e** Book Review: *The Lost Boy. The Inspiring Sequel to "A Child Called 'It'" The Story about David Pelzer.* http://adoption.about.com/od/guidereviews/fr/thelostboy.htm
Craven, Jim (1999) 29 September. *Masonic Bone Ritual shocks Aborigines; boys find skulls in store room.* http://archives.econ.utah.edu/archives/pen-l/1999m09.e/msg00267.html
Croce, Nannette (2006) 24 April. *Canadian Residential Schools: Allegations of Abuse in Aboriginal Schools.* http://www.suite101.com/content/canadianresidentialschools-a1300
Crosby, Karen (2007) 08 September. *Aboriginal traditions before the arrival of Europeans: Aboriginal tradition: The Story of the Blackfoot People: Alberta.* Online Encyclopedia: Glenbow Archives. http://ww.canada.com/calgaryherald/features/discoveringalberta/story.html?d=709d9e9-b33a-4846-9e57-0ef53e65e3c2
Cruckshank, Robert (2010) 31 May. *Texas Budget Deficit Shatters Myths about California Budget.* http://bigeducationape.blogspot.com/2010/05/texas-budget-deficit-shatters-myths.html
Cymal Canada.com (2006) *I am a Nanny Caregiver.* Canadian Caregivers Association. http://www.cca-acaf.ca/complaints3.htm

Cultural China (2011) 28 November. *Shanghai, China.* http://kaleidoscope.cultural-china.com/en/7Kaleidoscope9040.html

Dager, Al *(1991) Media Spotlight Special Report May. American Masonic History: What are America's True Roots?* http://www.rapidnet.com/~jbeard/bdm/Psychology/mashist.htm

Danster, Dan (2010) 22 October. *Report on A & W Restaurants* - Yum. Beijing, China. http://www.yum.com/company/china.asp

Davies, C.J. (2005) 27 July. *Robin Williams Tells World's Most Offensive Joke* http://www.hecklerspray.com/robin-williams-tells-worlds-most-offensive-joke/2005967.php

***D'Cruz**, Ann Beverly* (2010) 28 July, *Southern California wildfires still burning* http://www.theweathernetwork.com/news/storm_watch_stories3&stormfile=californiawildfire_28_07_2010

DearDeath.com (2007). *Japan.* http://www.deardeath.com/japan.htm

Deb, Sutapa (2013) 27 April. *What makes someone rape a child?* http://www.ndtv.com/article/india/what-makes-someone-rape-a-child-359599

Decian, Walsh (2011) 27 January. *US embassy official kills two men during 'robbery' in Pakistan.* http://www.guardian.co.uk/world/2011/jan/27/us-embassy-official-kills-pakistan

Department of Finance & Department of Budget Management. (2011) *Chapter 6: Causes of Poverty in the Philippines.* http://www.adb.org/Documents/Books/Poverty-in-the-Philippines/chap6.pdf

Department of Justice (2010) 8 January. *Victims Rights around the World.* http://www.justice.gc.ca/eng/pi/rs/rep-rap/2000/rr00_vic20/p422.html 14 September 2010.

Department of Labor (2011) *Fair Labor Standards Act (FLSA): The Employment of Workers with Disabilities at Special Minimum Wages Fact Sheet.* http://www.dds.ca.gov/WorkServices/docs/SpecialMinimumWageFactSheet.pdf

De Souza, Mike (2010) 18 February, *Political Benefits of Infrastructure Plan Highlighted,* CanWest News Services. http://www.canada.com/news/Political+benefits+infrastr

ucture+plan+highlighted/2578648/story.html
Dewar, Gwen (2008), *Music and intelligence: A guide for the science-minded parent.* http://www.parentingscience.com/music-and-intelligence.html
Dhammakaya Foundation (2011) February. *Dharma Meditation Peace Buddha Karma.* http://www.dmc.tv
DHH (2003) 20 November. *Living in Japan: Japan's Disturbing Superiority Complex.* http://yawandmog.wordpress.com/2005/11/20/japans-disturbing-superiority-complex/
Directessays (2011) *Theme of Motherhood in Obasan.* http://www.directessays.com/viewpaper/94140.html
Dixon, John (2011) 13 March. *Wild Plants ~ the useful and the beautiful.* Ojibwa from Port Dover, Ontario. http://www.albertburger.com/wild%20plants.htm.
Dobell, Graeme (2010) 8 February. *Mahathir's foreign policy surprises.* The Interpreter. Lowly Institute for International Policy. http://www.lowyinterpreter.org/post/2010/02/08/Mahathirs-foreign-policy-surprises.aspx
Dohrman, Paul, (2010) 18 November, *Why You Shouldn't Drink Stagnant Water.* http://www.ehow.com/way_5207456_shouldn_t-drink-stagnant-water.html, Ehow.Com
Donaghy, Greg (2007) 8 June. *Canada and the Early Cold War,* Foreign Affairs and International Trade Canadahttp://www.international.gc.ca/department/~history/coldwar_intro-en.asp
Dougan, Andry (1998) 28 November 2010, *Robin Williams.* Thunder's Mouth Press, New York, NY. http://www.adherents.com/people/pw/Robin_Williams.html
Dougherty, Steven (1989) 09 October, *A $90 Million Matter of Distrust Pits Billy Joel against His Ex-Manager,* Source. http://www.people.com/people/archive/article/0,,20121368,00.html
Dwivedi, Kedar Nath (2011) 1 January, *Buddhism and Mental Illness, AMIDA Trust: Culturally Engaged Buddhism.* Northampton.http://amidatrust.ning.com/group/buddhismandmentalillness

Ebert, Lawrence B. (2009) 05 September, *America's oldest newspaper apologizes for plagiarism.* http://ipbiz.blogspot.com/2009/09/americas-oldest-newspaper-apologizes.html.

EDCTP Secretariat the Hague (2009) 14 May. *European and Developing Countries Clinical Trials Partnership.* The Netherlands.http://www.edctp.org/Networks-of-Excellence.641.0.html

Edwards, Franklin G and Pettigrew, Thomas F. (2008) *Race Relations: World Perspectives.* http://www.encyclopedia.com/topic/Race_relations.aspx

EHow.com (2011) 15 January 2010, *How to Invest in Asian Property,* Bellevue, WA. http://www.ehow.com/how_2156817_invest-asian-property.html#ixzz19QbP8P2J

E-journal.com (2011) *Conceptual History of Ethnicity* .http://www.filepie.us/?title=Ethnicity

Elliott, Bill, PhD and Verdeyen, PhD (2002) *Game Over! Strategies for Redirecting Inmate Deception.* http://www.thefreelibrary.com/Game+Over!+Strategies+for+Redirecting+Inmate+Deception.-a0121937641

Ellis-Christensen, Tricia (2010) 11 October, *Roots of Empathy.* http://www.psychologynet.org/report/multple-sclerosis Wise Geek. 08 June 2010.

Entertaining YOUR GI (2005) 24 December, *It's Christmas Eve! Do You Know Who's Entertaining YOUR GI?* http://www.theleftcoaster.com/archives/006388.php

Ernst, Bruno (1981) *M. C. Escher Brief Biography: His Life and Complete Graphic Work.* http://users.erols.com/ziring/escher_bio.htm

Estep, Bill (2009) 27 March, *Clay County Judge Jailed until Trial.* http://www.kentucky.com/2009/03/27/740263/clay-county-judge-jailed-until.html

Expat Foreigner Meetup Groups (2011) *Expatriates Foreigner Meet-ups around the world.* http://expat-foreigner.meetup.com/

The Expatriate Group Inc. (2012) March. *Tax, banking, financial planning, investment, company profile.* http://www.expat.ca/main/page.php?page_id=1

Extra, Guus, and Yagmur Kutlay (2011) *Management of Social Transformations: Discussion Paper 63: Language Diversity in Multicultural Europe.*

http://www.unesco.org/most/dp63extra.pdf
Ewebwriter, eHow Member (2010) 05 April, *How to Get Married in Bangkok, Thailand.* http://www.ehow.com/how_6074318_married-bangkok_-thailand.html
Fairex Inc. (2011) 24 January. http://www.thefreedictionary.com/regimentations
Farlex Inc. The Free Library: (2002) January. *Cross-cultural leadership styles: a comparative study of U.S. and Nigerian financial institutions, Chapter 21.* Journal of International Business Research.http://www.thefreelibrary.com/Crosscultural+leadership+styles%3a+a+comparative+study+of+U.S.+and...-a01798l7825
Father Devine (1931) Indian Folklore; *Lake Ronkonkoa Legend the Curse.* http://truelegends.info/sayville/folklore.htm
Feder, Robert (2005) 17 July, *Magic Touch: Walt Disney's Vision of Family Amusement Remains Golden a half century later.* Chicago Sun-Times.http://www.highbeam.com/doc/1P2-1592323.html
Feinman, Robert D. (2009) *Society: Too Many People: Too Little Work.* http://robertdfeinman.com/society/people-work.html
Feng, Xin-Ming (2011), *Mulan's Near Execution: A Disney Fabrication. Mulan's Near Execution.* http://tsoidug.org/papers_mulan.php
Fenton, Andrew (2010) 19 August, *Robin Williams set for first ever stand-up comedy tour of Australia.* Herald Sunhttp://www.dailytelegraph.com.au/entertainment/robin-williams-set-for-first-ever-stand-up-comedy-tour-of-australia/story-e6frewyr-1225907225623
Feuer, Alan (2008) 19 March, *Dentist Pleads Guilty to Stealing Body.* http://www.nytimes.com/2008/03/19/nyregion/thecity/19bones.html
Fiero, Gian (2013) *The Difference between Being Smart, Educated, and Intelligent more*. Academia.comhttp://www.academia.edu/624021/The_Difference_Between_Being_Smart_Educated_and_Intelligent
Fieser, James (2011) 27 February, *Business Ethics.* http://www.utm.edu/staff/jfieser/vita/research/Busbook.htm

Flannery, Russell (2012) 28 May. *Hong Kong in Transition: Elite Family Businesses Are Facing Change.* http://www.forbes.com/sites/russellflannery/2012/05/28/hong-kong-in-transition-elite-family-businesses-are-facing-change/

Fox News (2007) O4 October. *Three Philadelphia-Area Funeral Directors Nabbed in Scheme Selling Body Parts.* Extracted from Associated Press. http://www.foxnews.com/story/0,2933,299508,00.html#ixzz1pfj36GVa

Freedom Magazine. (2011) *A Legacy of Drug Shattered Lives. 1996- 2006.* http://freedommag.scientology-tor.ca/vol4/9.html

Friedman, Emily and Weber, Vanessa (2009) 8 April, *More Auto and Car Insurance Fraud Cases in Bad Economy: Financial Problems Cause Cash-Strapped Owners to Illegally Ditch Cars.* http://abcnews.go.com/GMA/Economy/story?id=7283316&page=1

Gallagher, Erin (1997) *Face-Negotiation Theory.* http://oak.cats.ohiou.edu/~eg515298/face.htm.

Geohive (2012) 21 March. *Global Statistics / Population Statistics.* http://www.geohive.com/

Ginwright, Shawn and Cammarota (2002) 22 December, *New Terrain in Youth Development: The Promise of a Social Justice Approach.* http://www.highbeam.com/doc/1G1-99399475.html

Gmilburn, Geoff (2009) 15 June. *The Mystics and Realists of Quantum Physics.* http://www.gmilburn.ca/

Goodhand (2001) *Chapter 6: Causes of Poverty in the Philippines.* http://www.adb.org/Documents/Books/Poverty-in-the-Philippines/chap6.pdf

Google. (2011) 14 February and (2010) August, *World Media viewpoints on Former President of Taiwan Goes on Trial for Corruption*. Original Article: Chinese. http://www.intlhumanrights.com/CorruptionOfTaiwan.htm

Google (2001) October, *Understanding Poverty.* http://www.txtmania.com/articles/poverty.php

Google (2011) http://www.derbal.fr.gd/Cell-phones.htm 22 September 2010, *Algeria Tody Cell Phones.*

Google (2012) 20 March. *The Meaning of Magen David, the Star of David.*

http://www.youtube.com/watch?v=SrHb04Sb_FU
Gorman, Christine. (1998) 09 March. *Body Parts for Sale.* Time Magazine.
http://www.time.com/time/magazine/article/0,9171,987948,00.html#ixzz1pfcYvhwE
Got Questions Ministries (2011) *Why We Dress Up Nice For Church.*
http://www.gotquestions.org/dress-up-church.html
Government of Canada (2010) 21 June, *Aboriginal Canada Portal.*
http://www.aboriginalcanada.gc.ca/acp/site.nsf/eng/ao20017.html
Grand Lodge of British Columbia and Yukon, (2011) *Women in Freemasonry.*
http://freemasonry.bcy.ca/texts/women.html
Gristwood, Sarah, 18 June 1998
http://www.chico.mweb.co.z/mg/art/film/9806/980618,
Gristwood, Sarah (1998) 18 June. *The Religious Affiliation of Actor, Comedian. Robin Williams* and "Bobbin' Robin" in *Mail & Guardian* (Africa), Milwaukee Journal Sentinel. (http://www.chico.mweb.co.za/mg/art/film/9806/980618-robin.html; viewed 26 August 2005): and
http://www.jsonline.com/lifestyle/religon/feb01/scott09020801a.asp
Guide to Thailand.com. (2011) *Thailand's Domestic Airlines.*
http://www.guidetothailand.com/thailand-travel-information/air-travel.php
Global Gold (2010) 28 November, *Thailand Fetus Find Breaks Abortion Taboo.* Student Mid-Wife.net.
http://www.studentmidwife.net/smnet-community-15/midwifery-news-22/43676-thailand-foetus-find-breaks-abortion.html
Guyler Delva, Joseph (2011) 18 January, *Corruption, Theft Charges Filed Against Duvalier.*
http://www.nationalpost.com/Haiti+poised+arrest+Baby+Duvalier/4126190/story.html
Havighurst, Clark C. (1970) 10 July. *Compensating Persons Injured in Human Experimentation. p. 153-157. [DOI:10.1126/science.169.3941.153]*
http://hfs.sagepub.com/content/14/1/35.full.pdf+html
Harrin, Elizabeth (2007) 5 July, *Expatriate Experiences. Projects@work*
http://www.projectsatwork.com/content/articles/237153.cfm

Harris, Kevin (1995) *Quotes Albert Einstein.* http://rescomp.stanford.edu/~cheshire/EinsteinQuotes.html

Havana Journal Inc. (2006) 19 July, *What's it like being a "diplomat" living in Cuba.* http://havanajournal.com/politics/entry/whats-it-like-being-a-diplomat-living-in-cuba/

Hays, Jeffrey (2008), updated April 2010, *Chinese Media: Facts & Details.* http://factsanddetails.com/china.php?itemid=2378&catid=7&subcatid=43 06 June 2010.

Heidorn, Keith (2011) *List: Significant Weather Events Canada.* http://www.islandnet.com/~see/weather/almanac/diarymay.htm

Heinen, Tom (2001) 9 February, *New governor practices quiet faith: Christian Science's democratic tenets guide to Wisconsin's Governor.* *http://www2.ljworld.com/news/2001/feb/16/christian_sciences_democratic/*

Heller, Robert (2009) 20 March, *Rewards and incentives - when self-interest isn't enough* http://www.management-issues.com/2009/3/20/opinion/rewards-and-incentives----when-self-interest-isnt-enough.asp

Heyhoe, Kate (1999) October, *Monkey Feast: Kate's Virtual Journey: A Progressive Feast, Lopburi, Thailand.* http://www.globalgourmet.com/food/kgk/1099/kgk102399.html#ixzz1EmqUlcGk

Higginbotham, Peter (2010) August, *Poor Laws.*http://www.workhouses.org.uk/

Hindutstantimes.com (2010) 1 January, *Indian origin scientist gets Canada's highest civilian award.* http://www.hindustantimes.com/Indian-origin-scientist-gets-Canada-s-highest-civilian-award/Article1-492631.aspx

Historic UK (2012) *Druids.* http://www.historic-uk.com/HistoryUK/HistoryofWales/Druids/

Holy Mountain Trading Company (2011) *Water Rituals in Japan.* http://www.holymtn.com/fountain/rituals.htm

Homes Point2 (2007) Houston and Third Ward Demographic Data by Zip code http://homes.point2.com/Neighborhood/US/Texas/Harris-County/Houston/Third-Ward-Demographics.aspx

Hong, Doo-Seung (2013) May. *Current Sociology. Sage Journals. International Sociological Association.* http://csi.sagepub.com/content/50/5/729.abstract

Hopper, Rowan (2005) 26 January, *Evolutionary Take on Love.* The Japan Times. http://www.meditationblg.com/2005/01/26/love-story/

Howard, Gardner (2011) *What are Multiple Intelligences? Gardner, Howard Frames of Mind: The Theory of Multiple Intelligences.* Basic Books New York. http://www.multipleintelligencetheory.co.uk/

Hoyk, Robert and Hersey, Paul (2008), *Ethical executive: becoming aware of the root causes of unethical behavior, Traps Everyone Falls Into.*Stanford University Press. http://books.google.ca/books?id=WtS15XFhdcwC&pg=PA31&lpg=PA31&dq=self+interest+executive&source=bl&ots=kLFSJc8d03&sig=dvQck0JbqYZOE3BNg7dxh4hv30&hl=en&ei=6BZPTcCoBcG88gbfqpyxDg&sa=X&oi=book_result&ct=result&resnum=4&ved=0CCYQ6AEwAw#v=onepage&q=self%20interest%20executive&f=false

Hotnet Sdn.Bhd (2011) *Filipino Food.* http://www.marimari.com/content/philippines/food/main.html

Hugman, Barry (2013). Boxing Record. http://boxrec.com/

Hotnet Sdn.Bhd (2011) *National Dishes.*http://www.marimari.com/content/philippines/food/national_dishes.html

Hwang, Jaeho (2010) 30 September. *The Fifth Berlin Conference on Asian Security (BCAS). Session VI: Regional Formats of Military and Security Cooperation.* Hankuk University of Foreign Studies, Seoul, Korea. http:/www.swpberlin.org/fileadmin/contents/products/projekt_papiere/Hwang_BCAS2010_web_ks.PDF

IFAD (2011) *Statistics and key facts about indigenous people.* http://www.ruralpovertyportal.org/web/guest/topic/statistics/tags/indigenous%20peoples

IMDB (2011) *The Nanny (TV Series 1993–1999).* http://www.imdb.com/title/tt0106080/

India Parenting (2010) 26 November, *The Mentally Challenged Child.* http://www.indiaparenting.com/childs-healthcare/36_237/the-mentally-challenged-child.html

Indo-Asian News Service (2010) 1 January, *Indian Origin*

Scientist gets highest civilian award. http://www.hindustantimes.com/Indian-origin-scientist-gets-Canada-s-highest-civilian-award/Article1-492631.aspx

Inside Higher Ed (2008) 14 May, *Students Fail -- and Professor Loses Job - Who is to blame when students fail? If many students fail -- a majority even -- does that demonstrate faculty incompetence, or could it point to a problem with standards?* www.insidehighered.com/news/2008/05/14/aird

Institute of Hazard, Risk and Resilience Blog. (2010) 6 August 2010, *Landslide at Meager Creek, British Columbia, Canada.* http://daveslandslideblog.blogspot.com/2010/08/landslide-at-meager-creek-british.html

International Committee of the Fourth International (ICFI) (2009) 14 December, *Martial Law in the Philippines.* World Socialist. http://www.wsws.org/articles/2009/dec2009/pers-d14.shtml

International Work Group for Indigenous People. (2010) 27 May, *Russia: Indigenous peoples of Kamchatka prepare for protests.* www.iwgia.org/sw42052.asp

Intense Debate (2011), *U.S. Patent #3351836: Robert Kearns.* http://honoringtheinventor.blogspot.com/2008/09/us-patent-3351836.html

Internet Center for Corrupt Research (2012) October. *The 2004 Corruption Perceptions Index.* Innstr.27 - 94032 Passau - Germany. An Association for Cultural Heritage Interpretation. http://www.icgg.org/corruption.cpi_2004_data.html

Interpretation Canada (2011) 20 February, *Training Requirements Application*. Red Deer, AB. http://www.interpcan.ca/new/files/uplink/Training_Cmttee_Nom_Form.pdf

In-the-news.company.uk (2008) 30 May, *Lost tribe' discovered on Brazil-Peru border.* http://www.inthenews.co.uk/news/world/-lost-tribe-discovered-on-brazil-peru-border-$1225100.htm

Iraq Updates Limited. (2008) 5 January, *Sulaimaniya Airport Flights Stop Due to Bad Weather.* http://www.iraqupdates.com/p_articles.php/article/25839

Ismail, Wasiq (June 2010) *Express Tribute with the International Herald Tribune.* http://blogs.tribune.com.pk/story/502/ethical-dilemma-of-academics/Opinion Blog

Ivars Peterson's Math Trek (1998) 23 November, *Birthday Surprises.* http://www.maa.org/mathland/mathtrek_11_23_98.html

Jamieson, Don (2009) *Is there a literacy crisis in Canada? Janet Steffen Hagen, Canada, BC, literacy, early literacy, national strategy.* http://communities.canada.com/vancouversun/blogs/reportcard/archieve/2009/03/24/does-canada-have-a-literacy-problem.aspx

Japan-Guide.com (2008) 06 May, *Japanese Table Manners.* http://www.japan-guide.com/e/e2005.html

Judicial Circuit (2008) 19th*2008 Annual Report.* http://www.19thcircuitcourt.ste.il.us/annual/2008/Org/Adult/Org-Adult-Volunteer/ProbationSupportProgram.aspx

Jones, Del (2009) 2 January, *Women CEOs slowly gain on Corporate America.* http://www.usatoday.com/money/companies/management/2009-01-01-women-ceos-increase_N.htm

Kadmon-Telias, Ana (2003) *What Does Social Justice Mean and Require in the Rehabilitation of Ex-Convicts Addicts in the Era of Privatization.* http://www.psychosocial.com/IJPR_7/social_justice.html

Kawada, Fumiko (2011), Ibaraki, Satoshi, Yoshida, Yutaka, *Center for Research and Documentation on Japan's War Responsibility.* Chuo University, Kansai University, and Kanto Gakuin University. http://japanfocus.org/data/comwomappeal.abbrev.pdf

Kaewthep, Suttira (2010) 6 October, *Bathing Buddha in Phetchabun.* Tourism Authority of Thailand: Phetchabun's Public Relations Center http://www.thailand-travelonline.com/thailand-events-calendar/bathing-buddha-in-phetchabun/510/

Kalb, Rosalind, and Holland, Nancy (2011) *Common MS Related Cognitive Problems. Common MS Related Cognitive Problems.* http://www.dummies.com/how-to/content/common-multiple-sclerosisrelated-cognitive-rpblem.html

Kane, Joanne and Ven Boven (2011) Abstracts: *Emotional Intensity.* http://papers.ssm.com/sol3/papers.cfm?abstract_id1531661&http://www.goggle.ca/search?hl=en&source=hp&q

=feeling+closed+source+space+&aq=f8Feeling Close: Emotional Intensity Reduces Perceived Psychological Distance\Van Boven, Leaf (University of Colorado), Kane, Joanne (Princeton University

Kalpana (2011) 14 February, *Hot springs in Taiwan*. http://travel.hindustantimes.com/featured_destination/destination/taiwan.php

Kearns, Robert (2010) 26 August, http://en.Wikipedia./wki/Robert_Kearns

Keating Chisholm, Charlyn (2011) *Hotels and Resorts*. http://hotels.about.com/b/2004/09/22/the-royal-treatment-for-your-little-princess.htm

Keith, Barry, (2008) 09 September, *Greg Kinnear + Windshield Wiper*. Autopia. http://www.wired.com/autopia/2008/09/take-your-date/

Kelly, John (2008) 1 April, *Medicaid's Buried Treasure for Juvenile Justice*. http://www.youthtoday.org/view_article.cfm?article_id=1680

Khandro.Net (2011) 28 January, *Mythology: Inhabitants of Nagaland*. http://www.khandro.net/mysterious_naga.htm

Kiff, Joe (2011) Psychology Wikia, *Wilderness Therapy*. http://psychology.wikia.com/wiki/Probation

Kim, Hyung-Jin (2011) 03 January, *South Korea: North Korea builds up Special Forces*. http://www.wptv.com/dpp/news/world/south-korea%3A-north-korea-builds-up-special-forces-wcpo1294052361208. The Associated Press.

King, Stephen (2011) *Quote*, http://www.finestquotes.com/select_quote-category-Communication-page-0.htm

Kirsten, et al. (2003) 13 July, *Prisons are a Failed*. .http://www.prisonjustice.ca/politics/1012_failedexp.html

Knowledge Rush (2011) *All in the Family*, http://www.knowledgerush.com/kr/encyclopedia/Archie_Bunker/

Korff, Jens-Uwe (2005-2007) *Creative Spirits: Gambling and Aboriginal People*. http://www.creativespirits.info/aboriginalculture/people/aboriginal-gambling.html17 September 2010.

Korff, Jens-Uwe (2011) *Aboriginal Indigenous spirituality and beliefs*. http://www.creativespirits.info/aboriginalculture/spirituality/index.html

Klu Klux Klan Rally (1996) 21 January, *Rally Portage, IN.* http://www.youtube.com/watch?v=hjiFWeF2Bc4&NR=1&feature=fvwp

Kurashina, Yuko, and Lipari, Rachel (2011) *Social Construction of Peacekeeping in South Korea and Japan:* http://www.allacademic.com/meta/p_mia_apa_research_citation/1/0/6/8/1/p106818_inex.html

Lage-Otero, Eduardo, Delgadillo, Andres and Mitropoulos, Christina (2009) 03 October.

LaRocca, Nicholas and Kalb, Rosalind Kalb (2006) *Understanding the cognitive Challenges.* American Academy of Physical Medicine and Rehabilitation. http://www.demosmedpub.com/prod.aspx?prod_id-9781932603316

Leader-Post (2007) 24 August, *Kku Klux Klan History: The Ku Klux Klan has a long, patchy history in Saskatchewan.*http://www.canada.com/reginaleaderpost/news/story.html?id=d54ebac0-aeeb-4c39-84c4-7bfa855df2f3&k=61059

Lebovits, Susan Chaityn (2011) 24 March. *Irv Epstein: Patterns found in lab spark insight into nature, society.* http://www.brandeis.edu/now/2011/march/epstein.html

Lee Eun Joo (2011) *Han Cinema.* http://www.hancinema.net/korean_Lee_Eun-joo.php

Legett, Christopher *(1999) The Ford Pinto Case: The Valuation of Life as it applies to the negligence-efficiency argument. http://www.wfu.edu/~palmitar/Law&Valuation/Papers/1999/Leggett-pinto.html*

Levy, Jessica (2001) 3 December, *Japanese Civilization: Alcohol: Traditional Presence, Modern Threat.* Washington University St. Louis, MO. http://artsci.wustl.edu/~copeland/alcohol.html

Li and Karakowsky, Leonard (2011) *Handbook of Organizational Culture and Climate. International Themes in Organizational Culture Research, Second Edition. pp. 564-650. Sage Publications.* http://books.google.ca/books?id=HfqqeV9SumEC&pg=PA564&lpg=PA564&dq=Leonard+Karakowsky+culture+study&source=bl&ots=hSmOgeXS0N&sig=SEPGoimuu0fdLZwAapnznrdL8uQ&hl=en&sa=X&ei=7TcHUZWQDu6VjAL9oIEw&sqi=2&ved=0CEUQ6AEwAw#v=onepage&q=Leonard%20Karakowsky%20culture%20study&f=false

Liquid Generation Tube. (2011) 21 January, *10 Most Racist Moments in Television.*
http://www.youtube.com/watch?v=kMvfEdTUO6Q&feature=related
Lindseth, Shawn (2008) 27 March. *Robin Williams' Wife and Her Giant Mole Are Leaving Him.*
http://www.hecklerspray.com/robin-williams-wife-and-her-giant-mole-are-leaving-him/200813192.php
Liveonearth Journal (2009) 22 March. *Patch Adams spoke at NCNM.* http://liveonearth.livejournal.com/499299.html
Long, Dong (2008) 30 September, *The American Institute of Physics' Albert Einstein web site*. Albert Einstein and the Atomic Bomb. http://www.doug-long.com/einstein.htm
Lonely Planet (2011). *China Entertainment.*
http://www.lonelyplanet.com/china/hong-kong/entertainment-nightlife/bar/cafe-einstein
Los Angeles Times (1998) 17 February, *In the News: Weather Afghanistan.*
The Associated Press.
http://articles.latimes.com/keyword/weather-afghanistan
Louisiana Cultural Districts (2011) 12 January, *Department of Culture, Recreation and Tourism*.
http://www.crt.state.la.us/CULTURALDISTRICTS/
Lumberton USA (2008) 17 October, *Philippines To Seek Attack Helicopters (FI)*. http://www.airliners.net/aviation-forums/military/read.main/56103/
Love, Susan, MD (2013) January. *Dr. Susan Love is Back in Action*. Dr Susan Love's Research Foundation. Army of Women.
http://a4bc.wordpress.com/2013/01/24/dr-susan-love-is-back-in-action/
Madej, Krystina (2007) 19 November, *Characteristics of Early Narrative Experience: Connecting Print and Digital Game*. *Simon Fraser University*. School of Interactive Arts and Technology.
http://www.siat.sfu.ca/grad/theses/kmadej/
Malig, Jojo (2011) 24 January, *Philippines' global peace index ranking plunges.*
abs-cbnNEWS.comhttp://www.abs-cbnnews.com/-depth/01/24/11/philippines-global-peace-index-ranking-plunges
Manali Oak (2010) 18 November, *Famous People with Learning Disabilities.*
http://www.buzzle.com/articles/famous-people-with-

learning-disabilities.html
Manitoba Minister of Labor & Immigration (2011) *Cabinet Minister: Jennifer Howard: Biography.* http://www.gov.mb.ca/minister/minlab.htmlGovernment of Canada.
Manning, Martin (1999) September, *Hidden significance of a man's ring finger: Fluctuating Asymmetry, Relative Digit Length and Depression in Men, Evolution and Human Behavior 20: 203-214*. Iss: 2. University of Liverpool. http://www.liv.ac.uk/researchintelligence/issue2/finger.html
Mapsofworld.com (2007) *Weather Caribbean.* http://www.mapsofworld.com/referrals/weather/world-weather/weather-caribbean.html
Martin, Roger (2009) November, *Who Killed Canada's Education Advantage? Forensic Investigation into the Disappearance of Public.* http://www.walrusmagazine.com/articles/2009.11-policy-who-killed-canadas-education-advantage/
Mason, Lisa (2011) 2 February, *First Person: Bad Weather Hits Texas.* http://news.yahoo.com/s/ac/20110202/tr_ac/7767000_first_person_bad_weather_hits_texas
Massie, Meri (2008) *Our Legacy: Trapping and Trap line*. University of Saskatchewan. http://scaa.sk.ca/ourlegacy/exhibit_trapping
Masters Jeff (2006) 24 July. *Gulf of Mexico disturbance; Ultra-marathon today in Death Valley.* http://www.wunderground.com/blog/JeffMasters/comment.html?entrynum=432
Mateo, Stefano (2008) 29 March, *Greed, Lust, Pride and the Fading American Dream.* http://www.helium.com/knowledge/4766-greed-lust-pride-and-the-fading-american-dream
Matthews, Chris (2006) 03 June. *Discuss: The ten lessons of Winston Churchill.* http://www.msnbc.msn.com/id/11689933/
Mariana (2011) 17 November. *Cosmetic Surgery for Men and Women Seeing a Dramatic Rise in Popularity.* http://www.zimbio.com/Plastic+Surgery/articles/oC18ByM7OZZ/Cosmetic+Surgery+Men+Women+Seeing+Dramatic
Maxwell, Mary (2011) 12 February, *Organizing for America Part 2: Social Justice: NRA or Women Rights Amendments.*

http://my.barackobama.com/page/community/blog/marymaxwell
Maya Health (2013) Pinterest. *Lotus and Water Lilies.* http://pinterest.com/isiscat/lotus-water-lilies/
Mazloomian, Hoda and Moon, Bruce (2007) *Images from Purgatory: Art Therapy with Male Adolescent Sexual Abusers.* Art Therapy: Journal of the American Art Therapy Association, v24 n1 p16-21 2007, Milwaukee, WI, Eric Reference EJ777019.
http://www.eric.ed.gov/ERICWebPortal/search/detailmini.jsp?_nfpb=true&_&ERICExtSearch_SearchValue_0=EJ777019&ERICExtSearch_SearchType_0=no&accno=EJ777019
MBA Publishing Limited. (2010) 19 September. *HK Di Source*North Yorkshire, UK.
http://www.hkdlsource.com/park/history
McCain, John (2011) *On the Issues & Speak Out Foundation* Cambridge, MA.
http://www.ontheissues.org/john_mccain.htm
McConaghy, Tom (1997) *A Battle is Raging over Ontario Education*. Volume 78. *Phi Delta Kappan.*
http://www.questia.com/googleScholar.qst?docId=5000535679
McFadden, Patricia (2010) 22 January, *Emotional Intelligence in Early Childhood: Social Emotional Learning for the Preschool Child.*
http://www.suite101.com/content/emotional-intelligence-in-early-childhood-a192691
Medel, Brian (2011) 03 February, *Mancini: Priests' actions criminal.* The Chronicle Herald
Media Awareness Network (2010) *Beauty and Body Image in the Media.*
http://www.media-awareness.ca/english/issues/stereotyping/women_and_girls/women_beauty.cfm
Mercer, Jane (1970) *Label Game: The History of Labels.* http://www.labelgame.org/label.html
Merriam Webster (2013) January. *Definition of ethnic.* http://www.merriam-webster.com/dictionary/ethnic
Mills, Quinn D. (2005) 27 June, *Asian and American Leadership Styles: How Are They Unique?* Harvard Business School. http://hbswk.hbs.edu/item/4869.html
Mi Marketing Pty Ltd. (2010) 3 March, *Japanese Lifestyle: Geisha.*
http://www.japaneselifestyle.com.au/culture/geisha.html

Mitra, Robin (2004) 3 March, *India in America's Mind: A Contrast in Perception.* http://www.ivarta.com/columns/OL_040303.htm

Monitor, Redd (2010) 21 December, *President of the Amerindian Peoples Association gets death: Threats in Guyana.* www.redd-monitor.org/2010/12/21/president-of-the-amerindian-peoples-association-gets-death-threats-in-guyana/

Moore, George, Bro. RW (2010) 20 September. *Grand Lodge of British Columbia and Yukon* A.F. http://en.wikipedia.org/wiki/Freemasonry

Moore, Robert L. (2005) 22 September, *Generation KU: Individualism and China's millennial youth.* http://www.highbeam.com/doc/1G1-1487663e26.html

Moviefone (2012) *FBI Investigation: Michael Douglas FBI Financial Fraud PSA: 'Wall Street' Star Warns Of Insider.* http://news.moviefone.com/2012/02/27/michael-douglas-gordon-gekko-fbi-psa_n_1305118.html

Mshelizza, Ibrahim (2009) 28 July. *Fight for Sharia leaves dozens dead in Nigeria: Islamic militants resisting Western education extend their campaign of violence.* The Independent Worldttp://www.independent.co.uk/news/world/africa/fight-for-sharia-leaves-dozens-dead-in-nigeria-1763253.html

Muhammad, Jesse (2009) *Racial tension flares in Paris, Texas during rally over the dragging death of Brandon McClelland.*http://jessemuhammad.blogs.finalcall.com/2009/07/racial-tension-flares-in-paris-texas.html

Music Stack (2011) 12 March, *Popular Robin Williams CDs and Vinyl Records.* http://www.musicstack.com/records-cds/robin+williams

Museum of Hoaxes (2011) *Science Points to Six Sense.* http://www.museumofhoaxes.com/hoax/forum/forum_comments/2510/P20

Nakata, Hiroko (2009) 28 July, *FUNERAL: Japan's funerals deep-rooted mix of ritual, form* http://search.japantimes.co.jp/cgi-bin/nn20090728i1.html

Nam-Su, Kim, Je-Gyun, Kim, Jeong, Jae-Won (2010) 28 January, *Film Festivals: Harmony.* http://asianmediawiki.com/Harmony

National Institute for Literacy (2003) August, *Literacy in the United States: Almanac of Policy Issues.* http://www.policyalmanac.org/education/archive/literacy.shtml

National Park Service. Department of the Interior. (2013) History of Cherry Trees. Cherry Blossom Festival. Note: Cherry blossom origins.
http://www.nps.gov/cherry/cherry-blossom-history.htm

National Weather Service Weather Forecast Office (2010) 30 October, *Severe Weather in North & Central Georgia October 25-27, 2010.*
http://www.srh.noaa.gov/ffc/?n=tor102510

National White Collar Crime Center (2008) *Research Section. Insurance Fraud.*
http://www.nw3c.org/docs/whitepapers/insurance_fraud_(6-08).pdf?sfvrsn=7

Nauert, Rich, & Grohol, John M. (2008) 19 September, *Dominant Parents Influence Child's Passion.*
http://psychcentral.com/news/2008/09/19/dominant-parents-influence-childs-passion/2968.html

Nawojczyk, Steven (2010) 24 July *Gang War.* Little Rock, Arkansas. http://www.gangwar.com/dynamics.htm

Near Death Experiences (2011) *Edgar Casey on the Future.*
http://www.near-death.com/experiences/cayce11.html

Nessia, Rachelle M. & Government of Philippines. (2010) 19 November, *Philippines: Disaster council to inspect hazard-prone areas in Negros Oriental.*
http://www.reliefweb.int/rw/rwb.nsf/db900SID/JDUN-8BC8YA?OpenDocument&rc=3&emid=FL-2010-000107-PHL

NetCent Communications (2010) *Texas Drug Sheet: Drugs in the United States: Texas.*
http://www.ncbuy.com/health/drugs/us_tx.html

Nelson, William (2012) *Roots of American Bureaucracy, 1830.*
http://books.google.ca/books/about/The_Roots_of_American_Bureaucracy_1830.html?id=1RklcVws7PIC&redir_esc=y

Neuman, Scott (2012) 02 March. *Decoding Allure of the Almanac.*
http://www.npr.org/2012/03/02/147810046/decoding-the-allure-of-the-almanac

News Asia Pacific (2010) 10 November, *China's human rights 'getting worse.*
http://www.bbc.co.uk/news/world-asia-pacific-11730827

NewsMax.com (2004) 30 July. *China Threatens War With Taiwan by 2008.*
http://archive.newsmax.com/archives/articles/2004/7/30/111246.shtml

New York Times (2011) 22 March. *2010 Pakistan Floods.* http://topics.nytimes.com/top/reference/timestopics/subjects/f/floods/2010_pakistan_floods/index.html?scp=4&sq=pakistan%20flood&st=cse

Nineteenth Judicial Circuit (2009) *Robert W. Depke Juvenile Justice Complex: Minard E. Hulse Juvenile Detention Center.* Vernon Hills, Illinois. http://204.58.204.52/juvprob/juv_main.htm#guiding

Ngumuta, Stella (2008) 09 June, *Living and Working in Kenya.* http://www.devex.com/en/articles/a-guide-for-expatriates-practicalities-of-living-and-working-in-kenya

Nova Scotia Education (2002) *Racial Equity Policy.* (Remains consistent for 2011), The Ministry of Education.

Nova Scotia Office of Immigration (2011), *Honorable Marilyn More.* http://www.novascotiaimmigration.com/nova-scotia-office-of-immigration/minister-of-immigration-biography

NUS Entreprise (2012) 22 February. *Social Business Forum for Corporate Leaders: Using Social Business Models to serve the Bottom of the Pyramid: Lessons from Far-Sighted Corporate Leaders.* http://www.nusentrepreneurshipcentre.sg/initiatives/initiatives_article/social_business_week/social_business_forum_for_corporate_leaders

NYSED (2010) 22 April, *Chapter 515 Law: Adult Vocational Rehabilitation Service Delivery and Coordination.* University of the State of New York New York State Education Department. New York, NY. http://www.vesid.nysed.gov/current_provider_information/vocational_rehabilitation/chapter_515/chapter_515_Law.htm

Olson, O. (2010) 26 June. *1/3rd of Women in US Military Raped.* http://newsjunkiepost.com/2010/01/26/13rd-of-women-in-us-military-raped/

Onecle (2010) 5 March, *Arizona Revised Statutes - Title 23 Labor - Chapter 3 Employment Services.* http://Law.onecle.com/arizona/labor/ch3.html

OPPapers.com (2010) *Personality Types and Learning Styles.* http://www.oppapers.com/essays/Personality-types-And-Learning-Styles/250603?topic

Oweh, Innocent (2009) 8 September. *Nigeria: 776 Million Adults Illiterate Globally.* Unesco Report.

http://allafrica.com/stories/200909080739.html
Palmer, Diane (2003) *Manners and Etiquette.* Dictionary of American History
http://www.encyclopedia.com/doc/1G2-3401802520.html
Park, Kyeung IL (2001) *Global Alcohol Policy Alliance.* The Globe: Issues 3 & 4
http://www.ias.org.uk/resources/publications/theglobe/globe200103-04/gl200103-04_p30.html
Pavlina, Steve (2006) 13 April, *How to Squash Negative Thought Patterns.*
http://www.stevepavlina.com/blog/2006/04/how-to-squash-negative-thought-patterns/
Peltz, Jennifer (2011) 13 January, *NYC Juvenile Justice Worker's Sex Trial Opens.*
The Associated Press.
http://www.mercurynews.com/breaking-news/ci_17088618?nclick_check=1
Penre, Wes (1999) 26 February, *List of Significant Freemasons.* http://www.illuminati-news.com/famous-freemasons.htm
Peter (2011) 4 January, *North Korea boosts tanks and Special Forces, says South Korea: Military Spending, North Korea, Regional Arms Race,* Regional Security. South Korea. http://pacificfreeze.ips-dc.org/2011/01/north-korea-boosts-tanks-and-special-forces-says-south-korea/
Peteru, Chris (1996) October, *while challenging the traditional norms of masculinity, Western Samoa's drag queens find themselves in a world of near acceptance country: the gay Life.* GenderTalk Archive Pacific Islands Monthly.
http://www.gendertalk.com/articles/archive/samoaq.shtml
Pike, John (2005) 27 April, *Military Nigeria: Introduction.*
http://www.globalsecurity.org/military/world/war/nigeria-intro.htm
Pioch, Nicholas (2002) 14 October. *Bosch, Hieronymus: The Ship of Fools; Illustrated allegories* Musee du Louvre, Paris. http://www.ibiblio.org/wm/paint/auth/bosch/fools/
Pitzer Education (2010) *Comparing Minds and Facial Expressions of Japanese and Americans: Nonverbal Communication.*
http://dwardmac.pitzer.edu/faculty/jkaret/Classes/English3%20S96/Yusukenonver.html

PLQ (2011) *Yolande James Nelligan. Biography. Minister of Immigration and Cultural Communities National Assembly.*
http://www.plq.org/en/candidat/083yolandejames.php
Pornchokchai, Sopon (2010) 23 September, *President, Thai Appraisal Foundation Affairs: Bangkok Housing Market's Booms and Busts. What Do We Learn?* Christchurch, New Zealand.
http://www.prres.net/Papers/Pornchokchai_Bangkok_housing_markets_what_do_wee_learn.pdf
Pottie, Erin (2010) April, *Nova Scotia parishes raise millions for sex abuse victims.* Toronto Globe & Mail
http://www.theinquiry.ca/wordpress/rc-scandal/canada/nova-scotia-parishes-raise-millions-for-sex-abuse-victims/
Popular Occultism *(2003) 03 February. Symbols and Their Meanings: Introduction.*
http://www.radioliberty.com/Symbolsandtheirmeaning.html
Poverty Alleviation and Social Protection (2011) March. *Conference 2012, 8-10 March 2012,* Bangkok, Thailand.
http://www.tomorrowpeople.org/poverty-and-social-protection-conference-2012-html
Press, Eyal and Washburn, Jennifer Washburn (2000) 7 May, *Neglect for Sale: ResCare in Florida: What the Advocacy Center Missed.* The American Prospect.
http://www.prospect.org/cs/articles?article=neglect_for_sale_050700
PRWeb (2004) 12 February, Dr. William Glasser Endorses *Connections board game.* Morganton, North Carolina.
http://www.prweb.com/releases/2004/02/prweb107987.htm
Public Health Agency of Canada: (2001) 25 November, *Education Wife Assault and the National Clearinghouse on Family Violence FAQs.*
http://www.womanabuseprevention.com/html/question__1.html
Rajan, C.V. (2008) 18 December, *Understanding the relationship between business and ethics*. Helium Inc.
http://www.helium.com/items/1269994-understanding-the-relationship-between-business-and-ethics
Redman, Michael (2010) *4closureFraud.org: Open Letter to Ohio Attorney General Cordray RE: Chase Home Finance, LLC – Across America: Wrongful foreclosures & Corrupted Land*

*Records.*http://4closurefraud.org/2010/09/30/open-letter-to-ohio-attorney-general-cordray-re-chase-home-finance-llc-across-america-wrongful-foreclosures-amp-corrupted-land-records/

Reed, Johnson (2008) 03 October. *The cantankerous man behind the wipers.* *wipers.http://articles.latimes.com/2008/oct/03/entertainment/et-kearns3*

Reen at Big River (2013) *Traditional Aboriginal Bush Medicine.* http://www.aboriginalartonline.com/culture/medicine.php

Ridon, Terry (2011) 31 January, *LFS to Acquino: Learn from Arab-world protests, address roots of poverty to end insurgency (PR). National Chairperson of the League of Filipino Students.* http://bulalat.com/main/2011/01/31/lfs-to-acquino-learn-from-arab-world-protests-address-roots-of-poverty-to-end-insurgency-pr/

Right Management (2011) 15 November. *Poor Relationships Top Cause for Leader Failure.* http://www.right.com/news-and-events/press-releases/2011-press-releases/item22034.aspx

Roberts, Janet. (2011) 24 February, *Trichotillomani.* North American Hair Research Society. http://www.nahrs.org/home/Default.aspx?tabid=67

Robinson, James Foster (2004) 04 August, *History of Storytelling - In the Beginning.* http://www.suite101.com/article.cfm/the_art_of_storytelling/110011

Robinson, Viola, Honsberger, Fred, and Tax, Ted (2011), *Directions in Mi'Kmaq Justice: An Evaluation of the Mi'kmaq Justice Institute and its Aftermath.* Dalhousie University. http://sociologyandsocialanthropology.dal.ca/Files/FUTRE_DIRECTION_IN_M%27KMAQ_JUSTICE-EVALUATION_OF_MI%27KMAQ.JU.pdf

Roman, Moises (2012) 08 March. *Seizing a Teachable Moment.* http://kidslinkcares.com/tflblog/

Ross, Kevin (1995) *Son yeol-eum plays Mozart Volodos Turkish March.* http://www.youtube.com/watch?v=SRQxJkh4RSI

Runner, Night (2008) 3 September. *Palin cut Special Education budget by 62%.* http://www.dailykos.com/story/2008/09/03/584963/-Palin-

cut-Special-Education-budget-by-62
Ryall, Julian (2010) 14 May, *Japan Black Market.* Reports from Sydney Morning Herald. Japan Times, Hiroko Tabuchi, U.S. Department of State, he Star/Asia News and International Authentication Association. http://www.havoscope.com/regions-main/asia/japan/
Saberi, Roy (2010) 07 October, *Burmese General Elections: Another Sham?* http://globalpolitician.com/24201-culture
Sable (2008) 2 October. *"Tuskegee-like" experiments on Aboriginal children?* http://www.sableverity.com/tuskegee-like-experiments-on-aboriginal-children/
Sabol, William J. (2010) 21 December, *Prisoners in 2009.* Bureau of Justice Statistics http://bjs.ojp.usdoj.gov/index.cfm?ty=pbdetail&iid=2232
Sadeghian, Abbas (2007) 13 January. *The Neuropsychological of George W. Bush.* http://www.rense.com/general75/neur.htm
Sailorange, Jessie (2010) 17 June, For *Mentally Challenged Staten Island couple, a marriage worth wait,* http://community.livejournal.com/ontd_political/6451832.html
Saisan, Joanna, Segal, Jeanne Segal, Smith, Melinda Smith, and Robinson, Lawrence (2010) November. (2010) 6June, *Gambling Addiction and Problem Gambling: Signs, Symptoms and, Treatments.* http://helpguide.org/mental/gambling_addiction.htm
Salvador Dali Art Gallery (2011) Salvador Dali. http://dali-gallery.com/
Sang-Hun, Choe Sang-Hun (2005) 29 December, *After unsmiling centuries, Koreans need lessons to learn to laugh.* Asia Pacifichttp://www.nytimes.com/2005/12/29/world/asia/29iht-laugh.html
Schudel, Matt (2005) 26 February, page B01, *Accomplished, Frustrated Inventor Dies*. Washington Post. http://www.washingtonpost.com/wp-dyn/articles/A54564-2005Feb25.html
Schneider, Walter (2008) *Fathers for Life: Battered Women Shelter Index.* http://www.fathersforlife.org/fv/battered-women_shelters.htm

Science Daily (Sep. 22, 2005) *Impact of Global Warming On Weather Patterns Underestimated*
Science News.
http://www.sciencedaily.com/releases/2005/09/050922015634.htm
Scott, Elizabeth (2007) 1 November, *Music and Your Body: How Music Affects Us and Why Music Therapy Promotes Health: How and Why Is Music A Good Tool For Health?* http://stress.about.com/od/tensiontamers/a/music_therapy.htm
Scream Online (2003) 05 December. *Indigo.* http://thescreamonline.com/film/film4-1/indigo.html
Sekularac, Ivana (2011) 18 January, *Save the planet: Swap your steak for bugs and worms.* The Star Phoenix http://www.thestarphoenix.com/life/Save+planet+Swap+your+steak+bugs+worms/4125294/story.html
Sen, Amartya (2001) 8 December, Issue No. 22. *Human Rights: Human Rights Vision- Gender: Seven types of Inequality.* Asia Human Rights News.
http://www.ahrchk.net/news/mainfile.php/ahrnews_200112/2247/
Sen, Amartya (2011) 27 October, *Many Faces of Gender Inequality* India's National Magazine, Volume 18, Issue 22. The Hindu.
http://www.hinduonnet.com/fline/fl1822/18220040.htm
Service Ontario (2010) 19 August. *Vocational Rehabilitation Services Act. Regulations 1095. R.R.O. 1990, Reg. 1095, Form 2. Ontario, CA.*
http://www.eLaws.gov.on.ca/html/revokedregs/english/eLaws_rev_regs_901095_e.htm
Shakespeare, William (2013) *Hamlet Monologue* .http://www.monologuearchive.com/s/shakespeare_001.html
Shanghai Architecture (2011) *Photos Schramm, Paul.*http://www.chinese-architecture.info/SHANGHAI/SH.htm
Shanghais (2006) 23 February. *Tujiapizza proves that Chinese invented pizza.*
http://shanghaiist.com/2006/02/23/tujia_pizza_pro_1.php
Sherin, Lal Aqa Sherin (2009) 20 August, *Near-Epidemic of Land and Home Theft.*
http://www.ipsnews.net/news.asp?idnews=48150

Shores, Lucie (2010) 28 January, *Greed, Lust, Pride and the Fading American Dream* http://www.helium.com/knowledge/4766-greed-lust-pride-and-the-fading-american-dream

Shin, Hwa-Ji (2005) 12 August, *Trajectories of Nation: Citizenship, Immigration and National Self-identification in Japan*. American Sociological Associations. PA. http://www.alacademic.com/one/www/www/index.php?click_k=1

Siddiqi, Shibil (2010) 23 August, *Pakistan's Wages of Sin. Global Power and Politics*. Trent University. http://www.themarknews.com/articles/2071-pakistan-s-wages-of-sin

Simmons, Sue (1999) *Grief in a Family Context -- HPER F460/F560. Multicultural Interview - Grief in the Chinese Culture.* http://www.indiana.edu/~famlygrf/culture/simmons.html

Sina-English (2011) 9 January, *China works on smoke-free public environment.* http://english.sina.com/life/p/2011/0108/355158.html

Sina-English (2011) 16 January, *Hundreds punished in China's public servant exam.* http://english.sina.com/life/2011/0116/356109.html

Sivananda, Sri Swami (2005) 20 February, *Shintoism.* http://www.dlshq.org/religions/shintoism.htm

Skenny (2011) Soc. 3290 *Deviance: Homicide 2: Victims & Deviance: Victims of Crime and Labeling Theory.* http://www.ucs.mun.ca/-skenney/courses/3290/329class20.pdf

Siow, Maria (2011) October. *Luxury car owners draw public ire in China.* Lifestyle. http://www.channelnewsasia.com/stories/lifestylenews/view/1103069/1/.html

Slater, Steven (2009) 15 June, *Mount Fuji, Religion and Commercialism: Japan's Highest Peak Both a Symbol and a Commodity.* http://www.suite101.com/content/mount-fuji-a126651

Smart, Brief (2011) 5 January, *How do you think social media affects consumer complaints?* http://www.sciencedaily.com/releases/2005/09/050922015634.htm

Smith, Jennie (1992) *Japanese View of Americans.* Helvidius. http://www.helvidius.org/files/1992/1992_Smith.pdf

Smithe, Bob (2009) 16 April, *Most Dangerous Cities in America.* http://www.associatedcontent.com/article/1646896.top_10_most_dangerous_cities_in_the.html
Soccerphile Ltd. *Japan Tourist Information, Ferries in Japan.* (2010) 24.http://www.japanvisitor.com/index.php?cID=424&pID=1568&pName=japan-ferry
Socionics (2010) 22 November, *Relations between Psychological ("personality") Types.* http://www.socionics.com/rel/rel.htm
Spezzan, Guiseppe, C. (2010) 7 April. *Family Anatomy: Parenting & Relationship Information From a Trusted Source: Academics, Parenting Ideas.* http://www.familyanatomy.com/2010/04/07/can-parents-influence-their-childs-career-choice/
Spitzer, Nicholas R. (1999) *Louisiana Living Traditions: Louisiana Division of Arts*, Baton Rouge, Louisiana. http://www.louisianafolklife.org/LT/Articles_Essays/creole_art_creole_state.html
Squidoo (2011) *Black Presidents and the One Drop Rule?* http://www.squidoo.com/FiveBlackPresidentsoftheUSA
Squidoo (2011) *Color: Meaning, Symbolism and Psychology.* http://www.squidoo.com/colorexpert
Stachowiak, Julie (2010) 19 August, *Cognitive Dysfunction as a Symptom of Multiple Sclerosis.* Multiple Sclerosis Symptoms and Signs. Division.
Division of New York Times.
http://ms.about.com/od/signssymptoms/a/cognitive-over.htm
Statistics Canada (2006)
http://www12.statcan.gc.ca/census-recensement/2006/dp-pd/tbt/RP-
Statistics Canada (2010) 14 June, *Police-reported hate crimes 2008.* http://www.statcan.gc.ca/daily-quotidien/100614/dq100614b-eng.htm
Stein, Jason (2008) 30 May. *W. Edwards Deming: In simple terms, he's why Japanese carmakers flourished as North America's Big Three floundered.* http://autos.winnipegfreepress.com/news-article/id-458/
Stephney, Philip H.R. (2011) *Kingfisher.* Historical Dominion. http://www.thecanadianencyclopedia.com/index.cfm?PgNm=TCE&Params=A1ARTA0004317
Stephenson, Kelly (2010) 22 November, *Street Level Consulting.*

http://www.streetlevelconsulting.ca/biographies/patchadams.htm

Steven, David (2010) 4 March, *Ku Klux Klan 2010 Rally in South Georgia*. Global Dashboard. http://www.globaldashboard.org/2010/03/04/ku-klux-klan-2010-rally-in-south-georgia/

Stewart, Phil (2011) 26 October. *U.S. defense chief says North Korea "serious threat"* http://www.reuters.com/article/2011/10/26/us-korea-usa-panetta-idUSTRE79P2LH20111026

Stolyarov II, G (2006) 23 December, *Winston Churchill's welfare: Static and the dangers of democracy.* http://www.helium.com/items/105340-winston-churchills-welfare-statism-and-the-dangers-of-democracy

Straits Times (2010) 24 October, *Bad weather caused sinking.* http://www.straitstimes.com/BreakingNews/SEAsia/Story/STIStory_594710.html

Sudan Tribune (2008) 7 May, *South Korea mulling to join Darfur peacekeeping force.* http://www.sudantribune.com/South-Korea-mulling-to-join-Darfur,27027

Sundelin, Jenny (2008) 11 March, *Play: The Swedish Way.* The Society Guardian http://www.guardian.co.uk/society/2008/mar/11/children

Surrealism.org (2009) *Salvador Dali.* http://www.surrealism.org/

Sun Sentinel (2000) 1 May, *Caregivers Told: Avoid Neglect.* http://articles.sun-sentinel.com/keyword/neglect/featured/2

Sun Sentinel (1993) 24 July, *Man Sentenced In Neglect.* http://articles.sun-sentinel.com/keyword/neglect/featured/2

Support the Children Foundation (2006) 30 January. *About the Children.* Chaingmai, Thailand. http://support-the-children.org/

Swarthmore (2011) *Psycho-diagnosis in Question: A Brief Overview.* http://www.swarthmore.ed/Soc.Sci/kgergen1/Psychodianostics/biblio.html

Tajima, Asushi (2008) 21 May, *Trans-national & Domesticated Use of Racial Hierarchy: Representations of Blacks in Japan.* http://www.alacademic.com/one/www/www/index.ph

p?click_k=1
Tajima, Asushi (2009) 20 May, *Whites in a Non-White Mind: Ethnographic Study of White Perception in Japan.* http://www.alacademic.com/one/www/www/index.php?click_k=1
Taylor-Butts, Andrea (2008) 27 November, *Canada's Shelters for Abused Women, 2005/2006*, 85-002-XIE, Volume 27, No. 4, Canadian Centre for Justice Statistics, Statistics Canada. http://www.statcan.gc.ca/pub/85-002-x/85-002-x2007004-eng.htm
Texas Observer (2007) 17 March, *KKK Rally in Stephenville, TX.* http://www.youtube.com/watch?v=XXLqmnAnPg8&feature=related
Thai Boxing Camp Ltd. (2006) *Thailand Culture and the People of Thailand.* http://www.horizonmuaythai.com/Thailand/culture.html#time
The Associated Press (2010) 30 October, *Call for Britain's iconic telephone booths? Popularity of cell phones puts one-third of traditional kiosks in jeopardy.* http://www.msnbc.msn.com/id/27455972/ns/world_news-europe
The Associated Press (2005) 17 November, *Einstein robot the star of high-tech show: South Korea conference shows serious side with wireless test.* http://www.msnbc.msn.com/id/10085890/
The Associated Press (2011) March. *Hamz Hendaw & Maggie Michael, Reform leader calls for Egypt's Mubarak to resign as military boosts presence in chaotic Cairo.* News 1130. http://www.news1130.com/news/world/article/176591-egypt-s-military-steps-up-presence-in-chaotic-cairo-with-jets-and-tanks-protests-endure
The Associated Press (1998) 7 June, *Jasper, Texas: KKK Rally Stirs Racial Tension: Armed Militant Group Arrives To Protect Blacks.* http://www.cbsnews.com/stories/1998/06/27/national/main12722.shtml
The Associated Press (2008) 31 January, *Nurse Admits to Stealing Body Parts from 244 Corpses for Resale Thursday.* http://www.foxnews.com/story/0,2933,327007,00.html

The Canadian Press (2009) 4 October, *Halfway house slaying shocks community.* http://www.theprovince.com/news/Murderer+sought+Canada+wide+after+failing+show+Vancouver+halfway+house/3713207/story.html

The Canadian Encyclopedia (2011) Historical Dominica. http://www.thecanadianencyclopedia.com/index.cfm?gNm=TCE&Params=A1ARTA0008681

The Canadian Press (2011) 27 January, *Norbourg fraudster Lacroix out of prison and living in Montreal halfway house.* http://news.sympatico.ca/business/norbourg_fraudster_lacroix_out_of_prison_and_living_in montreal_halfway_house/760773e5

The Dui Hua Foundation (1994) *Advocating Rights Through Clemency.* http://duihua.org/wp/?page_id=1828

The Encyclopedia of Canada's Peoples/Canadian Culture and Ethnic Diversity (2011), *Aboriginal People.* http://www.multiculturalcanada.ca/Encyclopedia/A-Z/c2/1

The Governor General Canada (2011) 28 January, *His Excellency of the Right Honorable David Johnston. It's an Honor: Orders.* Ottawa, Ontario. http://www.gg.ca/document.aspx?id=72

The Global Post (2012) 22 March. *The Top 25 most-powerful world leaders according to their number of friends, likes and followers. Page links also include* 1, 2, 9, 11, 16, and 17. http://www.globalpost.com/photo-galleries/5660579/follow-the-leader?page=18

The Guardian and Media Limited (2013) *Data Blog: Corruption index 2011 from Transparency International: find out how countries compare.* http://www.guardian.co.uk/news/datablog/2011/dec/01/corruption-index-2011-transparency-international

The Hanoist (2010) 24 April, *Vietnam's guarded US embrace*: Asia Times. http://www.atimes.com/atimes/Southeast_Asia/LD24Ae01.html 21 September 2010.

The Heat is Online (2003) EXTREME WEATHER PROFILE: July-December, 2003. http://www.heatisonline.org/contentserver/objecthandlers/index.cfm?id=4190&method=full

The Hienrich Boll Stiftung Foundation (2011), www.boelf-cambodia.org/web/49-347.html

CIYA moving forward for networking, education and Indigenous Rights. Indigenous Association
The Times 100 (2011) *Business Environment.* http://www.thetimes100.co.uk/theory/theory--constraints--421.php
The Mozart Forum (2011). http://www.mozartforum.com/VB_forum/showthread.php?t=3613
The Physics Encyclopedia (2008) 10 July, *Disneyland.* http://www.physicsdaily.com/physics/Disneyland
The Times of India (2007) 18 October. *Symonds mistook antics for racism: Pawar.* http://articles.timesofindia.indiatimes.com/2007-10-18/top-stories/27958471_1_symonds-sharad-pawar-bcci-president
Think Weird Blog (2008) 21 April, *The Kang Bed in Northern Chinese Villages.* http://thinkweird.info/33/the-kang-bed-in-northern-chinese-villages
Thompson, Robert (2007) 28 September, *Chinese Bars, Karaoke in China, Nightlife in China KTV: Chinese Drinking Etiquette: Beer, Tea Etiquette, Bottled Water, Hard Liquor. What is Gross to Chinese People (and Vice Versa) Cultural Differences.* http://www.jazzviolin.com/china/2007/09/28/chinese-bars-karaoke-china-nightlife-in-china/
Tinker. John (2010). *War & armed conflict in Indonesia.* Last modification June 18, 2013. http://schema-root.org/region/asia/southeast_asia/indonesia/war/
Tjaden, Patricia and Thoennes, Nancy (2000) *Extent, Nature, and Consequences of Intimate Partner Violence.* America Bar Association. U.S. Department of Justice http://new.abanet.org/domesticviolence/Pages/Statistics.aspx#prevalence
Time Magazine (1984) 22 October, *Books: Eavesdropping on History.* http://www.time.com/time/magazine/article/0,9171,951370,00.html
Tripod (1998) *The Role of Self Interest in Political Philosophy.* http://ssscott.tripod.com/philosophy.html
TMCNet (2008) 26 September, *Cell Phones Worth Killing for in Africa: Google Patent Imagines a Freer World for Making Mobile Calls.*http://blog.tmcnet.com/wireless-mobility/cellular/cell-phones-worth-killing-for-in-africa.asp
TMZ (2012) 30 February. *Whitney Houston: Family Told She*

Died From RX Not Drowning.
http://www.tmz.com/2012/02/13/whitney-houston-cause-of-death-prescription-drugs-drowning-atlanta/

Toland-Frith, Katherine (2008) 26 January, *Cover Girls: White Models in Asia.*
http://covergirlsthedocumentary.blogspot.com/2008/06/white-models-in-asia.html

Tom.com.au (2005). *Taiwan's Population Distribution.*
http://www.taiwan.com.au/Soccul/People/Pop

TopRen.Net (2011), *China Culture Lifestyle.*
http://topren.net/travel/culture/lifestyle/index.htm

Toronto Star Staff (2010) 26 November, *Thestar.com. Japan turns to Mozart to improve sake taste.*
http://www.thestar.com/news/world/article/897657--japan-turns-to-mozart-to-improve-sake-taste

Trannoy, Alain (2010) *Internet, Literacy & Earnings Inequality: Economic Research of Louvain.* Cairn. Info De Boeck University, http://www.cairn.info/revue-recherché-economiques-d-Louvain-2002-1-page-125.htm

Treble, Patricia (2009) *The Rankings: Canada's most dangerous cities.* MacLean's
http://www2.macleans.ca/2009/03/05/the-most-dangerous-cities-in-Canada/

Trickey, Mike (2001) 21 March, *Mexico: Mexico's President Backs Drug Legalization.*
http://www.mapinc.org/drugnews/v01.n492.a02.html

Tucker, Bush (2011) *Indigenous Australian Foods.*
http://www.hiptravelguide.com/modules.php?name=News&file=article&id=381&site=8

Tudor, Allison and Ng. Jeffrey (2012) 28 May. *Li Weighs Bid to Buy ING Unit.* The Wall Street Journal.
http://www.forbes.com/profile/ka-shing-li/

Tvgasm (2010) 12 October, *Fran Drescher: Talk Show.*
http://igossip.com/gossip/Franny_The_Nanny_Is_Getting_Her_Own_Talk_Show_Fran_Drescher/1317367

UN (2004) *Sanitation Country Profile: Indonesia.*
http://www.un.org/esa/agenda21/natlinfo/countr/indonesa/sanitationIndonesia04f.pdf

United Nations Research for Social Development (2011) *Gender and Development.*
http://www.unrisd.org/80256B3C005BB128/(httpProgrammeAreasForResearchHome)/BAC527EAC4F1F59C8025718B003C2B65?OpenDocument

United Nations Research Institute Social Development 2006-2009 (2011) *Political and Social Economy of Care:*

Program Area: Gender and Development. http://www.unrisd.org/unrisd/website/projects.nsf/(httpProjectsForProgrammeAreaen)/37BD128E275F1F8BC1257296003210EC?OpenDocument

United States Department of Interior. US Geological Survey. (2012) 03 December. *Earthquake Hazards Program: Earthquakes with 50,000 or More Deaths.* http://earthquake.usgs.gov/earthquakes/world/most_destructive.php

United States Department of Statement (2007) *Trafficking in Persons Report 2007.* Secretary for Civilian Security, Democracy, and Human Rights. Bureau of Public Affairs. http://www.state.gov/j/tip/rls/tiprpt/2007/

USA Today (2008) 29 October, *Drug bust charges 41 people, nabs $22 million.* ttp://www.usatoday.com/news/nation/2008-10-29-drugbust_N.htm

United States Forces Website: **Iraq** (2008) 21 September, *Release No. 080918002. MoD hosts women's military intelligence panel: Operation New Dawn.* http//www.usf-iraq.com/?option=com_content&task=view&id=22497&Itemid=128

Urquhart, Conal (2007) 21 June, *Women Soldiers in their underwear: Israel's Image Boost*. The Guardian. http://www.guardian.co.uk/world/2007/jun/21/israel1.

Viacom International Inc. (2011) *Archie Bunker*. http://www.tvland.com/shows/all-in-the-family

Vilches, Nimfa Cuesta Honorable Judge (2011) February. *Thailand Law Forum: Law Analysis and Features of Southeast Asia. The Casa/Gal Volunteer Program*. The Philippine Judges Association. Manila, Philippines. http://www.thaiLawforum.com/articles/casavillches.html

Voigt, Keven (2012) 06 December. *Best, worst nations for corruption*. CNN. http://edition.cnn.com/2012/12/06/business/best-worst-corrupt-countries

Wang, Laurie (2008) 1 May. http://medicine.ucalgary.ca/about/order_of_canada*Faculty of Medicine celebrates Order of Canada recipients.* Faculty of Medicine, University of Calgary.

Wang, Xu-Ming (1996) 20 February, *Roles in Beijing Opera.* http://www.chinapage.com/xwang/roles.html

Warrior Tours (2010), *Chinese Alcohol.* http://www.warriortours.com/intro/alcohol.htm

Watts, Jonathan (2010) 20 June, *China devastated by floods: Over 130 dead and 800,000 displaced after torrential rain sees rivers swell and houses hit by landslides.* http://www.guardian.co.uk/world/2010/jun/20/china-devastated-floods

Webster, Timothy (2010) 4 June. *No Foreigner Allowed: Racial Discrimination in Japan.* The Law and Society Association. http://www.allacademic.com/meta/p_mia_apa_research_citation/1/7/7/5/1/p177512_index.html

Wehner, Chris C. (2010) 12 September, *More Teaching for Social Justice.* http://www.blog4history.com/2010/09/more-teaching-for-social-justice

Wikipedia (2011), *Buddhism: Details about 'Buddhist Terms and Concepts.* Wikipedia Foundation Inc., San Francisco. http://www.buddhismguide.com/buddhism/buddhist_terms_and_concepts.htm

Wikipedia (2010) 18 November, *Albert Einstein* Wikipedia Foundation Inc., San Francisco, CA. http://en.wikipedia.org/wki/Albert_Einstein

Wikipedia (2013) 13 May. *Batik.* Wikipedia Foundation Inc., San Francisco, CA http://en.wikipedia.org/wiki/Batik

Wikipedia, (2012) Vol.32, No.15. *Distrust.* http://en.wikipedia.org/wiki/Distrust

Wikipedia (2010)18 November. *Causes of Malaria.* Wikipedia Foundation Inc., San Francisco, CA. http://en.wikipedia.org/wiki/Malaria#Causes

Wikipedia (2010) 28 September, *Cell Phone Novel.* Wikipedia Foundation Inc., San Francisco, CA. http://en.wikipedia.org/wiki/Mobile_phone_novel.

Wikipedia (2011) 7 February, *1925 Charlevoix–Kamouraska earthquake.* Wikipedia Foundation Inc., San Francisco, CA. http://en.wikipedia.org/wiki/1925_Charlevoix-Kamouraska_earthquake.

Wikipedia (2011) *Children in jail in the Philippines.* Wikipedia Foundation Inc., San Francisco, CA. http://en.wikipedia.org/wiki/Children_in_jail_in_Philippines

Wikipedia (2010) 18 November, *Clementine Churchill, Baroness Spencer-Church.* Wikipedia Foundation Inc., San Francisco, CA. www.en.wikipedia.org/wiki/Clementine_Churchill_Barone

ss_Spencer-Churchill
Wikipedia (2011) 21 March, *Comfort Women*. Wikipedia Foundation Inc. San Francisco, CA. http://en.wikipedia.org/wiki/Comfort_women.
Wikipedia (2010) 18 November, *Dengue Fever*. Wikipedia Foundation Inc. San Francisco, CA. http://en.wikipedia.org/wiki/Dengue_fever
Wikipedia (2012) 19 March. *What Dreams May Come* (film) http://en.wikipedia.org/wiki/What_Dreams_May_Come_(film)
Wikipedia (2010) 18 November, *Einstein Family*. Wikipedia Foundation Inc. San Francisco, CA. http://en.wikipedia.org/wiki/Einstein_family
Wikipedia (2011) *Friendship Stores*. Wikipedia Foundation Inc. San Francisco, CA. http://en.wikipedia.org/wiki/Friendship_store
Wikipedia (2011) 19 March, *Gender Inequality*. Wikipedia Foundation Inc. San Francisco, CA. http://en.wikipedia.org/wiki/Gender_inequality
Wikipedia (2012) 18 May. *Giacomo Casanova*. Wikipedia Foundation Inc. San Francisco, CA. http://en.wikipedia.org/wiki/Giacomo_Casanova
Wikipedia (2010) 26 September, *Guilt Society*. Wikipedia Foundation Inc. San Francisco, CA. http://en.wikipedia.org/wiki/Guilt_society.
Wikipedia (2011) 15 March, *Harlem: Neighborhoods in the New York City Borough of Manhattan.* Wikipedia Foundation Inc. San Francisco, CA. http://en.wikipedia.org/wiki/Harlem.
Wikipedia (2013) 27 April. *Harris County Texas.* Wikipedia Foundation Inc. San Francisco, CA. http://en.wikipedia.org/wiki/Harris_County,_Texas
Wikipedia (2011) 7 March, *Income gender gap.* Wikipedia Foundation Inc. San Francisco, CA. Article originates from Wikipedia. http://www.ask.com/wiki/Income_gender_gap
Wikipedia (2011) 16 March, *Human rights in the People's Republic of China.* Wikipedia Foundation Inc. San Francisco, CA. http://en.wikipedia.org/wiki/Human_rights_in_the_People%27s_Republic_of_China.
Wikipedia (2011) 5 March, *Hurricane Hazel*. Wikipedia Foundation Inc. San Francisco,

CA.http://en.wikipedia.org/wiki/Hurricane_Hazel.
Wikipedia (2011) *Indigenous Movements in the Americas.* Wikipedia Foundation Inc., San Francisco, CA. http://en.wikipedia.org/wiki/Indigenous_movements_in_the_Americas.
Wikipedia (2011) 20 March, *Iraq War.* Wikipedia Foundation Inc. San Francisco, CA. http://en.wikipedia.org/wiki/Iraq_War.
Wikipedia (2011) 21 March, *Jurisprudence*. Wikipedia Foundation Inc. San Francisco, CA. http://en.wikipedia.org/wiki/Jurisprudence.
Wikipedia (2012) March. *Lady Randolph Churchill.* Wikipedia Foundation Inc. San Francisco, http://en.wikipedia.org/wiki/Lady_Randolph_Churchill
Wikipedia (2011) *List of countries by literacy rate.* Wikipedia Foundation Inc. San Francisco, CA. http://en.wikipedia.org/wiki/List_of_countries_by_literacy_rate.
Wikipedia (1968) June. *Margaret Mead.* http://en.wikiquote.org/wiki/Margaret_Mead
Wikipedia (2011) *Mozart and Freemasonry.* Wikipedia Foundation Inc. San Francisco, CA http://en.wikipedia.org/wiki/Mozart_and_Freemasonry
Wikipedia (2011) *Mugwump.* Wikipedia Foundation Inc. San Francisco, CA. http://en.wikipedia.org/wiki/Mugwump.
Wikipedia (2010) 18 November, *Michelle Malkin*. Wikipedia Foundation Inc. San Francisco, CA. http://en.wikipedia.org/wiki/Michelle_Malkin
Wikipedia (2011) *Mindfulness (Buddhism).* Wikipedia Foundation Inc. San Francisco, CA. http://en.wikipedia.org/wiki/Mindfulness_%28Buddhism%29
Wikipedia (2010) 18 November, *Michelle Malkin*. Wikipedia Foundation Inc. San Francisco, CA. http://en.wikipedia.org/wiki/Mindfulness#Continuous_mindfulness_practice
Wikipedia (2010) 11 March, *Multicultural Topics CSD: Taiwan.*Wikipedia Foundation Inc. San Francisco, CA. http://en.wikipedia.org/wiki/Multiculturalism
Wikipedia (2010) 18 November, *Multiple Sclerosis.* Wikipedia Foundation Inc. San Francisco, CA. http://en.wikipedia.org/wiki/Multiple_sclerosis
Wikipedia (2011) *Octavio Ocampo.* Wikipedia Foundation Inc. San Francisco, CA.

http://en.wikipedia.org/wiki/Octavio_Ocampo.
Wikipedia (2010) *Northern Hemisphere Summer Heat.* Wikipedia Foundation Inc. San Francisco, CA. http://en.wikipedia.org/wiki/2010_Northern_Hemisphere_summer_heat_wave.

Wikipedia (2011) 11 March, *Northern Hemisphere*. Wikipedia Foundation Inc. San Francisco, CA. http://en.wikipedia.org/wiki/Northern_Hemisphere#Continents_found_in_the_Northern_Hemisphere

Wikipedia (2011) *Organizational Development*. Wikipedia Foundation Inc. San Francisco, CA. http://en.wikipedia.org/wiki/Organizational_Development

Wikipedia (2011) 20 March, *Parti Quebecois*. Wikipedia Foundation Inc. San Francisco, CA. http://en.wikipedia.org/wiki/Parti_Qu%C3%A9b%C3%A9cois. .

Wikipedia (2012) 25 May. *Political positions of John McCain*. . Wikipedia Foundation Inc. San Francisco, CA. http://en.wikipedia.org/wiki/Political_positions_of_John_McCain

Wikipedia (2012) *Pope Benedict XVI*. . Wikipedia Foundation Inc. San Francisco, CA. http://en.wikipedia.org/wiki/Pope_Benedict_XVI

Wikipedia (2011) 30 January, *Poverty in Canada*.Wikipedia Foundation Inc. San Francisco, CA. http://en.wikipedia.org/wiki/Poverty_in_Canada

Wikipedia (2011) 14 February, *Poverty in Mexico*.Wikipedia Foundation Inc. San Francisco, CA http://en.wikipedia.org/wiki/Poverty_in_Mexico

Wikipedia (2011) 20 February. *Presidential Medal of Freedom*. Wikipedia Foundation Inc. San Francisco, CA. http://en.wikipedia.org/wiki/Presidential_Medal_of_Freedom.

Wikipedia (2011) *Public Health Care China*. Wikipedia Foundation Inc. San Francisco, CA.http://en.wikipedia.org/wiki/Public_health-care_in_China

Wikipedia (2012) *List of natural disasters by death toll*. . Wikipedia Foundation Inc. San Francisco, CA. http://en.wikipedia.org/wiki/List_of_natural_disasters_by_death_toll

Wikipedia (2011) *Race and ethnicity in the United States Census*. Wikipedia Foundation Inc. San Francisco, CA. http://en.wikipedia.org/wiki/Race_and_ethnicity_in_the_United_States_Census
Wikipedia (2011) *Racial Intermarriage*. Wikipedia Foundation Inc. San Francisco, CA. http://en.wikipedia.org/wiki/Racial_intermarriageJapan.
Wikipedia (2010) *Face: Sociological Concept*. Wikipedia Foundation Inc. San Francisco, CA, http://en.wikipedia.org/wiki/Face_(sociological_concept
Wikipedia (2011) 28 February, *Sakoku*. Wikipedia Foundation Inc. San Francisco, CA. http://en.wikipedia.org/wiki/Sakoku.
Wikipedia (2011) March, *Salvador Dalí*. Wikipedia Foundation Inc. San Francisco, CA. http://en.wikipedia.org/wiki/Salvador_Dal%C3%AD. .
Wikipedia (2011) *Southern Hemisphere*. Wikipedia Foundation Inc. San Francisco, CA. http://en.wikipedia.org/wiki/Southern_Hemisphere.
Wikipedia (2011) 07 March, *Special Forces*. Wikipedia Foundation Inc. San Francisco, CA. http://en.wikipedia.org/wiki/Special_Forces.
Wikipedia (2011) 12 February, *Thai Chinese*. Wikipedia Foundation Inc. San Francisco, CA. http://en.wikipedia.org/wiki/Thai_Chinese.
Wikipedia (2011) *The History of Jack and the Bean Stalk: Printed by Benjamin Tabart*. Wikipedia Foundation Inc. San Francisco, CA. http://en.wikipedia.org/wiki/Jack_and_the_Beanstalk.
Wikipedia (2011) 16 March, the *Nanny*. Wikipedia Foundation Inc. San Francisco, CA. http://en.wikipedia.org/wiki/The_Nanny_(TV_series).
Wikipedia (2011) *the New Face of Asian Pacific America: Numbers, Diversity, and Change in the 21st Century*, UCLA Asian American Studies Center. Wikipedia Foundation Inc. San Francisco, CA.
Wikipedia (201) 28 April. *Tornadoes striking downtown areas of large cities.* Wikipedia Foundation Inc. San Francisco, CA. http://en.wikipedia.org/wiki/List_of_tornadoes_striking_downtown_areas_of_large_cities
Wikipedia (2011) *Transfer of Sovereignty*. Wikipedia Foundation Inc. San Francisco, CA. http://en.wikipedia.org/wiki/Transfer_of_sovereignty_over_Hong_Kong

http://www.asian-nation.org/japanese.shtml
Wikipedia *(2013) 2 May. Religion (Buddhism) and Abortion* Wikipedia Foundation Inc. San Francisco, CA. http://en.wikipedia.org/wiki/Religion_and_abortion
Wikipedia (2011) 3 March, *Timeline of Taiwanese history.* Wikipedia Foundation Inc. San Francisco, CA. http://en.wikipedia.org/wiki/Timeline_of_Taiwanese_history.
Wikipedia (2011) 13 March, *Transport in Japan*. Wikipedia Foundation Inc. San Francisco, CA. http://en.wikipedia.org/wiki/Transport_in_Japan.
Wikipedia (2011) March, *Transport in Thailand*. Wikipedia Foundation Inc. San Francisco, CA. http://en.wikipedia.org/wiki/Transport_in_Thailand.
Wikipedia (2012) 12 March. *Tuskegee syphilis experiment.* http://en.wikipedia.org/wiki/Tuskegee_syphilis_experiment
Wikipedia (2011) *Typhoon Sepat 2007.* Wikipedia Foundation Inc. San Francisco, CA. http://en.wikipedia.org/wiki/Typhoon_Sepat_(2007).
Wikipedia (2011) *Japan – United Kingdom relations.* Wikipedia Foundation Inc. San Francisco, CA. http://en.wikipedia.org/wiki/Anglo-Japanese_relations.
Williams, Joseph (2010) *Poverty and Crime.* Christian Association for Prison Aftercare.http://capaassociation.org/newsletter_N009/Articles/PovertyCrime.htm
Williams, Robins. (2010) 18 November 2010, *Movie Review.*http://www.the-movie-times.com/thrsdir/actors/actorProfiles.mv?robin
Wong, Patty (1998) October. *The Chinese: Generations, Immigration and Length of U.S. Residency.* Berkeley Public Library. San Francisco, CA. http://www.library.ca.gov/services/docs/chinese.pdf
Wood, Laura (2010) 15 November, *The Thinking Housewife: The Loss of Maternal Love and Hook-up Culture.* Mount Carmel Church, CO http://www.thinkinghousewife.com/wp/2010/11/the-loss-of-maternal-love-and-hook-up-culture.
WordReference.com English Dictionary (2011) 24 January 2011,
Bureaucratic.
http://www.wordreference.com/definition/bureaucratic

World Association of Newspapers and News Publishers (2008) 08 February. *Journalist Li Chang Qing, winner of WAN's Golden Pen award, freed after three years in jail; WAN calls for further releases.* http://www.ifex.org/china/2008/02/05/journalist_li_chang qing_winner/
World Lingo (2011) *military of South Korea.*http://www.worldlingo.com/ma/enwiki/en/Military _of_South_Korea
WorldNetDaily.com (2004) 01 July, *Falun Gong sect accuses Beijing of torture, theft, sale of body parts: China selling organs of executed prisoners.* *http://www.indymedia.ie/article/74819&comment_limit= 0&condense_comments=false*
World Toilet Organization (2011). *Sanitation Project Indonesia: July 2006 - August 2008.*http://www.worldtoilet.org/sp.asp?no=2
Worsfold, Adrian (2006) 02 May, *Pluralist - Liberal and Thoughtful, Ethno methodology: Harold Garfinkel.* http://www.change.freeuk.com/learning/socthink/garfin kel.htm
Writers Weekly (2005) 30 March, *Whispers and Warnings.* http://www.writersweekly.com/whispers_and_warnings/0 02537_03302005.html
Xianchen Liu, Lianqi Liu, Owen, Judith, Kaplan, Debra L. (2005) 3 January. *Pediatrics Vol. 115 No. 1 pp. 241-249. Sleep Patterns and Sleep Problems among Schoolchildren in the United States and China.* Department of Family and Human Development and Prevention Research Center, Arizona State University, Tempe, Arizona. http://pediatrics.aappublications.org/cgi/content/full/11 5/1/S1/241
Xinhua News Agency (2008) 7 February. *Government Promotes Healthy Lifestyle.* http://www.china.org.cn/english/government/242281.ht m
Yau, Jo-Anne (2011) *Stealing What's Free: Exploring Compensation to Body Parts Sources for Their Contribution to Profitable* V5. No.1 http://Law.unh.edu/assets/pdf/pierce-Law-review-vol05-no1-yau.pdf
Yahoo (2011) *Is Robin Williams Weapons of self-destruction coming out on DVD? Amazon.* http://answers.yahoo.com/question/index?qid=20090304

151332AABb3E0

Yahoo Canada (2011) *Images Octavia Campo.* http://ca.images.search.yahoo.com/search/images;_ylt=A0oG75AS4HhNh0QBF1_rFAx.?ei=UTF-8&p=Octavio%20Ocampo&fr2=tab-web&fr=yfp-t-715

You Tube (2012) *Meaning of Magen David, The Star of David.* http://www.youtube.com/watch?v=SrHb04Sb_FU

Yearbook of the Republic of China (2005) *Taiwan's Population Distribution.* http://www.taiwan.com.au/Soccul/People/Pop/2005/200508a.html

Yishau, Olukorede (2011) 12 February. *Transparency International ranks Nigeria 143th on corruption index. The Nation.* *http://www.thenationonlineng.net/2011/index.php/news/28348-transparency-international-ranks-nigeria-143th-on-corruption-index.html*

Yi-Ying Lin, Serena (2010) July. *US in Focus: Taiwanese Immigrants in the United States.* Migration Policy Institute. http://www.migrationinformation.org/USFocus/display.cfm?ID=790

DVDs

Hopkins, Anthony and Hurt, John (2000). *The Elephant Man: Exposing Emotional Impact to Ridicule* Reprint of 1950.

About the Series

The Forgotten Waves

Volume 1 – Lily's Story: Walking in Lily's Shoes

Becoming Emotionally Intelligent: Lily's challenges & likenesses to celebrities

Dr. Patch Adams, Winston Churchill, Albert Einstein, Dr. Robert Kearns, Wolfgang Amadeus Mozart, Robin Williams and others.

Volume 2 – Lilies Talk to Lily in flowering fields

Treasure chest (Case studies & analysis)

Becoming Emotionally Intelligent: Challenges & Social justice around the world

Correlations to Volume 1.

Volume 3 – Practicing Lily's Walks and Talks

Gems in the Treasure chest (journals, analysis)

Increasing Intelligence: about the world

(Workshops, Questionnaires)

Correlations to Volume 1 and 2.

By: Frances Ludmer

Proof

Made in the USA
Charleston, SC
05 May 2014